BARRON'S

Military Flight Aptitude Tests

2nd Edition

Terry L. Duran
Major, U.S. Army

BARRON'S

All photographs in this book either are the property of the author
or have been released for public use by the Department of Defense.

All inquiries should be addressed to:
Barron's Educational Series, Inc.
250 Wireless Boulevard
Hauppauge, New York 11788
www.barronseduc.com

ISBN: 978-0-7641-4573-5

Library of Congress Catalog Card No. 2011004390

Library of Congress Cataloging-in-Publication Data
Duran, Terry L.
   Military flight aptitude tests / Terry Duran. — 2nd ed.
      p.   cm.
   Includes bibliographical references and index.
   ISBN: 978-0-7641-4573-5
   1. United States—Armed Forces—Aviation—Examinations—Study
guides. 2. Air pilots, Military—Training of—United States. I. Title.
   UG638.D87   2011
   153.9'4358400973—dc22   2011004390

PRINTED IN THE UNITED STATES OF AMERICA

9 8 7 6 5 4 3 2

This book is dedicated to the glory of God
and in honor of my wonderful, loving, supportive family—
my angelic, beautiful, talented, wise, and witty bride, June;
our awesome children, Heather, Amanda, and Jonathan;
and our wonderful grandchildren Jaycie and Jolie—
without whom I am nothing

and

in memory of fallen brothers:

Cadet Woodrow K. "Woody" Ratliff, Company S-2, TAMU '82
18 March 1960–2 September 1979

Staff Sergeant Shawn A. Graham
H Troop, 124th Cavalry (BRT)
25 March 1971–28 September 2005

Colonel Thomas H. Felts, Sr., U.S. Army
Formerly of 1st Battalion, 327th Infantry Regiment
5 March 1961–14 November 2006

Contents

PART III: FLIGHT APTITUDE QUALIFICATION TESTS

PART I:
AVIATION AND
THE ALL-VOLUNTEER
AMERICAN MILITARY

Officers and Aviators, Professionals All

CHAPTER 1

"We only have those rights that we can defend."

The Role of the American Military in Today's World

You're thinking of becoming a military aviator. Or maybe you already know that's what you want—and now you just have to figure out how to get there.

That's commendable—military aviation is a noble, worthwhile, and even exciting profession, and you have shown initiative and good judgment by choosing this book to improve your chances for selection.

You may already be a member of the U.S. military, or you may just be considering your options. Either way, you deserve to know . . . you *need* to know . . . the bigger picture. You will have to study hard and prepare well to be initially selected as a military aviator—and then you will have to successfully complete long periods of challenging training . . . just to get started.

Are you up for it? Can you measure up?

Great. That's your first lesson, right here at the beginning of this book—success comes to those who *want* it and are willing to *work* for it.

Let's get your education and preparation started right away by talking about *why* the job of military aviator exists at all.

The American military exists (as you already know, if you are a current service member) to defend and protect the people and freedoms of the United States of America. Its establishment is provided for in the Constitution, it is drawn from the nation it represents, and today's all-volunteer military ultimately reflects the best of the nation it defends—those who are willing to sacrifice or subordinate their own desires and comfort for the benefit and protection of all.

Today's American military is the world's largest "meritocracy," where those who achieve are rewarded based on their demonstrated merit and performance—not their background, social or economic status, race, ethnicity, connections, or other unearned qualities. It is, on average, somewhat better educated than the country it represents—maybe because it emphasizes the value of education and self-improvement—and it proportionately includes every possible race, religion, ethnicity, and the like . . . even non-U.S. citizens who think our principles and way of life are worth fighting for. It's not perfect, it's not instantaneous, and it definitely isn't easy—but it's better than anything else out there.

The military can be a harsh, no-excuses, results-only taskmaster that calls for its members to pledge their very lives if that's what it takes to get the job done—and yet it reaches out to and cares for its members and their families in ways no civilian corporation can even conceive of.

The U.S. service member—soldier, sailor, airman, Marine—is seen around the world as a representation of all that is essentially American: an individual human but yet an icon of freedom, a curiously contradictory but respected blend of foibles and nobility—no better friend in time of need, no fiercer foe when attacked or threatened.

Today's American military employs organizational practices and procedures that are imitated by businesses worldwide—because they work. In study after study, survey after survey, the U.S. military is one of the most respected American institutions, steeped in tradition and service and bound together by principles of honor, courage, and loyalty found nowhere else. It is by no means perfect—no human institution can be—but it holds itself and its members accountable and strives to make itself better—not only because those qualities are ingrained, but because it has to.

And make no mistake, at this writing the U.S. military is an organization at war—at war with those who declared war on us years *before* September 11, 2001. Months-long, repetitive deployments are the norm for units in all the services in the long struggle against those who hate our liberties and want to either dictate our thoughts, dress, speech, and manner of worship . . . or kill us. The Cold War lasted for 46 years, from the end of World War II in 1945 to the fall of the Soviet Union and the Warsaw Pact in 1991; anyone who thinks the causes of the current conflict can be solved as easily and quickly as a drive-through fast-food order is sadly mistaken. Even Reservists and Guardsmen—once recruited with the idea that "it's only one weekend a month and two weeks in the summer"—are called upon again and again to pack their rucksacks or seabags or duffles and report for active duty.

Within that framework, military aviation is a vital part of the air, sea, and land forces that defend our nation and our way of life. Aviation units are integrated into land and sea forces in the Army, Marine Corps, and Navy—and they are, of course, present in a "purer" sense in the air-oriented branch of the military, the Air Force.

The aircraft of the Air Force, Army, Navy, and Marine Corps are versatile, hard-hitting forces that can be employed swiftly anywhere in the world. These forces can quickly gain and maintain air superiority over regional aggressors and provide close air support for U.S. ground forces, permitting rapid air attacks on enemy targets while providing security for ground forces to conduct logistics, command and control, intelligence, and other functions.

Fighter/attack aircraft, operating from both land bases and aircraft carriers, take to the sky to oppose enemy fighters, as well as to attack ground and ship targets. Conventional bombers provide a worldwide capability to strike surface targets on short notice. Specialized aircraft supporting conventional operations perform functions such as airborne early warning and control, suppression of enemy air defenses, reconnaissance, surveillance, and combat search and rescue. In addition, the U.S. military operates a variety of transport planes, aerial-refueling aircraft, helicopters, and other support aircraft.

The Air Force, Navy, and Marine Corps keep part of their tactical air forces forward deployed (based outside the United States) at all times. These forces can be augmented as necessary with aircraft based in the United States.

The Air Force is capable of deploying, as part of its expeditionary forces, seven to eight fighter wings to a distant area or *theater of operations* in a matter of days as an initial response. Additional wings can follow within the first month. These forces can operate from local bases where infrastructure, such as airports and fuel resupply facilities, already exists and political agreements allow. Likewise, Navy and Marine Corps air wings can be employed during distant contingencies on very short notice, providing the unique ability to carry out combat operations even without access to regional land bases.

Naval aircraft missions are fleet air defense, strike warfare, antisubmarine warfare (ASW), electronic warfare, early warning, amphibious assault, training, and unmanned aerial vehicles (UAV). Each mission requires different capabilities; most Navy aircraft are able to perform more than one type of mission and may perform support functions as well. The Navy and Marine Corps have over six thousand active and reserve aircraft.

The fleet air defense mission performed by Navy and Marine Corps fighters is to defend the fleet from shore- and sea-based air attacks. Strike aircraft attack enemy surface targets such as ships and ground forces. Marine Corps aircraft emphasize vertical or short takeoff capability to provide airpower even where there are no airfields. Naval airborne early warning aircraft provide all-weather active and passive air and sea surveillance of enemy targets and maritime traffic. Electronic countermeasure aircraft reduce the electronic vision of the enemy by jamming the opposing force's sensors and communications. The Tactical Electronic Warfare Reconnaissance Force performs electronic support measures and signal intelligence functions. This includes interception of radio and other electromagnetic transmissions for intelligence purposes to support military operations. ASW platforms include several kinds of aircraft and helicopters designed to seek out and destroy enemy submarines.

The movement of troops and supplies from ship to shore is called *amphibious assault*. The Marine Corps uses both fixed-wing and rotary-wing aircraft to accomplish the airborne portion of this mission. Artillery pieces, support vehicles, troops, ammunition, and supplies must be brought ashore quickly, making aircraft an essential element in this mission.

Mine warfare ranges from denial of harbors or sea lanes to the enemy to destruction or neutralization of hostile minefields. A little-known but very important naval aviation mission is Fleet Ballistic Missile Communications. TACAMO (Take Charge and Move Out) aircraft fill the role of relaying very low frequency signals to strategic missile submarines.

The role of UAVs in both reconnaissance and attack missions is growing in all the services. Technological advances are enabling more and more capabilities to be placed on increasingly smaller airframes.

Bomber forces play a key role in delivering precision-guided munitions against point targets, such as small units, terrorist training camps, command and control facilities, and air defense sites. Bombers can also deliver large quantities of unguided general-purpose bombs and cluster munitions against area targets, such as ground units, airfields, and rail yards.

The ability of these forces to have an immediate impact on a conflict by precision attacks on selected enemy targets—slowing the advance of enemy forces, suppressing enemy air defenses, and inflicting massive damage on an enemy's strategic infrastructure—has expanded dramatically as an increasing proportion of "smart" munitions has been deployed.

Special aviation forces contribute to all phases of military operations. Some of their most important missions are insertion, support, and extraction of special operations forces; suppression of enemy air defenses; and aerial reconnaissance and surveillance.

U.S. military aviation began in 1861 during the Civil War when the Union Army used observers in hot-air balloons to keep an eye on Confederate troop movements and adjust artillery fire. The expansion of Army aviation continued to progress through the formation of the Army Air Corps in July 1926, which became the U.S. Air Force, a separate military branch, in 1947.

Modern Army aviation was born on June 6, 1942, seven months after the United States entered World War II. These assets were known as *organic Army aviation*, because they were "organic" (i.e., assigned) to units of the Army ground forces, and to distinguish them from the Army Air Corps. The primary aircraft used by organic Army aviation were light, fixed-wing aircraft such as the L-4 Piper Cub. These aircraft were utilized for adjusting artillery fire, command and control, medical evacuation (MEDEVAC), aerial photography, reconnaissance, and other purposes. The value of organic Army aviation proven during World War II was that its aircraft were accessible to ground commanders and therefore able to operate in close coordination with ground forces. Air Corps aircraft were often unable to fulfill these needs because they were more focused on missions directed by their headquarters with different goals.

The helicopter's potential was demonstrated to some extent during the Korean War, but rapid development and procurement of rotary-wing aircraft in the Army did not occur until the early 1960s. In 1963, the 11th Air Assault Division tested the airmobile concept at Fort Benning, Georgia, and in 1965 the 1st Cavalry Division was organized as the first "airmobile" division and sent to Vietnam.

With the arrival of the UH-1 Huey and two airmobile divisions, helicopter warfare became the most important innovation of the Vietnam conflict. Armed helicopter development was also greatly advanced during Vietnam. These gunships provided direct fire support to units that were operating outside the range of conventional artillery. The idea of armed helicopters also led to the specific development of more heavily armed attack helicopters.

Army aviation units have begun a transition from entire battalions organized around one mission—attack, assault, transport, cargo, and so on—to multifunctional battalions and brigades that are more self-sustaining and more in keeping with the increasingly expeditionary nature of current military operations. The multifunctional battalion structure includes AH-64D Apache attack helicopters, UH-60 Blackhawk utility helicopters, and other units dedicated to reconnaissance and support missions.

Coast Guard aviation elements work in conjunction with ship- and shore-based units to perform their missions of coastal security and rescue. Their aircraft are specially adapted to the needs of their missions and in wartime they provide an important contribution to Homeland Defense, in addition to their other duties.

The United States leads the world in manufacturing military aircraft and associated systems. Military aircraft are a key component of both national defense and power projection to encourage allies and deter enemies and potential adversaries.

Roles, Duties, and Opportunities of Military Officers

If you are going to be an American military aviator or pilot, you will also generally be a commissioned or warrant officer. An *officer*, in the broadest sense of the term, is someone in an organization who has both the authority and the obligation to *lead*—to exert influence over others to accomplish the mission . . . to get the job done.

Aviation units have proportionately more officers than other units, in all the services, simply because almost all pilots are either commissioned or warrant officers. Some maintain that the idea that aviators must be officers hearkens back to the days of the feudal nobility and, later, landed gentry who were leaders—officers—of the militias and regiments that they raised from their kingdom, the surrounding townships, or wherever. Whether that holds any merit or not, the simple fact is that military flying is a very technical *and* a very physical business, and the educational, age, and other requirements have evolved based on studies of the types of people who were successful in pilot training and beyond—and who were not.

We're going to discuss some very general aspects of being an officer and even just a member of the military in general. Then we'll focus on how you go from where you are now to the cockpit.

Military Rank Structure, Pay, and Benefits

There are three types of officers in the U.S. military: commissioned officers, warrant officers, and noncommissioned officers. The remaining members at the lower end of the hierarchy are known as "enlisted personnel." Every *rank*, though, officer or not, has a *pay grade* associated with it; many times the rank and the pay grade are used interchangeably, but not always. And, even though they do have leadership responsibilities, noncommissioned officers (NCOs for short) are also enlisted; the jump from "just enlisted" to NCO occurs at pay grade E-4 or E-5, depending on the service. The pay grades for enlisted members run from E-1 to E-9, for warrant officers from W-1 to W-5, and for officers from O-1 to O-10; you can see more detail in the charts that follow shortly.

Pay grades are especially useful for comparative purposes between the services because of the different rank titles in the various branches. For example, an Air Force staff sergeant is an E-5, whereas an Army or Marine staff sergeant is an E-6. Likewise, an Army or Marine captain is an O-3, but a Navy or Coast Guard captain is an O-6.

The bottom line is that the same pay grade with the same years of service will get paid the same base pay, no matter which service they are in or what position they are currently assigned. Aviators, however, frequently get extra pay on top of this—but more about that later.

A few other technicalities: the Navy and Coast Guard call their NCOs *petty officers*; the Air Force doesn't have any warrant officers; the commander of a Navy or Coast Guard ship is commonly called *captain* regardless of what pay grade/rank they hold; and the Navy and Coast Guard use the term *rate* instead of *rank* when referring to enlisted personnel. Here, though, we are going to use only the term *rank* to avoid confusion, and *captain* will be a rank unless it's specified to be the commander of a ship.

When people refer to "officers" as such, they are usually talking about commissioned officers, those who have a *commission* at the direction of the president of the United States to act on his behalf (the military falls under the executive branch of government). Sometimes, though, they are talking about commissioned officers *and* warrant officers; warrant officers have a *warrant* from the Secretary of their service to perform special technical and leadership functions. Just to make things more confusing, some warrant officers have commissions, also, but that's for legal reasons involving command authority that we don't need to get into here.

Officers of all three types have two types of authority: *general* and *organizational.* General authority means that service members of a lower rank/pay grade are obligated to follow the orders or directions of a higher-ranking service member, whether or not they are in the same organization or even service. Splitting hairs on authority between service members of the same pay grade depends on the *date of rank*— when the individual was promoted to that rank.

Organizational authority applies to service members within the same organization, where one individual may occupy a position over another individual, and the second individual is obligated to carry out the orders of the first, even if the higher-positioned member is the same rank as the lower.

Note: Army/Air Force/Marine officer rank insignia is silver unless otherwise noted; Navy/Coast Guard shoulder board insignia is gold on black.

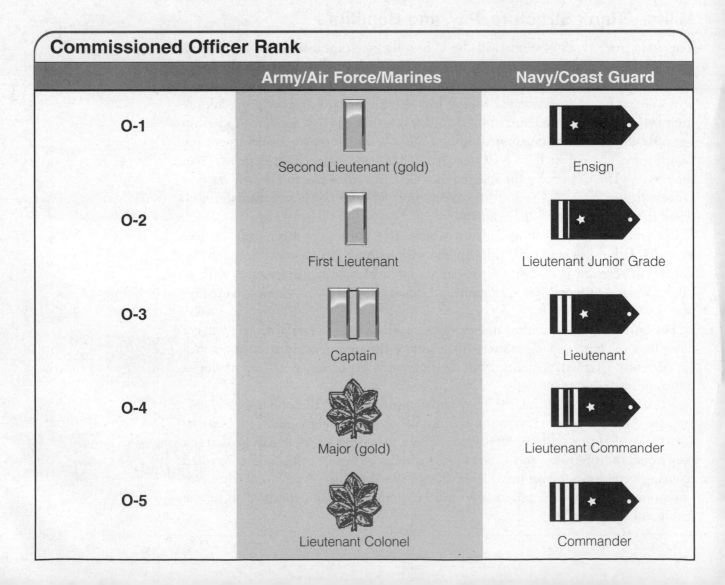

Commissioned Officer Rank

	Army/Air Force/Marines	Navy/Coast Guard
O-1	Second Lieutenant (gold)	Ensign
O-2	First Lieutenant	Lieutenant Junior Grade
O-3	Captain	Lieutenant
O-4	Major (gold)	Lieutenant Commander
O-5	Lieutenant Colonel	Commander

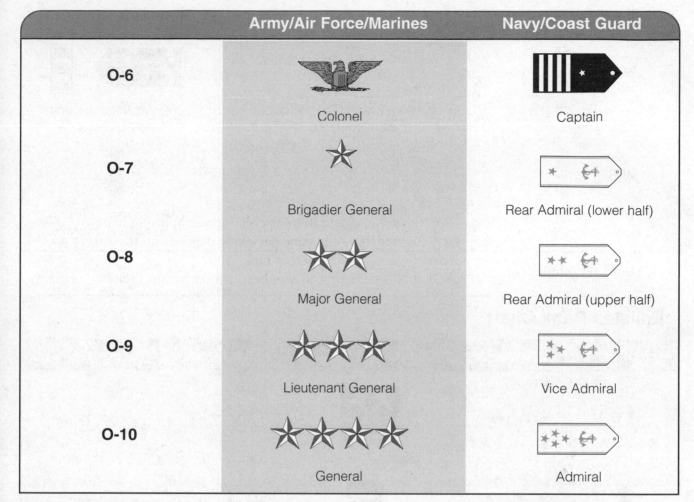

	Army/Air Force/Marines	Navy/Coast Guard
O-6	Colonel	Captain
O-7	Brigadier General	Rear Admiral (lower half)
O-8	Major General	Rear Admiral (upper half)
O-9	Lieutenant General	Vice Admiral
O-10	General	Admiral

Note: The Navy also uses Air Force/Army/Marine style rank on the collar of uniforms that do not use shoulder boards.

Warrant Officer Rank

	Army	Marines	Navy/Coast Guard
W-1	Warrant Officer 1 (black and silver)	Warrant Officer (red and gold)	The grade of Warrant Officer (W-1) is no longer used.
W-2	Chief Warrant Officer 2 (black and silver)	Chief Warrant Officer 2 (red and gold)	Chief Warrant Officer Two (blue and gold)
W-3	Chief Warrant Officer 3 (black and silver)	Chief Warrant Officer 3 (red and gold)	Chief Warrant Officer Three (blue and silver)

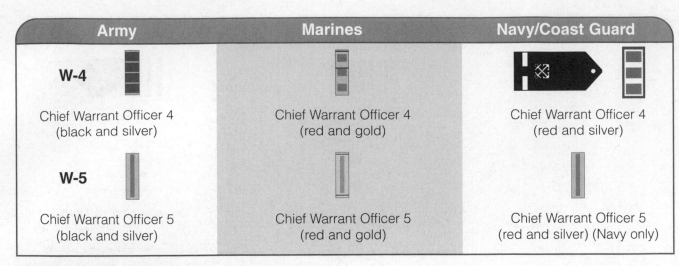

	Army	Marines	Navy/Coast Guard
W-4	Chief Warrant Officer 4 (black and silver)	Chief Warrant Officer 4 (red and gold)	Chief Warrant Officer 4 (red and silver)
W-5	Chief Warrant Officer 5 (black and silver)	Chief Warrant Officer 5 (red and gold)	Chief Warrant Officer 5 (red and silver) (Navy only)

Note: The Air Force does not have Warrant Officers.

Enlisted Rank Chart

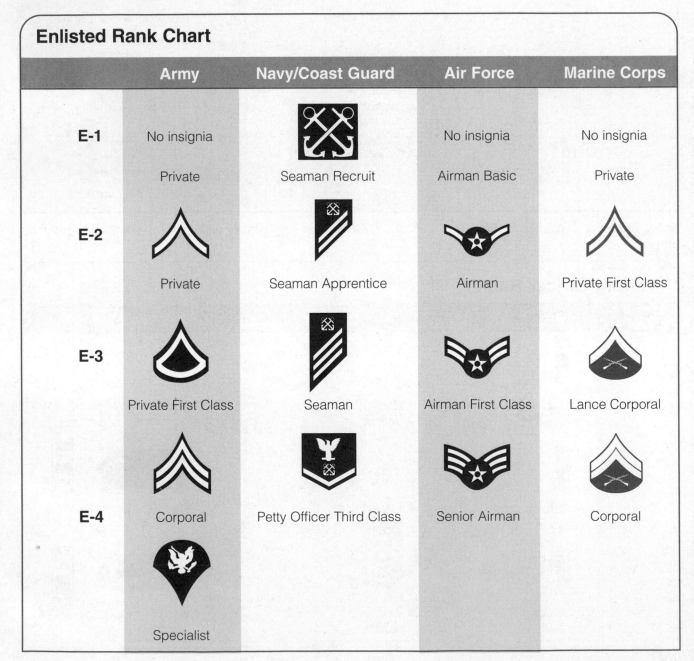

	Army	Navy/Coast Guard	Air Force	Marine Corps
E-1	No insignia Private	Seaman Recruit	No insignia Airman Basic	No insignia Private
E-2	Private	Seaman Apprentice	Airman	Private First Class
E-3	Private First Class	Seaman	Airman First Class	Lance Corporal
E-4	Corporal	Petty Officer Third Class	Senior Airman	Corporal
	Specialist			

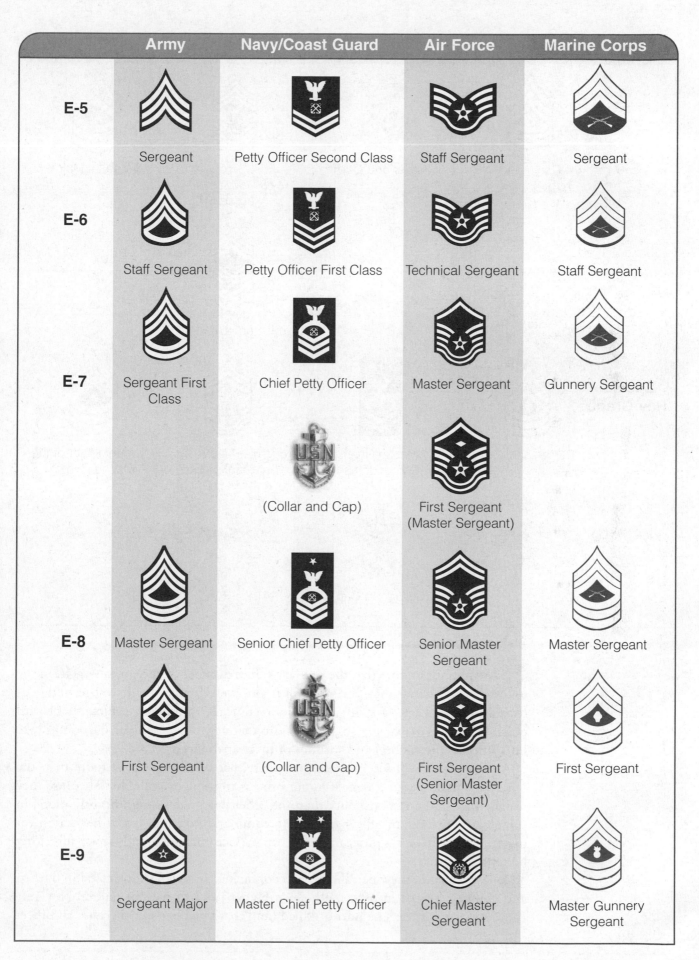

	Army	Navy/Coast Guard	Air Force	Marine Corps
E-5	Sergeant	Petty Officer Second Class	Staff Sergeant	Sergeant
E-6	Staff Sergeant	Petty Officer First Class	Technical Sergeant	Staff Sergeant
E-7	Sergeant First Class	Chief Petty Officer (Collar and Cap)	Master Sergeant First Sergeant (Master Sergeant)	Gunnery Sergeant
E-8	Master Sergeant First Sergeant	Senior Chief Petty Officer (Collar and Cap)	Senior Master Sergeant First Sergeant (Senior Master Sergeant)	Master Sergeant First Sergeant
E-9	Sergeant Major	Master Chief Petty Officer	Chief Master Sergeant	Master Gunnery Sergeant

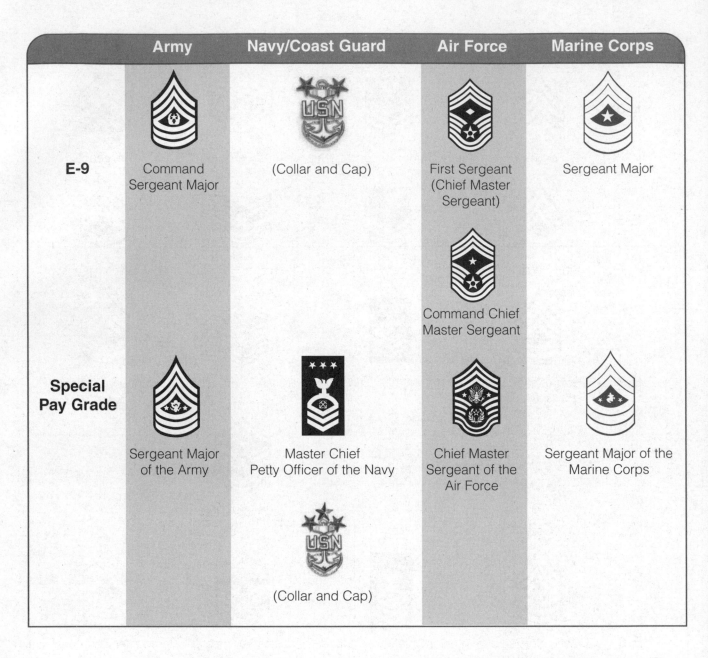

	Army	Navy/Coast Guard	Air Force	Marine Corps
E-9	Command Sergeant Major	(Collar and Cap)	First Sergeant (Chief Master Sergeant)	Sergeant Major
			Command Chief Master Sergeant	
Special Pay Grade	Sergeant Major of the Army	Master Chief Petty Officer of the Navy (Collar and Cap)	Chief Master Sergeant of the Air Force	Sergeant Major of the Marine Corps

It's important to note that the military values experience, as you can see from the following pay chart—they pay more for it. So, even though the newest second lieutenant or ensign (an O-1 in either case) technically outranks a senior NCO with possibly decades of experience, woe be unto that new officer if he or she doesn't take into account the counsel and wisdom of that experienced NCO!

And, yes, you will see from the pay chart that officers get paid more than the other pay grades, even the most junior officers to some extent. That's because they usually have more responsibility than the other pay grades—significantly more, in some cases. Even if an officer is not in a command position, his or her action (or inaction) can have a significant effect on service members and units, for either better or worse.

And, because of the "special trust and confidence in the patriotism, valor, fidelity, and abilities" placed in officers, there's a higher price to pay for failure. Not only could service members be hurt or killed (and that's bad enough) because an officer

Basic Pay—Effective January 2011

Pay Grade	2 or less	Over 2	Over 3	Over 4	Over 6	Over 8	Over 10	Over 12	Over 14	Over 16	Over 18
O-10[1]											
O-9[1]											
O-8[1]	9,530.70	9,842.70	10,050.00	10,107.90	10,366.50	10,798.20	10,899.00	11,308.80	11,426.40	11,779.80	12,291.00
O-7[1]	7,919.10	8,287.20	8,457.30	8,592.60	8,837.70	9,079.80	9,359.70	9,638.70	9,918.60	10,798.20	11,540.70
O-6[2]	5,869.50	6,448.50	6,871.50	6,871.50	6,897.60	7,193.40	7,232.40	7,232.40	7,643.40	8,370.30	8,796.90
O-5	4,893.00	5,512.20	5,893.80	5,965.80	6,203.70	6,346.20	6,659.40	6,889.20	7,186.20	7,640.70	7,856.70
O-4	4,221.90	4,887.30	5,213.40	5,286.00	5,588.70	5,913.30	6,317.40	6,632.10	6,851.10	6,976.50	7,049.10
O-3	3,711.90	4,208.10	4,542.00	4,951.80	5,188.80	5,449.20	5,617.80	5,894.70	6,039.00	6,039.00	6,039.00
O-2	3,207.30	3,652.80	4,207.20	4,349.10	4,438.50	4,438.50	4,438.50	4,438.50	4,438.50	4,438.50	4,438.50
O-1	2,784.00	2,897.40	3,502.50	3,502.50	3,502.50	3,502.50	3,502.50	3,502.50	3,502.50	3,502.50	3,502.50
O-3[3]				4,951.80	5,188.80	5,449.20	5,617.80	5,894.70	6,128.10	6,262.20	6,444.90
O-2[3]				4,349.10	4,438.50	4,580.10	4,818.60	5,002.80	5,140.20	5,140.20	5,140.20
O-1[3]				3,502.50	3,740.40	3,878.70	4,020.30	4,158.90	4,349.10	4,349.10	4,349.10
W-5											
W-4	3,836.10	4,126.50	4,245.00	4,361.40	4,562.10	4,760.70	4,961.40	5,264.40	5,529.60	5,781.90	5,988.30
W-3	3,502.80	3,648.90	3,798.60	3,847.80	4,004.70	3,313.70	4,635.00	4,786.20	4,961.10	5,142.00	5,466.00
W-2	3,099.90	3,393.00	3,483.30	3,545.40	3,746.40	4,059.00	4,213.50	4,366.20	4,552.50	4,698.00	4,838.10
W-1	2,721.00	3,013.50	3,092.40	3,258.90	3,456.00	3,745.80	3,881.40	4,070.40	4,256.70	4,403.10	4,530.00
E-9[4]							4,634.70	4,739.70	4,872.00	5,027.70	5,184.60
E-8						3,794.10	3,961.80	4,065.60	4,190.40	4,325.10	4,568.40
E-7	2,637.30	2,878.50	2,988.90	3,135.00	3,249.00	3,444.60	3,554.70	3,750.90	3,913.50	4,024.50	4,143.00
E-6	2,281.20	2,510.10	2,620.80	2,728.50	2,840.70	3,093.60	3,192.30	3,382.80	3,441.00	3,483.60	3,533.40
E-5	2,090.10	2,230.20	2,337.90	2,448.30	2,620.20	2,800.50	2,947.50	2,965.50	2,965.50	2,965.50	2,965.50
E-4	1,916.10	2,014.20	2,123.40	2,230.80	2,325.90	2,325.90	2,325.90	2,325.90	2,325.90	2,325.90	2,325.90
E-3	1,729.80	1,838.70	1,950.00	1,950.00	1,950.00	1,950.00	1,950.00	1,950.00	1,950.00	1,950.00	1,950.00
E-2	1,644.90	1,644.90	1,644.90	1,644.90	1,644.90	1,644.90	1,644.90	1,644.90	1,644.90	1,644.90	1,644.90
E-1[5]	1,467.60										

Pay Grade	Over 20	Over 22	Over 24	Over 26	Over 28	Over 30	Over 32	Over 34	Over 36	Over 38	Over 40
O-10[1]	15,400.80	15,475.80	15,797.70	16,358.40	16,358.40	17,176.20	17,176.20	18,034.80	18,034.80	18,936.90	18,936.90
O-9[1]	13,469.70	13,663.80	13,944.00	14,433.00	14,433.00	15,155.10	15,155.10	15,912.90	15,912.90	16,708.50	16,708.50
O-8[1]	12,762.30	13,077.30	13,077.30	13,077.30	13,077.30	13,404.30	13,404.30	13,739.40	13,739.40	13,739.40	13,739.40
O-7[1]	11,540.70	11,540.70	11,540.70	11,599.50	11,599.50	11,831.70	11,831.70	11,831.70	11,831.70	11,831.70	11,831.70
O-6[2]	9,222.90	9,465.60	9,711.30	10,187.70	10,187.70	10,391.10	10,391.10	10,391.10	10,391.10	10,391.10	10,391.10
O-5	8,070.30	8,313.30	8,313.30	8,313.30	8,313.30	8,313.30	8,313.30	8,313.30	8,313.30	8,313.30	8,313.30
O-4	7,049.10	7,049.10	7,049.10	7,049.10	7,049.10	7,049.10	7,049.10	7,049.10	7,049.10	7,049.10	7,049.10
O-3	6,039.00	6,039.00	6,039.00	6,039.00	6,039.00	6,039.00	6,039.00	6,039.00	6,039.00	6,039.00	6,039.00
O-2	4,438.50	4,438.50	4,438.50	4,438.50	4,438.50	4,438.50	4,438.50	4,438.50	4,438.50	4,438.50	4,438.50
O-1	3,502.50	3,502.50	3,502.50	3,502.50	3,502.50	3,502.50	3,502.50	3,502.50	3,502.50	3,502.50	3,502.50
O-3[3]	6,444.90	6,444.90	6,444.90	6,444.90	6,444.90	6,444.90	6,444.90	6,444.90	6,444.90	6,444.90	6,444.90
O-2[3]	5,140.20	5,140.20	5,140.20	5,140.20	5,140.20	5,140.20	5,140.20	5,140.20	5,140.20	5,140.20	5,140.20
O-1[3]	4,349.10	4,349.10	4,349.10	4,349.10	4,349.10	4,349.10	4,349.10	4,349.10	4,349.10	4,349.10	4,349.10
W-5	6,820.80	7,167.00	7,424.70	7,710.00	7,710.00	8,095.80	8,095.80	8,500.50	8,500.50	8,925.90	8,925.90
W-4	6,189.60	6,485.00	6,728.40	7,005.60	7,005.60	7,145.70	7,145.70	7,145.70	7,145.70	7,145.70	7,145.70
W-3	5,685.30	5,816.40	5,955.60	6,144.90	6,144.90	6,144.90	6,144.90	6,144.90	6,144.90	6,144.90	6,144.90
W-2	4,987.80	5,091.60	5,174.10	5,174.10	5,174.10	5,174.10	5,174.10	5,174.10	5,174.10	5,174.10	5,174.10
W-1	4,701.60	4,701.60	4,701.60	4,701.60	4,701.60	4,701.60	4,701.60	4,701.60	4,701.60	4,701.60	4,701.60
E-9[4]	5,436.60	5,649.30	5,873.40	6,215.70	6,215.70	6,526.20	6,526.20	6,852.90	6,852.90	7,195.80	7,195.80
E-8	4,691.70	4,901.70	5,017.80	5,304.60	5,304.60	5,411.10	5,411.10	5,411.10	5,411.10	5,411.10	5,411.10
E-7	4,189.20	4,342.80	4,425.60	4,740.00	4,740.00	4,740.00	4,740.00	4,740.00	4,740.00	4,740.00	4,740.00
E-6	3,533.40	3,533.40	3,533.40	3,533.40	3,533.40	3,533.40	3,533.40	3,533.40	3,533.40	3,533.40	3,533.40
E-5	2,965.50	2,965.50	2,965.50	2,965.50	2,965.50	2,965.50	2,965.50	2,965.50	2,965.50	2,965.50	2,965.50
E-4	2,325.90	2,325.90	2,325.90	2,325.90	2,325.90	2,325.90	2,325.90	2,325.90	2,325.90	2,325.90	2,325.90
E-3	1,950.00	1,950.00	1,950.00	1,950.00	1,950.00	1,950.00	1,950.00	1,950.00	1,950.00	1,950.00	1,950.00
E-2	1,644.90	1,644.90	1,644.90	1,644.90	1,644.90	1,644.90	1,644.90	1,644.90	1,644.90	1,644.90	1,644.90

Notes:

1. Basic pay for an O-7 to O-10 is limited by Level II of the Executive Schedule which is $14,975.10. Basic pay for O-6 and below is limited by Level V of the Executive Schedule which is $12,141.60.
2. While serving as Chairman, Joint Chief of Staff/Vice Chairman, Joint Chief of Staff, Chief of Navy Operations, Commandant of the Marine Corps, Army/Air Force Chief of Staff, Commander of a unified or specified combatant command, basic pay is $20,263.50. (See note 1 above).
3. Applicable to O-1 to O-3 with at least 4 years and 1 day of active duty or more than 1460 points as a warrant and/or enlisted member. See Department of Defense Financial Management Regulations for more detailed explanation on who is eligible for this special basic pay rate.
4. For the Master Chief Petty Officer of the Navy, Chief Master Sergeant of the AF, Sergeant Major of the Army or Marine Corps or Senior Enlisted Advisor of the JCS, basic pay is $7,489.80. Combat Zone Tax Exclusion for O-1 and above is based on this basic pay rate plus Hostile Fire Pay/Imminent Danger Pay which is $225.00.
5. Applicable to E-1 with 4 months or more of active duty. Basic pay for an E-1 with less than 4 months of active duty is $1,357.20.
6. Basic pay rate for Academy Cadets/Midshipmen and ROTC members/applicants is $974.40.

did something stupid or wrong, but the officer can be relieved and discharged from the service, as opposed to an enlisted member, who might even be reduced one or more pay grades but allowed to stay in the military.

Some other benefits to military service regardless of pay grade include: the structured pay raises over time (something you will very seldom see in the civilian world); the potential for extra, nontaxable allowances for subsistence (meals) and housing, depending on your situation; the opportunity for all of your basic pay to be tax free during those time periods that you are deployed to a combat zone; free or very low-cost medical care; and special pays such as flight pay, sea pay, parachutist pay (commonly known as "jump pay"), combat zone pay, and so on.

Requirements for Becoming an Officer and Aviator

All three branches of the military have three main sources of commissioned officers: their service academy, an officer candidate or training school, and the Senior Reserve Officer Training Corps. Requirements for the service academies include being between 17 and 23 at the time of enrollment, outstanding high school records and test results, and a nomination from a member of Congress or the Executive Branch. Requirements for commissioning and for pilot/aviator selection are similar among the services, with some benchmarks set by law and others by the particular service based on their needs.

U.S. Air Force

The U.S. Air Force has three pathways to becoming an officer first, after which you might be selected to become a pilot: the U.S. Air Force Academy (USAFA) at Colorado Springs, Colorado; Air Force Reserve Officer Training Corps (AFROTC), offered directly at 144 colleges and universities throughout the country; and Officer Training School (OTS), where current enlisted Air Force, Air Force Reserve, and Air National Guard members can be selected to undergo training and evaluations that can result in their commissioning as an officer.

The U.S. Air Force Academy at Colorado Springs, established in 1954, is the premier source of officers for the Air Force, graduating about a thousand second lieutenants a year. Applicants must compete for nominations and then appointments—usually sponsored by a U.S. representative or senator—based on their overall high school record, physical fitness scores, and military test scores. USAFA cadets are paid during their four years of attendance and incur a mandatory service obligation upon their graduation and commissioning as second lieutenants.

There are two primary routes to an Air Force commission for college students through AFROTC—the four-year program and the two-year program. Students in both programs attend AFROTC classes along with other college courses and normally receive elective academic credit. Cadets who successfully complete all requirements are commissioned as Air Force officers with a four-year active-duty service commitment. Those selected as pilots, navigators, and air battle managers have longer commitments upon completion of specialized training. If you want to be a pilot, you must be commissioned before you reach 29 years of age; you also have to meet Air Force height and weight requirements and pass a physical fitness test.

The Air Force conducts its Officer Training School at Maxwell Air Force Base (AFB), Alabama, for current Air Force enlisted members who meet the qualifications, have their commander's recommendation, and are chosen by a selection board. OTS is a 12-week course that graduates about a thousand new Air Force officers annually. Upon graduation, candidates are commissioned as Air Force second lieutenants and proceed to the technical training for their officer specialty.

Regardless of commissioning source, the Pilot composite score on the Air Force Officer Qualifying Test (AFOQT) will determine whether you are eligible and selected for pilot training. The Pilot composite score is made up of the scores on the Arithmetic, Math Knowledge, Instrument Comprehension, Table Reading, and Aviation Information subtests. This measures some of the knowledge and abilities the Air Force considers necessary for successful completion of pilot training. You still have to meet at least the minimums on the other subtests, though, so don't think you can just blow them off because they're not part of the Pilot composite score.

Nineteenth Air Force, with headquarters at Randolph AFB, Texas, conducts the Air Education and Training Command's (AETC) flying training. Air Force pilot candidates begin with Initial Flight Training, where civilian instructors provide up to 25 hours of flight instruction to pilot candidates. Pilot candidates then attend either Euro-NATO Joint Jet Pilot Training (ENJJPT) or Joint Specialized Undergraduate Pilot Training (JSUPT).

ENJJPT is at Sheppard AFB, Texas, and lasts about 54 weeks (yes, just over a year). Students learn with, and are taught by, U.S. Air Force officers as well as officers from various allies' air forces. Student pilots first fly the T-37 trainer, learning about contact, instrument, low-level, and formation flying. Next, they strap into the supersonic T-38 Talon and continue building the skills necessary to become a fighter pilot.

JSUPT students accomplish primary training in the T-6 Texan II at one of three Air Force bases: Columbus AFB, Mississippi; Laughlin AFB, Texas; Vance AFB, Oklahoma; or in the T-34C Turbomentor at Naval Air Station (NAS) Whiting Field, Florida. Joint training is conducted at Vance AFB and NAS Whiting Field for students from the Air Force and Navy. During the primary phase of JSUPT, students learn basic flight skills common to all military pilots. Most JSUPT students use the Joint Primary Aircraft Training System (JPATS) during the primary training phase. The aircraft portion of JPATS uses the T-6 Texan II.

After the primary phase of JSUPT, student pilots elect one of several advanced training tracks based on their class standing and train at Columbus AFB, Laughlin AFB, or Vance AFB. Prospective airlift and tanker pilots are assigned to the airlift/tanker track and train in the T-1A Jayhawk. Student pilots scheduled for bomber or fighter assignments are assigned to the bomber/fighter track and train in the T-38 Talon. Students assigned to the multi-engine turboprop track fly the T-44 turboprop trainers or TC-12B trainers at NAS Corpus Christi, Texas, and will eventually fly the C-130 Hercules. A small number may also be selected to undergo C-12 training at Elmendorf AFB, Alaska. Those students selected to fly helicopters are assigned to the helicopter track and fly the UH-1 Huey or the UH-60 Blackhawk at Fort Rucker, Alabama.

Nineteenth Air Force also provides follow-on training for most Air Force pilots in their assigned aircraft. Pilots assigned to fighter aircraft complete the introduction to fighter fundamentals course at Randolph AFB or Sheppard AFB in Texas, or Moody AFB, Georgia, flying the AT-38B, and then move on to train at either Tyndall AFB, Florida or Luke AFB, Arizona. Altus AFB, Oklahoma, hosts training for pilots assigned to C-5 Galaxy, KC-135 Stratotanker, and C-17 Globemaster III aircraft. Aircrews assigned to fly the C-130 train at Little Rock AFB, Arkansas, and pilots assigned to fly MC-130 Combat Talon, HC-130 aircraft, UH-1N, MH-53 Pave Low, or HH-60 Pave Hawk helicopters receive their training at Kirtland AFB, New Mexico. Keesler AFB, Mississippi, provides follow-on training for pilots assigned to the C-21, and the Army's Fort Rucker provides training in the C-12 Super King Air.

U.S. Army

The U.S. Army also has three primary sources of commissioned officers: the U.S. Military Academy at West Point, New York; Army Reserve Officer Training Corps (ROTC), offered directly at 272 colleges and universities nationwide; and Officer Candidate School, where current enlisted soldiers can be selected to undergo training and evaluations that can result in their commissioning as an officer.

The U.S. Military Academy at West Point, established in 1802, is the premier source of officers for the Army, graduating about a thousand highly trained second lieutenants a year. Applicants must compete for nominations and then appointments—usually sponsored by a U.S. representative or senator—based on their overall high school record, physical fitness scores, and military test scores. USMA cadets are paid during their four years of attendance, and incur a five-year mandatory service obligation upon their graduation and commissioning as second lieutenants.

Army ROTC commissions about four thousand new second lieutenants a year—well over half the active Army's requirement. Students in Army ROTC attend their military science classes along with other college courses and normally receive elective academic credit. Cadets who successfully complete all requirements are commissioned as Army officers with an eight-year total commitment, at least six of which must be in an active, Reserve, or National Guard unit. If you want to be a pilot, you must be commissioned before you reach 29 years of age, and you must enter flight school no later than your 30th birthday.

The Army conducts Officer Candidate School (OCS) at Fort Benning, Georgia, for the active Army, the U.S. Army Reserve, and selected members of the Army National Guard. Army OCS at Fort Benning is an intensive 14-week course whose graduates are commissioned in one of 18 branches. Army National Guard OCS is also conducted by most of the 54 states and territories, under the accreditation and approved curriculum of the U.S. Army Infantry School at Fort Benning, just as is the federal OCS. Upon graduation, candidates are commissioned as Army second lieutenants and proceed to the Basic Officer Leader Course for their branch. Army aviator requirements for OCS graduates are the same as for ROTC.

Warrant Officer Candidate School (WOCS) is an intensive six-week course conducted at Fort Rucker, Alabama. Only candidates preselected for follow-on aviator duty can enter WOCS without significant prior military experience in a particular field such as logistics, personnel, ordnance, and so on. Graduates are appointed a Warrant Officer One and proceed to their warrant officer basic course.

Army flight training, both basic and advanced, is conducted for both commissioned and warrant officers at Fort Rucker. The 1st Aviation Brigade at Fort Rucker conducts training for Army aviators (as well as other services and students from other friendly nations' militaries) on the OH-58A/C, TH-67A+, OH-58D, UH-1, UH-60, CH-47, and AH-64D. Initial training of an Army aviator can take up to a year before assignment to an operational unit.

U.S. Navy and Marine Corps

There are four main pathways to becoming a Naval or Marine officer: the U.S. Naval Academy, Naval ROTC, Navy OCS, and the Marine Corps' Platoon Leaders' Course (PLC) and Officer Candidate Course (OCC).

Like the other services, the U.S. Navy operates its own service academy, this one at Annapolis, Maryland, established in 1845. USNA midshipmen include prospective Marine officers, since the Marine Corps is a Naval Service and part of the Department of the Navy. The Naval Academy provides the Navy and Marine Corps with about a thousand new officers annually.

Likewise, Navy ROTC is offered at more than 160 colleges and universities nationwide. It is organized much as the other services' programs, with the exception that Marine Option cadets normally have extra training activities. More than 40 percent of the Navy's new officer needs are met by NROTC.

Navy OCS is one of five officer training schools located at Naval Station Newport in Rhode Island. The 12-week course not only assesses candidates to see if they have what it takes, but gives them a working knowledge of the Navy afloat and ashore, preparing them to assume the responsibilities of a naval officer. Graduates of Navy OCS are commissioned as ensigns and attend technical training at a Navy technical school before reporting to their first fleet assignment.

The Marine Corps' Platoon Leaders Course is designed for college students who have not yet received their degree, splitting up their training into two six-week summer training courses. OCC candidates have already received their bachelor's degree, and so undergo a rigorous 10-week training and evaluation that focuses on military and leadership tasks, rapid absorption of military knowledge, physical training, and sleep deprivation. Graduates of both courses are commissioned as Marine second lieutenants and attend another six months of demanding instruction at The Basic School (TBS), where (regardless of their eventual specialty) they will learn to become Marine platoon commanders. After completion of TBS, they proceed to technical schools for their particular assigned jobs, and from thence to the field.

Coast Guard officers receive their commissions as ensigns from either the U.S. Coast Guard Academy or Coast Guard OCS, both of which are located in New London, Connecticut. Generally, they are then integrated into the Navy's flight training program as appropriate to the kind of aircraft they will fly for the Coast Guard.

To become a naval or Marine aviator, you must be between the ages of 19 and 27 at the time you apply for flight training. Waivers of up to 24 months can be made on a month-for-month basis for those with prior active-duty military service, up to a maximum age of 29. The standards are the same for naval flight officers (such as Radar Intercept Officers or RIOs), except NFOs may be granted a waiver of up to 48 months for active duty served before their 27th birthday—again on a month-for-month basis—to a maximum age of 31.

Naval flight officers in both the Navy and Marine Corps are not pilots, but they undergo much of the same training. They perform many "copilot" functions in aircraft with multi-person crews, specializing in airborne weapons and sensor systems. They are by no means "second fiddle," however—they can serve as tactical mission commanders (although the pilot in command, regardless of rank, is always responsible for the safe piloting of the aircraft) of single or multiple air assets during a particular mission. They may also command squadrons, carrier- and shore-based air wings and groups, Marine aircraft wings and groups, air facilities and stations, aircraft carriers, and carrier strike groups, as well as numbered fleets.

The pilot training program for new naval aviators takes 18 months altogether to complete. All students undergo common training at NAS Pensacola, where they are screened for one of three primary pipelines: helicopters, multi-engine propeller-driven aircraft, or strike warfare (jets). Upon completion of training at Pensacola, Student Naval Aviators (SNAs) enter their primary training pipelines, where they learn the basics of flying.

The Primary SNA learns visual flight operations, basic instrument flying, introduction to aerobatics, radio instrument navigation, and formation flying, and has several solo flights. All SNAs go through the same curriculum for Primary. At the end of Primary, the SNAs request the intermediate flight training path they would like to enter: Tailhook (jets), electronic warfare, maritime propeller, helicopter, or E-6B Mercury.

Intermediate Flight Training is different for each of the five platforms. SNAs learn more about navigation and air traffic control by flying to other training bases. Intermediate training for single-seat aircraft such as jet platforms will focus on individual skills, whereas the multi-seat platforms (such as maritime propellers, helicopters, and electronic warfare) will focus on crew coordination.

Advanced Flight Training is the final stage in earning aviator's wings. SNAs learn skills specific to the chosen platform such as air-to-air combat, bombing, search and rescue, aircraft carrier qualifications, over-water navigation, and low-level flying.

American Military Aviation

Military aircraft exist to perform one or more of four basic tasks: *transporting* people and/or things from one place to another; *bombing* enemy forces, facilities, or ships on the ground or at sea; *shooting*, either at enemy aircraft in the air or at enemies on the ground or afloat; or *observing* enemy actions and reporting them to other friendly forces.

In most cases, military aircraft operate at some level in support of surface (ground or sea) forces, since the only way to control what's happening on the surface for more than a short time is to *be* there. Or, said another way, ground units and air units often work together to accomplish the mission at hand.

Military aircraft can be divided into two general categories: *fixed-wing* aircraft, commonly referred to as *airplanes*; and *rotary-wing* aircraft, commonly referred to as *helicopters*, with *choppers* being a frequently used slang term. Troop transport helicopters are also referred to sometimes as *slicks*, and attack helicopters are sometimes called *snakes*.

Fixed-Wing Aircraft (Airplanes)

Fixed-wing aircraft are just that—their wings are "fixed," meaning that they don't move. These aircraft get their ability to fly (a quality called *lift*) from air passing over their wings, and are either pulled through the air by a corkscrew-type propeller or pushed through the air by the thrust from one or more jet engines.

American fixed-wing military aircraft are referred to by an alphanumeric system that consists of three parts and a given name. The first part, which consists of one or two letters, refers to the function of the airplane. Here are some of the most common functional designators:

A—Attack	F/A—Fighter/attack
B—Bomber	O—Observation
C—Cargo	P—Patrol (maritime)
AC—Cargo plane modified to perform an attack mission	Q—Unmanned aerial vehicle
KC—Cargo plane modified to perform an aerial refueling mission	R—Reconnaissance
	S—Antisubmarine
E—Electronic	T—Trainer
F—Fighter	U—Utility
	V—Vertical takeoff and/or landing

The second part of the designation is the model or sequence number, which, in combination with the functional designation, yields the series designation. A letter that follows the sequence number denotes the exact model or version; successive letters designate upgrades, modifications, and/or improvements. Thus, we can tell that an F/A-18C is a fighter of the F/A-18 series, and that it is a later or modified (or at least different) version from, for instance, an F/A-18A.

For ease of reference (and it doesn't hurt crew morale, either), American military aircraft are also given a name of some sort, usually one that relates to its mission, warlike qualities, or special characteristics. Thus, we have the F-117 Nighthawk, a stealthy fighter named after a bird of prey; the heavily armed B-52 Stratofortress, the EA-6B Prowler—even the A-10 Thunderbolt II, nicknamed the "Warthog," not much to look at, but without question rugged and powerful.

Rotary-Wing Aircraft (Helicopters)

Rotary-wing aircraft don't have wings in the same sense as fixed-wing aircraft. They get their lift from air passing over rotor blades that are spun around at high speed in a circle by an engine; the tilt of the rotors relative to the helicopter's body or fuselage governs the aircraft's movement forward and backward, left and right, up and down. A notable difference between rotary- and fixed-wing aircraft is that rotary-wing craft can hover.

The inside joke at some rotary-wing aviator schools is "A helicopter doesn't fly—it beats the air into submission." A helicopter does not have the same stable tendencies while in flight that a well-designed conventional airplane does. It maintains its altitude and flight by a variety of forces and controls that are actually working in opposition to each other; the pilot's job is to balance (or nearly balance) these forces for the helicopter to go where he wants it to go.

By worldwide convention, helicopters are categorized by maximum gross weight (aircraft, fuel, crew, equipment, weapons, and so on—the most weight with which the aircraft can take off under normal conditions): "light," "medium lift," and "heavy lift." Light helicopters are generally considered to be those below 12,000 pounds. Medium-lift helicopters are those that weigh from about 14,000 to 45,000 pounds, and heavy-lift helicopters are usually considered to be those that weigh more than 50,000 pounds. Some in the field reserve the *heavy-lift* term for the very largest copters—above 80,000 pounds. The exact amount of load a helicopter can carry depends on the model, the fuel on board, the exact distance to be flown, and atmospheric conditions.

U.S. military helicopters are designated by a system that has three alphanumeric parts and a given name. The first part, which consists of letters, refers to the function of the helicopter. Here are some of the most common designations:

AH—attack helicopter
CH—cargo helicopter
HH—heavy-lift and large rescue helicopters not otherwise classified
MH—modified for special operations
OH—observation, reconnaissance, and courier
SH—antisubmarine warfare (ASW) helicopter
UH—utility/general purpose; can move internal or external ("sling") loads

The second part of the designation is the model or sequence number, which, in combination with the functional designation, yields the series designation. A letter that follows the sequence number denotes the exact model or version; successive letters designate upgrades, modifications, and/or improvements. Thus, we can tell that a UH-60L is a utility helicopter of the UH-60 series, and that it is a later or modified (or at least different) version from, for instance, a UH-60A.

Most Army helicopters are named after Native American tribes (such as Blackhawk, Apache, and Iroquois). Most Navy and Marine Corps helicopters have a maritime reference in their names, such as Sea Hawk, Sea Knight, and so on.

This section will acquaint you with the most common types of aircraft used by the U.S. military today. See the section titled "Aviation Information" in Chapter 7 for more technical information.

Advanced Early-Warning Aircraft

E-2C Hawkeye

The E-2C Hawkeye is the U.S. Navy's all-weather, carrier-based tactical airborne warning and control system platform. It provides all-weather airborne early warning and command and control functions for the carrier battle group. Additional missions

E-2C Hawkeye

Description	High-wing, two-engine, propeller-driven aircraft
Mission/branches	Carrier-based all-weather airborne early-warning and control aircraft—provides early warning of approaching enemy aircraft and vectors (guides) interceptors into attack position; U.S. Navy
Crew	Crew of five: two pilots and three operators/controllers
Length	58 ft. (17.5 m)
Height	18 ft., 5 in. (5.6 m)
Wingspan	81 ft. (24.6 m)
Empty weight	39,290 lbs. (17,859 kg)
Max. gross weight	51,597 lbs. (23,453 kg)
Maximum speed	389 mph (338 knots)
Cruising speed	298 mph (259 knots)
Maximum altitude	37,200 ft. (11,275 m)
Maximum range	1,725 miles (1,500 nautical miles)
Powerplant(s)	Two Allison T56-A-427 turboprop engines, each generating approximately 5,100 hp
Payload capacity	N/A
Armament	N/A
Manufacturer	Prime contractor Northrop Grumman; Westinghouse, Lockheed Martin
Variants	E2C+: upgraded engines, radar, and avionics

include surface surveillance coordination, strike and interceptor control, search and rescue guidance, and communications relay.

An integral component of the carrier air wing, the E-2C carries three primary sensors: radar, identification friend-or-foe (IFF), and a passive detection system. These sensors are integrated through a computer that enables the E-2C to provide early warning, threat analyses, and control of counterstrikes against air and surface targets. The E-2C incorporates the latest electronics and avionics.

The AN/APS-145 radar provides fully automatic overland detection and tracking of targets anywhere within a three-million-cubic-mile surveillance envelope while simultaneously monitoring maritime traffic. An enhanced high-speed processor, which expands the number of targets or contacts that can be tracked at the same time by 400 percent over previous versions, is incorporated into the mission computer. Each E-2C can maintain all-weather patrols, tracking more than 600 targets automatically and simultaneously, while still controlling more than 40 airborne intercepts.

Early Hawkeye versions served with distinction in Vietnam; during the 1991 Gulf War, only 27 airplanes completed 1,183 sorties without loss. The E-2D Advanced Hawkeye—with upgraded avionics, computers, satellite communications, engines, and a new in-flight refueling capability—is currently undergoing operational testing; the first squadron is scheduled to be operational in 2014. Meanwhile, the Hawkeye continues to provide critical support to the fleet during the Global War on Terror, as well as in fulfilling international commitments and participation in joint and coalition exercises.

E-3 Sentry (AWACS)

The E-3 Sentry is an airborne warning and control system (AWACS) aircraft that provides all-weather surveillance, command, control, and communications for commanders. It is the premier air battle command and control aircraft in the world today.

The E-3 Sentry is a modified Boeing 707 commercial airframe with a rotating radar dome mounted above the fuselage. The dome is 30 feet (9.1 m) in diameter, 6 feet (1.8 m) thick, and is mounted 11 feet (3.3 m) above the fuselage on two struts. It employs a radar subsystem that permits surveillance from the surface up to the stratosphere, over both land and water, for more than 200 miles (320 km) for low-flying targets, and even farther for aircraft or other targets at medium-to-high altitudes. The radar, combined with an IFF subsystem, can look down to detect, identify, and track enemy and friendly low-flying aircraft by eliminating ground clutter returns that confuse other radar systems.

Multiple video screens on the aircraft display computer-processed information in graphic and tabular format. Console operators perform surveillance, identification, weapons control, battle management, and communications functions.

The radar and computer subsystems on the E-3 Sentry can gather and present both broad and detailed real-time battlefield information. The information can be sent to major command and control centers in rear areas or aboard ships in the operational theater, or to national command authorities in the United States.

In support of air-to-ground operations, the E-3 Sentry can provide direct information for interdiction, reconnaissance, airlift, and close air support of friendly ground forces. It can also provide information for air operations commanders to

E-3 Sentry (AWACS)

Description	Four-engine jet with large rotating radome mounted above fuselage
Mission/branches	Airborne surveillance, command, control, and communications; U.S. Air Force
Crew	Flight crew of four plus mission crew of 13–19 specialists
Length	145 ft., 6 in. (44 m)
Height	41 ft., 4 in. (12.5 m)
Wingspan	130 ft., 10 in. (39.7 m)
Rotodome	Diameter: 30 ft. (9.1 m) thickness: 6 ft. (1.8 m); mounted 11 ft. (3.33 m) above fuselage
Empty weight	162,000 lbs. (73,480 kg)
Max. gross weight	347,000 lbs. (156,150 kg)
Maximum speed	530 mph (353 knots)
Maximum altitude	Above 29,000 ft. (8,788 m)
Maximum range	1,000 miles (1,610 km)
Powerplant(s)	Four Pratt and Whitney TF33-PW-100A turbofan engines, each generating 21,000 lbs. of thrust
Payload capacity	N/A
Armament	N/A
Manufacturer	Prime contractor Boeing Aerospace Co.; radar contractor Northrop Grumman
Variants	N/A

gain and maintain control of the air battle, as well as directing fighters to engage enemy aircraft.

The E-3 Sentry is a jam-resistant system that has performed missions while experiencing heavy electronic countermeasures, and can fly for more than eight hours without refueling. Its range and on-station time can also be increased through in-flight refueling.

E-3 Sentry aircraft were among the first to deploy during Operation Desert Shield in 1990, where they immediately established an around-the-clock radar screen. During Operation Desert Storm, E-3s flew more than 400 missions and logged more than 5,000 hours of on-station time, providing radar surveillance and control to more than 120,000 coalition sorties. On September 11, 2001, E-3 Sentry aircraft were ordered to patrol the airspace over the eastern United States, which continues to this day.

The E-3's surveillance capabilities are also used in support of other U.S. government agencies during counterdrug operations. E-3 variants are operated by not only the United States, but also the North Atlantic Treaty Organization (NATO), the United Kingdom, France, and Saudi Arabia. E-3B and E-3C aircraft are currently being upgraded with improved computers and software—shortening time needed to execute either combat or search-and-rescue missions—to become the E-3G.

Since 2001, the E-3 has deployed in support of Operation Enduring Freedom in Afghanistan and Operation Iraqi Freedom in Iraq, as well as other worldwide U.S. operations.

Attack Aircraft

AV-8B Harrier II

The AV-8B Harrier V/STOL (Vertical/Short Takeoff and Landing) strike aircraft was designed to replace the earlier AV-8A and the A-4M light attack aircraft. The Harrier's unique capabilities allow it to operate from a variety of places inaccessible to other fixed-wing aircraft—such as amphibious ships, rapidly constructed expeditionary airfields, roads, forward area refueling points (FARPs), and damaged conventional airfields—while also able to operate from aircraft carriers and conventional land-based airfields.

The AV-8B Harrier II is typically assigned to conduct close air support using conventional and "smart" weapons, as well as conducting deep air support, including armed reconnaissance and air interdiction. This includes combat air patrol, armed escort missions, and offensive missions against enemy ground-to-air defenses. It

AV-8B Harrier II

Description	Vertical/short takeoff and landing single-engine jet
Mission/branches	Attack and destroy surface and air targets, escort helicopters; U.S. Marine Corps
Crew	One (pilot)
Length	46 ft., 4 in. (14.12 m)
Height	11 ft., 7 in. (3.55 m)
Wingspan	30 ft., 4 in. (9.25 m)
Empty weight	14,867 lbs. (6,758 kg)
Max. gross weight	31,000 lbs. (14,091 kg)
Maximum speed	675 mph (587 knots)
Maximum altitude	Over 50,000 ft. (15,152 m)
Maximum range	1,380 miles (1,200 nautical miles)
Powerplant(s)	One Rolls Royce Pegasus F402-RR-408A turbofan engine generating 22,200 lbs. of thrust
Payload capacity	Can carry up to 9,000 lbs. of ordnance on seven stations
Armament	• One fuselage-mounted 25-mm gun system • Standard air-to-ground load: six Mk 82; 500-lb. bombs • Standard air-to-air load: four AIM-9L/M Sidewinder missiles
Manufacturer	Airframe prime contractor: McDonnell Douglas; engine prime contractor: Rolls Royce
Variants	TAV-8B (trainer)

can operate at night and under instrument flight conditions; aerial refueling capabilities make up somewhat for the weight and space taken up by V/STOL-specific structures.

Operation Desert Storm in 1991 was highlighted by expeditionary AV-8B operations. The Harrier II was the first Marine Corps tactical strike platform to arrive in theater; three squadrons, totaling 60 aircraft, and one six-aircraft detachment operated ashore from an expeditionary airfield, while one squadron of 20 aircraft operated from a carrier at sea. The AV-8B flew 3,380 sorties for a total of 4,083 flight hours, with a mission capable rate of over 90 percent. More recent operations in Iraq and Afghanistan have seen Harriers in both close air support and reconnaissance roles of Marine operations.

Although scheduled for eventual replacement by the F-35B Lightning II (formerly known as the Joint Strike Fighter), the Harrier continues to be deployed worldwide in support of the Global War on Terror, as well as in fulfilling international commitments and partnerships.

F-117A Nighthawk

The F-117A Nighthawk is the world's first operational aircraft designed to exploit low-observable stealth technology. With a radar signature small enough to make it practically undetectable, the Nighthawk's unique shape, using flat angular panels, was the result of extensive computer work analyzing reflected radar waves. Once a shape was found with a sufficiently small radar cross-section, it was up to aircraft designers to find a way to make it fly. This feat was accomplished by advances in "fly-by-wire" computerized control systems that make constant adjustments to the F-117's control surfaces to maintain stability.

Further increasing the F-117's stealthy characteristics are coatings of radar-absorbent materials and radar-absorbent screens covering the engine inlets. Even the door edges are serrated to scatter radar waves. The aircraft's infrared signature has also been reduced by mixing the hot exhaust gases from its turbofan engines with cool air and ducting the mixture through a flat "platypus" exhaust.

Though called the "stealth fighter," the air-refuelable F-117 is actually intended to be an attack plane carrying precision-guided bombs deep within enemy territory. Standard armament consists of two 2,000-pound (905 kg) laser-guided bombs, but reports indicate that Maverick and HARM missiles are also regularly carried.

The F-117A employs a variety of weapons and is equipped with sophisticated navigation and attack systems, integrated into a state-of-the-art digital avionics suite that increases mission effectiveness and reduces pilot workload. Detailed planning for missions into highly defended target areas is performed by an automated mission planning system developed specifically to take advantage of the Nighthawk's unique capabilities.

First seeing action in December 1989 during Operation Just Cause in Panama, the F-117 has seen remarkable success in combat, such as in Operation Desert Storm in 1991, when 42 aircraft flew only two percent of the combat sorties against Iraq, yet accounted for 40 percent of the strategic targets attacked. The only Nighthawk combat loss to date occurred early in the Kosovo conflict, when poor mission planning allowed a Serbian missile battery to predict when an F-117 would fly through a certain area.

F-117A Nighthawk

Description	Low-observable, twin-engine, computer-assisted flying wing with V tail
Mission/branches	Precision stealth attack; U.S. Air Force
Crew	One (pilot)
Length	65 ft., 11 in. (20.1 m)
Height	12 ft., 5 in. (3.8 m)
Wingspan	43 ft., 4 in. (13.2 m)
Empty weight	29,500 lbs. (13,381 kg)
Max. gross weight	52,500 lbs. (23,814 kg)
Maximum speed	High subsonic
Cruising speed	646 mph (561 knots) at altitude
Maximum altitude	Classified
Maximum range	1,311 miles (1,140 nautical miles) with maximum payload; unlimited with aerial refueling
Powerplant(s)	Two General Electric F404-F1D2 turbofans generating 21,600 lbs. of thrust each
Payload capacity	At least 5,000 lbs.
Armament	Two 2,000-lb. laser-guided bombs; may also carry Maverick and/or HARM missiles
Manufacturer	Lockheed Aeronautical Systems Co.
Variants	N/A

F-117 Nighthawk units continue to participate in deployments supporting worldwide commitments in the Global War on Terror and other operations.

AC-130H/U Gunship

The AC-130H/U gunship's primary missions are close air support, air interdiction, and force protection. Close air support missions include those against enemy forces in contact with friendly ground forces, convoy escort, and urban operations. Air interdiction missions are conducted against preplanned targets or targets of opportunity. Force protection missions include airbase and facilities defense.

Based on the venerable C-130 Hercules airframe designed in the 1950s, the AC-130H Spectre packs an amazing wallop with its side-firing 40-millimeter and 105-millimeter cannons; the AC-130U Spooky has an additional 25-millimeter chain gun. Both variants integrate their heavy weapons with sophisticated sensor, navigation, and fire control systems to provide pinpoint firepower or area saturation during extended periods "loitering" near a target, even at night or in adverse weather. Sophisticated radar, television, and infrared sensors allow the gunship to visually or electronically identify friendly ground forces and targets anyplace, anytime.

The first AC-130 gunship made its appearance in 1967 over Laos and South Vietnam. Continuous upgrades of avionics, engines, and armament have kept these

AC-130 Spectre/Spooky

Description	Four-engine high-wing turboprop monoplane
Mission/branches	Close air support, air interdiction, force protection; USAF
Crew	Five officers (pilot, copilot, navigator, fire control officer, electronic warfare officer) and eight enlisted (flight engineer, TV operator, infrared detection set operator, loadmaster, four aerial gunners)
Length	97 ft., 9 in. (29.8 m)
Height	38 ft., 6 in. (11.7 m)
Wingspan	132 ft., 7 in. (40.4 m)
Empty weight	79,469 lbs. (35,797 kg)
Max. gross weight	155,000 lbs. (69,750 kg)
Maximum speed	300 mph (261 knots)
Cruising speed	300 mph (261 knots) maximum
Maximum altitude	25,000 ft. (7,576 m)
Maximum range	Approx. 1,495 miles (2,411 km); unlimited with air refueling
Powerplant(s)	Four Allison T56-A-15 turboprop engines, each generating 4,910 shaft hp
Payload capacity	N/A
Armament	AC-130H/U: 40-mm cannon and 105-mm cannon; AC-130U: 25-mm gun
Manufacturer	Lockheed/Boeing Corp.
Variants	AC-130H, AC-130U

gunships in demand on target. The AC-130U, introduced in 1995, employs the latest technologies and can attack two targets simultaneously. It also has twice the munitions capacity of the AC-130H, which was introduced in 1972.

During Operation Urgent Fury in Grenada in 1983, AC-130s suppressed enemy air defense systems and attacked ground forces, enabling the successful assault of the Point Salines Airfield. AC-130s also had a significant role during Operation Just Cause in Panama in 1989, when they destroyed Panamanian Defense Force Headquarters and numerous command and control facilities. During Operation Desert Storm in 1991, AC-130s provided close air support and airbase defense for ground forces, most notably during the Battle of Khafji. AC-130 gunships were also used during Operations Restore Hope and United Shield in Somalia, as well as playing a pivotal role supporting the NATO mission in Bosnia-Herzegovina. The AC-130H provided air interdiction against key targets in the Sarajevo area.

More recently, both aircraft variants have been employed in support of Operations Enduring Freedom and Iraqi Freedom, providing armed reconnaissance, interdiction, and direct support of ground troops engaged with enemy forces. In 2007, U.S. special operations forces used the AC-130 in attacks on suspected al-Qaeda militants in Somalia. The AC-130 has the distinction of never having a base under its protection lost to the enemy.

A-10 Thunderbolt II

The A-10 Thunderbolt II is the first U.S. Air Force aircraft specifically designed for close air support of ground forces. It is a simple, effective, and survivable twin-engine jet aircraft that can be used against all ground targets, including tanks and other armored vehicles.

The A-10 has excellent maneuverability at low airspeeds and low altitude, and is a highly accurate weapons delivery platform. It can loiter near battle areas for extended periods of time and operate under 1,000-foot (305 m) ceilings with only 1.5-mile (2.4 km) visibility. Its wide combat radius and short takeoff and landing capability permit operations in and out of locations near front lines and, by using night vision goggles (NVGs), A-10 pilots can conduct their missions during darkness.

Thunderbolt II pilots are protected by titanium armor that also protects parts of the flight control system. The aircraft can survive direct hits from armor-piercing and high-explosive projectiles up to 23 millimeters. Self-sealing fuel cells are protected by internal and external foam, and manual systems back up redundant hydraulic flight control systems. This permits the pilot to fly and land when hydraulic power is lost due to malfunction or battle damage.

A-10 Thunderbolt II

Description	Twin-engine, twin-tail straight-wing jet
Mission/branches	Close air support of ground forces; U.S. Air Force
Crew	One pilot
Length	53 ft., 4 in. (16.2 m)
Height	14 ft., 8 in. (4.4 m)
Wingspan	57 ft., 6 in. (17.4 m)
Empty weight	21,519 lbs. (9,761 kg)
Max. gross weight	51,000 lbs. (22,950 kg)
Maximum speed	420 mph (Mach 0.56)
Maximum altitude	45,000 ft. (13,700 m)
Maximum range	800 miles (695 nautical miles)
Powerplant(s)	Two General Electric TF34-GE-100 turbofans, each generating 9,065 lbs. of thrust
Payload capacity	Up to 16,000 lbs. of mixed ordnance on eight under-wing and three under-fuselage pylon stations, potentially consisting of some combination of: 500-lb. Mk-82 or 2,000-lb. Mk-84 series low/high drag bombs; AIM-9 Sidewinder missiles; AGM-65 Maverick missiles; 2.75-in. rockets; incendiary cluster bombs; combined effects munitions; mine-dispensing munitions; laser- or electro-optically guided bombs; infrared countermeasure flares; electronic countermeasure chaff; electronic jamming pods; or illumination flares
Armament	One 30-mm GAU-8/A seven-barrel Gatling gun
Manufacturer	Fairchild Republic Co.
Variants	OA-10A (air controller), A-10C

The Thunderbolt II can be serviced and operated from bases with limited facilities near battle areas. Many of the aircraft's parts are interchangeable left and right, including the engines, main landing gear, and vertical stabilizers. The Thunderbolt II's 30-millimeter GAU-8/A Gatling gun can fire 3,900 rounds a minute and can defeat a variety of ground targets, including tanks and other armored vehicles.

The A-10's official name derives from the P-47 Thunderbolt of World War II, a heavily armed, reliable fighter that was particularly effective at close air support—but the A-10 is more commonly known by its nickname of "Warthog." As a secondary mission, it provides airborne forward air control, guiding other aircraft against ground targets. A-10s used primarily in this role are designated OA-10s.

In the Gulf War, A-10s flew 8,100 sorties and launched 90 percent of the Maverick missiles used in the entire conflict. In 2005, the entire A-10 fleet also began receiving upgrades to their fire control systems, electronic countermeasures, and ability to aim "smart" bombs; aircraft with this upgrade are redesignated A-10C. The Warthog continues to participate in an outstanding manner in ongoing worldwide operations in support of the Global War on Terror, and is not expected to be replaced until 2028 or later.

Bombers

B-1B Lancer

The B-1B is a stealthy, multi-role, swing-wing, long-range bomber, capable of flying a variety of conventional or nuclear missions at up to intercontinental distances without refueling, and then penetrating both present and predicted enemy air defenses. Although smaller than the B-52 it was designed to replace, it carries more weapons—but has only one-tenth the radar signature. The B-1B's electronic jamming equipment, infrared countermeasures, and radar warning systems add to its low radar cross-section to form a potent integrated aircraft defense system.

The first B-1 prototype in 1974 showed a then-unique design with movable wings that could sweep back along the blended geometry airframe, and four engines podded in pairs under the wing roots. Despite the plane's promising performance, the program was cancelled in 1977 to concentrate on production of air-launched cruise missiles. In 1981, then-president Ronald Reagan reactivated an improved program, and the B-1B was born, with a new mission (low-altitude/high-speed penetration) and new technology that gave it a radar cross-section of about three square feet—only a little larger than a swan.

The variable-geometry wing design and turbofan engines not only provide greater range and high speed at low levels, but they also enhance the bomber's survivability by allowing a short takeoff roll with the wing sweep at the "full forward" position. Once airborne, the wings are positioned for maximum cruise distance or high-speed penetration.

The B-1B's radar and inertial navigation systems enable aircrews to navigate globally, update mission profiles, and target coordinates while in flight, then deliver precision munitions without the need for ground-based navigation aids.

The B-1B holds almost 50 world records in its class for speed, payload, range, and time of climb. The B-1B was first used in combat in support of operations against Iraq during Operation Desert Fox in December 1998. In 1999, six B-1s were used in Operation Allied Force, delivering more than 20 percent of the total ordnance while flying less than two percent of the combat sorties. During the first six months of

B-1B Lancer

Description	Swing-wing four-engine heavy bomber
Mission/branches	Long-range, multi-role, heavy bomber; USAF, Air National Guard
Crew	Four (aircraft commander, pilot, offensive systems officer, defensive systems officer)
Length	146 ft. (44.5 m)
Height	34 ft. (10.4 m)
Wingspan	137 ft. (41.8 m) extended forward, 79 ft. (24.1 m) swept aft
Empty weight	Approximately 190,000 lbs. (86,183 kg)
Max. gross weight	477,000 lbs. (214,650 kg)
Maximum speed	900-plus mph (Mach 1.2 at sea level)
Maximum altitude	Over 30,000 ft. (9,144 m)
Maximum range	Intercontinental, unrefueled
Powerplant(s)	Four General Electric F-101-GE-102 turbofan engines with afterburner, generating 30,000-plus lbs. of thrust each
Payload capacity	Assorted conventional, precision, and/or nuclear capability, to include cruise missiles
Armament	Can deliver conventional and nuclear weapons, to include "smart" precision munitions
Manufacturer	Rockwell International, North American Aircraft
Variants	N/A

Operation Enduring Freedom, eight B-1s dropped nearly 40 percent of the total tonnage delivered by coalition air forces. This included nearly 3,900 Joint Direct Attack Munitions (JDAMs)—commonly known as "smart bombs" due to their integrated inertial guidance system connected to a Global Positioning System (GPS) receiver—or 67 percent of the total. In Operation Iraqi Freedom, B-1Bs have flown less than one percent of the combat missions while delivering 43 percent of the total JDAMs used. The B-1 continues to be deployed today in support of continuing operations.

B-2 Spirit Stealth Bomber

The B-2 Spirit is a multi-role stealth bomber capable of delivering conventional (including precision-guided standoff) and nuclear munitions. The combination of low-observable technologies with high aerodynamic efficiency and a large payload capacity gives the B-2 important advantages over other existing bombers.

The B-2's low observability—derived from a combination of reduced infrared, acoustic, electromagnetic, visual, and radar signatures—provides it greater freedom of action at high altitudes, increasing its range and providing a better field of view for the aircraft's sensors. Many aspects remain classified, but the B-2's composite materials, special coatings, and flying-wing design all contribute to its stealthiness. The fuselage is smoothly blended into the wings, and the four engines are mounted in pairs above the wings, ending well short of the W-shaped trailing edge to reduce the aircraft's infrared

B-2 Spirit Stealth Bomber

Description	Stealthy "flying wing" heavy bomber
Mission/branches	Multi-role stealth heavy bomber; USAF
Crew	Two pilots
Length	69 ft. (20.9 m)
Height	17 ft. (5.1 m)
Wingspan	172 ft. (52.12 m)
Empty weight	158,000 lbs. (71,668 kg)
Max. gross weight	336,500 lbs. (152,635 kg)
Maximum speed	High subsonic
Maximum altitude	50,000 ft. (15,152 m)
Maximum range	Approximately 6,000 miles, unrefueled
Powerplant(s)	Four General Electric F-118-GE-100 engines, generating 17,300 lbs. (7,847 kg) of thrust each
Payload capacity	Up to 40,000 lbs. (18,000 kg)
Armament	Variety of conventional, precision, and nuclear munitions
Manufacturer	Northrop Grumman Corp.
Variants	N/A

signature. There are no vertical stabilizers—advanced computerized fly-by-wire systems automatically provide stable flight for what is otherwise a purposely unstable design.

The B-2 has a crew of two, an aircraft commander and mission commander, compared to the B-1B's crew of four and the B-52's crew of five.

B-2s in a conventional role—staging from Whiteman Air Force Base (AFB) in Missouri, Diego Garcia, or Guam—can cover the entire world with just one refueling. B-2s made a stunning battlefield debut in the 1991 Gulf War and further proved their worth in Operation Allied Force, where they were responsible for destroying 33 percent of all Serbian targets in the first eight weeks, by flying nonstop to Kosovo from their home base in Missouri and back. In support of Operation Enduring Freedom, the B-2 flew one of its longest missions to date from Whiteman to Afghanistan and back. B-2s supporting early combat in Operation Iraqi Freedom flew 22 sorties from a forward operating location and 27 sorties from Whiteman AFB, releasing more than 1.5 million pounds of munitions. On February 1, 2009, the Air Force's newest command, Air Force Global Strike Command, assumed responsibility for the B-2 from Air Combat Command.

B-52 Stratofortress

The B-52H "BUFF" (translated in polite company as "Big Ugly Fat Fellow") is a long-range heavy bomber that can perform a variety of missions. Capable of high subsonic speeds at up to 50,000 feet (15,152 m), it can conduct aerial refueling and can carry nuclear or precision-guided conventional ordnance worldwide.

The aircraft's flexibility was evident during heavy use in the Vietnam War and Operation Desert Storm, and more recently in Operations Enduring Freedom and Iraqi Freedom.

A total of 744 B-52s of all models have been built, with the last, a B-52H, delivered in October 1962. Only the "H" model is still in the Air Force inventory, and all continue to be updated with improved avionics, radars, and other features. The H model can carry up to 20 air-launched cruise missiles.

B-52Hs can perform air interdiction, offensive counter-air, and even maritime operations. During Desert Storm, B-52s delivered 40 percent of all the munitions dropped by coalition forces. It is highly effective when used for ocean surveillance, and can assist the Navy in antiship and mine-laying operations. Two B-52s, in two hours, can monitor 140,000 square miles of ocean surface.

The B-52H was originally designed for nuclear standoff, but it now has the conventional warfare mission role, carrying different kinds of external pylons (and therefore different munition configurations) as needed under its wings.

All B-52s are equipped with an electro-optical viewing system that uses forward-looking infrared and high-resolution low-light television sensors to augment the targeting, battle assessment, flight safety, and terrain-avoidance system, thus further improving its combat ability and low-level flight capability. Pilots wear NVGs to enhance their night visual, low-level, terrain-following operations.

During the 1991 Gulf War, a B-52H flew what was then the world's longest bombing mission by flying nonstop from Barksdale AFB, Louisiana, to Baghdad,

B-52 Stratofortress

Description	High-wing eight-engine jet heavy bomber
Mission/branches	Conventional and nuclear bomber; USAF
Crew	Five: pilot, copilot, electronic warfare officer, radar navigator/weapons delivery officer, navigator
Length	159 ft., 4 in. (48.5 m)
Height	40 ft., 8 in. (12.4 m)
Wingspan	185 ft. (56.4 m)
Empty weight	Approximately 185,000 lbs. (83,250 kg)
Max. gross weight	488,000 lbs. (219,600 kg)
Maximum speed	650 mph (Mach 0.86)
Maximum altitude	50,000 ft. (15,152 m)
Maximum range	8,800 miles unrefueled (7,652 nautical miles)
Powerplant(s)	Eight Pratt & Whitney engines TF33-P-3/103 turbofans generating up to 17,000 lbs. of thrust each
Payload capacity	Up to 70,000 lbs. (31,500 kg)
Armament	Up to 27 internal weapons, 45–51 smaller munitions and 24–30 larger munitions; the external pylon holds nine weapons
Manufacturer	Boeing Military Airplane Co.
Variants	Only the B-52H is still in the USAF inventory.

releasing several cruise missiles, and returning to base unscathed—a 35-hour, non-stop combat mission.

Since 2001, B-52s have contributed to the success of Operation Enduring Freedom, providing the ability to loiter high above the battlefield and provide close air support with precision-guided munitions. And on March 21, 2003, at the beginning of Operation Iraqi Freedom, B-52Hs launched about 100 cruise missiles during a night mission.

While the B-52 original airframes exceed 40 years of age, new modifications and mission capabilities are constantly updating the aircraft. The current service life of the aircraft is projected to extend beyond 2040, and B-52s continue to support worldwide commitments and operations in the Global War on Terror.

Cargo Aircraft

C-2A Greyhound

The C-2A Greyhound, a twin-engine cargo aircraft designed to land on aircraft carriers, provides critical onboard delivery of passenger and cargo to the Navy's aircraft carriers. The cabin can readily accommodate cargo, passengers, or both; it is also equipped to accept litter patients in medical evacuation missions.

Priority cargo such as jet engines can be transported from shore to ship in a matter of hours. A cage system provides cargo restraint for loads during carrier launches and landings. The large aft cargo ramp and door and a powered winch allow straight-in rear cargo loading and offloading for fast turnaround.

C-2A Greyhound

Description	Twin-engine turboprop cargo aircraft capable of landing on aircraft carriers
Mission/branches	Carrier onboard cargo and passenger delivery; U.S. Navy
Crew	Four: pilot, copilot, crew chief, and loadmaster
Length	56 ft., 10 in. (17.3 m)
Height	15 ft., 10.5 in. (4.85 m)
Wingspan	80 ft., 7 in. (24.6 m)
Empty weight	73,746 lbs. (15,310 kg)
Max. gross weight	57,500 lbs. (26,082 kg)
Maximum speed	343 knots (394 mph/635 kph)
Maximum altitude	30,000 ft. (9,144 m)
Maximum range	1,300 nautical miles (1,495 miles)
Powerplant(s)	Two Allison T-56-A-425 turboprop engines, developing 4,600 shaft horsepower each
Payload capacity	10,000s lbs. (5,546 kg); can be configured for cargo, 26 passengers, 12 litter patients, or a combination thereof
Armament	N/A
Manufacturer	Grumman Aerospace Corp.
Variants	N/A

The C-2A's open-ramp flight capability also allows airdrop of supplies and personnel. This, plus its folding wings and an onboard auxiliary power unit for engine starting and ground power self-sufficiency in remote areas, provide an operational versatility found in no other cargo aircraft.

The C-2A even has a special operations mission role from time to time. These missions include personnel, combat rubber raiding craft (CRRC), and air cargo drops. The CRRC drops entail disembarking a team of divers and their equipment while airborne.

C-2As remain the mainstay of Carrier Onboard Delivery operations for the fleet worldwide, as they participate in not only Global War on Terror operations, but also international commitments, coalition exercises, and the like.

C-17 Globemaster III

The C-17, the newest airlift aircraft to enter the USAF inventory, is capable of rapid strategic delivery of troops and all types of cargo to main operating bases or directly to forward bases in theater. It is also able to perform theater airlift missions when required.

The aircraft is powered by the military version of the engine currently used on the Boeing 757. Cargo is loaded onto the C-17 through a large aft door that can accommodate military vehicles and palletized cargo. The C-17 can carry virtually all of the Army's air-transportable combat equipment, and can also airdrop paratroopers and cargo.

C-17 Globemaster III

Description	High-wing, four-engined jet cargo aircraft
Mission/branches	Cargo and troop transport; U.S. Air Force
Crew	Three: pilot, copilot, loadmaster
Length	173 ft., 11 in. (53.04 m)
Height	55 ft., 1 in. (16.8 m)
Wingspan	170 ft., 9 in. (to winglet tips) (51.81 m)
Empty weight	269,363 lbs. (122,181 kg)
Max. gross weight	585,000 lbs. (265,352 kg) (peacetime)
Maximum speed	More than 500 mph/450 knots (.77 Mach)
Maximum altitude	45,000 ft. (13,700 m) at cruising speed
Maximum range	2,800 miles (4,506.16 km) unrefueled; unlimited with in-flight refueling
Powerplant(s)	Four Pratt & Whitney F117-PW-100 turbofan engines producing 40,440 lbs. (18,343 kg) of thrust each
Payload capacity	102 troops/paratroops; 48 litter and 54 ambulatory patients and attendants; 170,900 lbs. (77,519 kg) of cargo
Armament	N/A
Manufacturer	Boeing [McDonnell Douglas Corp.]
Variants	N/A

The C-17's design allows it to operate from small, austere airfields—it can take off and land on runways as short as 3,000 feet (914.4 m) and as narrow as 90 feet (27.43 m). Even on such narrow runways, the C-17 can turn around by using its backing capability while performing a three-point turn.

In 1998, the C-17 was called upon to fly probably the most unusual humanitarian mission ever when a Globemaster III ferried Keiko, a 10,000-lb. (4,536 kg) killer whale, from his tank in Oregon to the Westman Islands off Iceland. The nonstop flight was uneventful and ultimately successful, although the C-17 blew several tires on landing. C-17s have delivered military cargo as well as humanitarian aid during Operation Enduring Freedom in Afghanistan, Operations Iraqi Freedom and New Dawn in Iraq, and elsewhere around the world. On March 26, 2003, 15 C-17s participated in the largest formation airdrop since World War II—the nighttime airdrop of 1,000 Army paratroopers over Bashur, Iraq, opening the northern front to combat operations. U.S. Air Force (USAF) C-17s have also been used to transport U.S. allies' military equipment, and a C-17 also accompanies the president of the United States on domestic and foreign visits.

The C-17 continues to provide critical movement of troops, supplies, and equipment worldwide in support of the Global War on Terror.

C-21A Learjet

The C-21A, the military version of the Learjet 35A, provides cargo and passenger airlift; it can also transport litters during medical evacuations. The C-21A's turbo-

C-21A Learjet

Description	Small low-wing twin jet engine passenger jet
Mission/branches	Passenger and cargo airlift; U.S. Army, U.S. Air Force
Crew	Two: pilot, copilot
Length	48 ft., 7 in. (14.7 m)
Height	12 ft., 3 in. (3.7 m)
Wingspan	39 ft., 6 in. (11.97 m)
Empty weight	10,119 lbs. (4,590 kg)
Max. gross weight	18,300 lbs. (8,235 kg)
Maximum speed	530 mph (Mach 0.81, 461 knots, 848 kph)
Maximum altitude	45,000 ft. (13,700 m)
Maximum range	2,306 miles (2,005 nautical miles)
Powerplant(s)	Two Garrett TFE-731-2-2B turbofan engines generating 3,500 lbs. (1,575 kg) thrust each
Payload capacity	Eight passengers and 42 cubic feet of cargo or luggage
Armament	N/A
Manufacturer	Learjet, Inc. (formerly Gates Learjet)
Variants	N/A

fan engines are pod-mounted on the sides of the rear fuselage. The swept-back wings have hydraulically actuated, single-slotted flaps. The aircraft has retractable tricycle landing gear, a single steerable nose gear, and multiple-disc hydraulic brakes.

The safety and operational capabilities of the C-21A are enhanced by the autopilot, color weather radar, and tactical air navigation system, as well as HF, VHF, and UHF radios.

C-130 Hercules

The C-130 Hercules' primary role is the intratheater (within theater) portion of the Air Force's airlift mission. The "Herc" or "Herky Bird" can operate from rough dirt strips and is the prime transport for dropping parachute troops and equipment into hostile areas. Basic and specialized versions accomplish a wide range of missions, including airlift support, Antarctic ice mission resupply, aeromedical missions, aerial spray missions, firefighting duties for the U.S. Forest Service, and disaster relief missions around the world.

The C-130 can deliver personnel, equipment, or supplies either by landing or by various aerial delivery modes. In its personnel carrier role, the C-130 can accommodate 92 combat troops or 64 fully equipped paratroops on side-facing seats. For medical evacuations, it carries 74 litter patients and two medical attendants. Paratroopers exit the aircraft through two doors on either side of the aircraft behind the landing gear fairings, while the rear ramp is used for airdrops.

C-130J Hercules

Description	High-wing four-engined turboprop cargo aircraft
Mission/branches	Airlift of cargo, passengers, or paratroops; USAF, USMC; other government agencies
Crew	Five to six: two pilots, navigator, flight engineer, and loadmaster, plus extra loadmaster for airdrop missions
Length	97 ft., 9 in. (29.3 m)
Height	38 ft., 10 in. (11.9 m)
Wingspan	132 ft., 7 in. (39.7 m)
Empty weight	76,469 lbs. (34,686 kg)
Max. gross weight	155,000 lbs. (69,750 kg) peacetime, 175,000 lbs. (79,379 kg) wartime
Maximum speed	417 mph (Mach 0.59) at 22,000 ft. (6,706 m)
Maximum altitude	28,000 ft. (8,615 m) with 42,000 lbs. (19,051 kg) of payload
Maximum range	2,071 miles (1,800 nautical miles)
Powerplant(s)	Four Rolls-Royce AE 2100D3 turboprops generating 4,700 hp each
Payload capacity	Up to 45,000 lbs. (20,412 kg) of cargo; up to 92 troops, 64 paratroops, or 74 litter patients
Armament	N/A
Manufacturer	Lockheed Aeronautical Systems Company

More than five decades have passed since the Air Force issued its original design specification, yet the remarkable C-130 remains in production. The versatile, high-wing turboprop has accumulated over 20 million flight hours. It is the preferred transport aircraft for many U.S. government services and over 60 foreign countries. The basic airframe has been modified to hundreds of different configurations to meet ever-changing mission requirements. Most earlier versions are now retired from the U.S. military, but many are still in use elsewhere.

The C-130J is the latest addition to the C-130 fleet, replacing the aging C-130Es and C-130Hs. The C-130J incorporates state-of-the-art technology (new propellers and engines, improved navigation and avionics) to reduce manpower requirements and operating costs. It climbs faster and higher, flies farther at a higher cruise speed, and takes off and lands in a shorter distance than older models. The C-130J-30 is a stretch version, adding 15 feet to the fuselage length for more cargo capacity.

The WC-130E/H and C-130J are used in weather reconnaissance and aerial sampling. The HC-130 is an extended-range combat rescue version. The U.S. Marine Corps has replaced its aging KC-130F tanker fleet with KC-130Js. The J tanker is capable of refueling both fixed-wing and rotary-wing aircraft, as well as conducting rapid ground refueling.

Fighter Aircraft

F-15 Eagle

The F-15 Eagle is an extremely maneuverable all-weather tactical fighter designed to gain and maintain aerial combat superiority through a combination of maneuverability, acceleration, range, weapons, and avionics.

The F-15's maneuverability and acceleration are achieved through high engine thrust-to-weight ratio and low wing loading (the ratio of aircraft weight to its wing area). The F-15's multimission avionics system includes a heads-up display—instrument readouts projected on the canopy in front of the pilot so that he or she doesn't have to look down into the cockpit.

The Eagle can be armed with combinations of four different air-to-air weapons: AIM-7F/M Sparrow missiles or AIM-120 Advanced Medium Range Air-to-Air Missiles (AMRAAM) on its lower fuselage corners, AIM-9L/M Sidewinder or AIM-120 missiles on two pylons under the wings, and an internal 20-millimeter Gatling gun with 940 rounds of ammunition in the right wing root. Low-drag conformal fuel tanks can also be attached to hug the sides of the fuselage under each wing, reducing the need for in-flight refueling and increasing time in the combat area.

The F-15C is an improved version of the original F-15A single-seat air superiority fighter with upgraded avionics, increased internal fuel capacity, and a higher gross takeoff weight. The F-15D is a two-seat student/instructor variant of the single-seat F-15C.

The two-seat, all-weather, day/night F-15E Strike Eagle is configured for deep strikes far behind enemy lines, attacking high-value targets with a variety of precision-guided "smart" munitions or more conventional "dumb" (unguided) bombs.

Export variations of the Eagle have been chosen by several foreign military customers to modernize their air forces—Japan, Israel, Saudi Arabia, South Korea, and Singapore notably among them.

F-15 Eagle

Description	Two-engine, high-wing, twin-tail jet fighter
Mission/branches	Tactical/air superiority fighter/USAF
Crew	F-15A/C: one pilot; F-15B/D: two pilots; F-15E: pilot and weapons systems officer (WSO)
Length	63 ft., 9 in. (19.4 m)
Height	18 ft., 8 in. (5.7 m)
Wingspan	42 ft.,10 in. (13.1 m)
Empty weight	30,300 lbs. (13,744 kg)
Max. gross weight	68,000 lbs. (30,600 kg) (C/D models)
Maximum speed	1,875 mph (Mach 2.5-plus) at 45,000 ft. (13,716 m)
Maximum altitude	65,000 ft. (19,697 m)
Maximum range	3,450 miles (3,000 nautical miles) ferry range with conformal fuel tanks and three external fuel tanks
Powerplant(s)	Two Pratt & Whitney F100-PW-100 turbofan engines with afterburners generating 25,000 lbs. (11,340 kg) of thrust each
Payload capacity	Varies based on model
Armament	Internal 20-mm multibarrel gun, up to eight missiles under wings and on fuselage corners; F-15E bomb load 8,000 lbs. (3,636 kg)
Manufacturer	Boeing (formerly McDonnell Douglas)
Variants	F-15A, B/D (two-seat trainer), C (upgraded air superiority), and E Strike Eagle (ground attack)

After the September 11, 2001, attacks an F-15E squadron was rerouted to Afghanistan to support Operation Enduring Freedom. Within weeks, it became hard to find meaningful targets because almost all of them had been destroyed. The most frequent targets during the rest of the war were small groups of enemy fighters, vehicles, and convoys, using not only bombs but the internal 20-millimeter gun as well.

During the active phase of the Iraq War in 2003, F-15Es were credited with destroying 60 percent of the Iraqi Medina Republican Guard; they also scored hits on 65 MiGs on the ground and destroyed key air defense and command and control facilities deep in well-defended areas of Baghdad. To date, no air superiority versions of the F-15 (A/B/C/D models) have ever been shot down by enemy forces, with F-15s of all nations' air forces compiling an impressing 106 kills to zero losses.

Although ongoing upgrades to F-15C and D models include digital engine controls and improved radar, they are slowly being replaced in USAF service by the F-22 Raptor. The F-15E Strike Eagle, however, will remain in service for years to come because of its different air-to-ground role and the lower number of hours on most E-model airframes. The F-15 is expected to be in service with the USAF until at least 2025.

F-16 Fighting Falcon

The F-16 Fighting Falcon is a relatively small, highly maneuverable multi-role fighter that has proven itself in both air-to-air and air-to-surface roles. In its air combat role, the F-16 can locate targets in all weather conditions and sort out low-flying aircraft from radar ground clutter. In its air-to-surface role, the F-16 can fly more than 500 miles (860 km), deliver its weapons with superior accuracy under any weather conditions, defend itself against enemy aircraft, and return to its starting point.

The successful F-16 series' origin had its birth in dissatisfaction with U.S. fighter performance in the Vietnam War. Despite the success of the small, maneuverable F-86 Sabrejet during the Korean War, U.S. fighter design philosophy after that had changed to emphasize speed, altitude, and radar capability at the expense of maneuverability, pilot vision, and other characteristics needed for close-up aerial combat—dogfighting. After unsatisfactory close-in performance by the F-4 Phantom over Vietnam, the Department of Defense began a program stressing low cost, small size, and very high performance at speeds below Mach 1.6 and altitudes below 40,000 feet (12,192 m).

The resulting design incorporated highly innovative technologies that matched or exceeded many capabilities of the more expensive, twin-engined F-15. This included

F-16 Fighting Falcon

Description	Single-engine jet fighter
Mission/branches	Multi-role fighter; USAF, USN (for adversary training)
Crew	One or two, depending on model
Length	49 ft., 5 in. (14.8 m)
Height	16 ft. (4.8 m)
Wingspan	32 ft., 8 in. (9.8 m)
Empty weight	19,200 lbs. (8,641 kg)
Max. gross weight	37,500 lbs. (16,875 kg)
Maximum speed	1,500 mph (Mach 2 at altitude)
Maximum altitude	Above 50,000 ft. (15,152 m)
Maximum range	Over 2,425 miles (3,900 km), depending on configuration
Powerplant(s)	F-16C/D: one Pratt & Whitney F100-PW-200/220/229 or GE F110-GE-100/129 engine generating 27,000 lbs. (12,247 kg) of thrust
Payload capacity	Varies based on model
Armament	One internal 20-mm multibarrel gun; up to six air-to-air missiles, conventional air-to-air and air-to-surface munitions, and electronic countermeasure pods
Manufacturer	Lockheed Martin Corp.
Variants	A/C models single-seat multi-role; B/D models two-seat; CJ/DJ models one- and two-place Suppression of Enemy Air Defense (SEAD) versions

"fly-by-wire" technology where the pilot's controls, instead of being physically connected to control surfaces with hydraulic assistance, were connected to quadruple-redundant computers that managed the elevators, ailerons, and rudder movements, enabling a highly efficient but aerodynamically unstable design to be flown safely.

Previous fighters were designed to take up to 7Gs (seven times the force of gravity due to acceleration), mainly because most pilots, even with a G-suit, could not handle more. The F-16 seatback was reclined 30 degrees instead of the usual 13 to let the pilot withstand up to 9Gs by reducing the vertical distance between head and heart. The traditional center-mounted control stick was replaced by a smaller stick on the right console, with an armrest to relieve the pilot of the need to support his arm when weighing nine times normal.

The F-16's bubble canopy also allows 360-degree horizontal vision and unprecedented vision over the sides. The single engine helped minimize weight and drag, and that engine being a turbofan rather than a pure jet engine yielded higher fuel efficiency. With more room for fuel and a fuel-efficient engine, the F-16 rolled back the thought that small aircraft have to be short-ranged.

Because the F-16 carries no radar-guided missiles, it can only fight within visual range, but it was given a technologically advanced small radar, with excellent lookdown capability. Most importantly, the radar was integrated with the head-up display (HUD) so that, by looking at that image, the pilot was looking exactly where the target would become visible as he approached it.

The F-16B is the tandem-seat student/instructor variant of the A model. Likewise, the single-seat C model, with its improvements in avionics, radar, range, and targeting capabilities, has its two-seat counterpart in the D model. The F-16CJ comes in C (single-seat) and D (two-seat) versions, and is designed for Suppression of Enemy Air Defense (SEAD). This specialized version of the F-16 became the sole provider for Air Force SEAD missions when the F-4G Wild Weasel was retired from the Air Force inventory.

The F-16 is currently operated by the United States and 25 other air forces worldwide. It provides a relatively low-cost, high-performance weapon system for the United States and allied nations. During the 1991 Gulf War, F-16s flew over 13,500 sorties with tremendous target success and only four losses, and it has served with similar success in operations in both Afghanistan and Iraq.

The F-16 is scheduled to remain in service with the U.S. Air Force until 2025. The planned replacement is the F-35 Lightning II, which will gradually begin replacing a number of multi-role aircraft among the program's member nations. The Fighting Falcon continues to operate worldwide in support of operations in the Global War on Terror.

F/A-18 Hornet/Super Hornet

The F/A-18 is a twin-engine, midwing, all-weather fighter and attack aircraft. It was designed to be able to perform traditional strike missions such as interdiction and close air support without compromising its fighter capabilities. In its fighter mode, the F/A-18 is used primarily as a fighter escort and for fleet air defense; in its attack mode, it is used for force projection, interdiction, and close and deep air support.

Currently flown by the Navy's Blue Angels flight demonstration squadron and most carrier-based Navy fighter squadrons, the F/A-18 demonstrated its capabilities

F/A-18 Super Hornet

Description	Multi-role, midwing, two-engine, twin-tailed jet fighter
Mission/branches	Fighter/attack (strike) carrier aircraft; U.S. Navy
Crew	A/C/E models: one; B/D/F models: two
Length	60 ft., 4 in. (18.5 m)
Height	16 ft. (4.8 m)
Wingspan	44 ft., 11 in. (13.7 m)
Empty weight	30,564 lbs. (13,864 kg)
Max. gross weight	66,000 lbs. (29,932 kg)
Maximum speed	Mach 1.7+
Maximum altitude	50,000+ ft. (15,152+ m)
Maximum range	(With external tanks) Fighter: 1,586 miles (2,537 km); Attack: 1,533 miles (2,453 km)
Powerplant(s)	Two General Electric F414-GE-400 engines generating 22,000 lbs. (9,977 kg) of thrust per engine
Payload capacity	17,750 lbs. of munitions
Armament	One M61A1/A2 20-mm Vulcan cannon; can carry a combination of AIM-9 Sidewinder, AIM-7 Sparrow, AIM-120 AMRAAM, Harpoon, Harm, Shrike, SLAM, SLAM-ER, Walleye, Maverick missiles; Joint Stand-Off Weapon (JSOW); Joint Direct Attack Munition (JDAM); various general purpose bombs, mines, or rockets
Manufacturer	McDonnell-Douglas

and versatility during Operation Desert Storm, shooting down enemy fighters and subsequently bombing enemy targets with the same aircraft on the same mission, and reportedly breaking records for tactical aircraft in availability, reliability, and maintainability. The aircraft's survivability was proven by Hornets taking direct hits from surface-to-air missiles, recovering successfully, being repaired quickly, and flying again the next day.

The F/A-18A and C were single-seat aircraft, while the B and D models were two-seaters. The bigger, more powerful E and F Super Hornet models entered service in the mid-1990s; the E model is a single-seater, whereas the F model is a two-seater. The E and F models have replaced almost all earlier models in active service. All F/A-18s can be configured quickly to perform either fighter or attack roles or both, through selective use of external equipment to accomplish specific missions.

F/A-18s performed superbly in the Persian Gulf War in 1990–1991, and Navy and Marine Super Hornets have continued the tradition of excellence in support of Operation Enduring Freedom in Afghanistan and Operation Iraqi Freedom in Iraq. With current and ongoing upgrades and modifications, the F/A-18 is expected to continue serving well into the 2020s, if not beyond.

F-22 Raptor

The F-22 is the newest air superiority fighter for the Air Force. Its combination of stealth, supercruise, maneuverability, and integrated avionics, coupled with improved supportability, represents an exponential leap in war-fighting capabilities. It is designed to penetrate enemy airspace and achieve a first-look, first-kill capability against multiple targets.

The Raptor's low-observable ("semi-stealthy") characteristics greatly increase the aircraft's survivability and lethality by making it very difficult for the enemy to successfully track or attack the F-22. Integrated avionics allow F-22 pilots unprecedented awareness of enemy forces through the fusion of on- and off-board information. The Raptor's "supercruise" capability—the ability to cruise at supersonic airspeeds (greater than 1.5 Mach) without using afterburner—enhances weapons effectiveness, allows rapid movement through the battle space, and reduces the enemy's time to counterattack. The F-22's engine is expected to be the first to provide the ability to fly faster than the speed of sound for an extended period of time without the high fuel consumption characteristic of aircraft that use afterburners to achieve supersonic speeds. It is expected to provide high performance and high fuel efficiency at slower speeds as well.

The F-22's combat configuration is "clean"—that is, all armament is carried internally, with no external weapons. This is an important factor in the F-22's

F-22 Raptor

Description	Single-seat, two-engine, twin-tailed fighter
Mission/branches	Air superiority fighter
Crew	One pilot
Length	62 ft., 1 in. (18.9 m)
Height	16 ft., 8 in. (5.1 m)
Wingspan	44 ft., 6 in. (13.6 m)
Empty weight	43,340 lbs. (19,700 kg)
Max. gross weight	83,500 lbs. (38,000 kg)
Maximum speed	Mach 2 class
Maximum altitude	Above 50,000 ft. (15,152 m)
Maximum range	More than 1,850 miles (29.77 km) ferry range with two external wing fuel tanks
Powerplant(s)	Two Pratt & Whitney F119-PW-100 engines generating 35,000 lbs. of thrust each
Payload capacity	(Not released)
Armament	One M61A2 20-mm cannon with 480 rounds; side weapon bays can carry two AIM-9 infrared air-to-air missiles and main weapon bays can carry (air-to-air loadout) six AIM-120 radar-guided air-to-air missiles or (air-to-ground loadout) two 1,000-lb. GBU-32 JDAMs and two AIM-120 radar-guided air-to-air missiles
Manufacturer	Lockheed-Martin/Boeing/Pratt & Whitney
Variants	N/A

stealth characteristics, and it improves the fighter's aerodynamics by dramatically reducing drag, which, in turn, improves the F-22's range. The F-22 has four under-wing hardpoints, each capable of carrying 5,000 pounds (2,268 kg).

In the air-to-ground configuration the aircraft can carry two 1,000-pound (452.5 kg) GBU-32 Joint Direct Attack Munitions (JDAMs) internally and will use onboard avionics for navigation and weapons delivery support. In the future, air-to-ground capability will be enhanced with the addition of an upgraded radar and up to eight small-diameter bombs. The Raptor will also carry two AIM-120s and two AIM-9s in the air-to-ground configuration.

Advances in low-observable technologies provide significantly improved survivability and lethality against air-to-air and surface-to-air threats. The F-22A brings stealth into the day, enabling it to protect not only itself but also other assets.

The F-22A is projected to have better reliability and maintainability than any fighter aircraft in history. An F-22A squadron will require less than half as much airlift capacity as an F-15 squadron to deploy. Increased F-22A reliability and maintainability will pay off in less manpower required to fix the aircraft and the ability to operate more efficiently.

F-35 Lightning II

The F-35 Lightning II is the result of the Defense Department's Joint Strike Fighter (JSF) program, which sought to build a multi-role fighter optimized for the air-to-ground role with secondary air-to-air capability. The JSF requirement was to meet the needs of the Air Force, Navy, Marine Corps, and allies, with improved survivability, precision engagement capability, and reduced costs. By using many of the same technologies developed for the F-22, the F-35 has the opportunity to capitalize on common parts and systems, as well as modularity, to maximize affordability.

Lockheed Martin developed four versions of the Joint Strike Fighter to fulfill the needs of the Navy, Marine Corps, Air Force, and the United Kingdom's Royal Air Force and Navy. All versions have the same fuselage and internal weapons bay, common outer mold lines with similar structural geometries, identical wing sweeps, and comparable tail shapes. The weapons are stored in two parallel bays aft of the main landing gear. The canopy, radar, ejection system, subsystems, and avionics are common among the different versions, as is the core engine, based on the F119 by Pratt & Whitney.

The Air Force expects to procure well over a thousand F-35As to complement the F-22 Raptor and eventually replace the F-16 as an air-to-ground strike aircraft. The A model includes an internal gun, infrared sensors, and a laser designator. This is the technologically simplest version of the F-35, in that it does not require hover or aircraft carrier capability. Therefore, it does not require the vertical thrust, ability to perform catapult launches, and strengthened structure to handle carrier-deck arrested landings. At the same time, because replacement of the F-16 series by the F-35A will entail a significant payload reduction, the F-35 faces a very demanding one-shot/one-kill requirement.

The distinguishing feature of the USMC version, the F-35B, is its short takeoff/vertical landing capability. There will not be an internally mounted gun, but an external gun can be fitted. This version requires controllability in all axes of movement while hovering, much like a helicopter. Another critical design feature is its impact on the ground surface beneath it during hover. The USMC expects this

F-35 Lightning II

Description	Stealthy, supersonic, two-engine STOVL strike fighter
Mission/branches	Multi-role (primarily air-to-ground) fighter; USAF, USN, USMC
Crew	One pilot
Length	50 ft., 6 in. (15.2 m)
Height	16 ft., 5 in. (5.1 m)
Wingspan	35 ft. (10.5 m)
Empty weight	30,697 lbs. (13,953 kg)
Max. gross weight	62,000 lbs. (28,123 kg)
Maximum speed	Over 1,500 mph
Maximum altitude	Over 65,000 ft. (21,000 m)
Maximum range	Over 1,000 miles (1,609 km)
Powerplant(s)	Interchangeable engines manufactured by Pratt & Whitney (F135) and General Electric (F136). Engine thrust rated at 17,600 lbs. (7,983 kg), roll nozzle thrust rated at 3,700 lbs. (1,678 kg), and lift fan thrust rated at 18,500 lbs. (8,392 kg) each
Payload capacity	Varies depending on model
Armament	Both internal weapons bays are capable of carrying one 2,000-lbs. (907.19 kg) class weapon and one AMRAAM each. Seven external stations provide an assortment of air-to-air and air-to-ground weapons, including the full range of "smart" (precision-guided) munitions
Manufacturer	Lockheed Martin/Northrop Grumman/British Aerospace
Variants	F-35A

stealthy, supersonic, multi-role STOVL strike fighter to eventually replace the AV-8B Harrier and F/A-18C/D Hornet, performing five of the six functions of marine aviation: offensive air support, anti-air warfare, electronic warfare, aerial reconnaissance, and control of aircraft and missiles.

The F-35C model, designed for the Navy, has larger wing and tail control surfaces for low-speed carrier approaches, as well as leading-edge flaps and foldable wing-tip sections. The larger wing area also provides the F-35C with an increased payload capability. To support the stresses of carrier landings and catapult launches, it has a strengthened internal structure, higher-load landing gear, and, of course, an arresting hook. The F-35C has twice the range on internal fuel as the F/A-18C. And, like the USAF version, the Navy version will incorporate an internal gun and sensors, making it a worthwhile complement to the F/A-18 Hornet.

The A model is expected to be in operational service about 2011, the B model in 2012, and the C model in 2014.

Special Purpose Aircraft

E-6B Mercury

The Boeing E-6 Mercury operates as an airborne command post and communications center, relaying instructions from the National Command Authority, for instance, to fleet ballistic missile submarines—giving it the semi-official suffix of TACAMO, for "Take Charge and Move Out."

Like the E-3 Sentry AWACS and KC-135 tanker aircraft, the E-6 Mercury is adapted from Boeing's 707-300 commercial airliner. Only one version of the E-6 currently exists, the E-6B; this upgraded version of the E-6A now includes a battle staff area for the U.S. Strategic Command Airborne Command Post and new flight deck systems, replacing the aging 1970s-style cockpit with an off-the-shelf Boeing 737NG cockpit. This greatly increases the situational awareness of the pilot and saves significant cost over a custom avionics package.

The E-6A was designed to replace the EC-130 and was accepted by the U.S. Navy in August 1989; 16 were delivered up to 1992. The first E-6B was accepted in December 1997, and the entire E-6 fleet was then modified to the E-6B standard.

EA-6B Prowler

The EA-6B Prowler provides a long-range, all-weather umbrella of advanced electronic countermeasures over strike aircraft, ground troops, and ships by jamming enemy radar, electronic data links, and communications.

E-6B Mercury

Description	Modified Boeing 707; four-engine low-wing jet
Mission/branches	Airborne command post/communications center; USN
Crew	22
Length	150 ft., 4 in. (45.8 m)
Height	42 ft., 5 in. (12.9 m)
Wingspan	148 ft., 4 in. (45.2 m)
Empty weight	106,500 lbs. (48,308 kg)
Max. gross weight	342,615 lbs. (154,400 kg)
Maximum speed	585 mph (960 kph)
Maximum altitude	39,650 ft. (12,200 m)
Maximum range	1,150 miles (1,850.75 km)
Powerplant(s)	Four CFMI CFM-56-2A-2 high-bypass turbofans
Payload capacity	N/A
Armament	N/A
Manufacturer	Boeing
Variants	N/A

To house the extra electronics, the basic A-6 airframe was stretched and strengthened to accommodate a four-seat (instead of the original two) cockpit, and a forward equipment bay and a pod-shaped fairing on the vertical fin were added. Capable of operating from both carriers and advanced bases, the EA-6B Prowler is included in every aircraft carrier deployment. After Department of Defense restructuring in the mid-1990s that saw the retirement of the Air Force's EF-111 Raven, the EA-6B was left as the U.S. military's only radar jammer. Five new squadrons were organized; four of these were dedicated to supporting Air Force expeditionary wings.

The Prowler can carry up to five pods (one belly-mounted and two on each wing) that each contain two jamming transmitters covering one of seven frequency bands. The EA-6B can carry a mix of pods, fuel tanks, and missiles, depending on mission requirements. The EA-6B's tail-fin pod houses sensitive surveillance receivers, capable of detecting hostile radar emissions at long range.

Carrier-based Marine Prowlers supported joint operations against Libya in 1986. During Desert Shield, the squadron flew 936 sorties for a total of over 2,100 hours. Marine Prowlers flew 495 combat missions totaling 1,622 hours, supporting the full spectrum of joint and combined missions.

The EA-6B has seen missions in Vietnam, the Middle East, Southwest Asia, and the Balkans, and is frequently flown in support of USAF missions. Prowlers have participated in a multitude of joint operations in Afghanistan and Iraq, as well as maintaining other U.S. commitments worldwide. According to news reports, the Prowler has been used in an anti-improvised explosive device (IED) role by jamming remote detonation devices such as garage door openers and cellular telephones.

EA-6B Prowler

Description	Twin-engine, midwing jet; variant of A-6 Intruder attack plane
Mission/branches	Electronic countermeasures; USN, USMC, USAF
Crew	Four: pilot and three electronic countermeasures officers
Length	59 ft., 10 in. (17.7 m)
Height	16 ft., 8 in. (4.9 m)
Wingspan	53 ft. (15.9 m)
Empty weight	33,600 lbs. (15,273 kg)
Max. gross weight	61,500 lbs. (27,921 kg)
Maximum speed	Over 500 knots (575 mph, 920 kph)
Maximum altitude	40,000 ft. (12,192 m)
Maximum range	1,150 m (1,000 nautical miles, 1,840 km)
Powerplant(s)	Two Pratt & Whitney J52-P408 turbofan engines, generating 10,400 lbs. (4,767 kg) of thrust per engine
Armament	AGM-88A HARM missile
Manufacturer	Northrup Grumman Aerospace Corporation

In 2009, the Navy EA-6B Prowler community began transitioning to the EA-18G Growler, a new electronic warfare variant of the F/A-18 Super Hornet. This transition is expected to be complete by 2014, but updated Marine Prowlers are scheduled to keep flying until at least 2019.

P-3 Orion

The P-3C is a land-based, long-range antisubmarine warfare (ASW) patrol aircraft. The avionics system integrates all tactical displays and monitors, coordinates navigation information, and accepts sensor inputs for tactical display and storage; it also can automatically launch ordnance and provide flight information to the pilots.

The P-3C can operate alone or as support to many different customers, including aircraft carrier battle groups and amphibious readiness groups. Infrared and long-range electro-optical cameras, plus special imaging radar, allow it to monitor activity from a comfortable distance. It can stay aloft for extremely long periods, and its four powerful Allison turboprop engines can fly at almost any altitude. And like all good hunters, it has no problem carrying weapons—it can carry a variety of weapons internally and on wing pylons, such as the Harpoon antisurface missile, the MK-50 torpedo, and the MK-60 mine.

Each maritime patrol aviation (MPA) squadron has nine aircraft and about 60 officers and 250 enlisted personnel. Each eleven-person crew includes both officer and enlisted personnel. In peacetime, MPA squadrons deploy to sites outside the United States for about six months and spend a year between deployments training at home.

P-3 Orion

Description	Four-engined low-wing turboprop
Mission/branches	Antisubmarine/antisurface warfare (ASW/ASUW); U.S. Navy
Crew	5 minimum flight crew; 11 normal crew; 21 max
Length	117 ft., 6 in. (35.6 m)
Height	33 ft., 11 in. (10.3 m)
Wingspan	100 ft., 3 in. (30.4 m)
Empty weight	61,360 lbs. (27,890 kg)
Max. gross weight	139,760 lbs. (63,527 kg)
Maximum speed	374 mph (411 knots)
Maximum altitude	28,500 ft. (8,625 m)
Maximum range	1,536 miles (1,690 nautical miles)
Powerplant(s)	Four T56-A-14 Allison turboprops generating 4,600 hp each
Armament	Up to approx. 20,000 lbs. (9,072 kg) internal and external loads of torpedoes, mines, depth bombs, missiles, sonobuoys, etc.
Manufacturer	Lockheed
Variants	EP-3 electronic surveillance

The P-3C Orion entered the inventory in July 1962, and over 30 years later it remains the Navy's only land-based ASW aircraft. Orions have flown missions during the Cuban Missile Crisis, the Vietnam War, Operation Desert Shield/Desert Storm, peacekeeping in Haiti and the former Yugoslavia, and currently support Operation Enduring Freedom in Afghanistan.

Tanker Aircraft

KC-10 Extender

The USAF KC-10 Extender tanker/cargo aircraft is a modified DC-10 commercial airliner, providing increased mobility for U.S. forces in contingency operations, without dependence on overseas bases and without depleting critical fuel supplies overseas. The KC-10 fleet provides in-flight refueling worldwide to aircraft from all branches of the U.S. armed forces, as well as those of other coalition forces.

Equipped with its own refueling receptacle, the KC-10A can support deployment of fighters, fighter support aircraft, and cargo aircraft from U.S. bases to any area in the world. The aerial refueling capability of the KC-10A nearly doubles the nonstop range of a fully loaded strategic transport aircraft. In addition, the Extender's cargo capability enables the United States to deploy some fighter squadrons and their unit support personnel and equipment with a single support aircraft type, instead of requiring both tanker and cargo aircraft.

KC-10 Extender

Description	Three-engine aerial refueler based on commercial DC-10
Mission/branches	Aerial refueling and transport/U.S. Air Force
Crew	Four (aircraft commander, pilot, flight engineer, and boom operator)
Length	181 ft., 7 in. (54.4 m)
Height	58 ft., 1 in. (17.4 m)
Wingspan	165 ft., 4 ½ in. (50 m)
Empty weight	240,026 lbs. (108,874 kg)
Max. gross weight	590,000 lbs. (265,500 kg)
Maximum speed	619 mph (Mach 0.825)
Maximum altitude	42,000 ft. (12,727 m)
Maximum range	4,400 miles (3,800 nautical miles) with cargo; 11,500 miles (10,000 nautical miles) without cargo
Powerplant(s)	Three General Electric CF-6-50C2 turbofans
Payload capacity	342,000 lbs. (155,129 kg) of fuel, all usable or transferable via either boom or probe and drogue refueling; some aircraft are modified with two wing-mounted air refueling pods, which allow simultaneous operations with probe-equipped aircraft
Armament	N/A
Manufacturer	McDonnell Douglas Aircraft Co.
Variants	N/A

The KC-10A tanker can deliver 200,000 pounds (90,718 kg) of fuel to a receiving aircraft 2,200 miles (3,540.56 km) from the home base and return, or it can carry a maximum cargo payload of 169,409 pounds (76,843 kg) a distance of 4,370 miles (7,032.84 km).

The KC-10A's boom operator controls refueling operations through a digital "fly-by-wire" (computer-assisted) system. Sitting in the rear of the aircraft, the operator can see the receiver aircraft through a wide window. During boom refueling operations, fuel is transferred at a maximum rate of 1,100 gallons (4,180 liters) per minute; the maximum hose and drogue refueling rate is 470 gallons (1,786 liters) per minute. The KC-10A can be air-refueled by a KC-135 or another KC-10A to increase its delivery range.

Several configurations exist for personnel and crew accommodations. One arrangement is for the crew of five, plus six seats for additional crew and four bunks for crew rest, with a curtain between bunks and the cargo net. The same area also has space for the installation of 14 more seats for support personnel. In another arrangement, the bunks, environmental curtain, and cargo net can be shifted rearward, making room for 55 more support people, along with the necessary utility, lavatory, and stowage modules, raising the personnel capacity to a total of 80 crew and support staff.

During Operations Desert Shield and Desert Storm in 1990 and 1991, the KC-10 fleet provided in-flight refueling to aircraft from U.S. and coalition armed forces. The KC-10 flew 409 missions throughout the entire NATO Allied Force campaign against Yugoslavia in 1999 and continued support operations in Kosovo.

KC-10s continue to participate in operations in Afghanistan in support of the Global War on Terror and other worldwide commitments.

KC-135 Stratotanker

The USAF KC-135 Stratotanker not only refuels long-range bombers, but also provides aerial refueling support to Air Force, Navy, Marine Corps, and allied/coalition aircraft.

Nearly all internal fuel can be pumped through the tanker's flying boom, the KC-135's primary fuel transfer method. A special shuttlecock-shaped drogue, attached to and trailing behind the flying boom, is used to refuel aircraft fitted with probes. An operator stationed in the rear of the plane controls the boom. A cargo deck above the refueling system holds passengers or cargo.

The KC-135 tanker fleet made an invaluable contribution to the success of Operations Desert Storm, Enduring Freedom, and Iraqi Freedom, flying around-the-clock missions to maintain coalition warplanes' operational abilities. KC-135s form the backbone of the Air Force tanker fleet, meeting the aerial refueling needs of bomber, fighter, cargo, and reconnaissance aircraft, as well as for Navy, Marine, and allied nations' aircraft.

To increase the efficiency and flexibility of the USAF refueling fleet, some KC-135R Stratotanker aircraft have been outfitted to accept wingtip hose-and-drogue and air refueling pods for refueling NATO and U.S. Navy aircraft. U.S. Navy and many NATO aircraft cannot be refueled using the boom and receptacle refueling method common to USAF aircraft, and instead use a probe-and-drogue system where probes on the receiver aircraft make contact with a hose that is reeled out behind a tanker aircraft. With the number of worldwide joint and combined

KC-135 Stratotanker

Description	Four-engine intercontinental jet tanker
Mission/branches	Aerial refueling; U.S. Air Force
Crew	Four or five; up to 80 passengers
Length	136 ft., 3 in. (40.8 m)
Height	38 ft., 4 in. (11.5 m)
Wingspan	130 ft., 10 in. (39.2 m)
Empty weight	119,231 lbs. (53,654 kg)
Max. gross weight	322,500 lbs. (145,125 kg)
Maximum speed	Maximum speed at 30,000 ft. (9,144 m): 610 mph (Mach 0.93)
Maximum altitude	50,000 ft. (15,152 m)
Maximum range	11,192 miles (9,732 nautical miles) with 120,000 lbs. (54,000 kg) of transfer fuel
Powerplant(s)	Four CFM International F108-CF-100 turbojets producing 22,224 lbs. (10,081 kg) of thrust each
Payload capacity	Up to 83,000 lbs. (37,350 kg), depending on configuration
Armament	N/A
Manufacturer	Boeing Military Airplanes
Variants	KC-135E (new engines)

military operations on the rise, the Department of Defense directed the Air Force to outfit part of its KC-135 fleet with the capability of refueling both probe-and-drogue and boom receptacle aircraft on the same mission. This also allows refueling up to two probe-and-drogue aircraft at the same time.

With projected modifications, the KC-135 series will continue to fly and refuel long into the twenty-first century. A new aluminum-alloy skin grafted to the underside of the wings will add 27,000 flying hours to each aircraft.

Attack Helicopters

AH-1W Super Cobra

The Marine Corps' AH-1W Super Cobra provides close-in all-weather fire support in aerial and ground escort operations during amphibious ship-to-shore movements and subsequent shore operations within the objective area. Additional missions include direct air support, antitank, armed escort, and air-to-air combat. The AH-1W is a two-place, tandem-seat, twin-engine helicopter capable of land- or sea-based operations.

The AH-1W Super Cobra is a direct descendant of the AH-1 series attack helicopter first used by the U.S. Army in Vietnam. The Army had gone through enough modifications and upgrades to get to the AH-1G—logging more than a million hours on various Cobra airframes—when the Marine Corps decided to procure a twin-engine version, resulting in the AH-1J Sea Cobra. The Marine Corps then identified a need for more armaments, so the AH-1T upgrade was initiated, with an extended tailboom and fuselage and upgraded transmission and engines.

By the early 1980s, USMC AH-1T inventory was declining because of attrition; the Marine Corps sought a fully navalized helicopter with the AH-1W. The AH-1W distinguished itself with its more powerful T700-GE-401 fully marinized engines and advanced electronic weapons capability. The AH-1W can fire TOW, Hellfire, and Sidewinder missiles and can be outfitted with Zuni rocket launchers. Each stub-like "wing" has two hardpoints, for a total of four stations. A representative mix when targeting armor formations would be eight TOW missiles, two 2.75-inch rocket pods, and 750 rounds of 20-millimeter ammunition. The armored cockpit can withstand small arms fire, and the composite blades and tailboom are able to withstand damage from 23-millimeter cannon hits and smaller.

The Marine Corps deployed four of six active Marine squadrons (48 AH-1Ws) to southwest Asia during Operation Desert Shield/Desert Storm. These helicopters destroyed 97 tanks, 104 armored personnel carriers and vehicles, 16 bunkers, and two anti-aircraft artillery sites without the loss of any aircraft. The deployment required no additional augmentation to squadron support personnel and only one Bell Helicopter technical representative.

Additional improvements in rotor blades, cockpit configuration, and other features continue to be planned and executed to upgrade the AH-1W to the AH-1Z

AH-1W Cobra

Description	Twin-engine tandem-seat attack helicopter, skid mounted
Mission/branches	Close-in all-weather fire support for aerial and ground escort; USMC
Crew	Two in tandem: copilot/gunner in front, pilot elevated in rear
Length	Overall: 57 ft., 11 in. (17.7 m); fuselage: 45 ft., 5 in. (13.9 m)
Height	14 ft., 6 in. (4.4 m)
Rotor diameter	47 ft., 11 in. (14.6 m)
Empty weight	10,283 lbs. (4,634 kg)
Max. gross weight	14,845 lbs. (6,690 kg)
Maximum speed	195 mph (170 knots); climb rate: 1,925 ft. (586.74 km) per minute
Maximum altitude	More than 14,750 ft. (4,540 m)
Maximum range	365 miles (317 nautical miles/598 km) (without drop tanks)
Powerplant(s)	Two GE T700-GE-401 turboshaft engines producing 1,690 hp each
Payload capacity	931 lbs. (2,065 kg)
Armament	One M197 three-barrel 20-mm gun mounted in chin turret; under-wing attachments for four TOW missiles, eight Hellfire missiles, or one AIM-9L Sidewinder missile; can also be equipped with Zuni rocket launchers
Manufacturer	Bell Helicopter Textron

King Cobra so that it can continue to serve the Marine Corps and the United States in the Global War on Terror and in its worldwide commitments.

OH-6A Cayuse and AH-6J/MH-6J Little Bird

The OH-6A was designed for use as a scout helicopter during the Vietnam War to meet the U.S. Army's need for an extremely maneuverable light observation helicopter. The Hughes OH-6A Cayuse was quite effective when teamed with the AH-1G Cobra attack helicopter as part of what were then known as "Pink Teams." The OH-6A "Loach" would find targets by flying low, "trolling" for fire, and then leading in a Cobra (nicknamed "Snake") to attack. The OH-6A could be armed with the M27 armament subsystem, the M134 six-barrel 7.62 mm "minigun," or the M129 40 mm grenade launcher.

AH-6J/MH-6J Little Bird

Description	Single-engine light attack/special operations helicopter, 4–5 bladed main rotor
Mission/branches	Fire support/personnel insertion for special operations/U.S. Army
Crew	One or two pilots
Length	Overall: 32 ft., 1 in. (9.8 m); fuselage: 23 ft., 11 in. (7.3 m)
Height	11 ft., 2 in. (3.4 m)
Rotor diameter	26 ft., 4 in. (8 m)
Empty weight	1,971 lbs. (896 kg)
Max. gross weight	3,542 lbs. (1,610 kg)
Maximum speed	170 mph (282 kph); climb rate: 2,063 ft. per minute
Maximum altitude	16,000 ft. (4,875 m)
Maximum range	288 miles (250 nautical miles/472 km)
Powerplant(s)	One 425-hp Allison 250-C30 turboshaft
Payload capacity	External load of 1,219 lbs. (550 kg); transports two or three service members or equivalent cargo internally, or six on external platforms in lieu of weapons
Armament	Combinations of: • two M134 7.62-mm six-barrel Gatling-type MG pods • two M260 2.75-in Hydra 70 rocket pods (7 or 12 each) • two .50 cal MG pods • two M75 40-mm grenade launchers • two MK19 40-mm grenade launchers • two TOW missile pods (2 each) • two Hellfire antitank guided missiles • two Stinger air-to-air missiles
Manufacturer	McDonnell Douglas
Variants	AH-6J, MH-6J, OH-6A

Two special operations versions of the OH-6A are the "Little Bird" AH-6J armed variant and the MH-6J insertion and extraction transport version, which can carry up to six personnel for quick insertion and extraction missions. Both versions feature a more powerful engine and improved avionics, including an embedded GPS/inertial navigation system and forward-looking infrared radar. The AH-6J can be armed with two seven-tube 2.75-inch (6.99 cm) rocket launchers and two 7.62-millimeter M134 miniguns. The Little Bird can also be armed with .50 caliber machine guns, the Mark 19 40-millimeter grenade machine gun, Hellfire missiles, and air-to-air Stinger missiles.

They are also equipped with mast-mounted sights which allow the pilot to expose only the sights instead of the entire aircraft, which can then hover in relative safety behind trees, buildings, hilltops, or the like.

AH-6 and MH-6 Little Bird variants have been used in increasing numbers since the late 1980s by U.S. special operations units, including service in Panama, the Persian Gulf War, Somalia, Afghanistan, and Iraq.

OH-58D Kiowa Warrior

The OH-58D Kiowa Warrior is a single-engine, four-bladed, multi-role helicopter used by the U.S. Army for reconnaissance, security, and attack missions. The Kiowa's advanced navigation, communication, and weapons systems enable it to locate targets at long ranges by day and night and in adverse weather.

OH-58D Kiowa Warrior

Description	Single-engine, four-bladed, helicopter
Mission/branches	Observation, utility, direct fire support; U.S. Army
Crew	Two: pilot, copilot/gunner
Length	33 ft., 4 in. (10.18 m)
Height	12 ft., 11 in. (3.69 m)
Rotor diameter	35 ft. (10.67 m)
Empty weight	3,289 lbs. (1,492 kg)
Max. gross weight	5,500 lbs. (2,495 kg) armed
Maximum cruising speed	128 mph
Maximum altitude	19,000 ft. (5,791 m)
Maximum range	300 miles (483 km)
Powerplant(s)	One Rolls-Royce T703-AD-700A or 250-C30R/3 turboshaft, 650 hp (485 kw) each
Payload capacity	2,000 lbs. (907 kg)
Armament	Combinations of air-to-air Stinger missiles; .50-cal. machine gun, seven-shot pod of Hydra 70 2.75" rockets; Hellfire missiles
Manufacturer	Bell Helicopter Textron/Rolls Royce/Boeing
Variants	Bell Jet Ranger (civilian)

The original OH-58, fielded in 1969, was an unarmed reconnaissance and artillery spotting helicopter used in Vietnam, and has a civilian counterpart, the Bell Jet Ranger. It was first armed in 1987 to protect oil tankers in the Persian Gulf from attacks by Iranian gunboats.

The current Kiowa Warrior is equipped with two quick-change universal weapons pylons, each of which can be fitted with an anti-armor Hellfire missile, a seven-tube Hydra rocket pod, an air-to-air Stinger missile, or a .50-cal. machine gun. It also sports a mast-mounted sight (MMS) resembling a beach ball perched on top of the rotor system hub containing a video camera, thermal imaging system, and a laser range-finder/designator—allowing the Kiowa Warrior to see the 360-degree battlefield while unobserved behind trees or terrain features, exposing only the MMS.

Kiowas were also the first Army helicopter to be fitted with the Wire Strike Protective System—knifelike extensions above and below the cockpit that protect 90 percent of the helicopter's frontal area from power lines and other wires encountered at low altitudes.

The Kiowa Warrior is rapidly deployable by air—two can be transported in a C-130 Hercules cargo plane—and can be fully operational within minutes of arrival. Normally deployed in coordination with AH-64D Apache gunships or with artillery batteries and fixed-wing attack aircraft, the Kiowa Warrior has seen action in the Persian Gulf (1987–1989), Operation Just Cause in Panama (1989), Operation Iraqi Freedom in Iraq (2003–2010), and Operation Enduring Freedom in Afghanistan (2001–present). It has also served well here at home with National Guard Reconnaissance and Aerial Interdiction Detachments (RAID) counterdrug efforts, as well as post-9/11 Border Patrol support missions.

AH-64 Apache

The AH-64 Apache is the Army's primary attack helicopter. It is a twin-engine, four-bladed, multimission attack helicopter that can fight in any weather, day or night, both close and deep, to destroy, disrupt, or delay enemy forces. The principal mission of the Apache is the destruction of high-value targets with the Hellfire missile. It is also capable of using its 30-millimeter chain gun and 2.75-inch rockets against a wide variety of targets. The Apache can withstand hits from rounds up to 23 millimeters in critical areas.

With a tandem-seated crew consisting of the pilot in the rear cockpit position and the copilot/gunner (CPG) in the front position, the Apache is self-deployable, highly survivable, and can deliver a lethal array of battlefield munitions. The Apache features a Target Acquisition Designation Sight and a Pilot Night Vision Sensor, which enables the crew to navigate and conduct precision attacks in day, night, and adverse weather conditions. The Apache has four articulating weapons pylons, two on either side of the aircraft, on which weapons or external fuel tanks can be mounted and it can carry up to 16 Hellfire laser-designated missiles.

The Apache has state-of-the-art optics that provide the capability to select from three different target acquisition sensors—daylight TV, thermal, and digital enhanced. An onboard video recorder has the capability of recording up to 72 minutes of either the pilot or CPG selected video, an invaluable tool for damage assessment and reconnaissance. The Apache's navigation equipment consists of a Doppler navigation system, and most aircraft are equipped with a GPS receiver.

AH-64 Apache

Description	Twin-engine, four-bladed, multimission attack helicopter
Mission/branches	Close air support of ground forces; U.S. Army
Crew	Two: copilot/gunner in front, pilot in back, elevated
Length	58 ft., 2 in. (17.7 m)
Height	A model: 15 ft., 3 in. (4.6 m); D model: 13 ft., 4 in. (4.1 m)
Rotor diameter	48 ft. (14.6 m)
Empty weight	11,800 lbs. (5,364 kg)
Max. gross weight	A model: 15,075 lbs. (6,838 kg); D model: 16,600 lbs. (7,530 kg)
Maximum speed	A model: 170 mph (279 kph); D model: 167 mph (273 kph)
Maximum altitude	20,500 ft. (6,248 m)
Maximum range	300 miles (483 km) on internal fuel
Powerplant(s)	Two T700-GE-701C engines generating 1,890 shp each
Payload capacity	Up to 16 Hellfire antitank missiles or 76 2.75-in. rockets
Armament	M230 33-mm Gun 70-mm (2.75-in.) Hydra-70 folding-fin aerial rockets AGM-114 Hellfire antitank missiles AGM-122 Sidearm antiradar missile AIM-9 Sidewinder air-to-air missiles
Manufacturer	Boeing/McDonnell Douglas Helicopter Systems, General Electric, Martin Marietta
Variants	AH-64D Apache Longbow

The AH-64A proved its capabilities in action during both Operation Restore Hope and Operation Desert Storm. Apache helicopters played a key role in the 1989 action in Panama, where much of its activity was at night, when the AH-64's advanced sensors and sighting systems were effective against Panamanian government forces. AH-64A Apaches also played a major role in the 1991 liberation of Kuwait and the conflicts in Bosnia and Kosovo in the 1990s.

The AH-64D Longbow Apache is a remanufactured and upgraded version of the AH-64A Apache attack helicopter. The primary modifications to the Apache are the addition of a millimeter-wave Fire Control Radar target acquisition system, the fire-and-forget Longbow Hellfire air-to-ground missile, updated engines, and a fully integrated cockpit. In addition, the D model has improved survivability, communications, and navigation capabilities.

AH-64s have been supporting Operation Enduring Freedom in Afghanistan since its beginning in 2001, as well as Operation Iraqi Freedom in Iraq from 2003 until its close in 2010. After initial major combat operations in Iraq were concluded, Apaches have been flying in both operations without their Longbow fire control radar, since there is no armored threat.

Apache variants are also flown by the British, Israeli, Dutch, Japanese, Greek, Egyptian, and Saudi Arabian militaries, among several others.

Apache models continue to support operations worldwide for the Global War on Terror.

Cargo Helicopters

CH-46 Sea Knight

The CH-46 Sea Knight's primary functions are troop assault and movement of supplies and equipment. It is also designed to provide the U.S. Marine Corps and Navy with a medium-lift helicopter capable of combat and assault support for evacuation operations and other maritime special operations; over-water search and rescue augmentation; support for mobile forward refueling and rearming points; and aeromedical evacuation of casualties from the battlefield to suitable medical facilities.

The CH-46 was originally procured in 1964 to meet the medium-lift requirements of the Marine Corps in Vietnam. The aircraft has since seen action in the 1983 invasion of Grenada and the 1991 Gulf War, where CH-46s flew 1,601 sor-

CH-46 Sea Knight

Description	Two-engine cargo helicopter with tandem rotors
Mission/branches	All-weather, medium-lift day/night assault transport of troops and cargo during amphibious and shorebound operations; U.S. Marine Corps
Crew	Normal: 4—pilot, copilot, crew chief, and first mechanic Combat: 5—pilot, copilot, crew chief, and two aerial gunners
Length	Rotors unfolded: 84 ft., 4 in. (25.7 m) Rotors folded: 45 ft., 7.5 in. (13.9 m)
Height	16 ft., 8 in. (5.1 m)
Rotor diameter	51 ft. (15.5 m)
Empty weight	15,537 lbs. (7,048 kg)
Max. gross weight	24,300 lbs. (11,032 kg)
Maximum speed	167 mph (145 knots)
Maximum altitude	Over 10,000 ft. (3,048 m)
Maximum range	151.8 miles (132 nautical miles, 249 km) for an assault mission
Powerplant(s)	Two GE-T58-16 engines, generating 1,770 shaft horsepower
Payload capacity	Combat: 14 troops with aerial gunners; medical evacuation: 15 litters and two attendants; cargo: maximum of 4,000 lbs. (2,270 kg) external load
Armament	Two .50-cal. machine guns
Manufacturer	Boeing Defense, Space & Security
Variants	N/A

ties from the amphibious assault ship USS *Guam*. The CH-46 continues to perform yeoman duties for the U.S. Marine Corps in support of operations during the Global War on Terror, as well as humanitarian and other missions worldwide.

CH-47D Chinook

The CH-47 is a twin-engine, tandem-rotor helicopter designed for transportation of cargo, troops, and weapons during all conditions. Development of the medium-lift Boeing Vertol CH-47 Series Chinook began in 1956. Since then the effectiveness of the Chinook has been continually upgraded by successive product improvements—the CH-47A, CH-47B, CH-47C, and CH-47D, and now the MH-47E.

The CH-47A was first delivered in 1962. Early production CH-47As operated with the 11th Air Assault Division during 1963, and in October of that year the aircraft was formally designated as the Army's standard medium-transport helicopter.

CH-47As deployed to Vietnam in 1965 had a maximum gross weight of 33,000 pounds (14,969 kg), allowing for a maximum payload of approximately 10,000 pounds (4,536 kg). The hot mountainous conditions of Vietnam limited the A model's performance capabilities, generating a requirement for increased payload and better performance.

CH-47D Chinook

Description	Twin-engine, three-bladed (per engine) tandem-rotor cargo helicopter
Mission/branches	Cargo/assault; U.S. Army
Crew	Four to five, depending on mission: two pilots, one flight engineer, and one or two crew chiefs
Length	Fuselage: 51 ft. (15.3 m); 100 ft. (30.5 m) from leading tip of forward rotor sweep to rear of aft rotor sweep
Height	18 ft., 8 in. (5.7 m)
Rotor diameter	60 ft. (18.3 m)
Empty weight	23,401 lbs. (10,637 kg)
Max. gross weight	50,000 lbs. (22,727 kg)
Maximum speed	163 mph (142 knots); max rate of climb 1,522 ft. per min.
Maximum altitude	8,500 ft. (2,591 m)
Maximum range	1,279 miles (2,058.35 km)
Powerplant(s)	Two Textron Lycoming T55-L712 engines
Payload capacity	33 troop seats, 24 litters, 26,000 lbs. (11,793 kg) of external cargo
Armament	N/A
Manufacturer	Boeing
Variants	(see text)

Subsequent upgrades eventually led to the CH-47D, introduced in 1982. The D model can carry twice the load of the A model, and can operate at night and in nearly all weather conditions.

The Chinook can accommodate a wide variety of internal payloads, including vehicles, artillery pieces, 33 to 44 troops, or 24 litters plus two medical attendants. It can also be equipped with two side-door-mounted 7.62-millimeter machine guns. The D model can carry up to 26,000 pounds (11,793 kg) externally on one or more of its three cargo hooks.

During Operation Desert Shield/Storm, the CH-47D was often the only mode of transportation available to rapidly shift large numbers of personnel, equipment, and supplies over the vast area in which U.S. forces operated.

The thin air of Afghanistan's mountains ruled out UH-60 Blackhawk operations in many instances, and the twin-rotor Chinook filled the gap (although not loaded anywhere near its normal full capacity).

The MH-47E is a special operations variant with a significantly increased fuel capacity, modified integrated avionics suites and multimode radars, and an aerial refueling boom.

Chinooks continue to perform heroic workhorse duties in support of the Global War on Terror and other U.S. commitments and operations worldwide, and are expected to continue doing so for many years to come.

CH-53E Sea Stallion

The CH-53E Sea Stallion transports equipment, supplies, and personnel during the assault phase of a Marine amphibious operation, as well as follow-on operations ashore. Capable of carrying supplies both internally and externally, the CH-53E is compatible with shipboard operations and can operate in adverse weather conditions day and night.

The Sea Stallion is capable of lifting 16 tons at sea level, transporting the load 50 nautical miles (57.5 miles), and returning. A typical load might be a 16,000-pound (7,258 kg) M198 howitzer or a 26,000-pound (11,793 kg) light armored vehicle. The CH-53E can also retrieve downed aircraft, including another CH-53E; it's equipped with a refueling probe and can be refueled in flight, giving it virtually indefinite range.

During Operation Eastern Exit in January 1990, two CH-53Es launched from amphibious ships and flew 463 nautical miles at night (refueling twice en route) to rescue American and foreign allies from the American Embassy in the civil war–torn capital of Mogadishu, Somalia. Two CH-53Es rescued Air Force Captain Scott O'Grady after he was shot down in Bosnia in June 1995.

The newest military version of Sikorsky's H-53E/S80 series, the MH-53E Sea Dragon, is the Western world's largest helicopter. The MH-53E is used primarily for airborne mine countermeasures, with a secondary mission of shipboard delivery. Additional mission capabilities include air-to-air refueling, search and rescue, and external cargo transport operations in both overland and seaborne environments. The MH-53E was derived from the CH-53E Super Stallion, but is heavier and has greater fuel capacity than its predecessor. The Sea Dragon can carry up to 55 troops or a 16-ton payload 50 nautical miles, or a 10-ton payload 500 nautical miles, and is also capable of towing a variety of minesweeping countermeasures systems.

CH-53E Sea Stallion

Description	Three-engine heavy-lift helicopter w/seven-bladed rotor
Mission/branches	Shipboard and onshore transport of supplies and personnel; USMC, USAF, USN
Crew	Six: two pilots, two flight engineers, two aerial gunners
Length	99 ft., ½ in. (30.2 m)
Height	28 ft., 4 in. (8.7 m)
Rotor diameter	79 ft. (24.1 m)
Empty weight	33,226 lbs. (16,613 kg)
Max. gross weight	73,500 lbs. (33,409 kg)
Maximum speed	173 mph (150 knots)
Maximum altitude	18,500 ft. (5,640 m)
Maximum range	552 miles (480 nautical miles)
Powerplant(s)	Three General Electric T64-GE-416/416A turboshaft engines generating 4,380 shp each
Payload capacity	Normal configuration: 37 passengers; 55 passengers with centerline seats installed; can be configured for up to 14 litters; cargo payload up to 32,000 lbs. (14,545 kg)
Armament	Three 7.62-mm miniguns
Manufacturer	Prime: Sikorsky; engines: General Electric
Variants	MH-53E Sea Dragon MH-53J Pave Low III

The MH-53J Pave Low III variation is the largest and most powerful helicopter in the Air Force inventory. Its mission is to perform low-level, long-range, undetected penetration into unfriendly areas, day or night, in adverse weather, for insertion, extraction, and resupply of special operations forces. Its terrain-avoidance radar and forward-looking infrared sensor, along with a projected map display, enable the crew to follow terrain contours and avoid obstacles, making low-level penetration much more feasible. It's equipped with armor plating and a combination of three 7.62-millimeter miniguns or .50-caliber machine guns. It can transport 38 troops or 14 litters, and has an external cargo hook with a 20,000-pound (9,000 kg) capacity.

The MH-53J Pave Low is a modified version of the HH-53 Super Jolly Green Giant helicopter used extensively in Vietnam for special operations and combat rescue. During the space program, the HH-53 was on duty at the launch site as the primary astronaut recovery vehicle. Under the Air Force's Pave Low IIIE program, nine MH-53Hs and 32 HH-53s were modified for night and adverse weather operations and designated MH-53Js.

MH-53Js were used in a variety of missions during Desert Storm. Pave Lows were among the first aircraft into Iraq when they led Army AH-64 Apaches to destroy Iraqi early-warning radars, and performed infiltration, exfiltration, and resupply of special operations teams throughout Iraq and Kuwait. Pave Lows also provided search-and-rescue coverage for coalition air forces in the entire region. An MH-53J made the first successful combat recovery of a downed pilot in Desert Storm.

CH-53s have been used by the Air Force, Navy, and Marine Corps in both Iraq and Afghanistan. A new variant, the CH-53K, is planned to replace Navy and Marine Corps CH-53Es by 2015.

Utility Helicopters

UH-1 Huey

The "Huey" helicopter, a legendary workhorse of the Vietnam War, has been produced in greater numbers than any aircraft since World War II; it is still operated by about 50 air forces around the world.

The first XH-40 prototype debuted in 1956 and could carry up to six combat-loaded soldiers or an equivalent amount of cargo. The first production models in 1959 were originally designated as the HU-1 Iroquois, but the "Huey" nickname (based on its initials) stuck fast even after it was redesignated as the UH-1.

Hueys were among the first modern helicopters to serve in Vietnam, and they became a common sight on a variety of missions, the most common being troop and cargo transport, medical evacuation, and attack gunship. During what were then known as "airmobile" operations (now doctrinally referred to as "air assaults"), UH-1Cs armed with machine guns and rocket pods swooped in low over landing

UH-1 Huey (Iroquois)

Description	Two-bladed single-engine transport/assault utility helicopter
Mission/branches	Utility transport; some Army, Air Force models remain
Crew	Up to five: pilot, copilot, crew chief, one or two gunners or medics
Length	57 ft., 1 in. with rotors (17.4 m)
Height	14 ft., 5 in. (4.4 m)
Rotor diameter	48 ft. (14.6 m)
Empty weight	5,215 lbs. (2,365 kg)
Max. gross weight	9,500 lbs. (4,318 kg)
Maximum speed	135 mph (220 km/hr)
Maximum altitude	12,700 ft. (4,097 m)
Maximum range	777 miles (1,275 km)
Powerplant(s)	One 1,400-hp Lycoming T53 turboshaft engine
Payload capacity	2,200 lbs. (990 kg)
Armament	Up to four 7.62-mm machine guns, two 40-mm grenade launchers, or six TOW antitank missiles
Manufacturer	Bell Helicopter
Variants	Medevac, gunship

zones while the more vulnerable troop transports remained out of range until the zone was declared safe. Afterward, medevac Hueys extracted the casualties to medical units that saved more lives than in any previous conflict. The various models of the UH-1 rendered outstanding service in their many roles, although the gunship versions were later replaced by the faster AH-1 Cobra.

To date, more than ten thousand Hueys have been built around the world, and more than 65 countries have used them at one time or another. Although largely replaced by UH-60 Black Hawks, the U.S. military still operates a handful for non-frontline duties.

UH-60 Black Hawk

The UH-60 Black Hawk is the U.S. Army's frontline utility helicopter used for air assault, transportation, air cavalry, and aeromedical evacuation missions; variants are also used for electronic countermeasures, command and control, and special operations missions. The Black Hawk is designed to carry up to 11 combat-loaded air assault troops, and it is capable of slingloading a 105-millimeter howitzer as well as 30 rounds of ammunition for it.

As the Army's primary division-level transport helicopter, the Black Hawk provided dramatic improvements in troop and cargo lift capability over the UH-1 "Huey" it replaced starting in 1978. The Black Hawk's protective armor—both pilot and copilot have armored seats—can withstand hits from up to 23-millimeter shells. The UH-60L conversion provided greater engine power, and an External Stores Support System consisting of removable four-station pylons that can carry external fuel tanks or 16 Hellfire missiles.

The UH-60 Firehawk provides both a wartime and peacetime firefighting capability by use of a detachable 1,000-gallon belly tank. The EH-60A Electronic Countermeasures variant has a unique external antenna designed to intercept and jam enemy communications. The UH-60Q medical evacuation variant provides significant enroute patient care enhancements: a six-patient litter system, onboard oxygen generation, cardiac monitoring, airway management, and a medical suction system.

The Air Force's HH-60G's primary wartime missions are combat search and rescue, infiltration, exfiltration, and resupply of special operations forces in day, night, or marginal weather conditions. Combat-equipped personnel can be covertly inserted and/or extracted in any terrain with precise GPS navigation accuracy. The HH-60G provides the capability of independent rescue operations in combat areas up to and including medium-threat environments. Recoveries are made by landing or by alternate means, such as rope ladder or the 200-foot hoist. The basic crew normally consists of five: pilot, copilot, flight engineer, and two parajumpers. The aircraft can also carry eight to ten troops, and has limited self-protection provided by side window-mounted M-60, M-240, or GAU-2B machine guns.

The MH-60G Pave Hawk is operated by the Air Force Special Operations Command, a component of the U.S. Special Operations Command. The MH-60G's primary wartime missions are infiltration, exfiltration, and resupply of special operations forces day or night in any weather, as well as combat search and rescue. MH-60Gs have all-weather radar, a retractable in-flight refueling probe, internal auxiliary fuel tanks, and a 200-foot rescue hoist with a 600-pound (272.16 kg) lift capacity. Pave Hawks are also equipped with folding rotor blades

UH-60 Black Hawk

Description	Twin-engine, medium-lift, four-bladed utility helicopter
Mission/branches	Air assault, utility airlift, aeromedevac, command and control; U.S. Army, Air Force, Navy
Crew	Up to four: pilot, copilot, crew chief/flight engineer, door gunner
Length	64 ft., 10 in. (19.7 m)
Height	16 ft., 10 in. (5.1 m)
Rotor diameter	53 ft., 8 in. (16.3 m)
Empty weight	11,516 lbs. (5,234.5 kg)
Max. gross weight	22,000 lbs. (10,000 kg)
Maximum speed	Up to 165 mph (150 knots)
Maximum altitude	Up to 11,125 ft. (3,400 m)
Maximum range	362 miles (315 nautical miles)
Powerplant(s)	Two GE T700-GE-701C turboshafts generating 2,000+ shp each
Payload capacity	9,000 lbs. (4,090 kg)
Armament	Two M60D 7.62-mm machine guns
Manufacturer	Sikorsky Aircraft Corp.
Variants	UH-60L (attack), UH-60Q (aeromedevac), MH-60G Pave Hawk (USAF special operations), MH-60K (Army special operations)

and a tail stabilator for shipboard operations and easier air shipment on large cargo planes. During Operation Desert Storm in 1991, Pave Hawks provided combat recovery for coalition air forces in Iraq, Saudi Arabia, Kuwait, and the Persian Gulf, as well as emergency evacuation coverage for U.S. Navy SEAL teams penetrating the Kuwait coast before the invasion—all capabilities that have been maintained and expanded in Operations Enduring Freedom and Iraqi Freedom.

The MH-60K, the Army special operations version of the Black Hawk, provides long-range airlifts deep into hostile territory in adverse weather conditions. Modifications include two removable 230-gallon (870.64 L) external fuel tanks, two .50-caliber machine guns, an air-to-air refueling probe, and an external hoist. The MH-60K can also be armed with two M134 7.62-millimeter miniguns. An upgraded avionics suite includes interactive Multi-Function Displays, Forward-Looking Infrared, digital map generator, and terrain-avoidance/terrain-following multimode radar. The MH-60K, like the MH-60G, has full shipboard operability, emphasizing the need for joint (multiservice) operations in today's environment.

The older MH-60L model can be adapted to the attack mission by attaching dual weapons pylons to both sides of the fuselage. Pylon-mounted cannon, rockets, or missiles can be supplemented by door- or port-mounting guns or launchers, limited mainly by the range, duration, cargo, or troops required to complete the mission.

HH-65A Dolphin

The U.S. Coast Guard's twin-engine HH-65A Dolphin helicopters operate up to 150 miles offshore and can fly comfortably at 120 knots for up to three hours. Though normally stationed ashore, Dolphins can be carried on board medium- and high-endurance Coast Guard cutters. They assist in search and rescue, drug interdiction, polar ice breaking, marine environmental protection, and military readiness operations. They also airlift supplies to ships and villages isolated by winter.

Made of corrosion-resistant composite materials, the Dolphin sports a unique shrouded tail rotor and computerized flight management system, which integrates state-of-the-art communications and navigation equipment to provide automatic flight control. The pilot can make the system bring the aircraft to a stable hover 50 feet (15.24 m) above a selected object. Selected search patterns can be flown automatically, freeing the pilot and copilot to concentrate on finding the object of their search.

HH-65A Dolphin

Description	Short-range recovery
Mission/branches	Twin-engine helicopter; U.S. Coast Guard
Crew	Three: pilot, copilot, crew chief
Length	38 ft. (12.3 m)
Height	13 ft. (4.2 m)
Rotor diameter	39 ft. (12.6 m)
Empty weight	6,092 lbs. (2,769 kg)
Max. gross weight	9,200 lbs. (4,182 kg)
Maximum speed	165 knots (190 mph)
Cruising speed	120 knots (138 mph)
Maximum altitude	12,000 ft. (3,658 m)
Maximum range	400 nautical miles (655 km)
Powerplant(s)	Two Lycoming LTS-101-750B-2 engines rated at 742 shp each
Payload capacity	2,000 lbs. slingload, 600-lb. hoist
Armament	N/A
Manufacturer	Aerospatiale Helicopter Corporation, Grand Prairie, Texas

PART II:
TESTING FORMATS AND
REVIEW INFORMATION

Test Information

CHAPTER 3

Test Formats

AIR FORCE OFFICER QUALIFYING TEST (AFOQT)

The Air Force Officer Qualifying Test (AFOQT) measures aptitudes used by the U.S. Air Force to select candidates for officer commissioning programs and specific officer training programs.

The AFOQT was revised in 2005 and now consists of 12 timed subtests (there were previously 16). The scores from the individual subtests are combined in different ways to generate up to five composite scores used to help predict success in selected USAF training programs.

Subtest	# of Items	Time Allowed (mins)
1. Verbal Analogies (VA)	25	8
2. Arithmetic Reasoning (AR)	25	29
3. Word Knowledge (WK)	25	5
4. Math Knowledge (MK)	25	22
5. Instrument Comprehension (IC)	20	6
6. Block Counting (BC)	20	3
7. Table Reading (TR)	40	7
8. Aviation Information (AI)	20	8
9. General Science (GS)	20	10
10. Rotated Blocks (RB)	15	13
11. Hidden Figures (HF)	15	8
12. Self-Description Inventory (SDI)	220	40

The five composite scores derived from the AFOQT subtest scores and the kinds of abilities and knowledge they measure are as follows:

1. **Pilot** (AR + MK + IC + TR + AI) This composite score measures some of the knowledge and abilities the Air Force considers necessary for successful completion of pilot training. The Pilot composite includes subtests that measure mathematical ability, aeronautical concept knowledge, the ability to determine aircraft attitude from instruments, and perceptual speed (how fast the test-taker can figure things out).

2. **Navigator-Technical** (VA + AR + MC + BC + TR + GS) This composite score measures some of the abilities and knowledge considered necessary for successful completion of navigator training. It shares some subtests with the Pilot composite, but tests that measure aeronautical knowledge and the ability to determine aircraft attitude from instruments are not included. However, additional subtests measure verbal aptitude, perceptual speed, some spatial abilities, and general science knowledge.

3. **Academic Aptitude** (VA + AR + WK + MK) The Academic Aptitude composite measures verbal and quantitative abilities and knowledge. It also combines all subtests that make up the Verbal and Quantitative composites.

4. **Verbal** (VA + WK) The Verbal composite measures verbal knowledge and abilities using subtests that measure the ability to reason, recognize relationships between words, and understand synonyms.

5. **Quantitative** (AR + MK) This composite measures math-related abilities and knowledge. It shares subtests with the Navigator-Technical subtest and includes subtests that measure the test-taker's ability to understand and reason with mathematical relationships, as well as using mathematical terms, formulas, and relationships.

Everyone who wants to become an Air Force officer of any type must take the AFOQT. The three commissioning sources—the US Air Force Academy, Air Force Reserve Officer Training Corps (AFROTC), and Officer Training School (OTS)—initially consider only the applicant's Verbal and Quantitative composite scores, so you could say that these parts of the AFOQT are the first gateway through which a prospective Air Force officer must pass. The three commissioning sources maintain their own standards for entry, which can and do change based on the needs of the Air Force at that time. It is only after an applicant gains entry to a commissioning program that further evaluation of other AFOQT composite scores determines the candidate's eventual eligibility for pilot, navigator, or other nonflying specialty areas.

It's important to make the best initial score possible on the AFOQT, because the scores are valid for life and applicants may only take the test twice (one original and one retest at least 180 days later). Additional retests are sometimes allowed, but require a waiver which is not guaranteed. Only the latest scores—not necessarily the highest—are used in selection consideration.

ARMY ALTERNATE FLIGHT APTITUDE SELECTION TEST (AFAST)

The Army's flight aptitude test is known as the Alternate Flight Aptitude Selection Test (AFAST). The AFAST is used to select men and women who have the best chance of successfully completing Army helicopter pilot training. Being an Army aviator requires an individual to have special abilities, high motivation, good coordination, leadership skills, and excellent physical conditioning. Studies have shown that people who score higher on the test are generally more successful in flight school than those who score lower. As in all the services, because flight training is so expensive, and because there are only a limited number of openings in flight school, the Army needs to screen flight school applicants to ensure that only those with the best chance of success in flight school are accepted for training.

The AFAST is not an intelligence test. Instead, just like the tests for the other services, it measures the special aptitudes, personality traits, and background characteristics that show that a person has a high probability of success in Army helicopter flight training. The AFAST has a total of 200 questions broken down into seven subtests, each with its own directions and time limits.

The seven subtests are as follows:

1. Background Information Form (25 questions, 10 minutes)
2. Instrument Comprehension (15 questions, 5 minutes)
3. Complex Movements (30 questions, 5 minutes)
4. Helicopter Knowledge (20 questions, 10 minutes)
5. Cyclic Orientation (15 questions, 5 minutes)
6. Mechanical Function (20 questions, 10 minutes)
7. Self-Description Form (75 questions, 25 minutes)

Your application for flight training will receive further consideration only if your AFAST score meets or exceeds the established cutoff score. Cutoff scores vary somewhat from time to time based on the needs of the Army, but it's not wise to count on the Army lowering the cutoff score just because they need pilots. And, once you meet the cutoff score, you will *not* be allowed to retest; therefore, it's in your best interest to score as high as possible the first time. If your test score just barely exceeds the cutoff score, your application will be ranked below other applicants who scored higher than you did.

When you go in to take the test, you will be given a test booklet, a separate answer sheet, and two soft-lead (usually No. 2) pencils. You will receive complete instructions for each test section and be told how to record your answers.

On some subtests, it's to your advantage to answer every question. On other subtests, a portion of the questions you answer incorrectly is counted against you, taking away from your credit for questions you answer correctly. Even in the second case, it's to your advantage to make the best choice you can, unless you have no idea and are purely guessing. Therefore, it's important that you listen carefully to the test administration instructions and that you read the instructions for each test section to yourself as the test administrator reads them out loud.

The answer sheet has a space for your name, Social Security number, and other identifying information. Following the identification section are the subtest sections, with a different answer circle for each question. The questions are numbered from 1 to 200. Be sure, as you go through the test, that you are marking the same answer on the answer sheet as the number of the question you are answering in the test booklet.

Here's an example of how to properly mark an answer:

Figure 3.1

If this was Question 1 on the test, and you decided that answer B was the best choice, you would carefully darken the circle marked B on your answer sheet. Remember to mark the circle heavily, completely filling in the circle. If your mark in the circle is too small or too light, the machine that scores the test may not read the mark. Likewise, if you decide to change an answer, you need to *completely* erase the answer you want to change, and then mark your new answer. Additionally, never have more than one answer marked for each question. Even if one of them is correct, you won't get credit for the answer.

NAVY AND MARINE CORPS/COAST GUARD AVIATION SELECTION TEST BATTERY (ASTB)

The Aviation Selection Test Battery (ASTB) is used by the Navy, Marine Corps, and Coast Guard as one factor in the selection of pilot and flight officer candidates; it is designed to predict successful performance or attrition through the beginning phases of aviation training. Aviation officer candidates and Navy intelligence officer applicants take the entire test, but all other Navy Officer Candidate School (OCS) candidates and Coast Guard Officer candidates take just the first three sections of the exam (math skills, reading skills, and mechanical comprehension).

The ASTB is administered at Navy recruiting offices, Navy Reserve Officer Training Corps units, Marine Corps Officer Selection Offices, and numerous other sites. The test is usually given in a paper format, but at many sites it can be administered on a computer through a web-based system called the Automated Pilot Examination System, or APEX.NET. There are three versions of the test: Form 3, Form 4, and Form 5. Each version of the test contains different questions, but all three versions have the same format, subtests, and number of questions. Taking the complete battery of tests requires approximately two hours and 30 minutes.

Navy, Marine, and Coast Guard recruiters contact 10,000 or more individual prospects each year in order to ultimately fill about 2,000 seats in aviation ground school classes; the complete flight training program costs more than a million dollars per student. Half of the individuals who take the ASTB don't achieve the minimum qualifying scores to enter pilot training. And even with this much prescreening, about one third of those who enter undergraduate pilot training still don't earn their wings. Aviation selection tests play an important early role in the screening of aviation officer applicants; the objective of testing is to select those applicants most likely to succeed in training.

In 2004, a lifetime limit of three tests was established. An examinee may take each version of the test (Form 3, Form 4, and Form 5) only once, which means that an individual will only be allowed to take the ASTB three times during his or her lifetime. Examinees must take a different version for each retest, but the forms can be taken in any order. However, this limit applies only to Forms 3, 4, and 5; therefore, if an individual took a previous version of the test (Form 1 or 2, which are no longer in use), it is not counted in this limit.

Examinees who want to improve their scores must wait until the 31st day after the last time they took the ASTB before retaking the test, and they must then take a different version. For example, an individual who takes Form 3 on his or her first attempt must take Form 4 or Form 5 during the second testing session. A third and final attempt is authorized on the 91st day after the first retest. These test interval requirements can't be waived, so it's important for examinees to be aware of which test version they took during previous administrations and the amount of time that has passed between administrations.

An examinee who retests too early or retests using a form that he or she has already taken will generate an "illegal" test, meaning that the individual will not receive valid scores for the testing attempt. However, the illegal test will still be counted against the individual's three-test lifetime limit.

The ASTB is primarily an aptitude test. It measures math skills and aptitude, the ability to understand written material, familiarity with mechanical concepts and simple machines, and the ability to perform mental rotations to determine the orientation of an aircraft in three-dimensional space.

The ASTB also measures the test-taker's knowledge of aviation and nautical terminology, familiarity with aircraft components and function, knowledge of basic aerodynamic principles, and grasp of basic flight rules and regulations. *You can definitely improve your performance on this part of the battery by studying.* Examinees with aviation experience—and, to a lesser extent, shipboard experience—will typically do well.

The entire test battery consists of six subtests:

- Math Skills Test (MST)—30 questions, 25 minutes
- Reading Skills Test (RST)—27 questions, 25 minutes
- Mechanical Comprehension Test (MCT)—30 questions, 15 minutes
- Spatial Apperception Test (SAT)—25 questions, 10 minutes
- Aviation and Nautical Information Test (ANIT)—30 questions, 15 minutes
- Aviation Supplemental Test (AST)—34 questions, 25 minutes (may have fewer than 34 questions; actual number of items depends on the form given)

Math Skills Test

The math skills measured by the ASTB subtests include arithmetic and algebra, with some geometry. The assessments include both equations and word problems. Some items require solving for variables, others are time and distance problems, and some require the estimation of simple probabilities. Skills assessed include basic arithmetic operations; solving for variables, fractions, roots, and exponents; and the calculation of angles, area, and perimeter of geometric shapes.

The Math Skills subtest consists of 30 questions, which you will have 25 minutes to answer.

Reading Skills Test

Reading comprehension items require ASTB examinees to understand the meaning of selected passages of text. Each item requires the test-taker to decide which of the possible answers can be inferred from the text in the passage. This is pretty straightforward, although it's very important for test-takers to remember that incorrect answer choices may still *appear* to be true—but that only one answer to each question can be derived exclusively from the information in the passage.

The Reading Skills subtest has 27 questions that must be answered in 25 minutes. Some questions will have a paragraph or passage that you must read and about which you must then answer one or more questions. Other questions will give you a word and ask you to choose a synonym from the choices given; still others will have you fill in the blank in a sentence, based on the context. Still others will give you a passage to read and ask you to pick out the word that is used incorrectly or that is inappropriate.

Mechanical Comprehension Test

Questions in the mechanical comprehension section of the ASTB include topics that would typically be found in a high school general physics course, as well as the application of this information in a variety of situations. The questions measure test-takers' knowledge of scientific principles dealing with gases and liquids, as well as their understanding of how these properties affect pressure, volume, and velocity. The subtest also includes questions about the components and performance of engines; principles of electricity, gears, and weight distribution; and the operation of simple machines, such as fulcrums and pulleys.

The Mechanical Comprehension subtest is made up of 30 questions, which you will have 15 minutes to answer.

Spatial Apperception Test

Spatial Apperception questions evaluate an examinee's ability to match external and internal views of an aircraft based on visual information about its direction and orientation relative to the ground. The subtest consists of 25 questions, which you will have 10 minutes to answer.

For each question, you will see a series of six illustrations. The first illustration will show a view of the landscape that a pilot would see when looking out the front of the cockpit. Your task is to determine whether the aircraft is diving, climbing, banking, or in level flight, and to choose the picture that best represents that same aircraft when viewed from the outside.

Aviation and Nautical Information Test

The Aviation and Nautical Information subtest (ANIT) measures an examinee's knowledge of aviation history, nautical terminology and procedures, and aviation-related concepts such as aircraft components, aerodynamic principles, and flight rules and regulations. Of all the ASTB subtests, ANIT scores are the most easily improved by studying, because this subtest is primarily a test of knowledge instead of aptitude. Examinees can prepare for this subtest by reviewing the first half of Chpater 7 in this book, Federal Aviation Administration and civilian aviation books, and handbooks and manuals about basic piloting, navigation, and seamanship. In addition to these sources, some examinees have successfully used commercially available study guides to prepare.

The subtest consists of 30 questions that you will have 15 minutes to answer.

Aviation Supplemental Test

The final ASTB subtest has a variety of questions that are similar in format and content to the items in the preceding subtests; it's basically a review of the previous five subtests. You may see questions that are exactly the same as questions you've previously answered; you may see questions that appear to be the same, but are slightly different; or you may see questions that are completely different from questions you saw in the previous subtests. The results of this subtest are input into a special algorithm that affects the composite scores used for pilot and flight officer selection.

The Aviation Supplemental Subtest has 34 questions, which you will have 25 minutes to answer.

Test Scores

Examinees who take the entire test receive four scores resulting from different combinations of the six subtests. Examinees who only take the first three subtests receive only one score, the Officer Aptitude Rating (OAR). The four scores for examinees taking the entire test are:

The **Academic Qualifications Rating (AQR)** is used to predict academic performance in aviation preflight instruction and the primary phase of ground school. This score is affected by the examinee's performance on all the subtests, but the strongest influence is made by his or her score on the Math Skills Test. The AQR ranges from 1 to 9 and is used to predict academic performance in Aviation Preflight Indoctrination and the primary phase of ground school. The minimum score to become a Navy pilot or flight officer is a 3.

The **Pilot Flight Aptitude Rating (PFAR)** ranges from 1 to 9 and is used to predict primary flight performance for student naval aviators. This score is affected by performance on all subtests, but the greatest contribution is made by scores on the Aviation and Nautical Information and Spatial Apperception tests. The minimum score to qualify as a Navy pilot is a 4.

The **Flight Officer Flight Aptitude Rating (FOFAR)**, again ranging from 1 through 9, is used to predict primary phase flight school performance for student naval flight officers. This score is affected by performance on all subtests, but the strongest influence is from the Math Skills Test. The minimum score to qualify as a Navy flight officer is a 4.

The **Officer Aptitude Rating (OAR)** is used by the Navy to predict academic performance in Navy Officer Candidate School. This score comes from performance on the first three subtests: Math Skills, Reading Skills, and Mechanical Comprehension. This score ranges from a minimum of 20 through a maximum of 80, with a mean score of 50.

After the tests are scored, you will receive notification (usually by e-mail) of your test results.

Test-Taking Strategies, Tips, and Techniques

"If you don't know where you are going, any path will take you there."
—Native American proverb

"…you just might not like where you wind up."
—Anonymous

"Plan the work, then work the plan."
—A senior NCO

Effective Studying

Many people hold two incorrect beliefs about test taking. First, they believe that the amount of time spent studying is the most important—or maybe even the only—factor in improving their test results. Likewise, many people believe that last-minute studying (commonly referred to as "cramming") will get the job done. Neither of these ideas is correct, at least not completely.

The proven truth is that *efficient* studying *ahead of time* is by far the best method—and the only really effective way to get significantly better results on whatever test you're preparing for. Although it is true that any time spent studying is better than none, the question you have to ask yourself is this: *Am I getting the most benefit possible out of the time I am spending studying?*

Because time is a finite resource—you're never going to be granted 25 hours in a day, nor 61 minutes in an hour—it makes sense to use it as wisely and efficiently as possible. Remember that you have the same number of minutes in an hour and hours in a day as Aristotle, Leonardo da Vinci, Michelangelo, Benjamin Franklin, Thomas Edison, and the Wright brothers did—and you have vastly more resources at your fingertips than they ever did!

To make the time you *do* have count for as much as possible, *plan* your studying, and do it as far ahead of time as possible; you've already taken an important step in that direction by buying and using this book. This will make the time you spend studying more effective, instead of just time spent reading (there's a difference). And, although the amount of time you spend studying is important, the amount of time you spend studying *effectively* is even more important—and it's what will help you get improved results on your test. Therefore, you need to develop a system.

Spending an hour a day in uninterrupted studying in a quiet, nondistracting place will pay off far more than spending twice that time in 15–20 minute segments, especially if you are in a place where there are distractions or interruptions. Contrary to what many people today think, studying with the TV on is *not* the most effective way to study; *any* distraction is, well . . . distracting. That is, it takes away from your focus on what you're studying, so it's bad. And, if you can start studying a week, two weeks, or more before your test—or, if not, as far ahead as possible—it will give your brain and memory time to shift the material from your short-term memory (think of a temporary file on your computer) to your long-term memory (think of a file permanently saved on your hard drive), where you will be able to access it more easily.

Studying Tips

Here are some important guidelines for successful, efficient, *effective* studying:

1. **Establish a study schedule and stick to it.** Don't put off studying until it's convenient, or for some time when you have nothing else to do. If the test is important enough for you to take, it's important enough to invest the time in it to do as well as you can. Make studying a priority, equal in importance at least to your social life or watching television. How many movies or concerts or music stars or actors have any chance at all to improve your future? Those celebrities are not going to take your test for you (and even if they did, you probably wouldn't like the results). Schedule your study time and make every effort not to let anything else interfere with that schedule.

2. **Concentrate your study efforts in your weakest areas.** Chances are you already have an idea of the general areas where you are weak, strong, or just so-so. The first practice test for your service will give you some more focused insight about the kinds of questions you do well on, as well as the ones where you need some work—but don't neglect your stronger areas and let them become your new "need work" categories! Go back and review the information in Chapter 3 in the specific areas where you realize that you need help; if some area is still not clear to you, do further research in a library or on the Internet. If you're in college, find a classmate who is strong in that area and ask for help, or go find a professor or graduate assistant in that subject and explain your goal; chances are they will make time to help you. Even if you're not enrolled in a college or university right now, you can still pick up the phone and call an expert in the field (maybe at that college you're not enrolled in) and ask for suggestions on sources appropriate to your level and the time you have available.

   When you're ready to take the second test, look back at how many questions in each section you got right and wrong, and decide that you are going to get every question right on the second practice test. Then take the second practice test for your preferred service and do what's necessary from there.

3. **Study without interruption or stopping for at least 30 minutes at a time.** Set up your schedule so that you can study for an uninterrupted period of at least 30 minutes. If you have set aside a couple of hours, for instance, take a short break (maybe five, no more than ten minutes) after 30–45 minutes—get a drink, go to the restroom, stretch briefly—but don't lose your focus! It's easy to get distracted during this time, so stay away from the TV, don't make any phone calls, don't start organizing your closet—don't do anything that's going to keep you from diving right back into your studying. BUT, when you are tak-

ing a practice test, do the complete examination in one sitting, just as you will have to do when it comes time to actually take the test.

4. **Make sure you understand the correct meaning of every word you read or hear.** Your ability to grasp and comprehend what you read is the key to doing well on the test—after all, it *is* a <u>written</u> test, right? If it was a test on making baskets from the free-throw line, would you practice more on dribbling and passing or on what you were going to be tested on? Remember (and you already know this), the flight aptitude test you're preparing for is not just a test to earn a numerical grade on a report card; it's a test to see if you have what it takes to take advantage of a whole wealth of opportunities . . . or not. So, starting now, every time you see a word whose meaning you aren't completely sure of (whether you're studying at that moment or not), make the effort to look it up. If you can't look it up right then, write it down and look it up when you can. This will require self discipline, but you will get the benefit not only on the test, but in your daily life.

5. **Keep a list of the words that you didn't know and had to look up.** Then go back and review them periodically. Try to use them in conversation when it's appropriate—not to make yourself sound like an egghead, but to be able to express yourself more precisely and concisely. Stretch your mental muscles by doing crossword puzzles.

6. **Write it down.** It is a well-proven fact that you retain things that you write down better and longer than those things that you just hear, even if you say them—so take the time and effort to write down the word and its definition. Not on a computer, but *longhand*. Okay, print it in block letters if you want, but *write it down*. Then write a sentence using that word as it might be used in a real conversation, or in an imaginary term paper. The mental and physiological effort you expend to write that word or concept down significantly reinforces your memory of it far above just hearing or even saying it. Even if you never see those notes again—and you *should* review them—you will still retain the material better.

7. **Simulate test conditions when studying—and especially when taking practice tests!** To the extent that you can, reproduce the same conditions you will encounter when you are taking the actual test. The more you do this when you are "just" studying—not to mention when you are taking a practice test—the more you will be used to this kind of environment when it comes time for the test that counts. If you have other people in the household, tell them that you are taking a practice test and ask for their support by not disturbing you; chances are they will be happy to comply.

8. **Follow the recommended techniques for answering multiple-choice questions.** This chapter will provide you with some very valuable techniques for maximizing your chances of getting multiple-choice questions right—and not just making it "multiple guess"!

9. **Time yourself when doing practice tests.** Running out of time on a multiple-choice test is a tragedy that you can avoid. Learn through practice how much time is reasonable to spend on any particular question, then stick to it.

10. **Exercise regularly and stay in good physical shape.** It's hard to remember sometimes that life is supposed to be about balance, especially when you have too many things to do and nowhere near enough time to do even half of them. However, the bottom line here is that if your body isn't in at least decent shape, you will not do as well as you could on the test. Do at least 20–30 *uninterrupted* minutes of aerobic exercise (something that makes you breathe hard) at least two to three times a week, and preferably more. Strength training (lifting some kind of weights) is good, but balance the amount of weight you can lift with how many repetitions you can do, and don't overdo things to the extent that you risk injury. Even a temporary injury is a distraction you don't need.

11. **Practice, practice, practice—stay in good <u>mental</u> shape, too.** After you take both practice tests for your preferred service, look at the sections in the other services' tests that are similar to the areas where you still need work. And even if you think vocabulary is a strong point for you, for instance, don't rest on your laurels; get everything out of this book that you can by looking at the language-related sections in the other tests. Look on the Internet for practice questions for your service's test. Look at practice SAT, ACT, and GRE tests that are available to you, even if they are older versions available in the library—the meaning of *indubitably* won't change, nor will the formula for the area of a circle or for calculating distance traveled when you know the velocity and the time elapsed. Do crossword and Sudoku puzzles. Keep learning, keep practicing, and keep your brain nimble.

Guidelines for Multiple-Choice Tests

This section lays out some specific test-taking techniques that will help you on this and other multiple-choice tests. Learn these techniques and then practice them so that they are second nature to you when it comes time to take the test.

1. **Read the directions.** Don't assume that you know what the directions are for a specific section, or for the test overall, without reading them. Make sure you read them through as thoroughly as if it was the first time you had seen them, and make sure you understand them fully. This is not *spending* time so much as *investing* it—and why take a chance on canceling out all the effort you've spent studying and otherwise preparing? Besides, the test monitor or proctor won't let you start until everyone has had plenty of time to read the directions—usually they read them aloud, too—so there's no reason *not* to read the directions. Pay special attention to whether there are different directions from one section of the test to another.

2. **Look closely at the answer sheet.** The answer sheets on your practice exams in this book are typical of what you should see when you take the test, but don't take anything for granted. Read the directions on the answer sheet carefully—that means all the way through—and make sure you understand the format.

3. **Be careful when you mark your answers.** Make sure that you mark your answers in accordance with the instructions on the answer sheet. Pay special attention to make sure that you do the following:

- **Mark only one answer for each question.**
- **Make <u>sure</u> you are marking the numbered answer for the question you think you are answering.** Although this may seem pretty obvious (and it is), lots of tests have been failed because of this kind of carelessness. All it takes is getting off track on one question. You probably won't notice it right away, so you'll continue being off for even more questions. If you do notice, you'll spend time you might not be able to afford trying to fix your mistake—and if you don't notice, you'll be baffled about why you did so poorly on that section that was supposed to be your strong area.
- **Don't make any extra or stray marks on your answer sheet;** most tests are machine graded, and it's not going to help you to confuse the scanner or optical character reader.
- **Completely fill in the allotted space** (circle, oval, rectangle) for the answer you choose.
- **Erase *completely*** any answers you want to change. This goes back to your preparation, in that you need to bring a good, fresh eraser that works; check it before the test to make sure it does the job. The machine grading the test won't know that you realized that choice B was really the right answer, and not choice A; it will just note that two choices were marked for Question 22, and grade you as WRONG. Ever hear the old saying, "Little things mean a lot"?
- **Make sure you understand what the question is really asking.** Read carefully what is normally called the root or stem of the question—the part before the answer choices—to make sure you know what the question really is. Don't be in such a galloping hurry that you slam through it and miss a *not* or *except* or some other small but important indicator. Read the question twice—and if none of the choices seem correct after the first time you look at them, read the question again.
- **Read all the choices before you choose an answer.** Don't fall into the trap of thinking that the best distractor—a plausible but still incorrect answer—is it because it's first and oh, boy, it seems right, and let's get on to the next question!
- **Know the key "tipoff" words that often signal a wrong answer.** Absolute words such as *never, nobody, nothing, always, all, only, any, everyone, everybody,* and the like are often clues that this answer is too broad and therefore wrong.
- **Know the key words that often signal a *possibly* correct answer.** Limiting words such as *usually, generally, sometimes, possible, many, some, occasionally, often,* and the like often signal a choice that at least *could* be correct—but read it carefully to be sure!
- **Look at how the meaning of the choices compare with each other.** If two choices have a conflicting or opposite meaning, chances are high that one of them is correct. And, if two choices are very close in meaning, chances are pretty good that *neither* of them is correct.
- **NEVER make a choice based on the frequency of lettered answer choices.** This is the same thing as rolling dice—the odds are stacked against you. If this is what you think will work, please just mail your money to the casino and don't waste time and taxpayer money taking the test.

- **Eliminate choices you recognize as being incorrect.** <u>This is the most important guideline to success on any multiple-choice test</u>. As you read through the choices, eliminate any choice you know is wrong. If you can eliminate all the choices except one, there's your answer! Read the choice one more time to make sure you haven't missed anything, then mark that answer on your answer sheet and move on to the next question. If you can, for example, eliminate only one or two of the possible choices, read through the question and the remaining choices once more. Many times the right answer will become apparent; if not—even if you have to flat-out guess between two or three possible choices that you think *could* be right—you will have significantly increased your odds of answering that question correctly.

- **Never reconsider answer choices that you have already eliminated.** If you thought it was wrong the first time through, you were probably correct. Focus on the ones that could be right.

- **Skip questions that are giving you too much trouble.** Don't dwell on any one question too long on your first trip through that section or subtest. If you've read the question twice, tried to eliminate any obviously incorrect answers, and still have no clue between three or four choices, it's time to go to the next question and come back when you get to the end of that section. There are two options on how to handle the question you're skipping. First, you can just plain skip it if you're reasonably certain you're going to get to the end of the subsection with time to spare; the trick here is to make sure that you leave that answer totally blank on your answer sheet and don't fill in the blank for the question that you skipped with the answer to the question *after* the one you skipped. The second option is to go ahead and fill in an answer for one of the choices you think might be right so that you stay in sequence, and also to hedge your bets in case you don't get to the end of the test with time enough to go back to questions that you skipped. Either way, if you are allowed to mark in your test booklet, or if you have scratch paper, circle the number of the question you skipped or write it down on the scratch paper.

- **Go back to the questions you skipped within a subtest after you get to the end.** Once you have answered all the questions you were at least reasonably sure of in a section or subtest, check to see how much time you have remaining. If you can, go back to the questions you skipped and reread the question and the choices. Sometimes a subsequent question will have jarred loose something in your memory and you will be able to make a good choice. If you read the question again and you still are having trouble, make the best guess you can, following the guidelines above.

- **Never leave any questions unanswered; there is no penalty for wrong answers, only credit for correct ones.** Enough said.

- **Be very reluctant to change answers.** Unless you have an <u>excellent</u> reason, *don't* change an answer you have already marked in the belief that it was correct. Studies have shown again and again and again that if you are still unsure and are just trying to use the really dependable intuition that has helped you so much up to this point (yes, that's sarcasm), you are far more likely to change a right answer to a wrong one than the other way around.

The Day of the Test

First, **get a good night's sleep** the night before the test. If you've established a plan and followed it, you won't be up until the wee hours cramming; if you haven't—well, good luck. Even better, try to get an adequate amount of sleep for several days before the test, and don't neglect an appropriate amount of physical exercise (and then keep that good habit *after* you take the test); this will help you sleep better at night, and you'll be more relaxed and have better stamina and resistance to stress during the day.

Organize your morning before you take the test for success. Lay out your clothes and test-taking materials the night before. Wake up early enough so that you can avoid rushing through your morning routine. Eat a good breakfast, but go easy on the carbs—some are okay, but just say "no" to that second stack of pancakes or second helping of hash browns. Your body won't realize that you need that blood to your brain, and it will be trying to divert more blood to your digestive system than you can afford during the test. Drink plenty of water early on, but not so much that you are guaranteed to need a restroom break after the first 15 minutes of the test.

If you have a choice, **wear comfortable clothes** to the test. If you are wearing a uniform, make sure you are wearing a fresh one, have a fresh haircut and shave, and generally look as if you are ready to be inspected by the local general or admiral. No one will give you points on the test for concluding from your rumpled, haggard appearance that you have been up studying nonstop for days—but *you* will feel more confident and therefore sharper if you look sharp and you know it. This applies whether you are wearing a uniform or not.

Take a light jacket or sweater that you can put on or take off easily. It might be cold in the testing area, and why subject yourself to an avoidable distraction?

Take a stopwatch or digital watch with a timer. Some proctors may give you a heads-up when your time for a certain section has almost elapsed, but some won't— the proctors for the ASTB are actually instructed *not* to give any warnings. When your time is down to a minute, you may want to seriously consider guessing your way through any remaining questions—if you still have a lot of questions left, you may want to just mark "B" or "C" (or whatever letter feels lucky) all the way through them. If you only have a few remaining questions, you can probably eliminate at least one or two wrong answers and guess between the ones that look plausible. Remember, you are not penalized for wrong answers; you just get credit for the right ones.

Get to the test location early. If you think it will take you 15 minutes to get there, allow 30. If you've been there a hundred times before and it's never taken longer than 30 minutes, allow an hour; this is the one day there will be road construction or a traffic jam in your way. If it's somewhere local but you haven't been there before, try to do a reconnaissance of the location, to include the room itself, in the week before you take the test. The one time that you get bad directions off the "always reliable" map-generating Internet site will be the time you need them, badly, to get to the test site on time. If you have to rush into the test site frustrated and out of breath, you are not setting yourself up for success—and in some circum stances, if you get there late, you'll be out of luck. If nothing else, get there with enough time to go to the restroom before you start the test, and to find a seat with a chair that doesn't make a distracting noise every time you move. Put yourself on Lombardi time: If you're not there early, you're late.

Tell yourself that you can do it. And, if you have been putting these principles into practice, chances are you'll be right.

Language Review Information

For officers to lead—which is, regardless of service or specialty, an officer's primary function—they must be able to communicate with the people they are trying to lead. The best plan in the world is worthless if the people who are supposed to execute it can't understand what they're supposed to do. If you want to be an officer in any service, you must be able to communicate at least reasonably well both orally and in writing—and, because officers are normally held to a higher standard, that "reasonably well" rating may be something at which you have to work.

This chapter reviews a wide array of language-related topics that help measure whether you can read and understand information presented to you. The flight aptitude tests evaluate this by a variety of multiple-choice questions dealing with synonyms and antonyms, analogies, and vocabulary—all of which add up to answering the question, *Can you comprehend what you read?*

Much of this information will, ideally, already be familiar to you. Going over it won't hurt you any—and chances are you will learn or reinforce something that will help you on whichever test you are taking.

Synonyms and Antonyms

A *synonym* is a word that has the same or almost the same meaning as another word. An *antonym* is a word that has the opposite or nearly opposite meaning of another word. A desk-size dictionary (not just a paperback version) will give you insight on some synonyms and maybe some antonyms; a thesaurus will give you the full range of both.

In determining whether a word has a similar or an opposite meaning to another word, it's necessary to understand the root of a word, as well as any prefixes or suffixes it may have. Go over the common roots, suffixes, and prefixes later in this chapter.

Verbal Analogies

The Air Force is the only service that tests flight aptitude test-takers on verbal analogies, but they are useful analytical tools in any case. Verbal analogies test your ability to determine the relationships between words. To do that, though, you not only need to know what the words mean, but you'll also have to apply logic to determine the relationships between the words in consideration.

There are two format types for verbal analogies on the AFOQT. The first type of analogy question contains three capitalized words in the stem, followed by five one-word choices. The first two of the three words will give you the base analogy (THIS is to THAT); your task then is to choose which of the five choices has the same relationship to the third word as is established in the base analogy.

Here's an example:

CAT is to KITTEN as WOLF is to

(A) dog
(B) cub
(C) lion
(D) puppy
(E) cougar

In this case, the correct answer would be **(B) cub**. A baby cat is a kitten, and a baby wolf is a cub. Therefore the relationship between the second capitalized word is the infant or baby form of the first capitalized word. A wolf's offspring are called cubs, and that represents the same relationship to the wolf as the kitten has to the cat.

The second type of verbal analogy on the AFOQT involves only two capitalized words—the first pair—in the stem of the question. Your task is then to choose which of the five pairs of words presented most closely resembles the same relationship as that shown in the first pair.

Here's an example of the first question recast in this format:

CAT is to KITTEN as

(A) puppy is to dog
(B) wolf is to cub
(C) lion is to lioness
(D) puppy is to kitten
(E) cougar is to panther

In this example, the only choice that represents the same relationship that CAT has to KITTEN is **(B) wolf is to cub**. Be careful to note that, in the base analogy, the adult form of the animal is listed first, so don't be thrown off by choice **(A) puppy is to dog**, because the younger form of the animal is listed first.

The most important part of correctly answering these analogy questions is to determine what kind of relationship exists between the first and second word in the first, or base, analogy, and then find a choice that closely reproduces that relationship between the two words used as the second analogy. Because there's no way to list every possible relationship that could exist, though, we will get the basics down by going over examples of the most common types of analogies you could see on the test.

Again, be sure to keep the order the same in the second pair as in the first—a common "distractor" choice is one where the relationship of the items in the second pair of words is the same as in the first, but the order is reversed.

Part to whole (correct): ROOM is to HOUSE as CABIN is to SHIP.
A room is an integral part of a house in the same way that a cabin is part of a ship.
Part to whole (incorrect): ROOM is to HOUSE as CABIN is to DECK.
The cabin and the deck are both parts of the ship; neither is a "whole" that the other is part of.
Part to whole (correct): GIRDER is to BUILDING as KEEL is to SHIP.
The girder and the keel are both structural components of the building and ship, respectively.
Part to whole (incorrect): GIRDER is to BUILDING as CABIN is to SHIP.
The girder is a structural component of the building; the cabin, although a component of the ship, is not so much the same kind of component—doesn't have the same relationship—as the girder is to the building.

Cause to effect (correct): SPARK is to FIRE as HURRICANE is to FLOOD.
The fire is the direct result of the spark, just as the flood is the direct result of the hurricane.
Cause to effect (incorrect): SPARK is to FIRE as HURRICANE is to DESTRUCTION.
The fire is the direct result of the spark, but the destruction is a result of the hurricane's wind or flooding, and not so much a direct result of the hurricane itself.

Source to product (correct): TREE is to ORANGE as FACTORY is to PRODUCT.
Source to product (incorrect): TREE is to BRANCH as FACTORY is to PRODUCT.
The branch is a part of the tree, but is not a product of it in the same way that a tree produces an orange or a factory produces its product.

Example to category (correct): CAR is to AUTOMOBILE as HOUSE is to DWELLING.
The first item is one of multiple items in the second item, which is the "next level up" category; trucks and vans are automobiles just like cars are, and caves and houseboats are dwellings in the same way that a house is.
Example to category (incorrect): CAR is to TRUCK as HOUSE is to DWELLING.
The car and the truck are both members of the same category—you could call this a "peer to peer" analogy—but the HOUSE is to DWELLING analogy is still an example-to-category exercise.
Example to category (incorrect): CAR is to AUTOMOBILE as HOUSE is to STRUCTURE.

This incorrect example is a little more subtle; STRUCTURE is a much broader, more inclusive category than DWELLING, including as it does structures that cannot be lived in as a house or a barn or a cave could, such as bridges, statues, gazebos, reviewing stands, and so on.

General to specific (correct): SHAPE is to TRIANGLE as PASTRY is to CROISSANT.

This could also be thought of as a "category to example" analogy, merely the mirror image of the previous example.

Object to function (correct): SHIELD is to PROTECT as CONTAINER is to HOLD.

Be sure the function word (almost certainly a verb) is the primary and definitive function of the noun/object that makes up the other word of the pair. If the function word is a minor or uncommon function of the object rather than a defining, typical function of the object, watch out!

Object to function (incorrect): WHEEL is to ROLL as SHIELD is to CARRY.

User to tool (correct): MECHANIC is to WRENCH as CARPENTER is to SAW.

Usually the tool mentioned in this kind of analogy is a defining or typical tool for the kind of user described, as it is in this example.

User to tool (incorrect): MECHANIC is to WRENCH as CARPENTER is to TROWEL. A stonemason might use a trowel, but a carpenter would not normally do so.

TIP

When one word of the pair is a verb, make sure that the verb tense (present, past, past participle, etc.) is the same for both word pairs. The same goes for the number of nouns—if one word pair mentions a singular object, chances are the correctly matching second pair will <u>not</u> have a plural noun for its object.

Doer to action (correct): FARMER is to PLANTING as DOCTOR is to HEALING.

Again, make sure that the action word or verb associated with the doer is something that is a typical or defining task for the doer. If not, then the relationship is something else!

Doer to action (incorrect): FARMER is to HARVEST as DOCTOR is to HEALING.

Numerical (correct): ONE is to TEN as FIVE is to FIFTY.

Note: The base analogy takes the first number and multiplies it by ten, so the second pair does the same thing.

Numerical (incorrect): ONE is to TEN as FIVE is to TEN.

Grammatical (correct): HOLD is to HELD as STOP is to STOPPED.
Grammatical (correct): DOG is to DOGS as CAT is to CATS.

The concept to watch out for here is nothing more difficult than identifying which choice has the analogy with the same grammatical relationship as the base analogy. If the base analogy goes from singular to plural, so too will the correct choice; if the base analogy goes from a present tense verb to a past or past perfect tense verb, so will the correct answer. Also, make sure you are going the right direction, i.e., have the terms in both the base and the matching analogy in the same or parallel order. And watch out for different tenses of the correct verb!

Grammatical (correct): RUN is to RAN as SING is to SANG.

Grammatical (incorrect): RUN is to RAN as SING is to SUNG.

Here, the base analogy is present/past, and the incorrectly matching analogy is present/past participle.

Geographic (correct): TEXAS is to OKLAHOMA as FLORIDA is to GEORGIA.

In both cases, the first of the pair is a U.S. state and the second is the state north of and adjacent to it.

Geographic (correct): AUSTIN is to TEXAS as MONTGOMERY is to ALABAMA.

Geographic (correct): BERLIN is to GERMANY as KABUL is to AFGHANISTAN.

Here we have the capital city of some U.S. states and some other nations, respectively. Sometimes you will have to bring other knowledge to bear to correctly match these analogies.

Geographic (incorrect): GEORGIA is to ALABAMA as MEXICO is to PARIS.

Geographic (incorrect): PARIS is to FRANCE as GERMANY is to MUNICH.

Here we have the base analogy with the capital of a country. The order of the countries is incorrectly matched, and a noncapital city is matched with Germany. This is wrong on two accounts: relationship and order.

Descriptive (correct): CANDY is to SWEET as ICE is to COLD

In this case, the second, descriptive term is something that defines the first word; sweetness and cold are inherent qualities of candy and ice, respectively.

Descriptive (incorrect): CANDY is to SWEET as TURKEY is to COLD.

Because a turkey can be any temperature, COLD is not a defining or frequently associated description of TURKEY, so this is not a valid analogy match.

Age (correct): CHILD is to ADULT as SEEDLING is to TREE.

Age (correct): PUPPY is to DOG as TADPOLE is to FROG.

Again, make sure the order (younger/older or older/younger) is the same for the second pair of words as for the first.

Age (incorrect): CHILD is to ADULT as MAN is to WOMAN.

Age (incorrect): CALF is to COW as CATERPILLAR is to WORM.

Some other analogy relationships with single examples:

Type of analogy	Example
Synonyms (same meaning)	HATE is to DESPISE
Antonyms (opposite meaning)	LOVE is to HATE
Homonyms (sound the same)	THERE is to THEIR
Measurement (time, distance, weight, volume, etc.)	MILE is to KILOMETER, MILLIMETER is to METER
Gender (one sex to the other)	COW is to BULL, GOOSE is to GANDER
Larger to smaller	LAKE is to POND
Degree/amount	COOL is to COLD, OLD is to ANCIENT
	AMUSING is to HILARIOUS

Remember, these categories are only examples to help you see the overall way that analogies are done, as well as for your convenience in studying and practice. The people who design the tests aren't bound by these categories! If the analogy you see on the test does not seem to fit into one of these categories, just remember these examples and guidelines, figure out what kind of relationship the base analogy demonstrates, and follow the lead of the base analogy.

Paragraph Comprehension

Understanding what you read involves being able to recognize the main idea, remember details, make conclusions or inferences, identify and understand factual relationships, and paraphrase or summarize. The Navy/Marine Corps ASTB will directly test you on these specific skills; the other tests will indirectly test you on these skills by your success in understanding and complying with their instructions. However, regardless of whether you are taking a test or just conducting daily operations, you should ideally be able to read a clearly written passage once and get the main idea; by referring to the passage, you should be able to easily do the other things.

The *main idea* is the most important point or idea that the writer wants the reader to know or understand. Sometimes the writer states the main idea clearly and directly; sometimes the main idea is implied or has to be inferred from what the passage *does* say. When a main idea is generalized across the entire passage, essay, book, and so on, it is known as the *theme*.

Whenever you are trying to determine a paragraph's main idea, it's a good idea to check the first (opening) and last (closing) sentences of the paragraph. Writers frequently use a *topic sentence* (often either at the beginning or end of a paragraph or essay, although they can be anywhere) that concisely addresses the main idea.

> To help you find the main idea in reading a passage or paragraph, ask these questions:
>
> 1. Who or what is this paragraph about?
> 2. What specific aspect or facet of this subject is the writer discussing?
> 3. What point is the writer trying to make about this subject or this particular aspect of it?

Look at this example paragraph:

> Making any of the eight errors common to transformation efforts can have serious consequences. In slowing down the new initiatives, creating unnecessary resistance, frustrating employees endlessly, and sometimes completely stifling needed change, any of these errors could cause an organization to fail to offer the products or services people want at prices they can afford. Budgets are then squeezed, people are laid off, and those who remain are put under great stress. The impact on families and communities can be devastating.

In this paragraph, the main idea is stated in the first sentence. You can tell that the paragraph will be about what happens when an organization makes any of the "eight errors common to transformation." In the same way as a headline or title, the topic sentence introduces the rest of the paragraph, setting the stage and getting you thinking about what's going to follow.

> During the latter years of the American Revolution, a government structured under the Articles of Confederation was formed. This government, which gave the states more power than the central national government, suffered severely and had many problems. The states distrusted each other and allowed the national or federal government to exercise very little authority. The Articles of Confederation produced a government that could not effectively raise money from taxes, prevent or stop Indian raids, or force the British out of the United States.

Can you identify the topic sentence in the paragraph above? Yes, the paragraph *is* about the Articles of Confederation. However, is the main idea in the first sentence, the second, or somewhere else? In this example, the *second* sentence does the best job of giving you an overall understanding of this paragraph: The lack of centralized authority under the Articles of Confederation caused lots of problems. The first sentence really just tells us *when* the items in the paragraph happened—it doesn't explain anything about what happened, much less the overarching idea. The sentences that follow give more details about this idea; they give you some of the reasons why the topic sentence was true. It's not a good idea to assume that the topic sentence is always the first sentence.

> With its smaller population and more agriculturally centered (and therefore manpower-intensive) economy, the Confederacy had fewer men available as soldiers. Less than one-third of the railroads and even fewer prewar United States industries were in the South. For most of the war, the ports and coastlines of Confederate states were blockaded by the Union Navy. It is considered in many circles a tribute to Confederate leadership and Southern courage that the rebels were not defeated sooner.

In this case, you can see that the passage builds up to its main point, which is in the last sentence.

And, as mentioned before, you may also find that the main idea is not stated directly at all, but can only be inferred or deduced from the whole passage or paragraph.

Finding Details

In developing the main idea of a paragraph or passage, the writer usually makes statements or shows action to support his or her point. They may give examples to illustrate the main idea, or they may mention facts or statistics to support it. The writer may give reasons why the main idea statement is true or correct; they might offer arguments for or against the position or idea that the main idea states. The writer can also define a complex term, cite different characteristics of a complex system or organization, classify objects within a larger category, or use descriptive details to develop an idea and help the reader understand or envision the situation. Also, the writer may *compare* two ideas, objects, or processes, to show how they are alike or similar, or the writer may *contrast* them—show how they are different.

Read how the writer of the following paragraph uses supporting details:

> My most hyperactive year was from June 1944 to June 1945. Arriving in England just in time for the invasion, my first mission as a new pilot in the 353rd Fighter Squadron was flying top cover over the invasion, combined with emptying my guns—strafing anything that moved in front of the Allied troops fighting for a secure beachhead. The reality of war became more complete on D+10 (June 16) when I landed our first P-51 at airstrip A2 at Criqueville, France. The reality of war meant being fired on during takeoff and landing. It seemed questionable to me to risk planes and pilots so close to the front; the rationale was more missions per plane per day, in addition to the advantage of avoiding the "London fog" weather of England, but France turned out to be just as bad. Our mission was to patrol the skies above and in front of the Third Army, keeping the Luftwaffe at bay, dive-bombing before each patrol and strafing afterward. We also flew escort for B-17, B-26, and B-25 bombers.

To help you understand what was "hyperactive" about the year from June 1944 to June 1945, the writer gives supporting details, detailing not only the amount of work or effort that went into his activities, but also some clues about the pace of the operations and the pilots' concerns about enemy fire.

When the test requires you to answer a question about some detail or details in the passage, you have to find words or phrases in the passage that specifically answer the question. In other words, considering the passage above, the test will *not* ask you about what kind of plane the writer flew before coming to Europe; the passage doesn't address that. Instead, it might ask you what kind of plane the writer flew when landing in France (P-51, fighter), when the writer landed in France (June 16, 1944), or who the writer's unit was up against (the Luftwaffe or German Air Force).

> Try the following techniques when a test asks you a specific question about details of the passage:
>
> 1. Look for key words (nouns and verbs) in the question stem and answer choices.
> 2. Read rapidly through the passage, looking for those key words or their synonyms.
> 3. Reread the part of the passage that contains the key word(s) or synonyms.

Understanding the Passage's Organization

Questions about a reading passage will also test your ability to understand the organization of the ideas in the passage and their relationship to each other. Writers usually organize their information in fairly predictable, logical ways to make it easier for the reader to understand. Recognizing common organizational patterns improves your understanding, memory, and reading speed—as well as helping you choose the right answer on the test.

Sequential Organization

A *sequence* is a series of events or steps where the order is important. If the sequence is *chronological* (time based), the events are described or listed in the order in which they occurred. Clues to help you spot sequential organization include ordinal numbers (*first, second, third*, etc.), cardinal numbers (*1, 2, 3*, etc.), transition words or phrases (*then, next, later, finally, ultimately*), and dates or other information referring to time (*this year, last month, in 1982, four days later*, and so on).

> If you are stung by a bee, the first thing you need to do is remove the stinger. Next, make a paste of baking soda and water and apply it to the sting site. Then, apply ice or cold water to help reduce the pain and minimize swelling. If the pain is severe or if you are allergic to the insect, find medical help immediately.

Physical or Spatial Organization

When the organization of a passage is physical or spatial, it describes the physical arrangement or situation of a place or object. Clues can include such words as *above, below, to the right of, to the left of, behind, in front of, next to,* and so on.

> Taste buds are distributed across the tongue, but the distribution is uneven, and certain areas of the tongue are more sensitive to certain basic tastes than other areas. The tip of the tongue is most sensitive to sweetness, but the area just behind the tip is the most sensitive to salty tastes. Only the sides of the tongue are very sensitive to sour tastes, and the back area specializes in bitter tastes.

Cause and Effect

A passage may include a description or statement that a particular thing happened, the reasons why it happened, and/or the results that came after the occurrence. For instance, a history passage may list the events that led up to a technological innovation, a social or political change, or a war; a scientific passage may explain tectonic plate shifts and how they affect mountain formation and earthquakes. Often, the relationship is presented as a chain of events, with one or more events leading to or resulting in one or more other events. Clues include *resulted in, because, consequently, since, therefore, thus,* and so on.

> By the year 2020, there will be approximately one retired American for every two working Americans. In these disproportionately large numbers, older Americans will therefore become an increasingly large and powerful political force, and political issues of concern to senior citizens and elderly people such as housing, medical benefits, and reduced employment levels will be taken more seriously by elected officials.

Comparing and Contrasting Ideas

A passage may present the similarities or differences between ideas, people, places, or other things. In a *comparison*, the passage will focus on similarities; clue words can include *like, likewise, also, in like manner, similarly,* and the like. The passage may instead focus on differences, presenting a *contrast*; clues for contrasting include *but, unlike, however, in contrast, on the other hand, versus,* and *nevertheless.*

> The American farm problem often centers on supply exceeding demand and farm policies that encourage surplus production. This is not true in most other parts of the world, where countries cannot produce enough food to support their own populations and have to import food or else face famine.

Solution to a Problem

In this pattern of organization, the writer presents the reader with a problem or describes a situation that is causing difficulty, and then presents or suggests a solution or a remedy. Clue words include *problem, cause, effects, consequences, answers, solutions,* and *remedy* or *remedies.*

> Students who lived in dormitories near an area in which earthquakes happened frequently, one study says, often just denied the seriousness of the situation and the potential danger they were in.

(In this case, the solution—although an unrealistic and ineffective one—was simply to ignore the problem.)

Drawing a Conclusion or Making an Inference

A conclusion is a logical inference based on information that is presented or implied. If you read a passage critically (which, in this case, doesn't mean *negatively,* but rather just *carefully while looking for errors*), you follow the writer's train of thought and arrive at logical conclusions. The writer may expect the readers to draw the conclusion by themselves, or the writer may explicitly say it, often using clue words such as *therefore, thus, hence,* or *in conclusion.*

The sample passage that follows is about Americans with disabilities. The reader can conclude that legislation has made progress in moving people with disabilities into society's mainstream, although the writer doesn't say so directly. Incidentally, note the sequence pattern in this passage.

> A major goal for the disabled is easier access to the mainstream of society. The 1973 Rehabilitation Act has moved them toward this goal, as has the Education for All Handicapped Children Act of 1975, which mandates that all children, however severe their disability, receive a free, appropriate education. Before the legislation, one million handicapped children were receiving no education and another three million were getting an inappropriate one (as in the case of a blind child who is not taught Braille or is not provided with instructional materials in Braille). In 1987, Congress enacted the Employment Opportunities for Disabled Americans Act, which allows disabled individuals to earn a moderate income without losing their Medicaid health coverage.

The Parts of a Word

When you first learned how to drive, you had to (among other things) learn the parts of an automobile and what they did, from the hood to the wheels to the engine to the controls and instruments to the trunk. Now you can use that automobile to transport yourself from one place to another.

In much the same way, if you want to transport your message to your listener, words are your vehicle—and the more you understand about how words are built, the better work they can and will do for you. You can (and should) flip this around, too: **For you to understand what the writers of the test you are preparing to take want you to do, you have to be able to understand the words they use.** This is not just for the part of the test dealing with language skills. The whole test is written, which means that you have to be able to read and understand what they are saying. You may be the world's best math whiz, but if you can't read the directions to a problem, you will never get a chance to demonstrate that skill.

The most important part of any word is the *root*. It may be a word in itself (for example, *flex*), or a word element from which other words are formed (*aud*, for instance). Knowing a large number of word roots is one way of multiplying your vocabulary's strength, because each root can lead you to the understanding of several words.

A *prefix* is a syllable or group of syllables added to the beginning of a word that changes its meaning. Let's go back to the previous example word, *flex*. By itself, it means "to bend or contract"; we'll say that the context is the human body, so you can flex a muscle, an arm, or the like. If you add the prefix *re* to the root word *flex*, you get a new word, *reflex*, with a new meaning: *reflex* describes an action you can't control, such as a sneeze.

We can further change the meaning of the root word *flex* by adding a suffix. A suffix is a syllable or group of syllables added to the end of a word that changes its meaning. If you add the suffix *ible* to the end of the root, you get another new word, *flexible*, with a new meaning: *flexible* means *able to bend without breaking* or, in a more general sense, *able to adjust to change*.

You can also add *both* a prefix and a suffix to a root and get still another word. If, for example, you add both the prefix *in* (meaning *not*) and the suffix *ible*, you get another word, *inflexible*, which means *unbending*—or, in a broader sense, *stubborn, unable to adapt to change*.

To extend the example, let's look at some more of the *flex* "family" of words. It's helpful to know in this case that *flect* is another form of *flex*; however, even though similar-sounding words often have the same root, don't be fooled that it is always the case—because it's not.

flexibility	deflect	inflection
circumflex	genuflect	reflection

If you're not sure of the exact meaning of some of these words, look them up—the effort you expend in doing so will help the meanings stick in your memory.

Following is a list of prefixes frequently used in English. Your task is to write down at least one word that uses the prefix and then check your dictionary to verify that you have used the prefix and the root word correctly.

<u>Prefix</u>	<u>Meaning</u>	<u>Complete Word(s)</u>
a	not, no, without	
ab	not, away from	
acantho	spiny, thorny	
acro	top, tip	
ad	to	
aero	air, gas	
amphi	both, around	
an	not	
ana	again, thoroughly	
andro/anthropo	man	
ante	before, prior to	
anti	against, not	
apo	away	
baro	weight	
be	completely	
bi	two	
biblio	book	
cent	hundred	
circum	around	
contra	against	
cosmo	universe	
cyto	cell	
dactylo	finger	
de	from, away	
dec/deca	ten	
dermo/dermato	skin	
di	two	
dia	across	
ergo	work	
eth/ethno	race, nation	
eu	well	
ex	out of	
extra	beyond	
fore	before, on the front	
gastro	stomach	
geronto	old age	
hema	blood	
hemi	half	
hepta	seven	
hex/hexa	six	
hyper	above	
hypo	under, below	
in	into	
in	not	
inter	between	
intra	within	
kilo	thousand	

Prefix	Meaning	Complete Word(s)
meso	middle	
meta	beyond, after, changed	
metro	measure	
mill	thousand	
milli	one-thousandth; very small	
mis	wrong, incorrect	
mono	one	
necro	dead, dead body	
non/nona	nine	
ob	against	
oct/octa	eight	
osteo	bone	
out	from, beyond	
over	above, too much	
para	beside, close, partial	
penta	five	
peri	around	
pneumo	lung, air	
poly	many	
post	after	
pre	before	
pro	forward or in favor of	
quadr	four	
quint	five	
re	back, do again	
retro	back	
se	apart	
semi	half	
sep/sept	seven	
sex	six	
sub	under	
super	above, beyond	
syn	together, with	
tetra	four	
tox/toxico	poison	
trans	across	
tri	three	
ultra	beyond	
un	not	
under	below	
uni	one	
xeno	foreign	
zoo	living	
zygo	double	

Following is a list of frequently used root words. Write down at least one word (make it up if you have to) using each listed root, then check your result in the dictionary. Try to combine the root with one of the prefixes listed earlier.

Root	Meaning	Complete Word(s)
ac/acr	sharp, bitter	
act	do	
amb	walk, go	
anim	life, spirit, breath	
ann/annu	year	
anthro	man	
aqua	water	
aud	hear	
bene	good, well	
cap/capit	head	
card/cord	heart	
carn	flesh	
cas	fall	
ced/cede	go	
chrom	color	
chron	time	
cid/cide	kill	
clud/clude	close	
cor	heart	
corp	body	
cred	believe	
curr	run	
dem	people	
demi	one-tenth	
dic/dict	say	
do/don	give	
duc/duct	lead	
fac/fact	make	
fer	carry, move	
fin	end	
flect/flex	bend	
flu/flux	flow	
fract	break	
frater	brother, brotherly	
graph	write	
gress	walk	
hetero	different	
homo	same	
hydr/hydro	water	
ject	throw	
jur/jure	swear	
litera	letter	
lith	stone	

Root	**Meaning**	**Complete Word(s)**
logo/logos	thought, study	
mag/magn	large, powerful	
mal	evil, incorrect	
man/manu	hand	
mar	sea	
mater	mother	
ment	mind	
met/meter	measure, measurement	
micro	very small	
mit	send	
mono	one	
mort	death	
mot	move	
multi	many	
norm	rule	
nov	new	
ortho	right, correct	
pan	all	
pater	father	
path	suffer, feel	
ped	foot, base	
pend	hang	
phil	like	
phon	sound	
psych	mind	
pug/pugn	fight	
rupt	break	
sci	know	
scrib	write	
sec/sect	cut	
sol	alone	
spec/spect	look	
struc/struct	build	
tele	far	
temp	time	
tract	draw	
vad	go	
ven/vent	come	
vert	turn	
vic/vict	conquer	
vis	see	
voc/voke	call	
volv	turn	

Following is a list of frequently used suffixes. Write down at least one word (make it up if you have to) using each listed root, then check your result in the dictionary. Try to combine the root with one of the prefixes listed earlier.

Suffix	Meaning	Complete Word(s)
androus	man	
archy	rule, government	
biosis	life	
cephalic/cephalous	head	
chrome	color	
cidal/cide	kill	
cracy/crat	rule, government	
derm	skin	
emia	blood	
fugal/fuge	run away from	
gamy	marriage	
gnosis	knowledge	
grade	walking	
gram/graph/graphy	writing	
hedral/hedron	sided	
iasis	disease	
iatrics, iatry	medical treatment	
itis	inflammation	
lepsy	seizure, fit	
lith	stone	
logy	science of, list	
machy	battle, fight	
mancy/mantic	foretelling	
mania/maniac	craving, strong desire	
meter/metry	measure	
morphic/morphous	shape	
nomy	science of, law of	
odont	tooth	
opsis	appearance	
pathy	suffering, disease	
phage/phagous	eating	
phany	manifestation	
phobe/phobia	fear	
phone/phony	sound	
plasm	matter	
rrhagia/rrhagic/rrhea	flow	
saur	lizard	
scope/scopy	observation	
soma/some	body	
taxis/taxy	order	
vorous	eating	

A Vocabulary Worthy of an Officer

Mark Twain is supposed to have said, "The difference between the right word and the almost right word is the difference between lightning and the lightning bug." Military officers, who are responsible for the lives of the people they lead—not to mention accomplishing the missions they are assigned—must be able to choose words that communicate the message they want to transmit. They have to be able to do it all the time, even in humdrum peacetime situations, so that they will be used to doing it all the time and therefore will be able to do it under pressure—or even under fire.

Additionally, a wide variety of studies have found that a good vocabulary is one of the most common characteristics that successful people in all professions share. This doesn't mean that you will automatically be successful if you have a good vocabulary, but it does suggest that it can help.

What's more, the AFOQT and ASTB will test you directly on your knowledge of what certain words mean; all three tests will indirectly measure if you know what words mean by your ability to follow their directions.

So, since words are the building blocks or bricks of language, you need to be sure you have enough of the right kind of bricks to construct your message so that it does its job well. The bigger your vocabulary, the more ideas you can express accurately. To help you build your vocabulary, this section has more than a thousand words you ought to know and be able to use correctly (especially if you want to have the credibility to lead other people). This will not only help you do well on your test, but help you perform your duties well after you get appointed as an officer!

Don't forget, though, that the absolute best way to improve your vocabulary is to *read*. Read the newspaper, read magazines, read books—read about things you're interested in, read about things you discover you need to know about, but *read*! And don't worry about reading things that are way above your level; read things that are only slightly above your level, and that level will begin to and continue to go up.

The other half of this equation is that you have to *write*. No one said you have to write for publication—no one's demanding that you win the Pulitzer Prize—but, in order for you to be able to apply what you're learning by reading, you need to write, go through it yourself after it's cooled off, and then have someone who is skilled and experienced in writing look at it and give you some pointers. It's the only way you will learn what you need to know, and it's the only way you will be able to significantly improve your vocabulary.

These words presented for your review are grouped into nouns, verbs, and adjectives. For each word, you'll find today's most common or widely used definition; however, that meaning may be a long way from the word's original or literal meaning. Some words have an alternate meaning that will be useful for you to know. It would be a good idea to study other meanings of the words, as well as to practice using them in sentences; this will help you remember the words and be able to use them correctly when you really need them.

TIP

You may look at these words and think that you already know them, but take the time to go through them and make *sure*. Many times the meaning you have deduced from seeing the word in context may not be quite right, or it may even be quite wrong. Remember another useful adage from Mark Twain: "It's not what we don't know; it's what we do know that ain't so."

Nouns

ABERRATION—a deviation from the standard; not typical

ACCESS—a means of approach or admittance (e.g., to an area or organization)

ACCORD—agreement

ADAGE—wise proverb or saying (e.g., "Too soon old, too late smart")

ADVERSARY—enemy, opponent

ADVOCATE—one who speaks in favor of or on behalf of another

AFFLUENCE—wealth or abundance

AGENDA—list of items to discuss or to accomplish

ALACRITY—cheerful willingness or ready response

ALIAS—an assumed name or pseudodym, used for purposes of deception, as a pen name, or the like

ALLUSION—an indirect reference to something else, especially in literature; a hint

AMITY—friendship

ANARCHY—lawlessness, disorder; a lack of government control or effectiveness

ANECDOTE—a brief, entertaining story

ANIMOSITY—bitter hostility or open hatred

ANOMALY—an abnormality or irregularity

ANTHOLOGY—collection of writings, songs, or other creative works

APATHY—indifference or lack of caring

APEX—highest point (e.g., of a triangle)

ARBITER—one who decides; a judge

ATLAS—book of maps

AUDACITY—boldness

AVARICE—greed, desire for wealth

AWE—deep feeling of respect and wonder

BASTION—stronghold, fortress, fortified place against opposition

BEACON—a guiding light to show the way or mark a spot

BENEDICTION—blessing; often a benediction is given at the end of an event, ceremony, or religious service

BIAS—prejudice or tendency in a certain direction; literally, a slant or tilt

BIGOT—a person who is prejudiced against someone else because of their race, skin color, religion, gender, and so forth; also, a person who is intolerant of others with different opinions or beliefs

BLASPHEMY—an insult to something held sacred

BLEMISH—defect, stain, or flaw that takes away from the quality of the rest of the area or item

BONDAGE—slavery

BOON—benefit or gift

BRAWL—a noisy fight

BREVITY—shortness, conciseness

BROCHURE—pamphlet

BULWARK—strong protection or barrier to enemy attacks

CACOPHONY—a harsh or unpleasant mixture of sounds, voices, or words

CALIBER—literally refers to size; the caliber or size of a bullet is referred to in hundredths of an inch, so a ".50 caliber" bullet is half an inch in diameter at the base, and a ".45 caliber" bullet is 45/100 of an inch across at the base; also used figuratively when referring to the *quality* of something or someone (British spelling: *calibre*)

CAMOUFLAGE—something that conceals people or things from the enemy by making them blend into their surroundings

CASTE—social class or category

CATASTROPHE—sudden disaster

CHAGRIN—embarassment or disappointment

CHRONICLE—historical record or listing, usually in sequential, chronological order

CHRONOLOGY—an order or listing of events, either written or spoken, in the order in which they happened

CLAMOR—uproar

CLEMENCY—mercy (e.g., on a prisoner or criminal)

CONDOLENCE—expression of sympathy to one who has suffered a loss

CONNOISSEUR—an expert judge of the best of something, such as wine, food, paintings, etc.

CONSENSUS—general or group agreement

CONTEXT—the words or ideas surrounding one particular word or idea that give clues or contribute depth to the word's meaning

CONUNDRUM—a perplexing puzzle or riddle

CRITERION—standard of judgment or comparison

CRUX—the essential point or central part

CYNIC—one who mocks or disbelieves the good intentions or values of others; one who believes people are motivated only by selfishness

DATA—facts or information

DEARTH—scarcity or lack of something

DEBACLE—large-scale defeat or complete failure

DEBUT—first appearance, especially before an audience

DEFERENCE—conceding to another's desire or will; respect or courtesy

DELUGE—great flood or overwhelming inflow

DEPOT—warehouse, large storage place

DEPRAVITY—moral corruption

DESTINY—predetermined fate

DETRIMENT—damage, loss, or disadvantage

DIAGNOSIS—analysis or determination of the cause of a disease or problem

DICTION—the way in which words are used by a speaker

DISCERNMENT—insight, ability to see things clearly

DISDAIN—arrogant scorn or contempt

DILEMMA—situation requiring a choice between two or more deeply held values, or between two or more possibly unpleasant courses of action

DIN—loud, pervasive, continuous noise

DIRECTIVE—a general order or instruction

DISCORD—disagreement, often noisy

DISCREPANCY—inconsistency or error

DISCRETION—freedom of choice; also refers to a judicious reserve in one's speech or behavior

DISSENT—difference of opinion, especially from a widely held opinion

DROUGHT—long period of dry weather or conditions

EFFLUVIUM—a disagreeable or bad-smelling vapor or gas

EGOTIST—self-centered person

ELITE—a part of the whole that is considered to be at or near the top. In society, *elite* usually refers to the wealthiest or best-educated group; in the military, *elite* usually refers to units who have special training and/or equipment, and are therefore capable of accomplishing particularly difficult missions

ENIGMA—mystery

ENTERPRISE—an important project or self-sufficient organization

ENVIRONMENT—general surroundings, either physical or referring to influences

EPITOME—a top-level representation of a quality, usually a virtue (e.g., "June is the *epitome* of beauty and wisdom.")

EPOCH—a particular period of history, especially one regarded in some way as remarkable or significant

ERA—a period of time, usually of significant length, identified by particular conditions, events, or the influence of a person or group

ESSENCE—basic nature

ETIQUETTE—generally accepted rules of social behavior and manners

EXCERPT—passage quoted from a book or other document

EXODUS—departure, usually referring to a group or large numbers

EXPOSITION—an explanation or expounding

FACET—a side or aspect of a problem or situation; also refers to a particular angled cut of a diamond or other precious stone

FACSIMILE—exact copy or representation

FALLACY—mistaken or erroneous idea, assumption, or conclusion

FANTASY—imagined scenario or situation

FERVOR—passion or enthusiasm

FEUD—long-term disagreement or open hatred between individuals or groups

FIASCO—disaster or complete failure

FIEND—cruel, hateful person

FINALE—the last part of a performance

FLAIR—natural-seeming talent or style

FLAW—defect or imperfection

FOCUS—central point

FOE—enemy, adversary, opponent

FORMAT—arrangement, especially of a document, book, or audiovisual presentation

FORTE (pronounced *fort* or *fortay*)—an area in which a person excels

FORTITUDE—steady courage or strength

FORUM—a gathering or place where ideas or situations are discussed

FOYER—the entrance hall to a building or dwelling

FRAUD—deliberate deception, especially an illegal one

FRICTION—the surface of one object rubbing against another

FUNCTION—the purpose served by a person, object, or organization

FUROR—an outburst of excitement or disagreement

GAMUT—an entire range or spectrum of possible outcomes or conditions

GENESIS—beginning or origin

GENRE (pronounced ***jhan-ruh***)—a class or category, especially when referring to arts or entertainment

GIST—essential content, central idea

GLUTTON—one who overeats or indulges in anything to excess

GRIEVANCE—a complaint made against an individual or an organization; also a grudge held over a period of time

GUILE—cunning, deceit, duplicity

HAVOC—great damage, destruction, or confusion (often used in the phrase "wreak havoc")

HAZARD—danger or risk of injury

HERESY—an opinion directly opposed to established beliefs, especially in a religious sense

HERITAGE—historical family, cultural, or organizational set of traditions, customs, and/or values; also can refer to an inheritance of either real property or traditions

HINDRANCE—obstacle or delaying obstruction

HOAX—deliberate attempt to trick someone, either as a joke or seriously

HORDE—multitude, great mass of people

HORIZON—farthest limit, usually referring to vision, knowledge, or experience

HUE—shade of color

HYSTERIA—excessive or uncontrollable fear or other strong emotion

IDIOM—a regional or group jargon, dialect, or manner of speech; can also mean a phrase or expression that has a different meaning than the literal meaning of the words that make it up

ILLUSION—an idea or impression that differs from reality

IMAGE—the likeness or reflected or interpreted impression of a person, object, or locale; can also refer to the general group of perceptions surrounding a person

IMPETUS—moving force or starting idea

INCENTIVE—motivation or benefit to doing something

INCUMBENT—present holder of an office or position

INCURSION—a hostile invasion

INDOLENCE—laziness

INFIRMITY—physical disease, injury, or defect

INFLUX—a flowing in of a substance, as of a wave or a flood

INFRACTION—violation of a rule, regulation, or law

INITIATIVE—desire, idea, or ability to take the first step in carrying out some action

INNOVATION—a new or improved way of doing something

INTEGRITY—moral and intellectual honesty and forthrightness; also refers to the quality of a structure or object to hold together

INTERIM—a period of time between one event, process, or period and another

INTERLUDE—a short feature or period of time coming between two other, longer events (such as acts of a play or movements of an opera) or time periods

INTRIGUE—secret plot or scheme

INTUITION—knowledge or conclusion obtained through instinct or feeling rather than conscious thought

INVECTIVE—insulting or abusive speech

IOTA—a very small amount or piece

IRONY—a significant and often unexpected difference between what might be expected and what actually occurs; also, the conscious use of words to convey the opposite of their literal meaning

ITINERARY—agenda or schedule of events or places visited during a trip

JEOPARDY—risk of danger or harm

KEYNOTE—main theme or idea, usually referring to the main speech at a convention or the like

LARCENY—theft, usually small

LAYMAN—a "regular" person who is not a member of a particular professional or technical specialty

LEGACY—material or spiritual inheritance or heritage; can also refer to the historical perceptions of someone after they have left their office or position of responsibility

LEGEND—unverified stories handed down from earlier times; can also refer to a person of great fame or reputation

LEGION—a large number of people; sometimes historically used as a designation of a military or paramilitary unit (e.g., French Foreign Legion)

LETHARGY—sluggishness, laziness, drowsiness

LEVEE—a raised embankment designed to prevent flooding from a river or other body of water

LEVITY—lightness, frivolity

LIAISON—contact or coordination between two or more individuals or groups

LITIGATION—legal proceedings

LORE—body of traditional or historical knowledge

MALADY—disease or illness

MANEUVER—movement of a unit or individual to achieve a goal

MANIA—abnormal concentration on or enthusiasm for something

MARATHON—a cross-country footrace of 26 miles, 385 yards named in commemoration of the messenger who ran that distance to bring news to Athens of the Greek victory over the Persians in 490 BC at Marathon; any contest or enterprise requiring unusual endurance or stamina

MAVERICK—a person who acts independently instead of in conformance with common organizational or expected behavior

MAXIM—an adage or proverb prescribing a rule or method of conduct, as in, "Measure twice, cut once."

MEDIUM—means of communication of presentation (e.g., radio, telephone, television, etc.); plural is *media*

MEMENTO—object that commemorates or reminds someone of a past event

METROPOLIS—a very large city

MILIEU—surroundings, environment

MORALE—the state of mind or attitude of an individual or group, usually in reference to how that attitude will either positively or negatively affect the future actions or success of that person or group

MORÉS—established customs or values of a group or segment of society

MULTITUDE—large number of something

MYRIAD—a vast number or great multitude of something, usually implying wide variations within that group

MYTH—a traditional story, usually attempting to explain a natural condition or occurrence, often involving supernatural influences

NEGLIGENCE—carelessness

NEOPHYTE—a beginner

NICHE—literally, a recess in a wall for holding a statue or other ornament; figuratively, an appropriate activity or situation that is especially well suited to a person's abilities or character

NOMAD—wanderer

NOSTALGIA—desire to return to a past experience or situation

OASIS—an isolated place or area of comfort surrounded by desolation or barrenness

OBJECTIVE—a goal

OBLIVION—a condition of complete ignorance, forgetfulness, or unawareness

OBSCURE—unclear, clouded, partially hidden

ODYSSEY—a long journey, usually involving significant challenges or obstacles; derived from the mythic ten-year journey home of Odysseus after the Trojan War chronicled in Homer's epic Greek poem "The Odyssey"

OMEN—a sign or event believed to foretell the future

OPTIMUM—the best possible condition or combination of factors

OVATION—applause of an audience, or any enthusiastically positive reception accompanied by applause

OVERSIGHT—an omission through error or carelessness; also can refer to a situation where one person or group supervises the activities of another, usually loosely

OVERTURE—first step, usually one that is intended to lead to others in action or discussion

PANACEA—a cure for all problems or diseases

PANORAMA—an unobstructed view of a wide area

PARADOX—a statement that contradicts or appears to contradict itself

PARSIMONY—stinginess or overzealous desire to be thrifty

PARTISAN—one who supports a particular cause, person, or idea; in a country occupied by an enemy, a *partisan* is one who opposes the occupying enemy by acts of defiance or sabotage

PASTIME—a way of spending leisure time

PATHOLOGY—the science of diseases; any deviation from a normal, healthy condition

PAUCITY—scarcity of a resource or condition

PAUPER—a very poor person

PEDAGOGUE—a strict, overly academic teacher or speaker

PEER—an equal in age, social standing, professional rank, or ability

PHENOMENON—an unusual, noticeable, or outstanding occurrence that is directly perceived by the senses or by results

PHILANTHROPY—love of mankind, usually exemplified by donations to charitable causes

PHOBIA—an unreasonable fear of something

PHYSIQUE—the build or physical condition of a human body

PILGRIMAGE—long journey to some place or condition worthy of respect or devotion

PINNACLE—highest point

PITFALL—trap or obstacle for the unwary

PITTANCE—very small amount, usually referring to money

PLATEAU—an elevated, relatively level expanse of land; also can refer to a leveling-off of progress or results

PLIGHT—an unfavorable condition or situation

POISE—calm and controlled behavior

POPULACE—the people living in a certain area; can also refer to "common" people, i.e., middle- and lower-class citizens

POSTERITY—future descendants or generations

PRECEDENT—event or law that serves as an example for later action

PREDECESSOR—someone or something that came before another

PREDICAMENT—unpleasant problem or situation, usually one that is difficult to escape

PREFACE—introductory statement or passage to a book, speech, or other communication

PRELUDE—something that is preliminary to some act or event that is more important

PREMISE—a statement or assumption from which a conclusion is drawn

PREMIUM—best quality; can also refer to an amount added to the usual price or payment

PRESTIGE—respect or status achieved through achievement or rank

PRETEXT—a reason given as a cover-up for the real purpose for an action

PRIORITY—something that comes before others in significance or importance

PROBITY—integrity, uprightness, honesty

PROCESS—a system or design for accomplishing a goal or objective

PRODIGY—an extremely talented or gifted child

PROPINQUITY—nearness

PROPRIETY—good manners, appropriately respectful and reserved behavior

PROSPECT—possibility for the future

PROVISO—a requirement that something specific is done, usually in writing

PROWESS—strength or superior ability

PROXIMITY—nearness

PSEUDONYM—an assumed name, usually a "pen name" taken by an author (e.g., Mark Twain was the *pseudonym* used by Samuel Clemens.)

PUN—a play on words that depends on two or more different meanings or sounds of the same word or phrase

PUNDIT—a knowledgeable person in a particular field; can also refer to a commentator who publicizes his opinions, whether or not he is actually an expert in that field

QUAGMIRE—literally, a bog or swamp that impedes movement or in which people or vehicles could be stuck or mired; figuratively, a difficult or dangerous situation from which there is limited hope of escape

QUALM—doubt or unease about some action or situation

QUANDARY—deep uncertainty or indecision about a choice between two or more courses of action; a dilemma

QUERY—a question or request for information

RAMPART—a fortification; bulwark or defense against attack

RAPPORT—a harmonious or mutually trusting relationship

RARITY—something that is infrequent or not commonly encountered

REFUGE—a place to which one can go for protection or separation from difficulty

REMNANT—remaining or left-over part of something

REMORSE—regret or guilt

RENAISSANCE (also RENASCENCE)—a rebirth or revival; a "Renaissance man" is one who is skilled in many different areas of learning

RENDEZVOUS—a meeting or location for a meeting

RENOWN—fame or wide acclaim, especially for accomplishments or skill

REPLICA—an exact copy or facsimile of something, although it may only be proportionate and not the same size

REPRIMAND—severe scolding or rebuke, usually from a superior to a subordinate

REPRISAL—retaliation for real or perceived injuries; often implies giving back more than was originally received

REPROBATE—a wicked, sinful, depraved person

RESERVE(S)—a fighting force kept uncommitted until the need arises

RESIDUE—the remainder of something after removal of a part; usually implies a small amount left, perhaps in a container, after the majority is removed

RESOURCES—assets that are available for use, either material or spiritual

RESPITE—a temporary break, usually one that brings relief

RESUMÉ—a written summary of work, education, and accomplishments, usually compiled for purposes of getting a particular job

REVERENCE—a feeling of great respect, usually religious in nature

ROSTER—list of names (e.g., of organization members, students in a class, etc.)

SABOTAGE—deliberate damage to facilities or equipment belonging to an enemy, usually performed by spies or an underground movement within an occupied country

SAGA—a long story or tale, usually involving heroic deeds

SALUTATION—a written or spoken greeting; also can refer to a person's title, such as *Dr., Mr., Mrs.,* etc.

SANCTION—approval, usually by a higher authority; can also mean a penalty for breaking a law or rule

SARCASM—cutting or insulting ironic remarks

SATIRE—criticism of someone or something by seeming approval cast in a light or taken to an extreme that makes the subject appear ridiculous

SCAPEGOAT—someone who is blamed, usually unjustly, for the mistakes or misdeeds of others

SCENT—distinctive aroma or smell

SCOPE—the complete area or extent of action or thought

SCROLL—a roll of paper or parchment with writing

SECT—a group of people having the same beliefs, usually religious; often has a slight to severe negative connotation

SEMBLANCE—outward appearance

SEQUEL—something that follows from what has happened before (e.g., a novel or movie)

SHAM—a false imitation; in slang, refers to avoiding work, sometimes by pretense

SHEAF—a bundle, usually either of papers or grain

SHEEN—shine or luster (e.g., of polished furniture)

SILHOUETTE—the outline of a person or object, usually without observable details because of low lighting

SITE—a location

SLANDER—spoken untruth that damages one's reputation

SLOGAN—motto or saying that sums up an individual or group's attitude

SLOPE—the angle of a surface that is neither vertical nor horizontal; measured between 0 and 90 degrees

SNARE—trap

SOLACE—comfort after loss or disappointment

SPONSOR—one who supports and approves of a person or activity; implies that the sponsor is at a higher level of status or authority than the sponsored person or group

STAGNATION—motionlessness or inactivity

STAMINA—endurance; physical or mental ability to withstand fatigue

STANZA—a section of a poem or song; a verse

STATURE—a height, measured either physically or in respect

STATUS—social or professional standing or level

STIGMA—mark or perception of disgrace or bad reputation

STIMULUS—an encouragement to act or react

STRATEGY—planning and coordination aimed at achieving a goal or objective; a way to get something done

STRIFE—conflict, disagreement, contention

SUMMIT—the highest point (e.g., of a mountain or a career)

SUPPLEMENT—an amount added to complete something

SURVEY—a general study of a topic or issue

SUSPENSE—tenseness brought on by uncertainty about an outcome; can also refer to a deadline

SYCOPHANT—one who flatters a superior in hope of getting preferential treatment

SYMBOL—a design or insignia that represents something, usually a value, action, or group identity

SYMPTOM—indication of a problem, usually referring to a disease or illness

SYNOPSIS—brief summary

SYNTHESIS—the combining of parts to form a whole, especially referring to ideas or procedures

TACIT—silent or unspoken (e.g., "His brief grin constituted his *tacit* approval."); implied

TACT—the ability to communicate a message without causing offense, especially an unpleasant message

TACTICS—specific actions used to achieve a purpose or accomplish an objective; in military terms, maneuvers by small or lower-level units in contact with the enemy

TALLY—a record of an account or score; any list that involves counting or enumeration

TECHNIQUE—a method or specific way of doing something

TEMERITY—recklessness, audacity; boldness verging on foolhardiness

TEMPERAMENT—overall attitude, disposition, or character

TEMPO—the pace or speed of an activity or series of activities

TENSION—mental or emotional strain, usually brought on by perceived or actual problems or conflicts

THEME—the main topic, as of a written work, movie, show, speech, etc.

THRESHOLD—the starting point of an activity; literally, the line that separates one area (such as a room or house) from another

THRIFT—an ability or desire to spend money wisely, to get the most value possible

TIMBRE—the quality of a sound, independent of pitch and volume

TINT—a shade of a color

TOKEN—a sign or object that signifies a greater feeling or whole (e.g., "a *token* of respect")

TRADITION—customs and beliefs common to a group that are passed down through time

TRAIT—characteristic or distinguishing feature

TRANSITION—movement from one condition or situation to another; implies some degree of change or transformation

TREPIDATION—fear, apprehension

TRIBUNAL—a place of judgment, usually legal in nature

TRIBUTE—a demonstration of respect or gratitude

TURMOIL—disturbance or upheaval

TURPITUDE—shameful wickedness or depravity

TUTOR—a private teacher, often for a student who needs extra or specialized help in a particular academic area

TYCOON—a very wealthy and powerful business leader

ULTIMATUM—a final demand or condition (e.g., "Get the dog out of the house or I'm leaving!")

UPHEAVAL—conflict or disturbance, usually characterized by changes in group membership, leadership, or goals

UTENSIL—an implement or tool to help the user accomplish something

UTOPIA—an ideal place or society, usually regarded as unachievable

VALOR—courage, heroism

VENTURE—a project or enterprise, usually one involving some degree of risk, although not necessarily physical risk

VICINITY—local area

VICTOR—winner

VIGOR—vitality or energy

VISIONARY—one with lofty, revolutionary, or sometimes impractical goals or ideas about the future

VOLITION—will or conscious choice

VOW—solemn pledge or promise

WAGER—bet

WELTER—confused mass; commotion or turmoil

WHIM—impulsive idea or desire, usually not thought out

WOE—great trouble or sorrow

WRATH—intense anger or fury

ZEAL—eager desire or enthusiasm

ZENITH—highest point

ZEST—enthusiasm

Verbs

ACQUIESCE—to give in; to agree

ALLEVIATE—to lessen or relieve discomfort or a bad situation, even if only temporarily

AMASS—to accumulate

AMELIORATE—to make better or more tolerable

APPEASE—to soothe; to pacify by giving in

ASSUAGE—to soothe or comfort; to lessen the pain of

ATROPHY—to waste away from lack of use

AUGMENT—to add to or increase

AUTHORITARIAN—in the same manner as an absolute ruler or dictator

BELITTLE—to insult or degrade

CENSOR—to limit communication to prevent the loss of secret information

CENSURE—to condemn severely for inappropriate or rule-breaking behavior

COALESCE—to come together as one; to unite

CONDESCEND—to patronize; to stoop to someone else's level in an offensive way

CONDONE—to approve of or allow to happen

DENOUNCE—to speak out against or condemn

DERIDE—to ridicule or laugh at contemptuously

DESECRATE—to profane a holy place

DETER—to prevent or stop someone from doing something

DIGRESS—to veer off the main topic

DISCRIMINATE—to differentiate or make a distinction based on some quality; in recent times, usually has the connotation of unfair racial, ethnic, or gender bias

DISPARAGE—to belittle or say uncomplimentary things about in an indirect way

DIVERT—to change the course or direction of

DRONE—to talk on and on in a dull way

EFFACE—to erase or rub away the features of

EMULATE—to imitate as a role model

ENGENDER—to create or produce

ENHANCE—to make better or improve

ENTHRALL—to hold spellbound; to captivate or charm completely

EXEMPLIFY—to serve as an example or representative of

EXPEDITE—to make faster or easier

EXTOL—to praise

FACILITATE—to make easier

HEED—to listen to and obey

INNOVATE—to create a new or better way of doing something

INSTIGATE—to provoke or stir up a controversy

LANGUISH—to become listless, hopeless, or depressed

MEANDER—to wander slowly or aimlessly

MITIGATE—to lessen the severity of something, such as a punishment or injury

NULLIFY—to cancel out or make very unimportant, as if nonexistent

PRECLUDE—to prevent or make impossible

REFUTE—to disprove

REJUVENATE—to give new energy or strength to, as if made young again

REPRESS—to hold down

REPROACH—to scold or rebuke

REPUDIATE—to reject or deny

RESCIND—to repeal, to take back formally

RETRACT—to take back or withdraw

REVERE—to worship or respect very deeply

SCRUTINIZE—to examine closely

SOLICIT—to ask for, to seek

SQUANDER—to waste

VACILLATE—to waver between alternatives; to be indecisive

VEER—to turn aside or swerve away from a course, direction, or purpose

VENERATE—to revere or treat as something or someone holy

VILIFY—to cast as a villain; to defame

Adjectives

ABSTRACT—theoretical or lacking substance; can also mean a brief summary of a scholarly article or paper

ACUTE—sharp, shrewd; also, an angle of less than 90 degrees

AESTHETIC—having to do with art or artistic beauty or sensibility; not to be confused with *ascetic*

AMBIGUOUS—unclear in meaning; confusing; able to be interpreted in more than one way

AMBIVALENT—undecided; wavering between alternatives

AMBULATORY—able to walk

AMIABLE—friendly, pleasant

ANIMATED—alive, lively

APOCRYPHAL—of doubtful or uncertain origin

APPREHENSIVE—worried, anxious

ARROGANT—feeling superior to others and not hiding your high opinion of yourself

ARTICULATE—well-spoken, having a good command of the language

ASCETIC—austere, self-denying

ASTUTE—perceptive, intelligent

AUSPICIOUS—favorable, seeming to point toward good results

AUSTERE—unadorned, forbiddingly bare

AUTHENTIC—real, genuine

BANAL—unoriginal, ordinary to a fault, boring

BELLIGERENT—combative, quarrelsome

BENEVOLENT—kind, generous

BENIGN—gentle; not harmful

BLITHE—carefree, cheerful

CANDID—honest, forthright, frank

CAUSTIC—like acid or corrosive; also, a very sharp or cutting insult or comment

COMPLACENT—smug, self-satisfied, content with the current situation

COMPLIANT—yielding, submissive

CONCILIATORY—peacemaking

CONCISE—succinct; brief and direct

CONGENIAL—agreeably pleasant

CONSPICUOUS—obvious, standing out, very noticeable

CONTRITE—genuinely and deeply apologetic or remorseful

CREDULOUS—believing something outrageous; gullible

CRYPTIC—mysterious, hard to understand

DIDACTIC—instructive

DIFFIDENT—timid; lacking in self-confidence

DILIGENT—hardworking

DISPARATE—different, varied; often with a connotation of incompatible

DISPASSIONATE—without emotion; neutral

DIVERSE—varied

DOGMATIC—arrogantly or overconfidently claiming the truth of unproven ideas, or claiming that a belief system is beyond dispute

DUBIOUS—doubtful or uncertain

ECCENTRIC—unconventional, irregular

ELABORATE—a result of great effort and attention to detail; intricate

ELUSIVE—hard to capture or pin down; can mean evasive

EPHEMERAL—short-lived, fleeting, temporary

ESOTERIC—hard to understand, cryptic

EXEMPLARY—setting a superior example; outstanding

EXHAUSTIVE—very thorough and complete, with great attention to detail

EXPEDIENT—meeting an immediate need; also, self-serving or granting immediate advantage

EXTRANEOUS—irrelevant, extra, unnecessary

FALLACIOUS—false

FANATICAL—extremely devoted to or passionate about a cause or idea

FASTIDIOUS—meticulous; insistent on attention to detail

FICKLE—not faithful or consistent; unpredictable

FLAGRANT—shocking or outrageous violation of a custom, expectation, rule, or law

FORTUITOUS—luckily coincidental; accidentally advantageous

FRIVOLOUS—not serious; with levity; inconsequential

FURTIVE—secretive, trying to remain hidden

FUTILE—hopeless, without effect or result

GULLIBLE—overly trusting; willing to believe anything

HACKNEYED—overused, trite

HEDONISTIC—pleasure seeking, overly indulgent

HYPOTHETICAL—unproven; used as a theoretical example for the purpose of discussion

IMMUTABLE—unchangeable, permanent

IMPARTIAL—fair, unbiased, neutral

INADVERTENT—accidental

INCESSANT—unceasing, never-ending; usually implies an unpleasant condition

INCOHERENT—jumbled, hard to understand

INCONGRUOUS—inconsistent or inappropriate

INDIFFERENT—not caring one way or the other; can also mean "mediocre"

INDULGENT—lenient, giving in to momentary desires or whims

INEVITABLE—unavoidable, especially when referring to a result of a course of action or decision

INFAMOUS—having a bad reputation; disgraceful

INNATE—inborn, inherent

INNOCUOUS—harmless, insignificant

INSIPID—dull, meaningless, empty

IRASCIBLE—irritable

IRONIC—marked by an unexpected difference between what might be expected and what acutally happens; using words so as to convey the opposite of their literal meaning; satiric

LAUDABLE—worthy of praise

LAX—careless, negligent, not diligent

LUCID—clear, easily understandable

MARRED—damaged or scarred

NOVEL—new or original

OBJECTIVE—without bias, analyzing logically based on facts (opposite: *subjective*)

OBSCURE—unclear, clouded, partially hidden; hard to understand

ORTHODOX—conventional, adhering to established principles or practices, especially in religious matters

PEDESTRIAN—common, ordinary

PERIPHERAL—unimportant, of little consequence

PERVASIVE—a quality of being present throughout; permeating

PIOUS—reverent or devout; depending on context, can also mean *falsely* devout

PIVOTAL—crucial, result changing

PRAGMATIC—practical, based on experience rather than theory

PRETENTIOUS—pompous, self-important

PRODIGAL—extravagant, rebellious, wasteful

PRODIGIOUS—enormous, of extraordinary size

PROFOUND—deep, insightful

PROFUSE—extravagant, free-flowing

PROSAIC—dull, unimaginative

PROVINCIAL—limited in outlook to one's own small area; narrow; implies that the *provincial* person also thinks that the rest of the world is just like his or her limited experience

PROVOCATIVE—exciting; attracting attention or sparking controversy

PRUDENT—careful, wisely cautious

RECALCITRANT—stubbornly defiant of authority or control

REDUNDANT—repetitive, unnecessary

RELEVANT—important to the matter at hand; pertinent

REPREHENSIBLE—worthy of blame; disgraceful

RESOLUTE—firm, determined, unwavering in the face of challenges or obstacles

RETICENT—restrained, uncommunicative

RIGOROUS—strict, harsh, severe

SACCHARINE—overly sweet or flattering

SAGE—wise or knowledgeable, usually from experience

SCANTY—inadequate, minimal

SCRUPULOUS—strict or careful in an ethical sense

SERVILE—submissive and subservient

SKEPTICAL—doubting

SOLEMN—grave, serious

STATIC—stationary or unmoving

STOIC—outwardly indifferent to circumstances, especially to bad or challenging times

STRINGENT—strict or restrictive

SUBTLE—not obvious; also, able to make fine distinctions

SUPERCILIOUS—haughty, insultingly patronizing

SUPERFICIAL—on the surface only; shallow; not thorough

TACITURN—untalkative by nature

TANGIBLE—touchable, not imagined or figurative

TEDIOUS—boring, overly detailed for no reason

TEMPERATE—moderate or restrained

TENACIOUS—dogged or determined in the pursuit of an objective

TENTATIVE—temporary; uncertain; experimental

TIMID—shy, afraid of attention

UNIFORM—consistent throughout; the same for everyone or in every situation

UNPRECEDENTED—happening for the first time; never seen before

VEHEMENT—strong, urgent, passionate

VERBOSE—wordy, overly talkative

VIRULENT—malignant, malicious, full of hate

VOLATILE—highly unstable, explosive

VOLUMINOUS—very large, spacious

WILLFUL—deliberate, obstinate, insistent on having one's own way

ZEALOUS—enthusiastically devoted to a cause or idea

Abbreviations

Technical language for any given field often contains many abbreviations, and the military is no exception. Fortunately, your flight aptitude test won't require you to learn all the military's abbreviations and acronyms (a word taken from the first letter or letters of a phrase; for instance, the term *scuba* is actually an acronym that stands for Self-Contained Underwater Breathing Apparatus). You will, however, need to be able to correctly use the most common abbreviations in everyday, official, and academic language—abbreviations that are often misused, misunderstood, or both.

A.D. (often seen in small capitals as A.D. or AD) is an abbreviation for the Latin phrase *anno Domini*, "in the year of our Lord"; measures time after the birth of Christ as established in the Middle Ages.

ASAP As Soon As Possible

B.C. (often seen in small capitals as B.C. or BC), "before Christ"

B.C.E. (often seen in small capitals as B.C.E. or BCE), "before Christian era" or "before common era"

e.g. is an abbreviation for the Latin phrase *exempli gratia*, which means "for example." This is the abbreviation you use when you want to give an example of a group of items or ideas, as in, "Not all Christmas tree decorations are expensive—e.g., candy canes—but they can all become family heirlooms."

etc. is an abbreviation for the Latin phrase *et cetera* which means "and so on"—or, literally, "and other things." You should use etc. only after a series of at least two or three things, as in, "We unpacked the Christmas tree lights, ornaments, tinsel, etc."

ibid. is short for the Latin term *ibidem*, meaning "in the same place."

i.e. is an abbreviation for the Latin phrase *id est*, "in other words." (This is the most misused abbreviation of the ones presented here.)

op. cit. is short for the Latin phrase *opere citato*, "in the work cited."

USS in front of a ship's name means it is a U.S. Navy vessel, a "United States Ship."

Mathematics Review Information

This section is a review of basic math terms and problem-solving methods taught in high school and lower-division college courses. You will find samples of math problems most often encountered in the various flight aptitude tests for the different services, with an explanation of how to solve each. You may find that you know one or more other ways to solve these problems, also—the more complex a math problem, the more chance that there's more than one way to solve it.

And, although there is a fair amount of basic concept review here, the chapter's purpose is <u>not</u> to *teach* the concepts to you for the first time, but rather just to remind you of "what right looks like." If you are completely unfamiliar with many of the concepts addressed in this chapter, you will probably want to do some special-emphasis math studying or get some math-focused tutoring.

And here's something else to consider: Most of us are so accustomed to using calculators that doing some pencil-and-paper calculations would be worthwhile to knock off the mental rust. Yes, it's a pain in the neck, and sure, you used to know how to do it—but why risk having a brain cramp during the test because you haven't done long division in a long time? Practice like it's game time and do it on paper—you won't have a calculator on the test!

Before you study the information in this section, consider these suggestions for effective math problem solving (and this includes those pesky word problems!):

1. Develop the habit of reading the problem carefully. Look for answers to these questions:
   a. What are the facts given in the problem?
   b. What is the unknown quantity or amount that the problem asks you to find? In what terms or units is it to be expressed (pure numbers, miles, square feet, number of children in the audience, etc.)?
   c. What method should you use to solve the problem? What is the best method or series of steps?
2. Pay close attention to each word, number, and symbol. In math, directions and operations are usually compressed into a very few words or symbols. The key to the problem or the principal direction can sometimes be expressed as a symbol.
3. How does one fact or idea lead to another? Which facts or ideas are connected, and which facts don't really contribute to the solution of the problem?

Mathematics Laws and Operations

The numbers 0, 1, and 2 are *whole numbers*. So are 3, 4, 5, and so on; in comparison, ⅓ is a *fraction*, and 5½ is a *mixed number*—a whole number plus a fraction. Mathematically speaking, when we combine two or more whole numbers, we call it performing an *operation* on them. Officially, there are two basic operations, *addition* and *multiplication*; *subtraction* is the opposite, or *inverse*, of addition, and *division* is the inverse of multiplication.

In addition, we combine two or more individual numbers (24 + 2, for instance) to produce an answer called the *sum*. In multiplication, we combine groups of numbers to produce an answer called the *product*. An example of multiplication would be "eight times two" (8×2), which simply means eight groups of two, or counting two items eight times; the answer, or product, is 16.

Subtraction and *division*, as mentioned earlier, are really opposite or inverse operations of addition and multiplication. Subtraction is performed to undo addition, and division is performed to undo multiplication. The answer in subtraction is called the *remainder*; in division, it's called the *quotient*. In both cases, we're going to presume that you know how to perform these basic mathematics operations and move on to make sure you're ready for your flight aptitude test.

Use of Parentheses: Order of Operations

Sometimes, math problems use parentheses to indicate which operation or operations are supposed to be done first. For example, in the problem $3 + (5 \times 2)$, you would first multiply 5×2, then add 3. Look at the different results you get when you work without the parentheses and then with them.

$$3 + 5 \times 2 = \qquad\qquad 3 + (5 \times 2) =$$
$$8 \times 2 = 16 \qquad\qquad 3 + 10 = 13$$

Even though we read a problem from left to right, there is an order in which we must perform arithmetic operations:

1. First, do all the operations within parentheses.
2. Next, do all multiplications and divisions. Do these in left-to-right order.
3. Finally, do additions and subtractions.

In the following example, notice the order in which arithmetic operations are carried out.

$(10 - 6) \times 5 - (15 \div 5) =$		(first do operations inside the parentheses)
$4 \times 5 -$	$3 =$	(next do multiplication)
$20 -$	$3 = 17$	(then do subtraction)

Rounding Off Numbers

Sometimes, a problem will call for you to round off the answer to the nearest ten, hundred, thousand, etc. We do this in everyday conversation when we say that a steak dinner listed on the menu at $21.95 costs "about $20," or that a laptop computer advertised at $695.99 was "about $700." *Rounding off, estimating,* and *approximating* all mean the same thing: You are making a statement about the approximate value of a number.

When rounding off numbers, the first thing to do is to look at the way the number is constructed or organized, and the second thing to do is to determine the level of accuracy at which you want to express or talk about that number.

Look at the way the number 282,535,321 is written below.

282,   535,   321

Here we can see that the whole nine-digit number is divided up into three-number segments that are more easily dealt with—"eating the elephant one bite at a time," so to speak. But let's break this number down into its most understandable form:

Hundreds of millions	2	200,000,000 (two hundred million)
Tens of millions	8	80,000,000 (eighty million)
Millions	2	2,000,000 (two million)
Hundreds of thousands	5	500,000 (five hundred thousand)
Tens of thousands	3	30,000 (thirty thousand)
Thousands	5	5,000 (five thousand)
Hundreds	3	300 (three hundred)
Tens	2	20 (twenty)
Ones	1	1 (one)

If you need to round off 282,535,321 to the nearest hundred, you would first find the number in the "hundreds" row (3), and then look at the number to its right (2). If the number to the right is 5, 6, 7, 8, or 9, you round off the hundreds to the next higher number (4) and replace the 21 with 00. By the same token, if it's *less* than 5, you would round *down*, as we do in this case—so we can say that 321 is *about* 300. Your answer would then be 282,535,300.

This same method works regardless of whether you go higher or lower within this particular number—and it works with any number, no matter how large or small. For instance, if we wanted to round 282,535,321 off to the nearest *million*, following the same procedure, since the first number to the right of the million is 5 or larger, we would round *up* the last "millions" number and replace everything to its right with zeroes, giving us 283,000,000.

Suppose your original amount was 763,219,846 and you needed to round this number to the nearest ten thousand. In this case, when you break down the number to its components, you find a 1 in the "ten thousands" position, and a 9 to its immediate right. Therefore, to round the complete number to the nearest ten thousand, we increase the 1 to a 2 and replace all numbers to its right with zeroes, giving us 763,220,000.

Prime and Composite Numbers

Whole numbers are classified as either *prime* or *composite* numbers. A prime number is one that can be divided evenly by itself and 1, but not by any other whole number.

EXAMPLES: 1, 2, 3, 5, 7, 11, 13

A composite number is one that can be divided evenly by itself, by 1, and by at least one other whole number.

EXAMPLES: 4, 6, 10, 15, 27, 82

Factors

When a whole number has other divisors besides 1 and itself, these other divisors are called *factors*. In other words, factors are numbers we use to multiply to form a composite (whole) number. Sometimes you will be asked to "factor" a number—for example, 6. The factors of 6 are the numbers that you multiply to produce 6. Since 3 times 2 equals 6, the factors of 6 are 3 and 2.

Exponents

The short way of writing *repeated factors* in multiplication—i.e., when a given number is multiplied by itself a certain number of times—is called using *exponents*. For example, you can write 5×5 as 5^2 or "five times five equals five squared." The smaller 2 written to the right of and slightly above the 5 is called an *exponent*; it tells us that 5 is used twice as a factor. You can read 5^2 as either "5 to the second power" or "5 squared." Note that 5^2 does *not* represent "five times two" (5×2). The expression 2^3 is read as "2 to the third power," "2 to the power of 3," or "2 cubed," and represents $2 \times 2 \times 2$.

n Factorial

Don't confuse exponents (expressions of repeated factors) with the term *factorial*. When you see "5 factorial," for example, it means "find the product of every number between 1 and 5 multiplied together." Thus, "5 factorial" means $5 \times 4 \times 3 \times 2 \times 1$. The symbol for 5 factorial is "5!"

Reciprocal

You may also need to find the *reciprocal* of a number. To find the reciprocal of 4, for instance, look for the number that you multiply by 4 to get 1. The easiest way to calculate this is to divide 1 by 4. You can express the answer either as $\frac{1}{4}$ or as 0.25 (see the following sections on fractions and decimals). Remember that the product of a number and its reciprocal is always 1: the reciprocal of $\frac{1}{4}$ is 4; the reciprocal of $\frac{2}{4}$ is 2.

Series and Sequences

A frequently asked type of test question involves a *series* or *sequence* of numbers. You are given several numbers arranged in a pattern, and are then asked to find the number that comes next. The way to solve this is to figure out the pattern; i.e., figure out what the relationship is between the first and second number, second and third, and so on. Try the following two examples:

(A) 2, 4, 6, 8, ?
(B) 3, 9, 4, 8, ?

Each number in Series (**A**) is 2 higher than the previous number. Thus, the next term in the series is 10. By testing the relationships between numbers in Series (**B**), you find the following pattern:

3 (+ 6) = 9	The first step is "add 6."
9 (−5) = 4	The next step is "subtract 5."
4 (+ 4) = 8	The next step is "add 4."

To continue the pattern, the next step will have to be "subtract 3." Therefore, the next number in the series is 5.

Fractions

Many problems in arithmetic have to do with fractions. (Decimals and percents are really just different ways of writing fractions.) There are at least four ways to think about fractions.

1. A fraction is a part or fragment of a whole. The fraction $\frac{2}{3}$ means that something has been divided into three parts, and we are working with two of those parts. The number written above the fraction line (2) is the *numerator*, and the number below it (3) is called the *denominator*.

2. A fraction can be the result of a multiplication operation. The fraction $\frac{3}{4}$ means 3 times $\frac{1}{4}$.

3. A fraction is an expression of division. Thus $\frac{2}{5}$ is the quotient (result) when 2 is divided by 5. This can also be written as $2 \div 5$.

4. A fraction is an expression of a ratio, which is a comparison between two quantities. For example, the ratio of 6 inches to 1 foot is $\frac{6}{12}$, since there are 12 inches in a foot.

Performing Mathematical Operations with Fractions

There are some special rules—and some shortcuts, too—for multiplying, dividing, adding, and subtracting fractions and mixed numbers. Remember, a *mixed number* is one that is made up of a whole number and a fraction—for example, $5\frac{1}{2}$.

Multiplying Fractions

The general rule for multiplying two or more fractions is to multiply the numerators by each other, and then multiply the denominators by each other.

EXAMPLE: $\frac{1}{2} \times \frac{3}{4} \times \frac{5}{8} = \frac{15}{64}$ $\frac{\text{(numerators)}}{\text{(denominators)}}$

EXPLANATION: $1 \times 3 \times 5 = 15$; $2 \times 4 \times 8 = 64$

Sometimes, the product you get when you multiply two fractions can be expressed in simpler terms than what originally results from your calculations. When you express a fraction in its *lowest terms,* you put it in a form in which the numerator and denominator no longer have a common factor by which they can be divided.

EXAMPLE: Reduce $\frac{24}{36}$ to lowest terms.

Step 1. Find a number that is a factor of both 24 and 36. Result: Both numbers can be divided by 4.

Step 2. Divide 24 by 4 and then divide 36 by 4.

$24 \div 4 = 6$

$36 \div 4 = 9$

Therefore, $\frac{24}{36} = \frac{6}{9}$

Step 3. Check again. Is there a number that is a factor of both 6 and 9? Yes, both numbers can be divided by 3. Divide 6 and then 9 by 3.

$6 \div 3 = 2$

$9 \div 3 = 3$

Therefore, $\frac{6}{9} = \frac{2}{3}$

ANSWER: $\frac{24}{36}$ can be reduced to the lowest terms of $\frac{2}{3}$.

Changing Improper Fractions to Mixed Numbers

When the numerator of a fraction is larger than its denominator, it is called an *improper fraction*. An improper fraction can be changed to a mixed number.

EXAMPLE: Change $\frac{37}{5}$ to a mixed number.

Because a fraction is also another way to express division, $\frac{37}{5}$ means $37 \div 5$. If 37 is divided by 5, the quotient is 7, and the remainder is 2—or, expressed another way, $\frac{37}{5} = 7\frac{2}{5}$.

Changing Mixed Numbers to Improper Fractions

To multiply or divide mixed numbers, it is necessary to change them into improper fractions.

EXAMPLE: Change $8\frac{3}{5}$ to an improper fraction.

Convert the whole number, 8, to fifths: $8 = \frac{40}{5}$

$\frac{40}{5} + \frac{3}{5} = \frac{43}{5}$, an improper fraction. A shortcut for changing a number from a mixed number to an improper fraction is to multiply the whole part of the mixed number by the fraction's denominator, and then add the result to the original numerator.

Therefore, $8\frac{3}{5} = \frac{8 \times 5 + 3}{5} = \frac{43}{5}$.

Multiplying Mixed Numbers

When multiplying or dividing with a mixed number, change the mixed number to an improper fraction before working out the problem.

$$2\frac{2}{3} \times \frac{5}{7} = \frac{8}{3} \times \frac{5}{7} = \frac{40}{21} = 1\frac{19}{21}$$

Cancellation

Cancellation is a shortcut you can use when you're multiplying or dividing fractions. For example, if you are going to multiply $\frac{8}{9}$ times $\frac{3}{16}$, you first multiply the numerators by each other, then the denominators by each other; this gives you an answer you have to reduce to lowest terms.

$$\frac{8}{9} \times \frac{3}{16} = \frac{24}{144} = \frac{1}{6}$$

There's an easier way to solve this problem: See if there is a number you can divide evenly into both a numerator and a denominator of the original problem. In this example, there is such a number: You can divide 8 into both itself and 16.

Step 1. $\dfrac{\overset{1}{\cancel{8}}}{9} \times \dfrac{3}{\underset{2}{\cancel{16}}} =$

You can also divide 3 into the numerator 3 and the denominator 9. Having found this, solve the problem by multiplying the new numerators and then the new denominators.

Step 2. $\dfrac{\overset{1}{\cancel{8}}}{\underset{3}{\cancel{9}}} \times \dfrac{\overset{1}{\cancel{3}}}{\underset{2}{\cancel{16}}} = \dfrac{1}{6}$

Dividing Fractions

Dividing fractions looks a lot like multiplying them, but there is an important extra consideration that we can use to manipulate the fractions in an equation: Dividing something by a number is the same as multiplying that something by 1 over that number. Therefore we can convert the division problem $\frac{1}{2} \div \frac{3}{1}$ into the multiplication problem $\frac{1}{2} \times \frac{1}{3}$.

To divide with fractions, you have to *invert* the second fraction (turn it upside down), and then change the division sign to a multiplication sign and solve as a multiplication of fractions. This is also called multiplying the first fraction by the *reciprocal* of the second fraction. Remember: Any whole number can be written as that number over 1; i.e., the number 5 can be written as $\frac{5}{1}$, 3 can be written as $\frac{3}{1}$.

$$\frac{1}{5} \div 4 = \frac{1}{5} \div \frac{4}{1} = \frac{1}{5} \times \frac{1}{4} = \frac{1}{20}$$

Adding and Subtracting Simple Fractions

There are some basic rules for adding and subtracting fractions:

1. Add or subtract only those fractions that have the same denominator.
2. Add or subtract only the numerators of the fractions, keeping the same denominator.
3. If two fractions you want to combine by adding or subtracting do not have the same denominator (a *common denominator*), find a way to change them so that both denominators are the same.

This last operation is easy if one of the denominators divides evenly into the other. To add $\frac{2}{3}$ and $\frac{3}{6}$, for instance, you can work with the fact that 3 goes into 6 evenly. You can change the $\frac{2}{3}$ to $\frac{4}{6}$, a fraction with the same value, and then work with the two fractions on an equitable basis.

If you can't divide one of the denominators into the other, then you have to find a number that both denominators will go into evenly. If you are working with three fractions or even more, you have to find a number that all the denominators can divide into evenly.

For instance, if you need to add $\frac{1}{4}$, $\frac{1}{5}$, and $\frac{1}{6}$, you need to find a common denominator that all three fractions can divide into evenly. One technique for finding a common denominator between several fractions is to take the largest denominator and start multiplying it by 2, 3, and so on, until you find a number that the other denominators will also divide into evenly. In this case, 6 is the largest denominator; multiply 6 times 2 and you get 12, a number that 5 does not divide into evenly. You have to keep trying until you reach 60, which is the first product that all three denominators divide into evenly.

And—don't forget—to convert a fraction expressed with one denominator, you have to multiply the numerator by the same number used to multiply the denominator.

Let's look at this example:

$$\frac{1}{4} = \frac{15}{60} \qquad \frac{1}{5} = \frac{12}{60} \qquad \frac{1}{6} = \frac{10}{60}$$

Now add the converted fractions:

$$\frac{15+12+10}{60} = \frac{37}{60}$$

Adding and Subtracting Mixed Numbers

To add mixed numbers (numbers consisting of whole numbers and fractions, such as $1\frac{2}{3}$), follow these steps:

1. Add the whole numbers.
2. Add the fractions. (Make sure that the denominator is the same!) If the sum of these is an improper fraction, change the sum to a mixed number.
3. Add the sum of the whole numbers to the sum of the fractions.

EXAMPLE: $3\frac{2}{3} + 12\frac{2}{3}$

Step 1. $3 + 12 = 15$

Step 2. $\frac{2}{3} + \frac{2}{3} = \frac{4}{3} = 1\frac{1}{3}$

Step 3. $15 + 1\frac{1}{3} = 16\frac{1}{3}$

The principles are the same when you subtract mixed numbers, but there are some additional wrinkles to watch out for. When you subtract mixed numbers, you may have to "borrow" in the same way that you do when you subtract whole numbers. For example, if you want to subtract $4\frac{3}{4}$ from $8\frac{1}{4}$, you realize you cannot take $\frac{3}{4}$ from $\frac{1}{4}$. (Kind of difficult to get $.75 out of a quarter!) Therefore, you have to borrow 1 (expressed in this case as $\frac{4}{4}$) from 8, and rewrite the problem.

$$8\frac{1}{4} = 7\frac{4}{4} + \frac{1}{4} = 7\frac{5}{4}$$

$$-4\frac{3}{4} = \qquad\qquad -4\frac{3}{4}$$

$$\overline{\qquad\qquad} \qquad\qquad \overline{\qquad\qquad}$$

$$3\frac{2}{4} = 3\frac{1}{2}$$

Decimal Fractions

Decimal fractions are special fractions whose denominators are powers (multiples) of ten. The *exponent* (smaller number to the upper right) tells you how many zeros there are in the power of ten. For instance:

$10^1 = 10$ $\qquad\qquad = 10 \times 1$
$10^2 = 100$ $\qquad\qquad = 10 \times 10$
$10^3 = 1,000$ $\qquad\qquad = 10 \times 10 \times 10$
$10^4 = 10,000$ $\qquad\qquad = 10 \times 10 \times 10 \times 10$

You can tell what the denominator of a decimal fraction is by counting the places (not just the zeros) in the number to the right of its decimal point. When it is written as a fraction, the denominator has the same number of zeros as this number of places; that is, it has the same power of ten. For example:

$$0.7 = \frac{7}{10^1} \text{ or } \frac{7}{10} \qquad \text{(seven tenths)}$$

$$0.07 = \frac{7}{10^2} \text{ or } \frac{7}{100} \qquad \text{(seven hundredths)}$$

$$0.007 = \frac{7}{10^3} \text{ or } \frac{7}{1,000} \qquad \text{(seven thousandths)}$$

Changing Fractions to Decimals

To change a fraction to a decimal, divide the numerator by the denominator. Place a decimal point to the right of the numerator, and add a zero for each decimal place you want to show in your answer. For example:

$$\frac{2}{5} = 5\overline{)2.0}^{\,0.4}$$

So we can see that $\frac{2}{5} = 0.4$ after we change the fraction to a decimal.

Changing Decimals to Fractions

Every decimal is really a fraction whose denominator is a power of ten. For example:

$$0.01228 = \frac{1,228}{100,000}$$

$$0.50 = \frac{50}{100} = \frac{1}{2}$$

$$6.1 = \frac{61}{10}$$

Dividing Decimals by Powers of 10

To divide a decimal by a power of ten, count the number of zeros in the power of ten, then move that many places to the left of the decimal.

EXAMPLES: $182.7 \div 10^1 = 182.7 \div 10 = 18.27$
$.47 \div 10^2 = 00.47 \div 100 = .0047$

Adding and Subtracting Decimals

To add or subtract decimals, line up the numbers so that the decimal points are directly under one another, then add or subtract in the same way that you would with whole numbers. Write zeros at the end of decimals if you find it easier to work with placeholders to keep things lined up.

EXAMPLE: Add the numbers 5.14, 11.7, 798.1, and 0.0327, and then subtract their sum from 2,790.59. Remember to include the decimal point in the answers.

5.14		5.1400
11.7	OR	11.7000
798.1		798.1000
+ 0.0327		0.0327
814.9727		814.9727

$$\begin{array}{r} 2790.59 \\ -\ 814.9727 \\ \hline 1975.6173 \end{array}$$

Multiplying Decimals

To multiply two decimals, line them up from the right as though they were whole numbers, regardless of how many digits there are to the right of the decimal in either number. Count the number of places to the right of the decimal in each number, then add them together. From right to left, count the same number of places in the answer as you got when you added the places together from the two numbers you multiplied—then insert a decimal point in the answer at that point.

$$
\begin{array}{r}
\boxed{1\ 2\ 3\ 4} \\
17.8592 \\
\times \quad\quad 2.3 \leftarrow \boxed{1} \\
\hline
41.07616 \\
\boxed{5\ 4\ 3\ 2\ 1}
\end{array}
$$

Dividing Decimals

To divide a decimal by a whole number, divide the numbers as though they were both whole numbers. Then place a decimal point in the answer directly above the decimal in the problem and solve the problem. Add zeros to the right of the dividend (the number inside the division sign) if you need to in order to finish the problem.

$$
\begin{array}{r}
7.0615 \\
2\overline{)14.123} \\
\underline{14} \\
12 \\
\underline{12} \\
3 \\
\underline{2} \\
10 \\
\underline{10}
\end{array}
$$

To divide one decimal by another, begin by making the divisor a whole number. To do this, move the decimal to the far right of the number, and count the number of places that you move it. Then move the decimal in the dividend (the other number) the same number of places (in the same direction, of course!). For example:

$$\frac{3.6}{0.3} = \frac{36}{3} = 12$$

Rounding Off Decimals

Many math problems require a process called *rounding off* to reach an answer, where one or more numbers are made shorter and therefore usually easier to deal with. The idea of rounding off also has to do with the accuracy or precision of the number or measurement—the longer the number (i.e., the more places used to the right of the decimal point), the more accurate or precise the number is considered to be.

Let's consider a measurement of 3.6 meters. Is this closer to 3 meters or to 4 meters? $3.6 = 3\frac{6}{10}$, which is closer to 4 meters than it is to 4. But what about 3.5 meters? This is exactly midway between 3 and 4 meters. The common, widely accepted method of rounding off a number of this type is that anything that is halfway or more between one level or amount and another is rounded up to the higher level; anything lower than half is rounded down. This means that 3.5 and 3.6 are rounded *up* to 4, but that 3.3 and 3.4 are rounded *down* to 3, simply because they are closer.

This rounding principle works in the same way regardless of where you are looking at a number relative to the decimal point. Thus,

0.35 meters rounded to the nearest tenth of a meter is 0.4 meters (four-tenths of a meter)

3.6 meters rounded to the nearest meter is 4 meters

37 meters rounded to the nearest 10 meters is 40 meters

380 meters rounded to the nearest hundred meters is 400 meters

Also, when you have long numbers, it's important to remember to do your rounding off from *right to left*. Look at the first number to the right of the position you must round to, and any number of 5 or over elevates the number to its left, whereas any number of less than 5 is dropped, along with any further numbers to the right. For example:

3.39 meters rounded to the nearest tenth of a meter is 3.4 meters

3.49 meters rounded to the nearest tenth of a meter is 3.5 meters

3.49 meters rounded to the nearest meter is 4 meters

3.267919 meters rounded to the nearest tenth of a meter is 3.3 meters

3.9847769034 meters rounded to the nearest hundredth of a meter is 3.98 meters

Percentages

A *percent* is a way to express a fraction that simply means a certain amount expressed in hundredths. To use a percent figure when solving a problem, change it to a fraction or a decimal. To change a percent to a fraction, drop the percent sign and multiply by $\frac{1}{100}$.

7% is the same as $7 \times \frac{1}{100}$ or $\frac{7}{100}$

25% is the same as $25 \times \frac{1}{100}$ or $\frac{25}{100}$

100% is the same as $100 \times \frac{1}{100}$ or $\frac{100}{100} = 1$

Changing a Percent to a Decimal

To change a percent figure to a decimal figure, drop the percent sign and move the decimal point two places to the left. Add extra zeros, if needed, to fill out the correct number of places. If the percent is given as a fraction, first change the fraction to a decimal. For example:

4% = .04	1.7% = .017
55% = .55	1/5% = .20% = .002
17% = .17	100% = 1.00 (or 1)

Changing a Decimal to a Percentage

To change a decimal to a percent, move the decimal point two places to the right and add the percent sign. For instance:

0.47 = 47%	0.03 = 3%
0.008 = .8%	3.27 = 327%

Percentages over 100% are often used to talk about an increase of twice as much or more.

Square Roots

The square root of a number is one of the two <u>equal</u> factors (numbers) that, when multiplied together, result in that number. In other words, to find a square root, ask yourself, "What number multiplied by itself (squared) will yield the original number?"

For instance, the square root of 9 is 3, because $3 \times 3 = 9$, and the square root of 25 is 5, since $5 \times 5 = 25$.

The square root of a number is indicated by using a radical sign ($\sqrt{}$). For example, $\sqrt{64}$ means "the square root of 64," or $\sqrt{64} = 8$. In the same way, $\sqrt{36} = 6$, $\sqrt{49} = 7$, and so on.

Square roots are often complex in the sense that they may be very long numerically, and may, in fact, not be able to be expressed completely as a decimal number. Numbers that have *exact* square roots are called *perfect squares*. The perfect squares with which you are probably most familiar are 1, 4, 9, 16, 25, 36, 49, 64, 81, and 100. Also, it's worth remembering that a "gross" of something is a dozen dozens, or 144—so the square root of 144 is 12.

Finding the Square Root of a Number

You may be asked to find the square root of a number that is not a perfect square, giving your answer rounded off to the nearest tenth, for example. You can use a trial-and-error method to find a square root to the nearest decimal place that the problem asks you for. For example, suppose you are asked to find $\sqrt{28}$ to the nearest tenth: $\sqrt{28}$ is between $\sqrt{25}$, which we know is 5, and $\sqrt{36}$, which we know is 6. And, we can infer that $\sqrt{28}$ is closer to $\sqrt{25}$ than it is to $\sqrt{36}$. So, to start, make an estimate (yes, a guess, but an informed, reasonable guess) that 5.2 is $\sqrt{28}$ to the nearest tenth, and then see how close you are by multiplying 5.2×5.2 and seeing that the result is 27.04—less than our goal of 28. Because that was too low, we can multiply 5.3×5.3 and see that the result is 28.09, which is pretty close but a little more than our goal of 28.

Because we now have a "bracket" of 28—one set of factors on each side, one more and one less—we know that the square root of 28 is between 5.2 and 5.3.

Further, we know that the actual exact $\sqrt{28}$ is closer to 5.3 than 5.2, so, since our objective was to find $\sqrt{28}$ rounded off to the nearest tenth, our job is done: The answer is 5.3.

Algebra

Algebra is a way to express a problem or mathematical relationship with a small set of symbols used to substitute for actual numbers. This is because we don't know what all the actual values are, or because the same relationship may apply to different sets of numbers.

Let's look at an example. We know that if a jacket is priced at $20, we have to pay $20 to buy one. If we want three jackets, we pay three times that amount, or $60. How do we find that answer of $60? We multiply two numbers together to find a third number. Using the style of algebra, we can express this operation briefly. Let p equal the price of one jacket, and let c (the "unknown") equal the cost of three jackets. This is the algebraic expression for how we find c.

$$c = 3 \times p \quad \text{or} \quad c = 3p$$

In this equation, the letters c and p are called *variables,* meaning that the numbers they stand for can change. In other words, if the price of the jacket is discounted to $18, then p will equal $18, and c will equal $54.

Arithmetic Operations in Algebra

All four arithmetic operations are possible in algebra: both basic operations (addition and multiplication) and both inverse operations (subtraction and division). We can express these operations algebraically:

1. The sum of two numbers x and y is $x + y$
2. The difference between two numbers x and y is $x - y$
3. The product of two numbers, x and y, is $(x) \times (y)$ or $x \cdot y$ or xy
4. The quotient of two numbers x and y is $x \div y$ (or) $\dfrac{x}{y}$

Equations

An *equation* is a statement that two quantities are equal. This is easily understandable and obvious when the quantities are expressed in numbers, such as these:

$$2 + 3 = 5$$
$$8 \times 2 = 16$$
$$24 - 7 = 17$$
$$99 \div 11 = 9$$

In algebra, however, equations will include *variables* (a letter or sign that can stand for more than one value) or *unknowns* (a letter or sign that stands for a quantity or idea that we don't know yet). Usually, you will be asked to *solve the equation* by finding or *solving for* the unknown number value, often represented as the letter *x*. In this sense, the *solution* to an equation is the number that proves that the equation is true, and you show that it's true by substituting the number for the variable. But how do you find the number?

Suppose you heard somebody say, "I can't afford to pay cash to buy a car for $9,000; that would leave me with only $500 to pay my bills for the rest of the month." What we don't know here is how much that person had originally; the other numbers are provided or given to us. How would we express his statement algebraically? (Remember, the "unknown" is the unstated amount *x* now in the bank account.) Here's one way of writing the expression:

$$x - \$9,000 = \$500$$

Now, how do we solve for *x*, the unknown?

Step 1. Think about what the expression now means: A certain number minus $9,000 equals $500.

Step 2. Decide how you want to express the solution: In this case, we have decided that *x* = the amount originally in the bank before we do any car buying or bill paying.

Step 3. For your solution, think about how to get the unknown *x* by itself on one side of the equal sign. This means you will have to manipulate the entire equation by performing the same operations on both sides of the equal sign to get *x* by itself. How do we clear the $9,000 from the side that shows *x*? Notice that the sign in front of $9,000 is a minus sign. Saying "*x* − $9,000" is the same as saying "*x* + (−$9,000)," otherwise known as adding a negative number to a positive number. So, if you *add* $9,000 to the left side of the equation, the two $9,000s will cancel each other out. However, remember that, because it's an *equation*, everything has to stay equal or balanced; this means that whatever you do to the left side of the equation you have to do to the right side—otherwise it wouldn't be an equation. If you add $9,000 to the left, you have to add it to the right. This, then, is how it looks:

$$x - \$9,000 = \$500$$
$$x - \$9,000 + \$9,000 = \$500 + \$9,000$$
$$x = \$9,500 \text{ (amount originally in the bank)}$$

How did we solve this equation? By performing an inverse operation on both sides of the equation. To solve for *x*, we went through three steps:

Step 1. We decided to solve for *x* by removing all other operations from the side of the equation where *x* is—we have to isolate *x*, or get *x* "by itself."

Step 2. We removed an operation (in this case, adding negative $9,000) from one side of the equal sign by performing its inverse or opposite operation (adding a positive $9,000) on the same side.

Step 3. We then performed the same operation on the other side of the equal sign. This resulted in isolating *x* on one side of the equation, which tells us that *x* equals $9,500.

This, then, is generally how we solve equations: We perform operations to both sides of the equation that will result in the unknown being "alone" on one side of the equation—and the other side of the equal sign shows us the answer.

Operations with More Complex Equations

Sometimes, an equation shows x as part of more than one operation. There may also be negative terms (terms with a minus sign). The same basic steps are involved in finding the solution, but may have to be repeated. Remember, the goal is always to isolate x on one side of the equation. Here's an example:

$$3x + 7 = -11$$

Step 1. Perform the inverse operation of + 7.

$$3x + 7 - 7 = -11 - 7$$
$$3x = -18$$

Step 2. Perform the inverse operation of $3x$, which can also be expressed as $(3 \cdot x)$; using the dot $(\cdot)$ instead of the multiplication sign $(\times)$ can sometimes help reduce confusion by reducing the number of x's in the equation.

$$\frac{3x}{3} = \frac{-18}{3}$$

$$x = -6$$

Remember, in multiplication and division, if the signs of both terms are plus or minus (positive or negative), the answer has a plus or positive sign. If the two terms are different, the answer has a minus or negative sign.

Sometimes, x appears on both sides of the original equation. In that case, the first step is to remove or factor out x from one side (also known as "collecting all x's on one side") of the equal sign.

Algebraic Expressions

An *algebraic expression* is any collection of numbers and variables. This collection may have more than one variable. For example, $2x + 3y$ is an algebraic expression meaning, "2 times one unknown number (x) plus 3 times another unknown number (y)."

Arithmetic Operations with Algebraic Expressions

To add or subtract algebraic expressions, remember that only *similar* or *"like"* terms can be combined. Terms are similar if they have the same variable, raised to the same power. For instance, we can subtract $3x$ from $5x$ to get $2x$, but we cannot get x^3 by adding x and x^2, or get $9zh$ from adding $4z$ and $5h$. For example, simplify the following series of terms:

$$3x + 2y - 4z + 2x - 5y$$

Start by arranging like terms together and combining them.

$$3x + 2x = 5x \text{ (first partial sum)}$$
$$2y - 5y = -3y \text{ (second partial sum)}$$

Therefore, the simplified expression is $5x - 3y - 4z$.

To multiply algebraic expressions, first multiply the numbers of similar terms, then multiply the variables (letters) of similar terms. When you multiply one power of x by another power of x, just add the exponents together. For instance:

$$(3x^2)\,(4x^3)$$

$$3 \times 4 = 12 \text{ (first partial product)}$$
$$x^2 \cdot x^3 = x^5 (\text{ second partial product})$$

Therefore, the product is $12x^5$.

The rules for multiplying more complex algebraic equations are basically the same—just take things step by step and stay organized. In the expression $x^2y(2x - 3y)$, the parentheses mean that x^2y is the multiplier for both $2x$ and $-3y$, so we work out the expression like this:

$$x^2y(2x - 3y)$$
$$x^2y(2x) + x^2y(-3y)$$

$x^2y(2x)$		$x^2y(-3y)$
$1 \cdot 2 = 2$ (first partial product)	+	$1 \cdot -3 = -3$
$x^2 \cdot x = x^3$ (second partial product)		$x^2 \cdot 1 = x^2$
$y \cdot 1 = y$ (third partial product)		$y \cdot y = y^2$

Therefore, the simplified expression is $2x^3y - 3x^2y^2$.

Evaluating Algebraic Expressions

To *evaluate* an algebraic expression means to replace the variables with numbers (usually given to you), and then simplify the expression by adding, multiplying, and so on. For instance, evaluate the expression $(x + 2a)$ if $x = 3$ and $a = 2$.

$$x + 2a$$
$$= 3 + 2(2)$$
$$= 3 + 4$$
$$= 7$$

Factoring in Algebra

Sometimes, you are given the answer to an algebraic multiplication problem and are then asked to find the original multipliers; this is called *factoring*. These kinds of problems can be of different types:

Type 1. Factor the *Highest Common Factor*

The highest common factor of an algebraic expression is the highest expression that will divide into every one of the terms of the expression.

EXAMPLE: $6x^2 + 3xy$

Step 1. The highest number that will divide into the numerical coefficients, 6 and 3, is 3.

Step 2. The highest literal factor that will divide into x^2 and xy is x. Notice that y is not contained in the first term at all.

Step 3. Divide the highest common factor, $3x$, into $6x^2 + 3xy$ to find the remaining factor. When we do this, we find that the factors are $3x(2x + y)$.

Type 2: Factor the *Difference of Two Squares*

This type of problem contains the square of one number minus the square of another number. Remember, the square of a number is the product that you get when you multiply a number by itself, and the square root of a number is the number that was multiplied by itself to get the square or original number. For example: Find the difference of two squares for $x^2 - 9$.

Step 1. Find the square root of x^2 and place it to the left within each of two shell or empty parentheses you've set up for this purpose. The square root of x^2, of course, is x.

$$(x \quad) (x \quad)$$

Step 2. Find the square root of 9 and place it on the right within each of the two parentheses you've set up. The square root of 9 is 3.

$$(x \quad 3) (x \quad 3)$$

Step 3. Put a plus sign between one pair of terms, and a minus sign between the other pair of terms.

$$(x + 3) (x - 3)$$

The factors of $x^2 - 9$ are $(x + 3)$, $(x - 3)$.

Type 3. Factor a *Quadratic Trinomial*

A quadratic trinomial is an algebraic expression of the form $ax^2 + bx + c$, where a, b, and c are numbers and a does not equal zero. Its factors are always two pairs of terms. The terms in each pair are separated by a plus or minus sign.

EXAMPLE: Factor $x^2 - 11x + 30$.

Step 1. Set up your two shell sets of parentheses, then find the factors of the first term in the trinomial; again, the factors of x^2 are x and x.

$$(x \quad) (x \quad)$$

Step 2. Look at the last term in the trinomial, which has in this case a plus sign. We now have to find the factors of the third term; because it is positive, we know that the factors are either both positive or both negative. Because the middle term is negative, we know that the factors must be both negative.

$$(x - \quad) (x - \quad)$$

Step 3. Find factors of the last term that will also add to get the number of the second term. In this case, although we know that 30 has several factors, only the factors 5 and 6 also add up to 11, which is the numerical part of the second term. We already know that both factors have to be negative, so the factors of 30 we are looking for are actually –5 and –6.

$$(x - 5)\ (x - 6)$$

Therefore, for our solution, the factors of $x^2 - 11x + 30$ are $(x - 5)\ (x - 6)$.

Solving Quadratic Equations

A *quadratic equation* is an equation that contains a term with the square of the unknown quantity and has no term with a higher power of the unknown. In a quadratic equation, the exponent is never higher than 2 (x^2, b^2, c^2, etc.). Examples of quadratic equations include the following:

$$x^2 + x - 5 = 0$$
$$2x^2 = 3x - 5$$
$$x^2 - 3 = 0$$
$$81 = x^2$$

To solve equations like this, factor them, and then set each factor equal to zero. After that, it's easy to solve for x. Let's take it step by step.

Solve: $x^2 = 3x + 10$

Step 1. Move all the terms onto one side of the equal sign so that the equation on that side is equal to nothing on the other side—in other words, zero. Don't forget inverse operations.

$$x^2 - 3x - 10 = 0$$

Step 2. Factor the equation.

$$(x - 5)(x + 2) = 0$$

Step 3. Set each factor equal to zero, then solve the resulting equations.

$$x - 5 = 0 \qquad\qquad x + 2 = 0$$
$$x = +5 \qquad\qquad x = -2$$

Step 4. To check the accuracy of the answer, substitute each answer in the original equation.

$$x^2 = 3x + 10 \qquad\qquad x^2 = 3x + 10$$
$$(5)^2 = 3(5) + 10 \qquad\qquad (-2)^2 = 3(-2) + 10$$
$$25 = 15 + 10 \qquad\qquad 4 = -6 + 10$$
$$25 = 25 \text{ (proof)} \qquad\qquad 4 = 4 \text{ (proof)}$$

The solution of the quadratic equation is proven to be $x = 5, -2$.

Geometry

Geometry is a useful tool in the world we live in. Geometry problems require a knowledge of both the principles and the application of arithmetic and algebra to arrive at the correct solution. Many geometry problems require you to make or infer some kind of measurement; they also use familiar terms such as *line*, *angle*, and *point*.

Lines

A *line* is made up of *points*; it can have a definite length, or it can be infinitely long. For purposes of our geometry problems, a line has no particular width. *Parallel lines* are lines that are equidistant (the same distance) from each other at every point along both lines so that, even if they were infinitely long, they would never touch.

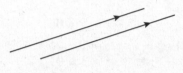

Perpendicular lines are lines that meet to form a right angle (90 degrees).

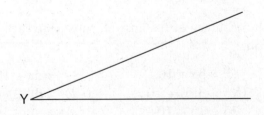

Angles

When two lines meet at a point, they form an *angle*. The point where the lines meet is called the *vertex* of the angle. Angles can be named or designated in one of three ways:

1. For the point at the vertex (in this case, angle Y).

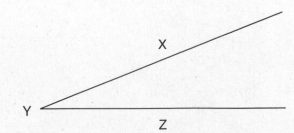

2. For the letter names of the lines that meet to form the angle, with the vertex in the middle (in this example, angle XYZ).

3. For a number written or displayed inside the angle (in the diagram below, angle #3).

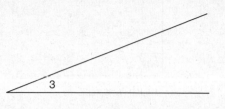

Measuring Angles

The best way to measure an angle is with a *protractor*. Angles are measured in *degrees*, up to 180°. Remember that a circle has 360°, and that half of that circle would be a semicircle with its bottom edge going from edge to edge through the middle of the circle. So we see that two lines joined at a "180° angle" would be no angle at all, but instead just one line joined to the other as a straight-out continuation.

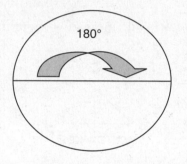

So, as we see the possible measures of an angle from 0° to 180°, we need to know that each degree is divided into 60 minutes (designated by a tick mark like this ′), and each minute of a degree is further divided into 60 seconds of arc (designated by a double tick mark ″).

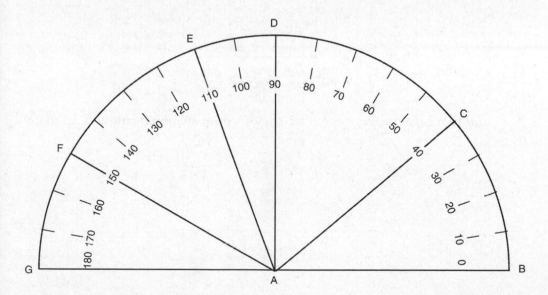

Further, we need to remember that a *right angle* is an angle of 90 degrees.

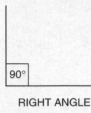

RIGHT ANGLE

Next, we need to remember that an *obtuse angle* is an angle measuring more than 90 degrees but less than 180 degrees . . .

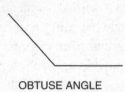

OBTUSE ANGLE

. . . and that an *acute angle* is one measuring more than 0 degrees but less than 90 degrees.

ACUTE ANGLE

We also need to remember that *complementary angles* are two angles that have measurements that add up to 90 degrees (a right angle) . . .

∠1 AND ∠2 ARE
COMPLEMENTARY ANGLES

. . . and that *supplementary angles* are angles whose measurements add up to 180 degrees.

∠3 AND ∠4 ARE
SUPPLEMENTARY ANGLES

Polygons

A *polygon* is made up of three or more lines that are connected so that an area is enclosed. There are, technically, an infinite number of different types of polygons; here are some of the most common:

1. A *triangle* has three sides.
2. A *quadrilateral* has four sides.
3. A *pentagon* has five sides.
4. A *hexagon* has six sides.
5. An *octagon* has eight sides.
6. A *decagon* has ten sides.

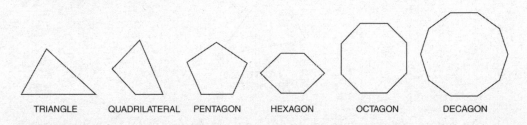

TRIANGLE   QUADRILATERAL   PENTAGON   HEXAGON   OCTAGON   DECAGON

Triangles

A *triangle* is a polygon with three straight sides. There are several ways to categorize triangles, but all triangles have three angles, and their measurements add up to 180 degrees.

1. An *equilateral triangle* is one where all three sides are of equal length, and whose angles are also equal at 60 degrees each.

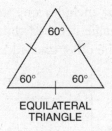

EQUILATERAL
TRIANGLE

2. An *isosceles triangle* is one in which only two sides are equal; this results in the angles opposite those sides also being equal.

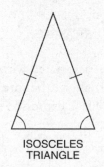

ISOSCELES
TRIANGLE

3. A *scalene triangle* is one in which all three sides (and therefore all three angles) are *un*equal.

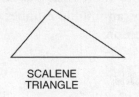

SCALENE
TRIANGLE

4. An *acute triangle* is one in which all three angles are less than 90 degrees.

ACUTE
TRIANGLE

5. An *obtuse triangle* is one where one angle is obtuse (more than 90 degrees).

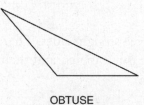

OBTUSE
TRIANGLE

6. A *right triangle* is one that includes one angle of exactly 90 degrees. The longest side of a right triangle is called the *hypotenuse*; it is always the side opposite the right angle. The other two sides of a right triangle are called *legs*.

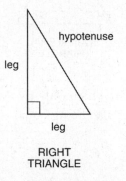

RIGHT
TRIANGLE

A very important, useful concept associated with right triangles is the *Pythagorean Theorem*. This says that in a right triangle, the sum of the squares of the legs is equal to the square of the hypotenuse. This is expressed in an equation like this:

$$a^2 + b^2 = c^2$$

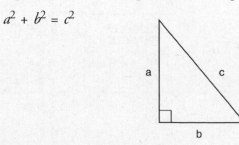

7. *Congruent triangles* are identical in every way—their sides are the same length, and their angles are exactly the same from one to the other.

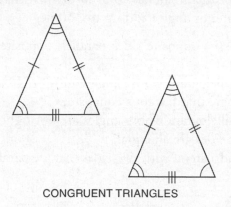

CONGRUENT TRIANGLES

8. *Similar triangles* are triangles with the same shape—whose sides are proportionate, but not the same measurement. The angles of similar triangles are identical.

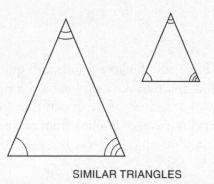

SIMILAR TRIANGLES

9. A special way to work with triangles is to calculate an *altitude*. In the diagram below, $\overline{BD}$ is an altitude . . .

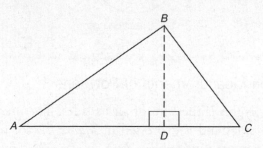

. . . and in this one, $\overline{CD}$ is an altitude, also. Notice that side *AB* has to be extended for the perpendicular *CD* to meet it at a right angle.

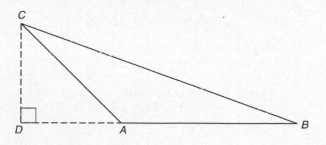

Quadrilaterals

There are several types of quadrilaterals, but all of them have four sides and the measurements of their interior angles add up to 360 degrees.

1. A *parallelogram* has its opposite sides parallel; opposite sides and angles are also equal.
2. A *rectangle* is a parallelogram whose angles are all right angles.
3. A *square* is a rectangle that has four equal sides.
4. A *rhombus* is a parallelogram whose angles are not right angles (i.e., it's not a square), but whose sides are all equal.
5. A *trapezoid* is a quadrilateral with two sides that are parallel and two sides that are not.

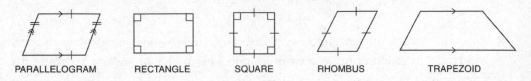

PARALLELOGRAM   RECTANGLE   SQUARE   RHOMBUS   TRAPEZOID

Circles

A *circle* is a closed curved line, all of whose points are equidistant from the center. A circle is divided into 360 degrees; its *circumference* is the equivalent of the perimeter of a polygon. The *radius* of a circle is a line drawn from its center to any point on the circumference. The circle's *diameter* is a line from one point on the circumference that passes through the circle's center; it is equal to twice the length of the radius.

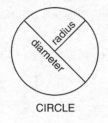

CIRCLE

Perimeter and Area Measurements of Polygons

The *perimeter* of a polygon is the sum of all its sides. The *area* of a polygon is the space enclosed by its sides and is expressed in *square feet* (or square inches, square yards, square meters, square centimeters, etc.)

1. The area of a parallelogram is equal to its base multiplied by its height.

h

b
PARALLELOGRAM
A = bh

2. The area of a rectangle is equal to its length multiplied by its width.

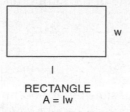

RECTANGLE
A = lw

3. The area of a square can be found by methods 1 or 2 above, or by simply multiplying the length of one side by itself (*squaring* it); if you take a moment, you will see that all three methods are the same for a square, because of its four equal sides.

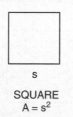

SQUARE
$A = s^2$

4. The area of a triangle is half the measurement of its base multiplied by its height.

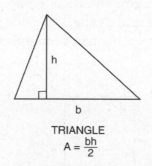

TRIANGLE
$A = \frac{bh}{2}$

Perimeter and Area Measurements of a Circle

To find the circumference of a circle, we need to use a new concept, the number π (pronounced "pi"), which is usually approximated as the fraction $\frac{22}{7}$. In geometry π expresses the unchanging relationship between the circumference of a circle and its diameter. Because the diameter is twice the length of the radius, we can also say that the circumference of a circle is π times twice the radius. Expressed mathematically it looks like this:

$C = \pi d$ (the circumference is equal to pi times the diameter)
$C = \pi 2r$ (the circumference is equal to pi times twice the radius)

Because π is an infinite, nonrepeating decimal, we can either approximate π's value by rounding it to 3.1415926 or even 3.14 for most problems. If a fraction is more appropriate, then we use the approximation $\frac{22}{7}$.

The area of a circle also has an unchanging relationship to π: The area of a circle equals π multiplied by the square of the radius, or

$$A = \pi(r^2)$$

Volume

Volume is the total, three-dimensional space occupied by a solid object, which has (for our mathematical purposes) flat sides of *length*, *width*, and *depth*. Volume measurements are expressed in *cubic* units. Therefore, the equation for the volume of a rectangular object is

$$V = lwh$$

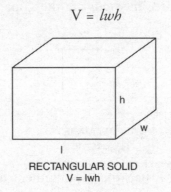

RECTANGULAR SOLID
V = lwh

A *cube* is a solid whose length, width, and height are all the same—a three-dimensional square. The volume of a cube is one side raised to the third power, i.e., one side multiplied by itself, then the result multiplied by itself again.

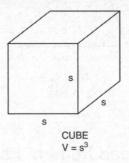

CUBE
V = s³

A solid where both bases are circles in parallel planes is called a *cylinder*. The volume of a cylinder is the area of its base (which is a circle) multiplied by its height, or, expressed mathematically,

$$V = (\pi)r^2h$$

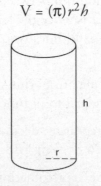
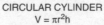

CIRCULAR CYLINDER
V = πr²h

A *sphere* is a perfectly round, three-dimensional object (e.g., a round ball). The volume of a sphere is found by multiplying $\frac{4}{3}$ times π times the cube of the radius.

$$V = \frac{4}{3}\pi r^3$$

Technical Knowledge and Science Review

This chapter will provide you with information on aviation basics, nautical knowledge, a general science review, and a walk-through of basic mechanical comprehension. This will help you on the AFOQT's Instrument Comprehension, Aviation Information, and General Science sections; the AFAST's Instrument Comprehension, Complex Movements, Helicopter Knowledge, Cyclic Orientation, and Mechanical Function sections; and the ASTB's Mechanical Comprehension, Spatial Apperception, Aviation and Nautical Information, and Aviation Supplemental Test sections.

Aviation Information

To do well on any of the aviation sections of these tests, you should have some basic knowledge of how airplanes and helicopters fly. It's a good idea, after you do some basic research of your own at the library or on the Internet, to take some time to visit an airport and talk with pilots to get some basic information about how to fly a plane. It might even be worth hiring a pilot for a few hours to take you up so you can see how the basic concepts are applied—if a picture is worth a thousand words, then direct experience is worth ten thousand (maybe a million in some cases). Even better, go through this book, write down any questions with which you had problems, and then ask the pilots for help. A hands-on demonstration will definitely help you remember the material.

This section covers the basics of flight for both fixed- and rotary-wing aircraft, including how aircraft are constructed; flight instruments and controls; flight theory and the flight envelope; basic aviation terminology; and basic flight maneuvers. We will go all the way through this sequence with fixed-wing aircraft, then come back and revisit how rotary-wing aircraft are similar and how they are different.

While you're working your way through this section, make a note when you come to a concept that you don't fully understand based on the explanation in that particular section, but try to continue: Some ideas have to be explained one piece at a time, and the explanation will become clearer as you go along. For instance, it's impossible to explain aircraft controls without mentioning the control surfaces and what they do, but explaining what they do isn't very clear until you know what the three axes of movement are, which in turn don't make much sense unless explained in the context of cockpit controls and the airplane's control surfaces.

It's like listening to a class on a subject that's new to you, but having to wait until the end to ask any questions. Many of the questions you have will be answered as the information is explained, part by part. If you get to the end, however, and some ideas aren't clear yet, go back to that section and reread it; you will probably understand it better now that you have some of the other pieces of the puzzle in place. If that idea is still not clear to you, talk to a licensed pilot or do some more research on your own. You'll get it.

Fixed-Wing Aircraft Structure

Although airplanes vary widely based on their design purposes and capacities, most have some version of the same basic components:

1. Fuselage
2. Wings
3. Tail assembly or empennage
4. Landing gear
5. Powerplant
6. Flight instruments/controls and control surfaces

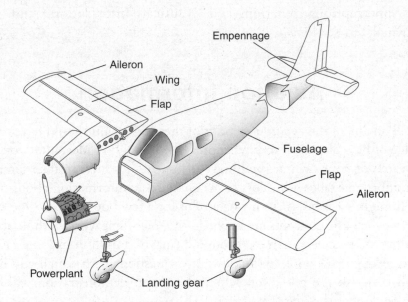

Figure 7.1 Basic fixed-wing aircraft construction

Fuselage

The *fuselage* or body of the airplane contains the cockpit, from which the pilots and flight crew control the aircraft's operations; the cabin, if the airplane carries any passengers; the cargo area if there is one; and attachment points for other major airplane components, such as the wings, tail section, and landing gear.

Single-engine propeller-driven airplanes usually have the engine in the front of the fuselage. There is a fireproof partition called a *firewall* between the engine compartment and the cockpit/cabin to protect the crew and passengers (if any) from a fire in the engine.

The two general design types of fuselage construction are *truss* and *monocoque*. Truss construction fuselages use steel or aluminum tubing in a series of triangular shapes (called trusses) to get the necessary strength and rigidity. Monocoque designs use bulkheads, stringers (running the length of the fuselage), and formers (perpendicular to the stringers) of various sizes and shapes to support a stretched or "stressed" skin.

Wings

The wings are airfoils attached to each side of the fuselage that serve as the main lifting surfaces supporting the airplane in flight. An *airfoil* is an aircraft part or surface (such as a wing, propeller blade, or rudder) that controls lift, direction, stability, thrust, or propulsion for the aircraft. Modern aircraft may have any one of a wide variety of wing designs, shapes, and sizes, based on the aircraft's purpose and design capabilities; the different types of wing shapes provide different capabilities, advantages, and disadvantages, but they all work basically the same way (we'll get into that shortly).

Wings may be attached to the fuselage at the top, middle, or bottom (hence the terms *high-wing*, *mid-wing*, and *low-wing*). How many wings an airplane has can also vary, but this is counted in pairs or sets (wouldn't want to have an airplane with only a left wing, for instance); airplanes with one set of wings are *monoplanes*, and those with two sets (usually stacked vertically) are called *biplanes*. There were a few triplanes early in the airplane's history, but you won't see them any more; there are still a few types of biplanes around (usually crop dusters and the like), but almost all planes today are monoplanes.

In terms of bracing and support, wings fall into one of two major categories, *cantilever* or *semi-cantilever*. A cantilever wing requires no external bracing, getting its support from internal wing spars, ribs, and stringers, as well as the construction of the wing's skin or covering. A semi-cantilever wing requires both internal bracing and external support from struts attached to the fuselage.

Attached to the rear (trailing) edges of the wings are two sets of control surfaces known as *ailerons* and *flaps* (see Figure 7.1). Ailerons extend from about the middle of the wing out toward the wingtip; they move in opposite directions to create aerodynamic forces that cause the airplane to roll. Flaps extend outward from near where the wing joins the fuselage (called the *wing root*) to about the middle of the wing's trailing edge. The flaps are usually flush with the rest of the wing surface during cruising (constant speed, neither climbing nor diving) flight; when they are extended, the flaps move downward together to increase the lift of the wing for takeoffs and landings.

In the flight theory section, we'll discuss in more detail how wings generate lift. For right now, though, let's hit the high points of how wings are shaped. First, we'll look at a cross section of a conventional wing shape or *airfoil*.

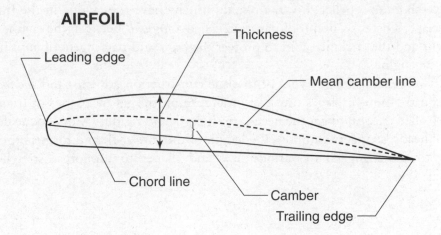

Figure 7.2 Airfoil cross section

Airfoil shapes are found on wings, fans, and propellers—any application where air needs to be moved. The airfoil shape provides lift when it splits the airstream through which it is moving. An airfoil has a thicker, rounded front or leading edge, and a thinner trailing edge. In between the leading and trailing edge, an airfoil is curved; the top surface usually has a greater curve than the bottom surface. When a surface is curved, we say it has *camber*.

An airfoil uses the aerodynamics identified by Bernoulli's Principle to provide lift to the aircraft. Because the top surface of the wing has more camber than the bottom surface, the air flows faster over the top of the wing than it does underneath. This means that there is less air pressure above the wing than there is underneath; the difference in air pressure above and below the wing causes lift.

Different airfoil shapes generate different amounts of lift and drag. If an airplane is designed to fly at low speeds (up to 100 mph), it will have a different airfoil shape than an airplane designed to fly at supersonic speed (above about 750 mph). That's because the airflow behaves in slightly different ways at different speeds and at different altitudes. In general, low- to medium-speed airplanes have airfoils with more thickness and camber.

The distance from the leading edge of the wing to the trailing edge is called the *chord*; the line from the middle of the leading edge to the trailing edge (as depicted in Figure 7.2) is the *chord line*, which cuts the airfoil into an upper surface and a lower surface. If we plot the points that lie halfway between the upper and lower surfaces, we obtain a curve called the *mean camber line*. For a symmetric airfoil, where the upper surface has the same shape as the lower surface, the mean camber line is the same as the chord line—but in most cases, since the airfoil surface has less curvature on the bottom than the top, these are two separate lines. The maximum distance between the two lines is called the *camber*, which is a measure of the curvature of the airfoil (high camber means high curvature); the maximum distance between the upper and lower surfaces is called the *thickness*.

The ends of the wings are called the *wingtips*, and the distance from one wingtip to the other is called the *wingspan*. The shape of the wing viewed from above is called a *planform*. For a rectangular wing, the chord length at every location along the span is the same. For most other planforms, the chord length varies along the span.

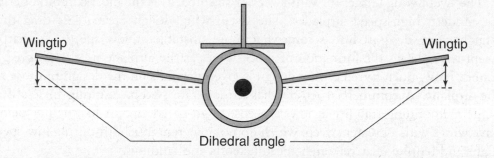

Figure 7.3 Front wing view showing dihedral

The front view of this wing shows that the left and right wings aren't truly horizontal (i.e., perpendicular to the fuselage), but instead meet at an angle called the *dihedral angle*. Dihedral is built into the design for roll stability; a wing with some dihedral will naturally return to its original position if it encounters a slight displacement. You may have noticed that most large airliner wings are designed with dihedral—you can tell by the fact that the wingtips are higher off the ground than the wing roots. Highly maneuverable fighter planes, on the other hand, don't have dihedral; in fact, some fighters have wingtips lower than the roots (called *anhedral*), giving the aircraft a higher roll rate.

Different wing planforms have different uses, characteristics, advantages, and so on. An airplane's speed, maneuverability, and handling qualities are all very dependent on the shape of the wings. There are three basic wing types used on modern airplanes: straight, sweep, and delta.

Straight wings are mostly found on small, low-speed airplanes, as well as gliders and sailplanes. These wings give the most efficient lift at low speeds, but are not very good for high-speed flight, especially that approaching the speed of sound.

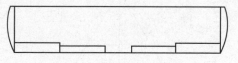

Figure 7.4 Straight-wing designs

The swept wing (either forward-swept or sweptback) is the most common design for modern high-speed airplanes. The swept-wing design creates less drag than straight-wing designs, but is somewhat more unstable at low speeds. A sharply swept wing delays the formation of shock waves as the airplane nears the speed of sound. How much sweep a wing design is given depends on the design purpose for the airplane. A commercial jetliner has a moderate sweep, resulting in less drag while maintaining stability at lower speeds. High-speed aircraft like fighter planes have wings with a greater sweep, which do not generate much lift during low-speed flight and require relatively high-speed takeoffs and landings.

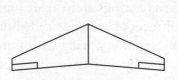 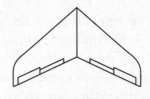 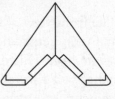

Slightly swept wing   Moderately swept wing   Sharply swept wing

Figure 7.5 Swept-wing designs

A delta wing looks like a large triangle viewed from above. It has a high angle of sweep with a straight trailing edge. Airplanes with this type of wing design are designed to reach supersonic speeds, and also land at high speeds. This type of plan-form is found on the supersonic transport Concorde and the shuttle Orbiters, as well as some experimental aircraft and European fighters; the delta wing design was also used on the now-obsolete F-102 Delta Dart and F-106 Delta Dagger American fighters and the B-58 Hustler bomber.

Simple delta wing

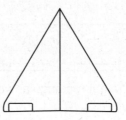

Complex delta wing

Figure 7.6 Delta wing designs

Landing Gear

The landing gear provide the main support for the airplane when it is on the ground. Landing gear usually consists of three wheels or sets of wheels—sometimes more for large or special-purpose aircraft—but airplanes can also be equipped with skis for landing on snow and ice, or floats to land on water.

Landing gear can be either retractable or nonretractable. Retractable gear can be mechanically pulled up into a cavity designed for them, with a door or doors closing over the opening to reduce drag and improve the airplane's performance. Nonretractable landing gear usually have fairings over their top half to reduce drag and improve the airplane's performance.

Two of the three wheels or sets of wheels are mounted either under the wings or at the outside edges of the fuselage. Sets of wheels, rather than single wheels, perform the same function as dual wheels on the back of a pickup truck or tractor-trailer rig: They support more weight. A few very large cargo and passenger airplanes even have more than two sets of landing gear, each with multiple wheels, mounted at the outside edges of the fuselage.

The third wheel or set of wheels is normally mounted either under the tail of the airplane or at the nose. Landing gear using a tailwheel are often called *conventional landing gear*, or the planes that have such landing gear may be referred to as *tailwheel airplanes*. Designs with the third wheel under the nose (a *nosewheel*) are commonly called *tricycle landing gear*. In either case, a steerable tailwheel or nosewheel allows the airplane to be controlled during ground movement.

Powerplant

There are two main types of fixed-wing aircraft propulsion systems we will discuss here: propellers and jets. Propeller- or "prop"-driven planes get their *thrust* by the corkscrew action of one or more propellers with two or more blades each rotating very fast at the front of the engine, which pushes air backward with the result that the airplane is "pushed" forward in accordance with Newton's third law. The propeller blades are curved or slanted in a certain way to achieve this effect, and often the amount of the slant or *pitch* is variable—that is, the pilot can control just how much "pull" or *thrust* he wants the propeller to exert. Various designs, including the Wright brothers' original 1903 model, have placed the propeller at the back of the plane, resulting in the name *pusher prop*, but these are by far in the minority.

The powerplant of a propeller-driven plane is usually considered to include both the engine and the propeller. The primary function of the engine is to turn the propeller, but it also generates electrical power, provides a vacuum source for some flight instruments, and provides a heat source for pilot and passengers in most small single-engine planes.

Propeller-driven airplanes may have either a *fixed-pitch* or *variable-pitch* propeller. A fixed-pitch propeller's pitch has a blade angle that can't be changed by the pilot. The propeller is connected directly to the engine's crankshaft; engine power rotates the crankshaft as well as the propeller, and the propeller converts the engine's rotary power into thrust. A variable-pitch propeller, also known as a *constant-speed* propeller, is more efficient than its fixed-pitch counterpart because the pilot can adjust the blade angle for the most efficient operation.

Single-engine propeller-driven airplanes usually have the engine attached to the front of the fuselage, covered by a cowling to streamline the airflow around the engine; it also helps cool the engine by ducting air around the cylinders. Multi-engine planes, whether propeller driven or jet, usually have the engines mounted under the wings in a nacelle, which surrounds the entire engine and performs the same functions as a cowling. Some jet engines are attached to the empennage, but these are in the minority.

Jet engines work by forcing incoming air into a tube or cylinder where the air is compressed, mixed with fuel, burned, and pushed exhausted at high speed to generate thrust. There are several variations of jet engines, including the turbojet, turbofan, and ramjet. These engines all operate by the same basic principles, but each has its own distinct advantages and disadvantages.

The critical part of a jet engine's operation is compressing the incoming air. Most jets employ a section of compressors, consisting of rotating blades that slow the incoming air to create high pressure. This compressed air is then forced into a combustion section, where it is mixed with fuel and burned. As the high-pressure gases are exhausted, they are passed through a turbine section with more rotating blades. In this region, the exhaust gases turn the turbine blades, which are connected by a shaft to the compressor blades at the front of the engine—which means that the exhaust turns the turbines that turn the compressors to bring in more air and keep the engine going. The combustion gases then continue to expand out through the nozzle, "pushing" backward to create a forward thrust.

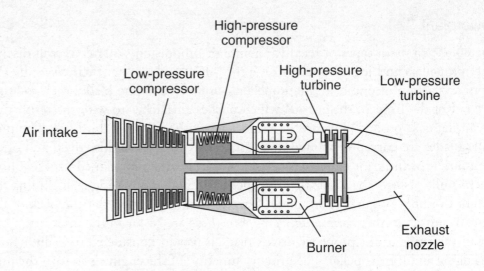

Figure 7.7 Turbojet engine cross section

Turbojets and turbofans can also be fitted with an *afterburner.* An afterburner is a tube placed between the turbine and the rear exhaust nozzle where additional fuel is added to the flow and ignited to provide increased thrust. However, afterburners greatly increase fuel consumption, so they can be used only for short periods.

Tail Assembly/Empennage

The technical name for the tail section of an airplane is the *empennage*; this includes the entire tail section, which consists of both fixed and movable control surfaces.

The fixed surfaces are the vertical and horizontal stabilizers, and the moveable surfaces include the elevators, the rudder, and any trim tabs.

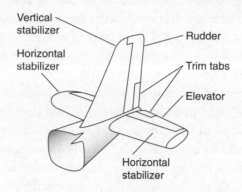

Figure 7.8 Conventional empennage

The elevators are movable control surfaces attached to the back or trailing edge of the horizontal stabilizers; they are used to move the nose of the airplane up or down during flight. Usually the two stabilizers are split, even at the back edge, by either the vertical stabilizer, the back end of the fuselage, or both; however, there are a few airplane designs where the trailing edge of the horizontal stabilizer is not split, and therefore there is only one elevator instead of two. For purposes of our discussion, however, we will consider the left and right horizontal stabilizers—and hence the attached elevators—to be split.

The rudder is a movable control surface attached to the back of the vertical stabilizer that is used to move the airplane's nose left and right during flight. The rudder is used in combination with the ailerons for turns while the airplane is flying. Some people incorrectly refer to the vertical stabilizer as the rudder, but now you know better.

Trim tabs are small movable segments of the trailing edge of the rudder, elevator(s), and ailerons. Controlled by the pilot in the cockpit, they reduce control pressures and decrease the pilot's workload.

Newton's Laws

British mathematician and philosopher Sir Isaac Newton put forth three basic laws of motion in the mid-1600s. Although we can be pretty confident that he wasn't thinking of aircraft flight characteristics when he propounded these laws, virtually everything that an aircraft does has something to do with one or more of his three laws of motion.

Newton's First Law of Motion (or Inertia), stated simply, maintains that a body at rest tends to remain at rest, and a body in motion tends to remain in motion (at the same speed and in the same direction) unless acted upon by an outside force. Stated differently, nothing in nature starts or stops moving until some outside force causes it to do so. This is connected with the concept of *inertia*, which is the property by which an object resists being accelerated in some different way from its current state.

Examples are the soccer ball that remains motionless (relative to the earth, anyway) upon the ground until it is kicked, and the same soccer ball that keeps rolling until friction with the ground and the air around it slow it down and finally stop it. Likewise, an airplane parked on the ramp will stay there until enough force to move it is applied by the engines, a vehicle, a tornado, or something else.

Newton's Second Law of Motion is represented by the equation F = *ma*, where F is the *force* acting on an object, *m* stands for an object's *mass*, and *a* is the object's acceleration. According to this law, when an object is acted upon by a force, its resulting acceleration is directly proportional to the applied force and inversely proportional to the mass of the object. This means that force must be applied to overcome the inertia of an object: The greater the mass of the object, the greater the force needed to produce a particular acceleration.

Newton's Third Law of Motion is usually summarized like this: "For every action there is an equal and opposite reaction." Stated differently, when one object exerts a force on a second object, the second object exerts an equal and opposite force on the first object. This law is most clearly demonstrated in the aerospace world by the operation of jets and rockets: As hot gases are pushed out the back, they exert a forward push on the object from which they escape (such as the jet engine connected to the aircraft).

These laws need to be considered in the context of another of Newton's laws, that of *universal gravitation*. This law says that two objects attract each other with a force that is proportional to the product of their masses (i.e., their masses multiplied together), and inversely proportional to the square of the distance between them. This attraction is commonly known as *gravity*. Gravity accounts for the weight of an object on Earth (or some other planet, for that matter), and usually measures the pull of the large body (the earth, in this case) in pounds or kilograms.

It needs to be noted here that, although *mass* and *weight* are both commonly referred to in pounds or kilograms, *mass* is a constant that is unaffected by local gravitational conditions, whereas *weight* is a function of the planet's gravity at that point. In other words, regardless of the fact that an object can weigh 6 pounds on Earth, 1 pound on the moon (where gravity is one-sixth of that on Earth), or nothing at all in far outer space, its mass remains the same regardless—it will take the same amount of force in any of those places to accelerate it the same amount.

Flight Theory and the Flight Envelope

Four forces act upon an aircraft in flight: *lift*, *gravity* (or weight), *thrust*, and *drag*. Lift pushes the aircraft up (i.e., away from the earth's surface); weight pulls the aircraft down toward the earth (or, more precisely, toward the earth's center); thrust pushes the aircraft forward; and drag tends to slow the aircraft, pushing back on it as it moves forward.

The *flight envelope* consists of the different combinations of these factors and others that allow the aircraft to be flown safely. "Flying outside the envelope" is usually slang for some unsafe condition that caused problems in maintaining stability or even the ability to fly at all.

An airfoil uses the aerodynamic forces identified by Bernoulli's Principle to provide *lift* to the wings and therefore the aircraft (Daniel Bernoulli, a Swiss mathematician, expanded on Newton's theories about the motion of fluids in his *Hydrodynamics*, published in 1783.) Bernoulli's Principle basically says that as the velocity of a fluid increases, the pressure exerted by that fluid decreases. You can think of it (simplistically) that the faster a fluid (and air is a fluid—not a liquid, but a fluid) travels over a surface, the less time it has to exert pressure on any given part of that surface.

Because the top surface of the wing has more camber (curvature) than the bottom surface, the air flows faster over the top of the wing than it does underneath;

this is because aerodynamic forces won't allow the air flowing over the upper surface to "lag behind," since it would create a vacuum at the trailing edge (and nature is very reluctant to allow vacuums to form). This faster airflow over the upper wing surface means that there is less air pressure above the wing than there is underneath; the difference in air pressure above and below the wing causes lift.

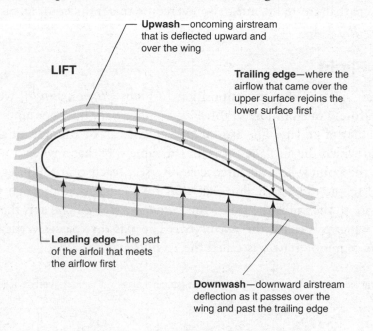

Upwash—oncoming airstream that is deflected upward and over the wing

LIFT

Trailing edge—where the airflow that came over the upper surface rejoins the lower surface first

Leading edge—the part of the airfoil that meets the airflow first

Downwash—downward airstream deflection as it passes over the wing and past the trailing edge

Figure 7.9 Airfoil produces lift

A *stall* is caused by the separation of airflow from the wing's upper surface, resulting in a rapid decrease in lift—possibly to the extent of falling out of the sky. This separation happens from the trailing edge moving forward toward the leading edge, and allows a reverse airflow to creep in that presses down on the wing. A stall usually occurs somewhat gradually, and the first indications may be provided by a mushiness in the controls or a slight buffeting of the aircraft; stall warning devices that detect the airflow separation may also provide notice. To recover from a stall or imminent stall, the pilot must restore the smooth airflow by decreasing the angle of attack below the stalling angle, allowing normal lift dynamics to resume.

Weight is the force produced by the mass of the airplane interacting with Earth's gravitational field; it is the force that must be counteracted by lift to maintain flight.

Different kinds of weight are discussed in aviation circles:

- Basic Weight—the weight of the basic aircraft plus weapons, unusable fuel, oil, ballast, survival kits, oxygen, and any other internal or external equipment on board the aircraft that will not be disposed of during flight.
- Operating Weight—the sum of basic weight and items such as crew, crew baggage, steward equipment, pylons and racks, emergency equipment, special mission fixed equipment, and all other nonexpendable items not included in basic weight.
- Gross Weight—the total weight of an aircraft, including its contents and externally mounted items, at any time.
- Landing Gross Weight—the weight of the aircraft, its contents, and external items when the aircraft lands.
- Zero Fuel Weight (ZFW)—the weight of the aircraft without any usable fuel.

Profile drag or *parasitic drag* is experienced by all objects in an airflow, and is caused by the airplane pushing the air out of the way as it moves forward. This can be experienced by putting your hand out the window of a moving vehicle.

The other type of drag is *induced drag*, which is the result of the production of lift. It is the part of the force produced by the wing that is parallel to the relative wind. Objects that create lift must also overcome this induced drag, also known as *drag-due-to-lift*.

Axes of Flight

Whenever an airplane changes its position in flight (*flight attitude*), we talk about movement around one or more of three *axes*—imaginary lines running through the airplane's center of gravity. The axes of an airplane can be thought of as imaginary axles around which the airplane turns, in the same way that a wheel rotates around its axle. At the point where all three axes intersect, each is at a 90-degree angle (a right angle) to the other two. The axis that runs lengthwise through the fuselage from the nose to the tail is the called the *longitudinal axis*. The axis that runs from wingtip to wingtip is called the *lateral axis*. The axis that passes vertically through the aircraft's center of gravity is called the *vertical axis*.

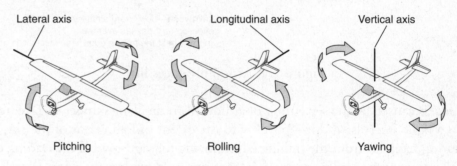

Figure 7.10 The three axes of flight

The airplane's motion around its longitudinal axis resembles the roll of a ship from side to side. In fact, the names used in describing movement around the airplane's three axes were originally nautical terms. Movement around the airplane's longitudinal axis is called *roll*; movement around its lateral axis is referred to as *pitch*; and movement around the vertical axis is known as *yaw*—a horizontal (left and right) movement of the airplane's nose. The three motions of the airplane (roll, pitch, and yaw) are controlled by three control surfaces: Roll is controlled by the ailerons; pitch is controlled by the elevators; and yaw is controlled by the rudder.

The Atmosphere

The atmosphere is composed of 78 percent nitrogen, 21 percent oxygen, and 1 percent other gaseous elements such as argon and helium. The heavier of these elements exhibit a natural tendency to remain closer to the surface of the earth, and the lighter elements are in the higher regions of the atmosphere. This explains why the vast majority of the atmosphere's oxygen, as one of the relatively heavier elements, is found below 35,000 feet from the surface.

The atmosphere—the air surrounding the earth—has mass and weight; for instance, the weight of the atmosphere at sea level results in an average pressure of

14.7 pounds on each square inch of an object's surface. At 18,000 feet, however, the weight of the atmosphere is only about half of what it is at sea level.

Temperature, air pressure (which is dependent in large part on altitude), and humidity play a part in an airplane's performance, largely by affecting the amount of lift produced by the airfoils. Warmer air, for instance, is less dense than cooler air and therefore produces less lift.

Flight Controls

A flight control system has two ends to it: the end where the pilot makes a change to a control in the cockpit, and the end where something on the outside of the aircraft changes and affects the airplane's performance (faster, slower, up, down, left, right, etc.). Implied in this, of course, are the mechanical, hydraulic, electronic, and other means of connecting these two ends—of having the expected result occur reliably from a certain movement of the cockpit controls.

There are two types of flight control systems, *primary* and *secondary*. The primary control systems are those needed to safely control an airplane during flight, including the ailerons, elevator/stabilator, and rudder. Secondary control systems, such as wing flaps and trim control systems, improve the airplane's performance or relieve the pilot of having to deal with excessive control forces.

In the cockpit, the pilot has three main ways to control the aircraft while in flight: the joystick or control wheel, the rudder pedals, and the throttle(s) for the engine(s).

The joystick controls *roll* (movement around the longitudinal axis, one wing up and one wing down) and *pitch* (movement around the lateral axis, nose up or nose down). Some airplanes (usually larger ones) have a movable control column with a control wheel mounted near the top; the functions are the same. Move the stick or wheel to the left, and the left wing goes down while the right one comes up. Push forward on the joystick or control column and the nose of the airplane moves downward; pull back toward you and the nose will rise.

The two rudder pedals control the *yaw* of the airplane, which is how much (or how little) the nose points to the left or right in a horizontal sense.

The engine throttles are considered flight controls because they are the main way for the pilot to regulate how much thrust the engine is producing. This is important because the pilot has to use all these controls in coordination to safely control the airplane; having the airplane at the proper attitude to climb higher, for example, does no good if the engine isn't producing enough thrust to accomplish the climb.

Primary Flight Controls

Airplane control systems are designed to provide the pilot a natural "feel"—one where the amount of force the pilot uses, as well as the resistance and other feedback felt by the pilot through the controls, are proportionate to the amount of actual movement by the control surfaces—but at the same time be adequately responsive to the pilot's inputs on the controls. At low airspeeds, the controls usually feel soft and sluggish, and the airplane responds slowly to the controls. At higher speeds, the controls feel firmer and the response is quicker.

Moving one or more of the three primary flight control surfaces changes the airflow and pressure distribution over and around the airfoil (wings). These changes affect the lift and drag produced by the airfoil/control surface combination, which allows a pilot to control the airplane around its three axes of rotation.

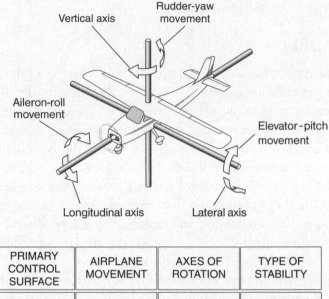

PRIMARY CONTROL SURFACE	AIRPLANE MOVEMENT	AXES OF ROTATION	TYPE OF STABILITY
Aileron	Roll	Longitudinal	Lateral
Elevator/ stability	Pitch	Lateral	Longitudinal
Rudder	Yaw	Vertical	Directional

Ailerons

Ailerons control the airplane's movement around the longitudinal axis, also known as *roll*. They are attached to the outboard trailing edge of each wing and move in opposite directions from each other.

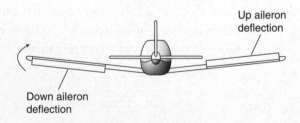

Figure 7.11 Ailerons

Moving the joystick or control wheel to the right causes the right aileron to move or *deflect* upward while the left aileron moves downward. The upward deflection of the right aileron decreases the camber of that wing, causing a decrease in lift that makes the right wing drop. The same aerodynamics in reverse on the left cause that wing to rise because of increased lift. The combined effects cause the airplane to roll to the right.

Rudder

The rudder controls the airplane's movement around its vertical axis, called *yaw*. Like the other primary control surfaces, the rudder is a movable surface hinged to a fixed surface—in this case, to the vertical stabilizer. Moving the left or right rudder pedal causes the rudder to move in the same direction as the depressed pedal, and to the same relative extent. When the rudder is deflected into the airflow, the airflow exerts a horizontal force in the opposite direction.

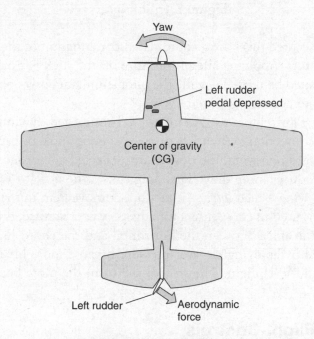

Figure 7.12 Rudder

By pushing the left pedal, the rudder moves left. This alters the airflow around the vertical stabilizer and rudder, creating a sideward force that moves the tail to the right and yaws the nose of the airplane to the left. Rudder effectiveness increases with speed, so large deflections at low speeds and small deflections at high speeds are usually what's required. In propeller-driven aircraft, any slipstream (rearward-flowing air pushed back by the propeller) flowing over the rudder increases its effectiveness.

Elevator

The elevator is a hinged control surface attached to the rear of the horizontal stabilizer. On most planes, the elevators are divided by the vertical stabilizer and rudder; however, on some designs, the elevators are far enough back so that they are not two separated surfaces but one, called a *stabilator*.

The elevator controls the airplane's movement around its lateral axis, called *pitch*. Moving the joystick or control column to the rear, toward the pilot, causes the elevators to move or *deflect* upward. The up-elevator position decreases the camber of the horizontal tail surface, creating a downward aerodynamic force greater than the slight tail-down force normal in most designs during straight and level flight. The overall effect causes the tail to move downward and the nose to pitch up, rotating around the plane's center of gravity (CG). Moving the joystick or control column forward, of course, has the opposite effect.

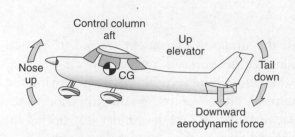

Figure 7.13 Elevator

All correctly executed turns are a coordinated combination of the use of ailerons, rudder, and elevators. Applying aileron pressure on the stick left or right is needed to achieve the desired bank angle, while the pilot simultaneously applies pressure on the rudder pedal to counteract adverse yaw.

Control surfaces are seldom used in isolation, because aerodynamic forces seldom work in only one direction. When left or right stick is applied, causing an aileron deflection that raises one wing, the downward-deflected aileron not only produces more lift, but produces more drag. This drag causes the nose to yaw in the direction of the raised wing, called *adverse yaw*. Rudder movement in the opposite direction of the bank is used to compensate for adverse yaw. Likewise, during a turn, the angle of attack (the angle between the horizontal and the chord line of the airfoil) must be increased by applying elevator pressure because more lift is required than during straight-and-level flight. The steeper the turn, the more back elevator pressure is needed.

Secondary Flight Controls

Secondary flight control systems may consist of flaps, leading edge devices, spoilers, and trim devices.

Flaps

Flaps are the most common high-lift devices. These surfaces, which are attached to the trailing edge of the wing, increase both lift and drag for any given angle of attack. Flaps allow a compromise between high cruising speed and low landing speed because they may be extended when needed and then retracted into the wing's structure when not needed.

Leading Edge Devices

High-lift devices also can be applied to the leading edge of the airfoil. The most common types are fixed slats, moveable slats, and leading edge flaps.

Spoilers

On some airplanes, high-drag devices called spoilers are deployed from the wings to spoil the smooth airflow, reducing lift and increasing drag. Spoilers are used for roll control on some aircraft, one of the advantages being the elimination of adverse yaw. To turn right, for example, the spoiler on the right wing is raised, destroying some of the lift and creating more drag on the right. The right wing drops, and the airplane banks and yaws to the right. Deploying spoilers on both wings at the same time allows the aircraft to descend without gaining speed. Spoilers are also deployed to help shorten the ground roll after landing—by destroying lift, they transfer weight to the wheels, improving braking effectiveness.

Trim Systems

Trim systems are used to relieve the pilot of the need to maintain constant pressure on the flight controls—just think how tired you would get if you had to hold the steering wheel a quarter turn to the right just to go *straight* down the highway. Trim systems usually consist of small hinged devices attached to the trailing edge of one or more of the primary flight control surfaces. They help minimize a pilot's workload by aerodynamically assisting movement and positioning of the flight control surface to which they are attached.

The most common trim system on small airplanes is a single trim tab attached to the trailing edge of the elevator, usually manually operated by a small control wheel or a crank. The cockpit control includes a tab position indicator; placing the trim control in nose-down position moves the tab to its full "up" position. With the tab up and into the airstream, the airflow over the horizontal tail surface forces the trailing edge of the elevator down. This causes the tail of the airplane to move up, and results in a nose-down pitch change.

In spite of the opposite direction movement of the trim tab and the elevator, trim control is natural to a pilot. If you have to exert constant back pressure on the control column, the need for nose-up trim is indicated. The normal trim procedure is to continue trimming until the airplane is balanced and the nose-heavy or tail-heavy condition is no longer apparent. Pilots normally establish the desired power, pitch, attitude, and configuration first, and then trim the airplane to relieve control pressures that may exist for that flight condition. Any time power, pitch, attitude, or configuration are changed, retrimming will normally be necessary to relieve the control pressures for the new flight condition.

Flight Instruments

Flight instruments enable a pilot to operate an airplane with optimal performance and increased safety, especially when flying long distances or in inclement weather conditions.

Altimeter

The altimeter measures height above a particular air pressure level, and therefore gives the pilot information about his altitude above the ground. Air is denser at sea level than at higher altitudes, so as altitude increases, atmospheric pressure decreases. The pressure altimeter is an anaeroid barometer that measures atmospheric pressure at the level where the altimeter is located, and presents an altitude in feet. Different altimeters can vary considerably, though, in how they show altitude; some have one pointer, whereas others have two or more. The dial of a typical altimeter is graduated, with numerals arranged clockwise from 0 to 9. The shortest hand indicates altitude in tens of thousands of feet, the intermediate hand in thousands of feet, and the longest hand in hundreds of feet.

Figure 7.14 Altimeter

This indicated altitude is precisely correct, though, only when the sea level barometric pressure is at what has been determined to be the "standard" (29.92 inches of mercury), the sea level free air temperature is "standard" (+15°C or 59°F), and the pressure and temperature decrease at a standard rate with an increase in altitude. Adjustments for nonstandard conditions are performed by setting the corrected pressure into a barometric scale on the face of the altimeter; only after this corrected setting is in place does the altimeter indicate the precise altitude.

Types of Altitude

Altitude is vertical distance above some point or level used as a reference. There are as many kinds of altitude as there are reference levels from which altitude is measured, and each may be used for specific reasons. Pilots are mainly concerned with five types of altitude:

- **Indicated Altitude**—The uncorrected altitude read directly from the altimeter when it is set to the current altimeter setting.
- **True Altitude**—The vertical distance of the airplane above sea level; the actual altitude. It is often expressed as feet above mean sea level (MSL); airport, terrain, and obstacle elevations on aeronautical charts are true altitudes.
- **Absolute Altitude**—The vertical distance of an airplane above the terrain, or above ground level.
- **Pressure Altitude**—The altitude indicated when the altimeter setting window (barometric scale) is adjusted to 29.92. This is the altitude above the standard datum plane, which is a theoretical level where air pressure (corrected to 15°C) equals 29.92 inches of mercury (Hg). Pressure altitude is used to compute density altitude, true altitude, true airspeed, and other performance data.
- **Density Altitude**—This altitude is pressure altitude corrected for variations from standard temperature. When conditions are standard, pressure altitude and density altitude are the same. If the temperature is above standard, the density altitude is higher than pressure altitude. If the temperature is below standard, the density altitude is lower than pressure altitude. This is an important altitude because it is directly related to the airplane's performance.

As an example, consider an airport with a field elevation of 5,048 feet MSL where the standard temperature is 5°C. Under these conditions, pressure altitude and density altitude are the same—5,048 feet. If the temperature changes to 30°C, the density altitude increases to 7,855 feet. This means an airplane would perform on takeoff as though the field elevation were 7,855 feet at standard temperature. Conversely, a temperature of –25°C would result in a density altitude of 1,232 feet.

An airplane would have much better performance under these conditions because the denser air would produce more lift.

Hypoxia is a condition caused by insufficient oxygen in the bloodstream (in this context usually caused by unpressurized flight at too high an altitude). Symptoms are impaired reaction, confused thinking, poor judgment, fatigue, headaches, and sometimes euphoria; a prolonged condition can cause loss of consciousness and eventually death. A person with hypoxia may also show bluish lips and fingernail beds. This is generally not an issue below 10,000 feet altitude above mean sea level (MSL), although some people do not experience problems until higher elevations, and mountain climbers may be able to acclimatize themselves to much higher altitudes over time. Federal Aviation Administration (FAA) regulations only require oxygen for flights above 12,500 feet, but the rule of thumb for military flight operations above 10,000 feet is to use oxygen.

Vertical Speed Indicator

The vertical speed indicator (VSI), sometimes called a vertical velocity indicator, indicates whether the airplane is climbing, descending, or in level flight. The rate of climb or descent is indicated in feet per minute. If properly calibrated, the VSI indicates zero in level flight. The vertical speed indicator is capable of displaying two different types of information:

- trend information that shows an immediate indication of an increase or decrease in the airplane's rate of climb or descent
- rate information that shows a stabilized rate of change in altitude

Figure 7.15 Vertical speed indicator

For example, if the airplane is maintaining a steady 500-foot-per-minute (fpm) climb and the nose is lowered slightly, the VSI immediately senses this change and indicates a decrease in the rate of climb. This first indication is called the *trend*. After a short time, the VSI needle stabilizes on the new rate of climb, which in this example is something less than 500 fpm. The time from the initial change in the rate of climb until the VSI displays an accurate indication of the new rate is called the *lag*. Some airplanes are equipped with an instantaneous vertical speed indicator (IVSI), which incorporates accelerometers to compensate for the lag in the typical VSI.

Airspeed Indicator

The airspeed indicator is a sensitive differential pressure gauge that measures and promptly shows the difference between *pitot* (impact) pressure and static pressure, the undisturbed atmospheric pressure at level flight. These two pressures will be equal when the airplane is parked on the ground in calm air. When the airplane moves through the air, the pressure on the pitot line becomes greater than the pressure in the static lines. This difference in pressure is registered by the airspeed pointer on the face of the instrument, which is calibrated in miles per hour, knots, or both.

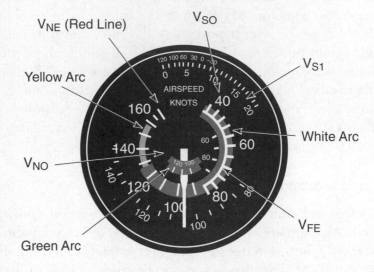

Figure 7.16 Airspeed indicator

There are four airspeed types, which you can remember by using the mnemonic **ICE-T**.

1. **I**ndicated airspeed—measures air pressure reading from the pitot tube.
2. **C**alibrated airspeed—airspeed calculated after accounting for aircraft mechanical and position errors (attitude).
3. **E**quivalent Airspeed—airspeed calculated after compensating for compression effects; usually only needed at speeds over 200 mph.
4. **T**rue Airspeed—airspeed calculated after accounting for temperature and atmospheric pressure changes.

- White arc—This arc is commonly referred to as the flap operating range, since its lower limit represents the full flap stall speed and its upper limit provides the maximum flap speed. Approaches and landings are usually flown at speeds within the white arc.
- Lower limit of white arc (V_{SO})—The stall speed or the minimum steady flight speed in the landing configuration. In small airplanes, this is the power-off stall speed at the maximum landing weight in the landing configuration (gear and flaps down).
- Upper limit of the white arc (V_{FE})—The maximum speed with the flaps extended.
- Green arc—Normal operating range of the airplane; most flying occurs within this range.
- Lower limit of green arc (V_{S1})—The stall speed or minimum steady flight speed in a specified configuration; for most airplanes, this is the power-off stall speed at the maximum takeoff weight in the clean configuration (gear up if retractable, and flaps up).
- Upper limit of green arc (V_{NO})—The maximum structural cruising speed; do not exceed this speed except in smooth air.

- Yellow arc—Caution range; fly within this range only in smooth air, and then only with caution.
- Red line (V_{NE})—Never-exceed speed; operating above this speed is prohibited, because it may result in damage or structural failure.

Turn Indicators

Airplanes use two types of turn indicators—the *turn-and-slip indicator* and the *turn coordinator*. Because of the way the gyro is mounted, the turn-and-slip indicator shows only the rate of turn in degrees per second. Because the gyro on the turn coordinator is set at an angle, or canted, it can initially also show roll rate. Once the roll stabilizes, it indicates the rate of turn. Both instruments indicate turn direction and quality (coordination), and also serve as a backup source of bank information in the event an attitude indicator fails. Coordination is achieved by referring to the *inclinometer*, which consists of a liquid-filled curved tube with a ball inside.

The inclinometer shows airplane yaw, the side-to-side movement of the airplane's nose. During coordinated, straight-and-level flight, gravity causes the ball to rest in the lowest part of the tube, centered between the reference lines. Coordinated flight is maintained by keeping the ball centered. If the ball is not centered, it can be centered by using the rudder. To do this, apply rudder pressure on the side where the ball is deflected. Use the simple rule of "step on the ball" to remember which rudder pedal to press.

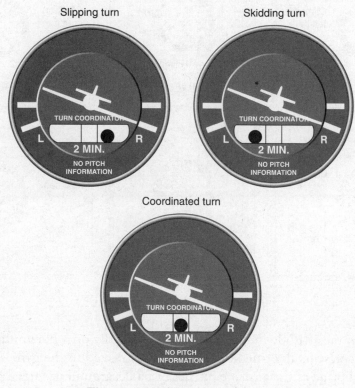

Figure 7.17 Turn coordinator

If aileron and rudder movements are coordinated during a turn, the ball remains centered in the tube. If aerodynamic forces are unbalanced, the ball moves away from the center of the tube.

Attitude Indicator

The attitude indicator, with its miniature airplane and horizon bar, displays a picture of the attitude of the airplane. The relationship of the miniature airplane to the horizon bar is the same as the relationship of the real airplane to the actual horizon. The instrument gives an instantaneous indication of even the smallest changes in attitude.

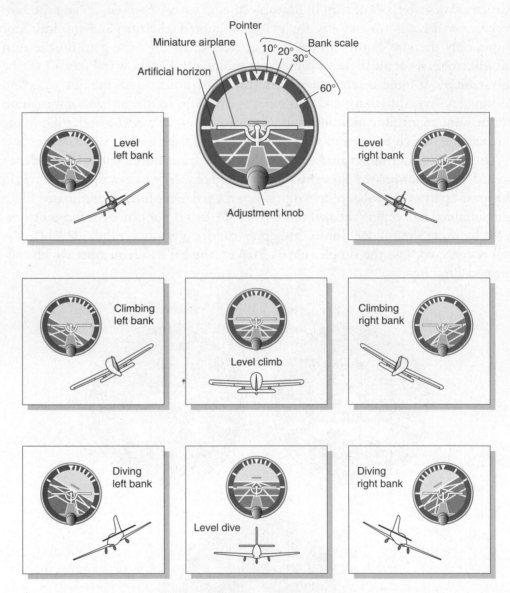

Figure 7.18 Attitude indicator

The gyro in the attitude indicator is mounted rigidly on a horizontal plane. The horizon bar represents the true horizon and is connected to the gyro, remaining in the horizontal plane as the airplane pitches or banks around its lateral or longitudinal axis, indicating the attitude of the airplane relative to the true horizon.

The pilot can use an adjustment knob to move the miniature airplane up or down to align it with the horizon bar as the pilot sees it from his position. Normally, the miniature airplane is adjusted so that the wings overlap the horizon bar when the airplane is in straight-and-level cruising flight.

Older models of attitude indicators have limits in the banking plane, usually from 100° to 110°; the pitch limits are usually from 60° to 70°. If either limit is exceeded, the instrument will tumble or spill and will give incorrect indications until restabilized. Most newer attitude indicators will not tumble.

The attitude indicator is reliable and the most realistic flight instrument on the instrument panel. What it shows are very close approximations of the actual attitude of the airplane.

Magnetic Compass

The magnetic compass, which is usually the only direction-seeking instrument in the airplane, is simple in construction. It has two magnetized steel needles fastened to a float, around which is mounted a compass card. The needles are parallel, with their north-seeking ends pointing in the same direction. The compass card has letters for cardinal headings, and each 30-degree interval is represented by a number, the last zero of which is omitted. For example, 30° appears as a 3 and 300° appears as a 30. Between these numbers, the card is marked in 5-degree increments. The magnetic compass is required equipment in all airplanes.

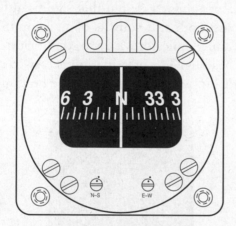

Figure 7.19 Magnetic compass

Although the earth's magnetic field lies *roughly* north and south, the magnetic poles don't exactly coincide with the geographic poles (which are used in the construction of aeronautical charts). Therefore, at most places on the earth's surface, the direction-sensitive steel needles that seek the earth's magnetic field will not point to true north, but instead to magnetic north. Furthermore, local magnetic fields from mineral deposits and other conditions may distort the earth's magnetic field and cause additional errors.

Heading Indicator

The *heading indicator* or *directional gyro* is a mechanical (not magnetic) instrument that backs up and supplements the magnetic compass. Frequent magnetic compass errors make straight flight and precision turns to exact headings (directions) hard to accomplish, especially in turbulent air. A heading indicator, however, being mechanical, is not affected by the forces that make the magnetic compass difficult to interpret precisely.

Figure 7.20 Heading indicator

Some heading indicators receive a magnetic north reference from a magnetic slaving transmitter, and generally need no adjustment. Heading indicators that don't have this automatic north-seeking capability are called "free" gyros, and require periodic adjustment.

Vertical Card Compass

The vertical card compass is a newer design that significantly reduces the inherent error of the older compass models. It consists of an azimuth on a rotating vertical card, and resembles a heading indicator with a fixed miniature airplane to accurately represent the airplane's heading. The presentation is easy to read, and the pilot can see the complete 360° dial in relation to the airplane heading.

Figure 7.21 Vertical card compass

Basic Flight Maneuvers

There are four fundamental flight maneuvers on which all flying tasks are based: straight-and-level flight, turns, climbs, and descents. All controlled flight consists of one or more of these basic maneuvers.

Straight-and-level flight is flight where the pilot maintains a constant heading and altitude. It is accomplished by making immediate, measured corrections for deviations in direction and altitude from unintentional slight turns, descents, and climbs.

An aircraft turns by banking the wings in the direction of the desired turn. The pilot chooses a specific bank angle and applies control pressure on the stick or control wheel to achieve it. Once the bank angle is established, the pilot continues to exert the pressure to maintain the desired angle.

All four primary controls are used in close coordination when making turns:

- The ailerons bank the wings and so determine the rate of turn at any given airspeed.
- The elevator moves the nose of the airplane up or down in relation to the pilot, and perpendicular to the wings. In doing so, it both sets the pitch attitude in the turn and "pulls" the nose of the airplane around the turn.
- The throttle controls the engine, which provides thrust that may be used for airspeed to tighten the turn.
- The rudder offsets any yaw effects developed by the other controls. The rudder does not turn the airplane, as many people believe.

For purposes of this discussion, we'll divide turns into three classes: shallow turns, medium turns, and steep turns.

- Shallow turns are those in which the bank is so shallow (less than about 20°) that the inherent lateral stability of the airplane acts to level the wings unless some aileron is applied to maintain the bank.
- Medium turns are those resulting from a degree of bank at which the airplane remains at a constant bank (approximately 20° to 45°).
- Steep turns are those resulting from a degree of bank (45° or more) at which the "over-banking tendency" of an airplane overcomes stability, and the bank increases unless aileron is applied to prevent it. Changing the direction of the wing's lift toward one side or the other causes the airplane to be pulled in that direction. The pilot does this by applying coordinated aileron and rudder to bank the airplane in the direction of the desired turn.

When an airplane is flying straight and level, the total lift force is acting perpendicular to the wings and to the earth. As the airplane is banked into a turn, the lift then becomes the result of two components. One, the vertical lift component, continues to act perpendicular to the earth and opposes gravity. Second, the horizontal lift component (centripetal force) acts parallel to the earth's surface and opposes inertia (apparent centrifugal force). These two lift components act at right angles to each other, causing the resultant total lifting force to act perpendicular to the banked wing of the airplane. It is the horizontal lift component that actually turns the airplane, not the rudder.

As the pilot applies aileron to bank the airplane, the lowered aileron (on the rising wing) produces a greater drag than the raised aileron (on the lowered wing). This increased aileron yaws the airplane toward the rising wing, or opposite to the direction of turn. To counteract this adverse yawing moment, the pilot must apply rudder pressure simultaneously with aileron in the desired direction to produce a coordinated turn.

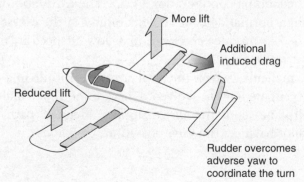

More lift

Additional induced drag

Reduced lift

Rudder overcomes adverse yaw to coordinate the turn

Climbs and Climbing Turns

When an airplane enters a climb, it changes its flight path from level flight to an inclined plane or *climb attitude*. In a climb, weight no longer acts in a direction perpendicular to the flight path, but instead in a rearward direction. This causes an increase in total drag, requiring an increase in thrust (power) to balance the forces. An airplane can sustain a climb angle only when there is sufficient thrust to offset increased drag; therefore, a climb is limited by the thrust available.

A *normal climb* is performed at an airspeed recommended by the airplane manufacturer, and is generally somewhat higher than the airplane's *best rate of climb*. The additional airspeed provides better engine cooling, easier control, and better visibility over the nose. Normal climb is sometimes referred to as *cruise climb*. Complex or high-performance airplanes may have a specified cruise climb in addition to normal climb.

An airplane's *best rate of climb* (V_y) is performed at an airspeed where the most excess power is available over that required for level flight. This condition of climb will produce the most gain in altitude in the least amount of time (maximum rate of climb in feet per minute). The best rate of climb made at full allowable power is a maximum climb.

An airplane's *best angle of climb* (V_x) is performed at an airspeed that will produce the most altitude gain in a given distance. Best angle-of-climb airspeed (V_x) is considerably lower than best rate of climb (V_y), and is the airspeed where the most excess thrust is available over that required for level flight. The best angle of climb will result in a steeper climb, although the airplane will take longer to reach the same altitude than it would at its best rate of climb. The best angle of climb, therefore, is used in such situations as clearing obstacles after takeoff.

Descents

When an airplane starts a descent, it changes its flight path from level to an inclined plane. There are three main categories of descents:

A *partial power descent* is the normal method of losing altitude, often called *cruise* or *enroute* descent. The airplane manufacturer normally recommends a setting of airspeed and power that will result in a target descent rate of 400–500 fpm. The airspeed may differ anywhere from cruise speed to that used on the downwind leg of the landing pattern. The pilot should keep the desired airspeed, pitch attitude, and power combination steady throughout the descent.

A *descent at minimum safe airspeed* (MSA) is a nose-high, power-assisted descent method mostly used for clearing obstacles during a landing approach to a short runway. The airspeed used for this type of approach is normally no more than 1.3 times the stall speed in the landing configuration (V_{S0}). The MSA approach is characterized by a steeper-than-normal descent angle, along with the excess power available that would be needed to produce acceleration at low airspeed if "mushing" and/or an excessive descent rate occur.

A *glide* is a basic maneuver where the airplane loses altitude in a controlled manner with little or no engine power involved. Forward motion is maintained by gravity pulling the airplane along its down-sloping inclined path; the descent is controlled as the pilot balances the forces of lift and gravity.

Power and Pitch

In addition to the dynamics already mentioned, the pilot must understand the effects of both power and elevator control as they work together during different flight conditions. Although there is a wide spectrum of combinations of conditions and settings, the overall rule of thumb for determining airspeed and altitude control runs something like this: *At any pitch attitude, the amount of power used will determine whether the airplane will climb, descend, or remain level at that altitude.*

In the majority of nose-down situations, a descent is the only possible flight condition. If you add power under these circumstances, it will only result in a descent at a faster airspeed. However, through a range of attitudes from only slightly nose-down to about 30° nose-up, a typical light aircraft can be made to climb, descend, or remain level based on the power used. In about the lower third of this range, the airplane will descend at idle power without stalling. As pitch attitude is increased, however, engine power is required to prevent a stall. Even more power will be required to maintain altitude, and yet more to climb. In a small plane, at a pitch attitude of about 30° nose-up, it will take all available power just to maintain altitude. A slight increase in the steepness of the climb, of a slight decrease in power, will result in a descent (whether the pilot intended it or not); again, this is known as "trying to fly outside the envelope." At that point, the slightest inducement will then further result in a stall.

Rotary-Wing Aircraft

A helicopter creates lift in a unique way. It has a rotary "wing," compared to the fixed, stationary wing on a "regular" airplane. Where a fixed-wing aircraft has to be moving to produce lift because of airflow over the airfoil or wing, a helicopter achieves it by manipulating the rapidly rotating main rotor blades, changing the angle at which they meet the air and subsequently the angle of attack.

The disadvantage with this arrangement is the need for *torque control* by a tail rotor, which uses some of the engine's power. Torque control is the compensation for the helicopter fuselage's tendency to rotate in the opposite direction from the rotor; the tail rotor continuously pulls the tail back the other way to maintain stability.

Helicopters in horizontal flight are subject to the same four forces as an airplane: lift, weight (or gravity), thrust, and drag. One difference, however, is that the thrust from a helicopter's rotors can be applied vertically, as when it's in a hover.

In stabilized horizontal flight, the force of lift equals weight and the force of thrust equals drag. The difference between hovering and horizontal flight is that, in horizontal flight, the thrust force and drag force are acting horizontally while the lift and weight act vertically. If thrust exceeds drag, then the helicopter increases its horizontal speed. If drag is greater than thrust, then the helicopter decreases its horizontal speed. If lift is greater than weight, then the helicopter climbs. If weight is greater than lift, then the helicopter descends. And, because of the helicopter's unique characteristics, horizontal flight is not limited to only the forward direction. This lift, weight, thrust, and drag relationship applies to any direction that the helicopter is moving (forward, sideways, or backward).

In a stabilized hover, the force of lift equals weight and the force of thrust equals drag. In addition, all four forces are acting vertically. If lift is greater than weight, the helicopter will climb; if weight is greater than lift, the helicopter will descend.

Helicopters are very sensitive to pilot input (the pilot in command normally sits on the right in a helicopter, as opposed to the left-hand seat in an airplane), and are therefore very responsive. Only slight control pressures are needed to master the techniques of hovering and landing.

Controlling a helicopter's flight path and position is a little more complex than a fixed-wing aircraft. The pilot has three major flight controls: the *cyclic*, whereby the pilot controls longitudinal and lateral movement with a joystick to his front center; the *collective*, which controls pitch by lifting or lowering the handle, as well as engine torque by means of a throttle that the pilot rotates around the collective handle; and the *directional control system*, where the pilot controls the tail rotor torque and how much or how little it is "pulling" or "pushing" the tail one way or the other. Let's examine these controls in a little more detail.

The cyclic controls the direction of the tilt of the main rotor. While the helicopter rotors are spinning, if you move the stick forward, the main rotor will tilt forward. If you move the stick backward, the main rotor will tilt backward; move the cyclic to one side and it will tilt the main rotor disc to that side. This control changes the lift and thrust forces. The three axes of movement are still the same, and the terms used to describe movement around (or *about*, as it is sometimes called) any of these axes are the same as with fixed-wing craft.

The collective is a long aluminum tube mounted at an angle to the cockpit floor to the left of the pilot; it controls the angle of the main rotor blades. If you pull the collective up, the angle of the main rotor blades increases (the leading edge of the rotor blades will move higher than the trailing edge of the rotor blade). This control affects the lift and thrust forces also. Wrapped around the collective is a throttle control the pilot operates by turning around the tube of the collective.

The tail rotor pedals at the pilot's feet control the pitch of the tail rotor blades.

To fly the helicopter, the pilot uses all of these controls in combination. By changing the lift and thrust of the main rotor with the cyclic and collective, the pilot can move the helicopter in any direction. Moving the cyclic forward moves the helicopter forward. Moving the cyclic to the left moves the helicopter to the left. Moving the cyclic to the left and forward moves the helicopter forward and to the left. Lifting the collective up causes the helicopter to climb. Lowering the collective causes the helicopter to descend. Moving the cyclic forward and lifting the collective causes the helicopter to increase its forward speed and may result in a climb, depending on how much the collective is raised. The pilot uses pressure from his feet on the tail rotor pedals to control whether the nose yaws left or right; left pedal moves the nose to the left, and right pedal moves the nose to the right.

If you increase the collective and the engine increases power (some helicopters have automatic engine controls that do this for you) to keep the same RPMs to the main rotor, the torque force that's trying to make the cabin spin around will also increase. This requires more left pedal (or pedal opposite to the direction that torque is trying to spin the helicopter) to keep the nose of the helicopter in the same place. So, an increase in collective needs to have an equal increase in pressure on the appropriate tail rotor pedal.

Transient torque occurs in single-rotor helicopters when lateral (left or right) cyclic is applied. At the rear half of the rotor disk, downwash is greater than for the forward half of the rotor disk. For conventional American helicopters, where the main rotor turns counterclockwise when viewed from above, a left cyclic input will cause a temporary increase in torque and a right cyclic input will cause a temporary drop in torque.

Autorotation is the action of turning a rotor system by airflow rather than engine power, which would be needed in, for instance, an engine failure situation. Airflow up through the rotor system during a power-off descent provides the energy to overcome blade drag and turn the rotor, slowing the descent of the helicopter to a manageable level.

The tail rotor is still important in an autorotation because the pilot needs to have some control over the yaw axis (left and right). During autorotation the tail rotor still turns because it is connected to the main rotor via a transmission; as long as the main rotor is turning (and the transmission is functioning properly), the tail rotor will be turning, too. Torque does not exist during an autorotation, but there is a little bit of drag/friction from the main rotors' and tail rotors' transmissions that causes the helicopter to turn in the direction of the main rotor spin. This is controlled by input from the pilot through the tail rotor.

Translational lift is the additional lift the helicopter gets when it flies out from its own downwash, which has a cushioning effect as long as the helicopter is low enough.

Gyroscopic precession, which applies to any spinning disc, means that a force applied to a spinning disc has its effect happen 90° later in the direction and plane of rotation.

Coriolis force (ice skater example): When an ice skater spins in a circle and her arms are out, they have a certain spin speed. If she pulls her arms in, the spin accelerates because the center of mass of the skater's arms is closer to the axis of rotation. The same thing happens in a helicopter if you replace the skater's arms with rotor blades.

The *transverse flow effect* is when air flowing over the rear portion of the main rotor disc is accelerated downward by the main rotor, which causes the rear portion to have a smaller angle of attack. This results in less lift to the rear portion of the rotor disc, but, because of gyroscopic precession, the result is felt 90 degrees later.

Aviation and Aerospace Historical Milestones

1783: The French Montgolfier brothers fly in a hot-air balloon for 5.5 miles in 25 minutes.

1861–65: Observation balloons are used in the Civil War.

1896: American scientist Samuel Langley flies the first (unmanned) powered aircraft.

Dec. 17, 1903: American brothers Orville and Wilbur Wright achieve first recognized powered, manned flight at Kitty Hawk, North Carolina.

Nov. 14, 1910: First airplane takeoff from a ship (USS *Birmingham*) by Eugene B. Ely.

Jan. 18, 1911: First successful shipboard landing (USS *Pennsylvania*) by Eugene B. Ely.

1913: Igor Sikorsky builds first multi-engined aircraft in Russia.

1914: First organized airline (St. Petersburg–Tampa, Florida Airboat Line).

1915: United States establishes National Advisory Committee for Aeronautics (NACA), first government-sponsored support of aviation research and development.

1919: First transatlantic air crossing by Navy and first nonstop transatlantic air crossing.

1920: Launch of first aircraft carrier, the USS *Langley*, CV-1.

1926: Robert H. Goddard, considered the father of American rocketry, launches the first liquid propellant rocket.

1927: Charles Lindbergh makes first solo flight across the Atlantic.

1930: First jet engine designed and patented by Great Britain's Frank Whittle; however, it is not tested on an airplane until a decade later.

1930: First practical helicopter design, developed by Russian Igor Sikorsky, has a large main rotor and a smaller vertical rotor on the tail boom, setting the standard for helicopter design still in use today.

1939–45: World War II ushers in mass production of aircraft, increasing from 500 a year to 50,000 a year by war's close. First jet aircraft, a German effort, flies in 1939. Coordination of airpower with ground troops in Europe and amphibious landings in the Pacific prove to be a significant advantage for the Allies. The Battles of the Coral Sea and Midway in the Pacific are the first battles where enemy ships never see each other, and all attacks are by naval aircraft; these U.S. victories begin to shift the momentum of the war. The P-51 Mustang's laminar-flow wing reduces drag and improves aerodynamics, helping give it the range to escort Allied bombers into Germany. German Luftwaffe deploys the first operational jet, the Me-262 fighter-bomber, in 1944. The B-29 Superfortress is the first bomber with crew cabin pressurization and remote-controlled powered turrets; two B-29s drop atomic bombs on Hiroshima and Nagasaki that end the war in August 1945.

1946: The FH-1 Phantom is the first jet combat aircraft to operate from the deck of a U.S. aircraft carrier and the Navy's first airplane to fly 500 mph.

1947: Chuck Yeager, in the Bell X-1 rocket-powered research aircraft, is the first man to verifiably break the sound barrier. The first swept-wing jet fighter (F-86 Sabrejet) and the first swept-wing multi-engine bomber (B-47 Stratojet) are introduced. The U.S. Air Force is established.

1948: Berlin Airlift supplies massive amounts of food, fuel, and other vital supplies to Allied West Berlin when East Germans and Soviets cut off ground access, keeping not only U.S. forces but West Berliners alive until tensions ease.

1950–53: Korean War, launched by North Korean invasion of South Korea, sees increasing use of jets and helicopters on a three-dimensional battlefield that, after seesaw defense and counterattack in 1950–51, settles down to a near-stalemate for the next two years.

1957: Soviet Union launches the first satellite into space, beginning space race between the United States and the U.S.S.R.

1958: United States launches Explorer I, first American satellite, into orbit.

1961: The Soviet Union's Yuri Gagarin becomes the first man in space on April 12, 1961, with a single orbit of the Earth. Alan Shepard becomes the first American in space when he was launched on a suborbital flight in a one-man Mercury space capsule.

1962: John Glenn is the first American to orbit the Earth.

1963: Mercury program ends, and Gemini program begins, using more sophisticated two-man capsules to develop space experience and skills leading to a lunar mission capability.

1965–75: Active phase of American involvement in the Vietnam War, characterized by increasing use of close air support, marginally effective strategic bombing of North Vietnam and Laos, and introduction of airmobile/air assault doctrine for Army, which increasingly uses transport and attack helicopters in coordination with ground forces. Near-total U.S. air superiority in the field does not make up for political blunders at home, and public support dwindles until withdrawal of troops is completed in 1974. North Vietnam attacks and takes over South Vietnam in 1975, uniting both under one Communist government.

1966: Gemini program concludes and Apollo program begins, with the chief goal of putting a man on the moon.

1967: Three American astronauts are killed in a flash fire on the launch pad in *Apollo 1.*

1968: *Apollo 8* orbits the moon and returns.

1969: *Apollo 11* lands two men, Neil Armstrong and Edwin "Buzz" Aldrin, on the moon on July 20, 1969. A British-French consortium conducts the first flight of the supersonic Concorde passenger jet.

1972: The first spacecraft to explore the outer solar system, *Pioneer 10*, is launched. After completing its study of Jupiter, its trajectory carried it outside the solar system—the first man-made craft to do so. *Pioneer 10* continued transmitting data until 2003, when its power source became too weak. By then, it was over 7.6 billion miles from Earth; in about two million years, it should reach the closest star on its trajectory, the red giant Aldebaran, about 71 light-years away.

1973–74: *Skylab*, an American orbital space station, has three crews spend several months each in orbit, providing proof that man could tolerate weightlessness for extended periods.

1975: NASA collaborates with Soviet space agency on the Apollo-Soyuz Test Project, where crews from each country rendezvoused and docked; last flight of the Apollo-Saturn hardware.

1981: First flight of the space shuttle *Columbia* on April 12, 1981.

1983: First American woman in space, Sally Ride, is a mission specialist on a space shuttle mission.

1986: Space shuttle *Challenger* explodes during liftoff; all aboard are killed.

1986: Russian space station *Mir* is launched.

1988: F-117 Nighthawk stealth fighter enters operational service.

1991: Persian Gulf War begins with a month-long aerial bombardment of Saddam Hussein's Iraqi forces that cuts their communication, resupply, and antiaircraft capabilities drastically, preparing the way for the ground phase of the war to only last four days.

1993: B-2 stealth bomber enters operational service.

1995: C-17 Globemaster III, a large four-engine jet transport, enters operational service.

1996: Launch of Mars Pathfinder.

1998: First components of International Space Station placed in orbit.

2000: Supersonic transatlantic passenger jet Concorde retired from service; first crew occupies International Space Station.

2003: Space shuttle *Columbia* breaks up during reentry; all seven aboard are killed.

2004: Mars exploration rovers *Spirit* and *Opportunity* land on Mars; mission still ongoing. *SpaceShipOne* becomes the first privately built craft to enter outer space.

2005: F-22 Raptor, a stealth air superiority fighter, enters USAF service; funding cut for 2010.

2006: First flight of F-35 Lightning II, a newer stealth fighter, which is planned to enter service around 2014–16 in three versions: F-35A, conventional takeoff/landing (USAF); F-35B, V/STOL variant for USMC; and F-35C, carrier-capable variant for USN.

2010: Space shuttle fleet scheduled for retirement.

Airport and Runway Information

A *runway* is a strip of land on which aircraft can take off and land; it is part of the *maneuvering* or *movement area*, which also includes taxiways and other areas controlled by the air traffic control tower. Runway surfaces can be composed of a man-made material (usually asphalt, concrete, or a mixture) or natural ones, such as grass, dirt, or gravel.

Runways are named from 01-36 for a one-tenth value of their heading or direction, rounded to the nearest 10 degrees—so a runway pointing east (90°) would be "runway 09," a runway pointing west (270°) would be "runway 27," and so on.

Runways in North America use true or geographic north (also known as grid north) instead of magnetic north because magnetic compass needles point toward the magnetic north pole, which is in the Arctic Ocean about a thousand miles south of the geographic north pole. The magnetic north pole also actually moves from 5 to 25 miles (9 to 41 km) per year because of currents in the magma far below the earth's surface.

Since most runways can be used coming from or going to either direction, they can be considered to have two identities. "Runway 30" would be coming in from the southeast or taking off to the northwest with a heading of 300°, whereas the same runway would be referred to as "runway 12," coming in from the northwest or taking off to the southeast. The numbers always differ by 18, indicating a difference of 180° or half of the compass, which is exactly opposite.

Runway numbers are also spoken one by one to avoid confusion. In the examples above, these would be spoken of as "runway three zero" and "runway one two" instead of "runway 30" and "runway 12."

If two or more runways are parallel, heading in the same direction (also known as "dual"), they are differentiated by adding "left," "center," or "right" to the number. For example, if two runways both run east-west, the northernmost runway when heading west (270°) would be runway 27R (spoken as "runway two seven right") and the other, runway 09L (spoken as "runway zero nine left"), when heading east (90°).

Fixed-wing aircraft usually try to take off and land into the wind to increase airflow over the wing and thereby increase lift, at the same time decreasing the ground speed needed.

Runways can vary in size from general aviation airports as small as 800 feet (244 m) long and 26 feet (8 m) wide to international airports as large as 18,000 feet (5,500 m) long and 260 feet (80 m) wide. At sea level, a 10,000-foot (3,000 m) runway can land virtually any aircraft. However, even an average size aircraft will need a longer runway at higher altitudes or in hotter, more humid conditions due to the decreased air density, which reduces lift and engine power.

A runway of at least 6,000 feet (1,800 m) in length is usually adequate for aircraft weighing less than about 200,000 lbs. (90,000 kg). Larger aircraft usually require at least 8,000 feet (2,400 m) at sea level and somewhat more at airports with higher altitudes. International "wide-body" flights, which carry substantial amounts of fuel and are therefore heavier, may also have landing requirements of up to 10,000 feet (3,000 m) or more and takeoff requirements of up to 13,000 feet (4,000 m) or more.

Runway markings are white, and may be outlined in black for greater visibility and contrast. Heliport landing area markings are also white, except for hospital heliports, which use a red "H" on a white cross. Markings for taxiways, areas not intended for use by aircraft, and holding positions—even if they are on a runway—are yellow.

There are three types of runways: *visual, nonprecision instrument,* and *precision instrument.* Visual runways such as those at small airstrips usually have no markings, but they may have threshold markings, designators, and centerlines. They do not provide an instrument-based landing procedure—pilots must be able to see the runway to use it. Also, radio communication may not be available, so pilots must be self-reliant.

Nonprecision instrument runways are most often seen at small- to medium-size airports. Depending on the surface, these runways may be marked with threshold markings, designators, centerlines, and sometimes a 1,000-foot (304.80 km) or 1,500-foot (457.20 km) mark known as an *aiming point.* They provide horizontal position guidance to planes on instrument approach.

Precision instrument runways, seen at medium- and large-size airports, usually consist of a blast pad/stopway, threshold, designator, centerline, aiming point, and touchdown zone marks at 500-foot intervals from 500 feet (152 m) to 3,000 feet (914 m). Precision runways provide pilots with both horizontal and vertical guidance for instrument approaches.

Airports that allow night landings use runway lighting to mark their runways, including some or all of the following, among others:

- Approach Lighting System (ALS): a series of lightbars, strobe lights, or a combination of the two that extends outward from the approach end of the runway.
- Runway End Identification Lights (REIL): a pair of synchronized flashing lights installed at the runway threshold, one on each side. They can face the approach direction or be omnidirectional (visible from all directions). They enhance identification of a runway surrounded by other lighting or lacking contrast with the surrounding terrain, as well as during reduced visibility.
- Runway end lights: a pair of four lights on each side of precision instrument runways, extending the full width of the runway. These lights show green when viewed by approaching aircraft and red when seen from the runway to indicate the end of the runway to a departing aircraft.

- Runway edge lights: white elevated lights running the length of the runway on both sides. On precision instrument runways, the edge lighting becomes yellow in the last 2,000 feet (610 m) or half the runway length, whichever is greater. Taxiways are differentiated by being bordered by omnidirectional blue lights, or by having green center lights, depending on the width of the taxiway and the complexity of the taxi pattern.
- Runway Centerline Lighting System (RCLS): white lights embedded in the surface of the runway along the centerline at 50-foot (15 m) intervals, changing to alternating red and white 3,000 feet (915 m) from the end of the runway, and then to red for the last 1,000 feet (305 m).

Larger airports may also have a Visual Approach Slope Indicator (VASI), which is a system of lights that provides descent guidance information during an approach to a runway. The system uses red lights to indicate the upper limits of the glide path and white lights for the lower limits. The VASI is visible for 3–5 miles during the day and up to 20 miles or more at night. The VASI's visual glide path provides safe obstruction clearance within 10 degrees plus or minus of the extended runway centerline and to up to 4 nautical miles from the runway threshold.

Runway lights are usually operated by the airport or airfield control tower. Smaller airports may not have lighted runways or runway markings; there may be nothing more than a wind sock beside a landing strip, particularly at small private airfields for light planes.

Nautical Information

The U.S. Navy was founded on October 13, 1775, and the Department of the Navy was established on April 30, 1798. The Department of the Navy has three principal components: the Navy Department, consisting of executive offices mostly in Washington, D.C.; the operating forces, including the Marine Corps, the reserve components, and, in time of war, the U.S. Coast Guard (which is a component of the Department of Homeland Security in peacetime); and the shore establishment.

The Naval Services comprise the U.S. Navy and the U.S. Marine Corps, two independent military services within the Department of the Navy. The Navy has a traditional pyramidal structure that is consistent with established principles of organizational design. The management of money, personnel, and materiel in the Navy is no different than that of most large corporations.

The Navy's operating forces are subordinate to the six multiservice or joint Unified Commands: Northern Command, Southern Command, European Command, Pacific Command, Central Command, and Africa Command.

The independent carrier battle group or strike group is usually considered the primary building block of projecting power or responding to any kind of crisis. Operating in international waters, the carrier battle group does not need the permission of host countries for landing or overflight rights, nor does it need to build or maintain bases in countries where a U.S. presence may cause political or other strains. Aircraft carriers are sovereign U.S. territory that can and do steam anywhere in international waters—and, it's useful to note, most of the surface of the globe is water. This characteristic is not lost on our political decision makers, who use Navy aircraft carriers as a powerful instrument of diplomacy, strengthening alliances or answering the fire bell of crisis.

By using the oceans both as a means of access and as a base, forward-deployed Navy and Marine forces are readily available to provide the United States with a flexible range of national response capabilities. These capabilities range from simply showing the flag—just a presence to let people in the region know that the United States is interested in what's going on—to insertion of power ashore. The unique contribution of aircraft carriers to our national security was best expressed by General John Shalikashvili, former chairman of the Joint Chiefs of Staff, who said during a visit to USS *Dwight D. Eisenhower*, "I know how relieved I am each time when I turn to my operations officer and say, 'Hey, where's the nearest carrier?' and he can say to me, 'It's right there on the spot.' For United States interests, that means everything."

As an example, on September 11, 2001, USS *Enterprise* (CVN 65) had just been relieved from being on station in support of Operation Southern Watch enforcing the southern no-fly zone in Iraq. She was heading south in the Indian Ocean, beginning her trip back to home port in Norfolk, Virginia, when the crew saw on television the live coverage of the attacks on the World Trade Center and the Pentagon. *Enterprise*, without an order from the chain of command, executed a 180-degree course change and headed back to the waters off southwest Asia. *Enterprise* then remained on station in support of Operation Enduring Freedom, launching air attacks against al-Qaeda terrorist training camps and Taliban military installations in Afghanistan. For the next three weeks, aircraft from *Enterprise* flew nearly 700 missions in Afghanistan, dropping hundreds of thousands of pounds of ordnance.

The typical air wing aboard a U.S. Navy aircraft carrier usually contains three to four FA-18 squadrons, one EA-6B squadron, one E-2C squadron, and one helicopter squadron. Up until 2009, a typical carrier air wing also included an S-3 squadron, but these have since been retired. However, since the ASTB questions have apparently not been updated since 1992, it might also be good to know the older organization.

Flight operations aboard a modern aircraft carrier resemble a well-choreographed ballet. Those involved in the "evolution" (one specific but multirole task, such as launching aircraft, landing aircraft, or refueling at sea) have specific, clearly defined roles, and are easily recognizable by the color of their jerseys.

Purple: aviation fuels (nicknamed "grapes")

Blue: plane handlers, aircraft elevator operators, airplane tractor drivers, messengers and phone talkers

Green: catapult and arresting gear crews, air wing maintenance personnel, cargo-handling personnel, ground support equipment troubleshooters, hook runners, photographer's mates, helicopter landing signal enlisted personnel

Yellow: aircraft handling officers, catapult and arresting gear officers, plane directors

Red: ordnancemen, crash and salvage crews, explosive ordnance disposal.

Brown: air wing plane captains, air wing line leading petty officers

White: air wing quality control personnel, squadron plane inspectors, landing signal officer, air transfer officers, liquid oxygen crews, safety observers, medical personnel

Marine Corps operating forces are provided from Marine Force, Atlantic (MAR-FORLANT) and Marine Force, Pacific (MARFORPAC). Each of the four Unified Commands is assigned a Marine Component for planning purposes and is provided task-organized Marine forces for execution of specific operational plans. The Marine Corps' principal operating force in the eastern United States is II Marine Expeditionary Force (II MEF), at bases in North and South Carolina; in the western United States, I MEF is based in California; in the western Pacific, III MEF, which was previously based in Okinawa and Japan, has been disbanded and replaced by the I MEF (Forward) Command Element, which retains all of the functions previously found in III MEF. The MEFs provide a Marine Expeditionary Unit–Special Operations Capable (MEU-SOC) for afloat forward deployment.

The Marine Corps is officially organized into three ground divisions and three aircraft wings, with a large combat support force formed into three service support groups. The Marine Corps Reserve consists of an additional ground division, aircraft wing, and support group. These divisions and wings can be considered the administrative structure for Marine units deployed in Marine Air-Ground Task Forces (MAGTFs). The MAGTF is the basic building block of Marine Corps operating forces, and is an integrated, combined-arms force made up of command, ground combat, aviation combat, and service support elements. Regardless of size— from relatively small, special purpose MAGTFs to multidivision-size Marine Expeditionary Forces—all MAGTFs are "expeditionary" forces, capable of carrying out specific missions. For example, MEFs, comprising 40,000 or more troops, are capable of amphibious assaults and sustained operations for up to 60 days without replenishment of ammunition, food, water, and other supplies.

Many nautical terms, phrases, and practices derive from situations and conditions that occurred in the days when naval vessels were made of wood and propelled by the wind in their sails. By no means will all of these terms be tested or even perhaps mentioned on the Navy/Marine Corps/Coast Guard Aviation Selection Test Battery (ASTB); however, since test questions are closely guarded secrets and change from version to version and time to time, it is wise for the examinee to be familiar with as much naval terminology as possible to gain the best possible understanding of a test question. Therefore, this section provides not only definitions but in some cases historical context and/or explanation.

Nautical Terms and Phrases

Ahoy—ship-to-ship or ship-to-shore combination greeting and attention-getting term, usually when one party is unknown to the other

Airdale—part of the aircraft-related crew

All hands—a directive or reference applying to everyone hearing the message, usually directing them to perform their specific function as part of a collective task for the ship to accomplish, as in "All hands to quarters," "All hands up anchor," etc.

Anchors aweigh—the anchor has broken contact with the floor or surface at the bottom of the body of water

Arresting cables—Each carrier-based aircraft has a tailhook, a hook bolted to an 8-foot bar extending from the after part of the aircraft. It is with the tailhook that the pilot catches one of the four steel cables stretched across the deck at 20-foot intervals, bringing the plane, traveling at 150 miles per hour, to a complete stop in about 320 feet. The cables are set to stop each aircraft at the same place on the deck, regardless of the size or weight of the plane.

Aye or **Aye Aye**—an acknowledgment of an order with the understanding that the receiver will execute the order

Barge—small boat used to transport personnel or light cargo

Before the mast—refers generally to the enlisted part of the crew, especially when comparing them with officers. On sailing ships, this was a literal term referring to the physical position of the enlisted sailors whose living quarters on the ship were in the forecastle (the part of the ship forward or "before" the foremast).

Belay—to make fast or secure to a pin or cleat, as in "belay that line"

"Belay that"—disregard the order or information referred to, or cease work if the order has already been partially executed

Bilge—water that has leaked into the ship and/or wastewater that can accumulate in a holding tank or empty space until it is pumped out

Binnacle list—a ship's sick list. On sailing ships, a binnacle was the stand on which the ship's compass was mounted; a list of men unable to report for duty was given to the officer or mate of the watch, who kept the list at the binnacle.

Black gang or **blackgang**—the engine room crew

Bluejacket—enlisted sailor

Boarding a small boat or entering a car—When boarding a small boat or entering a car, juniors enter first and take up the seats or the space beginning forward, leaving the most desirable seat for the senior. Seniors enter last and leave first.

Boatswain or **bosun**—the sailor or petty officer in charge of the deck force or a specific section of the ship's crew

Boot camp—Basic training given to new (recruit) sailors and Marines. During the Spanish-American War (1898–1902), sailors wore leggings called boots; this came to mean a Navy or Marine recruit.

Boot ensign—The most senior ensign of a Navy ship, squadron, or shore activity. In addition to his or her normal duties, the boot ensign teaches less-experienced ensigns about life at sea, planning and coordinating wardroom social activities, making sure that the officers' mess runs smoothly, and generally trying to make sure that the junior ensigns don't embarrass themselves or the Navy. Even though the position usually has little official authority, the boot ensign can also serve as the focus of the unit's expression of pride and spirit. Also called "bull ensign."

Bow—the front of the ship

Bravo Zulu—well done

Bridge—This is the primary control position for every ship when the ship is under way, and the place where all orders and commands affecting the ship, her movements, and routine originate.

Brightwork—Any trim or highly polished surface; this originally referred to polished metal objects, especially topside (on the deck of the ship). *Bright woodwork* is wood that is kept scraped and scrubbed. Both usually have a connotation of painstaking attention to detail in keeping something shipshape or clean.

"Bring ship to anchor"—Bring the ship to a halt and drop the anchor.

Bulkhead—a wall or other vertical surface, especially on a ship

Butterbar—someone with the lowest officer rank, pay grade O-1, ensign, whose rank insignia is one gold-colored rectangular bar; usually carries a connotation of a lack of experience

"Cast off all lines"—Disconnect or let go all lines connecting a ship with a dock or another ship.

Catapults — The four steam-powered catapults thrust a 48,000-lb. aircraft 300 feet, from zero to 165 miles per hour, in two seconds. On each plane's nose gear is a T-bar that locks into the catapult shuttle, which pulls the plane down the catapult's length. The flight deck crew can launch two aircraft and land one every 37 seconds in daylight, and one per minute at night.

Chit—a voucher or replacement for money or services, usually used on board ship

"Come left/right to course"—Make a slight change in course or heading, usually less than 15 degrees.

Course—the ship's direction or compass heading, expressed in degrees or, less frequently, in cardinal directions

Coxswain—the helmsman of a ship. Originally the coxswain (pronounced "coxun") was the swain (boy servant) in charge of the small cockboat kept aboard for the ship's captain, which was used to row him to and from the ship. With time this has come to mean the helmsman of any boat or ship, regardless of size.

Davy Jones' locker—the floor of the ocean

Deck—floor or other horizontal surface, especially on a ship

Dogwatch—The period of time at sea between 4 and 6 P.M. (first dogwatch) or 6 and 8 P.M. (second dogwatch).

Drill—a standardized sequence of actions designed to react to a possible situation; used to practice skills and improve proficiency

Duffle or **duffel**—a sailor's personal effects. Referring not only to the sailor's clothing but also the seabag in which he carries and stows it, the term comes from the Flemish town of Duffel near Antwerp, where a rough woolen cloth made there was often used to make the seabags.

Ease the rudder—Decrease the current rudder angle (with zero degrees being amidships). This command is normally given when the ship is turning too fast or is coming to the course required, e.g., "Ease your rudder to 5 degrees."

Elevators—Each of the four deck-edge elevators can lift two aircraft from the cavernous hangar deck to the 4.5-acre flight deck in seconds.

Fathom—a standardized nautical unit of measurement equaling 6 feet, usually referring to depth of water

"Gangway"—Get out of the way; make way for someone or something coming through an area.

General drills—emergency drills involving the entire ship's crew, such as abandon ship, general quarters, collision, and fire drills

General quarters—All hands man their battle stations on the double (at a run).

Handsomely—slowly and carefully

Hatch—doorway

Head—a ship's toilet, or, more generally, any toilet

Holystone—a soft sandstone used to scrub the decks of a ship; sailors had to kneel as if in prayer when scrubbing the decks. Also refers to the fact that holystone is full of holes, like a petrified sponge.

Jones, Captain John Paul (1747–1792)—Acknowledged as the "Father of the American Navy," Revolutionary War naval hero. As a ship's captain, he made daring raids along the British coast, including the famous victory of the *Bonhomme Richard* over HMS *Serapis*, where Jones is reputed to have said, "I have not yet begun to fight!" when asked to surrender.

Keelhaul—a naval punishment used by some European navies in the fifteenth and sixteenth centuries. In this practice, a rope was rigged from yardarm to yardarm passing under the bottom of the ship, and the offender was secured to it, sometimes with weights on his legs. He was hoisted up to one yardarm and then dropped suddenly into the sea, hauled underneath the keel or bottom of the ship, and then hauled up to the other yardarm. Because many ships accumulated barnacles and other rough places on the underside of the ship's hull—and because it took a significant amount of time to haul the offender underneath a larger ship, all underwater—not all recipients survived the procedure.

"Keep her so"—maintain the present course

Knot—a unit of speed measuring one nautical mile (1.15 statute miles, 1.85 km) per hour

Make a hole—Get out of the way; make way for someone or something coming through an area.

"Man overboard"—a command directing designated sailors to man their boat or boats and pick up the man as soon as possible; special conditions may apply for wartime

"Man your boat"—a command for all hands or designated sailors to take their stations in the boats used for abandoning ship or moving outside the ship to another ship, dock, etc.

Marine Corps Birthday—One of the most famous Marine customs is the observance of the Marine Corps Birthday. Since 1921, the birthday of the Marine Corps has been officially celebrated each year on November 10, since it was on this date in 1775 that the Continental Congress resolved "that two Battalions of Marines be raised." Over the years, the event has been celebrated in a wide variety of ways—depending on the circumstances of the Marine unit(s) involved—but the celebration generally involves the reading of an excerpt from the Marine Corps Manual and a birthday message from the commandant; the cutting of a birthday cake by the commanding officer; and the presentation of the first and second pieces of cake to the oldest and youngest Marines present. In recent years, the ceremony for the Marine Corps Birthday observance by large posts and stations has been incorporated into written directives.

Mayday—internationally recognized distress call used on voice radio for vessels and people in serious trouble at sea or in the air. Derived from the French *m'aidez* ("help me") and officially recognized by an international telecommunications conference in 1948.

"Meatball"—a series of lights that aids carrier pilots when lining up for landing. In the center are amber and red lights with Fresnel lenses. Although the lights are always on, the Fresnel lens makes only one light at a time seem to glow, as the angle at which the pilot looks at the lights changes. If the lights appear above the green horizontal bar, the pilot is too high. If it is below, the pilot is too low, and if the lights are red, the pilot is very low. If the red lights on either side of the amber vertical bar are flashing, it is a wave-off, meaning "don't land."

Nautical mile—unit of measurement used in air and sea navigation equal to 1,852 meters or about 6,076 feet; derived from the length of one minute of arc of a great circle

"Now hear this"—a phrase used to call attention to directions, information, or a command to follow

Officer of the Deck (OOD)—is always on the bridge when the ship is under way. Each OOD stands a four-hour watch and is the officer designated by the commanding officer to be in charge of the ship. The OOD is responsible for the safety and operation of the ship, including navigation, ship handling, communications, routine tests and inspections, reports, supervision of the watch team, and carrying out the Plan of the Day. Also on the bridge are the helmsman, who steers the ship, and the lee helmsman, who operates the engine order control, telling the engine room what speed to make. There are also lookouts, and the **boatswain's mate of the watch** (BMOW) who supervises the helmsman, lee helmsman, and lookouts. The **quartermaster of the watch** assists the OOD in navigation, reports all changes in weather, temperature, and barometer readings, and keeps the ship's log.

On the double—quickly, on the run

"Pipe down"—Be quiet.

Piping—On sailing ships, boatswains in charge of the deck force used whistle signals to coordinate and direct tasks such as setting sails, heaving lines, and hoisting anchors, including a pipe signal for hoisting distinguished or higher-ranking visitors aboard. Eventually, piping became a naval honor ashore as well as at sea.

Port—referring to the left side of a ship when facing the bow, or front

"Pri-Fly"—Primary Flight Control ("Pri-Fly") is the control tower for the flight operations on the carrier. Here, the "air boss" controls takeoffs, landings, aircraft in the air near the ship, and the movement of planes on the flight deck, which resembles a well-choreographed ballet.

Running lights—Required on all boats over 15 feet (5 m) by the International Regulations for Prevention of Collisions at Sea, these lights are red on the left (port) side, green on the right (starboard) side, and white to the rear. Side running lights are visible from both the side and front of the craft.

Rudder amidships—Orient the rudder along the long axis of the ship; straight ahead.

SCUBA—an acronym for "self-contained underwater breathing apparatus"

Scuttlebutt—gossip or rumors; because sailors stopped to talk and exchange gossip when they gathered at the cask of drinking water (called a "scuttlebutt") on board sailing ships, this became Navy slang referring to information or speculation, and eventually slang for any gossip or rumor. (A *butt* was a wooden cask for holding water or other liquids; to *scuttle* was to drill a hole, as when one taps a cask.)

Semper Fidelis—Latin for "always faithful," the motto of the Marine Corps

Semper Paratus—Latin for "always ready," the motto of the Coast Guard

Shipshape—in good order and function; squared away

Smoking lamp—If it's "lit," you have permission to smoke; if it's not, you don't. Seldom used literally.

Sonar—underwater detection device using sound and echo detection

Starboard—the right side as one is facing forward

"Steady as you go"—Maintain the course the ship is on at the moment the command is given.

Stern—the rear of the ship

Striking the colors/ensign/flag—Lowering or "striking" the ship's flag is the universally recognized sign of surrender.

Swab down—to wash something such as a deck, usually with the help of a water hose and mops

"Toe the line"—Once a literal command to gather on deck with one's toes on a line, now it means to give full obedience to orders or give extra attention to detail.

"Turn to"—begin ship's work

Uncover—to remove one's hat or headgear

"Very well"—an officer's response indicating that a report is understood

Up anchor—Raise the anchor and prepare to get under way.

Watches—Watches at sea are divided into four-hour intervals:

Morning watch: 4 A.M. to 8 A.M. (0400–0800 hours)

Forenoon watch: 8 A.M. to noon (0800–1200 hours)

Afternoon watch: noon to 4 P.M. (1200–1600 hours)

Dogwatch: 4 P.M. to 8 P.M. (1600–2000 hours) (also divided into first and second dogwatches)

Nightwatch: 8 P.M. to midnight (2000–2400 hours)

Midwatch: midnight to 4 A.M. (2400–0400 hours)

Wardroom—the officer's dining room that is also used for meetings and other functions

"What's your heading?"—a directive to report the course (compass heading) the ship is on

Major Naval Warship Classifications

Aircraft carriers
Multi-Purpose Aircraft Carrier	CV
Multi-Purpose Aircraft Carrier (Nuclear-Propelled)	CVN

Battleship	BB

Cruisers
Gun Cruiser	CA
Guided Missile Cruiser	CG
Guided Missile Cruiser (Nuclear-Propelled)	CGN

Destroyers
Destroyers	DD
Guided Missile Destroyer	DDG

Frigates
Frigate	FF
Guided Missile Frigate	FFG
Radar Picket Frigate	FFR

Attack Submarines
Submarine	SS
Submarine (Nuclear-Powered)	SSN

Ballistic Missile Submarines
Ballistic Missile Submarine (Nuclear-Powered)	SSBN

Amphibious Helicopter/Landing Craft Carriers
Amphibious Assault Ship (General Purpose)	LHA
Amphibious Assault Ship (Multi-Purpose)	LHD
Amphibious Command Ship	LCC
Amphibious Transport Dock	LPD
Amphibious Assault Ship (Helicopter)	LPH

Landing Craft Carriers
Amphibious Cargo Ship	LKA
Dock Landing Ship	LSD
Medium Landing Ship	LSM
Tank Landing Ship	LST

Combat Logistics Ships
Ammunition Ship	AE
Combat Store Ship	AFS
Oiler	AO
Fast Combat Support Ship	AOE
Replenishment Oiler	AOR

Mine Warfare Ships
Minesweeper—Ocean	MSO
Mine Countermeasures Ship	MCM
Mine Countermeasures Support Ship	MCS
Minehunter, Coastal	MHC

Coastal Defense Ships
Patrol, Coastal	PC

Naval Aviation Squadron Designations

VF	Fighter Squadron
VA	Attack Squadron
VFA	Strike Fighter Squadron
VAW	Carrier Airborne Early Warning Squadron
VS	Sea Control Squadron
HS	Carrier Helicopter Antisubmarine Squadron
HC	Helicopter Combat Support Squadron
HSL	Helicopter Antisubmarine Squadron Light
HM	Helicopter Mine Countermeasures Squadron
HT	Helicopter Training Squadron
HCS	Helicopter Combat Support Special Squadron
VP	Patrol Squadron

VR	Fleet Logistic Squadron
VRC	Fleet Logistic Support Squadron
VC	Fleet Composite Squadron
VQ	Fleet Air Reconnaissance Squadron
VX	Air Test and Evaluation Squadron
VXE	Antarctic Development Squadron
VXN	Oceanographic Development Squadron
VAQ	Tactical Electronic Warfare Squadron
VPU	Patrol Squadron Special Projects Unit
VFC	Fighter Squadron Composite
VT	Training Squadron

General Science

Science can generally be divided into life, physical, and earth sciences. *Biology* is the general term for the study of living things. It covers topics dealing with human health and medicine, and is closely related to *botany* (the study of plants) and *zoology* (the study of animals). *Earth science* covers conditions affecting the earth (weather, climate, the relationship of people to their environment). *Chemistry* is a physical science dealing with the composition, structure, and properties of matter; it's also concerned with changes in matter and the energy released during those changes. *Physics*, like chemistry, is a physical science that deals with matter and energy; however, physics gives more attention to mechanical and electrical forces in areas such as light, sound, heat, motion, and magnetism.

The Scientific Method

The commonly accepted problem-solving pattern of actions in all scientific disciplines is known as the *scientific method*, which involves five basic steps:

1. *Observation.* Observations, either of natural phenomena or of experimental results, require the accurate viewing and recording of a particular occurrence. The accuracy of one observation or set of observations is validated or *proved* when independent observers agree that they see the same set of circumstances, achieve the same experimental results, and so on.

2. *Hypothesis.* A temporary or working conclusion based on a set of observations, or *hypothesis*, is usually a very general statement about why (based on the observations to that point) the scientist thinks something happens in the way that it does. It usually suggests the need for a particular experiment.

3. *Experiment.* Scientists perform experiments to test a specific hypothesis. Reliable experiments require controlled conditions and careful recording of data.

4. *Theory.* A hypothesis becomes a theory when it is supported by one or more experiments; the original hypothesis is usually modified somewhat based on experimental data before it is acknowledged as a theory.

5. *Principle* or *law.* When a theory is repeatedly confirmed over a long period of time by multiple experiments, it is called a principle or law.

Life Science

Let's review some basic principles that biologists work with on a routine basis.

Homeostasis is the balanced internal situation of a cell and the organism as a whole; to stay alive and healthy, cells have to regulate their external and internal fluids based on temperature, acid/base balance, and the amount and type of a number of critical substances.

All known living species are said to share *unity* in that they have particular characteristics in common:

- All living cells come from preexisting living cells.
- All cells make and use *enzymes*, which are substances that start or speed up chemical reactions without themselves being affected or changed.
- The hereditary or genetic information of all cells is carried by *DNA* (deoxyribonucleic acid) molecules that give cells the ability to reproduce or *replicate*. DNA makes up *genes* contained in *chromosomes*, small rod-shaped bodies within a cell that control the characteristics that offspring receive from their parents.
- *Metabolism* refers to the biochemical activities necessary for life carried on by all cells, tissues, organs, and systems.
- A trait or characteristic that lends itself to the survival of an individual or a species is called *adaptation*.
- The basic unit of classification for living things is the *species*, which is a group of similar organisms that can mate and produce fertile offspring.

Life Functions

All living organisms, to be called "living," must be able to perform certain activities known as *life functions*.

1. *Nutrition* is the way an organism gets food or *nutrients* from its environment and uses it as fuel for growth and continued life. Nutrition includes the processes of *ingestion* (taking in food), *digestion* (chemical changes that convert nutrients into a usable form), and *assimilation* (changing nutrients into protoplasm).
2. *Synthesis* is the process whereby small molecules are built into larger ones; this causes *amino acids* (protein building blocks) to be changed into enzymes, hormones (chemical messengers produced by the endocrine gland that regulate and coordinate the body's activities), and protoplasm.
3. *Circulation* is the movement of fluid and the dissolved materials it carries throughout the cell or body.
4. *Regulation* includes all the processes that control and coordinate the activities of a living organism. Chemical activities inside cells are controlled by hormones, enzymes, vitamins, and minerals. The *endocrine* and *nervous* systems of higher (more complex) animals coordinate bodily activities. In plants, *auxins* and other growth-controlling substances are in charge.
5. *Respiration* is made up of *breathing* and *cellular respiration*. You know what breathing is; cellular respiration is a combination of processes that release energy from glucose (sugar).
6. *Excretion* is the way that the organism gets rid of waste products. In humans, the kidneys, lungs, and skin are involved in excretion, since they remove urea, carbon dioxide, and water from the blood and body tissues.

7. *Growth* is the increase of cell size and/or the increase of cell numbers in an organism. Cell numbers increase when cells divide (replicate) during a sequence of events called *mitosis*.

8. *Reproduction* is the way that new individuals are produced by parent organisms. It can be either *asexual* or *sexual*. Asexual reproduction involves only one parent, which may either divide into two or else produce a new organism from part of the parent cell. Sexual reproduction requires the participation of two parents of opposite sexes; each parent produces special reproductive cells called *gametes*, which combine with each other to form the starting point for the new individual organism.

Cells

The *cell* is the basic structural, functional, growth, and hereditary unit of all forms of life. Its various sizes and shapes give form to the body of more complex organisms. It is also the basic functional unit, acting as a biochemical factory to perform the basic metabolic life functions. As the basic unit of growth, it increases in size and multiplies to form an organism of a specific size and shape. As the basic unit of heredity, it produces cells identical to itself that carry the codes for all reproductive information.

Plant Life

The *plant kingdom* includes species ranging from single-celled organisms to multicellular plants, where different cells are "programmed" to carry out specialized functions. Lower (less complex) plant species, such as single-celled algae, can live in water; however, most species of plants (especially the more complex ones) are land-dwelling or *terrestrial*. These higher plants have roots, stems, and leaves. Roots anchor the plant in the soil and absorb nutrients (water and dissolved minerals) from the ground. Stems perform three functions: (1) they move water upward from the roots to the leaves and move dissolved food materials down from the leaves to the roots; (2) they produce and support leaves and flowers; and (3) they provide a way to store food.

Leaves carry out *photosynthesis*, the food-making process whereby inorganic materials are changed into nutrients. Green leaves have *chlorophyll*, which helps leaves use the sun's energy to make carbohydrates from carbon dioxide and water. These carbohydrates are the food used by the plants—*and* by the animals that eat the plants. During photosynthesis, oxygen needed by animals is released into the atmosphere.

Animal Life

All animals are multicellular, composed of cells without walls. Some forms reproduce through asexual means from an unfertilized egg, whereas others use a sperm and an egg from two different parents. About 90 percent of animals are *invertebrates*, animals without backbones.

Vertebrates have a true spine made of bone or cartilage and a noticeable development of the head, where the brain is enclosed in a *skull* or *cranium*. A closed *circulatory system* pumps blood throughout the body by means of a heart with two types of chambers, an *atrium* and a *ventricle*. Most vertebrates have a tail of some kind and a mouth closed by a moveable lower jaw.

Taxonomic Classification

The current system of living organism classification divides the million-plus kinds of plants and animals into seven levels, based mostly on relationships and similarities in physical structure. The top or broadest level, containing the most different kinds of organisms, is *kingdom* (as in *plant kingdom* and *animal kingdom*); the bottom or narrowest level, which contains the least number of different kinds of organisms, is the *species*.

From top to bottom, the levels are as follows:

1. Kingdom (plant, animal)
2. Phylum (e.g., chordates, echinoderms, mollusks, algae, mosses)
3. Class (e.g., mammals, birds, reptiles, crustaceans, ferns)
4. Order (e.g., primates, whales, rodents, grasses, roses)
5. Family (e.g., cats, salmon, earthworms, orchids, cacti)
6. Genus (e.g., conchs, rattlesnakes, dogs, oats, mulberries)
7. Species (e.g., spotted giraffe, bald eagle, corn, dandelion)

When we refer to an organism by its *scientific name*, we use the two most specific categories, the genus and the species; for instance, human beings are *Homo sapiens*, and house cats are *Felix domesticus*. In some cases, a subspecies may add extra specificity, as in the Siberian tiger, *Panthera tigris longipillis*.

The Human Animal

Humans belong to an order of vertebrates called *primates*, which have hands able to grasp objects, well-developed sight, and a relatively large brain. Humans are special primates: they are *bipedal* (walk on two legs instead of four); they can adapt to different environments; and they have the power of speech, along with the ability to remember events and make associations between ideas.

The key systems of the human organism are as follows:

Skeletal system—carries the body and supports and protects the vital organs

Muscular system—enables the body to move; about 40 percent of body weight

Nervous system—controls movement, provides communication between the individual and its environment

Endocrine system—includes glands that regulate growth, blood pressure, and other functions

Respiratory system—provides means to inhale air with oxygen and exhale carbon dioxide

Circulatory system—includes the heart and blood vessels, which transport oxygen and nutrients to cells throughout the body

Lymphatic system—assists with bringing oxygen to cells and removing waste products from them

Digestive system—processes and helps distribute nutrients

Excretory system—removes wastes from the body

Reproductive system—gives humans the means to reproduce and continue the species

Diseases

A *disease* is a disorder or problem that keeps the body or its organs from functioning as they are designed. Diseases can generally be classified as *infectious* or *noninfectious*.

Infectious diseases can be caused by germs or bacteria, fungi, viruses, or even parasitic worms. Viruses are inorganic, but grow within living cells. Most infectious diseases are contagious—they can be passed by contact of some sort between an infected individual and an uninfected individual.

Noninfectious diseases can be caused by malnutrition, poisoning, radiation, or the malfunction of a bodily system such as the endocrine system.

In humans, the skin itself kills most germs that land on it, as well as our saliva, stomach acid, and mucous membranes in our noses and throats. To take care of germs that get past these defenses, the body releases chemicals to surround and destroy them. Lymph cells, white blood cells, and *antibodies* (custom made by the body to fight specific invaders) are also part of this defense or *immune system*.

Genetics

Genetics is the study of the ways that characteristics are passed from parents to offspring. Different animals have differing numbers of chromosomes; human children develop from a fertilized egg that has 23 pairs of chromosomes or 46 total—half from each parent.

Three basic laws of heredity were identified by Austrian botanist and monk Gregor Mendel in 1866:

1. Law of segregation—individual hereditary traits, or units, separate in the gametes.
2. Law of independent assortment—each trait is inherited independently of other traits.
3. Law of dominance—when contrasting (i.e., conflicting) traits are both present, one trait is *dominant* and one is *recessive*.

Subsequent research has adjusted and expanded Mendel's original principles. We now know that Mendel's hereditary units are *genes*, which reside on *chromosomes*, and that genes are units of a DNA molecule that carries a code for the production of a specific protein needed by the organism. A change or disruption in the DNA coding is called a *mutation*, and is usually harmful to that organism.

Cloning

A clone is a new individual organism grown from a single cell of its parent and also genetically identical to that parent. This involves stimulating a parent cell to reproduce by asexual means. Since the mid-twentieth century, scientists have performed plant experiments where single nonembryonic cells were induced to develop in the same way as a fertilized egg. The results with certain species show that an entire plant can be reproduced from a single nonreproductive cell.

Among animals (including humans), *twinning* can occur naturally; this produces two separate organisms with the same genetic makeup. Beginning in the 1950s, scientists cloned frog tadpoles from frog embryonic cells by transferring the nucleus of one cell into another. In the 1980s, scientists created mammal clones by splitting embryos in a process called *artificial twinning*, or by transferring a nucleus between embryonic cells.

A major breakthrough in animal cloning occurred in 1997 when Scottish researchers cloned a sheep using genetic material from a nonembryonic cell. Once it was proven possible to clone a new animal from the cell of an adult animal, other groups began to experiment with cloning different species. Cloning from adult cells makes it possible to be surer ahead of time what the cloned animal will be like. So far, successfully cloned animals include frogs, mice, rats, sheep, cattle, pigs, goats, cats, rabbits, mules, horses, and deer.

Earth Science

Earth science includes several related disciplines such as *geology* (the study of the earth), *oceanography* (the study of the seas and oceans), *meteorology* (the study of weather and climate conditions), and *astronomy* (the study of Earth as part of the universe).

Geology

Geology is the study of the formation and composition of the earth. It relates to and borrows from other scientific disciplines such as chemistry, physics, and biology. And, because it is often necessary to understand how a geologic feature got to be the way it is before we can understand its present nature, the history of the earth is an integral part of understanding its current formation and structure.

The history of the earth is one of dramatic change—occasionally violent and swift, but more often over the course of many thousands or even millions of years. The surface of the earth is composed of irregularly shaped *tectonic plates* that fit together reasonably well but that ride on a shifting subsurface layer of molten rock called *magma*. When these plates bump or grind against each other, we experience earthquakes; holes in the surface layer that allow the molten rock (*lava*) to spew forth onto the surface are volcanoes. Collisions between these plates are thought to be responsible for most of the earth's mountain ranges.

The movement of the earth's seemingly solid crust is part of the theory of *continental drift*. According to this theory, at one time all the continents were joined into one large landmass called *Pangaea*. Gradually, this supercontinent split into two masses, with North America, Europe, and Asia in one mass, and the rest of today's continents in the other. Separations continued to form the continents as we know them today; the similarities in the Atlantic coastlines of Africa and South America seem to support this theory, as well as similar fossil remains in now widely separated areas (Africa and Antarctica, for example).

To provide a common frame of reference for studying this history, the time since the formation of the planet has been divided into *eras*, *periods*, and *epochs*.

The *Precambrian Era* ranged from the planet's formation, between about 3.5 and 4.5 billion years ago, to about 600 million years ago. This era was characterized by the formation of the earth, its cooling from its probable original molten state, and extensive seismic activity. Toward the end of this era, life is thought to have appeared on the planet in the form of amoebas, flagellates, sponges, worms, and jellyfish. The Precambrian Era is not divided into periods as are the other more recent eras.

The *Paleozoic Era* extended from about 600 million to about 230 million years ago. It saw the formation of many mountain ranges, the formation and disappearance of seas and oceans, and the appearance of life-forms ranging from trilobites to sharks to starfish to dragonflies and some reptiles.

The *Mesozoic Era* was from about 230 million to about 65 million years ago. Geologic features continued to appear, change, and disappear; this era saw the rise and fall of the dinosaurs and the introduction of ancient birds, snakes, and modern-type fish. The Mesozoic Era included the Triassic, Jurassic, and Cretaceous Periods.

The *Cenozoic Era* is what we are in now; the *Pleistocene Epoch* started about 500,000 years ago and saw the rise and fall of a global ice age that carved canyons and moved mountains. The *Holocene Epoch* started with the withdrawal of the glaciers about 11,000 years ago. This era has seen the appearance of most of the animal life that we recognize today—although you may have noticed some familiar names that have been around for quite some time.

Two opposite forces at work in today's geologic world are *sedimentation* and *erosion*. Sedimentation happens when flowing water deposits small particles along its path; over the course of time, these small particles build up and change the contours of the terrain. Erosion happens when wind, precipitation, water, and other phenomena gradually wear away portions of the surface, especially features that are higher than the surrounding surface.

Oceanography

Oceanography studies the earth's oceans and seas; like geology, it uses a variety of related scientific disciplines to pursue that investigation. Although water covers more than three-quarters of the earth's surface, only a relatively small amount has been explored at all by humankind.

The earth has four major oceans: the Atlantic, Pacific, Indian, and Arctic. An ocean can be divided into the *shoreline*, the *water* itself, and the *seabed* (also called the bottom or floor). These classifications, however, need further subdivision into zones or levels to be adequately studied, as shown here:

Marine Zones

Zone	Average Depth	Average Temperature	Comment
Shore (between high, low tides)	Varies	Varies by season	Wave action, light for photosynthesis
Water			
(1) shore to continental shelf	600 ft. (0–200 m)	41°– 77° F (5°– 25°C)	Waves, currents, greatest amount of plant and animal life
(2) downward slope from continental shelf	600–8,000 ft. (200–2,500 m)	41°– 59° F (5°– 15°C)	Currents, almost dark, fewer marine animals, no plants
(3) deeper plain	8,000–21,250 ft. (2,500–6,500 m)	27°– 35° F (3°– 4°C)	Dark, limited animal life, no plants
(4) deepest trenches or canyons	21,250–37,350 ft. (6,500–11,500 m)	34°– 37° F (1°– 3°C)	Dark, very limited animal life, no plants

Meteorology

Meteorology is the study of *weather* (the condition of the atmosphere at a certain time and place) and *climate* (the average of weather conditions in a particular place over a span of time).

Further, weather describes the interaction of several atmospheric conditions— temperature, air pressure, wind, humidity, and so on—that are themselves influenced by other factors.

1. The local temperature is affected by the angle of the sun's rays, what season it is currently (and therefore the position of the earth relative to the sun), the length of the daylight period (also affected by the season), the altitude, the nearness of any large bodies of water, and so on.

2. The local air pressure depends mostly on temperature and humidity; warm air is lighter than cold air, and moist air is heavier than dry air. Changes in atmospheric pressure are measured on a *barometer*.

3. Wind is air moving from one place to another; it is caused by differences in air pressure. Winds move from areas of higher pressure to areas of lower pressure.

4. Humidity is the amount of moisture in the air; *relative humidity* is a percentage of how much water vapor the local air *could* hold at a given temperature. When the air is warm and dry, moisture on the earth's surface tends to *evaporate* (turn into vapor); when the air is *saturated* or completely filled with moisture, a decrease in temperature will cause the moisture in the air to *condense* (form droplets) and *precipitate* (fall) as rain, sleet, snow, or hail.

Astronomy

Astronomy is related to and interwoven with both physics and earth science. The *rotation* of the earth on its *axis* (an imaginary line running between the North and South Poles) causes day and night as one side or the other of the planet faces the sun. The *revolution* of the earth around the sun and its path or *orbit* affect the seasons of the year. The earth is part of a *solar system* that includes seven other planets, and is part of a *galaxy* comprising many thousands of suns and their planets that is in turn part of the *universe* that includes all known and unknown matter and space.

There is also a band of *asteroids*—large, irregularly-shaped chunks of rock and other materials—between the orbits of Mars and Jupiter.

Solar System

Planet	Average distance from the sun (million miles)	Rank by size	Time for revolution	Number of moons
Mercury	36.0	8	88 days	0
Venus	67.1	6	225 days	0
Earth	93.0	5	365¼ days	1
Mars	141.7	7	687 days	2
Jupiter	483.4	1	12 years	63 (12 major, 51 minor)
Saturn	886.1	2	29 years	33 (9 major, 24 minor)
Uranus	1,783.0	3	84 years	27 (5 major, 22 minor)
Neptune	2,793.0	4	164 years	13 (2 major, 11 minor)

Basic Atomic Structure

Elements are the most basic materials in the universe. There are more than 120 elements, including some that have been made in the laboratory. Every known substance—solid, liquid, or gas—is composed of elements.

An *atom* is the smallest particle of an element that retains all the properties of that element. The inner part of an atom is called the *nucleus*, which is composed of very small particles called *protons* and *neutrons*. An atom also has an outer part, consisting of very small particles called *electrons*. The electrons orbit around the nucleus. (See Figure 7.22.)

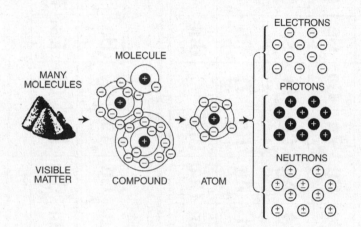

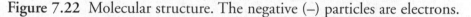

Figure 7.22 Molecular structure. The negative (–) particles are electrons.

Electricity is defined as the flow of electrons along a conductor. A *conductor* is an object that allows electrons to pass easily. That means electrons must be organized and pushed toward a goal, which can be done in a number of ways.

Protons have a positive charge and electrons have a negative charge; neutrons have no charge. Because of their charges, protons and electrons are particles of energy; these charges form an electric field of force within the atom. These charges are always pulling and pushing one other; this action produces energy in the form of movement.

The atoms of each element have a definite number of electrons, and they have the same number of protons. A hydrogen atom has one electron and one proton (Figure 17.23). The aluminum atom has 13 of each (Figure 17.24). The opposite charges—negative electrons and positive protons—attract each other and tend to hold electrons in orbit. As long as this arrangement is not changed, an atom is electrically balanced.

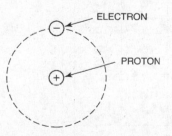

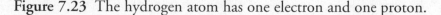

Figure 7.23 The hydrogen atom has one electron and one proton.

Periodic Table of the Elements

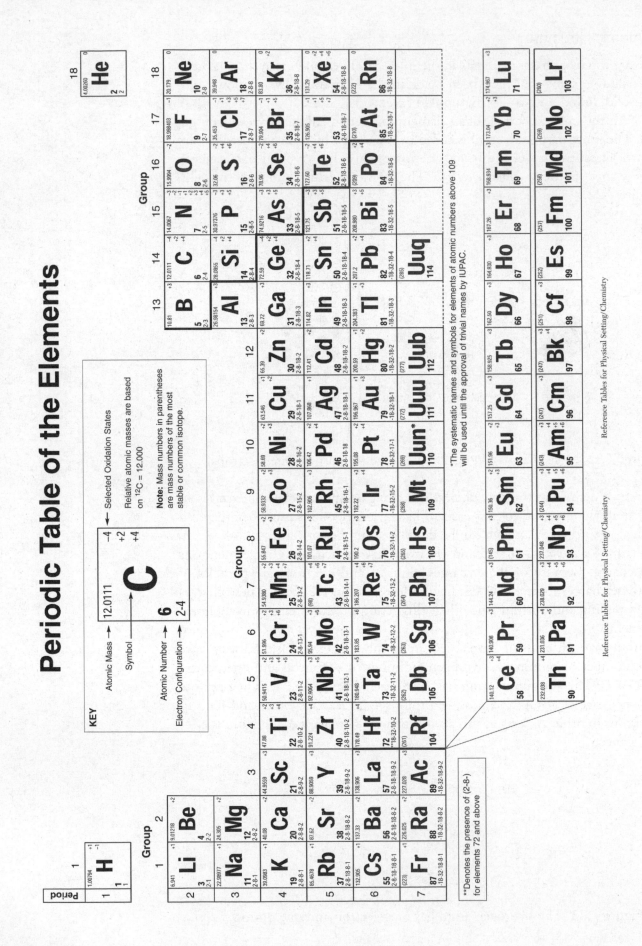

Reference Tables for Physical Setting/Chemistry

Reference Tables for Physical Setting/Chemistry

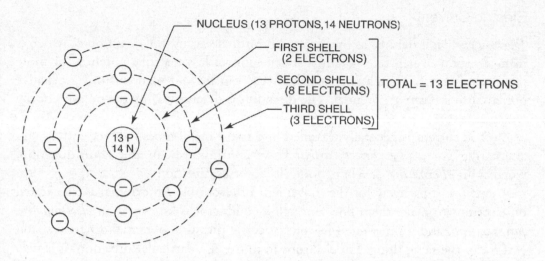

Figure 7.24 The aluminum atom has 13 electrons and 13 protons.

When electrons leave their orbits, they move from atom to atom at random, drifting in no particular direction; these are referred to as *free electrons*.

Heat is only one of the types of energy that can cause electrons to be forced from their orbits. A magnetic field can also be used to cause electrons to move in a given direction. Light energy and pressure on a crystal are also used to generate electricity by forcing electrons to flow along a certain path. So we can see that several types of forces can be used to cause electrons to move in a given direction; that's how electricity (the flow of electrons along a conductor) is generated. A *conductor* is any material that has many free electrons by virtue of its physical makeup.

Electric Energy

Electrons are incredibly small, measuring only about 0.00000000000022 inch (that's twenty-two hundred-trillionths) in diameter. You may wonder how anything so small can be a source of energy. Much of the answer lies in the fact that electrons move at nearly the speed of light, or 186,282 miles per second. In metric terms that's about 300 million meters per second. Billions of them can move at once through a wire. The combination of speed and concentration together produces great energy. When a flow of electrons along a conductor occurs, this is commonly referred to as *current flow.*

Magnetism and Electricity

Magnetism and electricity are closely related. Magnetism is used to generate electricity, and electricity produces a magnetic field.

Magnetism is a force that acts between certain objects. The area around a magnet where the force is felt is called a *magnetic field*. Electricity flowing through a wire sets up a magnetic field around the wire. A coil of current-carrying wire becomes an *electromagnet* with the magnetic field strongest at the two ends of the coil, the north and south *poles*. The electromagnet remains magnetic only as long as the electricity flows through it. A magnetic field can also produce electricity. If you pass a wire across a magnetic field, electricity will be generated in the wire; electric generators are based on this principle. The relationship between electricity and magnetism is also used in transformers, relays, solenoids, and motors.

Electric Current

Electron current is defined as the directed flow of electrons, the direction of which is from a region of negative potential to a region of less negative potential or more positive potential. Therefore, electric current can be said to flow from a negative potential to a positive potential. The direction is determined by the polarity of the voltage source.

Electric current is generally classified into two general types—direct current and alternating current. A *direct current* flows continuously in the same direction, whereas an *alternating current* periodically reverses direction.

A *circuit* is a pathway for the movement of electrons. An external force exerted on electrons to make them flow through a conductor is known as an *electromotive force,* or *emf,* and it's measured in volts. Electric pressure, potential difference, and emf mean the same thing. For electrons to move in a particular direction, it is necessary for a potential difference to exist between two points of the emf source. If 6,250,000,000,000,000,000 electrons pass a given point in one second, there is said to be one *ampere* (A) of current flowing. The same number of electrons stored on an object (a static charge) and not moving is called a *coulomb* (C).

The magnitude or "size" of a current is measured in *amperes.* A current of one ampere is said to flow when one coulomb of charge passes a point in one second. Expressed as an equation:

$$I = \frac{Q}{T}$$

Where: I = current in amperes
Q = charge in coulombs
T = time in seconds

Sometimes the ampere is too large a unit to be useful. Therefore the *milliampere* (mA), one-thousandth of an ampere, or the *microampere* (μA), one-millionth (0.000001) of an ampere, is used.

Current flow is assumed to be from negative (–) to positive (+) in the explanations here. Electron flow is negative (–) to positive (+), and we assume that current flow and electron flow are one and the same. This will make explanations simpler as we progress.

An *ammeter* is used to measure current flow in a circuit. A *milliammeter* is used to measure smaller amounts, and the *microammeter* is used to measure very small amounts of current. A *voltmeter* is used to measure voltage. In some instances it's possible to obtain a meter that will measure both voltage and current plus resistance. This is called a *multimeter,* or *volt-ohm-milliammeter.*

A material through which electricity passes easily is called a *conductor* because it has free electrons. In other words, a conductor offers very little resistance or opposition to the flow of electrons. All metals are conductors of electricity to some extent; some are much better than others. Silver, copper, and aluminum let electricity pass easily, and silver is a better conductor than copper. However, copper is used more frequently because it is cheaper. Aluminum is used as a conductor where light weight is important.

One of the most important reasons why some materials are good conductors— and some are not—is the presence of *free electrons.* If a material has many electrons that are free to move away from their atoms, that material will be a good conductor of electricity. Although free electrons usually move in a haphazard way, their movement can be controlled and results in the flow we call *electric current*.

Conductors may be in the form of bars, tubes, or sheets. The most familiar conductors are wire. Many sizes of wire are available; some are only the thickness of a hair, and other wire may be as thick as your arm.

To prevent conductors from touching at the wrong place, they are usually coated with plastic or cloth material called an *insulator*. An insulator is a material with very few, if any, free electrons. No known material is a perfect insulator; however, there are materials that are such poor conductors that they are classified as insulators, such as glass, dry wood, rubber, mica, and certain plastics.

In between the two extremes of conductors and resistors are *semiconductors*. Semiconductors in the form of transistors, diodes, and integrated circuits or chips are used every day in electronic devices. Materials used in the manufacture of transistors and diodes have a conductivity halfway between that of a good conductor and a good insulator. Therefore, the name *semi*conductor is given them. Germanium and silicon are the two most commonly known semiconductor materials. Through the introduction of small amounts of other elements (called impurities), these nearly pure (99.999999 percent) elements become *limited* conductors.

The opposite of conductors are *resistors*. Resistors are devices used to give a measured amount of opposition or resistance to the flow of electrons. This opposition to current flow is measured in ohms (Ω) and indicates the amount of resistance a piece of material offers to the flow of electrons.

The unit of conductance is the *siemen* (formerly the mho, which is *ohm* spelled backward). Whereas the symbol used to represent the magnitude of resistance is the Greek letter omega (Ω), the symbol used to represent conductance is *S*. The relationship that exists between resistance and conductance is a reciprocal one; the reciprocal of a number is one divided by that number.

If the resistance of a material is known, dividing its value into one will give its conductance. Also, if the conductance is known, dividing its value into one will give its resistance.

Ohm's Law

A German physicist by the name of Georg Ohm discovered the relationship between voltage, current, and resistance in 1827. He found that in any circuit where the only opposition to the flow of electrons is resistance, there is a relationship between the values of voltage, current, and resistance. The strength or intensity of the current is directly proportional to the voltage and inversely proportional to the resistance.

Power

Power is defined as the *rate* at which work is done. It is expressed in metric measurement terms of watts (W) for power and joules (J) for energy work. A *watt* is the power that gives rise to the production of energy at the rate of 1 joule per second (W = J/s). A *joule* is the work done when the point of application of force of 1 newton is displaced a distance of 1 meter in the direction of the force (J = N $\times$ m).

It has long been the practice in this country to measure work in terms of horsepower (hp). Electric motors are still rated in horsepower and probably will be for some time, since the United States did not adopt metric standards for everything.

Power can be electric or mechanical. When a mechanical force is used to lift a weight, *work* is done. The rate at which the weight is moved is called *power. One horsepower* is defined as 33,000 pounds being lifted 1 foot in one minute. Energy is consumed in moving a weight or when work is done. It takes 746 W of electric power to equal 1 hp.

The horsepower rating of electric motors is calculated by taking the voltage and multiplying it by the current drawn under full load. This power is measured in watts, so 1 volt times 1 ampere equals 1 watt. When put into a formula it reads as follows:

$$\text{Power} = \text{volts} \times \text{amperes or } P = E \times I$$
where E = voltage, or emf, and I = current, or intensity of electron flow

The kilowatt is commonly used to express the amount of electric energy used or available. Since the term *kilo* (k) means one thousand (1,000), a kilowatt (kW) is 1,000 watts. When the kilowatt is used in terms of power dissipated or consumed—by a home over a month, for instance—it is expressed in kilowatt hours. The unit kilowatt hour is abbreviated as kWh. It is the equivalent of one thousand watts used for a period of one hour. Electric bills are calculated or computed on an hourly basis and then read in the kWh units.

The *milliwatt* (mW) means one-thousandth (0.001) of a watt. The milliwatt is used in working with very small amplifiers and other electronic devices. For instance, a speaker used on a portable transistor radio could be rated as 100 milliwatts, or 0.1 W. Transistor circuits are designed in milliwatts, but power-line electric power is measured in kilowatts. Keep in mind that *kilo* means 1,000 and *milli* means 0.001 (one-thousandth).

Any time there is movement, there is resistance; this resistance is useful in electric and electronic circuits. Resistance makes it possible to generate heat, control electron flow, and supply the correct voltage to a device. Resistance in a conductor depends on four factors: material, length, cross-sectional area, and temperature. Resistance is measured by a unit called the *ohm*, symbolized by the Greek letter Ω (omega).

Some materials offer more resistance than others; it depends on the number of free electrons present in the material. The longer the wire or conductor, the more resistance it has, so resistance is said to vary *directly* with the length of the wire. However, resistance varies *inversely* with the size of the conductor in cross section—in other words, the larger the wire, the smaller the resistance per foot of length.

For most materials, the higher the temperature, the higher the resistance. However, the exceptions to this are devices known as *thermistors.* Thermistors change resistance with temperature. They *decrease* in resistance with an increase in temperature. Thermistors are used in certain types of meters to measure temperature.

Resistance causes a voltage drop across a resistor when current flows through it. The voltage is dropped or dissipated as heat and must be eliminated into the air. Some variable resistors can be varied, but can also be adjusted for a particular setting. Resistors are available in various sizes, shapes, and wattage ratings.

Mechanical Comprehension

This section reviews some basic principles of physics and how some simple machines make work easier.

Force

One of the basic concepts of physics is the concept of force. Force is something that can change the velocity of an object by making it start, stop, speed up, slow down, or change direction. When you take your foot off the gas pedal of a car, it doesn't suddenly come to a stop—it coasts on, only gradually losing its velocity. If you want the car to stop, you have to do something to it.

There are many types of force.

Friction

Your car has three controls whose function is to change its velocity: the gas pedal, the brake pedal, and the steering wheel. The brakes make use of the same force that stops your car if you just let it coast: friction.

Sliding friction is a force generated whenever two objects are in contact and there is relative motion between them. When something is moving, friction *always* acts in such a direction as to retard (slow down) the relative motion. Thus the direction of the force of friction on a moving object will always be directly opposite to the direction of the velocity. The brake shoes slow down the rotation of the wheels, and the tires slow the car until it comes to rest.

In the simplest case, the force of friction can be measured quite easily by means of a spring scale.

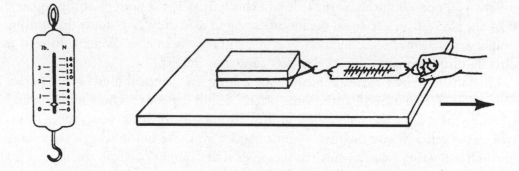

The spring scale can be used to measure all kinds of forces. Basically, it measures the force pulling on its shackle. A spring scale is calibrated in force units—*pounds* or *newtons*. A newton (abbreviated N) is a fairly small unit of force; it takes 4.45 newtons to equal 1 pound.

The figure on the right shows a spring scale being used to measure the force of sliding friction between a brick and the horizontal surface on which it is resting. The scale is pulling the brick along at constant speed. In this condition, the brick is said to be in *equilibrium*. Because its velocity is not changing, it follows that the net force acting on it is zero.

However, the spring scale is exerting a force, which is indicated on its face. This force is pulling the brick to the right. The brick can remain in equilibrium only if there is an equal force pulling it to the left, so that the net force acting on it is zero. In the situation shown, the only force pulling the brick to the left is the frictional force between the brick and the surface. Therefore the reading on the spring scale is equal to the force of friction.

Anyone who has ever moved furniture around or slid a box across the floor, knows that the frictional force is greater when the furniture or the box is heavier. The force of friction does not change much as the object speeds up, but it depends very strongly on how hard the two surfaces are pressed together.

When a solid moves through a liquid, such as a boat moving through the water, there is a frictionlike force retarding the motion of the solid; this is called *viscous drag*. Like friction, it always acts opposite to velocity. Unlike friction, however, it increases greatly with speed, and it depends more on the shape of the object and on the nature of the liquid than on the object's weight. Gases also produce viscous drag, and you are probably most familiar with this as the air resistance that acts on a car at high speed.

Gravity

Probably the first law of physics that everyone learns is this: If you drop something, it falls. Since its velocity keeps on changing as it falls, there must be a force acting on it during the time that it's falling—this is *gravity*.

You can measure gravity by balancing it off with a spring scale. When you hang something on a spring scale and read the scale in pounds or newtons, you usually call the force of gravity acting on the object by a special name. You call it the *weight* of the object.

Weight is not a fixed property of an object; it varies with location. A person who weighs 160 pounds at the North Pole will check in at 159.2 pounds at the equator. If he should step on a scale on the moon, it would read only 27 pounds. Everything weighs less where the acceleration caused by gravity is smaller. Weight, in fact, is directly proportional to the acceleration caused by gravity.

Obviously, weight also depends on something else, since things have different weights even if they are all at the same place. Weight depends on how much "stuff" (matter) there is in the object. If you buy 10 pounds of sugar, you expect to get twice as much as if you buy five pounds. And if you take both sacks to the moon, one will still weigh twice as much as the other. The amount of sugar, the *mass* of the sugar, did not change when it was brought somewhere else. And the more sugar you have, the more it weighs.

Weight, then, is proportional both to mass and to the acceleration caused by gravity.

This equation works nicely, without introducing any constants, if the units are carefully defined. Mass is measured by pounds in the English system and in kilograms in the metric system. By definition, when you multiply the mass in kilograms by the acceleration in meters per second squared, the weight comes out in newtons.

To summarize, weight—the force of gravity—is the product of mass and the acceleration caused by gravity.

Elastic Recoil

The basic feature of a solid, as opposed to a liquid or a gas, is that it has a definite shape. It resists changes in its shape and, in so doing, exerts a force against whatever force is applied to it.

Look, for example, at the meter bar supported at its ends, shown in Figure 7.25. If you push down on it, you bend it, and you can feel it pushing back on you. The harder you push, the more the bar bends and the harder it pushes back. It bends just enough to push on you with the same force that you exert on it. The force it exerts is called *elastic recoil*.

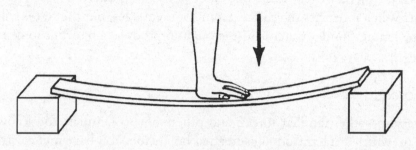

Figure 7.25

The same thing happens when you stand on the floor, or on the ground. You can't see the floor bend, but it bends just the same, just not very much. Even a feather resting on the floor bends it a little. The elastic recoil force needed to support the feather is very small, so the amount of bending is too small to detect.

A rope does not resist bending, but it certainly resists stretching. When a rope is stretched, it is said to be in a state of *tension*. The tension can be measured by cutting the rope and inserting a spring scale into it, as shown in Figure 7.26. The spring scale will read the tension in the rope, in pounds or newtons. If you pull with a force of 30 N, for example, the tension in the rope is 30 N, and that is what the scale will indicate. Something, such as the elastic recoil of the wall to which the scale is attached, must be pulling on the other end with a force of 30 N. The tension in the rope is the same throughout, and is equal to the elastic recoil force that the rope exerts at its ends.

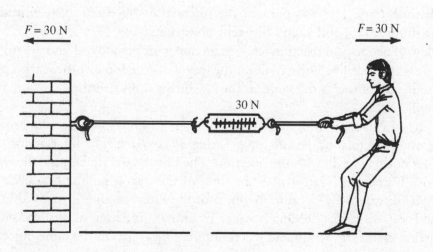

Figure 7.26

To summarize: A force applied to a solid distorts the shape of the solid, causing it to exert a force back on the force that distorted it.

Buoyancy

If you take a deep breath and dive into a pool, you will have trouble keeping yourself submerged—something keeps pushing you up. That force is called *buoyancy*.

The force of buoyancy acts in an upward direction on anything submerged in a liquid or a gas. Buoyancy is the force that makes ships float and helium-filled balloons rise. A rock sinks because its weight is greater than the buoyancy of the water. A submerged cork rises because the buoyancy of the water exerts a force greater than its weight. When it reaches the surface, some of it emerges, but the rest is still under water. The amount under water is just enough to produce a buoyant force equal to its weight, so it stays put.

Other Forces

There are some other familiar forces, and others not so familiar. You know about magnetism, which attracts iron nails to a red horseshoe. You have met electric force (static electricity), which makes a nylon shirt cling to you when you try to take it off. Airplanes stay up because of the lift force generated by the flow of air across their wings. A rocket takes off because of the force generated by the gases expanding in it and pushing out behind it.

Action and Reaction

The batter steps up to the plate and takes a healthy swing, sending the ball into left field. The bat has exerted a large force on the ball, changing both the magnitude and the direction of its velocity. But the ball has also exerted a force on the bat, slowing it down. The batter feels this when the bat hits the ball.

Next time up, he strikes out. He has taken exactly the same swing, but exerts no force on anything (air doesn't count). The batter has discovered that it is impossible to exert a force unless there is something there to push back. Forces exist *only* in pairs. When object A exerts a force on object B, then B must exert a force on A. The two forces are sometimes called *action* and *reaction,* although which is which is often somewhat arbitrary. The two parts of the interaction are equal in magnitude, are opposite in direction, and act on different objects.

The law of action and reaction leads to an apparent paradox, if you are not careful how it is applied. The horse pulls on the wagon. If the force of the wagon pulling the horse the other way is the same, as the law insists, how can the horse and wagon get started?

The error in the reasoning is this: If you want to know whether the horse gets moving, you have to consider the forces acting *on the horse.* The force acting on the wagon has nothing to do with the question. The horse starts up because the force he exerts with his hooves is larger than the force of the wagon pulling him back—and the wagon starts moving because the force of the horse pulling it forward is larger than the frictional forces holding it back. To know something moves, consider the forces acting *on* it. The action and reaction forces *never* act on the same object.

Balanced Forces

If a single force acts on an object, the velocity of the object must change. If two or more forces act, however, their effects may eliminate each other. This is the condition of equilibrium, in which there is no net force and the velocity does not change. We saw such a condition in the case in which gravity is pulling an object down and the spring scale, used for weighing it, is pulling it upward.

An object in equilibrium may or may not be at rest. A parachutist, descending at constant speed, is in equilibrium. His weight is just balanced by the viscous drag on the parachute, which is why he put it on in the first place. A heavier parachutist falls a little faster; his speed increases until the viscous drag just balances his weight.

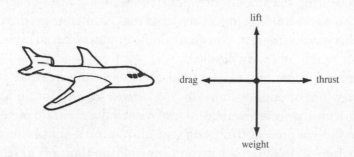

Balancing the vertical forces is not enough to produce equilibrium. An airplane traveling at constant speed is in equilibrium under the influence of four forces, two vertical and two horizontal. Vertical: Gravity (down) is just balanced by the lift (up) produced by the flow of air across the wing. Horizontal: Viscous drag (pulling back, slowing) is just balanced by the thrust of the engines (pushing forward). Both the vertical and the horizontal velocities are constant.

The brick in the illustration on page 205, resting on a tabletop and being pulled along at constant speed, is another example. Vertical: The downward force of gravity is balanced by the upward force of the elastic recoil of the tabletop. Horizontal: The tension in the spring scale, pulling to the right, is balanced by the friction pulling it to the left, opposite to the direction of motion.

If an object is in equilibrium—at rest or moving at a constant speed in a straight line—the total force acting on it in any direction is exactly equal in magnitude to the force in the opposite direction.

Simple Machines

"Simple machines" are devices that make work easier by changing either the direction or magnitude of an applied force. Without thinking about it, we all use a multitude of simple machines every day—a light switch, a water faucet, a doorknob, a hammer, a car, or a knife, just to name a few.

There are six basic simple machines recognized in mechanical physics—the lever, the inclined plane, the wedge, the wheel and axle, the screw, and the pulley—and all of them have been in use for thousands of years. In theory, all complex machines are made up of parts derived from these six simple machines. The principles behind some of them were quantified by Archimedes, the Greek mathematician, engineer, and inventor.

And, even though not on the "official" list, we will discuss the hydraulic jack, as well as a few complex machines that are good examples of combinations of simple machines.

Simple machines are useful because of their ability to perform *work*, which is defined as applying force over a distance. The effort multiplied by the effort distance is called the *work input*, and the load multiplied by the load distance (distance the load travels) is the *work output*. Machines create a greater output force than the amount of force input to them; the ratio of these forces is the *mechanical advantage* of the machine. Simple machines can also be used in combinations to create even greater mechanical advantages, as in the example of a bicycle.

The Work Principle

Work is done whenever a force moves something through or over a distance. The formula for measuring the amount of work done is $W = F \times d$ (force multiplied by distance). If you stand still holding a very large rock over your head, you might get tired, but in this physics context, you aren't doing any *work* because you aren't moving any load or weight over any distance.

The force to get something moved (and therefore result in work performed) is measured in newtons or pounds-force (lb_f). A *newton* (named for Sir Isaac Newton, English scientist) is the force required to move one kilogram one meter in one second. A *pound-force* (to prevent confusion with the pound as a *mass* unit of measurement) is equal to 4.44822162 newtons, or the amount of force required to accelerate one *slug* (32.17405 pounds-mass or lb_m) at a rate of 1 ft/sec^2.

The purpose of a machine is to make it possible to exert a large force on the load with a smaller effort. You could say that a machine magnifies force or effort. The amount of this magnification—the ratio of load to effort—is called the *mechanical advantage* of the machine. It can be shown algebraically like this:

$$MA = \frac{F_L}{F_E}$$

Something else to consider in this area is the direction of a force applied to an object, and how that direction affects the amount of work that is done on the object. One way to look at it is that only the amount of force that's in the direction of movement counts. For example, look at Figure 7.27 below (the child pulling a smaller child on a sled).

Figure 7.27

The tension in the rope held by the larger child is pulling the sled forward, but, because it is applied at an angle, it is also lifting the sled somewhat. Since neither the angle of the rope nor the upward force applied to it are enough to overcome the force of gravity, only the component or part of the forward-directed force is doing the work of moving the sled.

The angle between the direction of actual movement and the direction in which the force is applied is known as *theta* (Greek symbol θ) and is measured in degrees.

If we call the force that creates the tension in the rope to pull the sled T, the component of the force that actually pulls the sled forward is $T \cos \theta$, or T (tension) multiplied by the cosine of the angle theta.

You can probably understand just from the everyday intuitive application of these principles that the smaller the angle θ, the larger the effective force pulling the sled, and the smaller the amount of force that is spent trying to lift it. When θ = zero, the entire force contributes to moving the sled forward, and there is no effort spent lifting at all. On the other hand, when θ = 90°, the entire force is lifting the sled and nothing is pulling forward.

Most mechanical comprehension problems at this level are simplified—they do not, for instance, take into account the additional impact exerted by forces like friction with the ground, wind resistance (or the push from a tailwind), and so on. This leads us to the idea of a machine's *efficiency*: the ratio between the work output and the work input, expressed as a formula like this:

$$\text{efficiency} = \frac{W_{\text{out}}}{W_{\text{in}}}$$

Efficiency is usually expressed as a percentage that tells us what fraction of the work put into a machine comes out as useful work at the other end.

The next concept in this area that you need to know is the concept of *vectors*. A vector is any physical quantity that requires both a direction and an amount of force or *magnitude*. A vector is shown graphically as an arrow, where the length of the arrow represents the vector's magnitude, and the angle θ (sound familiar?) between the vector and a designated axis defines the vector's direction.

The Lever

Levers are a very common type of simple machine. A lever consists of a rigid bar that is supported at some point (the *fulcrum* or *pivot*), and has a load at some other point on the bar. The lever shown in Figure 7.28 is fairly typical. The load is the weight of the rock being lifted; the effort is the force exerted by the person trying to move the rock; and the fulcrum is the smaller rock supporting the lever.

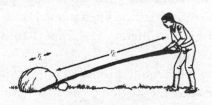

Figure 7.28

Applying a force to one end of the bar causes it to pivot about the fulcrum, causing a magnification of the force applied to the load at another point along the bar. The torque or force around the pivot that is exerted by the worker is $F_E r_E$, where r_E (the *effort arm*) is the distance from the point where the effort is applied to the pivot. Similarly, the torque produced by the weight of the rock is $F_L r_L$, where r_L is the load arm. If the system is rotating in equilibrium, these two torques must have the same magnitude, so

$$F_E r_E = F_L r_L$$

from which we find that the mechanical advantage, F_L/F_E, is given by

$$\text{MA}_{\text{lever}} = \frac{r_E}{r_L}$$

Or, in other words, in a lever the mechanical advantage is equal to the ratio of effort arm to load arm.

For many kinds of levers, friction at the pivot is quite small, so efficiencies approach 100 percent, and the arm ratio is very near the force ratio. Usually, no correction is needed.

Levers are classified according to the relative positions of the pivot, load, and effort. The three classes of levers are represented by the tools shown in Figure 7.29. In the pliers (first-class lever), the pivot is between the effort and the load. In the nutcracker (second-class lever), it is the load that is between the other two. And in the sugar tongs (third-class lever), the effort is in the middle.

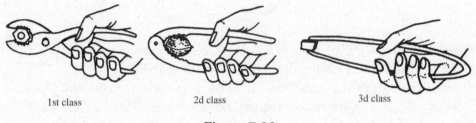

1st class   2d class   3d class

Figure 7.29

Note that in the third-class lever (the sugar tongs), the load arm is longer than the effort arm, so the mechanical advantage is less than 1. This lever magnifies distance at the expense of force.

Mechanical advantage is the ratio of load to effort; in a lever, it is equal to the ratio of effort arm to load arm.

The Inclined Plane

An inclined plane is a plane (flat) surface set at an angle to another surface. This results in using less effort to achieve the same results by applying the required force over a longer distance. The most basic inclined plane is a ramp; it requires less force to move up or down a ramp to a different elevation than it does to climb or lower oneself to that height vertically.

For example, a wagon rolls downhill, propelled only by its own weight. But gravity pulls straight down, not at the angle of the road going down the hill. What makes the wagon go is a *component* of its weight, a part of its weight acting downhill, parallel to the surface the wagon rests on. A component of a force can act in any direction, not just vertically or horizontally. On the inclined plane, the weight of the wagon has two different effects: It acts *parallel* to the surface of the hill, pushing the wagon downhill; and it acts perpendicular (also called *normal*) to the surface, pushing the wagon into the surface. As the hill gets steeper, the parallel component becomes larger and the perpendicular (normal) component decreases.

When the wagon is resting on the surface, the elastic recoil of the surface is just enough to cancel the normal component of the wagon's weight. If the wagon is to stay in equilibrium, you have to pull on it, uphill, to prevent it from rolling away.

If there is no friction, the uphill force needed is the same whether the wagon is standing still or going either uphill or downhill at a constant speed.

The situation is different if the wagon is moving and there is friction. If the wagon is going uphill, you have to pull harder, because the friction is working against you, holding it back. The total force you need to keep the wagon going is then equal to the parallel component of the weight plus the friction. On the other hand, if you are lowering the wagon down the hill, holding the rope to keep it from running away from you, friction is acting uphill, helping you hold the wagon back. Then the force you must exert is the parallel component of the weight *minus* the friction.

A ramp is a device commonly used to aid in lifting. To raise a heavy load a couple of feet onto a platform, it is common practice to place it on a dolly and wheel it up an inclined plane.

The work output of an inclined plane is the work that would have to be done to lift the load directly: the weight of the load times the vertical distance it goes. The work input is the actual force exerted in pushing the dolly up the ramp times the length of the ramp.

The ideal mechanical advantage of an inclined plane is equal to its length divided by its height.

The Wedge

A wedge—sometimes considered a specific type of inclined plane—is a double-inclined plane (i.e., both sides are inclined) that moves to exert a force along the lengths of its sides. The force is perpendicular to the inclined surfaces, so it pushes two objects (or portions of a single object) apart. Axes, knives, and chisels are all examples of wedges. The common door wedge used to keep an open door open uses the force on the surfaces of the door and floor to provide friction, rather than separate things, but it's still basically a wedge.

The Wheel and Axle

This simple machine involves a *wheel* attached to a rigid bar or *axle* in its center. A force applied to the wheel causes the axle to rotate, which can be used to magnify the output force (for example, by having a rope wind around the axle). Alternatively, a force applied to provide rotation to the axle translates into rotation of the wheel. The wheel and axle can be viewed as a type of lever that rotates around a center fulcrum. Ferris wheels, automobile wheels, and rolling pins are examples of wheel-and-axle machines.

The Screw

A screw is a shaft that has an inclined groove along its surface. It can also be thought of as an inclined plane wrapped around a cylinder. By rotating the screw (applying a *torque*), the force is applied perpendicular to the groove, thereby translating a rotational force into a linear one. Screws are frequently used to fasten objects together (as the hardware screw and bolt combination does), although the Babylonians developed a "screw" that could elevate water from a low-lying body to a higher one (which later came to be known as Archimedes' screw). Other examples of screws are propellers, fans, and most jar lids.

The Pulley

The pulley is a wheel with a groove along its edge where a rope or cable can be placed. It uses the principle of applying force over a longer distance—as well as the tension in the rope or cable—to reduce the magnitude of the force required to move the load. Complex systems of pulleys can be used to greatly reduce the force that must be applied to move an object.

For example, a piano mover, unable to fit the instrument into the staircase, decides to raise it outside the building to a window. He attaches it to a set of ropes and wheels that, somehow, make it possible for him to lift it with a force considerably smaller than the weight of the piano. How does this work?

Consider first the heavy block in Figure 7.30 suspended from two ropes. The upward force on the block is the tension (T) in the ropes, and the sum of the two tensions must equal the weight of the block. If the whole system is symmetrical, each rope is under tension equal to half the weight of the block.

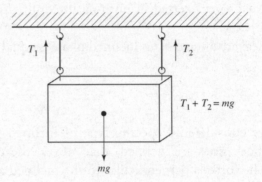

Figure 7.30

Now look at Figure 7.31, where the block has been attached to a wheel. There is now only one rope, which passes over the wheel. The tension in the rope is the same throughout; if it were different on one side than on the other, the wheel would turn until the tension on the two sides equalized. The tension in the rope is still only half the weight of the block, since it exerts *two* upward forces on the block. Now we have a system that helps in lifting things. Just fasten one end of the rope to a fixed support and pull on the other end (Figure 7.32). Now you can raise the block with a force equal to only half its weight.

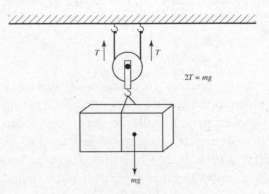

Figure 7.31

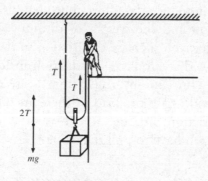

Figure 7.32

Are you getting something for nothing? Well, yes and no. True, you can now lift the weight with less force, but you have to pull the rope farther than you would if you lifted the block directly. Every time you pull 10 feet of rope through your hands, the block rises 5 feet. You might look at it this way: If the block rises 5 feet, *both* sides of the supporting rope have to shorten 5 feet, and the only way to accomplish this is to pull 10 feet of rope through. You raise the block with only half the force, but you have to exert the force through twice the distance.

You might prefer to pull in a downward direction rather than upward, and you can manage this by attaching a fixed wheel to the support and passing the rope around it as in Figure 7.33. The tension in the rope is still only half the weight of the block; the fixed pulley does nothing but change the direction of the force you exert.

Let's learn some vocabulary. The weight of the object being lifted is called the *load,* and the distance it rises is the *load distance.* The force you exert on the rope is the *effort,* and the distance through which you exert that effort is the *effort distance.* With a single moveable pulley in use, the effort is half the load and the effort distance is twice the load distance.

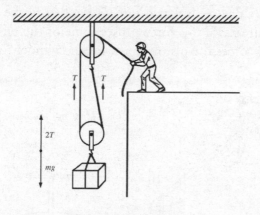

Figure 7.33

There are ways to string up a system of pulleys that will reduce the effort still further. Figure 7.34 shows how the same two pulleys can be connected to a rope in such a way as to divide the load among three strands of rope instead of two. This is done by fastening one end of the rope to the load instead of to the fixed support. Unfortunately, when you do this, you have to shorten all three strands when you raise the object, and the effort distance becomes three times the load distance. By using more pulleys you can reduce the effort still further. Unfortunately, there is a limit to how much you can reduce the effort. The analysis we did so far neglects a few things, such as friction and the weight of the moveable pulleys themselves. Every time you add a pulley, you increase the friction in the system; if it is a moveable pulley—the only kind that produces a reduction in force—you have to lift it along with the load. The effort in any real system is always larger than the ideal effort we calculated by dividing up the load. If there are a lot of pulleys, it may be considerably larger. And friction, although it increases the force you must exert, has no effect on the distance you have to pull that rope.

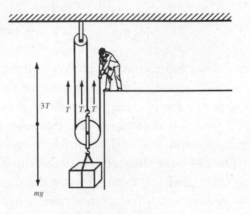

Figure 7.34

Effort distance is load distance times the number of supporting strands; effort is larger than load divided by the number of strands.

The Hydraulic Jack

Liquids are nearly incompressible. This property makes them suitable as a means of transforming work from one type to another.

A hydraulic jack is a device in which force is applied to the oil in a small cylinder. As shown in Figure 7.35, this force causes some of the oil to be transferred to a larger cylinder. This forces the piston in the larger cylinder to rise, lifting a load.

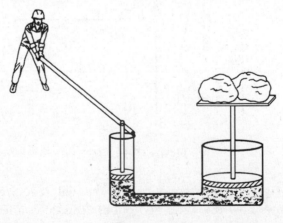

Figure 7.35

This device takes advantage of the fact that oil, being nearly incompressible, transmits whatever pressure is applied to it. The pressure applied in the small cylinder appears unchanged in the big one, pushing up its piston.

The ideal mechanical advantage is the ratio between effort distance and load distance; for a hydraulic jack, it is equal to the ratio of the area of the load piston to that of the effort piston.

You may see a test problem that involves an application of these principles by showing you two cylinders of different sizes, connected by a hydraulic line or the equivalent, and each containing a piston that is either forcing the fluid in one cylinder down or being pushed up by actions in the other cylinder; alternatively, you may see a problem where there is a piston in only one cylinder. In either case, you will have to be able to understand the effects of mechanical advantage in these different-sized cylinders.

TIP

The volume of the oil being transferred from one piston to another does not change—only the size of the piston will change.

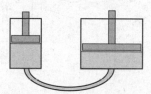

The question will give you some indication of the size of the cylinders, such as the diameter of the cylinder (or the piston within, which for purposes of the problem is assumed to be the same as the cylinder). It's good to remember that the volume of the oil being transferred from one piston to another does not change—only the dimensions of the piston change. Since the volume of a cylinder is $V = \pi r^2 d$ or ad (where a is the area of the circular part of the cylinder and d is the diameter of the cylinder), then $a_1 d_1 = a_2 d_2$, and the formula for mechanical advantage in this kind of problem is

$$\frac{a_2}{a_1} = \frac{d_1}{d_2}$$

where a_1 is the area of the smaller cylinder and a_2 is the area of the bigger cylinder, and d_1 is the vertical distance moved by the smaller cylinder and d_2 is the vertical distance moved by the larger cylinder. In a case where the smaller cylinder is two inches in diameter, for example, and the bigger one is eight inches, the mechanical advantage would be $(\frac{8}{2}) = 4$. Therefore, if the larger piston was pushed down one inch, the piston in the smaller cylinder would be correspondingly pushed upward four times that amount, or four inches. By the same token, if the piston in the smaller cylinder is pushed down four inches, for example, the piston in the larger cylinder would only be pushed upward one inch.

The Vise

The vise of Figure 7.36 is a complex machine in which the handle acts as a lever operating a different kind of machine: a screw. How can we calculate the constants of this gadget? It would be very difficult to calculate the ratio of the force the jaws apply to the force on the handle. The best we can do is work with the distances.

A screw consists of a single continuous spiral wrapped around a cylinder. The distance between ridges is known as the *pitch* of the thread, as shown in Figure 7.37. Every time the screw makes one complete turn, the screw advances a distance equal to the pitch. In the vise, one complete turn is made when the end of the handle travels in a circle whose radius is the length of the handle (l). Therefore, when the effort moves a distance $2\pi l$, the load moves a distance equal to the pitch of the thread. Therefore, for a screw,

$$\text{ideal MA} = \frac{2\pi(\text{length of handle})}{\text{pitch of thread}}$$

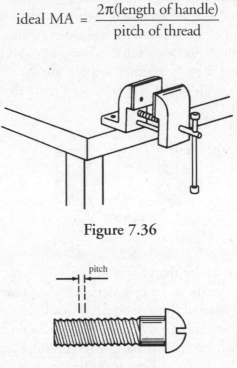

Figure 7.36

Figure 7.37

However, if you use this expression to calculate the forces, you will get it all wrong. The vise is a high-friction device. It has to be, for it is the friction that keeps it from opening when you tighten it. A vise is a self-locking machine because its efficiency is considerably under 50 percent.

Machines That Spin

What is the mechanical advantage of a winch, such as that shown in Figure 7.38? The principle is not much different from that of a lever. Because the crank and the shaft turn together, the torque exerted by the effort (the force on the handle) must be equal to the torque exerted by the load (the tension in the rope). The mechanical advantage, then, is the ratio of the radius of the crank to the radius of the shaft.

Figure 7.38

In mechanical devices, gears are commonly used to change torque. Consider the gears of Figure 7.39, for example. We assume that both gears are mounted on shafts of equal diameter, and that the small gear is driving the large one. What is the mechanical advantage of this combination?

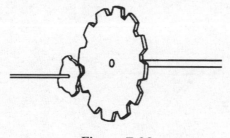

Figure 7.39

First of all, the teeth must have the same size and spacing on both gears for them to mesh properly. With 12 teeth in the large gear and only four in the small one, the small gear has to make three complete revolutions to make the big one turn once. The large *load* or *drive* gear moves only one-third as far as the smaller *effort* or *driving* gear, and the ratio of the two distances is the same as the ratio of the number of teeth in the two gears. Then we can say that the ideal mechanical advantage of a gear is the ratio of the number of teeth in the load gear to the number of teeth in the effort gear, in this case 3:1.

Power

When the piano mover rigs his tackle, he has to consider many factors. For one, the more pulley he puts in, the longer it will take him to get the job done. If he has to pull more rope—using less force, to be sure—he will have to keep pulling for a longer time.

There is a definite limit to the amount of work the mover can do in a given time. The rate at which he does work is called his *power*. Power is work done per unit time.

The English unit of power is the foot-pound per second, and it takes 550 of them to make one horsepower. The SI unit is the joule per second, or *watt* (W). A horsepower is 746 watts. The watt is a very small unit, and the kilowatt (= 1,000 W) is commonly used.

In all the machines we have discussed so far, work comes out the load end as it goes in at the effort end. Thus, the power output of any machine is equal to the power input. Machines do not increase your power. A pulley or a windlass will spread the work out over a longer period of time, so that you can do it with the power available in your muscles and without straining for a force larger than convenient.

Mental Skills

Both the AFOQT and the ASTB include subtests that measure your ability to visualize and understand the physical world around you. In addition, the AFAST will call on you to mentally visualize spatial relationship in two of its subtests. This chapter will help you review or develop the spatial-intelligence skills you need to be familiar with in order to score well on these tests:

- Block counting
- Rotated blocks
- Hidden figures
- Complex movements
- Cyclic orientation
- Spatial apperception

Block Counting

The Block Counting subtest on the AFOQT has 20 questions that test your ability to analyze the spatial relationships of a three-dimensional collection of blocks to determine how many other blocks are touched by designated numbered blocks. For purposes of the test, you can consider that every block in the stack is the same size and shape as the other blocks. A block is considered to be touching the numbered block if any part touches it, even if it's only a corner or an edge. The key to doing well on this test section is being methodical. *Choose one side or edge of the numbered block in question and work your way (mentally) all the way around your numbered block to see how many other blocks are in contact with it.*

Let's look at an example:

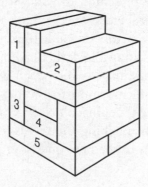

In this example, Block 1 is touching the block that is parallel to it (between Block 1 and Block 2), as well as the two blocks that are underneath and perpendicular (at right angles) to it, for a total of three blocks. Can you "see" that? Likewise, Block 2 is touching the block that is between it and Block 1, as well as the two blocks that are underneath and perpendicular, for a similar total of three blocks touched.

Block 3 is in a different circumstance, however; notice that Block 3 is edge-up at the back of this particular stack. Let's start at the top and work our way all the way around. First, notice the two blocks that are above and perpendicular to Block 3. Next, notice the two blocks (one of them numbered as Block 4) that are lying down where Block 3 is edge-up—both of them are in contact with Block 3's vertical face. Finally, there are the two blocks underneath and perpendicular to Block 3; one of them is numbered as Block 5. So, our total number of blocks in contact with Block 3 is six.

Before we look at the remaining numbered blocks, let's look at the way your possible answers are presented. This subtest is both like and unlike other multiple-choice tests. It is similar in that you will have several choices—in this case, five, designated as A through E—to pick from. Also, you will have to remain careful not to become confused between the several parallel lines of choices. However, there are no more or less attractive-sounding choices, nor are there clues you can deduce from the use of words such as *never* or *every*—there are only numbers in a table to pick from, with no difference between them except their value.

Now it's time to look at Block 4. Let's start at the back side of the stack, where we can readily see that Block 3 is touching Block 4. Then there is the block lying on top of Block 4, and then the one at the front of the stack that is perpendicular to Block 4 along its shorter axis, but parallel along the blocks' longer axis. Then, just as with Block 3, there are the two blocks at the bottom of the stack and perpendicular to Block 4's long axis. That's a total of five other blocks in the stack touching Block 4.

	KEY				
Block	A	B	C	D	E
1	2	3	4	5	6
2	1	2	3	4	5
3	2	3	4	5	6
4	4	5	6	7	8
5	4	5	6	7	8

The stack of blocks will be presented to you with the table of possible answer choices alongside. Find the numbered block you are analyzing in the left-hand column and then read horizontally across the table until you find the number 5, which was the number of blocks touching Block 4. Reading up from the 5, you can see that the correct answer for Question 4 (which dealt with Block 4) is B. You would, on the test, mark choice B and move on to the next question, which deals with Block 5. How many blocks are touching Block 5? Go ahead—we'll wait.

Right, the number of blocks touching Block 5 is four, so we would mark choice A for Question 5 and move on to the next question.

Rotated Blocks

This is one of the more challenging subtests of the AFOQT. It measures your ability to visualize an object and then mentally manipulate that object in space so that you can recognize and choose that same object when it has been rotated along one or more of the three-dimensional axes. You will be given an illustration—a 3D drawing—of a multipart block shape, followed by five other drawings. Your task is to identify and choose the one drawing of the five that represents the same object as the first graphic; the difference is that it will have been rotated into a different position.

You can use some techniques from more conventional multiple-choice tests to good advantage here. The first technique is to look at all the choices and see if one jumps out at you as being the one you're looking for. If one does, examine it carefully; try to rotate the original figure into the same position as the answer choice you (tentatively) think is correct. If it is, mark that answer and go on to the next question—you have only 13 minutes for 15 questions, so time management is critical.

The second technique you can use is to eliminate obvious wrong choices right away. In the same way that right answers sometimes stand up and beg to be noticed, there may be one or more figures that are so obviously wrong that you can eliminate them quickly. This may be because they are reversed or otherwise clearly impossible to manipulate so as to match the original figure.

Finally, unless the right answer has gotten your attention quickly—and whether or not you have been able to eliminate any choices—you will need to work your way through the choices one by one to find the correct answer. This is not quite as hard as it might sound, since the original drawing is presented immediately to the left of the five choices. Look at the example, pick a recognizable feature on the example figure as a landmark or mental handle (such as an angled cut or other unusually distinctive shape), then try to mentally twist or rotate it into the same position as the remaining choices you have not eliminated—choice A, then choice B, and so on.

If you can't get the original to match up with that choice fairly quickly, go to the next answer choice and try it. Keep going until you identify one that matches or until you run out of choices. If you have eliminated some choices early but none of the others seem to be right after a more thorough examination, go back and look again at the ones you eliminated. If you look at all the choices twice and still none of them seem to match, move to the next question; you can come back to it if you have time. If time is running out, go ahead and guess, since you're sure to miss the question if you don't mark any answer at all!

Let's try a practice problem.

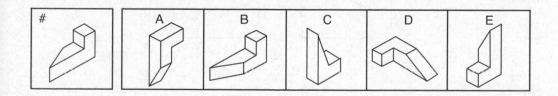

Okay, nothing jumps out as outstandingly right or wrong, so let's march through the choices one by one.

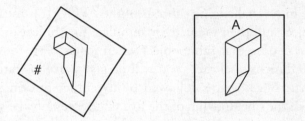

Nope, close but no cigar—this one seems to be a kind of twisted mirror image. Let's look at B.

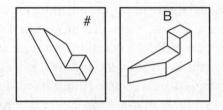

Nope, even worse—though we can't really show it on this two-dimensional page, you can see that when you bring the beveled edge of the example drawing "down" toward you, the angled cut will be on the top side, whereas in choice B the angled cut is on the right side as we face the drawing. And, when that's done, the square block sticking out from the side will be on the side, and not on the top as in choice B. Keep going . . .

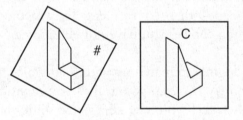

Same thing here—the block sticking out is on the wrong side, and the angled cut is different.

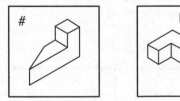

Well, the angled cut on these two is okay, but again, the square block sticking out is on the wrong side. That means it must be E, right? Well, let's check it out, just to be sure.

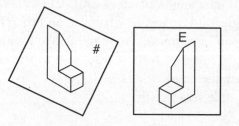

Well, choice E is no good, either—once again, the small square block sticking out on the wrong side is a clear indicator once you have the long portion with the angled cut oriented similarly to choice E. So, is "none of the above" a choice?

Wait a minute—something's bugging me about choice A. Let's look at it again.

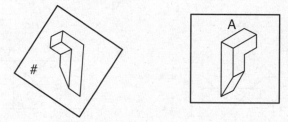

Hey, if we take the example figure and flip it over (mentally) toward us so that the angled cut is oriented properly, the square block sticking out is on the right side, too. So, the answer really is Choice A. Good thing we double-checked, right?

Hidden Figures

The Hidden Figures subtest measures your ability to identify a simple figure hidden within a complex drawing. You will be given a series of five lettered figures—A, B, C, D, and E—followed by five numbered drawings. Your objective is to determine which lettered figure is contained within which numbered drawing. Each numbered drawing contains only one of the lettered figures, and the correct figure in each numbered drawing is always the same size and in the same rotational position as it appears in the preceding lettered figure. However, you may find the lettered shape in more than one drawing, or you may not find it at all—in other words, in each series of five, you may have one or more lettered figures that are not found, and others that are to be found more than once.

Sometimes you will be able to spot the figure in the drawing quickly, and sometimes it will take significant study. The drawing with the hidden figures often has overlapping shapes and lines that can create optical illusions, or at a minimum, mask the shape you are looking for. If you can spot the figure quickly, mark that answer on your answer sheet. However, it's not always easy to spot the hidden figures; it requires trial and error, and sometimes even the process of elimination.

The best technique to use here is to let your eye focus briefly on the figure you want to find, and then look at the numbered drawing. Think of it as letting a bloodhound sniff something belonging to the person you want him to search for or track. If you don't see the figure you're looking for in the first numbered drawing, refocus briefly on the shape to be found and go to the next numbered drawing, and so on until you find the shape. Then mark that answer on your answer sheet.

It can also be helpful, especially when you are searching for a complex shape, to focus your search on unique angles or other unusual facets of the figure. If you can find that particular angle, odd corner, or whatever, and then find it in the numbered drawing, chances are you have found the shape you're looking for—but be sure to confirm that the rest of the figure is there, too, and in the same size and rotational position as in the lettered example.

Let's look at an example series of five:

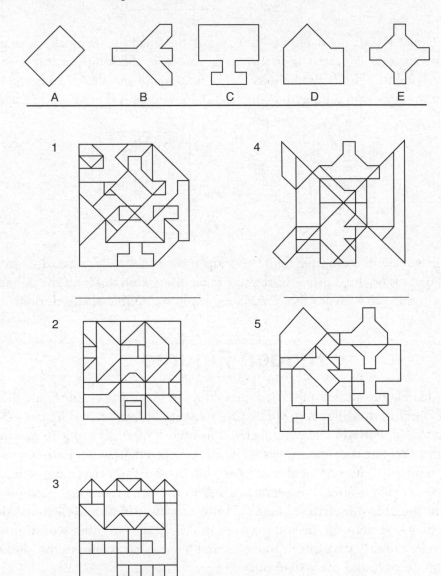

How did you do? The correct answers are as follows:

1. **A**
2. **B**
3. **C**
4. **B**
5. **D**

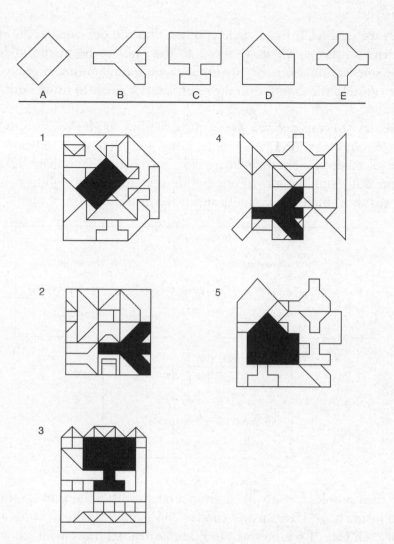

Complex Movements

The 30 questions in the Complex Movements subtest of the AFAST measure your ability to estimate distance and visualize motion. You are shown five pairs of symbols that represent a combination of distance and direction (one symbol in each pair represents distance, and the other direction). Your objective is to select the pair of symbols that represents the appropriate distance and direction to move a dot from outside a circle into the center of that circle. You will have only five minutes to complete this subtest, which comes out to just ten seconds per problem. However, with the practice you get here, you should be able to master this task sufficiently to do well on test day.

The first component of these questions is the circle and the dot.

You can see in the left-hand circle and dot that the dot outside the circle—the one you have to move—needs to move to the right to be in the middle of the circle. The smaller dot that is already in the circle is only meant to give you a point at which to aim. In the example on the right, the dot needs to move both down and to the left.

Now we have to consider *how far* to move the heavier dot to get it in the center of the circle. On the AFAST, you will be given a key like the one below that gives you three distances in approximately 1/8″ increments. You have to determine whether the dot should be moved one eighth of an inch, two eighths of an inch, or three eighths of an inch, horizontally and/or vertically.

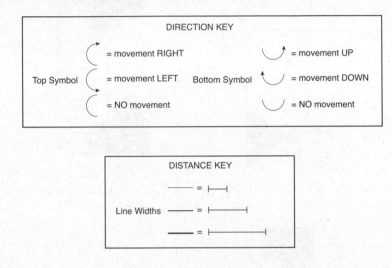

So, for each problem, you will be given a circle with a dot outside it that has to be moved inside it, and five answer choices consisting of pairs of symbols. The top symbol of each pair of symbols will indicate horizontal movement (movement left or right to get into the circle), and the bottom one will indicate vertical movement (movement up or down) needed to get the dot into the center of the circle. In both cases, the thickness of the curved lines indicates *how much* movement must be made—you can think of the three distance-indicating line widths as "a little bit," "some," and "a lot," if you want, but keep in mind that each increment represents only about an eighth of an inch. There's only so much room on the paper!

Also notice that there is a possibility of no movement needed in one or both categories; this is indicated by a line with no arrowhead on either end.

Now let's look at an example and walk through the best way to approach this kind of problem.

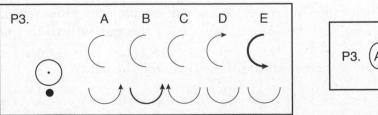 

We can see in the example problem above that the dot does not need to move left or right, but does need to move up a little. Remember that the answer key shows you that the top symbol deals with horizontal (left or right) movement, so let's look at that first. Since we don't need to move any left or right, we should consider only choices that show no movement (a thin, no-arrowhead line) as the top symbol; this lets us throw out choices D and E right away.

Now, of the remaining choices A, B, and C, which choices show movement going upward? Looking at the key, we see that movement upward is indicated by an arrowhead on the right-hand side of the curved line; this lets us eliminate choice C, since it has an arrowhead on the left-hand side of the curved line, indicating downward movement.

Of the two remaining choices, A and B, which shows upward movement of about an eighth of an inch ("a little")? This is choice A, because the distance indicated by the thicker curved line in choice B would move the dot above the center of the circle. Thus we see that choice A is the correct answer.

Cyclic Orientation

The Cyclic Orientation portion of the AFAST is a test of your ability to recognize simple changes in helicopter position and to indicate the corresponding cyclic (control stick) movement (see p. 176). Each question presents a series of three sequential pictures that represents the pilot's changing view through the cockpit windshield. The three pictures change from top to bottom, showing the pilot's view in a climb, dive, bank to the left or right, or a combination of these maneuvers. For purposes of simplicity in this test, the helicopter is assumed to have a constant engine power setting, and the cyclic is the only control mechanism considered. Your task is to determine which position the cyclic would be in to perform the maneuver shown.

The AFAST test has 15 questions of this type, which you have five minutes to answer; this means that you have an average of only about 20 seconds to answer each question, so preparation and practice beforehand will be extra important.

For purposes of this test, this is how the cyclic positions are indicated:

- To bank left, move the cyclic to the left.
- To bank right, move the cyclic to the right.
- To dive, push the cyclic forward.
- To climb, pull the cyclic back.
- To bank left and dive, push the cyclic to the front left.
- To bank right and dive, push the cyclic to the front right.
- To bank left and climb, pull the cyclic back and to the left.
- To bank right and climb, pull the cyclic back and to the right.

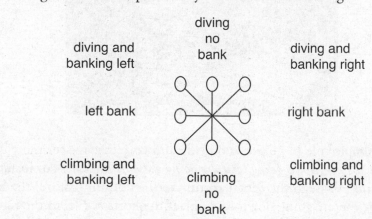

Accompanying each series of pictures is an illustration that you mark to indicate which position the cyclic should be in to answer the question. Just above is an illustration of the cyclic movement diagram and an indication of what each circle means. You are asked to fill in the circle that indicates in which direction you would move the cyclic to perform the maneuver indicated in the series of pictures.

Now let's work through a practice problem.

There is a simple rule to help you quickly and correctly answer these questions: *whichever way the horizon is going, you are going the opposite way.* For instance, if (as in the top picture through the center picture to the bottom picture) the horizon is going up, then you are going down (diving). If the horizon tilts to the right, or the "scenery" in the cockpit window moves from the left to the right, you are turning or banking to the left. So, in this example, as the horizon goes up and the right side of it goes down, you are diving and banking to the left.

That said, let's look at the example on the previous page. In it, starting at the first (top) picture and moving to the third (bottom) picture, the horizon both goes up and tilts to the right; therefore, you are diving and banking to the left, so your answer would look like this:

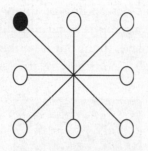

Another technique that may help you is to identify a significant topographical feature or landmark—an oddly shaped bend in the river, a distinctive building, a particularly noticeable building—and track its progress through the series of three pictures. In some pictures, it's possible that the horizon may not be easily distinguishable, either because of the things in the picture itself or the print quality of the test paper; you can use the placement and attitude (which way the feature is oriented) of the feature you choose as either a primary or secondary clue to which way the aircraft is going.

Spatial Apperception

The Spatial Apperception Test portion of the Navy and Marine Corps' ASTB measures your ability to perceive spatial relationships from differing orientations. The military uses scores from this subtest in calculating the Pilot Flight Aptitude Rating (PFAR) and the Flight Officer Flight Aptitude Rating (FOFAR). Specifically, this test measures your ability to determine the attitude or position of an airplane in flight by examining a representation of the view through the cockpit windshield. Studies have indicated for decades that skill in determining spatial orientation has a significant role in predicting success in flight training.

On the test, you will be presented with an aerial view of the horizon (as if you were in an airplane cockpit) and five drawings labeled A, B, C, D, and E showing planes flying in different attitudes relative to a coastline. Your task for each question is to determine which drawing of a plane in flight correctly matches the attitude that would result in the view that the pilot sees from the cockpit. The planes might be climbing, diving, banking, flying level, flying along the coastline or at an angle to it, flying out to sea or in to land, and so on. You are considered to be looking out from the middle of your windscreen (the front part of the canopy, directly in front of the pilot).

You should look for three important things as you answer the questions: whether the airplane is climbing or diving (pitch); whether the plane is "wings level" or banking left or right; and the airplane's heading (where it's going). If you use a systematic approach of analyzing the drawing representing the pilot's view from the cockpit, you will be less likely to get confused.

The first thing you should look for to determine pitch is the position of the horizon, which indicates whether the plane is climbing, diving, or in level flight. If the horizon is above the middle of the picture, the plane is diving or descending. If it's below the middle, the plane is climbing. If the horizon is about in the middle of the picture and level, the plane is in level flight. Or, another way to think of this is to compare the area above and below the horizon line. If there is more area above the horizon than below, the plane is climbing. If there is more area underneath the horizon than above it, the plane is descending or diving. And, if the area above and below are about the same, the aircraft is in level flight. This technique is especially helpful when the airplane is in level flight but is banking one way or the other, causing the horizon to appear to tilt accordingly relative to the edges of the picture.

Key

Dark Gray = Water
Light Gray = Land

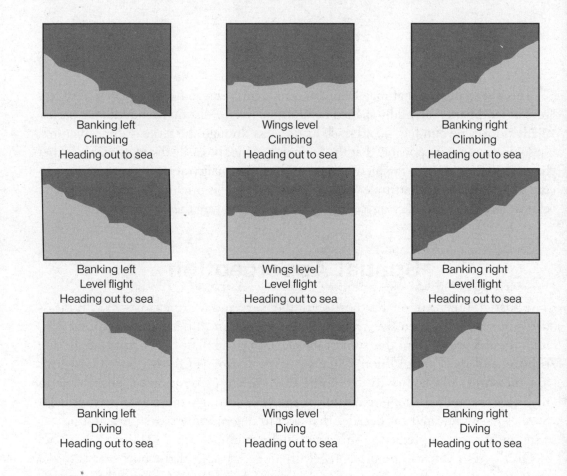

The next factor to consider is the horizon. If it's tilted to the left, the airplane is banking to the right; if the horizon is tilted to the right, the airplane is banking to the left. If the horizon is level—tilted neither left nor right—then the plane is in level flight, not banking either left or right.

The third thing to look for is the aircraft's heading (which direction it's going): out to sea, in from the sea, or along the coastline. This will be indicated by the representation of the land and water at the bottom of each of the five answer choices showing the airplane in flight. The lighter section is the land and the darker part represents the sea or ocean.

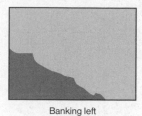

Banking left
Diving
Heading in to land

Wings level
Diving
Heading in to land

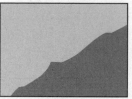

Banking right
Diving
Heading in to land

Key

Dark Gray = Water
Light Gray = Land

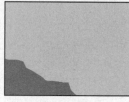

Banking left
Level flight
Heading in to land

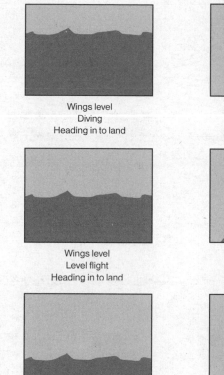

Wings level
Level flight
Heading in to land

Banking right
Level flight
Heading in to land

Banking left
Climbing
Heading in to land

Wings level
Climbing
Heading in to land

Banking right
Climbing
Heading in to land

Wings level
Level flight
Heading along coast

Now that we've discussed the view from the cockpit, let's talk about matching those views up to the external view of the airplane (looking at it from the outside).

Again, you have to approach this in a systematic way to maximize your chances for success. Determining whether the airplane is climbing, level, or diving is easy—if the nose is angled up relative to the page, then it's climbing; if it's headed straight across the page, it's level; if it's angled downward, then it's diving.

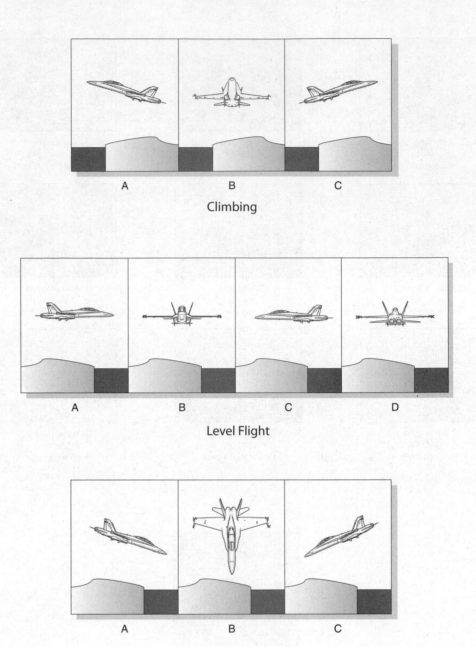

Determining the airplane's bank (or lack thereof) is as simple as seeing if the wings are level or not. If one wing is lower than the other, then that is the direction of bank.

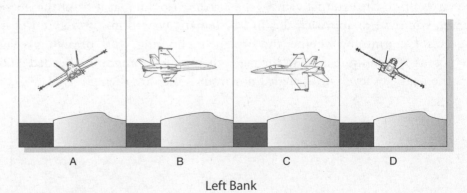

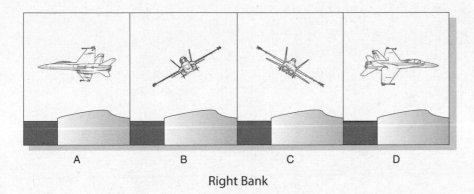

A   B   C   D

Right Bank

To determine whether the airplane is heading out to sea or in to land, look at the land and water "bar" at the bottom of the illustration. If the lighter section underneath the airplane is on the right side of the picture and the nose of the airplane is pointed to the left, then the airplane is headed out to sea. Or, to look at it another way, if the pilot's viewpoint picture has sea above land with the horizon line and coastline parallel to each other, you are heading out to sea.

If the lighter segment underneath the airplane drawing is on the left side of the picture and the nose of the airplane is pointed to the left, then the airplane is headed toward land. Said differently, if the picture has land above sea, with the horizon line and coastline parallel to each other, you are heading in to land.

If the horizon line and coastline are perpendicular to each other you are heading down the coast. Here you just need to be aware of which way the coastline is—to your left or right—to make sure that you select the correct external view of the airplane.

And, if the horizon line and coastline are neither parallel nor perpendicular, then you are heading at a 45-degree angle relative to the coastline, either heading in to land or out to sea.

PART III:
FLIGHT APTITUDE
QUALIFICATION TESTS

Practice Air Force Officer Qualifying Test (AFOQT) #1

TEST FORMAT

The Air Force Officer Qualifying Test (AFOQT) measures aptitudes used by the U.S. Air Force to select candidates for officer commissioning programs and specific officer training programs.

As discussed in Chapter 3, the AFOQT consists of 12 timed subtests. The scores from the particular subtests are combined in different ways to generate one or more of five composite scores used to help predict success in selected USAF training programs.

Subtest	# of Items	Time Allowed (mins)
1. Verbal Analogies (VA)	25	8
2. Arithmetic Reasoning (AR)	25	29
3. Word Knowledge (WK)	25	5
4. Math Knowledge (MK)	25	22
5. Instrument Comprehension (IC)	20	6
6. Block Counting (BC)	20	3
7. Table Reading (TR)	40	7
8. Aviation Information (AI)	20	8
9. General Science (GS)	20	10
10. Rotated Blocks (RB)	15	13
11. Hidden Figures (HF)	15	8
12. Self-Description Inventory (SDI)	220	40

The five composite scores derived from the AFOQT subtest scores and the kinds of abilities and knowledge they measure are as follows:

1. **Pilot** (AR + MK + IC + TR + AI) This composite measures some of the abilities and knowledge the Air Force considers necessary for successful completion of pilot training. The PILOT composite includes subtests that measure quantitative ability, knowledge of aeronautical concepts, the ability to determine aircraft attitude from instruments, and perceptual speed (how fast the candidate figures things out).

2. **Navigator-Technical** (VA + AR + MC + BC + TR + GS) This composite score measures some of the abilities and knowledge considered necessary for successful completion of navigator training. It shares some subtests with the PILOT composite, but tests that measure aeronautical knowledge and ability to determine aircraft attitude from instruments are not included. However, additional subtests measure verbal aptitude, perceptual speed, some spatial abilities, and general science knowledge.

3. **Academic Aptitude** (VA + AR + WK + MK) The ACADEMIC APTITUDE composite measures verbal and quantitative abilities and knowledge. It also combines all subtests that make up the VERBAL and QUANTITATIVE composites.

4. **Verbal** (VA + WK) The VERBAL composite measures verbal knowledge and abilities using subtests that measure the ability to reason, to recognize relationships between words, and to understand synonyms.

5. **Quantitative** (AR + MK) This composite measures math-related abilities and knowledge. It shares subtests with the NAVIGATOR-TECHNICAL subtest discussed above, and has subtests that measure the ability to understand and reason with arithmetic relationships, as well as using mathematical terms, formulas, and relationships.

SUBTEST #1: VERBAL ANALOGIES (25 QUESTIONS)

This part of the test measures your ability to reason and see relationships between words. Choose the answer that best completes the analogy developed at the beginning of each question.

1. GLOVE is to HAND as SHOE is to

   (A) SOCK.
   (B) LEG.
   (C) FOOT.
   (D) TOE.
   (E) HORSE.

2. AIRCRAFT is to FLY as BOAT is to

   (A) STEER.
   (B) SINK.
   (C) SHIP.
   (D) LAND.
   (E) SAIL.

3. PLAN is to STRATEGY as FIGHT is to

   (A) STRUGGLE.
   (B) HIT.
   (C) BLOW.
   (D) BATTLE.
   (E) CONQUER.

4. TRAVEL is to DESTINATION as WORK is to

   (A) GOAL.
   (B) OFFICE.
   (C) LABOR.
   (D) LEISURE.
   (E) COMMUTE.

5. PLOW is to FIELD as RACQUET is to

   (A) BALL.
   (B) COURT.
   (C) GANGSTER.
   (D) HAND.
   (E) JUDGE.

6. SALUTE is to RESPECT as HUG is to

   (A) SQUEEZE.
   (B) GESTURE.
   (C) ARM.
   (D) EMBRACE.
   (E) AFFECTION.

7. GRAVITY is to PLANET as ODOR is to

   (A) SKUNK.
   (B) AROMA.
   (C) NOSE.
   (D) DEATH.
   (E) SIGHT.

8. FISHING ROD is to HOOK as KNIFE is to

   (A) BLADE.
   (B) BULLET.
   (C) CUT.
   (D) STEAK.
   (E) HANDLE.

9. BOOT is to HIKE as VISOR is to

   (A) FACE.
   (B) SUIT.
   (C) MOTORCYCLE.
   (D) HEAD.
   (E) WELD.

10. PUSH is to SHOVE as CLIMB is to

    (A) MOUNTAIN.
    (B) FALL.
    (C) WALK.
    (D) LINGER.
    (E) CLAMBER.

11. GROW is to MATURE as BLOOM is to

    (A) ROSE.
    (B) PETAL.
    (C) FLOURISH.
    (D) DECAY.
    (E) BLOSSOM.

12. FUSELAGE is to BODY as

    (A) TURRET is to TANK .
    (B) LIFT is to DRAG.
    (C) DIVING is to FALLING.
    (D) WOOD is to OAK.
    (E) COMPASS is to DIRECTION.

13. CLIMB is to RISE as DIVE is to

(A) SWIMMING POOL.
(B) ARC.
(C) FALL.
(D) DECREASE.
(E) SLIDE.

14. ROPE is to KNOT as THREAD is to

(A) SANDWICH.
(B) FABRIC.
(C) NEEDLE.
(D) SEWING.
(E) THIMBLE.

15. WATCH is to OBSERVE as SWITCH is to

(A) LIGHT FIXTURE.
(B) RAILROAD TRACK.
(C) HIDE.
(D) MOVE.
(E) REPLACE.

16. OBEY is to COMPLY as REPLY is to

(A) QUESTION.
(B) STATEMENT.
(C) ANSWER.
(D) REPOSE.
(E) REWIND.

17. HONOR is to HONESTY as TRUST is to

(A) DEPENDABILITY.
(B) TREASON.
(C) PROMPTNESS.
(D) INTELLIGENCE.
(E) EMPATHY.

18. SPEED is to DECELERATION as VELOCITY is to

(A) DISTANCE.
(B) THRUST.
(C) RAPIDITY.
(D) BRAKING.
(E) URGENCY.

19. COMPRESSION is to RAREFACTION as DENSE is to

(A) THIN.
(B) APOGEE.
(C) IGNORANT.
(D) COMPACTED.
(E) PROTECTION.

20. DELAY is to POSTPONE as PREVENT is to

(A) DETER.
(B) DISCOURAGE.
(C) OFFEND.
(D) DEFEND.
(E) SWITCH.

21. ADD is to SUBTRACT as GROW is to

(A) DECAY.
(B) MATURE.
(C) SHRINK.
(D) HEIGHT.
(E) DIVIDE.

22. LEFT is to PORT as RIGHT is to

(A) STARBOARD.
(B) DEPARTED.
(C) HARBOR.
(D) RED.
(E) GREEN.

23. ODOMETER is to DISTANCE as ALTIMETER is to

(A) ALTITUDE.
(B) DISTANCE.
(C) FUEL.
(D) INSTRUMENT.
(E) READOUT.

24. ELEVATOR is to HEIGHT as THRUST is to

(A) STAIRWAY.
(B) CLIMBING.
(C) ROCKET.
(D) ALTITUDE.
(E) FLIGHT.

25. LOOK is to INSPECT as ARRIVE is to

(A) DEPART.
(B) TRAVEL.
(C) LOCATE.
(D) ATTEND.
(E) NOTICE.

SUBTEST #2: ARITHMETIC REASONING (25 QUESTIONS)

This part of the test measures your ability to use arithmetic to solve problems. Each problem is followed by five possible answers. You are to decide which of the choices is most nearly correct.

1. A theater contains x rows, with y seats in each row. How many total seats are there in the theater?

   (A) $x + y$
   (B) $x - y$
   (C) xy
   (D) $y - x$
   (E) $2x + y$

2. The sticker price of a new pickup truck was increased from $22,399 to $23,999 over last year's model. What was the approximate percentage of increase?

   (A) 1.07%
   (B) 7.1%
   (C) 9.3%
   (D) 71.4%
   (E) 93.3%

3. During one season, a high school football quarterback attempted 82 passes and completed 57 of them. What is his completion percentage?

   (A) 30.4%
   (B) 69.5%
   (C) 43.8%
   (D) 81.7%
   (E) 143.9%

4. Jaycie Marie has a 20-year term life insurance policy for $100,000. The annual premium is $12.00 per thousand. What is the total premium paid for this policy every six months?

   (A) $600
   (B) $1,200
   (C) $100
   (D) $2,400
   (E) $24,000

5. If 2 pounds of smoked deli turkey breast cost $13.98, what is the cost of a 5-oz. portion?

   (A) $0.44
   (B) $0.87
   (C) $1.40
   (D) $2.20
   (E) $4.36

6. If five shirts and four ties cost $173 and each tie costs $12, what is the cost of a shirt?

   (A) $15.00
   (B) $22.60
   (C) $32.20
   (D) $19.22
   (E) $25.00

7. What is the volume of a container that is 23 feet long, 15 feet wide, and 11 feet high?

   (A) 2,530 sq. ft
   (B) 3,450 cu. ft.
   (C) 3,795 sq. ft.
   (D) 3,795 cu. ft.
   (E) 5,280 cu. ft

8. The sister of a high school football player spent $119 on tickets for her family and friends to a playoff game. If tickets were $7 and $10, and she bought an equal number of both kinds of tickets, how many $7 tickets did she buy?

   (A) 4
   (B) 5
   (C) 7
   (D) 11
   (E) 17

9. Amanda earns an average of $22 an hour in tips as a waitress at the best steak restaurant in town. If her hourly wage is $2.50 and she has to pay a 10% tip share to the hostesses and busboys, how much does she take home at the end of a day when she worked from 10:30 A.M. to 5:30 P.M.?

   (A) $32.90
   (B) $121.11
   (C) $138.60
   (D) $156.10
   (E) $171.50

10. For a live performance of *The Nutcracker*, 76% of a 500-seat theater was occupied, and three-quarters of those attending were adults. How many children saw the performance?

    (A) 95
    (B) 100
    (C) 76
    (D) 285
    (E) 350

11. Jonathan spent four hours studying, one hour raking leaves, 30 minutes doing laundry, and two hours watching TV. What percentage of his time was spent studying?

    (A) 46.6%
    (B) 50.0%
    (C) 53.3%
    (D) 57.1%
    (E) 66.6%

12. June found a chandelier for the dining room for $1,400. However, since the model had been discontinued and the display had no factory packaging material, the store manager discounted the price to $1,150. What was the percentage of the reduction?

    (A) 1.78%
    (B) 13.0%
    (C) 15.0%
    (D) 17.9%
    (E) 21.7%

13. Heather bought a rectangular Persian rug with a perimeter measurement of 45 feet. If the long sides measure 15 feet each, how long is each short side of the rug?

    (A) 7.5 ft.
    (B) 10 ft.
    (C) 12.5 ft.
    (D) 15 ft.
    (E) 20 ft.

14. In a flooring outlet, four customer service representatives each receive $320 a week, and two sales managers each earn $12 per hour plus an average $100 per day commission. What is the average total weekly compensation paid to these six employees for a five-day, 40-hour work week?

    (A) $2,420
    (B) $3,240
    (C) $2,260
    (D) $4,520
    (E) $7,080

15. A submarine sails x miles the first day, y miles the second day, and z miles the third day. What is the average number of miles sailed per day?

    (A) $3xyz$
    (B) $3 \cdot (x + y + z)$
    (C) $(x + y + z) \div 3$
    (D) $(x + y + z)$
    (E) $xyz/3$

16. If a train can travel 500 miles in five hours, how far can it travel in 15 minutes?

    (A) 25 miles
    (B) 30 miles
    (C) 57 miles
    (D) 125 miles
    (E) 167 miles

17. Which of these is an example of similar figures?

    (A) a pen and a pencil
    (B) a motorcycle and a car
    (C) a bicycle and a motorcycle
    (D) an airplane and a scale model of that airplane
    (E) an equilateral triangle and an isosceles triangle

18. Upon his death, a man's life insurance policies paid $750,000 to his wife and three children. The policies were set up to pay the wife and children in the ratio of 5:1:1:1. How much did the children receive altogether?

    (A) $150,000
    (B) $200,000
    (C) $468,750
    (D) $250,000
    (E) $281,250

19. Although an air assault infantry company has 131 soldiers authorized, A Company has only 125 total soldiers assigned, of whom 4 percent are officers. How many enlisted soldiers are assigned to the company?

    (A) 114
    (B) 123
    (C) 120
    (D) 121
    (E) 126

20. An electronics store owner buys 20 DVD players for the listed wholesale price of $80 apiece, but receives a 25% discount because he is a frequent customer of the wholesale dealer. He sells these DVD players at a 20% markup above the original wholesale price. What is his profit on each DVD player?

    (A) $16
    (B) $720
    (C) $20
    (D) $360
    (E) $36

21. A mapmaker is told to prepare a map with a scale of 1 inch = 50 miles. If the actual ground distance between two points is 120 miles, how far apart should the mapmaker show them on the map?

    (A) 0.4 in.
    (B) 2.4 in.
    (C) 1.2 in.
    (D) 4.8 in.
    (E) 8.4 in.

22. In the city of Woodway, houses are assessed at 80% of the purchase price. If Mr. Thomas buys a house in Woodway for $120,000 and real estate taxes are $4.75 per $100 of assessed valuation, how much property tax must he pay per year?

    (A) $3,648
    (B) $5,472
    (C) $4,560
    (D) $4,845
    (E) $5,700

23. The fuel tank of a gasoline generator has enough capacity to operate the generator for one hour and 15 minutes. About how many times must the fuel tank be filled to run the generator from 6:15 P.M. to 7:00 A.M.?

    (A) 9.4
    (B) 10.2
    (C) 10.8
    (D) 11.5
    (E) 12.0

24. When a highway was converted from nonpaid to a toll road, the traffic declined from 11,200 cars per day to 10,044. What was the percent of the decline in traffic?

    (A) 10.3%
    (B) 11.5%
    (C) 10.1%
    (D) 8.9%
    (E) 79.3%

25. On Mr. Lee's trip, he first drives for two hours at 70 miles per hour. He then drives for another one and a half hours at 65 miles per hour. If his car gets 25 miles per gallon on the highway in this speed range, how many gallons of gas did he use for the trip?

    (A) 5.4 gals.
    (B) 8.2 gals.
    (C) 8.4 gals.
    (D) 9.5 gals.
    (E) 11.2 gals.

SUBTEST #3: WORD KNOWLEDGE (25 QUESTIONS)

This part of the test measures verbal comprehension involving your ability to understand written language. For each question choose the answer that means the same as the capitalized word.

1. TACIT

    (A) silent
    (B) sour
    (C) ornament
    (D) talkative
    (E) pleasing

2. ALTITUDE

    (A) direction
    (B) old saying
    (C) demeanor
    (D) height
    (E) distance

3. PORTEND

    (A) feign
    (B) give warning beforehand
    (C) develop pores or holes
    (D) assume a pose
    (E) inhabit

4. ITINERARY

    (A) migrant
    (B) not permanent
    (C) cure-all
    (D) schedule
    (E) character

5. VEXATIOUS

    (A) annoying
    (B) contagious
    (C) at a high volume
    (D) insatiably hungry
    (E) having a moral fault

6. EQUIVALENT

    (A) complicated
    (B) inferior
    (C) superior
    (D) evident
    (E) equal

7. CRITERION

    (A) standard
    (B) disaster
    (C) environment
    (D) criticism
    (E) excerpt

8. MERCURIAL

    (A) having compassion
    (B) specious
    (C) unpredictably changeable
    (D) metallic
    (E) containing mercury

9. CRITICAL

    (A) conversational
    (B) influencing
    (C) dying
    (D) less worthy
    (E) most important

10. TELEMETRY

    (A) mental communication
    (B) marketing goods or services by telephone
    (C) transmission of measurements made by automatic instruments
    (D) study of climactic variations
    (E) rashness, audacity

11. ANTAGONIST

    (A) ally
    (B) main character
    (C) soothing to the stomach
    (D) adversary
    (E) one who causes pain

12. DIAGNOSE

    (A) predict the outcome
    (B) cut in two
    (C) identify a situation
    (D) antagonize
    (E) speak about

13. KINETIC

    (A) relating to the motion of material bodies
    (B) referring to motion pictures
    (C) moving at a high speed
    (D) relating to sensory experience
    (E) referring to a relative

14. RECTIFY

    (A) dealing with the digestive system
    (B) cause trouble or havoc
    (C) get back
    (D) correct
    (E) give fresh life to

15. CAMOUFLAGE

    (A) substitute
    (B) conceal
    (C) redeem
    (D) divide
    (E) twist

16. EQUIVOCAL

    (A) equal
    (B) poised
    (C) overlapping
    (D) removed
    (E) evasive

17. CENTRIPETAL

    (A) away from a center or axis
    (B) relating to the feet
    (C) having more than 100 petals
    (D) toward a center or axis
    (E) circular

18. DISCONSOLATE

    (A) hopelessly sad
    (B) cease using
    (C) rearrange sloppily
    (D) uncover
    (E) recognize mentally

19. ANACHRONISTIC

    (A) chronologically out of place
    (B) cursed
    (C) dealing with organism structure
    (D) attribution of conscious thought to inanimate
        objects or animals
    (E) existing before a war

20. MODULATE

    (A) speak
    (B) decay
    (C) dry out
    (D) adjust
    (E) develop a mannerism

21. PICAYUNE

    (A) unnoticed
    (B) insignificant
    (C) intense
    (D) hot
    (E) unfortunate

22. TENACIOUS

    (A) annoying
    (B) persistent
    (C) religious
    (D) hot-tempered
    (E) cowardly

23. ENTENTE

    (A) relaxation of tensions
    (B) volition
    (C) agreement providing for joint action
    (D) freedom of entry or access
    (E) concentrated

24. REDUNDANT

    (A) brilliant
    (B) held back
    (C) repetitive
    (D) unruly
    (E) isolated

25. RECONNAISSANCE

    (A) surveying expedition
    (B) responsibility
    (C) obligation
    (D) resolution of differences
    (E) rebirth

SUBTEST #4: MATHEMATICS KNOWLEDGE (25 QUESTIONS)

This part of the test measures your ability to use learned mathematical relationships. Each problem is followed by five possible answers. Decide which one of the five answers is most nearly correct.

1. The expression "4 factorial" or 4! means

   (A) $\frac{1}{4}$

   (B) $\frac{1}{24}$
   (C) –2
   (D) 10
   (E) 24

2. An airplane is flying a circular or "racetrack" orbit around a 4,000-meter-high mountaintop. Assume the pilot flies a perfectly circular course. What is the distance in kilometers he travels each orbit if it is 40 kilometers from the mountaintop to the outer edge of his orbit? (use pi = $\frac{22}{7}$).

   (A) 13 km
   (B) 25 km
   (C) 126 km
   (D) 251 km
   (E) 503 km

3. The reciprocal of 7 to the nearest thousandth is

   (A) 0.143
   (B) 1.428
   (C) 14
   (D) 21
   (E) 49

4. The second digit of the square of 525 is

   (A) 2
   (B) 5
   (C) 6
   (D) 7
   (E) 0

5. The area of a square with a perimeter of 40 yards is

   (A) 100 sq. ft.
   (B) 180 sq. yds.
   (C) 300 sq. ft.
   (D) 300 sq. yds.
   (E) 900 sq. ft.

6. Solve the following equations for x.

   $$5x + 4y = 27$$
   $$x - 2y = 11$$

   (A) $x = \frac{5}{3}$
   (B) $x = 4.5$
   (C) $x = 9$
   (D) $x = 7$
   (E) $x = -3$

7. Find the square root of 85 correct to the nearest tenth.

   (A) 9.1
   (B) 9.2
   (C) 9.3
   (D) 9.4
   (E) 9.5

8. Solve for x: $8x - 2 - 5x = 8$

   (A) $x = 1.3$

   (B) $x = 3\frac{1}{3}$

   (C) $x = 2\frac{1}{2}$

   (D) $x = 7.0$
   (E) $x = -7.0$

9. $2(a - b) + 4(a + 3b) =$

   (A) $6a - 10b$
   (B) $6a + 2b$
   (C) $8a^2 + 2b^2$
   (D) $6a - 2b$
   (E) $6a + 10b$

10. Which of the following is the smallest prime number greater than 200?

   (A) 201
   (B) 205
   (C) 211
   (D) 214
   (E) 223

11. If a is a negative number, and ab is a positive number, then which of the following must be true?

(A) b is greater than a.
(B) a is greater than b.
(C) b is negative.
(D) b is positive.
(E) b is a whole integer

12. What is the product of $(a + 2)(a - 5)(a + 3)$?

(A) $a^3 + 2a^2 + 15a - 30$
(B) $a^3 + 6a^2 - 49$
(C) $a^3 - 19a - 30$
(D) $a^3 + 2a^2 - 15a + 30$
(E) $a^3 - 19a + 30$

13. Solve for z: $3z - 5 + 2z = 25 - 5z$

(A) $z = 1$
(B) $z = 3$
(C) $z = -3$
(D) $z = 0$
(E) no solution

14. An architect has won a contract to place a memorial sculpture at each of the corners of the Pentagon in Washington, D.C. How many sculptures will there be?

(A) 4
(B) 5
(C) 6
(D) 7
(E) 8

15. If one of the angles of a right triangle is 30 degrees, what are the measurements of the other two angles?

(A) 30 degrees, 120 degrees
(B) 60 degrees, 45 degrees
(C) 60 degrees, 90 degrees
(D) 45 degrees, 90 degrees
(E) 45 degrees, 120 degrees

16. Factor $x^2 - 11x + 30$

(A) $(x - 6), (x - 5)$
(B) $(x + 6), (x - 5)$
(C) $(x - 10), (x - 1)$
(D) $(x - 3), (x + 10)$
(E) $(x - 6), (y + 5)$

17. Solve $\dfrac{15a^3b^2c}{5abc}$

(A) $10abc$
(B) $3abc$
(C) $5a^2b^2$
(D) $3a^2b$
(E) $5a^2b^2c$

18. Two circles have the same center. If their radii are 7 cm and 10 cm, find the area that is part of the larger circle but not part of the smaller one.

(A) 3 sq cm
(B) 17 sq cm
(C) 51 pi sq cm
(D) 71 pi sq cm
(E) 91 pi sq cm

19. Amanda took five midterm tests for five different college classes; her average for all five tests was 88. That night at home, she could remember only her first four scores: 78, 86, 94, and 96. What was her score on the fifth test?

(A) 82
(B) 86
(C) 84
(D) 88
(E) 87

20. How many cubic yards of concrete are needed to make a concrete floor that measures $9' \times 12' \times 6''$?

(A) 2
(B) 18
(C) 54
(D) 210
(E) 648

21. A new wildlife preserve is laid out in a perfect circle with a radius of 14 kilometers. The lion habitat is shaped like a wedge and has an 8-foot-high razor wire fence around it. Two inner sides of the fence meet at a 90-degree angle in the center of the base. How much ground space (area) does the lion habitat have?

(A) 140 sq. km.
(B) 3.5 sq. km.
(C) 210 sq. km.
(D) 154 sq. km.
(E) 35 sq. km.

22. Factor $6x^2 + 3xy$.

    (A) $2x(3x - y)$
    (B) $x^2 + 3y$
    (C) $x + 3y$
    (D) $3x(2x + y)$
    (E) $6x(x + y)$

23. A cylindrical container has a radius of 7″ and a height of 15″. How many gallons of hydraulic fluid can it hold? (There are 231 cubic inches in a gallon.)

    (A) 15 gals.
    (B) 14 gals.
    (C) 140 gals.
    (D) 10 gals.
    (E) 23.1 gals.

24. A 10-foot-high ladder is resting against an 8-foot-high wall around a recreation area. If the top of the ladder is exactly even with the top of the wall, how far is the base of the ladder from the wall?

    (A) 18 ft.
    (B) 6 ft.
    (C) 12 ft.
    (D) 9 ft.
    (E) 8 ft.

25. A cook is mixing fruit juice from concentrate for a catered event. Ten ounces of liquid contain 20% fruit juice and 80% water. He then further dilutes the mixture by adding 40 additional ounces of water. What is the percent of fruit juice in the new solution?

    (A) 4%
    (B) 10%
    (C) 14%
    (D) 18%
    (E) 20%

SUBTEST #5: INSTRUMENT COMPREHENSION (20 QUESTIONS)

This part of the test measures your ability to determine the position of an airplane in flight from reading instruments showing its compass heading (direction), amount of climb or dive, and degree of bank to the right or left. In each problem, the left-hand dial is labeled ARTIFICIAL HORIZON. On the face of the dial, the small aircraft fuselage silhouette remains stationary, whereas the positions of the white line and the white pointer vary with changes in the position of the aircraft in which the instrument is located.

The white line represents the HORIZON LINE. The white pointer shows the degree of BANK to the right or left.

If the airplane is neither climbing nor diving, the horizon line is directly on the fuselage silhouette, as in dial 1 below.

If the airplane is climbing, the fuselage silhouette is seen between the horizon line and the pointer, as shown in dial 2 below. The greater the amount of climb, the greater the distance between the horizon line and the fuselage silhouette.

If the airplane is diving, the horizon line is seen between the fuselage silhouette and the pointer, as shown in dial 3 below. The greater the amount of dive, the greater the distance between the horizon line and the fuselage silhouette.

ARTIFICIAL HORIZON

Dial 1

ARTIFICIAL HORIZON

Dial 2

ARTIFICIAL HORIZON

Dial 3

If the airplane has no bank, the white pointer is seen to point to zero, as in dial 1 above.

If the airplane is banked to the pilot's right, the pointer is seen to the left of zero, as in dial 2 above.

If the airplane is banked to the pilot's left, the pointer is seen to the right of zero, as in dial 3 above.

The HORIZON LINE tilts as the aircraft is banked and is always at right angles to the pointer.

Dial 1 above shows an airplane neither climbing nor diving, with no bank.
Dial 2 above shows an airplane climbing and banked 45° to the pilot's right.
Dial 3 above shows an airplane diving and banked 45° to the pilot's left.

In each problem, the right-hand dial is labeled COMPASS. On this dial, the nose of the plane shows the compass direction in which the airplane is headed. Dial 4 shows the airplane headed north, dial 5 shows it headed west, and dial 6 shows it headed northwest.

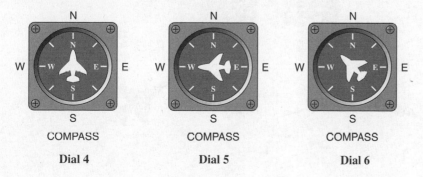

COMPASS   COMPASS   COMPASS

Dial 4   **Dial 5**   **Dial 6**

Each problem consists of two dials and four silhouettes of airplanes in flight. Your task is to determine which one of the four airplanes is MOST NEARLY in the position indicated by the two dials. You are always looking north at the same altitude as each of the four airplanes. East is always to your right as you look at the page. In the sample question below, the dial labeled ARTIFICIAL HORIZON shows that the airplane is NOT banked, and is neither climbing nor diving. The COMPASS shows that it is headed south. The only one of the four airplane silhouettes that meets these specifications is in the box lettered A, so the answer to the sample question is A.

ARTIFICIAL HORIZON   COMPASS

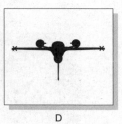

A   B   C   D

1.

ARTIFICIAL HORIZON   COMPASS

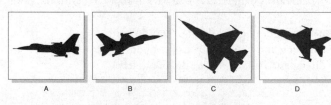

A   B   C   D

2.

ARTIFICIAL HORIZON   COMPASS

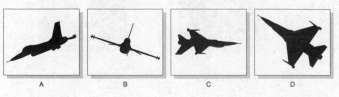

A   B   C   D

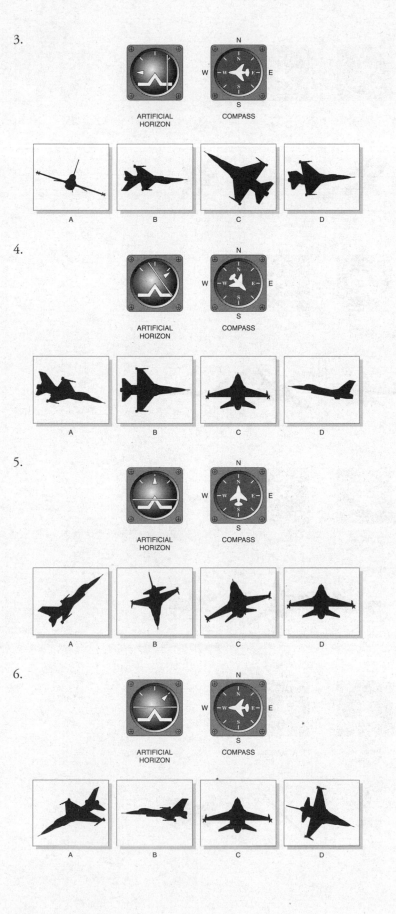

3.

ARTIFICIAL HORIZON   COMPASS

A   B   C   D

4.

ARTIFICIAL HORIZON   COMPASS

A   B   C   D

5.

ARTIFICIAL HORIZON   COMPASS

A   B   C   D

6.

ARTIFICIAL HORIZON   COMPASS

A   B   C   D

AFOQT #1

7.

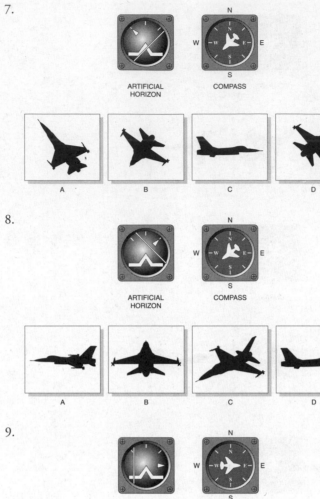

8.

9.

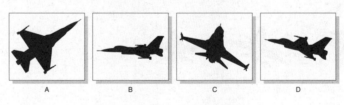

10.

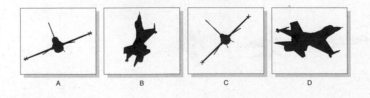

11.

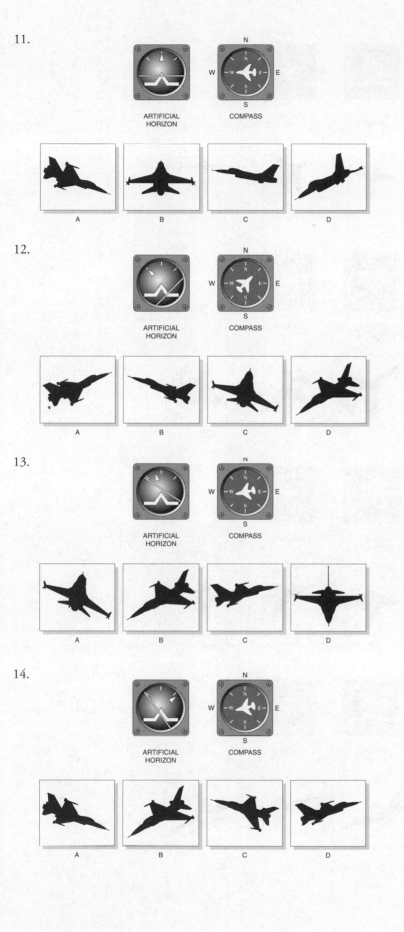

15.

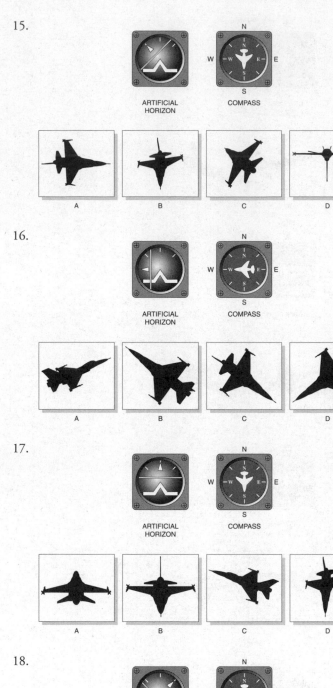

16.

17.

18.

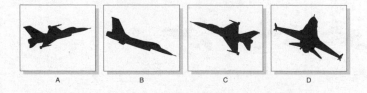

19.

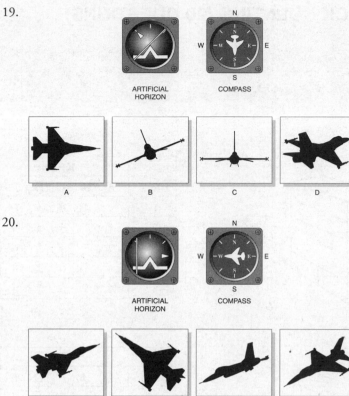

ARTIFICIAL HORIZON

COMPASS

A   B   C   D

20.

ARTIFICIAL HORIZON

COMPASS

A   B   C   D

SUBTEST #6: BLOCK COUNTING (20 QUESTIONS)

This part of the test measures your ability to "see into" a three-dimensional pile of blocks. Given a certain numbered block, your task is to determine how many other blocks it touches. *All of the blocks in each pile are the same size and shape.*

Questions 1–5

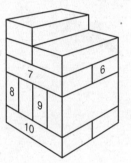

Block	KEY				
	A	B	C	D	E
1	2	3	4	5	6
2	1	2	3	4	5
3	2	3	4	5	6
4	4	5	6	7	8
5	4	5	6	7	8

Questions 6–10

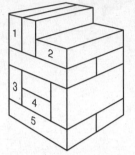

Block	KEY				
	A	B	C	D	E
6	4	5	6	7	8
7	3	4	5	6	7
8	4	5	6	7	8
9	4	5	6	7	8
10	2	3	4	5	6

Questions 11–15

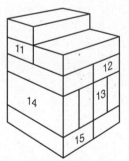

Block	KEY				
	A	B	C	D	E
11	3	4	5	6	7
12	3	4	5	6	7
13	3	4	5	6	7
14	3	4	5	6	7
15	2	3	4	5	6

Questions 16–20

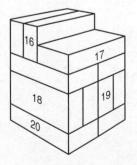

Block	KEY				
	A	B	C	D	E
16	3	4	5	6	7
17	2	3	4	5	6
18	3	4	5	6	7
19	3	4	5	6	7
20	1	2	3	4	5

SUBTEST #7: TABLE READING (40 QUESTIONS)

This part of the AFOQT measures your ability to read a table quickly and accurately. Questions 1–5 are based on the table below. Notice that the X values appear at the top of the table and the Y values are shown on the left side of the table. The X values are the column values and the Y values are the row values. For each test question, you are given an X value and a Y value; your task will be to find the box where the selected column and row meet, note the number that appears there, and then find that same number among the five answer options.

X VALUE

	−3	−2	−1	0	+1	+2	+3
+3	16	17	18	19	21	22	23
+2	19	20	22	23	23	24	25
+1	22	24	26	28	30	32	36
0	23	26	29	35	38	40	41
−1	24	26	28	30	32	34	36
−2	26	31	36	40	45	49	54
−3	28	31	34	37	40	43	46

Y VALUE (left side)

	X	Y	(A)	(B)	(C)	(D)	(E)
1.	+2	+1	34	32	24	21	49
2.	−1	0	26	30	35	28	29
3.	+3	−2	25	19	31	54	43
4.	+1	−3	40	18	34	21	22
5.	−2	−1	17	24	26	36	22

AFOQT #1

Questions 6–10 are based on the table below.

	Alpha Jet	F-1 Mirage	F-15 Eagle	F-16 Fighting Falcon	F/A-18 Hornet	FC-1	J-10	MiG-29	Su-27	Tornado	Eurofighter EF-2000 Typhoon
Australia					X						
Belarus								X	X		
Belgium	X			X							
Canada					X						
Cuba								X			
Egypt	X			X							
France	X	X									
Germany	X									X	X
Greece		X		X							
India								X			
Iran		X						X			
Israel			X	X							
Italy										X	X
Japan			X								
Kuwait		X			X						
Libya		X									
North Korea								X			
Pakistan						X	X				
People's Rep. of China						X	X		X		
Russia								X	X		
Saudi Arabia			X							X	
South Korea				X							
Spain		X		X	X						X
Taiwan			X								
Ukraine								X	X		
United Kingdom										X	X
United States of America			X	X	X						

6. According to this table, which countries currently use the F-15 Eagle?

    (A) France, Greece, Iran, Kuwait, Libya, Spain
    (B) Egypt, Greece, Israel, South Korea, Spain, USA
    (C) Israel, Japan, Saudi Arabia, Taiwan, USA
    (D) Israel, Japan, Kuwait, Saudi Arabia, Taiwan, USA
    (E) USA, Taiwan, Saudi Arabia, Greece, Egypt

7. Which fighters in this table are used by the People's Republic of China?

    (A) FC-1, J-10, Su-27
    (B) FC-1, J-10, MiG-29, Su-27
    (C) J-10, MiG-29, Su-27
    (D) FC-1, MiG-29, Su-27
    (E) FC-1, F-15, J-10, MiG-29, Su-27

8. Which countries do NOT use the F-1 Mirage?

   (A) Pakistan, Australia, Belarus, Canada, North Korea
   (B) Greece, North Korea, USA, Spain, Taiwan, Belgium
   (C) South Korea, Australia, Saudi Arabia, Libya, India
   (D) India, France, Pakistan, Iran, Ukraine, Belarus
   (E) Israel, Russia, USA, Italy, Australia, Kuwait

9. The MiG-29 is used by which of the following countries?

   (A) Belarus, Cuba, India, Iraq, North Korea, Russia
   (B) India, North Korea, Russia, Saudi Arabia, Libya
   (C) North Korea, Russia, India, Belarus, Israel, Japan
   (D) Russia, Cuba, India, Iran, North Korea, Belarus
   (E) Cuba, Russia, Iran, Iraq, India, North Korea

10. According to this table, which fighters are used by Spain?

    (A) F-1, F-15, F-18, EF-2000
    (B) Typhoon, Fighting Falcon, Mirage, Hornet
    (C) Hornet, Fighting Falcon, F-1, Tornado
    (D) F-16, F-18, Alpha, Tornado, EF-2000
    (E) Hornet, Mirage, EF-2000, Alpha

Questions 11–15 are based on the table below.

X VALUE

Y VALUE	-3	-2	-1	0	+1	+2	+3
+3	6	16	22	26	28	31	46
+2	13	15	17	19	21	23	25
+1	20	25	30	35	40	45	50
0	27	30	33	36	37	40	43
-1	34	36	38	40	42	44	45
-2	41	42	43	44	46	47	48
-3	47	58	69	80	91	102	203

	X	Y	(A)	(B)	(C)	(D)	(E)
11.	+3	-1	34	50	20	45	22
12.	-1	+2	17	43	46	40	15
13.	0	-3	26	36	80	27	40
14.	+2	-1	45	44	17	25	47
15.	-3	-2	41	13	48	25	58

Questions 16–20 are based on the table below.

COMMISSIONED OFFICERS MONTHLY BASE PAY

Pay Grade	<2 Yrs. SVC	2	3	4	6	8	10	12	14	16	18	20
O-10	0.00	0.00	0.00	0.00	0.00	0.00	0.00	0.00	0.00	0.00	0.00	13365.00
O-9	0.00	0.00	0.00	0.00	0.00	0.00	0.00	0.00	0.00	0.00	0.00	11689.50
O-8	8271.00	8541.90	8721.60	8772.00	8996.10	9371.10	9458.10	9814.20	9916.20	10222.80	10666.20	11075.40
O-7	6872.70	7191.90	7339.80	7457.10	7669.80	7879.50	8122.50	8364.90	8607.90	9371.10	10015.80	10015.80
O-6	5094.00	5596.20	5963.40	5963.40	5985.90	6242.70	6276.60	6276.60	6633.30	7263.90	7634.10	8004.00
O-5	4246.50	4783.50	5115.00	5177.10	5383.50	5507.40	5779.20	5978.70	6236.10	6630.60	6818.10	7003.80
O-4	3663.90	4241.40	4524.30	4587.60	4850.10	5131.80	5482.20	5755.80	5945.40	6054.30	6117.60	6117.60
O-3	3221.40	3651.90	3941.70	4297.50	4503.00	4728.90	4875.30	5115.90	5240.70	5240.70	5240.70	5240.70
O-2	2783.10	3170.10	3651.00	3774.30	3852.00	3852.00	3852.00	3852.00	3852.00	3852.00	3852.00	3852.00
O-1	2416.20	2514.60	3039.60	3039.60	3039.60	3039.60	3039.60	3039.60	3039.60	3039.60	3039.60	3039.60

16. What is the base pay for a second lieutenant (O-1) with three years' service?

    (A) $3,221.40
    (B) $2,514.60
    (C) $3,039.60
    (D) $3,651.00
    (E) $3,170.10

17. Based on this table, what is the maximum monthly base pay for a captain (O-3)?

    (A) $5,240.70
    (B) $6,117.60
    (C) $3,039.60
    (D) $4,875.30
    (E) $5,755.80

18. What is the base pay for a major (O-4) with 12 years' service?

    (A) $5,115.90
    (B) $5,755.80
    (C) $5,945.40
    (D) $5,978.70
    (E) $5,482.20

19. What is the minimum monthly base pay for a first lieutenant (O-2)?

    (A) $3,170.10
    (B) $2,514.60
    (C) $2,783.10
    (D) $2,416.20
    (E) $3,170.00

20. What is the monthly base pay for a colonel (O-6) with 18 years' service?

    (A) $7,634.00
    (B) $6,818.10
    (C) $7,634.10
    (D) $10,015.00
    (E) $7,263.90

Questions 21–25 are based on the table below.

X VALUE

		−3	−2	−1	0	+1	+2	+3
Y VALUE	+3	10.0	12.5	15.1	17.5	21.4	19.0	25.7
	+2	77	33	41	22.8	101	36	124
	+1	22.1	22.2	22.3	22.4	22.5	22.7	22.9
	0	0.75	0.77	0.79	0.82	0.60	0.86	0.89
	−1	1.7	2.77	3.14	6.1	7.3	8.5	9.9
	−2	3.3	101.20	40.00	49.04	136.8	36.40	124.02
	−3	21	33	59	78	25	34	15

	X	Y	(A)	(B)	(C)	(D)	(E)
21.	−1	+3	9.9	15.1	25	59	9.9
22.	+2	0	0.86	22.8	0.79	49.04	12.5
23.	−3	−2	3.3	124.02	124	77	33
24.	−2	0	0.86	49.04	22.8	0.77	78
25.	0	−1	22.4	0.79	6.1	49.04	1.7

AFOQT #1

Questions 26–30 are based on the table below.

inches Hg	mm Hg	millibars
26	660	880
26.5	673	897
27	686	914
27.5	699	931
28	711	948
28.5	724	965
29	737	982
29.5	749	999
30	762	1015
30.5	775	1033
31	787	1050
31.5	800	1066
32	813	1083

26. 27 inches of mercury (chemical symbol Hg) equals how many millibars?

(A) 914
(B) 931
(C) 686
(D) 699
(E) 897

27. 749 millimeters of mercury equals how many inches?

(A) 999
(B) 30
(C) 982
(D) 29
(E) 29.5

28. 931 millibars of Hg equals how many inches of mercury?

(A) 699
(B) 27
(C) 27.5
(D) 948
(E) 28

29. How many millibars Hg equal 31.5 inches of mercury ?

(A) 800
(B) 1066
(C) 787
(D) 1050
(E) 1066

30. How many inches of mercury equal 673 millimeters Hg?

(A) 897
(B) 26
(C) 26.5
(D) 660
(E) 27

Questions 31–35 are based on the virtual pressure conversion table below.

Unit of measure	lb/in² (psi)	kg/cm²	feet of H₂O	inches of Hg	mm of Hg	atmospheres	mbar
lb/in² (psi)	1	0.0703	2.3067	2.0360	51.7149	0.0681	68.9476
kg/cm²	14.2233	1	32.8093	28.9590	735.5588	0.9678	1013.2500
feet of H₂O	0.4335	0.0305	1	0.8827	22.4192	0.0295	29.6890
inches of Hg	0.4912	0.0345	1.1330	1	25.4000	0.0334	33.8639
mm of Hg	0.0193	0.0014	0.0446	0.0394	1	0.0013	1.3332
atmospheres	14.6960	1.0332	33.8995	29.9213	760.0000	1	1013.2500
millibars	0.0145	0.0010	0.0035	0.0295	0.7501	0.0010	1

31. How many inches of mercury equal 1 millimeter Hg?

(A) 25.4000
(B) 1.0000
(C) 0.0394
(D) 0.0295
(E) 0.8827

32. How many pounds per square inch equal 1 atmosphere?

(A) 14.6960
(B) 0.0681
(C) 0.0193
(D) 1.0000
(E) 0.0010

33. How many millibars make up 1 atmosphere?

(A) 0.0010
(B) 0.7501
(C) 760.0000
(D) 1013.2500
(E) 68.9476

34. How many feet of water equal the pressure of 1 atmosphere?

(A) 0.0295
(B) 14.6060
(C) 32.8093
(D) 33.8995
(E) 33.8639

35. How many kilograms per square centimeter are equivalent to 1 millibar?

(A) 0.0014
(B) 0.0703
(C) 0.0010
(D) 735.5588
(E) 1013.2500

Questions 36–40 are based on the table below.

X VALUE

	−3	−2	−1	0	+1	+2	+3
+3	1.1	3.1	3.7	5.0	7.5	10.0	12.5
+2	2.4	3.3	6.0	16.9	98.2	17.7	29.6
+1	4.5	5.1	5.5	33.3	55.4	46.2	77.1
0	6.7	7.0	7.2	7.7	2.5	19.2	3.3
−1	9.4	10.1	11.8	23.4	9.9	26.9	27.1
−2	12.0	12.1	12.2	12.4	12.3	11.0	3.9
−3	15.3	16.1	18.0	87.3	71.2	88.0	15.4

Y VALUE is the left-hand column.

	X	Y	(A)	(B)	(C)	(D)	(E)
36.	0	+2	12.4	16.9	7.0	19.2	11.0
37.	−1	−3	3.7	7.5	71.2	77.1	18.0
38.	+2	0	16.9	7.0	19.2	12.4	3.3
39.	−3	−2	12.0	2.4	16.1	3.9	88.0
40.	+1	+2	12.3	6.0	46.2	5.1	98.2

SUBTEST #8: AVIATION INFORMATION (20 QUESTIONS)

1. When in the down (extended) position, wing flaps provide

   (A) increased lift and decreased drag.
   (B) decreased lift and increased drag.
   (C) increased lift and increased drag.
   (D) increased lift only.
   (E) decreased wing camber (curvature).

2. Municipal airports often provide at least one extended or unusually long runway to facilitate the takeoff of

   (A) heavily loaded aircraft in calm conditions.
   (B) lightly loaded aircraft taking off in a crosswind.
   (C) small aircraft in rainy weather.
   (D) aircraft with higher than average climbing speeds.
   (E) rotary-wing aircraft in trail formation.

3. The small hinged section on the elevator of most airplanes is known as the

   (A) aileron.
   (B) flap.
   (C) stabilator.
   (D) elevon.
   (E) trim tab.

4. The rearward retarding force on the airplane known as drag is opposed by

   (A) lift.
   (B) thrust.
   (C) weight.
   (D) laminar air flow.
   (E) compression.

5. At night, airport taxiways are identified by omnidirectional edge lights that are _____ in color.

   (A) red
   (B) white
   (C) alternating red and white
   (D) blue
   (E) green

6. A runway with the Approach Lighting System (ALS) would show an incoming pilot

   (A) a pair of synchronized flashing lights at the runway threshold.
   (B) a series of lightbars and/or strobe lights extending outward from the runway approach end.
   (C) white elevated lights running the length of the runway on both sides.
   (D) white lights embedded in the runway centerline at 50-foot intervals.
   (E) unidirectional blue lights.

7. The thrust of a turbojet is developed by compressing air in the inlet and compressor, mixing the air with fuel and burning it in the combustor, and

   (A) venting the combusted air through side nozzles.
   (B) rerouting the airflow through the compressor for extra power.
   (C) expanding the gas stream through the turbine and nozzle.
   (D) using the resulting accelerated airflow to turn the propeller shaft.
   (E) diffusing the gas stream through the designated relief valves.

8. A ramjet engine consists of

   (A) an intake, a compressor, a combustion chamber, and an outlet.
   (B) an inlet, a turbine, a compressor, and a nozzle.
   (C) an intake, a compression chamber, and a nozzle.
   (D) an inlet, a combustion zone, and a nozzle.
   (E) an inlet, a compression chamber, a turbine, and a nozzle.

9. The four forces that act on an aircraft in flight are

   (A) lift, gravity, thrust, and drag.
   (B) lift, mass, propulsion, and resistance.
   (C) aerodynamics, mass, propulsion, and drag.
   (D) lift magnitude, mass, thrust, and drag.
   (E) roll, pitch, yaw, and magnitude.

10. For a fixed-wing aircraft, lift is generated _____ to the direction of flight.

   (A) parallel
   (B) reciprocal
   (C) proportionate
   (D) vectored
   (E) perpendicular

11. The angle formed by the chord of an airfoil or wing and the direction of the relative wind is known as the

   (A) critical angle.
   (B) stall angle.
   (C) angle of pitch.
   (D) delta angle.
   (E) angle of attack.

12. Pitot tubes furnish data to an instrument that is used by aircraft pilots in about the same way that a(n) _____ is used by an automobile driver.

    (A) pressure transducer
    (B) odometer
    (C) speedometer
    (D) tachometer
    (E) ohmmeter

13. The part of an airplane that holds the cargo and/or passengers—as well as providing a base for the other aircraft parts—is known as the

    (A) fuselage.
    (B) empennage.
    (C) cargo compartment.
    (D) cockpit array.
    (E) static line.

14. On a conventional fixed-wing aircraft, the _____ maintain(s) pitch and the _____ maintain(s) yaw.

    (A) elevators, rudder
    (B) horizontal stabilizers, vertical stabilizer
    (C) elevons, stabilator
    (D) rudder, elevators
    (E) trim tabs, wing flaps

15. _____ are additional hinged rear sections mounted to the wing near the body that are deployed downward on takeoff and landing to increase the amount of force produced by the wing.

    (A) Ailerons
    (B) Elevators
    (C) Flaps
    (D) Trim tabs
    (E) Elevons

16. Which one of the following does not affect density altitude?

    (A) Temperature
    (B) Atmospheric pressure
    (C) Humidity
    (D) Wind velocity
    (E) Altitude

17. The degree of movement of an aircraft around its longitudinal axis is known as

    (A) pitch.
    (B) sideslip.
    (C) yaw.
    (D) angle of attack.
    (E) bank.

18. The Venturi theory of lift says that faster airflow over the curved upper portion of a wing surface causes

    (A) decreased pressure according to Bernoulli's equation.
    (B) increased pressure according to Avogadro's constant.
    (C) increased drag proportionate to crosswinds.
    (D) decreased drag proportionate to the thrust vector.
    (E) decreased drag perpendicular to the thrust vector.

19. The maneuver in which a rotary-wing aircraft (helicopter) is maintained in nearly motionless flight over a ground reference point at a constant altitude and heading (direction) is known as

    (A) feathering.
    (B) autorotation.
    (C) hovering.
    (D) torque balance.
    (E) freewheeling.

20. The ratio of the speed of an aircraft to the speed of sound in the air around it is the aircraft's

    (A) compressibility factor.
    (B) Mach angle.
    (C) Mach number.
    (D) aerodynamic heating ratio.
    (E) isentropic threshold.

SUBTEST #9: GENERAL SCIENCE (20 QUESTIONS)

This part of the test measures your knowledge in the area of science. Each of the questions or incomplete statements is followed by five choices. Your task is to decide which one of the choices best answers the question or completes the statement.

1. What is energy called that is derived from the sun?

   (A) hydroelectric
   (B) solar
   (C) geothermal
   (D) volcanic
   (E) kinetic

2. Cells that can be easily scraped from the lining of the mouth are

   (A) connective tissue.
   (B) epithelial tissue.
   (C) supporting tissue.
   (D) voluntary tissue.
   (E) excess tissue.

3. The DNA of a cell is found mainly in its

   (A) membrane.
   (B) cytoplasm.
   (C) chromosomes.
   (D) vacuoles.
   (E) mitochondria.

4. The reaction between sodium, metal, and water can be classified as

   (A) single replacement.
   (B) double replacement.
   (C) decomposition.
   (D) synthesis.
   (E) aggregation.

5. The beneficial relationship between termites and the protozoa that inhabit their digestive system is called

   (A) parthenogenesis.
   (B) meiosis.
   (C) mitosis.
   (D) symbiosis.
   (E) phagocytosis.

6. Which substance can be used to treat drinking water of questionable purity?

   (A) ammonia
   (B) iodine
   (C) chlorine
   (D) hydrogen chloride
   (E) ethylene glycol

7. In the International System of Units, the way to measure mass is known as the

   (A) kilogram.
   (B) kilometer.
   (C) ampere.
   (D) ohm.
   (E) henry.

8. The end product(s) of protein digestion consist(s) of

   (A) glucose.
   (B) fatty acids.
   (C) amino acids.
   (D) glycerol.
   (E) sucrose.

9. The number of atoms in a molecule of $CuSO_4 \cdot 5H_2O$ is

   (A) 15.
   (B) 18.
   (C) 21.
   (D) 29.
   (E) 33.

10. A magnetic compass points in the direction of

   (A) true north.
   (B) the geographic north pole.
   (C) the magnetic north pole.
   (D) the local magnetic field.
   (E) grid north.

11. Compounds that include fat and oils found in foods and the human body are

   (A) vitamins.
   (B) carbohydrates.
   (C) lipids.
   (D) minerals.
   (E) proteins.

12. The kinetic energy of a 1-kilogram mass, dropped from a height of 1 meter, just before it hits the ground is

   (A) 1 Joule.
   (B) 10 Joule.
   (C) 100 Joule.
   (D) 1,000 Joule.
   (E) 10,000 Joule.

13. A 120-V electrical power supply produces 1/2 A to the load. The power delivered is

 (A) 60 watts.
 (B) 60 ohms.
 (C) 120 watts.
 (D) 240 watts.
 (E) 240 ohms.

14. Resistance—the tendency for a material to oppose the flow of electrons—is measured in

 (A) volts.
 (B) watts.
 (C) ohms.
 (D) amperes.
 (E) current.

15. Most cells without a cell wall would also lack

 (A) vacuoles.
 (B) chloroplasts.
 (C) mitochondria.
 (D) a cell membrane.
 (E) a nucleus.

16. A magnifying glass is what kind of lens used on objects how far away?

 (A) convex lens used beyond one focal length
 (B) convex lens used closer than one focal length
 (C) concave lens used beyond one focal length
 (D) concave lens used closer than one focal length
 (E) none of the above

17. The glucose content of the blood is regulated by

 (A) ACTH
 (B) nerve stimulation
 (C) corticosteroids
 (D) insulin and adrenaline
 (E) progesterone

18. Frictional forces usually do NOT

 (A) oppose motion.
 (B) decrease kinetic energy.
 (C) increase kinetic energy.
 (D) increase potential energy.
 (E) produce wear.

19. For a solar eclipse to take place, the

 (A) moon must be between the sun and the earth.
 (B) earth's axis of rotation must point toward the sun.
 (C) moon must be in its last crescent phase.
 (D) earth must be between the sun and the moon.
 (E) earth and moon must be on opposite sides of the sun.

20. The function of an enzyme is to

 (A) become hydrolyzed during a chemical reaction.
 (B) provide energy for a chemical reaction.
 (C) speed up a chemical reaction.
 (D) serve as an organic catalyst.
 (E) slow down a chemical reaction.

SUBTEST #10: ROTATED BLOCKS (15 QUESTIONS)

This part of the test measures your ability to visualize and manipulate objects in space. In each problem you are shown a picture of a block. Your task is to find a second block which is just like the first.

Look at the two blocks below. Although they are in different positions, the blocks are exactly the same.

Now look at the next two blocks below. They are not alike. They can never be turned in such a way that they will be alike.

Now look at sample S1 below. Which of the five choices is just like the first block?

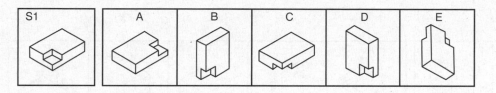

The correct answer is D. It is the same block placed in a different position.

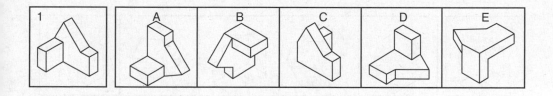

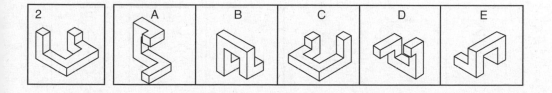

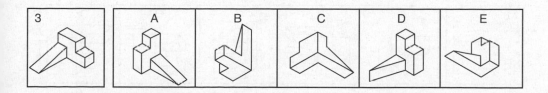

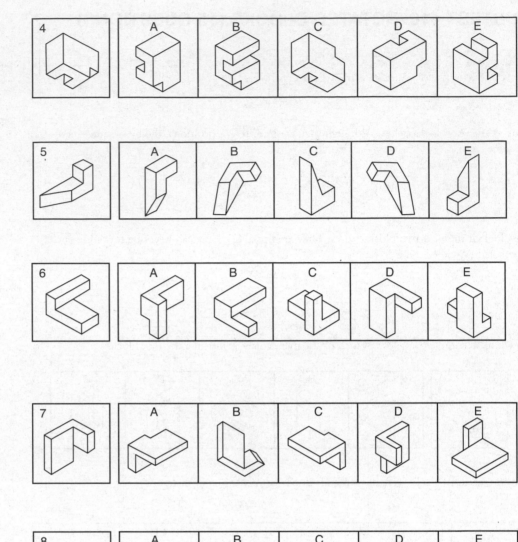

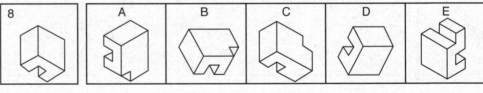

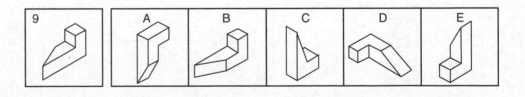

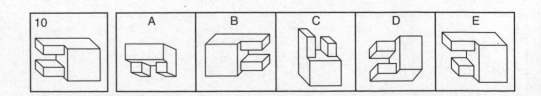

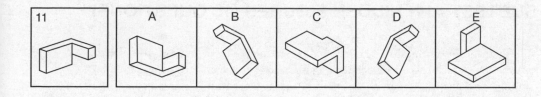

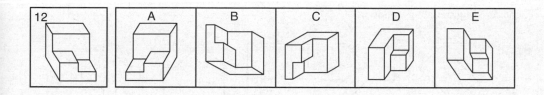

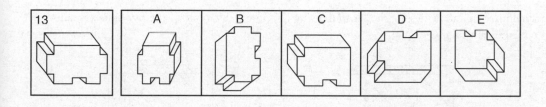

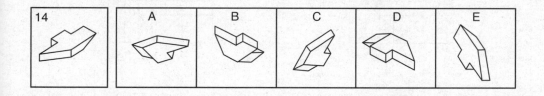

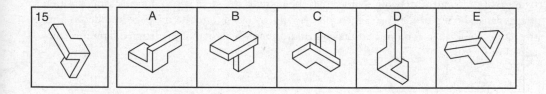

SUBTEST #11: HIDDEN FIGURES (15 QUESTIONS)

This part of the test measures your ability to see a simple figure in a complex drawing. At the top of each page are five lettered figures. Below these on each page are several numbered drawings. You are to determine which lettered figure is contained in each of the numbered drawings.

The lettered figures are as follows:

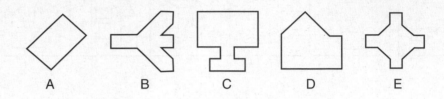

The numbered drawings are similar to drawing X below. Which one of the five figures is contained in drawing X?

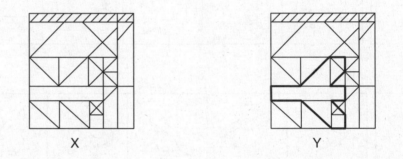

Figure B is contained in drawing X; therefore, B is the answer to sample question X. Drawing Y is exactly like drawing X except that the outline of figure B has been darkened to show that *all* of figure B appears in the drawing. Notice that the figure is the same size and in the same position as it appears at the top of the page. Therefore, you do not need to rotate the page in order to find the figure. Look at each numbered drawing and decide which one of the lettered figures is contained in it.

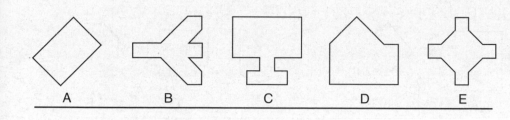

A   B   C   D   E

1

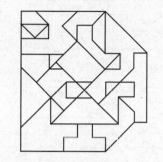

4

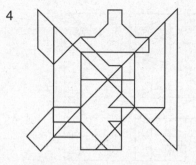

2

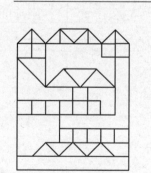

5

3

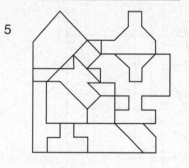

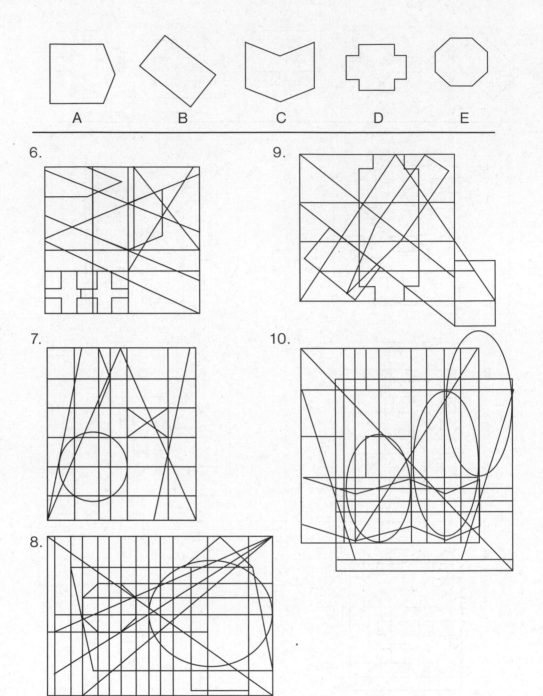

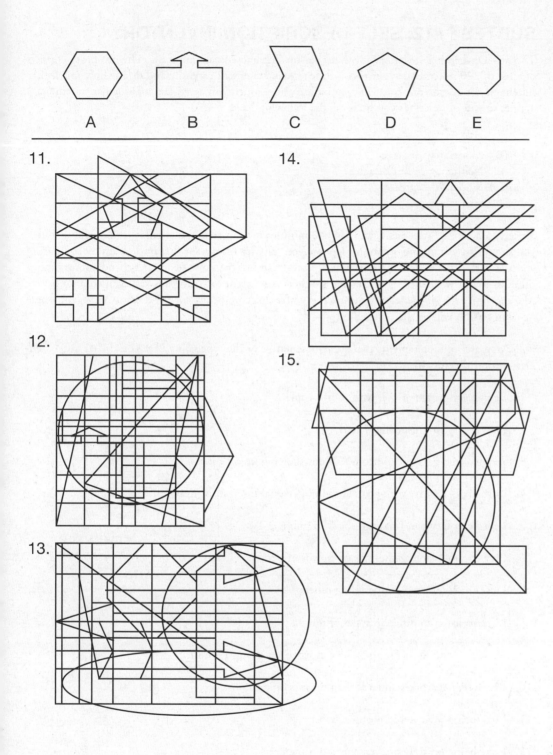

SUBTEST #12: SELF-DESCRIPTION INVENTORY

The Self-Description Inventory measures personal characteristics and traits. The inventory consists of a list of 220 statements; your task is to read each statement carefully and decide how much that statement applies to you. You will then indicate how much you agree that a particular statement applies to you or describes you by using the following scale:

(A) Strongly disagree
(B) Moderately disagree
(C) Neither agree nor disagree
(D) Moderately agree
(E) Strongly agree

Since you have 220 statements and only 40 minutes for this test, you should work quickly—but you should answer all the questions. Choose your answer from your first impression by comparing yourself with other people in your same age group and of the same sex. Don't spend a long time thinking about what the "right" answer is—there is no right or wrong answer to any question. Mark a choice for all the statements, even if you're not completely sure of the answer. Again, your first impression will be the best indicator.

Following are some statements that are representative of the type you will see on the AFOQT Self-Description Inventory.

1. I generally get along well with most people.

2. I always try to finish what I start.

3. People often get upset with me for not showing up on time.

4. I usually place my work goals ahead of personal interests or hobbies.

5. I get nervous when I have to speak in public.

6. I try to avoid large gatherings or crowds of people if I can.

7. I am not comfortable supervising others.

8. I like to listen to different types of music.

9. I usually wind up being the leader in whatever group I am in.

10. I have higher work standards than most people I know.

11. I like being involved in group activities.

12. I like being on time or even ahead of time.

13. I like meeting new people.

14. I like being where the action is.

15. I am pleased when friends stop by to see me.

16. I am reluctant to turn in an assignment unless it is perfect.

17. I am neater than most people I know.

18. I am usually afraid to voice my opinion because others may disagree.

19. I prefer an evening at home alone to a night on the town with friends.

20. I like new challenges.

ANSWERS AND EXPLANATIONS

Subtest #1: Verbal Analogies

Check your answers below and refer to the explanation for each question you missed. Use the table to record right and wrong answers.

	✔	✘		✔	✘		✔	✘		✔	✘		✔	✘
1. C			6. E			11. E			16. C			21. C		
2. E			7. A			12. A			17. A			22. A		
3. D			8. A			13. C			18. D			23. A		
4. A			9. E			14. B			19. A			24. D		
5. B			10. E			15. E			20. A			25. D		

1. **C** GLOVE is to HAND as SHOE is to **FOOT.** This is a "tool to user" analogy; a shoe is a protective, warming cover for the foot in the same way that a glove performs the same functions for the hand.

2. **E** AIRCRAFT is to FLY as BOAT is to **SAIL.** This is an "object to function" analogy; an aircraft is a means of conveyance or transportation used to fly, just as a boat is a means of transportation used to sail.

3. **D** PLAN is to STRATEGY as FIGHT is to **BATTLE.** This is an "action to result" analogy; one does the first to make the second happen or come into being.

4. **A** TRAVEL is to DESTINATION as WORK is to **GOAL** This is another "action to result" analogy—you travel to reach your destination, and you work to get to or achieve your goal.

5. **B** PLOW is to FIELD as RACQUET is to **COURT.** A plow is a tool or implement to be used on a field, just as a racquet is an implement used on a court.

6. **E** SALUTE is to RESPECT as HUG is to **AFFECTION.** This is a form of a "result to cause" analogy; a salute is a physical gesture resulting from respect held for another, and a hug is a physical symbol of affection (the cause of the result or physical action).

7. **A** GRAVITY is to PLANET as ODOR is to **SKUNK.** Another "result to cause" analogy; gravity is caused by the presence of a planet in roughly the same way that odor is caused by or comes from a skunk.

8. **A** FISHING ROD is to HOOK as KNIFE is to **BLADE.** This is a "whole to part" analogy. A hook is the part of a fishing rod that actually enables the rod's function to be fulfilled (to catch fish), in the same way that the blade is the part of a knife that fulfills the function of a knife (to cut). Choice E is not correct because, even though a handle *is* part of a knife, it is not the part that performs the primary function of the tool in the way that the blade is.

9. **E** BOOT is to HIKE as VISOR is to **WELD.** In the same way that a boot protects and helps the hiker, a visor protects and helps the welder—an "object to function" analogy.

10. **E** PUSH is to SHOVE as CLIMB is to **CLAMBER.** This is an analogy of language; *push* and *shove* mean nearly the same thing, as do *climb* and *clamber.*

11. **E** GROW is to MATURE as BLOOM is to **BLOSSOM.** *Grow* and *mature* mean very nearly the same thing, as do *bloom* and *blossom*—another language-based analogy.

12. **A** FUSELAGE is to BODY as TURRET is to **TANK.** This is a "part to whole" analogy. *Fuselage* is a specific term for the main part of the body of an airplane; *turret* is a term for the main part of a tank.

13. **C** CLIMB is to RISE as DIVE is to **FALL.** Although it may at first appear to be a language analogy—these word pairs almost seem like synonyms—this is actually an "action to result" analogy. A pilot causes his airplane to climb in order to rise, whereas he causes the plane to dive in order to fall or lose altitude.

14. **B** ROPE is to KNOT as THREAD is to **FABRIC**. This is a "part to whole" analogy; a rope is used to make a knot, just as a thread is manipulated to make fabric.

15. **E** WATCH is to OBSERVE as SWITCH is to **REPLACE**. Here we have an analogy of language—both these pairs of words are synonyms.

16. **C** OBEY is to COMPLY as REPLY is to **ANSWER**. Both these pairs of words are synonyms—another language analogy.

17. **A** HONOR is to HONESTY as TRUST is to **DEPENDABILITY**. This is an "action to result" analogy; honor is a result of consistent honesty, just as trust is a by-product of consistent dependability.

18. **D** SPEED is to DECELERATION as VELOCITY is to **BRAKING**. This is an "action to result" analogy. When an automobile driver, for instance, decreases his speed in a car (usually by stepping on the brake pedal), it is called *deceleration*; decreased velocity, similarly, is usually caused by braking.

19. **A** COMPRESSION is to RAREFACTION as DENSE is to **THIN**. Sound is made up of successive compression and rarefaction waves in the air—respectively, thickened and thinned areas resulting from the source of the sound. This is an analogy of language—these are opposites, or antonyms.

20. **A** DELAY is to POSTPONE as PREVENT is to **DETER**. *Delay* and *postpone* mean the same thing, to put something off or do it later; *prevent* and *deter* both mean to stop something from happening. This is another analogy of language, since these are basically synonyms.

21. **C** ADD is to SUBTRACT as GROW is to **SHRINK**. *Add* and *subtract* are opposite concepts, as are *grow* and *shrink*. This is an analogy of language, since they are antonyms.

22. **A** LEFT is to PORT as RIGHT is to **STARBOARD**. This is an analogy of language; *port* is an aviation and nautical term for *left*, and *starboard* refers to the right side or direction.

23. **A** ODOMETER is to DISTANCE as ALTIMETER is to **ALTITUDE**. In the same way that an odometer measures road distance traveled, an altimeter measures an aircraft's altitude above the earth. Although a compass needle points to the north because of magnetic attraction, it does not *measure* where the user is. This is an "object to function" analogy.

24. **D** ELEVATOR is to HEIGHT as THRUST is to **ALTITUDE**. This is a somewhat tricky "cause to effect" analogy; in the same way that an elevator on an airplane (or an elevator in a building) causes you to gain or lose height above the ground, thrust from a rocket or jet engine determines your altitude. "STAIRWAY is to BUILDING" is not the right answer—even though it could be thought of as close—because a stairway is static and does not move; the user must furnish the moving power (his or her legs), rather than being moved by an external source of power. Test-takers need to be aware of possible multiple meanings for certain words.

25. **D** LOOK is to INSPECT as ARRIVE is to **ATTEND**. This is an "action to result" analogy; one must first look in order to inspect, in the same way that one has to arrive before one can attend (a meeting, for example).

Subtest #2: Arithmetic Reasoning

Check your answers below and refer to the explanation for each question you missed. Use the table to record right and wrong answers.

	✔	✘		✔	✘		✔	✘		✔	✘		✔	✘
1. C			6. E			11. C			16. A			21. B		
2. B			7. D			12. D			17. D			22. C		
3. B			8. C			13. A			18. E			23. B		
4. A			9. D			14. B			19. C			24. A		
5. D			10. A			15. C			20. E			25. D		

1. **C** To calculate the number of total seats in the theater, multiply the number of rows (x) by the number of seats in each row (y). This equation is written as xy.

2. **B** First, find the amount of the price increase.

$$\$23,999 - \$22,399 = \$1,600$$

Multiply the amount of the increase by 100, then divide by the original price.

3. **B** Multiply the number of completed passes by 100, then divide it by the number of attempted passes. The result will be the percentage.

$$57 \times 100 = 5700$$
$$\frac{5700}{82} = 69.5 = 69.5\%$$

4. **A** There are 100 units of $1,000 in $100,000. Thus, Jaycie Marie pays $100 \times \$12$ (or $1,200) every year in premiums, or $100 every month. Therefore, every six months, Jaycie Marie pays $\frac{1}{2}$ of $1,200 (or six times $100), which equals $600.

5. **D** There are 16 ounces in 1 pound. Therefore, if 2 pounds of smoked deli turkey breast cost $13.98, then 1 pound costs $6.99.

1 oz. costs $\$6.99 \div 16 = \$0.44$
5 oz. cost $\$0.44 \times 5 = \$2.20$

6. **E** Find the cost of four ties:
$$4 \times \$12 = \$48$$
Find the cost of the shirts alone:
$$\$173 - \$48 = \$125$$
Find the cost of one shirt:
$$\$125 \div 5 = \$25.00$$

7. **D** The formula for the volume of an object with parallel sides and right-angle corners is

Length $l \times$ width $w \times$ height h or
$l \times w \times h$
23 ft. $\times$ 15 ft. $\times$ 11 ft. = 3,795 cu. ft. ("cubic feet")

8. **C** Let x be the number of tickets bought at each price (remember, the sister bought the same number of both kinds of tickets). So,

$$7x + 10x = 119$$

Now combine the terms and continue solving the equation for x.

$$17x = 119$$
$$\frac{17x}{17} = \frac{119}{17}$$
$$x = \frac{119}{17}$$
$$x = 7$$

9. **D** First, calculate the amount of Amanda's hourly wages for a shift of 10:30 A.M. to 5:30 P.M., which is seven hours.

$$7 \times \$2.50 = \$17.50$$

Next, calculate the amount of Amanda's tips for her seven-hour shift.

$$7 \times \$22 = \$154$$

Now, calculate the amount of her tips she has to share with the busboys and hostesses.

$$\$154 \times .10 = \$15.40$$

Now add everything up.

Wages	$17.50
Tips	+$154.00
Tip share	− $15.40
Net pay	$156.10

10. **A** First, calculate the number of total attendees by multiplying the total seats available by the percentage.

$$500 \times .76 = 380$$

Since "three quarters" (75%) of those attending were adults, that means that one quarter or 25% were children (which is the final result we are trying to find). Therefore, multiply the number of total attendees by the percentage of children to find out how many children saw the performance.

$$380 \times .25 = 95 \text{ children}$$

11. **C** Add all the blocks of time together.

$$4 + 1 + .5 + 2 = 7.5 \text{ hours total}$$

Now multiply the time spent studying (four hours) by 100 and divide it by the total time.

$$4 \times 100 = 400$$
$$400 \div 7.5 = 53.3\%$$

12. **D** Subtract the discounted price from the original price.

$$\$1,400 - \$1,150 = \$250$$

Now multiply the amount of the discount by 100 and divide it by the original price.

$$\$250 \times 100 = 25,000$$
$$25,000 \div 1,400 = 17.857142 = 17.9\%$$

13. **A** The formula for the perimeter of a rectangle is

$$P = 2l \times 2w$$

If the long sides of the rug measure 15 feet each, then both long sides together equal 30 feet. Subtract the length of both long sides from the total perimeter measurement.

$$45 - (2 \times 15) - 45 - 30 = 15 \text{ ft.}$$

Now we have the part of the perimeter made up by the short sides, but we need to divide it by two to get the length of each short side.

$$15 \text{ ft.} \div 2 = 7.5 \text{ ft.}$$

14. **B** First add up the wages made by the four customer service reps.

$$\$320 \times 4 = \$1,280$$

Now calculate how much the two sales reps make each week.

2 sales reps × [(\$12 per hr. × 40 hrs.) + (5 days per week × \$100)] =

2 sales reps × (\$480 + \$500) =

2 sales reps × \$980 = \$1,960 per week

Now add the pay for the four customer service reps to the pay for the two sales managers.

$$\$1,280 + \$1,960 = \$3,240$$

15. **C** To find an average, add the values for each day together and then divide by the total number of days. $(x + y + z) \div 3$

16. **A** First find the number of miles per hour the train travels.

500 miles ÷ 5 hours = 100 miles per hour (mph)

Now calculate how many miles the train travels in one minute.

100 mph ÷ 60 minutes = 1.67 miles per minute

Now multiply the train's speed in miles per minute by the number of minutes in question.

1.67 miles per minute × 15 minutes = 25 miles

17. **D** Two figures are "similar" in the mathematical sense if they have the same shape; they may or may not have the same size. An airplane and a scale model of that plane have the same shape and are therefore similar.

18. **E** Start by letting x equal one share of the insurance money. According to the ratio, the wife received five shares ($5x$) and the children received one share (x) apiece for a total of eight shares. Divide the total amount by the total number of shares.

$$\$750,000 \div 8 = \$93,750 \text{ per share}$$

Now multiply the amount of each share by the total number of shares received by the children.

$$\$93,750 \times 3 = \$281,250$$

19. **C** If 4% of the unit are officers, then the percent of enlisted men is

$$100\% - 4\% = 96\%$$

To find the number of enlisted men, multiply the total number by 96% or .96.

125 total soldiers × 0.96 = 120 enlisted soldiers

20. **E** First find the discount received from the wholesale dealer for each DVD player by multiplying the listed price by the discount percentage.

$$\$80 \times .25 = \$20$$

Now find the final price per DVD player paid to the wholesale dealer.

$$\$80 - \$20 = \$60$$

Now find the retail markup by multiplying the markup percentage by the original wholesale price.

$$\$80 \times .20 = \$16$$

Now find the retail price for which the electronics store owner sells the DVD players to his customers by adding the markup amount to the listed wholesale amount.

$$\$80 + \$16 = \$96$$

To find the profit, subtract the retail price from the actual price paid to the wholesale dealer.

$$\$96 - \$60 = \$36 \text{ profit per DVD player}$$

21. **B** Since 1 inch represents 50 miles, divide the ground distance (120 miles) by the scale (50 miles to the inch) to find the number of inches required to represent 120 miles.

$$120 \div 50 = 2.4$$

22. **C** Multiply the purchase price of the home by the assessment rate to find the assessed value.

$$120,000 \times .80 = \$96,000 \text{ (assessed value)}$$

Find the number of hundreds in the assessed value.

$$\$96,000 \div 100 = 960 \text{ (hundreds)}$$

Multiply the number of hundreds by the tax rate.

$$960 \times \$4.75 = \$4,560 \text{ (property tax)}$$

23. **B** First find the total time needed to run the generator = 12 hours and 45 minutes or 12.75 minutes. Now divide the total time needed to run the generator by the amount of time each tank of fuel will last.

$$12.75 \div 1.25 = 10.2 \text{ tanks of fuel}$$

AFOQT #1

24. **A** First find the amount of the decline in traffic.

11,200 cars – 10,044 = 1,156 fewer cars per day

Now multiply the amount of traffic decrease by 100 and then divide it by the amount of original traffic. This will yield the percentage decrease without further calculation.

$$1,156 \times 100 = 115,600$$

$$115,600 \div 11,200 = 10.3\% \text{ decrease}$$

25. **D** First calculate the distances driven during the two legs of the trip.

Leg 1: 2 hours × 70 mph = 140 miles

Leg 2: 1.5 hours × 65 mph = 97.5 miles

140 miles + 97.5 miles = 237.5 miles

Now divide the total distance traveled by the car's gas mileage rate.

$$237.5 \text{ miles} \div 25 \text{ mpg} = 9.5 \text{ gals.}$$

Subtest #3: Word Knowledge

Check your answers below and refer to the explanation for each question you missed. Use the table to record right and wrong answers.

	✔	✘		✔	✘		✔	✘		✔	✘		✔	✘
1. A			6. E			11. D			16. E			21. B		
2. D			7. A			12. C			17. D			22. B		
3. B			8. C			13. A			18. A			23. C		
4. D			9. E			14. D			19. A			24. C		
5. A			10. C			15. B			20. D			25. A		

1. **A** TACIT means **silent.**

2. **D** ALTITUDE means **height**, which *is* a measure of distance, but height is more specific and therefore the most accurate answer.

3. **B** To PORTEND is to **give warning beforehand**, as when building storm clouds portend a storm. To *feign* is to *pretend*; to assume a pose is to *portray*.

4. **D** ITINERARY means **schedule.**

5. **A** VEXATIOUS means to be **annoying**. A contagious disease is said to be *virulent*; someone who is insatiably hungry is *voracious.*

6. **E** EQUIVALENT means **equal.**

7. **A** CRITERION means a **standard** of judgment.

8. **C** MERCURIAL means **unpredictably changeable**, referring both to the speed of the mythical Roman god Mercury and the unpredictable physical nature of the element itself—mercury on a supposedly flat surface will flow in unexpected directions with the smallest provocation. Someone who is *merciful* is said to be compassionate; *specious* means tawdrily attractive or *meretricious.*

9. **E** CRITICAL means **most important**. A seriously ill or injured patient may be classified as "critical," but that does not necessarily mean the patient is dying. It just means that they are at risk of dying; therefore this is the **most important** classification, and the hospital staff pays extra attention to their status and needs.

10. **C** TELEMETRY means **the transmission of measurements made by automatic instruments**. Mental communication is *telepathy*; marketing goods or services by telephone is *telemarketing*; the study of climactic variations (i.e., weather) is *meteorology*; and *temerity* means "acting with rashness or audacity."

11. **D** ANTAGONIST means **adversary.** A main character is a *protagonist.*

12. **C** DIAGNOSE means to **identify a situation**. A prognosis is a prediction of the outcome.

13. **A** KINETIC means **relating to the motion of material bodies**. Something relating to the movies may be referred to as *cinematic*; someone moving at a high speed may be called *frenetic*; and things relating to a sensory experience are *kinesthetic.*

14. **D** RECTIFY means to **correct.**

15. **B** CAMOUFLAGE means to **conceal**.

16. **E** EQUIVOCAL means **evasive**. Another word for *equal* is *equivalent*.

17. **D** CENTRIPETAL means **moving toward a center or axis**. Moving away from an axis is *centrifugal*; having two feet is *bipedal*.

18. **A** DISCONSOLATE means **hopelessly sad.** To cease using is to *discontinue*; to rearrange sloppily is to *disarrange*; to uncover is to *discover*; and to recognize mentally is to *discern*.

19. **A** ANACHRONISTIC means **chronologically out of place**. To be cursed is to be *anathematized*; *anatomy* deals with an organism's physical structure; the attribution of conscious thought to inanimate objects or animals is *animism*; and things or situations existing before a war are described as *antebellum*.

20. **D** MODULATE means to **adjust**. To speak is to *enunciate*; to dry out is to *desiccate*.

21. **B** PICAYUNE means exceedingly small or **insignificant**. When something is intense—such as an emotion or a jalapeño pepper—we may say that it is "piquant."

22. **B** TENACIOUS means **persistent**. A hot-tempered person may be called "pugnacious."

23. **C** ENTENTE means **an agreement providing for** (or leading to) **joint action**. The relaxation of tensions or disagreements, especially between nations, is known as *détente*; *volition* means the same as *intent*, which is the state of mind with which an act is done; *freedom of entry or access* is often known as *entrée*.

24. **C** REDUNDANT means **repetitive** or having more than needed of something.

25. **A** RECONNAISSANCE means a **surveying expedition** or scouting trip to see how an area is set up, or the like. A rebirth or revival (especially cultural) is a *renaissance*.

Subtest #4: Mathematics Knowledge

Check your answers below and refer to the explanation for each question you missed. Use the table to record right and wrong answers.

	✔	✘		✔	✘		✔	✘		✔	✘		✔	✘
1. E			6. D			11. C			16. A			21. D		
2. D			7. B			12. C			17. D			22. D		
3. A			8. B			13. B			18. C			23. D		
4. D			9. E			14. B			19. B			24. B		
5. E			10. C			15. C			20. A			25. A		

1. **E** A factorial is the product of all the positive integers from 1 to a given number. The expression "4 factorial" or 4! means $1 \times 2 \times 3 \times 4 = 24$.

2. **D** The formula for the circumference of a circle is

$$d \text{ (diameter)} \times \pi = \text{circumference}$$

The pilot flies in a circle with a radius of 40 km and therefore a diameter of 80 km.

$$80 \text{ km} \times \frac{22}{7} = \text{circumference}$$

$$\frac{80 \times 22}{7} = \text{circumference}$$

$$\frac{1760}{7} = \text{circumference}$$

$$251 \text{ km} = \text{circumference}$$

3. **A** The reciprocal of any number is 1 over that number. The reciprocal of 7 to the nearest thousandth is $\frac{1}{7} = 0.143$.

4. **D** The square of any number is that number times itself. The square of 525 is

$$\begin{array}{r} 525 \\ \times\ 525 \\ \hline 27{,}625 \end{array}$$

Therefore the second digit of the square of 525 is 7.

5. **E** The area of a square with four sides of length *s* is $s \times s$ or s^2. A square with a perimeter of 40 yards has four sides where length = 10 yards. This means that

the area of this square is 10 yds. × 10 yds. = 100 sq. yds. Since this is not one of the choices, let's convert it to square feet:

$$\frac{100 \text{ yds.}^2}{1} \times \frac{9 \text{ ft.}^2}{1 \text{ yd.}^2} = 900 \text{ ft.}^2$$

The tricky part to remember here is that there are 9 square feet in a square yard (3ft. times 3 ft.), not just the 3 feet to 1 yard we are used to thinking about in linear terms.

6. **D** To solve these equations for x, start by finding a way to get rid of y. Multiply both sides of the second equation by 2.

$$2(x - 2y) = 2 \times 11$$
$$2x - 4y = 22$$

Then add the new form of the second equation to the first equation and solve for x.

$$\begin{array}{ll} 5x + 4y = 27 & \\ \underline{2x - 4y = 22} & \text{(+4 cancels out − 4)} \\ 7x \qquad = 49 & \\ \qquad x = 7 & \end{array}$$

7. **B** One way to solve this is to square each of the possible answers to see which one is closest to 85.

9.1	9.2	9.3	9.4	9.5
× 9.1	× 9.2	× 9.3	× 9.4	× 9.5
91	184	279	376	475
819	828	837	846	855
82.81	84.64	86.49	88.36	90.25

The squares of 9.2 and 9.3 are closer to 85 than the squares of 9.1, 9.4, or 9.5. Now find the difference between the square of each of the closest numbers and 85.

(9.2)	85.00	(9.3)	86.49
	− 84.64		− 85.00
	0.36		1.49

The square of 9.2 is closer to 85 than the square of 9.3. Therefore, the square root of 85 to the nearest tenth is 9.2.

8. **B** To solve for x, combine all similar terms and set the equation equal to 0.

$$(8x - 5x) + (-2 - 8) = 0$$

Do the operations inside the parentheses first.

$$(3x) + (-10) = 0 \quad \text{or}$$
$$3x - 10 = 0$$

Next, add 10 to each side to undo the subtraction.

$$3x - 10 + 10 = 0 + 10$$
$$3x = 10$$

Finally, divide each side by 3 to find the value of x. You are undoing the multiplication to find the value of a single x.

$$\frac{3x}{3} = \frac{10}{3}$$

$$x = 3\frac{1}{3}$$

9. **E** Clear the parentheses by multiplying $(a - b)$ by 2 and $(a + 3b)$ by 4. Line up similar terms and add.

$$\begin{array}{l} 2(a - b) + 4(a + 3b) = \\ 2a \;- 2b \\ \underline{+4a \;+12b} \\ 6a + 10b \end{array}$$

10. **C** A prime number is a number larger than 1 that has only itself and 1 as factors—i.e., it can be evenly divided only by itself and 1. The number 201 is divisible by 3. The number 205 is divisible by 5. The number 211, however, is a prime number.

11. **C** The product of a negative number and a positive number is always negative. The result of multiplying (product) two negative numbers is always a positive number. Since ab is positive, and a is negative, b must be negative, too.

12. **C** Set this up as a two-stage multiplication problem. Remember that when you multiply terms with opposite signs, the product is negative (i.e., it has a minus sign).

$$\begin{array}{r} a + 2 \\ \times \; a - 5 \\ \hline -5a - 10 \\ \underline{a^2 + 2a} \\ a^2 - 3a - 10 \end{array}$$

$$\begin{array}{r} a^2 - 3a - 10 \\ \times \qquad a + 3 \\ \hline 3a^2 - 9a - 30 \\ \underline{a^3 - 3a^2 - 10a} \\ a^3 - 19a \qquad - 30 \end{array}$$

13. **B** Begin by combining like terms.

$$3z - 5 + 2z = 25 - 5z$$
$$5z - 5 = 25 - 5z$$

Next, add $5z$ to each side, to eliminate the $-5z$ from the right side.

$$5z - 5 + 5z = 25 - 5z + 5z$$
$$10z - 5 = 25$$

Now, add 5 to each side to cancel out the remaining subtraction.

$$10z - 5 + 5 = 25 + 5$$
$$10z = 30$$
$$z = 3$$

14. **B** A pentagon is a five-sided figure, which therefore has five corners. If the architect places a sculpture at each corner, there will be five sculptures.

15. **C** Every right triangle contains an angle of 90 degrees. This particular right triangle also has an angle of 30 degrees. To find the third angle, subtract the sum of these two angles from 180 degrees.

$$180 - (30 + 90) =$$
$$180 - 120 =$$
$$60 = \text{degrees in third angle}$$

The other two angles are 60 and 90 degrees.

16. **A** Find the factors of the first term in the trinomial—the factors of x^2 are x and x.

$$(x \quad)(x \quad)$$

Then, look at the last factor in the trinomial—in this case, it has a plus sign. This means that both factors of the trinomial are either positive or negative. Which one, though? Since we see that the middle term ($-11x$) has a minus sign, both factors must have minus signs.

$$(x- \quad)(x- \quad)$$

The next step is to find the factors of 30. There are several numbers you can multiply to get 30—30×1, 10×3, 15×2, etc. However, the two multipliers that you use have to also combine somehow to give you the middle term, which is 11. When 5 and 6 are multiplied, they give you 30; when they're added, they give you 11. We know the factors have minus signs, so the factors of 30 are actually -6 and -5.

$$(x - 6)(x - 5)$$

17. **D** Divide only similar terms. First divide numbers, then letters. When dividing powers of a letter (variable), just subtract the exponents.

$$\frac{15a^3b^2c}{5abc} = \frac{15}{5} \times \frac{a^3}{a} \times \frac{b^2}{b} \times \frac{c}{c} = 3a^2b$$

18. **C** The formula for the area of a circle is $\pi \times r^2$. Find the area of the larger circle first.

$$\pi \times 10^2 = 100(\pi) \text{ sq in}$$

Then find the area of the smaller circle.

$$\pi \times 7^2 = 49(\pi) \text{ sq in}$$

To find the part of the larger circle that the smaller one doesn't touch, subtract the smaller area from the larger one.

$$100 - 49 = 51(\pi) \text{ sq in}$$

19. **B** The simplest way to solve this is to form an equation with x as the unknown grade.

$$\frac{78 + 86 + 96 + 94 + x}{5} = 88$$

$$\frac{354 + x}{5} = 88$$

Multiply both sides by 5. This will cancel out the division so you will no longer have a fraction to deal with, but instead whole numbers.

$$5 \times \frac{354 + x}{5} = 88 \times 5$$

Simplify both sides of the equation.

$$354 + x = 440$$
$$x = 440 - 354$$
$$x = 86 \text{ (missing grade)}$$

20. **A** First, change all measurements to yards.

$$9' = 3 \text{ yds} \quad 12' = 4 \text{ yds} \quad 6'' = \frac{1}{6} \text{ yd}$$

To find the volume of the concrete (the volume of a rectangle), multiply the length times the width times the height.

$$3 \times 4 \times \frac{1}{6} =$$

$$12 \times \frac{1}{6} = 2 \text{ cu. yds.}$$

21. **D** First, find the area of the entire new wildlife preserve. Since the preserve is in the shape of a circle, use the formula for the area of a circle (area = π times the square of the radius or A = $\pi \times r^2$).

$$A = \pi \times r^2$$
$$A = \frac{22}{7} \times (14)^2 = \frac{22}{7} \times 196$$
$$= 616 \text{ sq. km.}$$

The lion habitat area is a wedge formed by a 90-degree angle at the center of the circle.

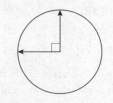

Since a circle has 360 degrees, we can find the part of the preserve that belongs to the lion habitat.

$$\frac{90}{360} = \frac{1}{4}$$

(reduce the fraction to simplest terms)
Next find what this fraction of the whole equals in square kilometers.

$$\frac{1}{4} \times \frac{616}{1} = 154 \text{ sq. km.}$$

22. **D** Find the highest common factor that will divide into the numerical coefficients, 6 and 3, which is 3. Then find the highest literal factor that will divide into x^2 and xy, which is x (note that y is not contained in the first term at all). The next step is to divide the highest common factor, $3x$, into $6x^2 + 3xy$ to find the remaining factor. Thereby we see that the factors are $3x (2x + y)$.

23. **D** To find the volume (V) of a cylinder, multiply π times the square of the radius (r) times the height (h).

$$V = \pi \times r^2 \times h$$
$$V = \frac{22}{7} \times \left(\frac{7}{1} \times \frac{7}{1}\right) \times 15/1$$
$$V = 154 \times 15$$
$$V = 2{,}310 \text{ cu. in. (volume)}$$

To find the number of gallons this cylinder will hold, divide its volume by 231.

$$2{,}310 \div 231 = 10 \text{ gals.}$$

24. **B** The wall, the ladder, and the ground in the recreation area form a right triangle. The ladder is on a slant and is opposite the right angle formed by the wall and the ground. In this position, the ladder is the "hypotenuse" of the right triangle. In geometry, the Pythagorean Theorem states that the square of the hypotenuse (c^2) of a right triangle equals the sum of the squares of the other two sides ($a^2 + b^2$).

Thus, $a^2 + b^2 = c^2$
$$8^2 + b^2 = 10^2$$

Solve by doing the arithmetic operations and by clearing one side of the equation for b^2.

$$64 + b^2 = 100$$
$$b^2 = 100 - 64$$
$$b^2 = 36$$

Then find the square root of b^2 and of 36.

$$b = 6$$

The base of the ladder is 6 feet away from the wall.

25. **A** First find how many ounces of the original mixture were fruit juice.

$$10 \times 20\% = 10 \times .2 = 2 \text{ oz.}$$

Next, find the total number of ounces in the new mixture.

$$10 + 40 = 50 \text{ oz.}$$

Then find what part of the new mixture is fruit juice and convert that to a percentage.

$$\frac{2}{50} = \frac{4}{100} = 4\%$$

Subtest #5: Instrument Comprehension

Check your answers below. Use the table to record right and wrong answers.

	✔	✗		✔	✗		✔	✗		✔	✗
1. B			6. B			11. C			16. D		
2. B			7. A			12. A			17. B		
3. C			8. C			13. B			18. D		
4. A			9. A			14. C			19. B		
5. D			10. D			15. B			20. B		

Answer	Nose	Bank	Heading	Answer	Nose	Bank	Heading
1. **B**	UP	LEFT	NE	11. **C**	UP	ZERO	W
2. **B**	LEVEL	LEFT	S	12. **A**	UP	RIGHT	NE
3. **C**	UP	RIGHT	W	13. **B**	DOWN	LEFT	WSW
4. **A**	DOWN	LEFT	SE	14. **C**	UP	LEFT	WSW
5. **D**	UP	ZERO	N	15. **B**	DOWN	RIGHT	S
6. **B**	LEVEL	LEFT	W	16. **D**	DOWN	RIGHT	W
7. **A**	UP	RIGHT	SW	17. **B**	DOWN	ZERO	S
8. **C**	DOWN	LEFT	SW	18. **D**	UP	LEFT	S
9. **A**	UP	LEFT	E	19. **B**	LEVEL	RIGHT	S
10. **D**	LEVEL	RIGHT	ENE	20. **B**	UP	LEFT	W

Subtest #6: Block Counting

Check your answers below. Use the table to record right and wrong answers.

	✔	✗		✔	✗		✔	✗		✔	✗
1. B			6. D			11. B			16. B		
2. C			7. E			12. D			17. B		
3. E			8. B			13. D			18. A		
4. B			9. C			14. A			19. D		
5. A			10. D			15. C			20. D		

Subtest #7: Table Reading

Check your answers below. Use the table to record right and wrong answers.

	✔	✘		✔	✘		✔	✘		✔	✘		✔	✘
1. B			9. D			17. A			25. C			33. D		
2. E			10. B			18. B			26. A			34. D		
3. D			11. D			19. C			27. E			35. C		
4. A			12. A			20. C			28. C			36. B		
5. C			13. C			21. B			29. B			37. E		
6. C			14. B			22. A			30. C			38. C		
7. A			15. A			23. A			31. C			39. A		
8. A			16. C			24. D			32. A			40. E		

Subtest #8: Aviation Information

Check your answers below and refer to the explanation for each question you missed. Use the table to record right and wrong answers.

	✔	✘		✔	✘		✔	✘		✔	✘
1. C			6. B			11. E			16. D		
2. A			7. C			12. C			17. E		
3. E			8. D			13. A			18. A		
4. B			9. A			14. B			19. C		
5. D			10. E			15. C			20. C		

1. **C** Being in the down or extended position means that the wing flaps are pivoted downward from hinged points on the trailing edge of the wing. This effectively increases the wing camber or curvature, resulting in increased lift and increased drag; this allows the airplane to climb or descend at a steeper angle or a slower airspeed.

2. **A** Heavily loaded aircraft are slower and therefore take longer to achieve flying speed, so a longer runway is needed to develop the lift required for takeoff. Also, a takeoff in calm or nearly calm air takes away the increased wind speed advantage derived from taking off into the wind. Therefore, many municipal or regional airports have a longer runway to accommodate airplanes needing a longer takeoff roll because of one or both of these conditions.

3. **E** The small hinged section on the elevator of most airplanes is called the **trim tab**. The trim tab helps prevent or minimize pilot fatigue by relieving control pressure at the desired flight angle—in other words, the pilot does not have to spend physical and mental energy keeping the elevator at a certain angle to maintain a certain attitude (climbing, level flight, or diving).

4. **B** The rearward retarding force on the airplane known as drag is opposed by **thrust**, which propels the aircraft through the air.

5. **D** At night, airport taxiways are identified by omnidirectional edge lights that are **blue** in color.

6. **B** A runway with the Approach Lighting System (ALS) would show an incoming pilot a series of light-bars and/or strobe lights extending outward from the runway approach end.

7. **C** The thrust of a turbojet is developed by compressing air in the inlet and compressor, mixing the air with fuel and burning it in the combustor, and **expanding the gas stream through the turbine and nozzle.**

8. **D** The ramjet engine consists of **an inlet, a combustion zone, and a nozzle.** The ramjet does not have a compressor and turbine as the turbojet does. Air enters the inlet, where it is compressed; it then enters the combustion zone, where it is mixed with fuel and burned. The hot gases are then expelled through the nozzle, developing thrust. Ramjet operation depends on the inlet to decelerate the incoming air to increase the pressure in the combustion zone. The pressure increase makes it possible for the ramjet to operate: The higher the velocity of the incoming air, the more the pressure increase. It is for this reason that the ramjet operates best at high supersonic velocities. At subsonic velocities, the ramjet is inefficient, and, to start the ramjet, air must first enter the inlet at a relatively high velocity.

9. **A** The four forces that act on an aircraft in flight are **lift, gravity, thrust, and drag**.

10. **E** For a fixed-wing aircraft, lift is generated **perpendicular** to the direction of flight.

11. **E** The angle formed by the chord of an airfoil or wing and the direction of the relative wind is known as the **angle of attack**.

12. **C** Pitot tubes furnish data to an instrument that is used by aircraft pilots in about the same way that a **speedometer** is used by an automobile driver.

13. **A** The part of an airplane that holds the cargo and passengers—as well as providing a base for the other aircraft parts—is known as the **fuselage**.

14. **B** On a conventional fixed-wing aircraft, the **horizontal stabilizers** maintain pitch and the **vertical stabilizer** controls yaw. If the pilot wishes to *change* pitch or yaw, he uses the elevators and rudder, respectively.

15. **C** **Flaps** are additional hinged rear sections mounted to the wing near the body deployed downward on takeoff and landing to increase the amount of force produced by the wing. *Ailerons* are mounted farther out on the wing, away from the body, and can change or control the roll of the aircraft. *Elevators* are the hinged rear part of the horizontal stabilizer and can change the aircraft's pitch (up and down orientation). *Trim tabs* are small hinged surfaces on the rear of the elevators that help prevent or minimize pilot fatigue by relieving control pressure at the desired flight angle. *Elevons* are movable flight surfaces on delta wing aircraft that help control roll and pitch.

16. **D** Density altitude is a theoretical air density that exists under standard conditions at a certain altitude—a "rule of thumb" guideline. The four factors that affect density altitude are altitude, atmospheric pressure, humidity, and temperature.

17. **E** The degree of movement of an aircraft around its longitudinal axis is known as **bank**; the movement itself is known as "roll."

18. **A** The Venturi theory of lift says that faster airflow over the curved upper portion of a wing surface causes **decreased pressure according to Bernoulli's equation**. Although this has been the widely accepted explanation for many years, emerging research is beginning to account for inconsistencies between theoretical and actual airfoil pressures and other performance results. However, the still widely recognized Venturi theory is correct in many major aspects and does accurately describe some airfoil performance characteristics.

19. **C** The maneuver in which a rotary-wing aircraft (helicopter) is maintained in nearly motionless flight over a ground reference point at a constant altitude and heading (direction) is known as **hovering**. It is usually done at a relatively low altitude.

20. **C** The ratio of the speed of an aircraft to the speed of sound in the air around it is the aircraft's **Mach number**, named in honor of Ernst Mach, a late-nineteenth-century physicist who studied gas dynamics.

Subtest #9: General Science

Check your answers below and refer to the explanation for each question you missed. Use the table to record right and wrong answers.

	✔	✘		✔	✘		✔	✘		✔	✘
1. B			6. B			11. C			16. D		
2. B			7. A			12. B			17. D		
3. C			8. C			13. A			18. D		
4. A			9. C			14. C			19. A		
5. D			10. D			15. B			20. C		

1. **B** Energy that is derived from the sun is called **solar energy**. *Hydroelectric power* is derived from the movement of water—for example, water pouring over the top of a dam, turning one or more turbines, and thereby generating electricity. *Geothermal* energy is energy produced by harnessing heat from the earth, usually from deep below the surface.

2. **B** There are four principal types of tissue in the human body: epithelial, connective, muscular, and nervous. **Epithelial tissue** forms the skin and inner lining for the organs. *Connective tissue* protects, supports, and binds together various organs; it also separates structures such as skeletal muscles and, in some cases, stores energy. *Supporting, voluntary*, and *excess* are not generally recognized categories of human tissue.

3. **C Chromosomes** are composed of DNA and protein and are usually found in the nucleus.

4. **A** Chemical reactions may be classified into four main types. In composition (direct combination), two or more elements or compounds combine to form a more complex substance. *Decomposition* (the reverse of composition) occurs when a complex compound breaks down to simpler compounds of basic elements. **Replacement** takes place when one substance in a compound is freed and another takes its place. *Double* (or ionic) *replacement* occurs when ions in a solution combine to form a new product that then leaves the solution. $2Na + 2HOH \rightarrow 2NaOH + H_2$ is a *single replacement* reaction where one sodium atom replaces just one of the hydrogen atoms in each water molecule.

5. **D Symbiosis** is a nutritive relationship in which organisms of different species live together and benefit each other. *Parthenogenesis* is the development of a new individual from an unfertilized, usually female, sex

cell. *Meiosis* is the process of cell division in gamete-producing cells in which the number of chromosomes is reduced by half. *Mitosis* is the process that takes place in the nucleus of a dividing cell that results in the formation of two new nuclei. *Phagocytosis* is the process by which cells (phagocytes) ingest and destroy microbes, cell debris, and other foreign matter.

6. **B Iodine** crystals in a small bottle of water make a saturated aqueous solution; a few milliliters of this solution added to a quart of water will destroy most organisms in an hour.

7. **A** The **kilogram** is the unit of mass used by the International System of Units, or SI (for Systéme International d'Unités). The *kilometer* is a unit of length (1,000 meters); the *ampere* is a unit of electric current; the *ohm* measures electrical resistance; and the *henry* is a unit of electrical inductance, which is the ability of a coil to oppose any change in circuit current.

8. **C** Proteins are synthesized from a variety of **amino acid** building blocks. Digestion breaks down these complex protein structures.

9. **C** The hydrate $CuSO_4 \cdot 5H_2O$ contains 6 atoms in the salt $CuSO_4$ (1Cu + 1S + 4O). The 5 loosely bonded water molecules contain 15 atoms (10H + 5O). The total number of atoms is 6 + 15 = 21.

10. **D** A magnetic compass is influenced by all magnetic sources in its vicinity and aligns itself according to the net **local magnetic field**; normally, this means pointing to the *magnetic north pole,* but not when there is a stronger magnetic influence nearby.

11. **C** Compounds that include fat and oils found in foods and the human body are **lipids**. *Vitamins* are

organic molecules needed in very small amounts that act as catalysts for normal metabolic processes in the body. *Carbohydrates* are organic compounds containing carbon, hydrogen, and oxygen and made up of sugar subunits. *Minerals* are inorganic solid substances—such as calcium, potassium, iron, and phosphorus—that often perform a function vital to key metabolic processes. *Proteins* are organic compounds consisting of carbon, hydrogen, oxygen, nitrogen, and sometimes sulfur and phosphorus, and made up of amino acids linked by peptide bonds.

12. **B** In this example, gravitational potential energy is converted into kinetic energy. The kinetic energy is equal to the mass of the object, *m*, multiplied by the acceleration caused by the force of gravity, *g*, multiplied by the distance or height involved, *h*. Thus,

$$m \times g \times h = 1 \text{ kilogram} \times 9.8 \text{ m/sec} \times 1 \text{ meter} = 9.8 \text{ J}$$
(approximately 10 J).

13. **A** The power delivered when a 120-volt electrical power supply produces $\frac{1}{2}$ amp to the load is **60 watts**. This is calculated by the formula

Power (measured in watts) = volts (measuring electricity) × amperes (measuring intensity)
or
$$P = E \times I$$
$$P = 120V \times 0.5A$$
$$P = 60W$$

14. **C** Resistance, which is the tendency for a material to oppose the flow of electrons, is measured in **ohms**, named after German physicist Georg Ohm, who discovered the relationship between voltage, current, and resistance in 1827.

15. **B** The cell wall, composed mainly of cellulose, is an important characteristic of plant cells. **Chloroplasts** contain energy-accumulating pigments and are found only in plant cells. Cells without cell walls would not be plant cells and would therefore not have *chloroplasts*, either.

16. **D** A magnifying glass is a **concave lens used for objects closer than one focal length**. The object held closer than one focal length from a convex lens will produce a virtual magnified image.

17. **D** The glucose content of the blood is regulated by insulin and adrenaline. The relative concentration of glucose is maintained by the combined action of insulin from the pancreas and adrenaline from the adrenal medulla. *ACTH* is adrenocorticotropic hormone, a pituitary gland hormone that stimulates secretion of hormones containing cortisone. *Progesterone* is a hormone secreted by the ovaries of the female.

18. **D** Frictional forces usually do NOT increase potential energy. The friction force *does* tend to *oppose motion*, slow the object down, and *produce wear* between contacting surfaces.

19. **A** For a solar eclipse to take place, the **moon must be between the sun and the earth**. Because the moon is directly between the earth and the sun—and because the earth and the moon are still moving and line up only relatively briefly—the moon only seems to block out the sun from a certain perspective; the moon's shadow (umbra) is very narrow, only about 170 miles in width.

20. **C** Enzymes are organic (protein) catalysts that **affect the speed of chemical reactions** without being used up themselves.

Subtest #10: Rotated Blocks

Check your answers below. Use the table to record right and wrong answers.

	✔	✘		✔	✘		✔	✘
1. D			6. B			11. D		
2. B			7. C			12. C		
3. C			8. D			13. B		
4. A			9. A			14. E		
5. D			10. B			15. A		

Subtest #11: Hidden Figures

Check your answers below. Use the table to record right and wrong answers.

	✔	✘		✔	✘		✔	✘
1. A			6. C			11. D		
2. B			7. A			12. B		
3. C			8. E			13. C		
4. B			9. B			14. D		
5. D			10. C			15. E		

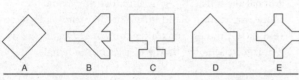

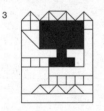

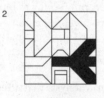

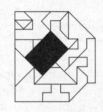

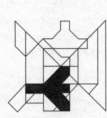

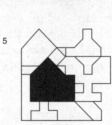

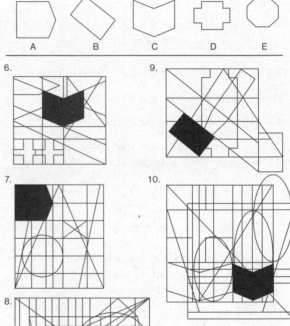

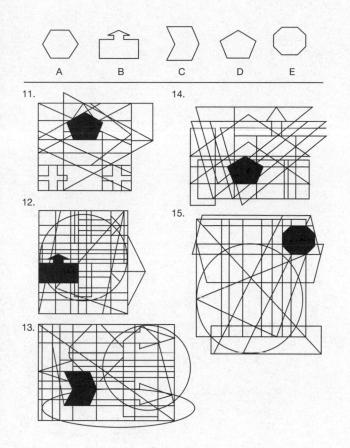

Subtest #12: Self-Description Inventory

There are no right or wrong answers to this subtest.

Answer Sheet

A F O Q T # 2

Subtest 1: Verbal Analogies

1 Ⓐ Ⓑ Ⓒ Ⓓ Ⓔ	8 Ⓐ Ⓑ Ⓒ Ⓓ Ⓔ	15 Ⓐ Ⓑ Ⓒ Ⓓ Ⓔ	22 Ⓐ Ⓑ Ⓒ Ⓓ Ⓔ
2 Ⓐ Ⓑ Ⓒ Ⓓ Ⓔ	9 Ⓐ Ⓑ Ⓒ Ⓓ Ⓔ	16 Ⓐ Ⓑ Ⓒ Ⓓ Ⓔ	23 Ⓐ Ⓑ Ⓒ Ⓓ Ⓔ
3 Ⓐ Ⓑ Ⓒ Ⓓ Ⓔ	10 Ⓐ Ⓑ Ⓒ Ⓓ Ⓔ	17 Ⓐ Ⓑ Ⓒ Ⓓ Ⓔ	24 Ⓐ Ⓑ Ⓒ Ⓓ Ⓔ
4 Ⓐ Ⓑ Ⓒ Ⓓ Ⓔ	11 Ⓐ Ⓑ Ⓒ Ⓓ Ⓔ	18 Ⓐ Ⓑ Ⓒ Ⓓ Ⓔ	25 Ⓐ Ⓑ Ⓒ Ⓓ Ⓔ
5 Ⓐ Ⓑ Ⓒ Ⓓ Ⓔ	12 Ⓐ Ⓑ Ⓒ Ⓓ Ⓔ	19 Ⓐ Ⓑ Ⓒ Ⓓ Ⓔ	
6 Ⓐ Ⓑ Ⓒ Ⓓ Ⓔ	13 Ⓐ Ⓑ Ⓒ Ⓓ Ⓔ	20 Ⓐ Ⓑ Ⓒ Ⓓ Ⓔ	
7 Ⓐ Ⓑ Ⓒ Ⓓ Ⓔ	14 Ⓐ Ⓑ Ⓒ Ⓓ Ⓔ	21 Ⓐ Ⓑ Ⓒ Ⓓ Ⓔ	

Subtest 2: Arithmetic Reasoning

1 Ⓐ Ⓑ Ⓒ Ⓓ Ⓔ	8 Ⓐ Ⓑ Ⓒ Ⓓ Ⓔ	15 Ⓐ Ⓑ Ⓒ Ⓓ Ⓔ	22 Ⓐ Ⓑ Ⓒ Ⓓ Ⓔ
2 Ⓐ Ⓑ Ⓒ Ⓓ Ⓔ	9 Ⓐ Ⓑ Ⓒ Ⓓ Ⓔ	16 Ⓐ Ⓑ Ⓒ Ⓓ Ⓔ	23 Ⓐ Ⓑ Ⓒ Ⓓ Ⓔ
3 Ⓐ Ⓑ Ⓒ Ⓓ Ⓔ	10 Ⓐ Ⓑ Ⓒ Ⓓ Ⓔ	17 Ⓐ Ⓑ Ⓒ Ⓓ Ⓔ	24 Ⓐ Ⓑ Ⓒ Ⓓ Ⓔ
4 Ⓐ Ⓑ Ⓒ Ⓓ Ⓔ	11 Ⓐ Ⓑ Ⓒ Ⓓ Ⓔ	18 Ⓐ Ⓑ Ⓒ Ⓓ Ⓔ	25 Ⓐ Ⓑ Ⓒ Ⓓ Ⓔ
5 Ⓐ Ⓑ Ⓒ Ⓓ Ⓔ	12 Ⓐ Ⓑ Ⓒ Ⓓ Ⓔ	19 Ⓐ Ⓑ Ⓒ Ⓓ Ⓔ	
6 Ⓐ Ⓑ Ⓒ Ⓓ Ⓔ	13 Ⓐ Ⓑ Ⓒ Ⓓ Ⓔ	20 Ⓐ Ⓑ Ⓒ Ⓓ Ⓔ	
7 Ⓐ Ⓑ Ⓒ Ⓓ Ⓔ	14 Ⓐ Ⓑ Ⓒ Ⓓ Ⓔ	21 Ⓐ Ⓑ Ⓒ Ⓓ Ⓔ	

Subtest 3: Word Knowledge

1 Ⓐ Ⓑ Ⓒ Ⓓ Ⓔ	8 Ⓐ Ⓑ Ⓒ Ⓓ Ⓔ	15 Ⓐ Ⓑ Ⓒ Ⓓ Ⓔ	22 Ⓐ Ⓑ Ⓒ Ⓓ Ⓔ
2 Ⓐ Ⓑ Ⓒ Ⓓ Ⓔ	9 Ⓐ Ⓑ Ⓒ Ⓓ Ⓔ	16 Ⓐ Ⓑ Ⓒ Ⓓ Ⓔ	23 Ⓐ Ⓑ Ⓒ Ⓓ Ⓔ
3 Ⓐ Ⓑ Ⓒ Ⓓ Ⓔ	10 Ⓐ Ⓑ Ⓒ Ⓓ Ⓔ	17 Ⓐ Ⓑ Ⓒ Ⓓ Ⓔ	24 Ⓐ Ⓑ Ⓒ Ⓓ Ⓔ
4 Ⓐ Ⓑ Ⓒ Ⓓ Ⓔ	11 Ⓐ Ⓑ Ⓒ Ⓓ Ⓔ	18 Ⓐ Ⓑ Ⓒ Ⓓ Ⓔ	25 Ⓐ Ⓑ Ⓒ Ⓓ Ⓔ
5 Ⓐ Ⓑ Ⓒ Ⓓ Ⓔ	12 Ⓐ Ⓑ Ⓒ Ⓓ Ⓔ	19 Ⓐ Ⓑ Ⓒ Ⓓ Ⓔ	
6 Ⓐ Ⓑ Ⓒ Ⓓ Ⓔ	13 Ⓐ Ⓑ Ⓒ Ⓓ Ⓔ	20 Ⓐ Ⓑ Ⓒ Ⓓ Ⓔ	
7 Ⓐ Ⓑ Ⓒ Ⓓ Ⓔ	14 Ⓐ Ⓑ Ⓒ Ⓓ Ⓔ	21 Ⓐ Ⓑ Ⓒ Ⓓ Ⓔ	

Subtest 4: Math Knowledge

1 Ⓐ Ⓑ Ⓒ Ⓓ Ⓔ	8 Ⓐ Ⓑ Ⓒ Ⓓ Ⓔ	15 Ⓐ Ⓑ Ⓒ Ⓓ Ⓔ	22 Ⓐ Ⓑ Ⓒ Ⓓ Ⓔ
2 Ⓐ Ⓑ Ⓒ Ⓓ Ⓔ	9 Ⓐ Ⓑ Ⓒ Ⓓ Ⓔ	16 Ⓐ Ⓑ Ⓒ Ⓓ Ⓔ	23 Ⓐ Ⓑ Ⓒ Ⓓ Ⓔ
3 Ⓐ Ⓑ Ⓒ Ⓓ Ⓔ	10 Ⓐ Ⓑ Ⓒ Ⓓ Ⓔ	17 Ⓐ Ⓑ Ⓒ Ⓓ Ⓔ	24 Ⓐ Ⓑ Ⓒ Ⓓ Ⓔ
4 Ⓐ Ⓑ Ⓒ Ⓓ Ⓔ	11 Ⓐ Ⓑ Ⓒ Ⓓ Ⓔ	18 Ⓐ Ⓑ Ⓒ Ⓓ Ⓔ	25 Ⓐ Ⓑ Ⓒ Ⓓ Ⓔ
5 Ⓐ Ⓑ Ⓒ Ⓓ Ⓔ	12 Ⓐ Ⓑ Ⓒ Ⓓ Ⓔ	19 Ⓐ Ⓑ Ⓒ Ⓓ Ⓔ	
6 Ⓐ Ⓑ Ⓒ Ⓓ Ⓔ	13 Ⓐ Ⓑ Ⓒ Ⓓ Ⓔ	20 Ⓐ Ⓑ Ⓒ Ⓓ Ⓔ	
7 Ⓐ Ⓑ Ⓒ Ⓓ Ⓔ	14 Ⓐ Ⓑ Ⓒ Ⓓ Ⓔ	21 Ⓐ Ⓑ Ⓒ Ⓓ Ⓔ	

Subtest 5: Instrument Comprehension

1 Ⓐ Ⓑ Ⓒ Ⓓ	6 Ⓐ Ⓑ Ⓒ Ⓓ	11 Ⓐ Ⓑ Ⓒ Ⓓ	16 Ⓐ Ⓑ Ⓒ Ⓓ
2 Ⓐ Ⓑ Ⓒ Ⓓ	7 Ⓐ Ⓑ Ⓒ Ⓓ	12 Ⓐ Ⓑ Ⓒ Ⓓ	17 Ⓐ Ⓑ Ⓒ Ⓓ
3 Ⓐ Ⓑ Ⓒ Ⓓ	8 Ⓐ Ⓑ Ⓒ Ⓓ	13 Ⓐ Ⓑ Ⓒ Ⓓ	18 Ⓐ Ⓑ Ⓒ Ⓓ
4 Ⓐ Ⓑ Ⓒ Ⓓ	9 Ⓐ Ⓑ Ⓒ Ⓓ	14 Ⓐ Ⓑ Ⓒ Ⓓ	19 Ⓐ Ⓑ Ⓒ Ⓓ
5 Ⓐ Ⓑ Ⓒ Ⓓ	10 Ⓐ Ⓑ Ⓒ Ⓓ	15 Ⓐ Ⓑ Ⓒ Ⓓ	20 Ⓐ Ⓑ Ⓒ Ⓓ

Answer Sheet
AFOQT #2

Subtest 6: Block Counting

1 Ⓐ Ⓑ Ⓒ Ⓓ Ⓔ	6 Ⓐ Ⓑ Ⓒ Ⓓ Ⓔ	11 Ⓐ Ⓑ Ⓒ Ⓓ Ⓔ	16 Ⓐ Ⓑ Ⓒ Ⓓ Ⓔ
2 Ⓐ Ⓑ Ⓒ Ⓓ Ⓔ	7 Ⓐ Ⓑ Ⓒ Ⓓ Ⓔ	12 Ⓐ Ⓑ Ⓒ Ⓓ Ⓔ	17 Ⓐ Ⓑ Ⓒ Ⓓ Ⓔ
3 Ⓐ Ⓑ Ⓒ Ⓓ Ⓔ	8 Ⓐ Ⓑ Ⓒ Ⓓ Ⓔ	13 Ⓐ Ⓑ Ⓒ Ⓓ Ⓔ	18 Ⓐ Ⓑ Ⓒ Ⓓ Ⓔ
4 Ⓐ Ⓑ Ⓒ Ⓓ Ⓔ	9 Ⓐ Ⓑ Ⓒ Ⓓ Ⓔ	14 Ⓐ Ⓑ Ⓒ Ⓓ Ⓔ	19 Ⓐ Ⓑ Ⓒ Ⓓ Ⓔ
5 Ⓐ Ⓑ Ⓒ Ⓓ Ⓔ	10 Ⓐ Ⓑ Ⓒ Ⓓ Ⓔ	15 Ⓐ Ⓑ Ⓒ Ⓓ Ⓔ	20 Ⓐ Ⓑ Ⓒ Ⓓ Ⓔ

Subtest 7: Table Reading

1 Ⓐ Ⓑ Ⓒ Ⓓ Ⓔ	11 Ⓐ Ⓑ Ⓒ Ⓓ Ⓔ	21 Ⓐ Ⓑ Ⓒ Ⓓ Ⓔ	31 Ⓐ Ⓑ Ⓒ Ⓓ Ⓔ
2 Ⓐ Ⓑ Ⓒ Ⓓ Ⓔ	12 Ⓐ Ⓑ Ⓒ Ⓓ Ⓔ	22 Ⓐ Ⓑ Ⓒ Ⓓ Ⓔ	32 Ⓐ Ⓑ Ⓒ Ⓓ Ⓔ
3 Ⓐ Ⓑ Ⓒ Ⓓ Ⓔ	13 Ⓐ Ⓑ Ⓒ Ⓓ Ⓔ	23 Ⓐ Ⓑ Ⓒ Ⓓ Ⓔ	33 Ⓐ Ⓑ Ⓒ Ⓓ Ⓔ
4 Ⓐ Ⓑ Ⓒ Ⓓ Ⓔ	14 Ⓐ Ⓑ Ⓒ Ⓓ Ⓔ	24 Ⓐ Ⓑ Ⓒ Ⓓ Ⓔ	34 Ⓐ Ⓑ Ⓒ Ⓓ Ⓔ
5 Ⓐ Ⓑ Ⓒ Ⓓ Ⓔ	15 Ⓐ Ⓑ Ⓒ Ⓓ Ⓔ	25 Ⓐ Ⓑ Ⓒ Ⓓ Ⓔ	35 Ⓐ Ⓑ Ⓒ Ⓓ Ⓔ
6 Ⓐ Ⓑ Ⓒ Ⓓ Ⓔ	16 Ⓐ Ⓑ Ⓒ Ⓓ Ⓔ	26 Ⓐ Ⓑ Ⓒ Ⓓ Ⓔ	36 Ⓐ Ⓑ Ⓒ Ⓓ Ⓔ
7 Ⓐ Ⓑ Ⓒ Ⓓ Ⓔ	17 Ⓐ Ⓑ Ⓒ Ⓓ Ⓔ	27 Ⓐ Ⓑ Ⓒ Ⓓ Ⓔ	37 Ⓐ Ⓑ Ⓒ Ⓓ Ⓔ
8 Ⓐ Ⓑ Ⓒ Ⓓ Ⓔ	18 Ⓐ Ⓑ Ⓒ Ⓓ Ⓔ	28 Ⓐ Ⓑ Ⓒ Ⓓ Ⓔ	38 Ⓐ Ⓑ Ⓒ Ⓓ Ⓔ
9 Ⓐ Ⓑ Ⓒ Ⓓ Ⓔ	19 Ⓐ Ⓑ Ⓒ Ⓓ Ⓔ	29 Ⓐ Ⓑ Ⓒ Ⓓ Ⓔ	39 Ⓐ Ⓑ Ⓒ Ⓓ Ⓔ
10 Ⓐ Ⓑ Ⓒ Ⓓ Ⓔ	20 Ⓐ Ⓑ Ⓒ Ⓓ Ⓔ	30 Ⓐ Ⓑ Ⓒ Ⓓ Ⓔ	40 Ⓐ Ⓑ Ⓒ Ⓓ Ⓔ

Subtest 8: Aviation Information

1 Ⓐ Ⓑ Ⓒ Ⓓ Ⓔ	6 Ⓐ Ⓑ Ⓒ Ⓓ Ⓔ	11 Ⓐ Ⓑ Ⓒ Ⓓ Ⓔ	16 Ⓐ Ⓑ Ⓒ Ⓓ Ⓔ
2 Ⓐ Ⓑ Ⓒ Ⓓ Ⓔ	7 Ⓐ Ⓑ Ⓒ Ⓓ Ⓔ	12 Ⓐ Ⓑ Ⓒ Ⓓ Ⓔ	17 Ⓐ Ⓑ Ⓒ Ⓓ Ⓔ
3 Ⓐ Ⓑ Ⓒ Ⓓ Ⓔ	8 Ⓐ Ⓑ Ⓒ Ⓓ Ⓔ	13 Ⓐ Ⓑ Ⓒ Ⓓ Ⓔ	18 Ⓐ Ⓑ Ⓒ Ⓓ Ⓔ
4 Ⓐ Ⓑ Ⓒ Ⓓ Ⓔ	9 Ⓐ Ⓑ Ⓒ Ⓓ Ⓔ	14 Ⓐ Ⓑ Ⓒ Ⓓ Ⓔ	19 Ⓐ Ⓑ Ⓒ Ⓓ Ⓔ
5 Ⓐ Ⓑ Ⓒ Ⓓ Ⓔ	10 Ⓐ Ⓑ Ⓒ Ⓓ Ⓔ	15 Ⓐ Ⓑ Ⓒ Ⓓ Ⓔ	20 Ⓐ Ⓑ Ⓒ Ⓓ Ⓔ

Subtest 9: General Science

1 Ⓐ Ⓑ Ⓒ Ⓓ Ⓔ	6 Ⓐ Ⓑ Ⓒ Ⓓ Ⓔ	11 Ⓐ Ⓑ Ⓒ Ⓓ Ⓔ	16 Ⓐ Ⓑ Ⓒ Ⓓ Ⓔ
2 Ⓐ Ⓑ Ⓒ Ⓓ Ⓔ	7 Ⓐ Ⓑ Ⓒ Ⓓ Ⓔ	12 Ⓐ Ⓑ Ⓒ Ⓓ Ⓔ	17 Ⓐ Ⓑ Ⓒ Ⓓ Ⓔ
3 Ⓐ Ⓑ Ⓒ Ⓓ Ⓔ	8 Ⓐ Ⓑ Ⓒ Ⓓ Ⓔ	13 Ⓐ Ⓑ Ⓒ Ⓓ Ⓔ	18 Ⓐ Ⓑ Ⓒ Ⓓ Ⓔ
4 Ⓐ Ⓑ Ⓒ Ⓓ Ⓔ	9 Ⓐ Ⓑ Ⓒ Ⓓ Ⓔ	14 Ⓐ Ⓑ Ⓒ Ⓓ Ⓔ	19 Ⓐ Ⓑ Ⓒ Ⓓ Ⓔ
5 Ⓐ Ⓑ Ⓒ Ⓓ Ⓔ	10 Ⓐ Ⓑ Ⓒ Ⓓ Ⓔ	15 Ⓐ Ⓑ Ⓒ Ⓓ Ⓔ	20 Ⓐ Ⓑ Ⓒ Ⓓ Ⓔ

Subtest 10: Rotated Blocks

1 Ⓐ Ⓑ Ⓒ Ⓓ Ⓔ	5 Ⓐ Ⓑ Ⓒ Ⓓ Ⓔ	9 Ⓐ Ⓑ Ⓒ Ⓓ Ⓔ	13 Ⓐ Ⓑ Ⓒ Ⓓ Ⓔ
2 Ⓐ Ⓑ Ⓒ Ⓓ Ⓔ	6 Ⓐ Ⓑ Ⓒ Ⓓ Ⓔ	10 Ⓐ Ⓑ Ⓒ Ⓓ Ⓔ	14 Ⓐ Ⓑ Ⓒ Ⓓ Ⓔ
3 Ⓐ Ⓑ Ⓒ Ⓓ Ⓔ	7 Ⓐ Ⓑ Ⓒ Ⓓ Ⓔ	11 Ⓐ Ⓑ Ⓒ Ⓓ Ⓔ	15 Ⓐ Ⓑ Ⓒ Ⓓ Ⓔ
4 Ⓐ Ⓑ Ⓒ Ⓓ Ⓔ	8 Ⓐ Ⓑ Ⓒ Ⓓ Ⓔ	12 Ⓐ Ⓑ Ⓒ Ⓓ Ⓔ	

Subtest 11: Hidden Figures

1 Ⓐ Ⓑ Ⓒ Ⓓ Ⓔ	5 Ⓐ Ⓑ Ⓒ Ⓓ Ⓔ	9 Ⓐ Ⓑ Ⓒ Ⓓ Ⓔ	13 Ⓐ Ⓑ Ⓒ Ⓓ Ⓔ
2 Ⓐ Ⓑ Ⓒ Ⓓ Ⓔ	6 Ⓐ Ⓑ Ⓒ Ⓓ Ⓔ	10 Ⓐ Ⓑ Ⓒ Ⓓ Ⓔ	14 Ⓐ Ⓑ Ⓒ Ⓓ Ⓔ
3 Ⓐ Ⓑ Ⓒ Ⓓ Ⓔ	7 Ⓐ Ⓑ Ⓒ Ⓓ Ⓔ	11 Ⓐ Ⓑ Ⓒ Ⓓ Ⓔ	15 Ⓐ Ⓑ Ⓒ Ⓓ Ⓔ
4 Ⓐ Ⓑ Ⓒ Ⓓ Ⓔ	8 Ⓐ Ⓑ Ⓒ Ⓓ Ⓔ	12 Ⓐ Ⓑ Ⓒ Ⓓ Ⓔ	

Practice Air Force Officer Qualifying Test (AFOQT) #2

CHAPTER 10

Please turn to the beginning of Chapter 9, page 241, for more information about the breakdown and scoring attributes of the Air Force Officer Qualifying Test (AFOQT).

SUBTEST #1: VERBAL ANALOGIES (25 QUESTIONS)

This part of the test measures your ability to reason and see relationships between words. Choose the answer that best completes the analogy developed at the beginning of each question.

1. CROWDED is to URBAN as SPARSE is to

    (A) SLOWER.
    (B) RURAL.
    (C) SUBURBAN.
    (D) INDUSTRIAL.
    (E) CALM.

2. WATCH is to WATCHED as THROW is to

    (A) THROWED.
    (B) THROWN.
    (C) THROWER.
    (D) THREW.
    (E) TOSSED.

3. WRENCH is to PLUMBER as HAMMER is to

    (A) NAIL.
    (B) CARPENTER.
    (C) CONSTRUCTION.
    (D) BUILDING.
    (E) FOREMAN.

4. NATURAL is to ARTIFICIAL as

    (A) COOK is to WAITER.
    (B) BIRTH is to MATURITY.
    (C) CREATE is to DESTROY.
    (D) CUT is to DISSECT.
    (E) TEAR is to WATER.

5. BACON is to PIGS as HAMBURGER is to

    (A) VEAL.
    (B) BEEF.
    (C) FOWL.
    (D) HORSES.
    (E) CATTLE.

6. KANGAROO is to POUCH as

    (A) BEAR is to CAVE.
    (B) GLOVE is to BALL.
    (C) WEB is to SPIDER.
    (D) BUTTERFLY is to COCOON.
    (E) FISH is to SCHOOL.

7. BEHAVE is to CANDY as DISOBEY is to

    (A) RELINQUISH.
    (B) REPRIMAND.
    (C) ARGUMENT.
    (D) DISHONESTY.
    (E) DISRUPTION.

8. XXII is to IXXX as 22 is to

    (A) 29
    (B) 31
    (C) 32
    (D) 51
    (E) 13

9. AMUSING is to FUNNY as ODD is to

    (A) EVEN.
    (B) EXTRA.
    (C) FELLOW.
    (D) DISTINCT.
    (E) UNUSUAL.

10. HONOR is to COURAGE as

    (A) LIGHT is to DARKNESS.
    (B) KNOWLEDGE is to WISDOM.
    (C) SELFISHNESS is to GREED.
    (D) DUTY is to COUNTRY.
    (E) KEY is to IGNITION.

11. ATLANTA is to GEORGIA as DALLAS is to

    (A) FORT WORTH.
    (B) BIRMINGHAM.
    (C) COWBOYS.
    (D) TEXAS.
    (E) LOUISIANA.

12. CLOCK is to WATCH as

    (A) LAKE is to STREAM.
    (B) OCEAN is to RIVER.
    (C) WATER is to FISH.
    (D) BOAT is to SAIL.
    (E) LAKE is to POND.

13. STABLE is to HORSE as

  (A) HOUSE is to HUMAN.
  (B) MOTHER is to DAUGHTER.
  (C) BOOK is to LIBRARY.
  (D) SEAMSTRESS is to CLOTH.
  (E) WATER is to DUCK.

14. SQUIRREL is to TREE as GOPHER is to

  (A) FOREST.
  (B) BUSH.
  (C) LAKE.
  (D) GROUND.
  (E) HOLLOW.

15. INFANCY is to CHILDHOOD as ENGAGEMENT is to

  (A) DRIVE TRAIN.
  (B) LOVE.
  (C) MARRIAGE.
  (D) RING.
  (E) BRIDE.

16. TRAVEL is to AUTO as

  (A) TRAIN is to WHISTLE.
  (B) WATER is to DRINK.
  (C) SOLDIER is to SAILOR.
  (D) EAT is to SPOON.
  (E) MEAT is to POTATOES.

17. ABU DHABI is to MUSCAT as

  (A) CAIRO is to INCIRLIK.
  (B) BEIRUT is to DAMASCUS.
  (C) AUSTIN is to BATON ROUGE.
  (D) OMAN is to YEMEN.
  (E) LONDON is to HAMBURG.

18. SURGEON is to SCALPEL as FIREMAN is to

  (A) SIREN.
  (B) DALMATIAN.
  (C) HELMET.
  (D) WATER HOSE.
  (E) POLICEMAN.

19. FRAME is to PAINTING as

  (A) FENCE is to YARD.
  (B) CLOUD is to SKY.
  (C) BOOK is to COVER.
  (D) PARK is to RANGER.
  (E) JACK is to TIRE.

20. CASCADE is to WATERFALL as

  (A) FISH is to RIVER.
  (B) WARN is to HURRICANE.
  (C) LAKE is to SAIL.
  (D) CROSS is to OCEAN.
  (E) MEANDER is to STREAM.

21. INFORM is to ENLIGHTEN as SING is to

  (A) MELODY.
  (B) ENTERTAIN.
  (C) REFRAIN.
  (D) CONFESS.
  (E) WHISTLE.

22. PECAN is to PIE as CHOCOLATE is to

  (A) BROWN.
  (B) FROSTING.
  (C) CHIPS.
  (D) CAKE.
  (E) DESSERT.

23. WALK is to MARCH as

  (A) READ is to STUDY.
  (B) FOOT is to TREAD.
  (C) RUN is to STOP.
  (D) WALTZ is to RUMBA.
  (E) RAP is to JAZZ.

24. KABUL is to AFGHANISTAN as

  (A) PENSACOLA is to FLORIDA.
  (B) CALCUTTA is to INDIA.
  (C) JAPAN is to KOREA.
  (D) CAIRO is to EGYPT.
  (E) CANCUN is to HONDURAS.

25. PERPLEX is to ENLIGHTEN as MIXTURE is to

  (A) INDIVIDUAL.
  (B) ADDITIVE.
  (C) SETTLE.
  (D) SOLIDIFY.
  (E) SOCIAL.

SUBTEST #2: ARITHMETIC REASONING (25 QUESTIONS)

This part of the test measures your ability to use arithmetic to solve problems. Each problem is followed by five possible answers. You are to decide which of the choices is most nearly correct.

1. A particular flight is composed of 11 enlisted men and one noncommissioned officer. A squadron of 132 enlisted men is to be divided into flights. How many noncommissioned officers will be needed?

   (A) 11
   (B) 12
   (C) 13
   (D) 10
   (E) 14

2. An employee earns $350 per week. A total of $27.75 is withheld for federal income taxes, $5.65 for FICA (Social Security taxes), $9.29 for state income taxes, and $3.58 for the employee's retirement fund. How much will her net pay for the week be?

   (A) $314.73
   (B) $304.73
   (C) $303.73
   (D) $313.73
   (E) $305.73

3. Temperature readings on a certain day ranged from a low of −4°F to a high of 16°F. What was the average temperature for the day?

   (A) 10°
   (B) 6°
   (C) 12°
   (D) 8°
   (E) 20°

4. On a scale drawing, $\frac{1}{4}$ inch represents 1 foot. How long would a line on the drawing have to be to represent a length of $3\frac{1}{2}$ feet?

   (A) $\frac{3}{4}$ in.

   (B) $\frac{7}{8}$ in.

   (C) $1\frac{7}{8}$ in.

   (D) $1\frac{1}{4}$ in.

   (E) $1\frac{3}{4}$ in.

5. During a sale, an auto dealership offers a 15% discount on the list price of a used car. What would be the discount on a car that lists for $13,620?

   (A) $900.00
   (B) $11,577.00
   (C) $204.30
   (D) $2,043.00
   (E) $20.43

6. The price of gasoline rose from $2.90 to $3.08 per gallon. What was the percent of increase?

   (A) 3.2%
   (B) 6.2%
   (C) 6.4%
   (D) 10.6%
   (E) 1.6%

7. A team won 70% of the 40 games it played. How many games did it lose?

   (A) 28
   (B) 30
   (C) 22
   (D) 12
   (E) 7

8. A flight is scheduled for departure at 3:50 P.M. If the flight takes 2 hours and 55 minutes, at what time is it scheduled to arrive at its destination?

   (A) 5:05 P.M.
   (B) 6:05 P.M.
   (C) 6:15 P.M.
   (D) 6:45 P.M.
   (E) 6:50 P.M.

9. How many 4-oz. candy bars are there in a 3-lb. package of candy?

   (A) 12
   (B) 16
   (C) 48
   (D) 9
   (E) 24

10. What is the fifth term of the series $2\frac{5}{6}, 3\frac{1}{2}, 4\frac{1}{6}, 4\frac{5}{6}, \ldots$?

    (A) $5\frac{1}{6}$

    (B) $5\frac{1}{2}$

    (C) $5\frac{5}{6}$

    (D) $6\frac{1}{6}$

    (E) $5\frac{1}{4}$

11. In a restaurant, Tony orders an entree with vegetables for $12.50, dessert for $3.50, and coffee for $1.25. If the tax on meals is 8%, what tax should be added to his check?

    (A) $.68
    (B) $.80
    (C) $1.00
    (D) $1.28
    (E) $1.38

12. A 55-gallon drum of oil is to be used to fill cans that hold 2 quarts each. How many cans can be filled from the drum?

    (A) 55

    (B) $27\frac{1}{2}$

    (C) 110
    (D) 220
    (E) 165

13. In a factory that makes wooden spindles, a lathe operator takes 45 minutes to do the finish work on nine spindles. How many hours will it take him to finish 96 spindles at the same rate?

    (A) 8
    (B) 72
    (C) 9
    (D) 10
    (E) 45

14. A triangle has two equal sides. The third side has a length of 13 feet, 2 inches. If the perimeter of the triangle is 40 feet, what is the length of one of the equal sides?

    (A) 13 ft., 4 in.
    (B) 26 ft., 10 in.
    (C) 13 ft., 11 in.
    (D) 13 ft., 5 in.
    (E) 10 ft., 3 in.

15. A lawn is 21 feet wide and 39 feet long. How much will it cost to weed and feed it if a gardening service charges $.40 per square yard for this treatment?

    (A) $109.20
    (B) $36.40
    (C) $327.60
    (D) $24.00
    (E) $218.40

16. Amanda drove for 7 hours at a speed of 48 miles per hour. Her car gets 21 miles per gallon of gas. How many gallons of gas did she use?

    (A) 24
    (B) 14
    (C) 18
    (D) 16
    (E) 21

17. Two partners operate a business that shows a profit for the year of $63,000. Their partnership agreement calls for them to share the profits in the ratio 5:4. How much of the profit should go to the partner who gets the larger share?

    (A) $35,000
    (B) $28,000
    (C) $32,000
    (D) $36,000
    (E) $24,000

18. A purchaser paid $17.16 for an article that had recently been increased in price by 4%. What was the price of the article before the increase?

    (A) $17.00
    (B) $17.12
    (C) $16.50
    (D) $16.47
    (E) $17.20

19. In a clothing factory, 5 workers finish production of 6 garments each per day, 3 others turn out 4 garments each per day, and one worker turns out 12 per day. What is the average number of garments produced per worker per day?

 (A) $2\frac{2}{9}$
 (B) 6
 (C) 4
 (D) $7\frac{1}{3}$
 (E) $5\frac{1}{9}$

20. A man makes a 255-mile trip by car. He drives the first two hours at 45 miles per hour. At what speed must he travel for the remainder of the trip in order to arrive at his destination five hours after he started the trip?

 (A) 31 mph
 (B) 50 mph
 (C) 51 mph
 (D) 55 mph
 (E) 49 mph

21. A contractor bids $300,000 as his price for erecting a building. He estimates that $\frac{1}{10}$ of this amount will be spent for masonry materials and labor, $\frac{1}{3}$ for lumber and carpentry, $\frac{1}{5}$ for plumbing and heating, and $\frac{1}{6}$ for electrical and lighting work. The remainder will be his profit. How much profit does he expect to make?

 (A) $24,000
 (B) $80,000
 (C) $60,000
 (D) $50,000
 (E) $48,000

22. The list price of a TV set is $325, but the retailer offers successive discounts of 20% and 30%. What price would a customer actually pay?

 (A) $182.00
 (B) $270.00
 (C) $162.50
 (D) $176.67
 (E) $235.50

23. A certain brand of motor oil is regularly sold at a price of two quart cans for $1.99. On a special sale, a carton containing six of the quart cans is sold for $5.43. What is the saving per quart if the oil is bought at the special sale?

 (A) $.27
 (B) $.09
 (C) $.54
 (D) $.5425
 (E) $.18

24. A worker earns $7.20 an hour. She is paid time and a half for overtime beyond a 40-hour week. How much will she earn in a week in which she works 43 hours?

 (A) $295.20
 (B) $320.40
 (C) $432.00
 (D) $464.40
 (E) $465.12

25. A tree 36 feet high casts a shadow 8 feet long. At the same time, another tree casts a shadow 6 feet long. How tall is the second tree?

 (A) 30 ft.
 (B) 27 ft.
 (C) 24 ft.
 (D) 32 ft.
 (E) 28 ft.

SUBTEST #3: WORD KNOWLEDGE (25 QUESTIONS)

This part of the test measures verbal comprehension involving your ability to understand written language. For each question choose the answer that means the same as the capitalized word.

1. SIMULTANEOUS

    (A) versatile
    (B) imitation
    (C) false appearance
    (D) concurrent
    (E) indefinite

2. PARAGON

    (A) triangular structure
    (B) prototype
    (C) wax figure
    (D) partially departed
    (E) peacemaker

3. DEMONSTRABLE

    (A) evident
    (B) able to be refuted
    (C) able to be torn down
    (D) possessed by demons
    (E) countable

4. CONTROVERSY

    (A) vehicles moving together
    (B) a school of music
    (C) armed police force
    (D) disagreement
    (E) agreement to commit wrong

5. TEMERITY

    (A) automatic readings
    (B) presumptuous daring
    (C) mental communication
    (D) tiresome
    (E) story prepared for television

6. SCRUTINY

    (A) point of conscience or ethics
    (B) obligation
    (C) revolt of a ship's crew
    (D) careful inspection
    (E) a room adjoining the kitchen

7. JETTISON

    (A) discard
    (B) long pier
    (C) uninteresting or empty
    (D) build shoddily
    (E) compete for advantage

8. CONCILIATE

    (A) speak briefly
    (B) form in the mind
    (C) placate
    (D) set apart as sacred
    (E) confuse

9. ARBITRARY

    (A) orderly
    (B) fervent
    (C) lacking consistency
    (D) disputed
    (E) selected at random

10. ENVISAGE

    (A) conceive
    (B) wrap around
    (C) articulate
    (D) designate
    (E) paint one's face

11. SCLEROTIC

    (A) mentally disturbed
    (B) having hardened arteries
    (C) remote
    (D) despicable
    (E) educational

12. PARTISAN

    (A) adherent
    (B) divided
    (C) not complete
    (D) over-hasty
    (E) part of speech

13. INCEPTION

   (A) careful examination
   (B) divine guidance
   (C) ever-present feature
   (D) beginning
   (E) revolt against authority

14. DERIVATIVE

   (A) having a bad reputation
   (B) disconnected
   (C) serving to prove
   (D) deprived of vitality
   (E) following from

15. PERVASIVE

   (A) influential
   (B) focused on wrong
   (C) lasting indefinitely
   (D) on the outer part
   (E) permeating

16. INANITY

   (A) mental unbalance
   (B) exemption from penalty
   (C) statement lacking sense
   (D) dishonesty
   (E) official approval

17. PLAUSIBLE

   (A) unemotional
   (B) deniable
   (C) believable
   (D) great quantity
   (E) flexible

18. CONDUCIVE

   (A) able to transmit electricity
   (B) contributive
   (C) compressed
   (D) simultaneous
   (E) ignitable

19. ENSEMBLE

   (A) coordinated group or outfit
   (B) bring together
   (C) naval officer rank
   (D) rake with gunfire
   (E) tail section

20. DELETERIOUS

   (A) with careful thought
   (B) behind schedule
   (C) very tasty
   (D) harmful
   (E) removed from the total

21. LITIGATION

   (A) marking or outlining
   (B) coastland waters
   (C) governmental ruling
   (D) legal case
   (E) chemical test for acid or base

22. IMPRIMATUR

   (A) not having to do with monkeys
   (B) improper
   (C) signature
   (D) official policy
   (E) controversial decision

23. DECELERATE

   (A) belittle
   (B) remove approval
   (C) speed up
   (D) slow down
   (E) deny

24. UNILATERAL

   (A) obligating one side only
   (B) the same throughout
   (C) sideways motion
   (D) wavelike motion
   (E) having one compartment

25. INTRANSIGENT

   (A) doing things in a new way
   (B) knowing without being told
   (C) in between boundaries
   (D) courageous
   (E) uncompromising

SUBTEST #4: MATHEMATICS KNOWLEDGE (25 QUESTIONS)

This part of the test measures your ability to use learned mathematical relationships. Each problem is followed by five possible answers. Decide which one of the five answers is most nearly correct.

1. What is 4% of 0.0375?

   (A) 0.0015
   (B) 0.9375
   (C) 0.0775
   (D) 0.15
   (E) 0.015

2. What number multiplied by $\frac{2}{3}$ will give a product of 1?

   (A) $-\frac{2}{3}$

   (B) $-\frac{3}{2}$

   (C) $\frac{3}{2}$

   (D) 4/6

   (E) $\frac{2}{3}$

3. What is the value of the expression $x^2 - 5xy + 2y$ if $x = 3$ and $y = -2$?

   (A) −25
   (B) −27
   (C) 32
   (D) 35
   (E) −32

4. Solve the following inequality: $x - 3 < 14$

   (A) $x < 11$
   (B) $x < 17$
   (C) $x = 11$
   (D) $x > 17$
   (E) $x > 11$

5. Multiply $7a^3b^2c$ by $3a^2b^4c^2$.

   (A) $10a^5b^6c^3$
   (B) $21a^5b^6c^2$
   (C) $21a^6b^8c^2$
   (D) $21a^5b^6c^3$
   (E) $10a^6b^8c^2$

6. A floor is made up of hexagonal tiles, some of which are black and some of which are white. Every black tile is completely surrounded by white tiles. How many white tiles are there around each black tile?

   (A) 4
   (B) 5
   (C) 6
   (D) 8
   (E) 7

7. The value of 8^0 is

   (A) 8
   (B) 0
   (C) 1
   (D) $\frac{1}{8}$
   (E) 80

8. If $2x - 3 = 37$, what is the value of x?

   (A) 17
   (B) 38
   (C) 20
   (D) 80
   (E) 34

9. An audience consists of M people. $\frac{2}{3}$ of the audience are adults. Of the adults, $\frac{1}{2}$ are males. How many adult males are in the audience?

   (A) $\frac{1}{6}M$

   (B) $M - \frac{2}{3} - \frac{1}{2}$

   (C) $\frac{1}{3}M$

   (D) $M - \frac{1}{3}$

   (E) $\frac{2}{3}M$

10. What is the value of $(0.2)^3$?

    (A) 0.008
    (B) 0.8
    (C) 0.006
    (D) 0.6
    (E) 0.06

11. If $x^2 + x = 6$, what is the value of x?

    (A) 6 or –1
    (B) 1 or –6
    (C) 2 or –3
    (D) 3 or –2
    (E) 0 or –3

12. What is the number of square inches in the area of a circle whose diameter is 28 inches? (Use $\frac{22}{7}$ for the value of *pi*.)

    (A) 616
    (B) 88
    (C) 44
    (D) 1,232
    (E) 22

13. The expression $\frac{x^2 + 2x - 3}{x + 3}$ cannot be evaluated if x has a value of

    (A) 0.
    (B) –1.
    (C) 3.
    (D) –3.
    (E) 1.

14. If $\sqrt{x + 11} = 9$, what is the value of x?

    (A) –2
    (B) –8
    (C) 70
    (D) 7
    (E) 10

15. The points A (2,7) and B (5,11) are plotted on coordinate graph paper. What is the distance from A to B?

    (A) 7
    (B) 5
    (C) 25
    (D) 14
    (E) 5

16. Solve the following equation for y: $ay - bx = 2$

    (A) $\frac{x + bx}{a}$

    (B) $2 + bx - a$

    (C) $\frac{2}{a - bx}$

    (D) $\frac{2}{a} - bx$

    (E) $bx - 2a$

17. For a special mission, one soldier is to be chosen at random from among three infantrymen, two artillerymen, and five tank crewmen. What is the probability that an infantryman will be chosen?

    (A) $\frac{3}{10}$

    (B) $\frac{1}{10}$

    (C) $\frac{1}{3}$

    (D) $\frac{3}{7}$

    (E) $\frac{1}{7}$

18. A cylindrical post has a cross section that is a circle with a radius of 3 inches. A piece of cord can be wound around it exactly seven times. How long is the piece of cord? (Use $\frac{22}{7}$ as the value of *pi*.)

    (A) 66 in.
    (B) 42 in.
    (C) 198 in.
    (D) 132 in.
    (E) 84 in.

19. A naval task force is to be made up of a destroyer, a supply ship, and a submarine. If four destroyers, two supply ships, and three submarines are available from which to choose, how many different combinations are possible for the task force?

    (A) 9
    (B) 24
    (C) 8
    (D) 12
    (E) 16

20. The basis of a cylindrical can is a circle whose diameter is 2 inches. Its height is 7 inches. How many cubic inches are there in the volume of the can? (Use $\frac{22}{7}$ for the value of *pi*).

    (A) $12\frac{4}{7}$ cu. in.
    (B) 22 cu. in.
    (C) 44 cu. in.
    (D) 88 cu. in.
    (E) 66 cu. in.

21. A rectangular vegetable garden 16 yards long and 4 yards wide is completely enclosed by a fence. To reduce the amount of fencing used, the owner replaced the garden with a square one having the same area. How many yards of fencing did he save?

    (A) 4
    (B) 6
    (C) 8
    (D) 16
    (E) 12

22. The value of $\sqrt{164}$ to the nearest integer is

    (A) 18
    (B) 108
    (C) 42
    (D) 13
    (E) 26

23. What is the maximum number of boxes, each measuring 3 inches by 4 inches by 5 inches, that can be packed into a storage space measuring 1 foot by 2 feet by 2 feet, 1 inch?

    (A) 120
    (B) 60
    (C) 15
    (D) 48
    (E) 24

24. A circle passes through the four vertices of a rectangle that is 8 feet long and 6 feet wide. How many feet are there in the radius of the circle?

    (A) 14
    (B) $2\frac{1}{2}$
    (C) 10
    (D) 5
    (E) $7\frac{1}{2}$

25. There are 12 liters of a mixture of acetone in alcohol that is $33\frac{1}{3}$% acetone. How many liters of alcohol must be added to the mixture to reduce it to a mixture containing 25% acetone?

    (A) 1
    (B) 2
    (C) 4
    (D) 6
    (E) 8

SUBTEST #5: INSTRUMENT COMPREHENSION (20 QUESTIONS)

This part of the test measures your ability to determine the position of an airplane in flight from reading instruments showing its compass heading (direction), amount of climb or dive, and degree of bank to the right or left. In each problem, the left-hand dial is labeled ARTIFICIAL HORIZON. On the face of the dial, the small aircraft fuselage silhouette remains stationary, whereas the positions of the white line and the white pointer vary with changes in the position of the aircraft in which the instrument is located.

The white line represents the HORIZON LINE. The white pointer shows the degree of BANK to the right or left.

If the airplane is neither climbing nor diving, the horizon line is directly on the fuselage silhouette, as in dial 1 below.

If the airplane is climbing, the fuselage silhouette is seen between the horizon line and the pointer, as shown in dial 2 below. The greater the amount of climb, the greater the distance between the horizon line and the fuselage silhouette.

If the airplane is diving, the horizon line is seen between the fuselage silhouette and the pointer, as shown in dial 3 below. The greater the amount of dive, the greater the distance between the horizon line and the fuselage silhouette.

ARTIFICIAL HORIZON

Dial 1

ARTIFICIAL HORIZON

Dial 2

ARTIFICIAL HORIZON

Dial 3

If the airplane has no bank, the white pointer is seen to point to zero, as in dial 1 above.

If the airplane is banked to the pilot's right, the pointer is seen to the left of zero, as in dial 2 above.

If the airplane is banked to the pilot's left, the pointer is seen to the right of zero, as in dial 3 above.

The HORIZON LINE tilts as the aircraft is banked and is always at right angles to the pointer.

Dial 1 above shows an airplane neither climbing nor diving, with no bank.
Dial 2 above shows an airplane climbing and banked 45° to the pilot's right.
Dial 3 above shows an airplane diving and banked 45° to the pilot's left.

In each problem, the right-hand dial is labeled COMPASS. On this dial, the nose of the plane shows the compass direction in which the airplane is headed. Dial 4 shows the airplane headed north, dial 5 shows it headed west, and dial 6 shows it headed northwest.

COMPASS

Dial 4

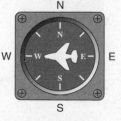

COMPASS

Dial 5

COMPASS

Dial 6

Each problem consists of two dials and four silhouettes of airplanes in flight. Your task is to determine which one of the four airplanes is MOST NEARLY in the position indicated by the two dials. You are always looking north at the same altitude as each of the four airplanes. East is always to your right as you look at the page. In the sample question below, the dial labeled ARTIFICIAL HORIZON shows that the airplane is NOT banked, and is neither climbing nor diving. The COMPASS shows that it is headed south. The only one of the four airplane silhouettes that meets these specifications is in the box lettered A, so the answer to the sample question is A.

ARTIFICIAL HORIZON   COMPASS

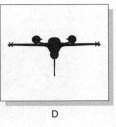

A   B   C   D

1.
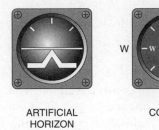

ARTIFICIAL HORIZON   COMPASS

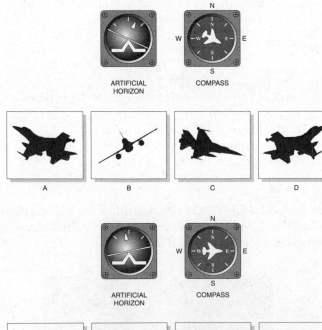

A   B   C   D

2.
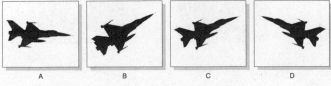

ARTIFICIAL HORIZON   COMPASS

A   B   C   D

3.

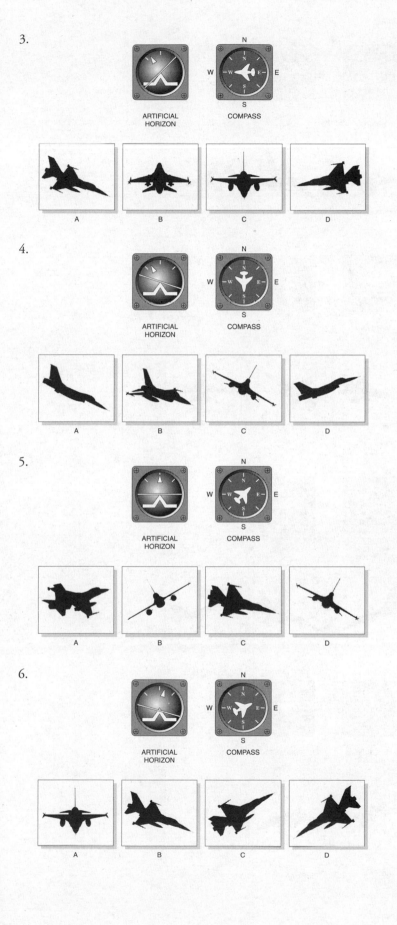

ARTIFICIAL HORIZON

COMPASS

A   B   C   D

4.

ARTIFICIAL HORIZON

COMPASS

A   B   C   D

5.

ARTIFICIAL HORIZON

COMPASS

A   B   C   D

6.

ARTIFICIAL HORIZON

COMPASS

A   B   C   D

7.

ARTIFICIAL HORIZON   COMPASS

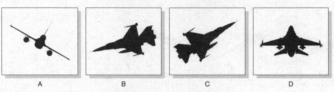

A   B   C   D

8.

ARTIFICIAL HORIZON   COMPASS

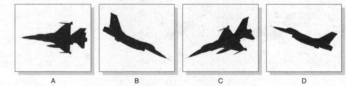

A   B   C   D

9.

ARTIFICIAL HORIZON   COMPASS

A   B   C   D

10.

ARTIFICIAL HORIZON   COMPASS

A   B   C   D

AFOQT #2

11.

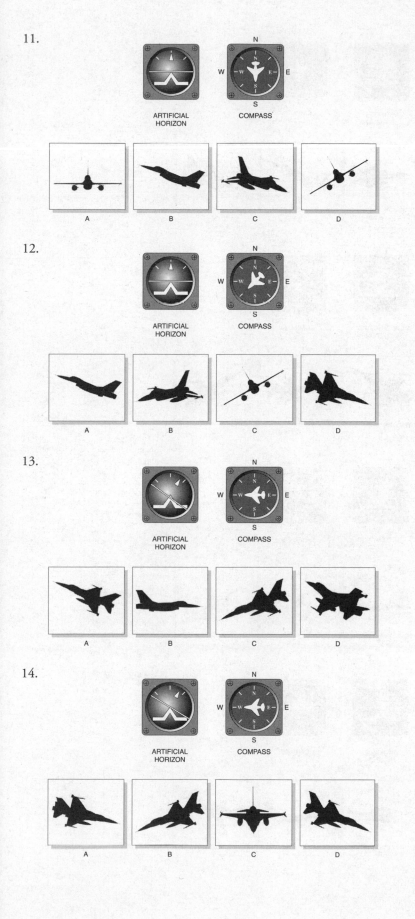

15.

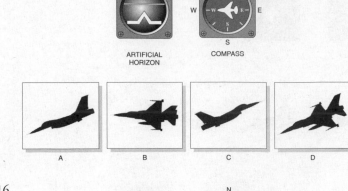

ARTIFICIAL
HORIZON

COMPASS

A   B   C   D

16.

ARTIFICIAL
HORIZON

COMPASS

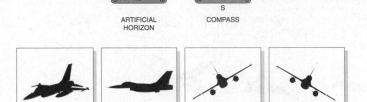

A   B   C   D

17.

ARTIFICIAL
HORIZON

COMPASS

A   B   C   D

18.

ARTIFICIAL
HORIZON

COMPASS

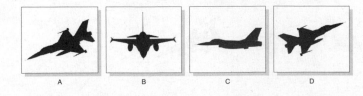

A   B   C   D

19.

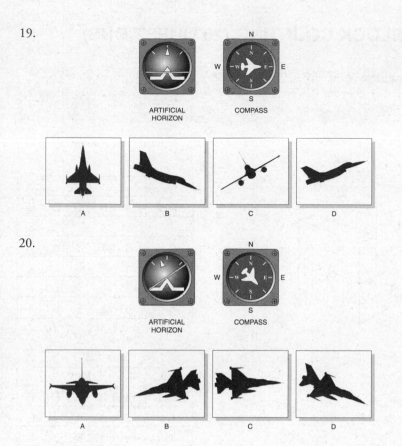

20.

SUBTEST #6: BLOCK COUNTING (20 QUESTIONS)

This part of the test measures your ability to "see into" a three-dimensional pile of blocks. Given a certain numbered block, your task is to determine how many other blocks it touches. *All of the blocks in each pile are the same size and shape.*

Questions 1–5

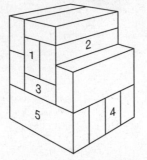

	KEY				
Block	A	B	C	D	E
1	2	3	4	5	6
2	3	4	5	6	7
3	4	5	6	7	8
4	3	4	5	6	7
5	3	4	5	6	7

Questions 6–10

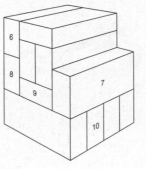

	KEY				
Block	A	B	C	D	E
6	2	3	4	5	6
7	4	5	6	7	8
8	4	5	6	7	8
9	4	5	6	7	8
10	4	5	6	7	8

Questions 11–15

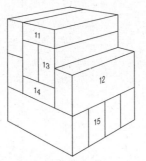

	KEY				
Block	A	B	C	D	E
11	3	4	5	6	7
12	4	5	6	7	8
13	3	4	5	6	7
14	4	5	6	7	8
15	3	4	5	6	7

Questions 16–20

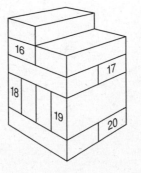

	KEY				
Block	A	B	C	D	E
16	3	4	5	6	7
17	3	4	5	6	7
18	4	5	6	7	8
19	3	4	5	6	7
20	2	3	4	5	6

SUBTEST #7: TABLE READING (40 QUESTIONS)

This part of the AFOQT measures your ability to read a table quickly and accurately. Questions 1–5 are based on the table below. Notice that the X values appear at the top of the table and the Y values are shown on the left side of the table. The X values are the column values and the Y values are the row values. For each test question, you are given an X value and a Y value; your task will be to find the box where the selected column and row meet, note the number that appears there, and then find that same number among the five answer options.

X VALUE

		–3	–2	–1	0	+1	+2	+3
	+3	0.01	0.24	0.37	0.38	0.59	0.77	0.81
	+2	2.3	3.2	3.7	4.8	4.9	4.9	5.1
	+1	17	18	19	20	21	22	23
Y VALUE	0	1.36	13.36	56.0	101.1	124.5	327.1	636.3
	–1	3	16	19	26	45	46	72
	–2	73	78	83	92	96	99	100
	–3	74	79	82	91	95	98	99

	X	Y	(A)	(B)	(C)	(D)	(E)
1.	–1	+2	0.37	3.7	46	18	19
2.	+2	+1	4.9	96	22	3.7	18
3.	0	–2	91	92	13.36	327.1	26
4.	–2	+3	70	79	100	0.24	3.2
5.	+1	0	124.5	20	56.0	21	26

Questions 6–10 are based on the table below.

	Austria/ Austria-Hungary	France	Germany	Italy	Japan	Russia/ USSR	Ottoman Empire/ Turkey	United Kingdom	USA
WW I Entente Powers		X		X	X	X		X	X
WW I Central Powers	X		X				X		
WW II Allied Powers		X				X	X	X	X
WW II Axis Powers	X		X	X	X				
Cold War NATO		X	X				X	X	X
Cold War Warsaw Pact						X			

6. Which country was a member of the World War I Entente Powers?

    (A) Ottoman Empire
    (B) Germany
    (C) Austria
    (D) Italy
    (E) Belgium

7. Which country was not a member of NATO during the Cold War?

    (A) Italy
    (B) Germany
    (C) France
    (D) United Kingdom
    (E) Turkey

8. Which country was a member of the World War II Axis Powers?

    (A) Italy
    (B) Russia
    (C) United Kingdom
    (D) France
    (E) Greece

9. Which national power was a member of the Central Powers during World War I?

    (A) United Kingdom
    (B) France
    (C) Ottoman Empire
    (D) Italy
    (E) Japan

10. During World War I, Japan was a member of which coalition of national powers?

    (A) Axis Powers
    (B) Entente Powers
    (C) Central Powers
    (D) NATO
    (E) Warsaw Pact

Questions 11–15 are based on the table below.

X VALUE

Y VALUE		-3	-2	-1	0	+1	+2	+3
	+3	9	12	15	18	21	24	25
	+2	2	4	6	8	10	12	14
	+1	1	3	5	7	9	11	13
	0	17	27	47	57	67	87	96
	-1	1.2	2.4	4.8	9.6	19.2	14.8	13.1
	-2	12	26	39	57	43	36	22
	-3	2	5	7	13	19	23	27

	X	Y	(A)	(B)	(C)	(D)	(E)
11.	+3	-1	15	13.1	13	96	14
12.	-1	+2	4.8	14.8	57	6	11
13.	0	-3	18	17	13	96	27
14.	+2	-1	11	14.8	3	5	2.4
15.	-3	-2	12	2	22	14	11

Questions 16–20 are based on the table below.

COMMISSIONED OFFICERS MONTHLY BASE PAY

Pay Grade	<2 Yrs. SVC	2	3	4	6	8	10	12	14	16	18	20
O-10	0.00	0.00	0.00	0.00	0.00	0.00	0.00	0.00	0.00	0.00	0.00	13365.00
O-9	0.00	0.00	0.00	0.00	0.00	0.00	0.00	0.00	0.00	0.00	0.00	11689.50
O-8	8271.00	8541.90	8721.60	8772.00	8996.10	9371.10	9458.10	9814.20	9916.20	10222.80	10666.20	11075.40
O-7	6872.70	7191.90	7339.80	7457.10	7669.80	7879.50	8122.50	8364.90	8607.90	9371.10	10015.80	10015.80
O-6	5094.00	5596.20	5963.40	5963.40	5985.90	6242.70	6276.60	6276.60	6633.30	7263.90	7634.10	8004.00
O-5	4246.50	4783.50	5115.00	5177.10	5383.50	5507.40	5779.20	5978.70	6236.10	6630.60	6818.10	7003.80
O-4	3663.90	4241.40	4524.30	4587.60	4850.10	5131.80	5482.20	5755.80	5945.40	6054.30	6117.60	6117.60
O-3	3221.40	3651.90	3941.70	4297.50	4503.00	4728.90	4875.30	5115.90	5240.70	5240.70	5240.70	5240.70
O-2	2783.10	3170.10	3651.00	3774.30	3852.00	3852.00	3852.00	3852.00	3852.00	3852.00	3852.00	3852.00
O-1	2416.20	2514.60	3039.60	3039.60	3039.60	3039.60	3039.60	3039.60	3039.60	3039.60	3039.60	3039.60

16. What is the base pay for a first lieutenant (O-2) with three years' service?

    (A) $3,221.40
    (B) $3,651.00
    (C) $3,039.60
    (D) $3,941.70
    (E) $3,170.10

17. Based on this table, what is the maximum monthly base pay for a major (O-4)?

    (A) $6,117.60
    (B) $5,240.70
    (C) $3,039.60
    (D) $4,875.30
    (E) $5,755.80

18. What is the base pay for a captain (O-3) with 12 years' service?

    (A) $3,852.00
    (B) $5,755.80
    (C) $5,945.40
    (D) $5,978.70
    (E) $5,115.90

19. What is the maximum monthly base pay for a lieutenant colonel (O-5)?

    (A) $6,170.10
    (B) $7,634.10
    (C) $8,004.00
    (D) $6,117.60
    (E) $7,003.80

20. What is the monthly base pay for a captain (O-3) with ten years' service?

(A) $3,039.60
(B) $6,818.10
(C) $5,482.20
(D) $4,875.30
(E) $3,852.00

Questions 21–25 are based on the table below.

		X VALUE						
		–3	–2	–1	0	+1	+2	+3
	+3	2	4	7	8	13	15	17
	+2	22	23	23	24	25	26	27
	+1	3	5	7	9	11	12	14
Y VALUE	0	16	19	26	3	45	46	21
	–1	5	10	15	20	25	30	35
	–2	9	3	2	4	16	5	25
	–3	10	20	30	40	50	60	70

	X	Y	(A)	(B)	(C)	(D)	(E)
21.	+1	+2	16	12	25	23	4
22.	–2	–3	10	20	4	15	60
23.	0	–3	40	8	16	21	3
24.	–1	–1	7	11	25	15	50
25.	0	+1	20	26	45	21	9

Questions 26–30 are based on the aircraft fuel consumption table below.

	ENGINE NAME	# ENG	FUEL FACTOR 1	FUEL FACTOR 2	FUEL (KG)	CATEGORY
KC-135R	TF33-P-5&9	4	0.5216	1.1290	2,095,550	J
A-4 SKYHAWK	J52-P-8B	2	0.2900	0.7720	2,972	J
C-130E HERCULES	T56-A-7	4	0.1110	0.2292	17,522	J
C-141 STARLIFTER	TF33-P-7	4	0.5022	0.9616	144,084	J
C-5 GALAXY	TF39-GE-1C	4	1.3201	1.5802	36,626	J
F/A-18 HORNET	F404-GE-400	2	0.3270	0.7462	43,102	J
DC 9-10	JT8D-7B	2	0.2861	0.8113	20,608	J
GULFSTREAM IV	TAY Mk611-8	2	0.2300	0.6300	240,706	J

26. What is the fuel factor 1 (FF1) for the F/A-18 Hornet?

    (A) 0.3270
    (B) 0.7462
    (C) 1.3201
    (D) 0.2861
    (E) 1.5802

27. How many engines and what type does the C-141 Starlifter have?

    (A) 4, TF33-P-5&9
    (B) 2, TF33-P-7
    (C) 2, F404-GE-400
    (D) 4, T56-A-7
    (E) 4, TF33-P-7

28. How much fuel does the C-5 Galaxy hold?

    (A) 144,084 kg.
    (B) 36,626 lb.
    (C) 36,626 kg.
    (D) 2,095,550 kg.
    (E) 20,608 lb.

29. How many F404-GE-400 engines does the DC 9-10 have?

    (A) 4
    (B) 3
    (C) 2
    (D) 0
    (E) 1

30. What is the FF1 for the C-130E Hercules?

    (A) 0.2292
    (B) 0.5022
    (C) 0.9616
    (D) 0.1110
    (E) 0.2300

Questions 31–35 are based on the table below.

	X VALUE						
	−3	−2	−1	0	+1	+2	+3
+3	1	2	3	5	7	8	9
+2	13	15	17	19	21	22	23
+1	14	16	18	20	22	24	25
Y VALUE 0	23	24	45	57	63	77	83
−1	8	9	10	11	12	13	14
−2	1.4	3	4.2	5	6.1	7.3	8.5
−3	3	36	101	327	49	144	136

	X	Y	(A)	(B)	(C)	(D)	(E)
31.	+2	−2	15	22	7.3	3	24
32.	−3	−1	1	8	49	14	25
33.	+1	0	20	11	5	45	63
34.	+2	−1	13	24	17	4.2	16
35.	−1	+3	101	3	14	25	9

Questions 36–40 are based on the table below.

Model	DC8-63	DC 9-10	MD-81	MD-82	MD-83	MD-87
Length (m)	55.70	27.91	41.30	41.30	41.30	36.30
Wingspan (m)	45.23	27.25	32.87	32.87	32.87	32.87
Max. seats (single class)	30.00	24.00	24.50	24.50	24.50	24.50
Vert Tail Area (m²)	23.60	14.96	15.60	15.60	15.60	18.50
Vert Tail Height (m)	6.40	3.90	4.10	4.10	4.10	4.20
Horiz Tail Span (m)	14.48	11.23	12.24	12.24	12.24	12.24
No. of wheels (nose; main)	2;8	2;4	2;4	2;4	2;4	2;4

36. What is the wingspan of the MD-81?

(A) 27.91
(B) 24.50
(C) 41.30
(D) 32.87
(E) 24.00

37. What is the vertical tail area of the DC 9-10?

(A) 15.60 m²
(B) 24.00 m
(C) 23.60 m²
(D) 14.96 m
(E) 14.96 m²

38. How many main landing-gear wheels does the MD-83 have?

(A) 2
(B) 3
(C) 4
(D) 5
(E) 6

39. How many passenger seats can be carried by the MD-82?

(A) 24
(B) 24.5
(C) 15.6
(D) 25
(E) 33

40. What is the horizontal tail span of the DC 9-10?

(A) 14.48 m
(B) 15.60 m²
(C) 12.24 m
(D) 12.24 m²
(E) 11.23 m

SUBTEST #8: AVIATION INFORMATION (20 QUESTIONS)

1. In a level turn, the acceleration experienced by the aircraft and its pilot in the direction perpendicular to the wing is solely determined by the

   (A) relative airspeed.
   (B) angle of attack.
   (C) bank angle.
   (D) altitude.
   (E) local air density and temperature.

2. The flight envelope of an aircraft is

   (A) the airspeed at which it achieves takeoff.
   (B) the region of altitude and airspeed in which it can be operated.
   (C) the volume of air it displaces in flight.
   (D) the envelope containing the aircraft registration documents.
   (E) the geographical area covered by the officially filed flight plan.

3. The locus of points equidistant from the upper and lower surfaces of an airfoil is called the

   (A) angle of attack.
   (B) leading airfoil edge.
   (C) upper camber measurement.
   (D) mean camber line.
   (E) wing chord.

4. The straight line joining the ends of the mean camber line is called the

   (A) lower camber curve.
   (B) mean airfoil throughpoint.
   (C) wing chord.
   (D) angle of attack.
   (E) relative lift threshold line.

5. A(n) _____ is the point at which the airflow over the wings ceases to be a smooth (laminar) flow and the wing starts to lose lift.

   (A) Mach threshold
   (B) tactile feedback
   (C) relative wind camber
   (D) maximum bank limit
   (E) aerodynamic stall

6. The two basic types of drag are

   (A) parasitic and induced.
   (B) simple and complex.
   (C) high pressure and low pressure.
   (D) induced and incidental.
   (E) parasitic and peripheral.

7. An airfoil's efficiency, either a wing or a rotor blade, is _____ at high altitudes by the _____ air density.

   (A) increased, lesser
   (B) increased, greater
   (C) decreased, lesser
   (D) decreased, greater
   (E) increased, stable

8. The degree of movement of an aircraft around its lateral axis is known as

   (A) yaw.
   (B) roll.
   (C) bank.
   (D) pitch.
   (E) sideslip.

9. When the flaps are extended, the camber of the wing is

   (A) enlarged proportionate to the airspeed.
   (B) decreased proportionate to the angle of attack.
   (C) unchanged.
   (D) decreased.
   (E) increased.

10. A helicopter's cyclic control is a mechanical linkage used to change the pitch of the main rotor blades

    (A) all at the same time.
    (B) at a selected point in its circular pathway.
    (C) proportionate to the engine rpm's.
    (D) in conjunction with the desired speed.
    (E) for vertical flight only.

11. When the rotor blades of a helicopter are spinning fast enough in a clockwise direction to generate lift, a phenomenon known as _____ causes the body of the helicopter to have a tendency to turn in a counter-clockwise direction.

    (A) centrifugal force
    (B) centripedal force
    (C) lateral roll
    (D) torque
    (E) autorotation

12. Pulling back (toward the pilot) on the control column or joystick of a fixed-wing aircraft will cause the aircraft to

    (A) increase its rpm's.
    (B) decrease its rpm's.
    (C) maintain its angle of attack.
    (D) pitch down.
    (E) pitch up.

13. Contra-rotating propellers, a complex way of applying the maximum power of a single piston or turboprop aircraft engine, uses two propellers

    (A) rotating in the same direction arranged one behind the other.
    (B) rotating in opposite directions arranged one behind the other.
    (C) rotating in opposite directions on opposite sides of the engine nacelle.
    (D) rotating in the same direction on opposite sides of the engine nacelle.
    (E) rotating asynchronously in the same direction.

14. The abbreviation VTOL, applied to aircraft other than helicopters, means

    (A) Vertical Transmission Of Lift.
    (B) Very Turbulent Opposite Launching.
    (C) Vertical Take-Off and Landing.
    (D) Velocity Transmitted to Onboard Lines.
    (E) Virtual Transmission Operation Line.

15. Delta wing aircraft have a wing in the form of a triangle, named after the Greek uppercase letter delta (Δ), and no

    (A) vertical stabilizer.
    (B) flaps.
    (C) horizontal stabilizer.
    (D) stabilizing canard.
    (E) ogival structure.

16. The Visual Approach Slope Indicator (VASI) is a system of lights designed to provide visual descent guidance information to the pilot during a runway approach. The system uses _____ lights to indicate the upper limits of the glide path and _____ lights for the lower limits.

    (A) red, white
    (B) white, red
    (C) blue, white
    (D) red, green
    (E) green, red

17. A biplane has

    (A) two wings arranged one behind the other.
    (B) two wings arranged one above the other.
    (C) two horizontal stabilizers, one above the other.
    (D) two horizontal stabilizers, one in front of the other.
    (E) two engines, one on each wing.

18. A coordinated turn (change of heading direction) includes both _____ of the airplane.

    (A) pitch and yaw
    (B) roll and bank
    (C) roll and pitch
    (D) pitch and roll
    (E) roll and yaw

19. _____ is induced by use of a movable rudder controlled by _____ in the cockpit.

    (A) Roll, ailerons
    (B) Bank, control column
    (C) Change of pitch, collective
    (D) Yaw, rudder pedals
    (E) Power dive, trim tabs

20. Moving the control column or joystick to the left or right affects the _____ rather than indicating the

    (A) angle of pitch, angle of attack.
    (B) angle of bank, rate of roll.
    (C) rate of roll, angle to which the aircraft will roll.
    (D) degree of bank, relative airspeed.
    (E) degree of roll, angle of yaw.

SUBTEST #9: GENERAL SCIENCE (20 QUESTIONS)

This part of the test measures your knowledge in the area of science. Each of the questions or incomplete statements is followed by five choices. Your task is to decide which one of the choices best answers the question or completes the statement.

1. The most accurate description of the earth's atmosphere is that it is made up of

    (A) 78% oxygen, 19% nitrogen, and 2% carbon dioxide, with trace amounts of nitrogen, water vapor, and dust particles.
    (B) 3% water vapor, 78% ozone, and 20% nitrogen.
    (C) 20% oxygen, 77% hydrogen, 3% carbon dioxide, and some water vapor.
    (D) 21% oxygen, 78% nitrogen, .03% carbon dioxide, trace amounts of rare gases, water vapor, and some dust particles.
    (E) 77% oxygen, 21% hydrogen, and 2% carbon dioxide, with trace amounts of nitrogen, water vapor, and dust particles.

2. A vibrating tuning fork, placed in a vacuum under a bell jar, will

    (A) have the pitch of its sound raised.
    (B) have the pitch of its sound lowered.
    (C) be inaudible.
    (D) crack the thick glass of the bell jar.
    (E) experience no change in its audible tone or pitch.

3. The three ingredients found most often in commercial fertilizers are

    (A) iron, calcium, and magnesium.
    (B) nitrogen, phosphorus, and potassium.
    (C) sulfur, phosphorus, and iron.
    (D) magnesium, iron, and calcium.
    (E) iron, sulfur, and magnesium.

4. To which organism is the whale most closely related?

    (A) shark
    (B) turtle
    (C) brachyiosaurus
    (D) horse
    (E) sparrow

5. What is the correct formula for "dry ice"?

    (A) HO_2
    (B) CO_2
    (C) H_2O_2
    (D) C_2O
    (E) $H_6O_6C_6$

6. When an airplane is in flight, the air pressure on the bottom surface of the wing is

    (A) less than on the top surface.
    (B) more than on the top surface.
    (C) either more or less than the top surface, depending on the speed of the airplane.
    (D) either more or less than the top surface, depending on the shape of the wing.
    (E) the same, regardless of airspeed or attitude.

7. In a vacuum, radio waves and visible light waves have the same

    (A) frequency.
    (B) speed.
    (C) intensity.
    (D) wavelength.
    (E) appearance.

8. Which structure in the human eye performs the same function as the film in a camera?

    (A) lens
    (B) cornea
    (C) retina
    (D) optic nerve
    (E) sclerotic membrane

9. A cloned organism is

    (A) an individual organism grown from a single body cell of its parent.
    (B) genetically identical to its parent.
    (C) a result of stimulating the parent cell to reproduce by asexual means.
    (D) all of the above.
    (E) none of the above.

10. Parallel rays of light, after reflection from a plane (flat) mirror, will be

    (A) converged.
    (B) parallel.
    (C) diffused.
    (D) absorbed.
    (E) invisible.

11. Object 1, with a mass of 4 kilograms, and Object 2, with a mass of 10 kilograms, are dropped simultaneously from a resting position 500 meters high. Neglecting air resistance, what is the ratio of the speed of Object 1 to the speed of Object 2 at the end of four seconds?

 (A) 2:5
 (B) 1:1
 (C) 1:4
 (D) 1:8
 (E) 2:1

12. Which of the following determines the sex of a human baby?

 (A) egg cell
 (B) polar body
 (C) sperm cell
 (D) mitochondrion
 (E) meiotic membrane

13. Isotopes of the same element have the same number of

 (A) electrons.
 (B) protons.
 (C) electrons and protons.
 (D) neutrons and protons.
 (E) electrons and neutrons.

14. Erosion and depletion are problems associated with

 (A) blood circulation.
 (B) baldness.
 (C) soil conservation.
 (D) cardiovascular exercise.
 (E) ozone hole maintenance.

15. An insulator is a material with

 (A) many free electrons.
 (B) few free electrons.
 (C) few free protons.
 (D) many free ions.
 (E) a variable number of neutrons.

16. Which of the following is a chemical change?

 (A) Vaporizing 1 gram of water
 (B) Melting ice
 (C) Magnetizing an iron rod
 (D) Mixing graphite flakes with oil
 (E) Burning 1 kilogram of wood

17. Spiders can be differentiated from insects by the fact that spiders have

 (A) eight legs in four pairs.
 (B) large abdomens.
 (C) biting mouth structures.
 (D) jointed legs.
 (E) a tough outer covering.

18. In atomic structure, what is the negative particle that orbits the atom's nucleus?

 (A) neutron
 (B) proton
 (C) meson
 (D) isotope
 (E) electron

19. Light from the sun takes approximately how long to reach the earth?

 (A) eight days
 (B) four hours
 (C) eight minutes
 (D) two years
 (E) nine seconds

20. The human shoulder joint is which type of joint?

 (A) gliding
 (B) hinge
 (C) pivot
 (D) ball-and-socket
 (E) fixed

SUBTEST #10: ROTATED BLOCKS (15 QUESTIONS)

This part of the test measures your ability to visualize and manipulate objects in space. In each problem you are shown a picture of a block. Your task is to find a second block that is just like the first.

Look at the two blocks below. Although they are in different positions, the blocks are exactly the same.

Now look at the next two blocks below. They are not alike. They can never be turned in such a way that they will be alike.

Now look at sample S1 below. Which of the five choices is just like the first block?

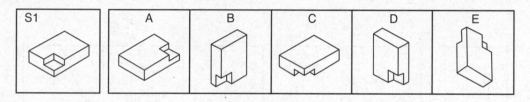

The correct answer is D. It is the same block placed in a different position.

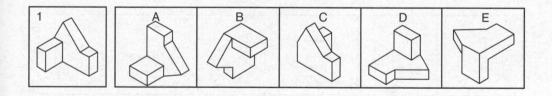

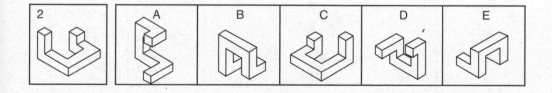

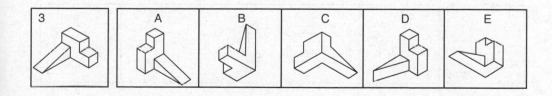

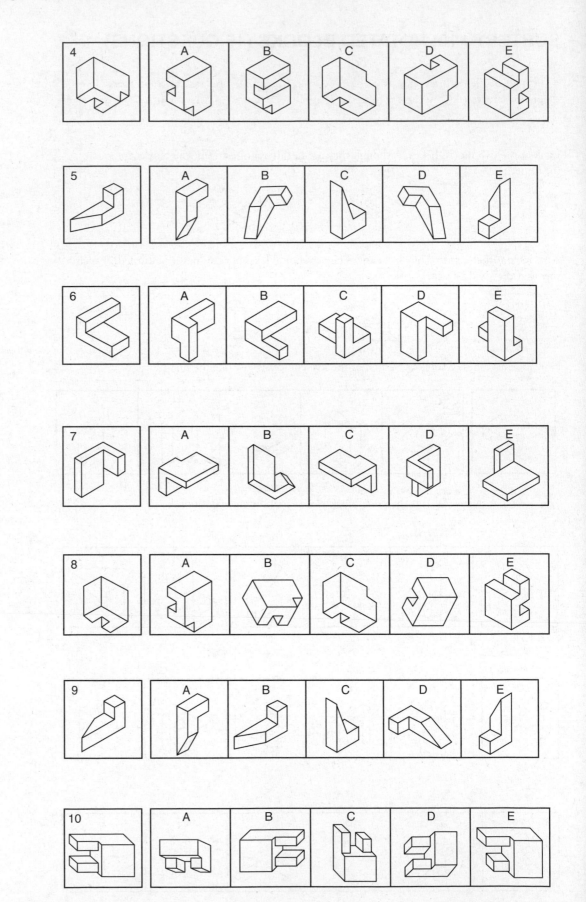

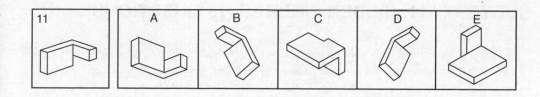

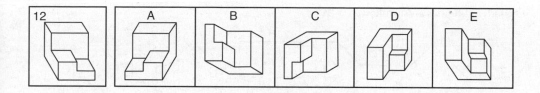

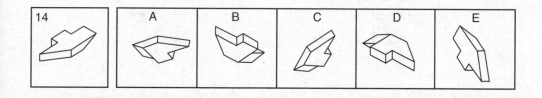

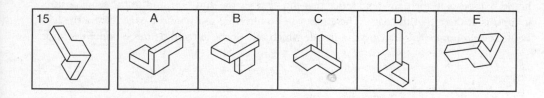

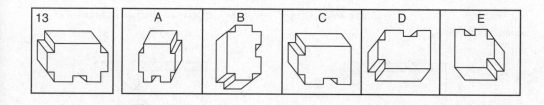

SUBTEST #11: HIDDEN FIGURES (15 QUESTIONS)

This part of the test measures your ability to see a simple figure in a complex drawing. At the top of each page are five lettered figures. Below these on each page are several numbered drawings. You are to determine which lettered figure is contained in each of the numbered drawings.

The lettered figures are as follows:

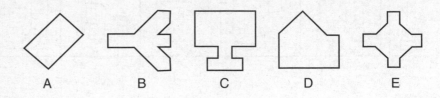

The numbered drawings are similar to drawing X below. Which one of the five figures is contained in drawing X?

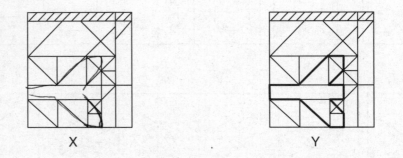

Figure B is contained in drawing X; therefore, B is the answer to sample question X. Drawing Y is exactly like drawing X except that the outline of figure B has been darkened to show that *all* of figure B appears in the drawing. Notice that the figure is the same size and in the same position as it appears at the top of the page. Therefore, you do not need to rotate the page to find the figure. Look at each numbered drawing and decide which one of the lettered figures is contained in it.

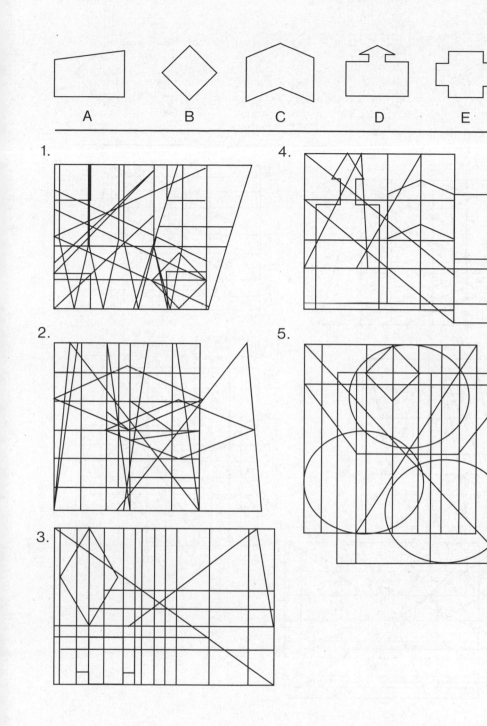

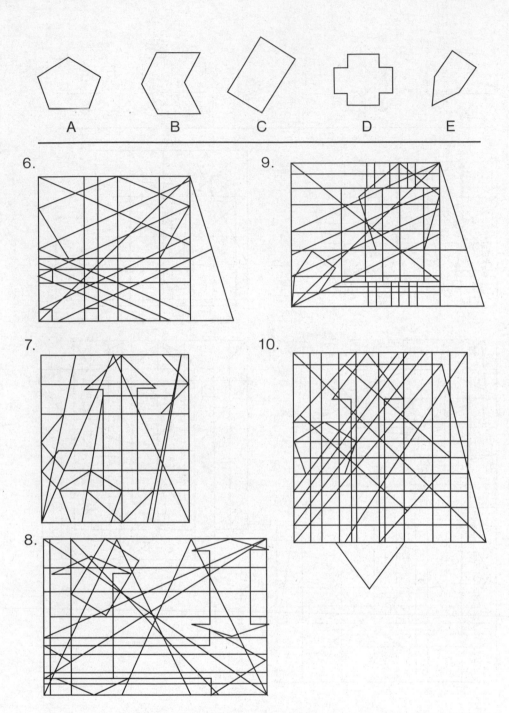

A   B   C   D   E

6.

7.

8.

9.

10.

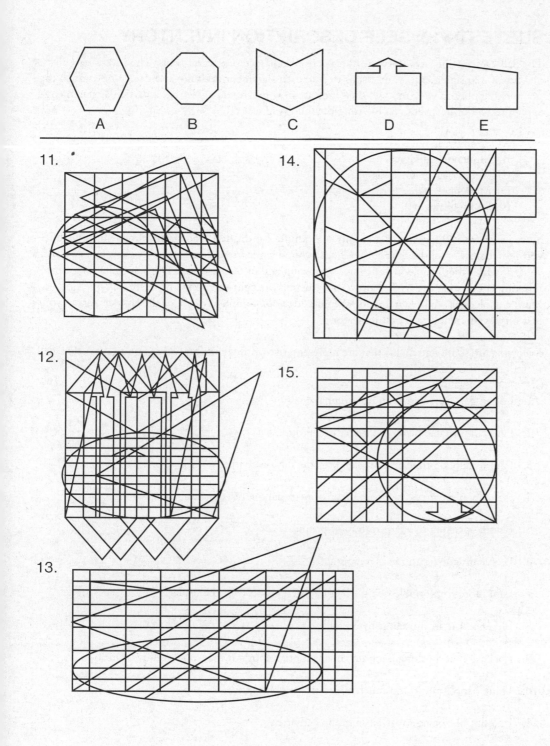

SUBTEST #12: SELF-DESCRIPTION INVENTORY

The Self-Description Inventory measures personal characteristics and traits. The inventory consists of a list of 220 statements; your task is to read each statement carefully and decide how much that statement applies to you. You will then indicate how much you agree that a particular statement applies to you or describes you by using the following scale:

(A) Strongly disagree
(B) Moderately disagree
(C) Neither agree nor disagree
(D) Moderately agree
(E) Strongly agree

Since you have 220 statements and only 40 minutes for this test, you should work quickly—but you should answer all the questions. Choose your answer from your first impression by comparing yourself with other people in your same age group and of the same sex. Don't spend a long time thinking about what the "right" answer is—there is no right or wrong answer to any question. Mark a choice for all the statements, even if you're not completely sure of the answer. Again, your first impression will be the best indicator.

Following are some statements that are representative of the type you will see on the AFOQT Self-Description Inventory.

1. I often get distracted from my original goals.

2. I am comfortable being the leader of a group.

3. I am usually on time and prepared for the day's activities.

4. I usually place my work goals ahead of personal interests or hobbies.

5. I enjoy speaking to a large group of people.

6. People often refer to me as a natural leader.

7. I am more comfortable being a member of a group than the leader.

8. I like to visit art museums by myself.

9. I believe that finishing a job on time is more important than how well it's done.

10. Many people put in too much effort on little things.

11. I do not like being involved in group activities.

12. I expect other people to show up on time.

13. I dislike having to meet new people.

14. I like being the center of attention.

15. I am annoyed when people drop in without advance notice.

16. I have a hard time getting along with people unless I know them well.

17. My personal interests and hobbies are very important to me.

18. I am seldom reluctant to voice my opinion in a group setting.

19. It is easy and enjoyable for me to learn new things.

20. I like going new places.

ANSWERS AND EXPLANATIONS

Subtest #1: Verbal Analogies

Check your answers below and refer to the explanation for each question you missed. Use the table to record right and wrong answers.

	✔	✘		✔	✘		✔	✘		✔	✘		✔	✘
1. B			6. D			11. D			16. D			21. B		
2. D			7. B			12. E			17. B			22. D		
3. B			8. A			13. A			18. D			23. A		
4. C			9. E			14. D			19. A			24. D		
5. E			10. C			15. C			20. E			25. A		

1. **B** CROWDED is to URBAN as SPARSE is to **RURAL.** This can be viewed as an analogy of description or an analogy of association; an urban area can be described as crowded with people in the same way that a rural area has only a sparse amount of people. Stated another way, an urban area is commonly associated with being crowded, whereas a rural area is usually associated with being sparsely populated. Both descriptive words (adjectives) refer to the amount of people in a given area, but the other adjective choices (slower, industrial, calm) describe other possible conditions of an urban or rural area. A suburban area is another category altogether, in between urban and rural.

2. **D** WATCH is to WATCHED as THROW is to **THREW.** This is an association of language; *watched* is the past tense of *watch*, so the correct choice to complete the analogy with *throw* is its past tense, *threw.* THROWED is not a standard conjugation of the verb *throw* (or *to throw*)—otherwise known as "improper English," and therefore not a correct choice. *Thrown* is the past participle form of *throw*—it needs the auxiliary or helping verb *has* to be used properly. A *thrower* is the person who throws—not a form of the verb itself—and *tossed* is not a form of *throw* at all, just a word that is close in meaning.

3. **B** WRENCH is to PLUMBER as HAMMER is to **CARPENTER.** This is a "tool to user" analogy. Pliers are the plumber's primary tool in the same way that a hammer is one of the carpenter's primary tools. A nail is used by a carpenter, but it becomes part of the structure the carpenter builds, as opposed to being a tool used on many different jobs. None of the other choices is a tool used by anyone.

4. **C** NATURAL is to ARTIFICIAL as **CREATE is to DESTROY.** This is an analogy of language—in this case, we have opposites or antonyms. *Cook* to *waiter* is a relationship, but not one of opposites. *Birth* and *maturity* are at different places on the spectrum of age, but not completely opposite ends of that spectrum. *Cut* and *dissect* are basically synonyms, and a *tear* is partially made out of *water*, so they can't be anything approaching opposites.

5. **E** BACON is to PIGS as HAMBURGER is to **CATTLE.** This is a "part to whole" analogy. Bacon comes from pigs and hamburger comes from cows or cattle; both are a certain way to prepare meat from the source animal. *Veal* is a special kind of beef, coming as it does from young cows (i.e., calves). *Beef* is a general term for the meat that comes from cattle; *fowl* is another word for birds (the implication is edible ones in this case); horses are an animal, but not normally used as a meat source.

6. **D** KANGAROO is to POUCH as **BUTTERFLY is to COCOON.** This is an analogy of association, although it may seem to be a "part to whole"—the pouch and the cocoon are protective coverings that help the kangaroo and butterfly, respectively, to develop physically and mature. A *bear* can enter a *cave*, but the cave is a shelter or hiding place, not a covering. A *ball* can go into a *glove*, but this analogy is not equivalent because neither the ball nor the glove is living, and therefore the glove can't be a developmental aid. The *web* is something made by the *spider* to catch its prey, and a *fish* can be a member of a *school*—but that's a group, not a covering.

7. **B** BEHAVE is to CANDY as DISOBEY is to **REPRIMAND.** This is an "action to result" analogy: if a child, for instance, behaves well, he or she may be rewarded with candy—whereas a child who disobeys will likely receive a **reprimand**. *Relinquish* means to let go of something, which doesn't make sense as a result of disobedience. An *argument* may ensue if directions are disobeyed, but the weak correlation (i.e., relationship) between cause and effect (it may or may not happen, very uncertain) makes this answer not nearly as strong as **reprimand**; besides, the implication is strong in the first analogy of a parent- or adult-to-young-child relationship, which doesn't really fit with the *argument* answer. *Dishonesty* and *disruption* may in fact be associated with disobedience, but there is again not nearly as clear a path of relationship as between **disobey** and **reprimand**.

8. **A** XXII is to IXXX as 22 is to **29**. This is a very easy numerical or mathematical analogy; all we are really asked to do is reproduce the relationship of XXII (22) to IXXX (29) in Arabic numerals rather than Roman.

9. **E** AMUSING is to FUNNY as ODD is to **UNUSUAL**. This is an association of language, since **amusing** and **funny** are basically synonyms. *Even* is an antonym (opposite) of **odd**, even though it is an opposite of a different meaning of **odd**. *Extra* is almost a synonym for yet another meaning of **odd**—as used in, "He picked up the odd scrap of bread here and there"; in this context, **odd** means *occasional* or *scattered*. *Fellow* has no relevant relationship to **odd** except as a distraction, because of the common phrase or cliché of *odd fellow*. *Distinct*, like *fellow*, is only a distracting filler choice—so don't fall for it.

10. **C** HONOR is to COURAGE as **SELFISHNESS is to GREED.** You can look at this analogy either as one of association or as "action to result"—when one has **honor** in one's character, one is likely to exhibit **courage**; in the same way, when a person has **selfishness** as part of their internal makeup, they will probably show some degree of **greed**. *Light* and *darkness* are opposites, rather than such associated qualities as **honor** and **courage**. *Knowledge* and *wisdom* are without doubt associated qualities, but *knowledge* is not a character trait—it is something one either has or doesn't. By the same token, *duty* is usually viewed as an externally imposed obligation; even if one feels *duty* to one's *country*, that is the object of the obligation, not the external manifestation of the inner quality. And, of course, a *key* does go into an *ignition* to start a car, but these are inanimate objects, not qualities of living beings.

11. **D** ATLANTA is to GEORGIA as DALLAS is to **TEXAS.** This is a geographical analogy (city-state/city-state); **Atlanta** is a very large metropolitan city in **Georgia**, just as **Dallas** is a very large metropolitan city in **Texas**. *Fort Worth* is another city in **Texas**, but this doesn't fit the city-state/city-state pattern; *Birmingham* is a large city in Alabama; *cowboys* (either the real kind or the football team) are associated with **Dallas** but don't fit the pattern; and *Louisiana*, although adjacent to Texas, does not fit the pattern, either.

12. **E** CLOCK is to WATCH as **LAKE is to POND**. This is an analogy of association; a **clock** is a larger version of a **watch** in much the same way that a **lake** is a larger version of a **pond**. *Stream* does not properly complete the analogy pattern, since it has a current and can be said to move "from" one place to another, whereas a *lake* does not have an appreciable current and stays in one place, so to speak. Viewed another way, a stream is a linear feature, whereas a lake is not; either way, *stream* is an incorrect choice. For much the same reasons, *ocean* and *river* are incorrect choices. *Water* and *fish* fit the pattern even less, since *fish* is either a verb or denotes a living thing—and *boat* and *sail* fit the pattern even more poorly (a *sail* is either part of a boat or it is a verb), even though they are associated terms.

13. **A** STABLE is to HORSE as **HOUSE is to HUMAN**. This is an analogy of association; for the second pair, we are looking for something that is a dwelling place or shelter for a living thing. The only choice here that is even close is **house** and **human**. *Water* and *duck* are the closest contenders, but, although water is certainly associated with ducks, it is not a shelter or dwelling for them.

14. **D** SQUIRREL is to TREE as GOPHER is to **GROUND**. Here we have yet another analogy of association; a **squirrel** lives in a **tree**, so we are looking for where in the wild a **gopher** lives. Since gophers live in holes in the **ground**—and not in the *forest* (too broad of a general area), nor in a *bush* or *lake* or *hollow* (either in a particular tree or in a forest)—**D** is the correct choice here.

15. **C** INFANCY is to CHILDHOOD as ENGAGEMENT is to **MARRIAGE**. This may best be viewed as an analogy of association; each of the first terms are immediate preparatory stages for the conditions mentioned as second terms. *Drive train* is a nonsense distracter choice; *love* usually comes before **engagement**, not after; a *ring* traditionally comes as a symbol of **engagement** rather than a stage; and a *bride* is what results from a **marriage**, but is a person and not a stage of development.

16. **D** TRAVEL is to AUTO as **EAT is to SPOON**. This is a "function to object" analogy, since **travel** can be done in an **auto**, just as **eat**ing can be done with a **spoon**. A *train* does *whistle*, but that's not its primary function; in addition, the order is reversed ("object to function" instead of "function to object"), so it doesn't fit the pattern, either. *Water* is something that is consumed in the act of its use as a *drink*, so that doesn't fit the pattern, either; *soldiers* and *sailors* are different categories of military personnel—just as *meat* and *potatoes* are different food items, so those choices don't fit, either.

17. **B** ABU DHABI is to MUSCAT as **BEIRUT is to DAMASCUS**. This is a geographical analogy; Abu Dhabi and Muscat are capitals of adjacent countries (United Arab Emirates and Oman, respectively), and **Beirut** and **Damascus** are likewise capitals of adjacent countries (Lebanon and Syria, respectively). *Cairo* is the capital of Egypt and *Incirlik* is the capital of Turkey, but those countries are not adjacent; *London* is the capital of England, but the German city of *Hamburg* is not that country's capital and England and Germany aren't adjacent. *Austin* and *Baton Rouge* are state capitals but not national capitals; and *Oman* and *Yemen* are countries, not cities.

18. **D** SURGEON is to SCALPEL as FIREMAN is to **WATER HOSE**. This is a "user to tool" analogy; a **surgeon** uses a **scalpel** to do his job (perform surgery), just as a **fireman** uses a **water hose** to put out fires. A *siren* is also a tool used by a fireman, but it is used to get to the scene of a fire, not to do the fireman's job of putting out the fire; likewise, a fireman may use a *helmet* for protection, but, again, he does not use it to perform his primary function. The *dalmatian* is a dog traditionally associated with firehouses, but it is not used to put out fires, either—and a *policeman* is a different type of emergency responder, by no means a tool used by the **fireman**.

19. **A** FRAME is to PAINTING as **FENCE is to YARD**. This is an analogy of association—specifically, the first object outlines and contains the second object. A *cover* does contain the pages of a *book*, but it does not outline the book in the same way as the correct choices. A *cloud* is an object in the *sky* ("part to whole"); a *park* is watched over by a *ranger* (an analogy of association but not the right kind); and a *jack* is used to change a *tire*—again, an analogy of association, but not the right kind.

20. **E** CASCADE is to WATERFALL as **MEANDER is to STREAM**. This is a "function to object" analogy— what the **waterfall** does is **cascade**, and what the **stream** does is **meander**; these are transitive, move-ment-oriented functions of inanimate things. *Fish* are living things that live in the water of a *river* in this case, but that water is the only connection to the analogy to which we are supposed to relate. *Warn* is something that the authorities do before a *hurricane*—there is no direct connection between the verb *warn* and the noun *hurricane*, because the hurricane neither warns nor gets warned; there must exist the help of people to complete the connection, such as it is. *Lake* is to *sail* also has a water-based connection, but this is an object that moves on top of the water, rather than the way the body of water itself moves. And, finally, *cross* is to *ocean* requires the presence of an implied direct object (whatever is crossing the ocean), which means again that there is not a direct connection, and that the analogy is not the correct choice.

21. **B** INFORM is to ENLIGHTEN as SING is to **ENTERTAIN**. This is an "action to result" analogy; when you *inform* someone of new information, you *enlighten* them. In the same way, when you *sing* for or to someone, you can *entertain* them (depending on the quality of the singing!). A *melody* and a *refrain* are things that you can sing—"whats" and not "results." *Confess* is a distracter choice, and *whistle*, although still musical, is in a "next-door-neighbor" category to singing—it's not a result.

22. **D** PECAN is to PIE as CHOCOLATE is to **CAKE**. This is an analogy of association where the first term of the base analogy is a main ingredient of the dessert named as the second term. *Brown* describes **chocolate** but nothing more—it is not an ingredient. *Frosting* denotes an optional outer part of a dessert, but, again, it is not an ingredient of that dessert. **Chocolate** *chips* can be an ingredient of a dessert, but are unlikely to be the primary ingredient. And *dessert*, of course, rather than being an appropriate second half of the analogy, is a general term for a sweet eaten after the main meal.

23. **A** WALK is to MARCH as **READ is to STUDY**. This is a "general to specific" analogy pattern—a certain type of **walking** is **marching**, just as a certain type of **reading** is **studying**. A *tread* is either one impact on the ground of a *foot*, or it's the sound that *foot* makes; *run* and *stop* are opposites; *waltz* and *rumba* are two different types of dance, just as *rap* and *jazz* are different types of music—in this context, you could call these two "specific to specific" analogies, if there were such a category.

24. **D** KABUL is to AFGHANISTAN as **CAIRO is to EGYPT**. This is a geographical analogy; **Kabul** is the capital of **Afghanistan**, just as **Cairo** is the capital of the country of **Egypt**. *Pensacola* is a city (not even the capital) of the state of *Florida*, which is not, of course,

a country unto itself. *Calcutta* is a large city—but, again, not the capital—of *India; Japan* and *Korea* are two different countries; and *Cancun* is a resort city in Mexico, which is a different Central American country than its neighboring country *Honduras.*

25. **A** PERPLEX is to ENLIGHTEN as MIXTURE is to **INDIVIDUAL.** This is an analogy of language. **Perplex** means to confuse or otherwise fail to gain understanding, whereas to **enlighten** is to grant or help achieve that understanding; these are opposites

(antonyms). Likewise, **mixture** and **individual** are opposite terms. An *additive* is something that might result in a **mixture**; a poorly combined mixture might have some of its components *settle* to the bottom of its container. Those same components that settled might eventually *solidify,* but in any case we can't tell whether the new solid was a **mixture** or a pure, **individual** material; and *social* is a distracter choice, meant to cause the test-taker to think of a **mixture** of different people instead of **mixture**'s opposite, **individual.**

Subtest #2: Arithmetic Reasoning

Check your answers below and refer to the explanation for each question you missed. Use the table to record right and wrong answers.

	✔	✘		✔	✘		✔	✘		✔	✘		✔	✘
1. A			6. B			11. E			16. D			21. C		
2. C			7. D			12. C			17. A			22. A		
3. B			8. D			13. A			18. C			23. B		
4. B			9. A			14. D			19. B			24. B		
5. D			10. B			15. B			20. D			25. B		

1. **A** The total number of airmen in the squadron (132) divided by the total number in each flight (11 airmen plus one NCO equals 12 total) gives the number of flights in the squadrons.

    $$132 \div 12 = 11$$

    Eleven noncommissioned officers are needed, one for each flight.

2. **C** Find the total of all the amounts withheld.

    $$\$27.75 + \$5.65 + \$9.29 + \$3.58 = \$46.27$$

    Net pay is the salary for the week minus the total of all withholdings.

    $$\text{Net pay} = \$350.00 - \$46.27$$
    $$= \$303.73$$

3. **B** The average is the sum of the high and low temperatures divided by two. However, we have to be careful not to get tangled up in the fact that the high and low temperatures cross the "zero" line, giving us positive and negative numbers. There are 20 degrees between $-4°$ and $16°$F,

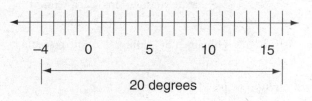

20 degrees

so when we divide 20 by 2, we get 10 degrees, which we have to add to $-4°$ to give us the final answer of 6°F.

4. **B** If $\frac{1}{4}$ inch represents 1 foot, then $\frac{3}{4}$ inch will represent 3 feet. $\frac{1}{2}$ foot will be represented by one-half of $\frac{1}{4}$ inch, or $\frac{1}{8}$ inch. Thus, $3\frac{1}{2}$ feet will be represented by $\frac{3}{4}$ inch plus $\frac{1}{8}$ inch, or $\frac{7}{8}$ inch.

5. **D** The discount will be 15% (or 0.15) of the list price, $13,620.

    $$\$13,620 \times 0.15 = \$2,043.00$$

6. **B** Find the increase in price by subtracting the original price from the new price per gallon.

Increase in price = $3.08 – $2.90 = $0.18

The percent of increase is the rise in price, multiplied by 100, divided by the original price.

($.18 × 100) ÷ $2.90 = 6.2%

7. **D** The number of games won is 70% (or 0.70) of the number of games played, 40.

Number of games won = 0.70(40) = 28

The number of games lost is the total number played minus the number won.

Number of games lost = 40 – 28 = 12

8. **D** The time of arrival is 2 hours and 55 minutes after the departure time of 3:50 P.M. By 4:00 P.M., the flight has taken 10 minutes of the total flight time of 2 hours and 55 minutes. 2 hours and 45 minutes remain, and 2 hours and 45 minutes after 4:00 P.M. is 6:45 P.M.

9. **A** There are 16 oz. in 1 lb. Therefore, 4 of the 4-oz. candy bars will make 1 lb. A 3-lb. package will hold 3 times 4 or 12 bars.

10. **B** Find the relationship between each pair of successive numbers in the series. It is helpful to change $3\frac{1}{2}$ to $3\frac{1}{6}$ to see the relationships. Each term of the series is obtained by adding $\frac{4}{6}$ to the preceding term. The fifth term is $5\frac{3}{6}$ or $5\frac{1}{2}$.

11. **E** First add the prices of the three items ordered to get the cost of the meal before the tax.

$12.50 + $3.50 + $1.25 = $17.25

The tax is 8% (or 0.08) of the cost of the meal.

0.08 × $17.25 = $1.38

12. **C** There are 4 quarts in 1 gallon; therefore, a 55-gallon drum holds 4 × 55 quarts.

4 × 55 qts. = 220 qts.

If each can holds 2 quarts, the number of cans filled is 220 divided by 2.

220 ÷ 2 = 110 cans

13. **A** Since it takes 45 minutes to finish nine spindles, it takes five minutes to finish each spindle (45 ÷ 9 = 5). So, the number of minutes it takes to finish 96 spindles is

5 × 96 = 480

480 minutes ÷ 60 minutes = 8 hours

14. **D** The perimeter, 40 feet, is the sum of the lengths of all three sides. The sum of the lengths of the two equal sides is the difference between the perimeter and the length of the third side. The sum of the lengths of two equal sides

= 40 ft. – 13 ft., 2 in.
= 39 ft., 12 in. – 13 ft., 2 in.
= 26 ft., 10 in.

The length of one side is obtained by dividing the sum by 2.
The length of one equal side

= 13 ft., 5 in.

15. **B** Since 3 feet = 1 yard, convert the length and width to yards by dividing their dimensions in feet by 3. The area of a rectangle is the product of its length and width.

Area = 7 × 13 = 91 sq. yds.

The cost for the entire lawn is obtained by multiplying the area in square yards by the cost per square yard.

91 × $.40 = $36.40

16. **D** Find the number of miles traveled by multiplying the rate, 48 mph, by the time, seven hours.

48 × 7 = 336 miles

The number of gallons of gas used is the number of miles driven divided by the number of miles per gallon.

336 ÷ 21 = 16

17. **A** If the profits are shared in the ratio 5:4, one partner gets $\frac{5}{9}$ of the profits and the other gets $\frac{4}{9}$. Note that $\frac{5}{9} + \frac{4}{9} = 1$, the whole profit. The larger share is $\frac{5}{9}$ of the profit, $63,000, or $35,000.

18. **C** Consider the original price as 100%. Then the price after an increase of 4% is 104%. To find the original price, divide the price after the increase, $17.16, by 104% (or 1.04).

$$\$17.16 \div 1.04 = \$16.50$$
$$\$16.50 = \text{original price}$$

19. **B** 5 workers making 6 garments each = 30 garments per day plus 3 workers making 4 garments each = 12 garments per day plus 1 worker making 12 garments each = 12 garments per day = 54 garments per day

Divide the total number of workers (5 + 3 + 1 = 9) into the total number of garments produced per day:

$$54 \text{ garments per day} \div 9 \text{ workers} =$$
$$6 \text{ garments per worker per day}$$

20. **D** The distance traveled by driving at 45 mph for 2 hours is 2 × 45 = 90 miles. The remainder of the 255-mile trip is 255 − 90, or 165 miles.

To finish the trip in 5 hours, the driver has 5 − 2 = 3 hours still to drive. To find the rate of travel for a distance of 165 miles driven in 3 hours, divide the distance by the time.

$$165 \text{ miles} \div 3 \text{ hours} = 55 \text{ mph}$$

21. **C** Calculate and add up the contractor's expenses:

Masonry materials and labor	$300,000 ÷ 10 =	$ 30,000
Lumber and carpentry	$300,000 ÷ 3 =	$100,000
Plumbing and heating	$300,000 ÷ 5 =	$ 60,000
Electrical and lighting work	$300,000 ÷ 6 =	$ 50,000
Total		$240,000

Subtract his expenses from the total bid:

$$\$300,000 - \$240,000 = \$60,000 \text{ profit}$$

22. **A** The first discount of 20% means that a customer actually pays 80% (or $\frac{4}{5}$) of the list price. The second successive discount of 30% means that a customer actually pays 70% (or $\frac{7}{10}$) of the price determined after the first discount. The price the customer actually pays is the list price multiplied by the portions determined from each discount or $182.00.

23. **B** At 2 quarts for $1.99, each quart costs

$$\$1.99 \div 2 = \$.995 \text{ per qt.}$$

At 6 quarts for $5.43, each quart costs

$$\$5.43 \div 6 = \$.905 \text{ per qt.}$$

The savings per quart is

$$\$.995 - \$.905 = \$.09 \text{ per qt. savings}$$

24. **B** For the regular 40 hours, the worker earns $7.20 × 40 = $288.00. If the regular wage is $7.20 per hour, then overtime paid at time and a half is $7.20 × 1.5 = $10.80. The three hours of overtime earn the worker a total of $32.40. Add the regular time wages to the overtime wages:

$$\$288.00 + \$32.40 = \$320.40 \text{ total pay}$$

25. **B** The ratio of the heights of the two trees will be the same as the ratio of the lengths of their shadows. The ratio of the length of the shadow of the second tree to the length of the shadow of the first tree is $\frac{6}{8}$ or $\frac{3}{4}$.

Thus, the height of the second tree is $\frac{3}{4}$ of the height of the 36-foot tree.

$$36 \text{ ft.} \times \frac{3}{4} = 27 \text{ ft.}$$

Subtest #3: Word Knowledge

Check your answers below and refer to the explanation for each question you missed. Use the table to record right and wrong answers.

	✔	✘		✔	✘		✔	✘		✔	✘		✔	✘
1. D			6. D			11. B			16. C			21. D		
2. B			7. A			12. A			17. C			22. C		
3. A			8. C			13. D			18. B			23. D		
4. D			9. E			14. E			19. A			24. A		
5. B			10. A			15. E			20. D			25. E		

1. **D** SIMULTANEOUS means **concurrent** or happening at the same time. *Versatile* means having the ability to change from one task to another, or to be used in more than one way; an *imitation* or *false appearance* could be thought of as a *simulation*, which has the same root as *simultaneous* but a different final meaning; *indefinite* means "having no precise limits" or "vague."

2. **B** PARAGON means a **prototype** or original example. A *triangular structure* is a pyramid; a *wax figure* is made from paraffin.

3. **A** DEMONSTRABLE means **evident** or provable. *Able to be refuted* is deniable; something that is *able to be torn down* is something that can be demolished; and another word for *countable* is denumerable.

4. **D** CONTROVERSY means **disagreement** or argument. *Vehicles moving together* are a convoy; a *school of music* is a conservatory; an *armed police force* is a constabulary; and an *agreement* by people *to commit* a crime or *wrong* act is a conspiracy.

5. **B** TEMERITY means **presumptuous daring** or rash boldness. *Automatically* transmitted readings are telemetry; *mental communication* is telepathy; and a *story prepared for television* is a teleplay.

6. **D** SCRUTINY means a **careful inspection**, often at close range or with a critical attitude. A *point of conscience or ethics* is a scruple; an *obligation* is a duty; a *revolt of a ship's crew* is a mutiny; and the *room adjoining the kitchen*—especially in a large, older-style house or mansion—is a scullery.

7. **A** To JETTISON an object is to **discard** it. A *long pier* is known as a jetty; something that is *uninteresting or empty* is jejune; to *build shoddily* is to jerry-build; to *compete for advantage* or position, especially in a crowd, is to jostle.

8. **C** CONCILIATE means to **placate**. To *speak briefly* is to speak in a concise way; to *form in the mind* is to conceive; to *set apart as sacred* is to consecrate; and to *confuse* is to confound.

9. **E** ARBITRARY means **selected at random**, as opposed to an orderly or arranged manner. *Fervent* means ardent or intense; one who is *lacking consistency* could be thought of as erratic; and *disputed* could be thought of as arguing or controversial.

10. **A** ENVISAGE means **conceive**. To *articulate* is to enunciate or explain; to *designate* is to set apart or mark. To *paint one's face* is a distracter choice, because it has an indirect reference to a common root, *visage* (meaning "face"), which still, however, does not apply to this question.

11. **B** SCLEROTIC means **having hardened arteries**. *Mentally disturbed* is neurotic.

12. **A** PARTISAN means an **adherent** or "one who takes the part of another"; by World War II, this had grown to include resistance members or guerillas in an occupied country, such as France when it was occupied by Nazi Germany. *Divided* means to be partitioned; *not complete* means partial; *over-hasty* could be thought of as precipitant; and a participle is one type of a *part of speech.*

13. **D** INCEPTION means **beginning**. A *careful examination* is an inspection; *divine guidance* is often thought of as inspiration; an *ever-present feature* is often referred to as an institution; and a *revolt against authority* is an insurrection.

14. **E** DERIVATIVE means **following** (or **deriving) from** something that has gone or occurred before. A synonym for *serving to prove* is demonstrative; and something that is *deprived of vitality* is said to be deanimated.

15. **E** PERVASIVE means **permeating**—as when an odor goes all through a room, to every corner, it is said to be **pervasive**. Being *influential*, on the other hand, is much the same as being persuasive; something that is *on the outer part* can be said to be peripheral.

16. **C** An INANITY is a **statement lacking sense**, as when someone wakes from a dream and says, "The sinks can't fly back to the kitchen because their lacquer has expired." This word (**inanity**) is often confused with insanity, which is *mental unbalance.*

17. **C** PLAUSIBLE means **believable**. Someone who is *unemotional* could be said to be phlegmatic, and something that is *flexible* is considered pliable.

18. **B** CONDUCIVE means **contributive**—it sets up the conditions for something that follows, as when you have a comfortable, quiet setting that is **conducive** to studying this book. This is often confused with being *able to transmit electricity*, which is conductive, and *ignitable*, which is another word for combustible. A synonym for *simultaneous* is also concurrent.

19. **A** ENSEMBLE means a **coordinated group or outfit**. To *bring together* is to assemble; the lowest *naval officer rank* is an ensign; to *rake with gunfire* along its length is to enfilade the enemy position; and an airplane's *tail section* is also known as the empennage.

20. **D** DELETERIOUS means **harmful**. This is another word that sounds a little like several other words, so some people get them confused. To do something *with careful thought* is to deliberate; someone who is *behind schedule* is delinquent; a dish that is *very tasty* is said to be delectable; and, when a part is *removed from the total*, it has been deleted.

21. **D** LITIGATION is nothing more than a **legal case.** *Marking or outlining* is called lineation; *coastland waters* are referred to as a littoral area or littorals; a *governmental ruling* by an elected body is known as legislation; and a *chemical test for acid or base* is known as a litmus test.

22. **C** IMPRIMATUR means a **signature**, usually one meaning approval by an authority. It has nothing to do with primates.

23. **D** DECELERATE means to **slow down**. To *belittle* someone is to denigrate them; to *remove or withdraw approval* in an official capacity is to decertify; to *speed up* is to accelerate; and to *deny* is to denegate.

24. **A** UNILATERAL means **obligating one side only**. Being *the same throughout* is to be uniform; a *sideways motion* can involve a common root, lateral; making a *wavelike motion* is to undulate; and an object or thing that *has one compartment* can be correctly called unilocular or unicameral.

25. **E** INTRANSIGENT means **uncompromising**. *Doing things in a new way* can be thought of as innovative; *knowing without being told* is intuitive; something that is *in between boundaries* is interstitial; and a *courageous* act can also be called intrepid.

Subtest #4: Mathematics Knowledge

Check your answers below and refer to the explanation for each question you missed. Use the table to record right and wrong answers.

	✔	✘		✔	✘		✔	✘		✔	✘		✔	✘
1. A			6. C			11. C			16. A			21. C		
2. C			7. C			12. A			17. A			22. D		
3. D			8. C			13. D			18. D			23. A		
4. B			9. C			14. C			19. B			24. D		
5. D			10. A			15. B			20. B			25. C		

1. **A** Multiply 0.0375 by 4% (or 0.04).

    $$0.0375 \times 0.04 = 0.001500 = 0.0015$$

    Note that the product has as many decimal places as there are in the multiplicand and multiplier combined, but the two final zeros may be dropped, since they are to the right of the decimal point and at the end.

2. **C** If a number is multiplied by its reciprocal (also called its multiplicative inverse), the product is 1. The reciprocal of a fraction is found by inverting the fraction.

    The reciprocal of $\frac{2}{3}$ is $\frac{3}{2}$, that is, $\frac{2}{3} \times \frac{3}{2} = 1$.

3. **D** Substitute 3 for x and -2 for y in the expression $x^2 - 5xy + 2y$.

    $$(3)^2 - 5(3)(-2) + 2(-2)$$
    $$9 - 15(-2) - 4$$
    $$9 + 30 - 4$$
    $$35$$

4. **B** $x - 3 < 14$ is an inequality that states that x minus 3 is less than 14. To solve the inequality, add 3 to both sides of it.

    $$x - 3 + 3 < 14 + 3$$
    $$x < 17$$

The result says that the inequality is true for any value of x less than 17. Try it for some value of x less than 17—for example, $x = 10$.

$$10 - 3 < 14$$
$$7 < 14 \text{ is a true statement}$$

5. **D** To multiply $7a^3b^2c$ by $3a^2b^4c^2$, first multiply the numerical coefficients, 7 and 3.

$$7 \times 3 = 21$$

Powers of the same base, such as a^3 and a^2, are multiplied by adding their exponents; thus, $a^3 \times a^2 = a^5$.

$$(a^3b^2c) \times (a^2b^4c^2) = a^5b^6c^3$$

Note that c should be regarded as c^1 when adding exponents. The combined result for $(7a^3b^2c) \times (3a^2b^4c^2) = 21a^5b^6c^3$.

6. **C** A hexagon has six sides. Each of the six sides of the black tile must touch a side of a white tile, so there are six white tiles surrounding each black tile.

7. **C** x^0 is defined as always equal to 1, provided that x does not equal 0; therefore, $8^0 = 1$.

8. **C** The equation $2x - 3 = 37$ means that "twice a number minus 3 is equal to 37." To arrive at a value for x, we first eliminate -3 on the left side. This can be done by adding 3 to both sides of the equation, thus undoing the subtraction.

$$2x - 3 + 3 = 37 + 3$$
$$2x = 40$$

To eliminate the 2 that multiplies x, we undo the multiplication by dividing both sides of the equation by 2.

$$\frac{2x}{2} = \frac{40}{2}$$

9. **C** If $\frac{2}{3}$ of M people are adults, then $\frac{2}{3}M$ represents the number of adults. If $\frac{1}{2}$ of $\frac{2}{3}M$ are males, then

$\frac{1}{2} \times \frac{2}{3}M$ represents the number of adult males.

10. **A** $(0.2)^3$ means $0.2 \times 0.2 \times 0.2$.
Multiply the first two numbers:

$$0.2 \times 0.2 \times 0.2 = 0.04 \times 0.2$$

Now multiply the remaining two numbers:

$$0.04 \times 0.2 = 0.008.$$

11. **C** Rewrite the equation as $x^3 + x - 6 = 0$. The left side of the equation can now be factored:

$$(x + 3)(x - 2) = 0$$

This result says that the product of two factors, $(x + 3)$ and $(x - 2)$, equals 0. But if the product of two factors equals 0, then either or both must equal 0:

$$x + 3 = 0 \text{ or } x - 2 = 0$$

Subtract 3 from both sides of the left equation to isolate x on one side, and add 2 to both sides of the right equation to accomplish the same result:

$$x + 3 - 3 = 0 \qquad x - 2 + 2 = 0 + 2$$
$$x = -3 \qquad\qquad x = 2$$

12. **A** The area of a circle is πr^2 where $\pi = \frac{22}{7}$ and r represents the length of the radius. A radius is one-half the length of a diameter. Therefore, if the diameter is 28 inches, the radius of the circle is 14 inches.

$$\text{Area of circle} = \frac{22}{7} \times \frac{14}{1} \times \frac{14}{1}$$

$$= \frac{44}{1} \times \frac{14}{1}$$

$$= \frac{616}{1}$$

$$= 616 \text{ sq. in.}$$

13. **D** If $x = -3$, the denominator of

$$\frac{x^2 + 2x - 3}{x + 3}$$

will equal 0. Division of 0 is undefined, so x cannot equal -3.

14. **C** The given equation means that a number is added to 11, the square root of the result is taken, and the result equals 9. The square root sign (or radical sign) can be removed by squaring both sides of the equation.

$$(\sqrt{x + 11})^2 = 9^2$$
$$x + 11 = 81$$

Isolate x on one side of the equation by subtracting 11 from both sides.

$$x + 11 - 11 = 81 - 11$$
$$x = 70$$

15. **B**

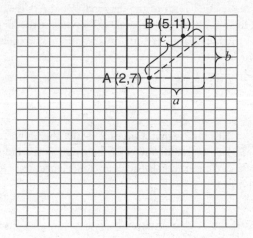

Plot the points. When a pair of numbers is given as the coordinates of a point, the first number is the x-value (the distance right or left from the origin or 0,0 point). The second number is the y-value (or distance up or down). Form the right triangle as shown in the diagram. The horizontal leg has a length of 5 − 2, or 3; the vertical leg has a length of 11 − 7, or 4. The distance A to B is the hypotenuse of the right triangle. Let $x = \overline{AB}$. By the Pythagorean Theorem, the square of the length of the hypotenuse equals the sum of the squares of the lengths of the legs.

$$x^2 = 3^2 + 4^2$$
$$x^2 = 9 + 16$$
$$x^2 = 25$$

The equation $x^2 = 25$ means that x times x equals 25. Therefore, $x = 5$.

16. **A** The given equation, $ay - bx = 2$, is to be solved for y. Isolate the y term on one side of the equation by adding bx to both sides.

$$ay - bx + bx = 2 + bx$$
$$ay = 2 + bx$$

This gives us y multiplied by a. To obtain y alone, undo the multiplication by dividing both sides of the equation by a.

$$\frac{ay}{a} = \frac{(2 + bx)}{a}$$

$$y = \frac{(2 + bx)}{a}$$

17. **A** The probability of a particular event occurring is the number of favorable outcomes divided by the total possible number of outcomes. Because there are three

possible infantrymen to choose, there are three possible favorable outcomes for choosing an infantryman. A choice may be made from among three infantrymen, two artillerymen, and five tank crewmen, so there are 3 + 2 + 5, or 10, possible outcomes in total. The probability of choosing an infantryman is, therefore, $\frac{3}{10}$.

18. **D** A length of cord that will wind around once is equal to the circumference of the circle whose radius is 3 inches. The circumference of a circle equals $2\pi r$ where $\pi = \frac{22}{7}$ and r is the radius.

$$\text{Circumference} = \frac{2}{1} \times \frac{22}{7} \times \frac{3}{1}$$

$$= 13\frac{2}{7} \text{ inches}$$

If the cord can be wound around the post seven times, its length is seven times the length of one circumference.

Length of cord = 132 inches

19. **B** There are four possible choices for the destroyer. Each of these choices may be coupled with any of the two choices for the supply ship. Each such destroyer-supply ship combination may in turn be coupled with any of the three possible choices for the submarine. Thus, there are $4 \times 2 \times 3$, or 24, different combinations possible.

20. **B** The volume of a cylinder is equal to the product of its height and the area of its base. The base is a circle. The area of a circle is πr^2, where $\pi = \frac{22}{7}$ and r is the radius. Since the diameter is 2 inches, the radius (which is one-half the diameter) is 1 inch.

A = Area of the base
$A = \pi (r^2)$
$A = \frac{22}{7}(1^2)$
$A = \frac{22}{7}$

V = Volume of the cylinder
h = height of the cylinder
$V = A \cdot h$
$V = \frac{22}{7}$ sq. in. · 7 in.
$V = 22$ cu. in.

21. **C**

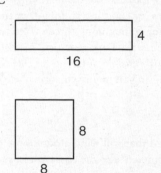

The area of the rectangular garden is equal to the product of its length and width.

Area of rectangle = 16 × 4 = 64 square yards.

For the square to have the same area, 64 square yards, its sides must each be 8 yards long, since 8 × 8 = 64 square yards. The fence around the rectangular garden has a length of 16 + 4 + 16 + 4, or 40, yards. The fence around the square garden has a length of 4 × 8, or 32, yards. Thus, the saving in fencing material is 40 – 32, or 8, yards.

22. **D** $\sqrt{164}$ stands for the square root of 164, or the number that when multiplied by itself equals 164. We know that 12 × 12 = 144 and that 13 × 13 = 169. Therefore, $\sqrt{164}$ lies between 12 and 13. It is nearer to 13 since 164 is nearer to 169 than it is to 144.

23. **A** The storage space measurements of 1 foot × 2 feet × 2 feet, 1 inch can be converted to inches as 12 inches × 24 inches × 25 inches. Boxes measuring 3 inches × 4 inches × 5 inches can be stacked so that four of the 3-inch sides make up the 12-inch storage dimension, six of the 4-inch sides fill the 24-inch storage dimension, and five of the 5-inch sides fill the 25-inch storage dimension. There will therefore be 4 × 6 × 5, or 120, boxes packed into the storage space.

24. **D**

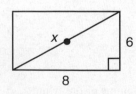

If the circle passes through all four vertices of the rectangle, its diameter will be a diagonal of the rectangle. Since a rectangle's angles are right angles, the diagonal

forms a right triangle with two sides of the rectangle. Let x = the length of the diagonal. By the Pythagorean Theorem, in a right triangle the square of the length of the hypotenuse is equal to the sum of the squares of the legs.

$$x^2 = 8^2 + 6^2$$
$$x^2 = 64 + 36$$
$$x^2 = 100$$

$x^2 = 100$ means that x times $x = 100$; therefore, $x = 10$ feet. But 10 is a diameter of the circle, and a radius of a circle is one-half the diameter. Hence, the radius is 5 feet.

25. **C** If the original mixture is $33\frac{1}{3}$ % (or $\frac{1}{3}$) acetone, then $\frac{1}{3}$ of the mixture of 12 liters, or 4 liters, is acetone. We can express $\frac{1}{3}$ as $\frac{4}{12}$ to represent the ratio of acetone to the total mixture; this wil be easier to deal with as we make our calculations, since there are 12 liters in the total mixture. If the total mixture is increased by x liters, the ratio of acetone to the total mixture becomes $\frac{4}{(12+x)}$. To solve this problem, we then have to set this as equal to 25%, which we will still express here as $\frac{1}{4}$ to make our calculations easier.

$$\frac{4}{(12+x)} = \frac{1}{4}$$

Our next objective is to solve for x by getting it by itself on one side of the equation. To undo the division on both sides of the equation, first multiply both sides by 4 and then by $(12 + x)$.

$$4 \times \left(\frac{4}{(12+x)}\right) = 4 \times \left(\frac{1}{4}\right)$$

$$\frac{16}{12+x} = 1$$

$$\frac{(12+x) \times 16}{12+x} = (12+x) \times 1$$

$$16 = 12 + x$$

$$16 - 12 = 12 + x - 12$$

$$4 = x$$

Subtest #5: Instrument Comprehension

Check your answers below. Use the table to record right and wrong answers.

	✔	✘		✔	✘		✔	✘		✔	✘
1. C			6. C			11. A			16. D		
2. A			7. B			12. B			17. D		
3. D			8. D			13. A			18. C		
4. C			9. B			14. B			19. D		
5. A			10. D			15. A			20. D		

Answer	Nose	Bank	Heading	Answer	Nose	Bank	Heading
1. C	DOWN	LEFT	SE	11. A	LEVEL	ZERO	S
2. A	LEVEL	RIGHT	E	12. B	LEVEL	ZERO	SW
3. D	DOWN	LEFT	W	13. A	UP	LEFT	W
4. C	UP	LEFT	S	14. B	DOWN	LEFT	W
5. A	LEVEL	ZERO	NE	15. A	DOWN	ZERO	W
6. C	UP	RIGHT	NE	16. D	UP	RIGHT	W
7. B	DOWN	ZERO	S	17. D	LEVEL	RIGHT	N
8. D	UP	ZERO	N	18. C	LEVEL	ZERO	W
9. B	DOWN	ZERO	E	19. D	UP	ZERO	E
10. D	LEVEL	RIGHT	S	20. D	DOWN	RIGHT	SE

Subtest #6: Block Counting

Check your answers below. Use the table to record right and wrong answers.

	✔	✘		✔	✘		✔	✘		✔	✘
1. D			6. B			11. A			16. B		
2. B			7. C			12. C			17. A		
3. E			8. D			13. B			18. B		
4. A			9. E			14. E			19. C		
5. B			10. B			15. C			20. D		

Subtest #7: Table Reading

Check your answers below. Use the table to record right and wrong answers.

	✔	✘		✔	✘		✔	✘		✔	✘		✔	✘
1. B			9. C			17. A			25. E			33. E		
2. C			10. B			18. E			26. A			34. A		
3. B			11. B			19. E			27. E			35. B		
4. D			12. D			20. D			28. C			36. D		
5. A			13. C			21. C			29. D			37. E		
6. D			14. B			22. B			30. D			38. C		
7. C			15. A			23. A			31. C			39. B		
8. A			16. B			24. D			32. B			40. E		

Subtest #8: Aviation Information

Check your answers below and refer to the explanation for each question you missed. Use the table to record right and wrong answers.

	✔	✘		✔	✘		✔	✘		✔	✘
1. C			6. A			11. D			16. A		
2. B			7. C			12. E			17. B		
3. D			8. D			13. B			18. E		
4. C			9. E			14. C			19. D		
5. E			10. B			15. C			20. C		

1. **C** The acceleration experienced by the aircraft and its pilot in the direction perpendicular to the wing is solely determined by the **bank angle**. Regardless of the aircraft type, its altitude, the density of the air, the temperature, or any other factor, the G-load (or load factor) experienced by the aircraft and pilot is related only to the bank angle. A Cessna 150 at 100 knots in a 60° bank will experience 2 G, just as an F-16 will at 500 knots at the same bank angle.

2. **B** The flight envelope of an aircraft is **the region of altitude and airspeed in which it can be operated**.

3. **D** The locus of points equidistant from the upper and lower surfaces of an airfoil is called the **mean camber line**.

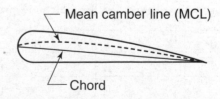

4. **C** The straight line joining the ends of the mean camber line is called the **wing chord**.

5. **E** A(n) **aerodynamic stall** is the point at which the airflow over the wings ceases to be a smooth (laminar) flow and the wing starts to lose lift.

6. **A** The two basic types of drag are **parasitic drag and induced drag.** Parasitic drag is the resistance of the aircraft to the air through which it moves; it increases with the square of the object's speed through the air. The second basic type of drag is called induced drag; it's related to the wing's production of lift. At low airspeed and high angles of attack, induced drag increases and becomes a large factor.

7. **C** An airfoil's efficiency, either a wing or a rotor blade, is **decreased** at high altitudes by the **lesser** air density.

8. **D** The degree of movement of an aircraft around its lateral axis is known as **pitch.**

9. **E** When the flaps are extended, the camber of the wing is **increased.** Effectively, the wing becomes larger and more curved. The flaps, mounted inboard of the ailerons, are probably the most commonly used lift device. They increase the lift capability of the airfoil (wing) to its maximum potential, which means an aircraft can become or remain airborne at lower speeds. They also permit a shorter ground roll on landing when used as airbrakes.

10. **B** A helicopter's cyclic control is a mechanical linkage used to change the pitch of the main rotor blades **at a selected point in its circular pathway.** For instance, if the pilot adjusts the cyclic pitch so that the rotor blades have more "bite" into the air (i.e., more lift) when they pass over the tail than when they pass over the nose of the helicopter, the aircraft travels forward.

11. **D** When the rotor blades of a helicopter are spinning fast enough in a clockwise direction to generate lift, a phenomenon known as **torque** causes the body of the helicopter to have a tendency to turn in a counter-clockwise direction.

12. **E** Pulling back (toward the pilot) on the control column or joystick of a fixed-wing aircraft will cause the aircraft to **pitch up**, that is, for the nose to rise.

13. **B** Contra-rotating propellers, a complex way of applying the maximum power of a single piston or turbo-prop aircraft engine, uses two propellers **rotating in opposite directions arranged one behind the other.** Power is transferred from the engine via a planetary gear transmission. When airspeed is low, the air mass going back through the propeller disk (thrust) causes a significant amount of tangential or rotational airflow to be created by the spinning blades; the energy of this tangential airflow is wasted in a single-propeller design. To use this wasted resource, the placement of a second propeller behind the first takes advantage of the already-disturbed airflow.

14. **C** The abbreviation VTOL, applied to aircraft other than helicopters, means **Vertical Take-Off and Landing.**

15. **C** Delta wing aircraft have a wing in the form of a tri-angle, named after the Greek uppercase letter delta (Δ) and no **horizontal stabilizer**. The primary advantage of this design is that the wing's leading edge remains behind the shock wave generated by the aircraft's nose when flying at supersonic speeds, which is an improvement on traditional wing designs.

16. **A** The Visual Approach Slope Indicator (VASI) is a system of lights designed to provide visual descent guidance information during a runway approach. The system uses **red** lights to indicate the upper limits of the glide path and **white** lights for the lower limits. It is visible from 3–5 miles during the day and up to 20 miles or more at night. The visual glide path of the VASI provides safe obstruction clearance within ±10 degrees of the extended runway centerline and to 4 nautical miles from the runway threshold.

17. **B** A biplane has **two wings arranged one above the other**.

18. **E** A coordinated turn (change of heading direction) includes both **roll and yaw** of the airplane.

19. **D** **Yaw** is induced by use of a movable rudder controlled by **rudder pedals** in the cockpit.

20. **C** Moving the control column or joystick to the left or right affects the **rate of roll** rather than indicating the **angle to which the aircraft will roll**.

Subtest #9: General Science

Check your answers below and refer to the explanation for each question you missed. Use the table to record right and wrong answers.

	✔	✗		✔	✗		✔	✗		✔	✗
1. D			6. B			11. B			16. E		
2. C			7. B			12. C			17. A		
3. B			8. C			13. C			18. E		
4. D			9. D			14. C			19. C		
5. B			10. B			15. B			20. D		

1. **D** The most accurate description of the earth's atmosphere is that it is made up of **21% oxygen, 78% nitrogen, .03% carbon dioxide, trace amounts of rare gases, water vapor, and some dust particles.**

2. **C** Since sound consists of vibrations passed through a medium such as air, in an environment where there is nothing to transmit the sound there will be no sound—so the tuning fork will **be inaudible.**

3. **B** Most plants need **nitrogen**; they also need **phosphorus and potassium**. Plants need only traces of other elements, so they are not a priority for companies that produce fertilizers.

4. **D** The whale and the **horse** are most closely related because they are both mammals with four-chambered hearts, mammary glands, and air-breathing lungs. They also both bear their young live, not as eggs. Sharks, turtles, and dinosaurs are all cold-blooded; turtles and dinosaurs are (or, in the dinosaur's case, were) egg-bearing.

5. **B** "Dry ice" is solid carbon dioxide (CO_2), made by cooling this gas to –80 degrees Celsius. In this case, CO_2 goes directly from a gaseous state to a solid—and then, when it warms above the temperature needed to keep it a solid, it goes directly back to a gas.

6. **B** An airplane wing is curved on the top and relatively flat on the bottom (this shape is called an airfoil). Because nature avoids having a vacuum whenever possible (the cliché is that "nature abhors a vacuum"), air flowing over the top surface is forced to flow faster over the top of the wing than under the bottom surface to avoid having a partial vacuum at the trailing (back) edge of the wing. This faster-flowing air results in less air pressure on the top surface of the wing than underneath. The scientific principle behind this was first described by Swiss mathematician Daniel Bernoulli (1700–1782): in any flowing fluid, as the speed of the fluid becomes greater, the pressure becomes less.

7. **B** Radio waves and visible light waves are two forms of electromagnetic radiation. Therefore, they have the same **speed** as all electromagnetic waves in a vacuum—that is, the speed of light.

8. **C** The lens of the eye focuses visible light on the **retina**, which records the image—the same function as the film in a camera. Impulses are then sent along the optic nerve to the brain. The cornea is the transparent tissue covering the eyeball.

9. **D** A clone is an individual organism grown from a single body cell of its parent, and is genetically identical to that parent. The cloned organism is a result of stimulating the parent cell to reproduce by asexual means.

10. **B** Parallel light rays each strike the mirror at a different point. Because the mirror has a plane (flat) surface, the rays are still **parallel** after reflection.

11. **B** All freely falling objects, regardless of their mass, fall toward the earth with equal acceleration. Any two objects that begin to fall at the same instant will have equal velocities at the end of four seconds, or at any other time interval. Therefore, the ratio of their speeds will be **1:1**.

12. **C** The **sperm cell** carries either an X or a Y chromosome, whereas all eggs normally have one X chromosome. When a sperm cell has an X chromosome, the two X chromosomes result in a female baby, whereas the union of an X chromosome with a Y chromosome results in a male.

13. **C** All atoms of the same element have the same number of protons. Neutral atoms have the same number of **electrons and protons** (protons are inside the atom's nucleus, and electrons are outside of it). Atoms of the same element may differ in the number of neutrons.

14. **C Soil** is eroded by the action of wind, water, and ice; it can also be depleted by the removal of organic matter or minerals.

15. **B** An insulator is a material that has tightly held electrons and very **few** (if any) **free electrons**. This means that it can be used to protect the conductor, since the insulator will not allow free electrons from the conductor to knock loose any tightly held electrons of the insulator material.

16. **E** Combustion (**burning**) is a chemical process; the others listed are not.

17. **A** Spiders have **four pairs of legs, for a total of eight**; true insects have only three pairs of legs for a total of six.

18. **E** The **electron** is the negatively charged particle that circles the nucleus of an atom. A *neutron* is neutral (has no charge), and a *proton* is positively charged; a *meson* has both positive and negative charges. An *isotope* is an atom of the same element that has a different number of neutrons.

19. **C** Light travels in a vacuum at 186,282 miles per second, and the earth is 92,955,807 miles from the sun. This means that light from the sun reaches the earth in about **eight minutes** and 19 seconds. (Even if you rounded off the speed of light to 186,000 mps and the earth-sun distance to 93,000,000 miles, the result would be only one second different—eight minutes and 20 seconds.)

20. **D** The human shoulder joint is a **ball-and-socket** joint. Ball-and-socket joints allow movement in almost any direction, similar to a universal joint on an automobile.

Subtest #10: Rotated Blocks

Check your answers below. Use the table to record right and wrong answers.

	✔	✗		✔	✗		✔	✗
1. D			6. B			11. D		
2. B			7. C			12. C		
3. C			8. D			13. B		
4. A			9. A			14. E		
5. D			10. B			15. A		

AFOQT #2

Subtest #11: Hidden Figures

Check your answers below. Use the table to record right and wrong answers.

	✔	✗		✔	✗		✔	✗
1. B			6. D			11. B		
2. A			7. A			12. D		
3. E			8. C			13. E		
4. C			9. E			14. C		
5. B			10. A			15. B		

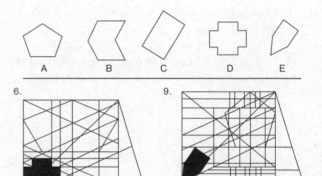
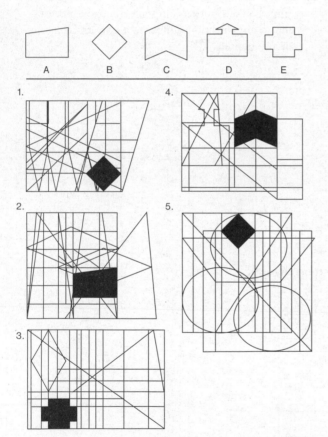
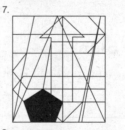
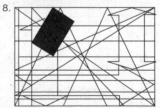
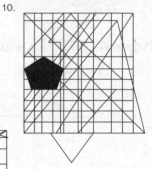

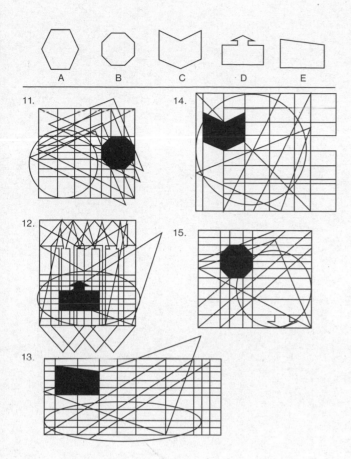

Subtest #12: Self-Description Inventory

There are no right or wrong answers to this subtest.

Answer Sheet
AFAST #1

Subtest 2: Instrument Comprehension

26 Ⓐ Ⓑ Ⓒ Ⓓ   30 Ⓐ Ⓑ Ⓒ Ⓓ   34 Ⓐ Ⓑ Ⓒ Ⓓ   38 Ⓐ Ⓑ Ⓒ Ⓓ
27 Ⓐ Ⓑ Ⓒ Ⓓ   31 Ⓐ Ⓑ Ⓒ Ⓓ   35 Ⓐ Ⓑ Ⓒ Ⓓ   39 Ⓐ Ⓑ Ⓒ Ⓓ
28 Ⓐ Ⓑ Ⓒ Ⓓ   32 Ⓐ Ⓑ Ⓒ Ⓓ   36 Ⓐ Ⓑ Ⓒ Ⓓ   40 Ⓐ Ⓑ Ⓒ Ⓓ
29 Ⓐ Ⓑ Ⓒ Ⓓ   33 Ⓐ Ⓑ Ⓒ Ⓓ   37 Ⓐ Ⓑ Ⓒ Ⓓ

Subtest 3: Complex Movements

41 Ⓐ Ⓑ Ⓒ Ⓓ Ⓔ   49 Ⓐ Ⓑ Ⓒ Ⓓ Ⓔ   57 Ⓐ Ⓑ Ⓒ Ⓓ Ⓔ   65 Ⓐ Ⓑ Ⓒ Ⓓ Ⓔ
42 Ⓐ Ⓑ Ⓒ Ⓓ Ⓔ   50 Ⓐ Ⓑ Ⓒ Ⓓ Ⓔ   58 Ⓐ Ⓑ Ⓒ Ⓓ Ⓔ   66 Ⓐ Ⓑ Ⓒ Ⓓ Ⓔ
43 Ⓐ Ⓑ Ⓒ Ⓓ Ⓔ   51 Ⓐ Ⓑ Ⓒ Ⓓ Ⓔ   59 Ⓐ Ⓑ Ⓒ Ⓓ Ⓔ   67 Ⓐ Ⓑ Ⓒ Ⓓ Ⓔ
44 Ⓐ Ⓑ Ⓒ Ⓓ Ⓔ   52 Ⓐ Ⓑ Ⓒ Ⓓ Ⓔ   60 Ⓐ Ⓑ Ⓒ Ⓓ Ⓔ   68 Ⓐ Ⓑ Ⓒ Ⓓ Ⓔ
45 Ⓐ Ⓑ Ⓒ Ⓓ Ⓔ   53 Ⓐ Ⓑ Ⓒ Ⓓ Ⓔ   61 Ⓐ Ⓑ Ⓒ Ⓓ Ⓔ   69 Ⓐ Ⓑ Ⓒ Ⓓ Ⓔ
46 Ⓐ Ⓑ Ⓒ Ⓓ Ⓔ   54 Ⓐ Ⓑ Ⓒ Ⓓ Ⓔ   62 Ⓐ Ⓑ Ⓒ Ⓓ Ⓔ   70 Ⓐ Ⓑ Ⓒ Ⓓ Ⓔ
47 Ⓐ Ⓑ Ⓒ Ⓓ Ⓔ   55 Ⓐ Ⓑ Ⓒ Ⓓ Ⓔ   63 Ⓐ Ⓑ Ⓒ Ⓓ Ⓔ
48 Ⓐ Ⓑ Ⓒ Ⓓ Ⓔ   56 Ⓐ Ⓑ Ⓒ Ⓓ Ⓔ   64 Ⓐ Ⓑ Ⓒ Ⓓ Ⓔ

Subtest 4: Helicopter Knowledge

71 Ⓐ Ⓑ Ⓒ Ⓓ Ⓔ   76 Ⓐ Ⓑ Ⓒ Ⓓ Ⓔ   81 Ⓐ Ⓑ Ⓒ Ⓓ Ⓔ   86 Ⓐ Ⓑ Ⓒ Ⓓ Ⓔ
72 Ⓐ Ⓑ Ⓒ Ⓓ Ⓔ   77 Ⓐ Ⓑ Ⓒ Ⓓ Ⓔ   82 Ⓐ Ⓑ Ⓒ Ⓓ Ⓔ   87 Ⓐ Ⓑ Ⓒ Ⓓ Ⓔ
73 Ⓐ Ⓑ Ⓒ Ⓓ Ⓔ   78 Ⓐ Ⓑ Ⓒ Ⓓ Ⓔ   83 Ⓐ Ⓑ Ⓒ Ⓓ Ⓔ   88 Ⓐ Ⓑ Ⓒ Ⓓ Ⓔ
74 Ⓐ Ⓑ Ⓒ Ⓓ Ⓔ   79 Ⓐ Ⓑ Ⓒ Ⓓ Ⓔ   84 Ⓐ Ⓑ Ⓒ Ⓓ Ⓔ   89 Ⓐ Ⓑ Ⓒ Ⓓ Ⓔ
75 Ⓐ Ⓑ Ⓒ Ⓓ Ⓔ   80 Ⓐ Ⓑ Ⓒ Ⓓ Ⓔ   85 Ⓐ Ⓑ Ⓒ Ⓓ Ⓔ   90 Ⓐ Ⓑ Ⓒ Ⓓ Ⓔ

Subtest 5: Cyclic Orientation

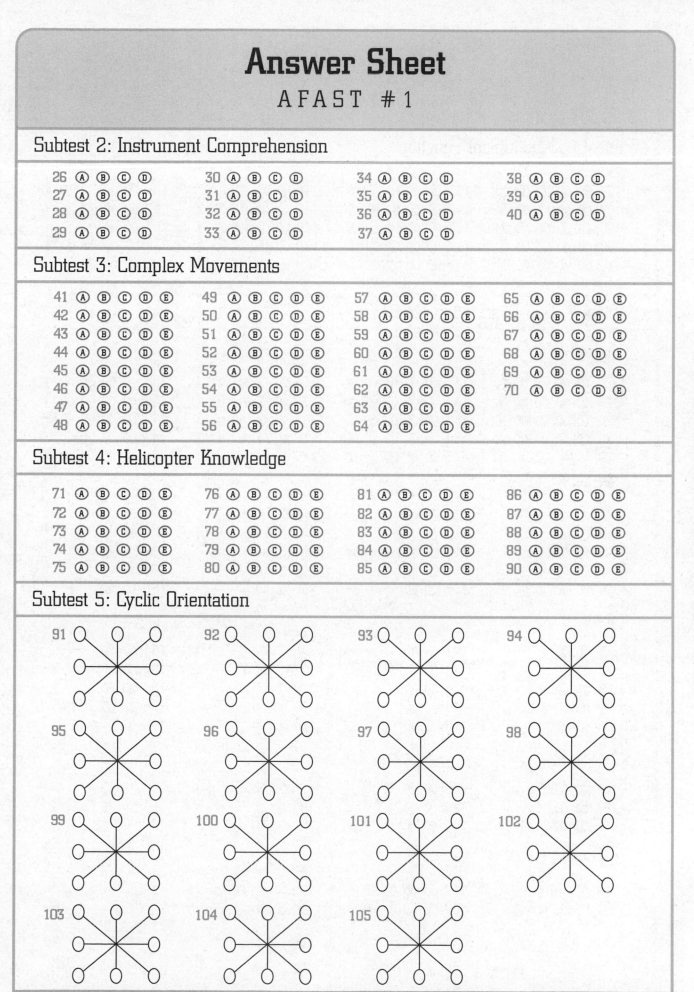

Answer Sheet
AFAST #1

Subtest 6: Mechanical Function

106 Ⓐ Ⓑ Ⓒ Ⓓ Ⓔ   111 Ⓐ Ⓑ Ⓒ Ⓓ Ⓔ   116 Ⓐ Ⓑ Ⓒ Ⓓ Ⓔ   121 Ⓐ Ⓑ Ⓒ Ⓓ Ⓔ
107 Ⓐ Ⓑ Ⓒ Ⓓ Ⓔ   112 Ⓐ Ⓑ Ⓒ Ⓓ Ⓔ   117 Ⓐ Ⓑ Ⓒ Ⓓ Ⓔ   122 Ⓐ Ⓑ Ⓒ Ⓓ Ⓔ
108 Ⓐ Ⓑ Ⓒ Ⓓ Ⓔ   113 Ⓐ Ⓑ Ⓒ Ⓓ Ⓔ   118 Ⓐ Ⓑ Ⓒ Ⓓ Ⓔ   123 Ⓐ Ⓑ Ⓒ Ⓓ Ⓔ
109 Ⓐ Ⓑ Ⓒ Ⓓ Ⓔ   114 Ⓐ Ⓑ Ⓒ Ⓓ Ⓔ   119 Ⓐ Ⓑ Ⓒ Ⓓ Ⓔ   124 Ⓐ Ⓑ Ⓒ Ⓓ Ⓔ
110 Ⓐ Ⓑ Ⓒ Ⓓ Ⓔ   115 Ⓐ Ⓑ Ⓒ Ⓓ Ⓔ   120 Ⓐ Ⓑ Ⓒ Ⓓ Ⓔ   125 Ⓐ Ⓑ Ⓒ Ⓓ Ⓔ

Subtest 7: Self-Description Form

Section A

126 Ⓐ Ⓑ Ⓒ Ⓓ Ⓔ   131 Ⓐ Ⓑ Ⓒ Ⓓ Ⓔ   136 Ⓐ Ⓑ Ⓒ Ⓓ Ⓔ   141 Ⓐ Ⓑ Ⓒ Ⓓ Ⓔ
127 Ⓐ Ⓑ Ⓒ Ⓓ Ⓔ   132 Ⓐ Ⓑ Ⓒ Ⓓ Ⓔ   137 Ⓐ Ⓑ Ⓒ Ⓓ Ⓔ   142 Ⓐ Ⓑ Ⓒ Ⓓ Ⓔ
128 Ⓐ Ⓑ Ⓒ Ⓓ Ⓔ   133 Ⓐ Ⓑ Ⓒ Ⓓ Ⓔ   138 Ⓐ Ⓑ Ⓒ Ⓓ Ⓔ   143 Ⓐ Ⓑ Ⓒ Ⓓ Ⓔ
129 Ⓐ Ⓑ Ⓒ Ⓓ Ⓔ   134 Ⓐ Ⓑ Ⓒ Ⓓ Ⓔ   139 Ⓐ Ⓑ Ⓒ Ⓓ Ⓔ   144 Ⓐ Ⓑ Ⓒ Ⓓ Ⓔ
130 Ⓐ Ⓑ Ⓒ Ⓓ Ⓔ   135 Ⓐ Ⓑ Ⓒ Ⓓ Ⓔ   140 Ⓐ Ⓑ Ⓒ Ⓓ Ⓔ   145 Ⓐ Ⓑ Ⓒ Ⓓ Ⓔ

Section B

146 Ⓨ Ⓝ   151 Ⓨ Ⓝ   156 Ⓨ Ⓝ   161 Ⓨ Ⓝ
147 Ⓨ Ⓝ   152 Ⓨ Ⓝ   157 Ⓨ Ⓝ   162 Ⓨ Ⓝ
148 Ⓨ Ⓝ   153 Ⓨ Ⓝ   158 Ⓨ Ⓝ   163 Ⓨ Ⓝ
149 Ⓨ Ⓝ   154 Ⓨ Ⓝ   159 Ⓨ Ⓝ   164 Ⓨ Ⓝ
150 Ⓨ Ⓝ   155 Ⓨ Ⓝ   160 Ⓨ Ⓝ   165 Ⓨ Ⓝ

Section C

166 Ⓛ Ⓓ   171 Ⓛ Ⓓ   176 Ⓛ Ⓓ   181 Ⓛ Ⓓ
167 Ⓛ Ⓓ   172 Ⓛ Ⓓ   177 Ⓛ Ⓓ   182 Ⓛ Ⓓ
168 Ⓛ Ⓓ   173 Ⓛ Ⓓ   178 Ⓛ Ⓓ   183 Ⓛ Ⓓ
169 Ⓛ Ⓓ   174 Ⓛ Ⓓ   179 Ⓛ Ⓓ   184 Ⓛ Ⓓ
170 Ⓛ Ⓓ   175 Ⓛ Ⓓ   180 Ⓛ Ⓓ   185 Ⓛ Ⓓ

Section D

186 Ⓐ Ⓑ   189 Ⓐ Ⓑ   192 Ⓐ Ⓑ
187 Ⓐ Ⓑ   190 Ⓐ Ⓑ   193 Ⓐ Ⓑ
188 Ⓐ Ⓑ   191 Ⓐ Ⓑ   194 Ⓐ Ⓑ

Section E

195 Ⓐ Ⓑ Ⓒ Ⓓ   197 Ⓐ Ⓑ Ⓒ Ⓓ   199 Ⓐ Ⓑ Ⓒ Ⓓ
196 Ⓐ Ⓑ Ⓒ Ⓓ   198 Ⓐ Ⓑ Ⓒ Ⓓ   200 Ⓐ Ⓑ Ⓒ Ⓓ

Practice Army Alternate Flight Aptitude Selection Test (AFAST) #1

CHAPTER 11

TEST FORMAT

The AFAST answer sheet has a space for your name, Social Security number (SSN), and other identifying information. After the identification section come the subtest sections, with a different answer circle to fill in for each question. The questions are numbered from 1 through 200. As you go through the test, be certain you are marking the same answer on the answer sheet as the number of the question you are answering in the test booklet.

Here's an example of how to properly mark an answer:

Figure 1

If this was Question 1 on the test, and you decided that Answer B was the best choice, you would carefully fill in the circle marked B on your answer sheet. Remember to mark the circle heavily, completely filling in the circle. If your mark in the circle is too small or too light, the machine that scores the test may not read the mark. Likewise, if you decide to change an answer, completely erase the answer you want to change, and then mark your new answer. Also, never mark more than one answer for any one question. Even if one of them *is* correct, you won't get credit for the answer; your answer will be counted as incorrect.

SUBTEST 1: BACKGROUND INFORMATION FORM

This section has 25 questions about your background. You will have 10 minutes to complete this section. Just answer the questions honestly, but be sure to read each question carefully so that you answer the question as it is written.

SUBTEST 2: INSTRUMENT COMPREHENSION

In this subtest, you will have to determine the position of an aircraft in flight by looking at two dials—one showing the artificial horizon, the other showing the compass heading. From the ARTIFICIAL HORIZON dial you will determine the amount of climb or dive and the degree of bank to the left or right; the COMPASS dial will show you the aircraft's heading or direction. The test booklet will show four airplane silhouettes; you will choose the one that most nearly represents the position indicated on the instrument dials for that question. There are 15 questions, and you will have five minutes for this subtest.

Shown below are two sets of dials, one labeled ARTIFICIAL HORIZON and the other labeled COMPASS. The white line on the ARTIFICIAL HORIZON represents the horizon line—simulating what the pilot would see looking straight ahead from the cockpit. If the airplane is above the white line representing the horizon, it's climbing (nose up); if it's below the horizon, it's diving (nose down). The greater the amount of climb or dive, the farther up or down the airplane is relative to the horizon line. The ARTIFICIAL HORIZON dial also has a white pointer showing the degree of bank to the left or to the right. If the airplane has no bank, the pointer points to zero. If the airplane is banked to the left, the pointer points to the right of zero. If the airplane is banked to the right, the pointer points to the left of zero.

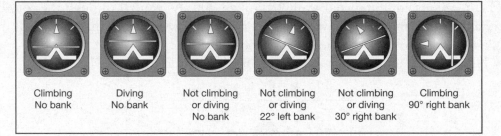

Figure 2. Examples of the Artificial Horizon Dial

The COMPASS dial shows the cardinal or semicardinal direction (north, southeast, west-northwest, etc.) that the aircraft is headed at that moment.

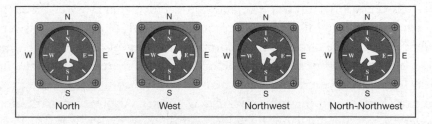

Figure 3. Examples of the Compass Dial

Look at the practice problem and decide which aircraft is in the position shown by the dials. You, as the examinee, are always looking north and at the same altitude as the airplane in the illustrations. East is always to your right as you look at the page; south is toward the bottom of the page, and west is to your left as you look at the page.

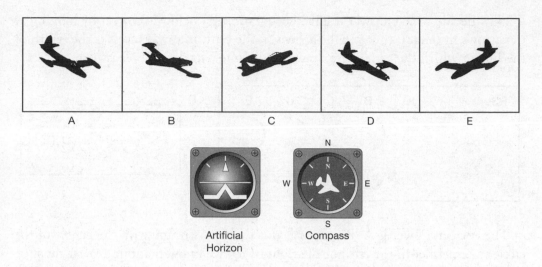

Artificial Horizon   Compass

The correct answer is C.

SUBTEST 3: COMPLEX MOVEMENTS

The 30 questions in this subtest measure your ability to judge distance and visualize motion. Five pairs of symbols are given representing direction and distance. Your task is to choose the one pair that represents the amount and direction of movement to move a dot from outside a circle into the center of the circle. You will have five minutes to complete this section.

Look at the heavy dark dot below the circle in the example. Your task is to move this dot to the center of the circle. You will have to decide which direction or directions the dot has to be moved (right or left and up or down), as well as the distance in each direction moved, for the dot to reach the center of the circle.

Look at the keys. These show the meaning of the symbols in the test. There is a **Direction Key**, which shows the meaning of the top row of symbols for movement left or right (horizontal movement) and the bottom row of symbols for movement up or down (vertical movement). Notice that, in each group, there is a symbol for "no movement." The **Distance Key** shows the three line widths in which the arrows can be drawn. The thinnest line width represents movement of about $\frac{1}{8}$ inch. The medium-width line represents movement of approximately $\frac{2}{8}$ inch, and the thickest line represents about $\frac{3}{8}$ inch.

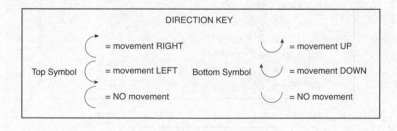

Now decide which answer in practice question P3 below is correct by looking at the arrows in the top row *and* the arrows in the bottom row, as well as the width of the line in which the arrows are drawn. Only one pair of symbols is correct.

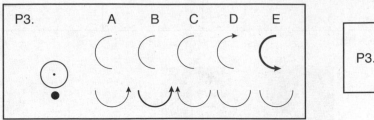

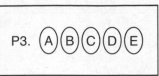

The correct answer is A. Because the dot is already in line with the center of the circle (i.e., neither to the left nor the right of it), we know that our answer must be one that shows no movement left or right; that eliminates Choices D and E. Looking at the picture and the remaining choices, we can see that we need to move the dot up a small amount to get it in the center of the circle; therefore, we can eliminate Choice C, since it shows us moving the dot downward, which would in this case be *away* from the center of the circle. And, since we can see that the dot is already very close to the outer edge of the circle, we know that we don't have to move it far; the amount of distance indicated by the thinnest line looks like it will be enough to move the dot into the center of the circle, and the greater distance represented by the heavier line in Choice B looks like it will move the dot past the center of the circle and onto the far edge, so A is correct.

SUBTEST 4: HELICOPTER KNOWLEDGE

This subtest deals with your general understanding of the principles of helicopter flight. It contains 20 incomplete statements, each followed by five choices. You have to decide which one of the five choices best completes the statement. You will have ten minutes to complete this subtest.

The incomplete statement in practice question P4 is followed by five choices; decide which one of the choices best completes the statement.

P4. You are in a helicopter in straight and level flight with a constant power setting. When the nose of the helicopter is pulled up, the altitude will:

A) Remain the same
B) Initially increase
C) Initially decrease
D) None of the above

P4. (A) (B) (C) (D)

AFAST #1

The correct answer is B. The helicopter's momentum will result in an initial increase in altitude, even if engine rpm's are not increased.

SUBTEST 5: CYCLIC ORIENTATION

This is a test of your ability to recognize simple changes in helicopter position and to indicate the corresponding cyclic (stick) movement. You will look at a series of three sequential pictures that represent the pilot's view out of the windshield of the helicopter cockpit. The three pictures change from top to bottom, showing a view from an aircraft in a climb, dive, bank to the left or right, or a combination of these maneuvers. You will determine which position the cyclic would be in to perform the maneuver indicated by the pictures. This subtest contains 15 questions, and you will have five minutes to answer them.

Instructions: You are the pilot of a helicopter with a constant power setting going through a maneuver as shown in the following pictures. The helicopter can be climbing, diving, banking (turning) to the left or right, or in a climbing or diving bank. Look at the pictures from top to bottom and decide what maneuver the aircraft is going through. Next, you must decide which position the cyclic (stick) would be in to perform the maneuver.

For questions in this subtest, the cyclic movements are as follows:

For banks: To bank left, move the cyclic stick to the left. To bank right, move the cyclic to the right.

For climbing and diving maneuvers: To dive, push the cyclic forward. To climb, pull the cyclic back.

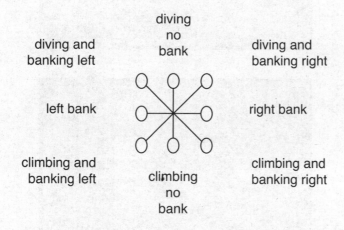

Figure 4. Example of Cyclic Movements

Now look at the pictures below in practice problem P5 and choose the cyclic position for the maneuver shown.

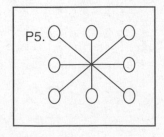

The correct answer is shown below because the aircraft is in a climbing bank to the left. We can tell this because the initial horizon goes down relative to the pilot's perspective; the initial view slides away to the right and down, and the pilot's view tilts to the left in the sequence from the top picture to the bottom. Because the horizon appears to go down, that means the nose of the aircraft is increasingly pointed up, or above the horizon—hence a climb, or increase in altitude. And, because the left side of the horizon goes down and the right side goes up during the sequence of pictures, we know we are turning or banking more to the left. Combine the two, and you have a climbing bank to the left.

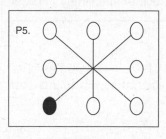

SUBTEST 6: MECHANICAL FUNCTION

This subtest measures your understanding of general mechanical principles by showing you pictures and asking you questions on the mechanical principles that are illustrated. There are 20 questions on this subtest, and you have ten minutes to answer them.

Instructions: Looking at the picture in practice problem P6, choose the best answer based on the mechanical principle or situation that is being illustrated. There is only one right answer.

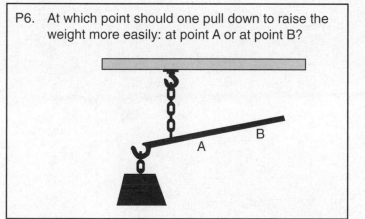

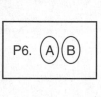

The correct answer is B. Pulling down at point B makes more leverage available because of the longer length of the lever. (The distance from the fulcrum—the point of attachment to the hanging chain—is farther to point B than point A, resulting in a longer effective lever length, and hence requiring less force to raise the weight at B than at A.)

SUBTEST 7: SELF-DESCRIPTION FORM

This section has 75 questions dealing with your interests, likes, and dislikes. You will have 25 minutes to complete this section. Read the question, then pick the one answer that applies most to you.

P7. From each pair, select the one activity you would prefer:

A) keeping a set of files in order
B) keeping a piece of machinery in order

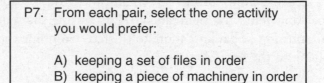

Either Answer A or B is correct, based on your personal preferences. The correct answer is the one that most accurately represents your interests, likes, or dislikes.

SUBTEST 1: BACKGROUND INFORMATION FORM

Questions 1–25: Self-explanatory.

SUBTEST 2: INSTRUMENT COMPREHENSION TEST

26.

27.

28.

AFAST #1

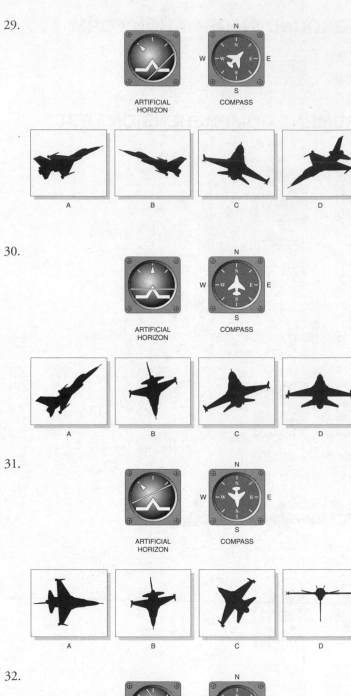

29.

ARTIFICIAL HORIZON   COMPASS

A   B   C   D

30.

ARTIFICIAL HORIZON   COMPASS

A   B   C   D

31.

ARTIFICIAL HORIZON   COMPASS

A   B   C   D

32.

ARTIFICIAL HORIZON   COMPASS

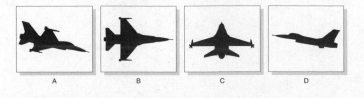

A   B   C   D

33.

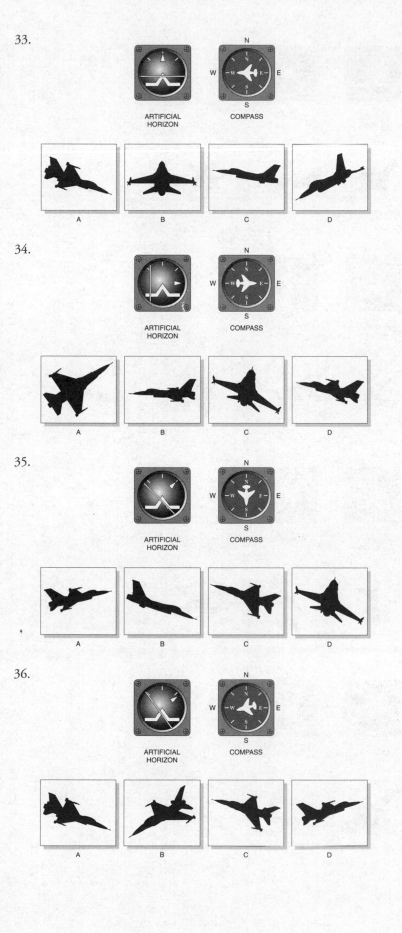

34.

35.

36.

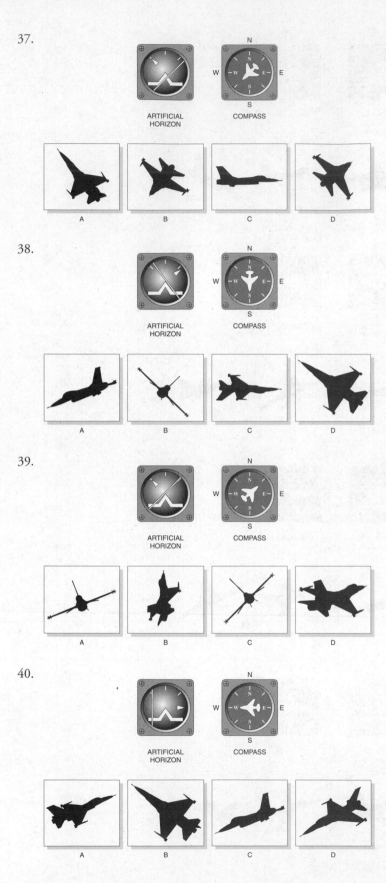

37.

ARTIFICIAL HORIZON

COMPASS

A   B   C   D

38.

ARTIFICIAL HORIZON

COMPASS

A   B   C   D

39.

ARTIFICIAL HORIZON

COMPASS

A   B   C   D

40.

ARTIFICIAL HORIZON

COMPASS

A   B   C   D

SUBTEST 3: COMPLEX MOVEMENTS TEST

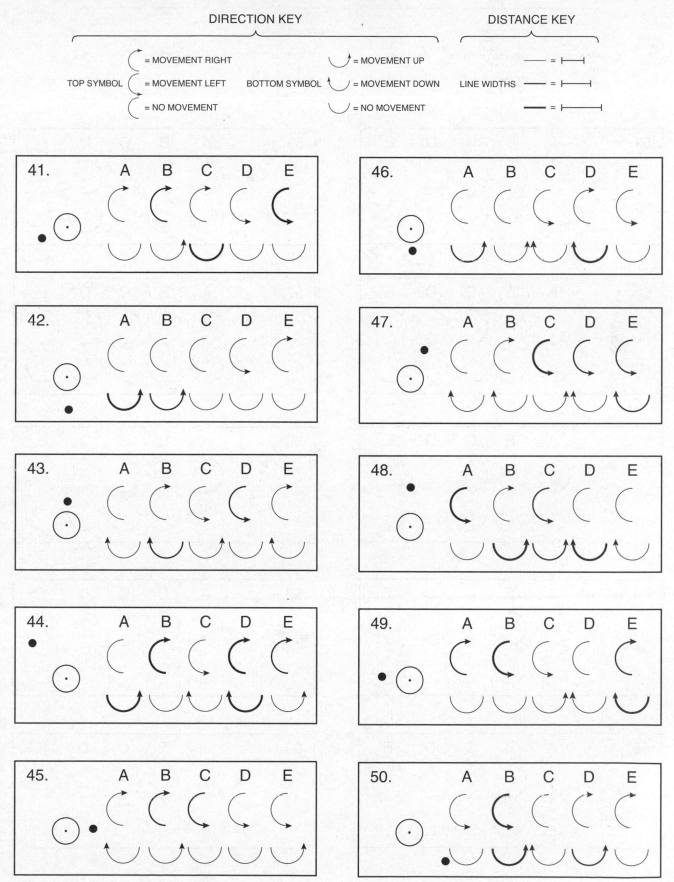

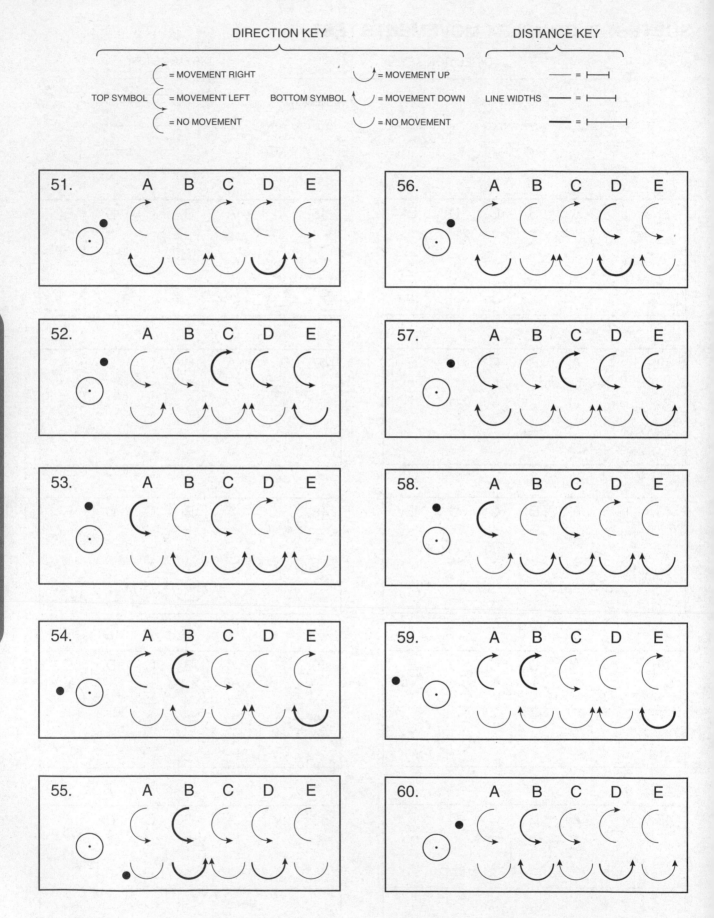

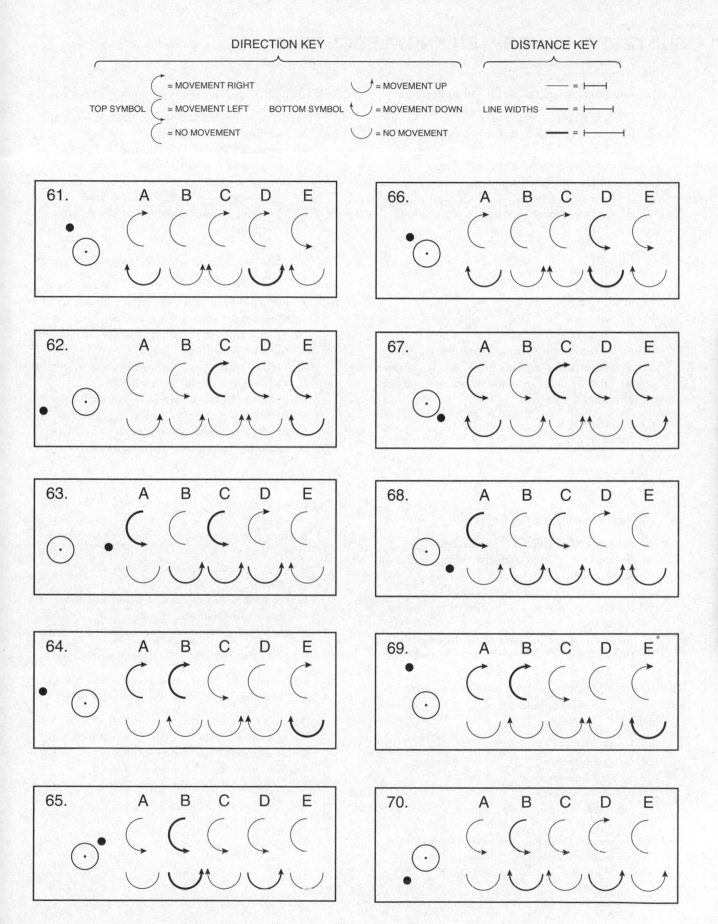

SUBTEST 4: HELICOPTER KNOWLEDGE TEST

71. The four forces that act on an aircraft in flight are

    (A) lift, gravity, thrust, and drag.
    (B) lift, mass, propulsion, and resistance.
    (C) aerodynamics, mass, propulsion, and drag.
    (D) lift magnitude, mass, thrust, and drag.
    (E) roll, pitch, yaw, and magnitude.

72. Which one of the following does not affect density altitude?

    (A) temperature
    (B) atmospheric pressure
    (C) humidity
    (D) wind velocity
    (E) altitude

73. The maneuver in which a rotary-wing aircraft (helicopter) is maintained in nearly motionless flight over a ground reference point at a constant altitude and heading (direction) is known as

    (A) feathering.
    (B) autorotation.
    (C) hovering.
    (D) torque balance.
    (E) freewheeling.

74. The flight envelope of an aircraft is

    (A) the airspeed at which it achieves takeoff.
    (B) the region of altitude and airspeed in which it can be operated.
    (C) the volume of air it displaces in flight.
    (D) the envelope containing the aircraft registration documents.
    (E) the geographical area covered by the officially filed flight plan.

75. An airfoil's efficiency, either a wing or a rotor blade, is _____ at high altitudes by the _____ air density.

    (A) increased, lesser
    (B) increased, greater
    (C) decreased, lesser
    (D) decreased, greater
    (E) increased, stable

76. The degree of movement of an aircraft around its lateral axis is known as

    (A) yaw.
    (B) roll.
    (C) bank.
    (D) pitch.
    (E) sideslip.

77. The primary purpose of the tail rotor system is to

    (A) maintain the aircraft's stability during pitch up and down maneuvers.
    (B) provide additional thrust during level flight.
    (C) provide additional lift during climbing and diving.
    (D) correct dissymmetry of lift during flight.
    (E) balance or counteract the torque effect of the main rotor.

78. Takeoff from a slope in a helicopter with skid-type landing gear is normally done by

    (A) turning the tail upslope to reduce the danger of the tail rotor striking the ground.
    (B) making a smooth running takeoff if the ground surface is smooth.
    (C) simultaneously applying downslope cyclic control and collective pitch.
    (D) bringing the aircraft to a level attitude before completely leaving the ground.
    (E) rapidly increasing collective pitch and upslope cyclic controls to avoid sliding downslope.

79. "True altitude" is defined as

    (A) the horizontal distance of the aircraft above the coastline.
    (B) the vertical distance of the aircraft above mean sea level.
    (C) the vertical distance of the aircraft above the terrain.
    (D) the uncorrected distance of the aircraft above the pressure gradient.
    (E) the adjusted vertical distance measured by density altitude.

80. A helicopter's cyclic control is a mechanical linkage used to change the pitch of the main rotor blades

    (A) all at the same time.
    (B) at a selected point in its circular pathway.
    (C) proportionate to the engine rpm's.
    (D) in conjunction with the desired speed.
    (E) for vertical flight only.

81. When the rotor blades of a helicopter are spinning fast enough in a clockwise direction to generate lift, a phenomenon known as _____ causes the body of the helicopter to have a tendency to turn in a counterclockwise direction.

    (A) centrifugal force
    (B) centripedal force
    (C) lateral roll
    (D) torque
    (E) autorotation

82. "Absolute altitude" is defined as

    (A) the vertical adjustment corrected for variations from standard conditions.
    (B) the vertical distance of the aircraft above the density pressure gradient.
    (C) the vertical distance of the aircraft above sea level.
    (D) the vertical distance of the aircraft above the terrain or ground level.
    (E) the horizontal distance of the aircraft above mean sea level.

83. The differential in lift between that of the advancing rotor blade and that of the retreating rotor blade is called

    (A) translational lift.
    (B) transitional torque.
    (C) dissymmetry of lift.
    (D) centripedal differential.
    (E) translating tendency.

84. Foot pedals in the helicopter cockpit give the pilot the ability to

    (A) smoothly enter transitional lift.
    (B) stabilize rotor rpm's.
    (C) be prepared to autorotate at any time.
    (D) control engine rpm's.
    (E) control the torque effect.

85. "Density altitude" is defined as

    (A) the pressure altitude reading corrected for variations from standard temperature.
    (B) the true altitude reading corrected for variations in inches of mercury.
    (C) the uncorrected standard reading listed on the standard datum plane.
    (D) the vertical distance of the aircraft above the highest obstacle.
    (E) the vertical distance of the aircraft above the nearest sea level reading.

86. The cyclic controls the

    (A) pitch of the helicopter.
    (B) engine rpm's.
    (C) torque effect.
    (D) direction of the tilt of the main rotor.
    (E) gyroscopic precession of the rotor blades.

87. Moving the cyclic forward and significantly raising the collective will cause the helicopter to

    (A) increase its forward speed.
    (B) increase its forward speed and begin to climb.
    (C) immediately increase its altitude without increasing forward velocity.
    (D) nose over.
    (E) stall.

88. Conventional American helicopters have a main rotor that

    (A) turns in a counterclockwise direction.
    (B) turns in a clockwise direction.
    (C) defeats translational torque.
    (D) experiences two stages of gyroscopic precession.
    (E) has two rotor blades of fixed pitch only.

89. Translational lift is

    (A) the lift needed to initially leave the ground.
    (B) the cushioning effect encountered in a low hover.
    (C) another name for Coriolis force.
    (D) the additional lift gained when the helicopter leaves its downwash.
    (E) the decreased lift suffered when the helicopter leaves its downwash.

90. Gyroscopic precession happens when

    (A) a force applied to a spinning disc has its effect 90 degrees later in the opposite direction of rotation.
    (B) a force applied to a spinning disc has its effect 180 degrees later in the opposite direction of rotation.
    (C) a force applied to a spinning disc has its effect 90 degrees later in the direction and plane of rotation.
    (D) a force applied to a spinning disc has its effect 180 degrees later in the direction and plane of rotation.
    (E) none of the above

SUBTEST 5: CYCLIC ORIENTATION TEST

91.

92.

93.

94.

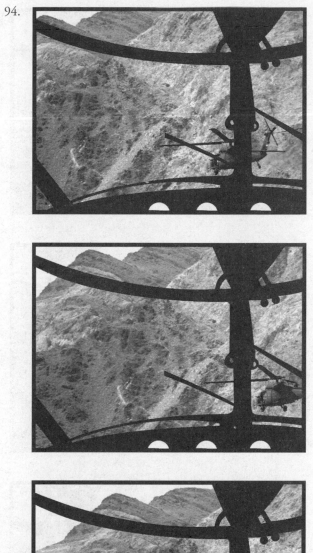

95.

96.

97.

98.

AFAST #1

99.

100.

101.

102.

103.

104.

105.

SUBTEST 6: MECHANICAL FUNCTIONS TEST

This subtest evaluates your understanding of general mechanical principles by showing you drawings or pictures, and then asking questions about the mechanical principles indicated. There are 20 questions on the subtest, which you will have ten minutes to answer. For each question, choose the best answer; there is only *one* right answer to every question.

106. Gear B is intended to mesh with

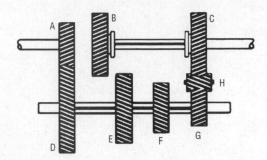

(A) gear A only.
(B) gear D only.
(C) gear E only.
(D) gear F only.
(E) all of the above gears.

107. As cam A makes one complete turn, the setscrew hits the contact point how many times?

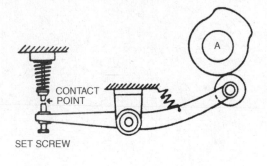

(A) once
(B) twice
(C) three times
(D) four times
(E) not at all

108. If gear A makes 14 revolutions, gear B will make

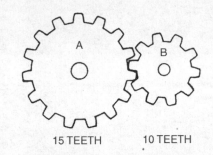

(A) 21 revolutions.
(B) 28 revolutions.
(C) 14 revolutions.
(D) 17 revolutions.
(E) 9 revolutions.

109. Which of the other gears is moving in the same direction as gear 2?

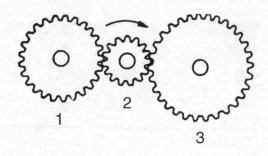

(A) gear 1
(B) gear 3
(C) neither of the other gears
(D) gears 1 and 3
(E) both of the other gears

110. Floats X and Y are measuring the specific gravity of two different liquids. Which float indicates the liquid with the highest specific gravity?

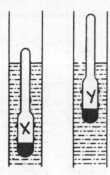

(A) Y
(B) X
(C) neither X nor Y
(D) both X and Y are the same
(E) cannot determine from the information given

111. The wheelbarrow is an example of a

(A) first-class lever
(B) second-class lever
(C) third-class lever
(D) load-bearing mechanism
(E) first- and third-class lever

112. In the figure, the angle θ is important because when it is

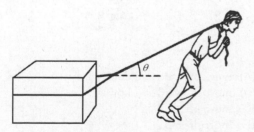

(A) 0 (zero) degrees, the entire force is dragging the box.
(B) 90 degrees, the entire force is lifting the box.
(C) 45 degrees, it is equally lifting and dragging the box.
(D) both lifting and dragging to some extent between 0 and 90 degrees.
(E) all of the above

113. Pliers are an example of a

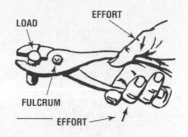

(A) first-class lever.
(B) second-class lever.
(C) third-class lever.
(D) first- and second-class lever.
(E) second- and third-class lever.

114. The follower is at its highest position between points

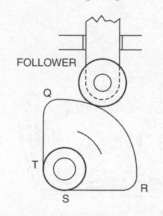

(A) Q and R
(B) R and S
(C) S and T
(D) T and Q
(E) T and R

115. If pulley A is the driver and turns in direction 1, which pulley turns faster?

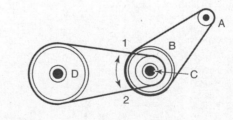

(A) A
(B) B
(C) C
(D) D
(E) A and D are equal.

116. Which shaft or shafts are turning in the same direction as shaft X?

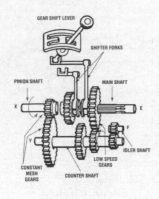

(A) Y
(B) Y and E
(C) F
(D) E and F
(E) E, F, and Y

117. The human arm as depicted below is an example of a

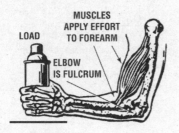

(A) first-class lever.
(B) second-class lever.
(C) third-class lever.
(D) second- and third-class lever.
(E) first- and second-class lever.

118. If arm H is held fixed as gear B turns in direction 2, gear

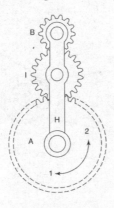

(A) A will turn in direction 1.
(B) A will turn in direction 2.
(C) I must turn in direction 2.
(D) A must be held fixed.
(E) B will spin freely.

119. Two 30-pound blocks are attached to the ceiling using ropes, as shown below. Which of the following statements are true?

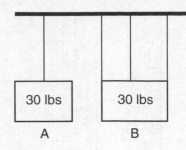

(A) All the ropes are under the same amount of tension.

(B) The rope holding block A is under $\frac{1}{3}$ of the tension of the ropes holding block B.

(C) The ropes supporting block B are under $\frac{1}{3}$ of the tension of the rope holding block A.

(D) The rope supporting block A is under twice the tension of the ropes holding block B.

(E) The ropes supporting block B are under $\frac{1}{6}$ of the tension of the rope holding block A.

120. As the shaft in the illustration below spins faster in a clockwise direction, balls A and B will

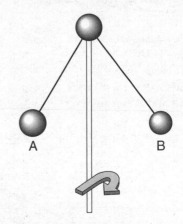

(A) move outward and downward.
(B) move outward and upward.
(C) move up.
(D) move down.
(E) stay at the same level.

121. Water flows into a water tower at a rate of 120 gallons per hour and flows out at the rate of 2 gallons per minute. The level of water in the tower will

    (A) remain the same.
    (B) lower.
    (C) rise.
    (D) rise initially, then lower.
    (E) lower initially, then rise.

122. In the illustration below, if the fulcrum is moved farther away from the weight on the resistance arm, the result will be that

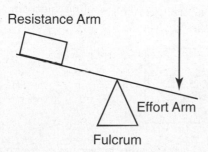

    (A) the weight will be easier to lift, and will travel higher.
    (B) the weight will be easier to lift, and will not travel as high.
    (C) the weight will take more effort to lift, and will travel higher.
    (D) the weight will take more effort to lift, and will not travel as high.
    (E) the weight will take the same amount of effort to lift, and will travel the same height.

123. What is the difference between weight and mass?

    (A) Weight can be changed by buoyancy, but mass is relative to gravity.
    (B) Mass remains constant, but weight depends on altitude.
    (C) Weight remains constant, but mass depends on altitude.
    (D) Mass can be changed by buoyancy, but weight is relative to gravity.
    (E) There is no difference between mass and weight.

124. In the illustration below, if pulley A is rotating in the direction indicated, then pulley C will

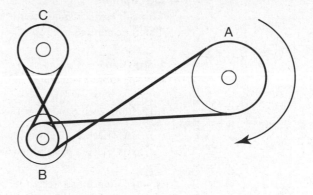

    (A) rotate in the same direction as pulley B.
    (B) rotate in the same direction as pulleys A and B.
    (C) rotate in the opposite direction of pulleys A and B.
    (D) rotate in the same direction as pulley A.
    (E) none of the above

125. In the pulley system shown in Problem 124, which pulley will rotate the fastest?

    (A) pulley A
    (B) pulley B
    (C) pulley C
    (D) They will all rotate at the same speed.
    (E) This depends on the speed of the drive pulley.

SUBTEST 7: SELF-DESCRIPTION FORM

Description
This subtest has 75 questions dealing with your interests, likes, and dislikes.
The time allotted is 25 minutes.

Instructions
On this subtest you will read the question, then pick the one answer that applies best to you.

1. From each pair, select the one activity you would prefer.

   (A) Keep a set of office files in order
   (B) Keep a piece of machinery in order

If you would rather keep a set of office files in order than keep a piece of machinery in order, choose Choice A and mark it in the appropriate space.

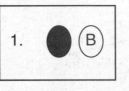

If your preference would be to keep a piece of machinery in order rather than a set of office files, select Choice B and mark it in the appropriate space.

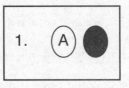

The 75 questions on this subtest are divided into five sections:

Section A: Questions 126–145 (5-choice questions)
Section B: Questions 146–165 (2-choice questions)
Section C: Questions 166–185 (2-choice questions)
Section D: Questions 186–194 (2-choice questions)
Section E: Questions 195–200 (4-choice questions)

When you begin, ensure that you start with Question 126 in Section A of your test booklet and number 126 in Section A on your answer sheet.

AFAST #1

Section A: Questions 126–145

The questions in this section consist of sets of five descriptive words from which you are to select the choice that *most* accurately describes you or the choice that *least* accurately describes you, as indicated.

126. Which of the following *most* accurately describes you?

  (A) thrifty
  (B) extravagant
  (C) sensible
  (D) lavish
  (E) economical

127. Which of the following *least* accurately describes you?

  (A) thrifty
  (B) extravagant
  (C) sensible
  (D) lavish
  (E) economical

128. Which of the following *most* accurately describes you?

  (A) skilled
  (B) gifted
  (C) competent
  (D) intelligent
  (E) adaptive

129. Which of the following *least* accurately describes you?

  (A) skilled
  (B) gifted
  (C) competent
  (D) intelligent
  (E) adaptive

130. Which of the following *most* accurately describes you?

  (A) sincere
  (B) sensitive
  (C) tolerant
  (D) empathetic
  (E) generous

131. Which of the following *least* accurately describes you?

  (A) sincere
  (B) sensitive
  (C) tolerant
  (D) empathetic
  (E) generous

132. Which of the following *most* accurately describes you?

  (A) patient
  (B) contemplative
  (C) impulsive
  (D) methodical
  (E) prudent

133. Which of the following *least* accurately describes you?

  (A) patient
  (B) contemplative
  (C) impulsive
  (D) methodical
  (E) prudent

134. Which of the following *most* accurately describes you?

  (A) friendly
  (B) polite
  (C) condescending
  (D) reserved
  (E) judgmental

135. Which of the following *least* accurately describes you?

  (A) friendly
  (B) polite
  (C) condescending
  (D) reserved
  (E) judgmental

136. Which of the following *most* accurately describes you?

  (A) investigative
  (B) courteous
  (C) analytical
  (D) considerate
  (E) patronizing

137. Which of the following *least* accurately describes you?

  (A) investigative
  (B) courteous
  (C) analytical
  (D) considerate
  (F.) patronizing

138. Which of the following *most* accurately describes you?

    (A) analytical
    (B) emotional
    (C) logical
    (D) sentimental
    (E) innovative

139. Which of the following *least* accurately describes you?

    (A) analytical
    (B) emotional
    (C) logical
    (D) sentimental
    (E) innovative

140. Which of the following *most* accurately describes you?

    (A) whimsical
    (B) dry
    (C) affable
    (D) reserved
    (E) serious

141. Which of the following *least* accurately describes you?

    (A) whimsical
    (B) dry
    (C) affable
    (D) reserved
    (E) serious

142. Which of the following *most* accurately describes you?

    (A) impetuous
    (B) impulsive
    (C) headstrong
    (D) adventurous
    (E) restless

143. Which of the following *least* accurately describes you?

    (A) impetuous
    (B) impulsive
    (C) headstrong
    (D) adventurous
    (E) restless

144. Which of the following *most* accurately describes you?

    (A) loyal
    (B) honorable
    (C) driven
    (D) open-minded
    (E) suspicious

145. Which of the following *least* accurately describes you?

    (A) loyal
    (B) honorable
    (C) driven
    (D) open-minded
    (E) suspicious

Section B: Questions 146–165

146. Do you generally start each new calendar year with a large amount of enthusiasm?

    (Y) yes
    (N) no

147. Do you trust people easily?

    (Y) yes
    (N) no

148. Do you often find yourself finishing sentences for other people?

    (Y) yes
    (N) no

149. Do you have a significant amount of time to devote to hobbies and other pastimes?

    (Y) yes
    (N) no

150. Do you like playing sports?

    (Y) yes
    (N) no

151. Do you often feel low or down?

    (Y) yes
    (N) no

152. Do you get very frustrated when traffic stops on a highway or major street?

    (Y) yes
    (N) no

153. Do you like watching sports on television?

    (Y) yes
    (N) no

154. Do you generally sleep well at night?

    (Y) yes
    (N) no

155. Have you ever built a model airplane?

    (Y) yes
    (N) no

156. Have you ever built a model airplane that could fly?

    (Y) yes
    (N) no

157. Have you ever flown in an airplane?

    (Y) yes
    (N) no

158. Have you ever flown in a helicopter?

    (Y) yes
    (N) no

159. Have you ever flown in a glider or piloted a hang glider?

    (Y) yes
    (N) no

160. Did you enjoy going to school dances?

    (Y) yes
    (N) no

161. Do you like pushing yourself to improve your abilities?

    (Y) yes
    (N) no

162. Do you have difficulty making decisions under pressure?

    (Y) yes
    (N) no

163. Do you often lose your temper when things don't go your way?

    (Y) yes
    (N) no

164. Do you wish you could change some of the things you have done?

    (Y) yes
    (N) no

165. Do you find vulgar or off-color language offensive?

    (Y) yes
    (N) no

Section C: Questions 166–185

The questions in this section consist of a listing of many different occupations. Some may appeal to you or sound desirable or fun; others might not. For each of the listed occupations you would like to have as a lifetime career, answer by selecting "like." For each of the listed occupations that you would *not* like as a lifetime career, answer by selecting "dislike."

166. Artist

    (L) like
    (D) dislike

167. Auditor

    (L) like
    (D) dislike

168. Air traffic controller

    (L) like
    (D) dislike

169. Bus driver

    (L) like
    (D) dislike

170. Cardiologist

    (L) like
    (D) dislike

171. Computer programmer

    (L) like
    (D) dislike

172. Farmer

    (L) like
    (D) dislike

173. Home appliance repairer

    (L) like
    (D) dislike

AFAST #1

174. Market research analyst

    (L) like
    (D) dislike

175. Medical technician

    (L) like
    (D) dislike

176. Probation officer

    (L) like
    (D) dislike

177. Payroll clerk

    (L) like
    (D) dislike

178. Sales representative

    (L) like
    (D) dislike

179. Substance abuse counselor

    (L) like
    (D) dislike

180. Teacher

    (L) like
    (D) dislike

181. Travel agent

    (L) like
    (D) dislike

182. Undertaker

    (L) like
    (D) dislike

183. Veterinarian

    (L) like
    (D) dislike

184. Video editor

    (L) like
    (D) dislike

185. Woodworker

    (L) like
    (D) dislike

Section D: Questions 186–194

This section consists of pairs of statements describing personal characteristics and preferences. For each question, select the statement that describes you better.

186. (A) I enjoy watching athletic events and sports.
    (B) I enjoy actively participating in athletic events and sports.

187. (A) I enjoy exercising for recreation in my spare time.
    (B) I enjoy playing video games in my spare time.

188. (A) I enjoy playing a musical instrument.
    (B) I enjoy listening to music.

189. (A) I tend to be calm and collected at all times.
    (B) I have a tendency to get upset easily.

190. (A) I appreciate input that can help me do something better.
    (B) I don't appreciate someone telling me how to do something.

191. (A) I am usually the center of attention in a group of people.
    (B) I am usually not the center of attention in a group of people.

192. (A) I generally put other people's needs ahead of my own.
    (B) I believe it is important to take care of myself and my own needs.

193. (A) Being organized is not one of my strong points.
    (B) I like having my environment organized and orderly.

194. (A) I enjoy solving complex puzzles as relaxation.
    (B) I enjoy watching old movies on television to relax.

Section E: Questions 195–200

This section of the test consists of statements that might be considered somewhat controversial. Choose one of the following choices that best describes how much you agree or disagree with each statement:

(A) strongly agree
(B) somewhat agree
(C) somewhat disagree
(D) strongly disagree

195. Global warming is one of the top three environmental problems facing us today.

    (A) strongly agree
    (B) somewhat agree
    (C) somewhat disagree
    (D) strongly disagree

196. Success at work depends mostly on who you know, not how hard you work.

    (A) strongly agree
    (B) somewhat agree
    (C) somewhat disagree
    (D) strongly disagree

197. Most people worry too much about themselves and not enough about others.

    (A) strongly agree
    (B) somewhat agree
    (C) somewhat disagree
    (D) strongly disagree

198. Breaking the law is all right if there is a justifiable reason.

    (A) strongly agree
    (B) somewhat agree
    (C) somewhat disagree
    (D) strongly disagree

199. Too much money is spent on welfare programs.

    (A) strongly agree
    (B) somewhat agree
    (C) somewhat disagree
    (D) strongly disagree

200. People seldom get the praise or recognition they deserve.

    (A) strongly agree
    (B) somewhat agree
    (C) somewhat disagree
    (D) strongly disagree

ANSWERS AND EXPLANATIONS

Subtest 1: Background Information Form

1–25. Self-explanatory.

Subtest 2: Instrument Comprehension Test

Check your answers below and refer to the explanation for each question you missed. Use the table to record right and wrong answers.

	✔	✗		✔	✗		✔	✗
26. B			31. B			36. C		
27. B			32. A			37. A		
28. C			33. C			38. B		
29. A			34. A			39. D		
30. D			35. D			40. B		

Answer	Nose	Bank	Heading	Answer	Nose	Bank	Heading
26. B	LEVEL	RIGHT	S	34. A	UP	LEFT	E
27. B	LEVEL	ZERO	W	35. D	UP	LEFT	S
28. C	DOWN	LEFT	SW	36. C	UP	LEFT	WSW
29. A	UP	RIGHT	NE	37. A	UP	RIGHT	SW
30. D	UP	ZERO	N	38. B	LEVEL	LEFT	S
31. B	DOWN	RIGHT	S	39. D	LEVEL	RIGHT	NE
32. A	DOWN	LEFT	SE	40. B	UP	LEFT	W
33. C	UP	ZERO	W				

Subtest 3: Complex Movements Test

	✔	✗		✔	✗		✔	✗		✔	✗		✔	✗
41. B			47. E			53. B			59. B			65. C		
42. A			48. D			54. A			60. B			66. C		
43. A			49. A			55. B			61. A			67. B		
44. D			50. B			56. E			62. C			68. C		
45. C			51. E			57. A			63. A			69. E		
46. B			52. E			58. E			64. B			70. D		

AFAST #1

Subtest 4: Helicopter Knowledge Test

	✔	✗		✔	✗		✔	✗		✔	✗
71. A			76. D			81. D			86. D		
72. D			77. E			82. D			87. B		
73. C			78. D			83. C			88. A		
74. B			79. B			84. E			89. D		
75. C			80. B			85. A			90. C		

71. **A** The four forces that act on an aircraft in flight are **lift, gravity, thrust, and drag.**

72. **D** Of the five factors listed, **wind velocity** does not affect density altitude.

73. **C** The maneuver in which a rotary-wing aircraft (helicopter) is maintained in nearly motionless flight over a ground reference point at a constant altitude and heading (direction) is known as **hovering.**

74. **B** The flight envelope of an aircraft is **the region of altitude and airspeed in which it can be operated.**

75. **C** An airfoil's efficiency, either a wing or a rotor blade, is **decreased** at high altitudes by the **lesser** air density.

76. **D** The degree of movement of an aircraft around its lateral axis is known as **pitch.**

77. **E** The primary purpose of the tail rotor system is to **balance or counteract the torque effect of the main rotor.**

78. **D** For a takeoff from a sloping surface, the pilot should first increase engine rpm's to takeoff level and move the cyclic stick so that the rotor cone is parallel to the true horizon instead of the slope. Apply up-collective pitch and apply pedal to maintain heading. As the downslope skid rises and the helicopter approaches a level attitude, move the cyclic stick back to the neutral position and take the helicopter straight up to a hover before moving away from the slope. The tail should not be turned upslope because of the danger of the tail rotor striking the surface.

79. **B** True altitude is defined as **the vertical distance of the aircraft above mean sea level.**

80. **B** A helicopter's cyclic control is a mechanical linkage used to change the pitch of the main rotor blades **at a selected point in its circular pathway.**

81. **D** When the rotor blades of a helicopter are spinning fast enough in a clockwise direction to generate lift, a phenomenon known as **torque** causes the body of the helicopter to have a tendency to turn in a counterclockwise direction.

82. **D** "Absolute altitude" is defined as **the vertical distance of the aircraft above the terrain or ground level.**

83. **C** The differential in lift between that of the advancing rotor blade and that of the retreating rotor blade is called **dissymmetry of lift.**

84. **E** Foot pedals in the helicopter cockpit give the pilot the ability to **control the torque effect.**

85. **A** "Density altitude" is defined as **the pressure altitude reading corrected for variations from standard temperature.**

86. **D** The cyclic controls the **direction of the tilt of the main rotor.**

87. **B** Moving the cyclic forward and significantly raising the collective will cause the helicopter to **increase its forward speed and begin to climb.**

88. **A** Conventional American helicopters have a main rotor that **turns in a counterclockwise direction.**

89. **D** Translational lift is **the additional lift gained when the helicopter leaves its downwash.**

90. **C** Gyroscopic precession happens when **a force applied to a spinning disc has its effect 90 degrees later in the direction and plane of rotation.**

AFAST #1

Subtest 5: Cyclic Orientation Test

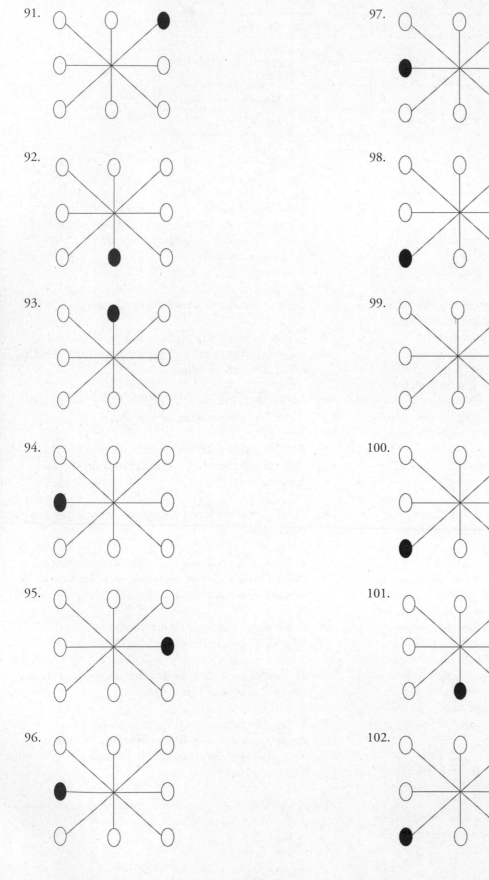

103.

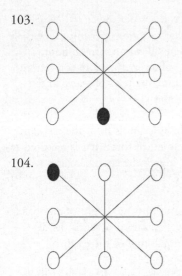

104.

105.

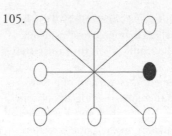

Subtest 6: Mechanical Functions Test

	✔	✘		✔	✘		✔	✘		✔	✘
106. C			**111. B**			**116. D**			**121. A**		
107. A			**112. E**			**117. C**			**122. C**		
108. A			**113. A**			**118. B**			**123. B**		
109. C			**114. A**			**119. C**			**124. D**		
110. A			**115. A**			**120. B**			**125. B**		

106. **C** Gears A and D are in constant mesh, and F is too small.

107. **A** When the lobe (high spot) on cam A makes contact with the follower (roller) on the contact arm, the contact will close. Since cam A has only one lobe, the contacts will close one time per revolution.

108. **A** To calculate the revolutions of gear B, use this formula: $r = \dfrac{(D \times R)}{d}$ where

   D = number of teeth on gear A;
   R = revolutions of gear A;
   d = number of teeth on gear B;
   r = revolutions of gear B;

   $r = \dfrac{(D \times R)}{d}$

   $r = \dfrac{(15 \times 14)}{10}$

   $r = \dfrac{210}{10}$

   $r = 21$

109. **C** Gears that are meshed turn in opposite directions. Gear 2 is turning clockwise; gears 1 and 3 are turning counterclockwise.

110. **A** Hydrometers use floats to measure specific gravity. Specific gravity is the weight of a liquid compared with the weight of the water. The liquid with the highest specific gravity will cause the float to rise higher in the glass tube.

111. **B** On a second-class lever, the fulcrum is at one end, the effort is at the other end, and the load is in between.

112. **E** The angle of the rope, θ, determines if the box is being pulled or dragged along the floor or being lifted from the floor. That means it can be both lifted and pulled along any angle that is more than 0 degrees and less than 90 degrees.

113. **A** The fulcrum is positioned between the effort and the load on a first-class lever.

114. **A** The shaft of the pivot is at T and S. The high spot (lobe) of the cam is between Q and R.

115. **A** When a series of pulleys is connected by drive belts, the pulley with the smallest diameter rotates at the highest speed; the smallest pulley will turn the fastest.

116. **D** When gears are meshed, they turn in opposite directions. X and Y are therefore turning in opposite directions. However, because both E and F are meshed with Y, they are both turning in the same direction as X.

117. **C** On a third-class lever, the fulcrum is at one end, the load is at the other, and the effect is between the fulcrum and the load.

118. **B** Two meshed gears turn in opposite directions. When an idler gear (gear I is the idler in this example) is placed between the two, both turn in the same direction. The idler gear turns in direction 1.

119. **C** Because there are three ropes supporting block B, they are under $\frac{1}{3}$ the tension as the rope supporting block A.

120. **B** Centrifugal force from the spin (it doesn't matter which direction) will cause the balls to move outward, and the tension on the strings holding them will result in the balls moving upward.

121. **A** Water is flowing into the water tower at 120 gallons per hour. To convert that to gallons per minute, we divide 120 gallons by the 60 minutes in an hour, resulting in a rate of 2 gallons per minute coming into the water tower. Therefore, the level of water in the tower will remain the same.

122. **C** The farther away the fulcrum is from the resistance arm, the greater the amount of force that is required to lift the weight and the higher the resistance arm will travel.

123. **B** Mass remains constant, but the weight of an object depends on its altitude—or, said differently, its distance from the gravitational pull of the earth.

124. **D** Pulley C will rotate in the same direction as pulley A. Pulley A causes pulley B to rotate in the opposite direction from pulley A, and pulley B causes pulley C to rotate in the opposite direction from pulley B—which (there being only two directions of rotation available) is the same direction as pulley A.

125. **B** Pulley B will rotate the fastest. In the same way as meshing gears, the smaller the pulley in a system, the faster it rotates.

Subtest 7: Self-Description Form

There are no right or wrong answers to the questions on this subtest; just answer them as honestly and accurately as possible.

Answer Sheet
A F A S T # 2

Subtest 2: Instrument Comprehension

26 Ⓐ Ⓑ Ⓒ Ⓓ   30 Ⓐ Ⓑ Ⓒ Ⓓ   34 Ⓐ Ⓑ Ⓒ Ⓓ   38 Ⓐ Ⓑ Ⓒ Ⓓ
27 Ⓐ Ⓑ Ⓒ Ⓓ   31 Ⓐ Ⓑ Ⓒ Ⓓ   35 Ⓐ Ⓑ Ⓒ Ⓓ   39 Ⓐ Ⓑ Ⓒ Ⓓ
28 Ⓐ Ⓑ Ⓒ Ⓓ   32 Ⓐ Ⓑ Ⓒ Ⓓ   36 Ⓐ Ⓑ Ⓒ Ⓓ   40 Ⓐ Ⓑ Ⓒ Ⓓ
29 Ⓐ Ⓑ Ⓒ Ⓓ   33 Ⓐ Ⓑ Ⓒ Ⓓ   37 Ⓐ Ⓑ Ⓒ Ⓓ

Subtest 3: Complex Movements

41 Ⓐ Ⓑ Ⓒ Ⓓ Ⓔ   49 Ⓐ Ⓑ Ⓒ Ⓓ Ⓔ   57 Ⓐ Ⓑ Ⓒ Ⓓ Ⓔ   65 Ⓐ Ⓑ Ⓒ Ⓓ Ⓔ
42 Ⓐ Ⓑ Ⓒ Ⓓ Ⓔ   50 Ⓐ Ⓑ Ⓒ Ⓓ Ⓔ   58 Ⓐ Ⓑ Ⓒ Ⓓ Ⓔ   66 Ⓐ Ⓑ Ⓒ Ⓓ Ⓔ
43 Ⓐ Ⓑ Ⓒ Ⓓ Ⓔ   51 Ⓐ Ⓑ Ⓒ Ⓓ Ⓔ   59 Ⓐ Ⓑ Ⓒ Ⓓ Ⓔ   67 Ⓐ Ⓑ Ⓒ Ⓓ Ⓔ
44 Ⓐ Ⓑ Ⓒ Ⓓ Ⓔ   52 Ⓐ Ⓑ Ⓒ Ⓓ Ⓔ   60 Ⓐ Ⓑ Ⓒ Ⓓ Ⓔ   68 Ⓐ Ⓑ Ⓒ Ⓓ Ⓔ
45 Ⓐ Ⓑ Ⓒ Ⓓ Ⓔ   53 Ⓐ Ⓑ Ⓒ Ⓓ Ⓔ   61 Ⓐ Ⓑ Ⓒ Ⓓ Ⓔ   69 Ⓐ Ⓑ Ⓒ Ⓓ Ⓔ
46 Ⓐ Ⓑ Ⓒ Ⓓ Ⓔ   54 Ⓐ Ⓑ Ⓒ Ⓓ Ⓔ   62 Ⓐ Ⓑ Ⓒ Ⓓ Ⓔ   70 Ⓐ Ⓑ Ⓒ Ⓓ Ⓔ
47 Ⓐ Ⓑ Ⓒ Ⓓ Ⓔ   55 Ⓐ Ⓑ Ⓒ Ⓓ Ⓔ   63 Ⓐ Ⓑ Ⓒ Ⓓ Ⓔ
48 Ⓐ Ⓑ Ⓒ Ⓓ Ⓔ   56 Ⓐ Ⓑ Ⓒ Ⓓ Ⓔ   64 Ⓐ Ⓑ Ⓒ Ⓓ Ⓔ

Subtest 4: Helicopter Knowledge

71 Ⓐ Ⓑ Ⓒ Ⓓ Ⓔ   76 Ⓐ Ⓑ Ⓒ Ⓓ Ⓔ   81 Ⓐ Ⓑ Ⓒ Ⓓ Ⓔ   86 Ⓐ Ⓑ Ⓒ Ⓓ Ⓔ
72 Ⓐ Ⓑ Ⓒ Ⓓ Ⓔ   77 Ⓐ Ⓑ Ⓒ Ⓓ Ⓔ   82 Ⓐ Ⓑ Ⓒ Ⓓ Ⓔ   87 Ⓐ Ⓑ Ⓒ Ⓓ Ⓔ
73 Ⓐ Ⓑ Ⓒ Ⓓ Ⓔ   78 Ⓐ Ⓑ Ⓒ Ⓓ Ⓔ   83 Ⓐ Ⓑ Ⓒ Ⓓ Ⓔ   88 Ⓐ Ⓑ Ⓒ Ⓓ Ⓔ
74 Ⓐ Ⓑ Ⓒ Ⓓ Ⓔ   79 Ⓐ Ⓑ Ⓒ Ⓓ Ⓔ   84 Ⓐ Ⓑ Ⓒ Ⓓ Ⓔ   89 Ⓐ Ⓑ Ⓒ Ⓓ Ⓔ
75 Ⓐ Ⓑ Ⓒ Ⓓ Ⓔ   80 Ⓐ Ⓑ Ⓒ Ⓓ Ⓔ   85 Ⓐ Ⓑ Ⓒ Ⓓ Ⓔ   90 Ⓐ Ⓑ Ⓒ Ⓓ Ⓔ

Subtest 5: Cyclic Orientation

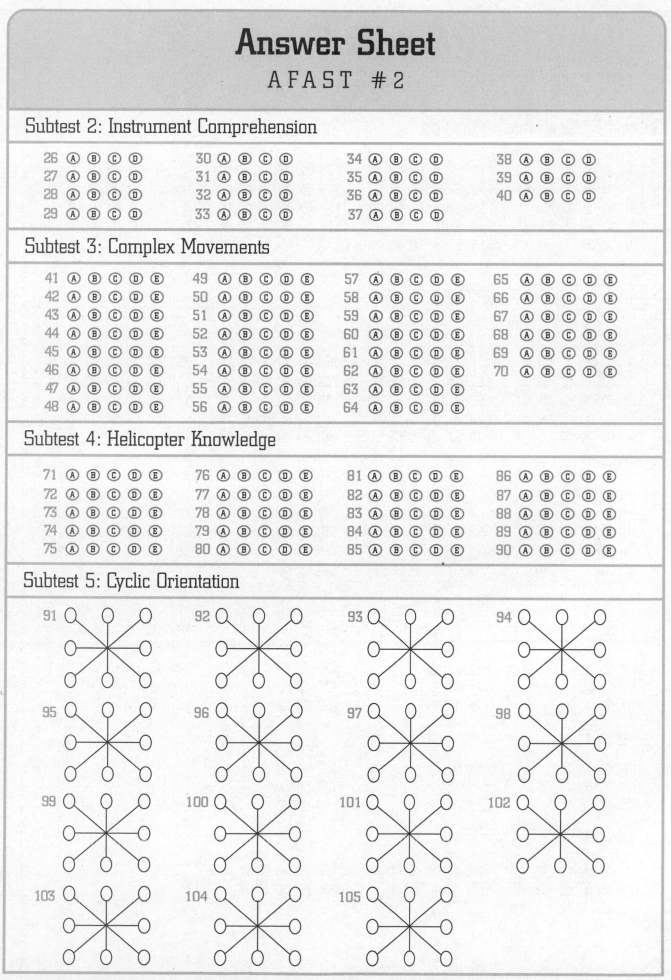

Answer Sheet
AFAST #2

Subtest 6: Mechanical Function

106 Ⓐ Ⓑ Ⓒ Ⓓ Ⓔ	111 Ⓐ Ⓑ Ⓒ Ⓓ Ⓔ	116 Ⓐ Ⓑ Ⓒ Ⓓ Ⓔ	121 Ⓐ Ⓑ Ⓒ Ⓓ Ⓔ
107 Ⓐ Ⓑ Ⓒ Ⓓ Ⓔ	112 Ⓐ Ⓑ Ⓒ Ⓓ Ⓔ	117 Ⓐ Ⓑ Ⓒ Ⓓ Ⓔ	122 Ⓐ Ⓑ Ⓒ Ⓓ Ⓔ
108 Ⓐ Ⓑ Ⓒ Ⓓ Ⓔ	113 Ⓐ Ⓑ Ⓒ Ⓓ Ⓔ	118 Ⓐ Ⓑ Ⓒ Ⓓ Ⓔ	123 Ⓐ Ⓑ Ⓒ Ⓓ Ⓔ
109 Ⓐ Ⓑ Ⓒ Ⓓ Ⓔ	114 Ⓐ Ⓑ Ⓒ Ⓓ Ⓔ	119 Ⓐ Ⓑ Ⓒ Ⓓ Ⓔ	124 Ⓐ Ⓑ Ⓒ Ⓓ Ⓔ
110 Ⓐ Ⓑ Ⓒ Ⓓ Ⓔ	115 Ⓐ Ⓑ Ⓒ Ⓓ Ⓔ	120 Ⓐ Ⓑ Ⓒ Ⓓ Ⓔ	125 Ⓐ Ⓑ Ⓒ Ⓓ Ⓔ

Subtest 7: Self-Description Form

Section A

126 Ⓐ Ⓑ Ⓒ Ⓓ Ⓔ	131 Ⓐ Ⓑ Ⓒ Ⓓ Ⓔ	136 Ⓐ Ⓑ Ⓒ Ⓓ Ⓔ	141 Ⓐ Ⓑ Ⓒ Ⓓ Ⓔ
127 Ⓐ Ⓑ Ⓒ Ⓓ Ⓔ	132 Ⓐ Ⓑ Ⓒ Ⓓ Ⓔ	137 Ⓐ Ⓑ Ⓒ Ⓓ Ⓔ	142 Ⓐ Ⓑ Ⓒ Ⓓ Ⓔ
128 Ⓐ Ⓑ Ⓒ Ⓓ Ⓔ	133 Ⓐ Ⓑ Ⓒ Ⓓ Ⓔ	138 Ⓐ Ⓑ Ⓒ Ⓓ Ⓔ	143 Ⓐ Ⓑ Ⓒ Ⓓ Ⓔ
129 Ⓐ Ⓑ Ⓒ Ⓓ Ⓔ	134 Ⓐ Ⓑ Ⓒ Ⓓ Ⓔ	139 Ⓐ Ⓑ Ⓒ Ⓓ Ⓔ	144 Ⓐ Ⓑ Ⓒ Ⓓ Ⓔ
130 Ⓐ Ⓑ Ⓒ Ⓓ Ⓔ	135 Ⓐ Ⓑ Ⓒ Ⓓ Ⓔ	140 Ⓐ Ⓑ Ⓒ Ⓓ Ⓔ	145 Ⓐ Ⓑ Ⓒ Ⓓ Ⓔ

Section B

146 Ⓨ Ⓝ	151 Ⓨ Ⓝ	156 Ⓨ Ⓝ	161 Ⓨ Ⓝ
147 Ⓨ Ⓝ	152 Ⓨ Ⓝ	157 Ⓨ Ⓝ	162 Ⓨ Ⓝ
148 Ⓨ Ⓝ	153 Ⓨ Ⓝ	158 Ⓨ Ⓝ	163 Ⓨ Ⓝ
149 Ⓨ Ⓝ	154 Ⓨ Ⓝ	159 Ⓨ Ⓝ	164 Ⓨ Ⓝ
150 Ⓨ Ⓝ	155 Ⓨ Ⓝ	160 Ⓨ Ⓝ	165 Ⓨ Ⓝ

Section C

166 Ⓛ Ⓓ	171 Ⓛ Ⓓ	176 Ⓛ Ⓓ	181 Ⓛ Ⓓ
167 Ⓛ Ⓓ	172 Ⓛ Ⓓ	177 Ⓛ Ⓓ	182 Ⓛ Ⓓ
168 Ⓛ Ⓓ	173 Ⓛ Ⓓ	178 Ⓛ Ⓓ	183 Ⓛ Ⓓ
169 Ⓛ Ⓓ	174 Ⓛ Ⓓ	179 Ⓛ Ⓓ	184 Ⓛ Ⓓ
170 Ⓛ Ⓓ	175 Ⓛ Ⓓ	180 Ⓛ Ⓓ	185 Ⓛ Ⓓ

Section D

186 Ⓐ Ⓑ	189 Ⓐ Ⓑ	192 Ⓐ Ⓑ
187 Ⓐ Ⓑ	190 Ⓐ Ⓑ	193 Ⓐ Ⓑ
188 Ⓐ Ⓑ	191 Ⓐ Ⓑ	194 Ⓐ Ⓑ

Section E

195 Ⓐ Ⓑ Ⓒ Ⓓ	197 Ⓐ Ⓑ Ⓒ Ⓓ	199 Ⓐ Ⓑ Ⓒ Ⓓ
196 Ⓐ Ⓑ Ⓒ Ⓓ	198 Ⓐ Ⓑ Ⓒ Ⓓ	200 Ⓐ Ⓑ Ⓒ Ⓓ

Practice Army Alternate Flight Aptitude Selection Test (AFAST) #2

CHAPTER 12

Please turn to the beginning of Chapter 11, page 363, for more information about the breakdown and scoring attributes of the Army Alternate Flight Aptitude Selection Test (AFAST).

AFAST #2

405

SUBTEST 1: BACKGROUND INFORMATION FORM

Questions 1–25: Self-explanatory.

SUBTEST 2: INSTRUMENT COMPREHENSION TEST

26.

27.

28.

29.

ARTIFICIAL HORIZON   COMPASS

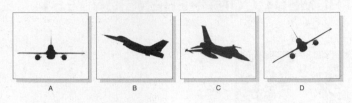

A   B   C   D

30.

ARTIFICIAL HORIZON   COMPASS

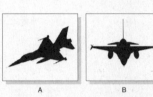

A   B   C   D

31.

ARTIFICIAL HORIZON   COMPASS

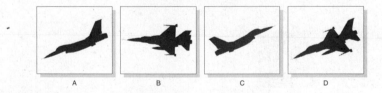

A   B   C   D

32.

ARTIFICIAL HORIZON   COMPASS

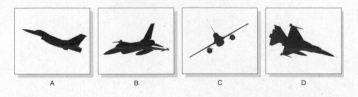

A   B   C   D

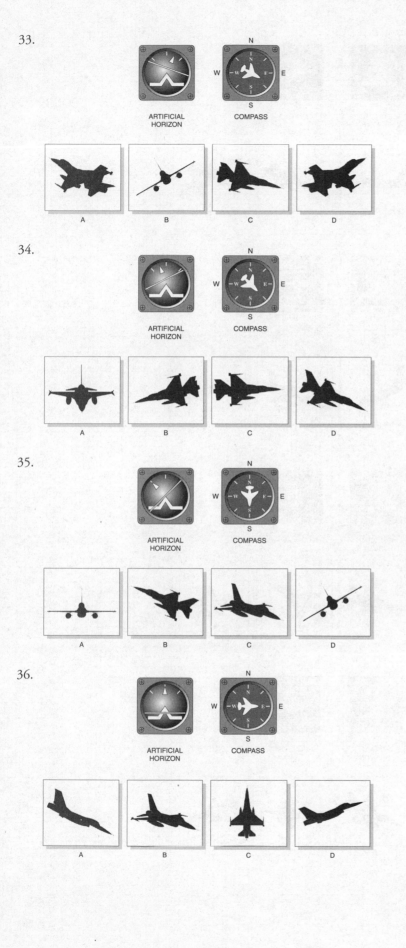

33.

ARTIFICIAL HORIZON   COMPASS

A   B   C   D

34.

ARTIFICIAL HORIZON   COMPASS

A   B   C   D

35.

ARTIFICIAL HORIZON   COMPASS

A   B   C   D

36.

ARTIFICIAL HORIZON   COMPASS

A   B   C   D

AFAST #2

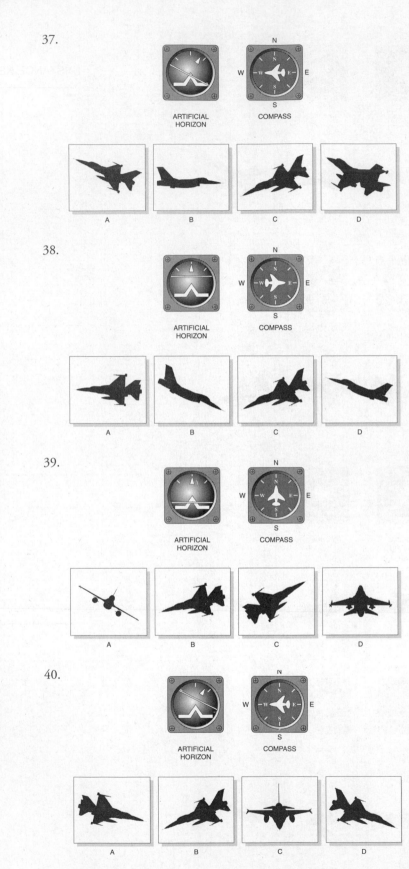

37.

ARTIFICIAL HORIZON   COMPASS

A   B   C   D

38.

ARTIFICIAL HORIZON   COMPASS

A   B   C   D

39.

ARTIFICIAL HORIZON   COMPASS

A   B   C   D

40.

ARTIFICIAL HORIZON   COMPASS

A   B   C   D

SUBTEST 3: COMPLEX MOVEMENTS TEST

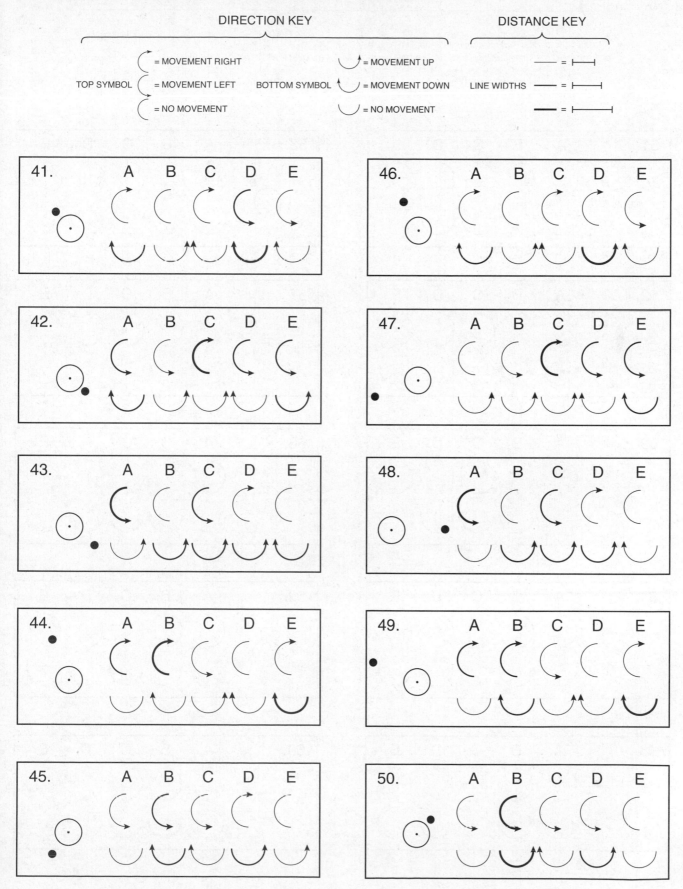

AFAST #2

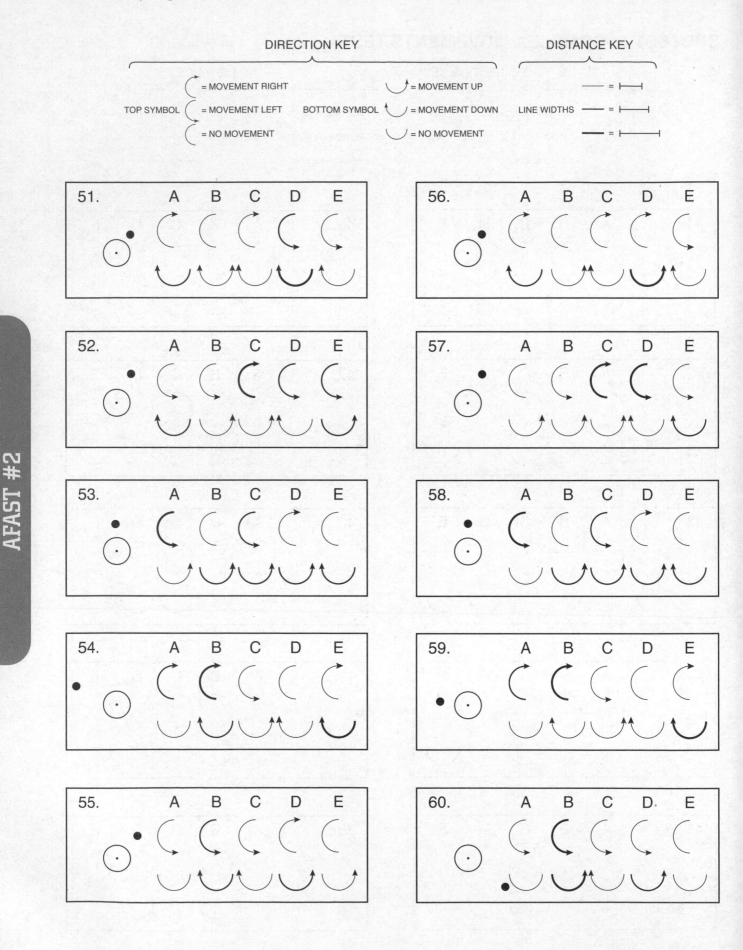

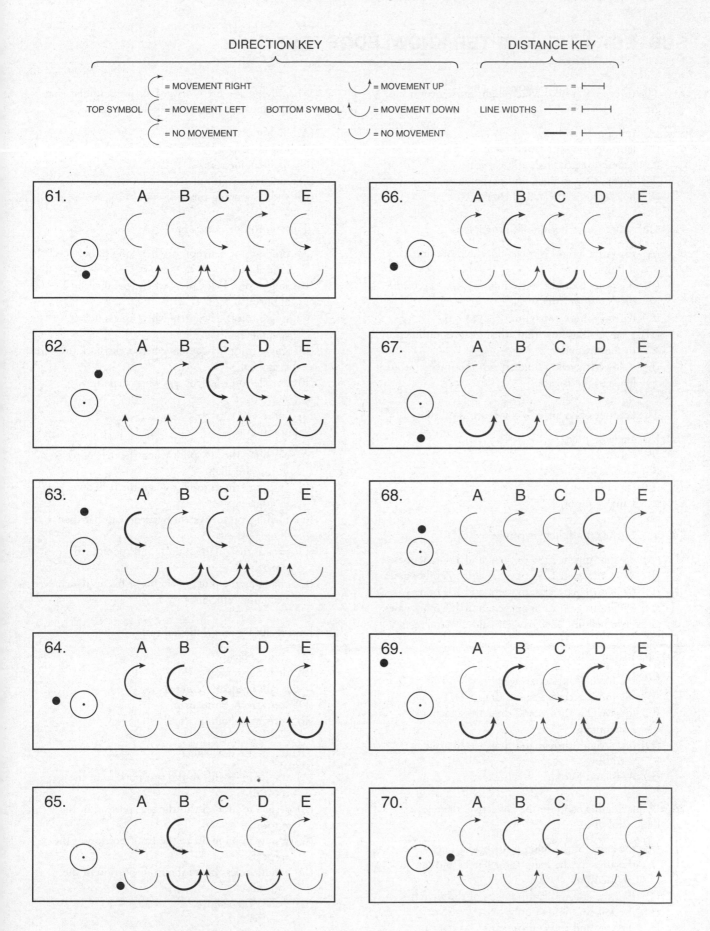

AFAST #2

SUBTEST 4: HELICOPTER KNOWLEDGE TEST

71. The three axes around which flight movement occurs are

    (A) roll, pitch, and yaw.
    (B) latitude, longitude, and vector.
    (C) lateral, longitudinal, and vertical.
    (D) lateral, longitudinal, and perpendicular.
    (E) horizontal, vertical, and lateral.

72. One way to state Bernoulli's Principle is

    (A) the faster a fluid is traveling, the more smoothly it flows.
    (B) the faster a fluid is traveling, the less its pressure on the supporting surface.
    (C) nature abhors a vacuum.
    (D) a slower-traveling fluid stream causes turbulence in the stream.
    (E) a slower-traveling fluid stream minimizes turbulence in the stream.

73. The amount of an airfoil's curvature is called its

    (A) angle of attack.
    (B) chord.
    (C) camber.
    (D) lift ratio.
    (E) Langley number.

74. The earth's atmosphere is composed of

    (A) 78% nitrogen, 21% oxygen, and 1% other gases.
    (B) 87% nitrogen, 12% oxygen, and 1% other gases.
    (C) 67% nitrogen, 31% oxygen, and 2% other gases.
    (D) 77% nitrogen, 22% oxygen, and 1% other gases.
    (E) 76% helium, 22% oxygen, and 2% other gases.

75. In a stabilized hover,

    (A) the force of lift equals weight.
    (B) the force of thrust equals drag.
    (C) lift, weight, thrust, and drag are all acting horizontally.
    (D) lift, weight, thrust, and drag are all acting vertically.
    (E) A, B, and D only.

76. By placing his hand on the collective, the pilot is in control of

    (A) the angle of the main rotor blades only.
    (B) the angle of the main rotor blades and the engine rpm's.
    (C) the yaw and roll components of the aircraft.
    (D) the roll component only.
    (E) the yaw and roll components and the tail rotor rpm's.

77. When flying at a high forward airspeed, under what condition is retreating blade stall more likely?

    (A) high gross weight
    (B) low gross weight
    (C) high engine rpm's
    (D) low density altitude
    (E) wide, sweeping turns

78. Transient torque occurs in

    (A) single-rotor helicopters when longitudinal cyclic is applied.
    (B) single-rotor helicopters when lateral cyclic is applied.
    (C) single-rotor helicopters when excess power is applied.
    (D) single-rotor helicopters when cyclic back pressure is applied.
    (E) double-rotor helicopters when making a sharp turn.

79. Autorotation is

    (A) engaging the autopilot when the helicopter is in forward flight.
    (B) engaging the autopilot when the helicopter is in a hover.
    (C) turning a rotor system by airflow rather than engine power.
    (D) part of the engine shutoff and spooldown procedure.
    (E) changing the pitch of the rotor blades to achieve maximum efficiency.

80. During autorotation, the tail rotor

    (A) is not a factor.
    (B) does not rotate.
    (C) is still needed to control yaw.
    (D) spins freely on its own.
    (E) is regulated automatically.

81. The transverse flow effect

    (A) results in less lift to the rear portion of the rotor disc.
    (B) results in more lift to the rear portion of the rotor disc.
    (C) results in more lift to the front portion of the rotor disc.
    (D) results in less lift to the front portion of the rotor disc.
    (E) none of the above.

82. A lighted heliport can be identified by

    (A) a white, yellow, and green rotating beacon.
    (B) a white, yellow, and red rotating beacon.
    (C) blue lights around a square landing area.
    (D) red and green alternating flashing lights.
    (E) red and blue alternating flashing lights

83. When a helicopter in a hover has a tendency to drift in the direction of tail rotor thrust, this is called

    (A) gyroscopic regression.
    (B) gyroscopic progression.
    (C) gyroscopic precession.
    (D) translating tendency.
    (E) transverse flow effect.

84. The best way to perform a quick stop is to

    (A) raise the collective and push forward on the cyclic.
    (B) lower the collective and pull back on the cyclic.
    (C) pull back on the cyclic and decrease engine rpm's.
    (D) push forward on the cyclic and decrease engine rpm's.
    (E) return all controls to the neutral position.

85. The collection of factors that facilitates maximum helicopter performance is

    (A) low altitude, low temperature, and high humidity.
    (B) low altitude, low temperature, and low humidity.
    (C) low altitude, high temperature, and high humidity.
    (D) high altitude, low temperature, and high humidity.
    (E) high altitude, high temperature, and high humidity.

86. The cyclic controls the

    (A) pitch of the helicopter.
    (B) engine rpm's.
    (C) torque effect.
    (D) direction of the tilt of the main rotor.
    (E) gyroscopic precession of the rotor blades.

87. Moving the cyclic forward and significantly raising the collective will cause the helicopter to

    (A) increase its forward speed.
    (B) increase its forward speed and begin to climb.
    (C) immediately increase its altitude without increasing forward velocity.
    (D) nose over.
    (E) stall.

88. Conventional American helicopters have a main rotor that

    (A) turns in a counterclockwise direction.
    (B) turns in a clockwise direction.
    (C) defeats translational torque.
    (D) experiences two stages of gyroscopic precession.
    (E) has two rotor blades of fixed pitch only.

89. Translational lift is

    (A) the lift needed to initially leave the ground.
    (B) the cushioning effect encountered in a low hover.
    (C) another name for Coriolis force.
    (D) the additional lift gained when the helicopter leaves its downwash.
    (E) the decreased lift suffered when the helicopter leaves its downwash.

90. Gyroscopic precession happens when

    (A) a force applied to a spinning disc has its effect 90 degrees later in the opposite direction of rotation.
    (B) a force applied to a spinning disc has its effect 180 degrees later in the opposite direction of rotation.
    (C) a force applied to a spinning disc has its effect 90 degrees later in the direction and plane of rotation.
    (D) a force applied to a spinning disc has its effect 180 degrees later in the direction and plane of rotation.
    (E) none of the above.

SUBTEST 5: CYCLIC ORIENTATION TEST

91.

92.

93.

94.

AFAST #2

95.

96.

97.

98.

AFAST #2

99.

100.

101.

102.

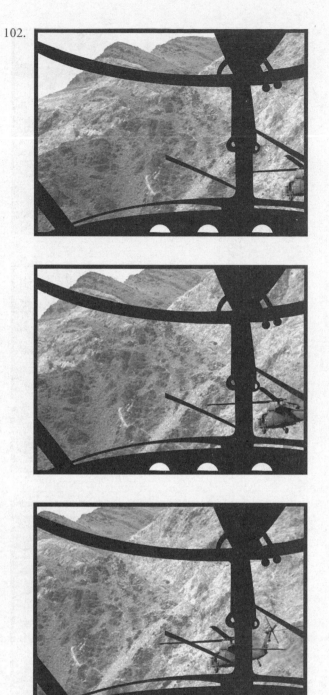

103.

104.

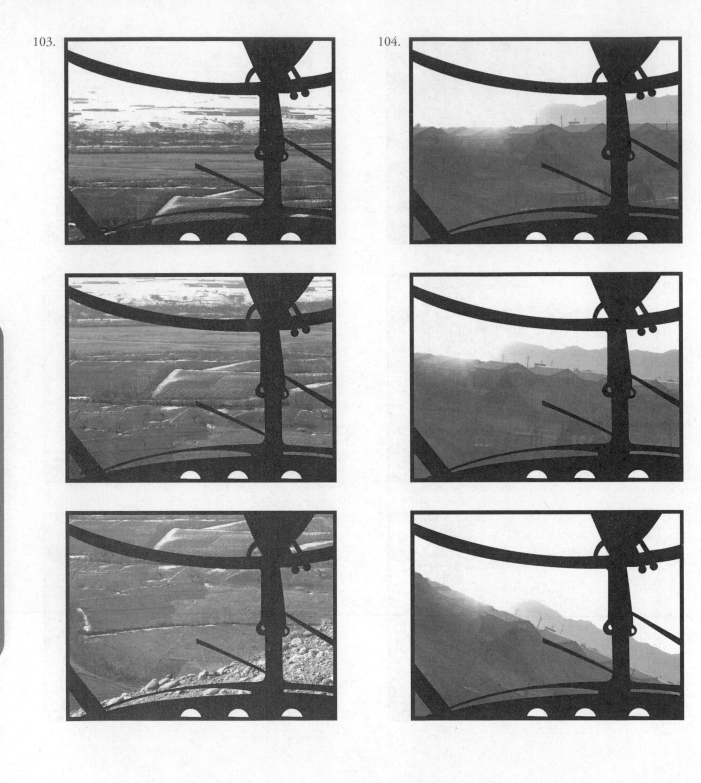

105.

SUBTEST 6: MECHANICAL FUNCTIONS TEST

This subtest evaluates your understanding of general mechanical principles by showing you drawings or pictures, and then asking questions about the mechanical principles indicated. There are 20 questions on the subtest, which you will have ten minutes to answer. For each question, choose the best answer; there is only *one* right answer to every question.

106. If gear B is the driving gear and it makes 10 revolutions, how many revolutions will gear A make?

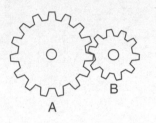

(A) 10
(B) 14
(C) 15
(D) 20
(E) 21

107. If block A, on which the lever is resting, is moved closer to block B,

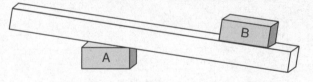

(A) there will be no change in the effort required to lift block B to the same height.
(B) it will be harder to lift block B but it will go higher.
(C) it will be easier to lift block B and it will go higher.
(D) it will be harder to lift block B and it will not be lifted to the same height.
(E) it will be easier to lift block B but it will not be lifted as high.

108. If pulley C is rotating clockwise, what direction will pulley A rotate?

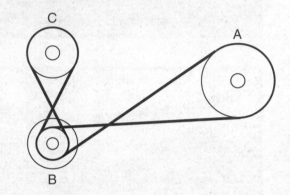

(A) clockwise
(B) counterclockwise
(C) insufficient information to answer
(D) pulley A will not rotate

109. In the pulley system above, which pulley will rotate the fastest?

(A) pulley A
(B) pulley B
(C) pulley C
(D) all will rotate at the same speed

110. If the cisterns of both water towers A and B are the same size and the same height above the ground, and both begin with a full water level, which water tower will be able to provide more water to the thirsty troops below?

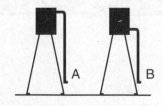

(A) water tower A
(B) water tower B
(C) both will provide the same amount
(D) unable to tell from the information provided

111. Which weight exerts more pull on the horizontal bar from which both weights hang by strings as shown?

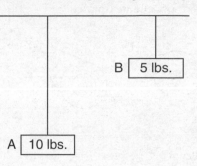

(A) A
(B) B
(C) both exert the same pull
(D) cannot tell from the information given
(E) none of the above

112. The wheels below are connected by a belt as shown. If the larger wheel makes 2 revolutions, how many revolutions will the smaller wheel make?

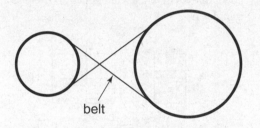

belt

(A) less than one
(B) one
(C) two
(D) more than two
(E) none of the above

113. The force required to balance the lever shown below would be

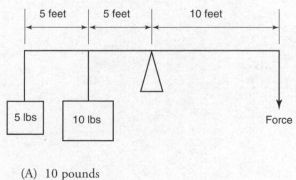

(A) 10 pounds
(B) 15 pounds
(C) 20 pounds
(D) 25 pounds
(E) 30 pounds

114. Which pendulum takes more time to make one complete swing?

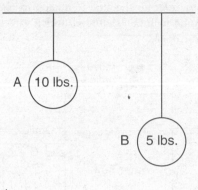

(A) A
(B) B
(C) both take the same amount of time
(D) insufficient information to answer

115. In the diagram above, if pendulum A was the same length as pendulum B, which pendulum would take less time to make one swing?

(A) A
(B) B
(C) both would take the same amount of time
(D) insufficient information to answer

116. When the plug in the tube is removed, water will flow

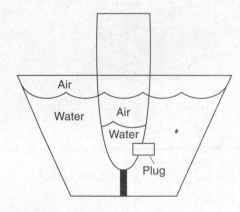

(A) into the tube.
(B) out of the tube.
(C) in neither direction.
(D) impossible to tell

117. In the water system below, assume that the main tank begins in an empty state and that all the valves are closed. In order for the tank to fill approximately halfway and maintain that level, which valves would have to be open?

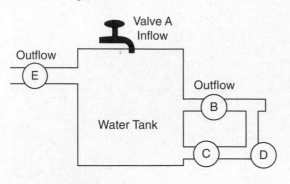

(A) A, B, and C.
(B) A, B, and D.
(C) A, E, and B.
(D) A, E, and C.
(E) B, C, and D.

118. You balance a wooden beam on a fulcrum at its center of gravity (CG). If you then mark the CG and cut the beam in two at that point, which section will weigh more?

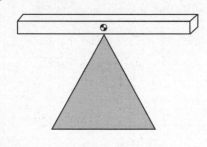

(A) the lefthand portion
(B) the righthand portion
(C) the bigger segment
(D) the smaller segment
(E) both segments will weigh the same

119. In the depicted arrangement of pulleys and belts, which pulley will have the highest number of revolutions per minute (rpm)?

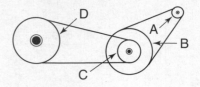

(A) pulley A
(B) pulley B
(C) pulley C
(D) pulley D
(E) unable to tell from information given

120. Two cylinders containing hydraulic fluid, A and B, are connected by a hydraulic line as shown. If the diameter of cylinder A is 3 inches and the diameter of cylinder B is six inches, and the piston in cylinder B presses down one inch, what will happen to the piston in cylinder A?

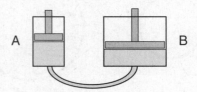

(A) It will rise one-half inch.
(B) It will rise one inch.
(C) It will rise two inches.
(D) Nothing; the fluid will compress.
(E) cannot tell from the information given

121. In the diagram below, if gear A is the driving gear turning clockwise, what directions will gears B, C, and D turn?

   (A) B counterclockwise, C counterclockwise, and D counterclockwise.
   (B) B clockwise, C clockwise, and D clockwise.
   (C) B clockwise, C counterclockwise, and D clockwise.
   (D) B counterclockwise, C clockwise, and D counterclockwise.
   (E) B counterclockwise, C counterclockwise, and D clockwise.

122. In the diagram above, what is the mechanical advantage of gear A to gear D?

   (A) 1:1
   (B) 1:2
   (C) 1:4
   (D) 1:8
   (E) 1:24

123. When two or more forces act in such a way that their combination has a net effect of zero, what is this condition called?

   (A) similarity
   (B) equilibrium
   (C) equilateral
   (D) notionality
   (E) equestrianism

124. The descent of an airborne paratrooper is primarily affected by what physical forces?

   (A) Gravity and thrust.
   (B) Gravity and temperature.
   (C) Thrust and temperature.
   (D) Drag and gravity.
   (E) Lift and drag.

125. Most of the lift on an aircraft's wings is because of

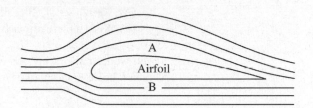

   (A) a decrease in pressure on the upper side of the wing (A).
   (B) a decrease in pressure on the bottom side of the wing (B).
   (C) a vacuum created under the wing at point B.
   (D) an increase in pressure on the upper side of the wing (A).
   (E) none of the above.

SUBTEST 7: SELF-DESCRIPTION FORM

Description

This subtest has 75 questions dealing with your interests, likes, and dislikes.
The time allotted is 25 minutes.

Instructions

On this subtest you will read the question, then pick the one answer that applies best to you.

1. From each pair, select the one activity you would prefer.

   (A) Keep a set of office files in order
   (B) Keep a piece of machinery in order

If you would rather keep a set of office files in order than keep a piece of machinery in order, choose Choice A and mark it in the appropriate space.

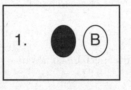

If your preference would be to keep a piece of machinery in order rather than a set of office files, select Choice B and mark it in the appropriate space.

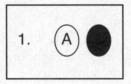

The 75 questions on this subtest are divided into five sections:

Section A: Questions 126–145 (5-choice questions)
Section B: Questions 146–165 (2-choice questions)
Section C: Questions 166–185 (2-choice questions)
Section D: Questions 186–194 (2-choice questions)
Section E: Questions 195–200 (4-choice questions)

When you begin, ensure that you start with Question 126 in Section A of your test booklet and number 126 in Section A on your answer sheet.

Section A: Questions 126–145

The questions in this section consist of sets of five descriptive words from which you are to select the choice that *most* accurately describes you or the choice that *least* accurately describes you, as indicated.

126. Which of the following *most* accurately describes you?

    (A) polite
    (B) direct
    (C) courteous
    (D) rude
    (E) outspoken

127. Which of the following *least* accurately describes you?

    (A) polite
    (B) direct
    (C) courteous
    (D) rude
    (E) outspoken

128. Which of the following *most* accurately describes you?

    (A) calm
    (B) unstable
    (C) easily stressed
    (D) moody
    (E) temperamental

129. Which of the following *least* accurately describes you?

    (A) calm
    (B) unstable
    (C) easily stressed
    (D) moody
    (E) temperamental

130. Which of the following *most* accurately describes you?

    (A) sympathetic
    (B) sensitive
    (C) tolerant
    (D) judgmental
    (E) detached

131. Which of the following *least* accurately describes you?

    (A) sympathetic
    (B) sensitive
    (C) tolerant
    (D) judgmental
    (E) detached

132. Which of the following *most* accurately describes you?

    (A) analytical
    (B) creative
    (C) impulsive
    (D) methodical
    (E) cautious

133. Which of the following *least* accurately describes you?

    (A) analytical
    (B) creative
    (C) impulsive
    (D) methodical
    (E) cautious

134. Which of the following *most* accurately describes you?

    (A) disciplined
    (B) indulgent
    (C) tolerant
    (D) free-spirited
    (E) determined

135. Which of the following *least* accurately describes you?

    (A) disciplined
    (B) indulgent
    (C) tolerant
    (D) free-spirited
    (E) determined

136. Which of the following *most* accurately describes you?

    (A) easily worried
    (B) optimistic
    (C) fatalistic
    (D) flexible
    (E) resigned

137. Which of the following *least* accurately describes you?

    (A) easily worried
    (B) optimistic
    (C) fatalistic
    (D) flexible
    (E) resigned

138. Which of the following *most* accurately describes you?

    (A) thrifty
    (B) extravagant
    (C) economical
    (D) moderate
    (E) impulsive

139. Which of the following *least* accurately describes you?

    (A) thrifty
    (B) extravagant
    (C) economical
    (D) moderate
    (E) impulsive

140. Which of the following *most* accurately describes you?

    (A) aggressive
    (B) reserved
    (C) even-tempered
    (D) moody
    (E) friendly

141. Which of the following *least* accurately describes you?

    (A) aggressive
    (B) reserved
    (C) even-tempered
    (D) moody
    (E) friendly

142. Which of the following *most* accurately describes you?

    (A) random
    (B) thoughtful
    (C) willful
    (D) adventurous
    (E) restless

143. Which of the following *least* accurately describes you?

    (A) random
    (B) thoughtful
    (C) willful
    (D) adventurous
    (E) restless

144. Which of the following *most* accurately describes you?

    (A) self-sufficient
    (B) dependent
    (C) ambitious
    (D) reliable
    (E) team-oriented

145. Which of the following *least* accurately describes you?

    (A) self-sufficient
    (B) dependent
    (C) ambitious
    (D) reliable
    (E) team-oriented

Section B: Questions 146–165

146. Do you generally start each new school year with a large amount of enthusiasm?

    (Y) yes
    (N) no

147. Do you have a difficult time relying on other people?

    (Y) yes
    (N) no

148. Do you often find yourself becoming the leader of a discussion?

    (Y) yes
    (N) no

149. Do you sometimes wish you had more time to devote to your professional pursuits?

    (Y) yes
    (N) no

150. Do you like watching sports?

    (Y) yes
    (N) no

151. Do you usually feel happy and optimistic?

    (Y) yes
    (N) no

152. Do you get angry when another driver cuts you off in traffic?

    (Y) yes
    (N) no

153. Do you like playing team sports?

    (Y) yes
    (N) no

154. Do you often find yourself arriving late to scheduled events?

    (Y) yes
    (N) no

155. Do you like to work crossword puzzles?

    (Y) yes
    (N) no

156. Have you ever built a model airplane that could fly?

    (Y) yes
    (N) no

157. Have you ever jumped from an airplane with a parachute?

    (Y) yes
    (N) no

158. Have you ever flown in a helicopter?

    (Y) yes
    (N) no

159. Have you ever flown in a glider or piloted a hang glider?

    (Y) yes
    (N) no

160. Do you like going to large parties?

    (Y) yes
    (N) no

161. Do you think of yourself as generous?

    (Y) yes
    (N) no

162. Do you like being responsible as the leader of a group?

    (Y) yes
    (N) no

163. Do you often do the opposite of what is requested?

    (Y) yes
    (N) no

164. Do you wish you could change some of the things you have done?

    (Y) yes
    (N) no

165. Do you seek out challenges to improve your abilities?

    (Y) yes
    (N) no

Section C: Questions 166–185

The questions in this section consist of a listing of many different occupations. Some may appeal to you or sound desirable or fun; others might not. For each of the listed occupations you would like to have as a lifetime career, answer by selecting "like." For each of the listed occupations that you would *not* like as a lifetime career, answer by selecting "dislike."

166. Bartender

    (L) like
    (D) dislike

167. Cartographer

    (L) like
    (D) dislike

168. Cell-phone service representative

    (L) like
    (D) dislike

169. Truck driver

    (L) like
    (D) dislike

170. Auto mechanic

    (L) like
    (D) dislike

171. Network manager

    (L) like
    (D) dislike

172. Rancher

    (L) like
    (D) dislike

173. Hotel desk clerk

    (L) like
    (D) dislike

AFAST #2

174. Waiter/waitress

    (L) like
    (D) dislike

175. X-ray technician

    (L) like
    (D) dislike

176. Police officer

    (L) like
    (D) dislike

177. High school coach

    (L) like
    (D) dislike

178. Elementary school teacher

    (L) like
    (D) dislike

179. Family violence counselor

    (L) like
    (D) dislike

180. Nurse

    (L) like
    (D) dislike

181. Pharmacy technician

    (L) like
    (D) dislike

182. Advertising sales representative

    (L) like
    (D) dislike

183. Radio disc jockey

    (L) like
    (D) dislike

184. Carpenter

    (L) like
    (D) dislike

185. Photographer

    (L) like
    (D) dislike

Section D: Questions 186–194

This section consists of pairs of statements describing personal characteristics and preferences. For each question, select the statement that describes you better.

186. (A) I am more theoretical.
    (B) I am more practical.

187. (A) I like to have lots of projects going on at any one time.
    (B) I like to finish one project before I start another.

188. (A) I like to watch the latest music videos.
    (B) I like to read for relaxation.

189. (A) I tend to be more passive.
    (B) I have a tendency to get upset easily.

190. (A) I appreciate input that can help me do something better.
    (B) I don't appreciate someone telling me how to do something.

191. (A) I am usually the center of attention in a group of people.
    (B) I am usually not the center of attention in a group of people.

192. (A) I generally put other people's needs ahead of my own.
    (B) I believe it is important to take care of myself and my own needs.

193. (A) Being organized is not one of my strong points.
    (B) I like having my environment organized and orderly.

194. (A) I enjoy solving complex puzzles as relaxation.
    (B) I enjoy watching old movies on television to relax.

Section E: Questions 195–200

This section of the test consists of statements that might be considered somewhat controversial. Choose one of the following choices that best describes how much you agree or disagree with each statement:

(A) strongly agree
(B) somewhat agree
(C) somewhat disagree
(D) strongly disagree

195. Global warming is one of the top three environmental problems facing us today.

(A) Strongly agree
(B) Somewhat agree
(C) Somewhat disagree
(D) Strongly disagree

196. Success at work depends mostly on who you know, not how hard you work.

(A) Strongly agree
(B) Somewhat agree
(C) Somewhat disagree
(D) Strongly disagree

197. Most people worry too much about themselves and not enough about others.

(A) Strongly agree
(B) Somewhat agree
(C) Somewhat disagree
(D) Strongly disagree

198. Breaking the law is all right if there is a justifiable reason.

(A) Strongly agree
(B) Somewhat agree
(C) Somewhat disagree
(D) Strongly disagree

199. Too much money is spent on welfare programs.

(A) Strongly agree
(B) Somewhat agree
(C) Somewhat disagree
(D) Strongly disagree

200. People seldom get the praise or recognition they deserve.

(A) Strongly agree
(B) Somewhat agree
(C) Somewhat disagree
(D) Strongly disagree

AFAST #2

ANSWERS AND EXPLANATIONS

Subtest 1: Background Information Form

1–25. Self-explanatory.

Subtest 2: Instrument Comprehension Test

Check your answers below and refer to the explanation for each question you missed. Use the table to record right and wrong answers.

	✔	✘			✔	✘			✔	✘
26. B			31. C				36. D			
27. A			32. B				37. A			
28. A			33. C				38. B			
29. A			34. D				39. D			
30. C			35. D				40. B			

Answer	Nose	Bank	Heading	Answer	Nose	Bank	Heading
26. B	DOWN	ZERO	S	34. D	DOWN	RIGHT	SE
27. A	LEVEL	RIGHT	E	35. D	LEVEL	RIGHT	S
28. A	LEVEL	ZERO	NE	36. D	UP	ZERO	E
29. A	LEVEL	ZERO	S	37. A	UP	LEFT	W
30. C	LEVEL	ZERO	W	38. B	DOWN	ZERO	E
31. C	UP	ZERO	E	39. D	UP	ZERO	N
32. B	LEVEL	ZERO	SW	40. B	DOWN	LEFT	W
33. C	DOWN	LEFT	SE				

Subtest 3: Complex Movements Test

	✔	✘			✔	✘			✔	✘			✔	✘			✔	✘
41. C			47. C				53. E				59. A				65. B			
42. B			48. A				54. B				60. B				66. B			
43. C			49. B				55. B				61. B				67. A			
44. E			50. C				56. E				62. E				68. A			
45. D			51. E				57. E				63. D				69. D			
46. A			52. A				58. E				64. A				70. C			

Subtest 4: Helicopter Knowledge Test

	✔	✘		✔	✘		✔	✘		✔	✘
71. C			76. B			81. A			86. D		
72. B			77. A			82. A			87. B		
73. C			78. B			83. D			88. A		
74. A			79. C			84. B			89. D		
75. E			80. C			85. B			90. C		

71. C The three axes around which flight movement occurs are **lateral, longitudinal, and vertical.**

72. B One way to state Bernoulli's Principle is **the faster a fluid is traveling, the less its pressure on the supporting surface.**

73. C The amount of an airfoil's curvature is called its **camber.**

74. A The earth's atmosphere is composed of **78% nitrogen, 21% oxygen, and 1% other gases.**

75. E In a stabilized hover, **the force of lift equals weight, the force of thrust equals drag,** and lift, weight, thrust, and drag are all acting vertically (Choices A, B, and D).

76. B By placing his hand on the collective, the pilot is in control of **the angle of the main rotor blades and the engine rpm's.** Lifting the collective affects the angle of the main rotor blades, and the throttle can be twisted with the same hand holding the collective.

77. A When flying at a high forward airspeed, retreating blade stall is likely under conditions of **high gross weight,** low rpm's, high density altitude, steep or abrupt turns, and turbulent air.

78. B Transient torque occurs in **single-rotor helicopters when lateral** (left or right) **cyclic is applied.**

79. C Autorotation is **turning a rotor system by airflow rather than engine power,** such as during an engine failure.

80. C During autorotation, the tail rotor **is still needed to control yaw.**

81. A The transverse flow effect occurs when air flowing over the rear portion of the main rotor disc is accelerated downward by the main rotor, which causes the rear portion to have a smaller angle of attack. This **results in less lift to the rear portion of the rotor disc,** but, because of gyroscopic precession, the result is felt 90 degrees later.

82. A A lighted heliport can be identified by **a white, yellow, and green rotating beacon.**

83. D When a helicopter in a hover has a tendency to drift in the direction of tail rotor thrust, this is called **translating tendency.**

84. B The best way to perform a quick stop is to **lower the collective and pull back on the cyclic.**

85. B The collection of factors that facilitates maximum helicopter performance is **low altitude, low temperature, and low humidity.**

86. D The cyclic controls the **direction of the tilt of the main rotor.**

87. B Moving the cyclic forward and significantly raising the collective will cause the helicopter to **increase its forward speed and begin to climb.**

88. A Conventional American helicopters have a main rotor that **turns in a counterclockwise direction.**

89. D Translational lift is **the additional lift gained when the helicopter leaves its downwash.**

90. C Gyroscopic precession happens when **a force applied to a spinning disc has its effect 90 degrees later in the direction and plane of rotation.**

AFAST #2

Subtest 5: Cyclic Orientation Test

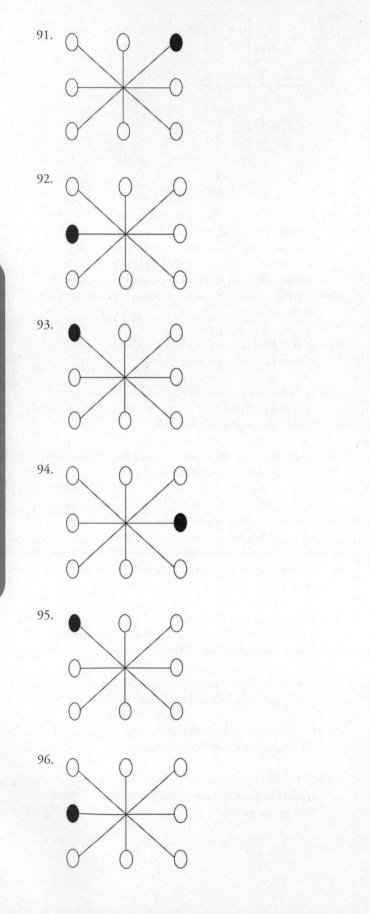

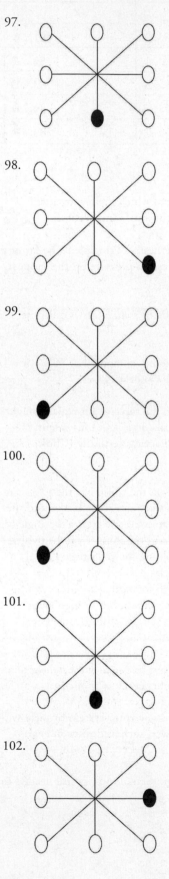

103.

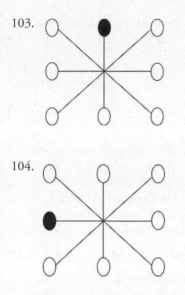

104.

105.

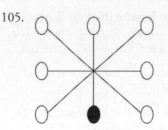

Subtest 6: Mechanical Functions Test

	✔	✘		✔	✘		✔	✘		✔	✘
106. C			111. A			116. A			121. D		
107. E			112. D			117. B			122. A		
108. A			113. A			118. E			123. B		
109. B			114. B			119. A			124. D		
110. B			115. C			120. C			125. A		

106. **C** Gear A will turn 15 times. Counting the number of teeth in the two gears tells us that the mechanical advantage of the larger gear A is 3:2, since gear A has 15 teeth and gear B has 10 teeth. Knowing that and knowing that gear B will make 10 revolutions, we divide 10 by 2 to get 5, then multiply that 5 by 3 to get 15.

107. **E It will be easier to lift block B but it will not be lifted as high.** If block A under the lever beam is moved toward block B on top of the lever beam, the moment for a particular force exerted will increase, since the fulcrum is now further from the force; this will make block B easier to lift. However, the height to which block B on the end of the lever beam can be raised decreases the closer block A is moved toward block B.

108. **A** By rotating clockwise, pulley C will cause pulley B to rotate counterclockwise, which will in turn cause pulley A to rotate **clockwise**.

109. **B Pulley B** will rotate the fastest because it is the smallest.

110. **B** Water tower B will be able to provide the most water, because its outlet pipe is near the bottom and can let almost all of its contents out, while the outlet pipe on tower A is near the top and will stop providing water as soon as A's water level drops below where the pipe leaves the cistern.

111. **A** The string holding the 10-lb. weight exerts more pull; the fact that that string is longer makes no difference.

112. **D** We are not told the sizes of the two wheels, but we can see that one is larger than the other. If the two wheels are connected by a belt, the small wheel will be forced to turn faster and complete more turns than the larger wheel.

113. **A** The force required to balance the lever shown would be **10 lb.** because the sum of the moments on each side of the fulcrum must be zero. To calculate this, we would set it up like this:

$$F \times d = F \times d$$

Where F is the force or weight involved and d is the distance from the fulcrum. Therefore,

$$(5 \text{ lb} \times 10 \text{ ft}) + (10 \text{ lb} \times 5 \text{ ft}) = F \times 10 \text{ ft}$$
$$50 \text{ ft-lb} + 50 \text{ ft-lb} = F \times 10 \text{ ft}$$
$$100 \text{ ft-lb}/10 \text{ ft} = F$$
$$10 \text{ lb} = F$$

114. **B** The length of time taken for one swing depends on the length of the string, not the weight.

115. **C** Both would take the same amount of time to make one swing; the length of time taken for one swing depends on the length of the string, not the weight at the end of it.

116. **A** When the plug is removed, water will flow **into the tube** to equalize the water level both inside and outside the tube.

117. **B** Valves A, B, and D must be open for the tank to fill halfway and maintain that level. Water flows in through valve A (so any choice not including valve A is a non-starter), and flows out when the tank is half full through valve B—but, for that water to leave the system, valve D must also be open.

118. **E** Both segments will weigh the same. If this were not the case, then you would not have been able to balance the beam at its CG because gravity would have been acting unequally on the two (still-joined) segments of the beam; the center of gravity wouldn't have been the center of gravity at all if you couldn't balance the beam there. Also, if the beam was regularly proportioned, both segments will be very close to the same size, allowing only for density variations in the wood itself.

119. **A** Pulley A will have the highest number of RPMs (i.e., **will turn the fastest**). In any arrangement of connected pulleys, the smaller pulley will turn faster than the larger pulley—it has to "keep up" and therefore turns faster. Pulleys B and D appear to be of the same size, while pulley A is the smaller of the connected pulleys and therefore turns fastest.

120. **C** The piston in cylinder A will rise two inches. The formula for mechanical advantage in this kind of problem is

$$\frac{a_2}{a_1} = \frac{d_1}{d_2}$$

where a_1 is the area of the smaller cylinder and a_2 is the area of the bigger cylinder, and d_1 is the vertical distance moved by the smaller cylinder and d_2 is the vertical distance moved by the larger cylinder. In this case the smaller cylinder is 3 inches in diameter and the bigger one is 6 inches Therefore, the mechanical advantage is $\left(\frac{6}{3}\right) = 2$. Therefore we take the one inch moved by the larger cylinder and multiply it by the mechanical advantage to see that the piston in the smaller cylinder A will be forced upwards by two inches.

121. **D** B counterclockwise, C clockwise, and D counterclockwise. Each driven gear in succession turns in the opposite direction from the gear that is driving it.

122. **A** The mechanical ratio of gear A to gear D is 1:1 because all four gears have the same number of teeth and will therefore turn at the same rate.

123. **B** When two or more act in such a way that their combination has a net effect of zero (i.e., they cancel each other out), the condition is called **equilibrium**.

124. **D** The descent of a paratrooper under his parachute is **primarily** affected by **drag** (air resistance) **and gravity**.

125. **A** When oncoming air meets the leading edge of the airfoil (wing), part goes over the top and part flows underneath. The air flowing over the top of the wing has to go farther than the air underneath, because it must meet again at the far side of the wing—physical laws act together to prevent or minimize vacuums in most cases. Because the air flowing over the top must go faster than that underneath, the pressure on the top of the wing is decreased, whereas the pressure underneath the wing remains relatively unchanged. Therefore, most of the lift on an aircraft's wing is because of a decrease in pressure on the wing's upper side.

Subtest 7: Self-Description Form

There are no right or wrong answers to the questions on this subtest; just answer them as honestly and accurately as possible.

Answer Sheet
ASTB #1

Subtest 1: Math Skills

1 Ⓐ Ⓑ Ⓒ Ⓓ Ⓔ	9 Ⓐ Ⓑ Ⓒ Ⓓ Ⓔ	17 Ⓐ Ⓑ Ⓒ Ⓓ Ⓔ	25 Ⓐ Ⓑ Ⓒ Ⓓ Ⓔ
2 Ⓐ Ⓑ Ⓒ Ⓓ Ⓔ	10 Ⓐ Ⓑ Ⓒ Ⓓ Ⓔ	18 Ⓐ Ⓑ Ⓒ Ⓓ Ⓔ	26 Ⓐ Ⓑ Ⓒ Ⓓ Ⓔ
3 Ⓐ Ⓑ Ⓒ Ⓓ Ⓔ	11 Ⓐ Ⓑ Ⓒ Ⓓ Ⓔ	19 Ⓐ Ⓑ Ⓒ Ⓓ Ⓔ	27 Ⓐ Ⓑ Ⓒ Ⓓ Ⓔ
4 Ⓐ Ⓑ Ⓒ Ⓓ Ⓔ	12 Ⓐ Ⓑ Ⓒ Ⓓ Ⓔ	20 Ⓐ Ⓑ Ⓒ Ⓓ Ⓔ	28 Ⓐ Ⓑ Ⓒ Ⓓ Ⓔ
5 Ⓐ Ⓑ Ⓒ Ⓓ Ⓔ	13 Ⓐ Ⓑ Ⓒ Ⓓ Ⓔ	21 Ⓐ Ⓑ Ⓒ Ⓓ Ⓔ	29 Ⓐ Ⓑ Ⓒ Ⓓ Ⓔ
6 Ⓐ Ⓑ Ⓒ Ⓓ Ⓔ	14 Ⓐ Ⓑ Ⓒ Ⓓ Ⓔ	22 Ⓐ Ⓑ Ⓒ Ⓓ Ⓔ	30 Ⓐ Ⓑ Ⓒ Ⓓ Ⓔ
7 Ⓐ Ⓑ Ⓒ Ⓓ Ⓔ	15 Ⓐ Ⓑ Ⓒ Ⓓ Ⓔ	23 Ⓐ Ⓑ Ⓒ Ⓓ Ⓔ	
8 Ⓐ Ⓑ Ⓒ Ⓓ Ⓔ	16 Ⓐ Ⓑ Ⓒ Ⓓ Ⓔ	24 Ⓐ Ⓑ Ⓒ Ⓓ Ⓔ	

Subtest 2: Reading Skills

1 Ⓐ Ⓑ Ⓒ Ⓓ Ⓔ	9 Ⓐ Ⓑ Ⓒ Ⓓ Ⓔ	17 Ⓐ Ⓑ Ⓒ Ⓓ Ⓔ	25 Ⓐ Ⓑ Ⓒ Ⓓ Ⓔ
2 Ⓐ Ⓑ Ⓒ Ⓓ Ⓔ	10 Ⓐ Ⓑ Ⓒ Ⓓ Ⓔ	18 Ⓐ Ⓑ Ⓒ Ⓓ Ⓔ	26 Ⓐ Ⓑ Ⓒ Ⓓ Ⓔ
3 Ⓐ Ⓑ Ⓒ Ⓓ Ⓔ	11 Ⓐ Ⓑ Ⓒ Ⓓ Ⓔ	19 Ⓐ Ⓑ Ⓒ Ⓓ Ⓔ	27 Ⓐ Ⓑ Ⓒ Ⓓ Ⓔ
4 Ⓐ Ⓑ Ⓒ Ⓓ Ⓔ	12 Ⓐ Ⓑ Ⓒ Ⓓ Ⓔ	20 Ⓐ Ⓑ Ⓒ Ⓓ Ⓔ	
5 Ⓐ Ⓑ Ⓒ Ⓓ Ⓔ	13 Ⓐ Ⓑ Ⓒ Ⓓ Ⓔ	21 Ⓐ Ⓑ Ⓒ Ⓓ Ⓔ	
6 Ⓐ Ⓑ Ⓒ Ⓓ Ⓔ	14 Ⓐ Ⓑ Ⓒ Ⓓ Ⓔ	22 Ⓐ Ⓑ Ⓒ Ⓓ Ⓔ	
7 Ⓐ Ⓑ Ⓒ Ⓓ Ⓔ	15 Ⓐ Ⓑ Ⓒ Ⓓ Ⓔ	23 Ⓐ Ⓑ Ⓒ Ⓓ Ⓔ	
8 Ⓐ Ⓑ Ⓒ Ⓓ Ⓔ	16 Ⓐ Ⓑ Ⓒ Ⓓ Ⓔ	24 Ⓐ Ⓑ Ⓒ Ⓓ Ⓔ	

Subtest 3: Mechanical Comprehension

1 Ⓐ Ⓑ Ⓒ Ⓓ Ⓔ	9 Ⓐ Ⓑ Ⓒ Ⓓ Ⓔ	17 Ⓐ Ⓑ Ⓒ Ⓓ Ⓔ	25 Ⓐ Ⓑ Ⓒ Ⓓ Ⓔ
2 Ⓐ Ⓑ Ⓒ Ⓓ Ⓔ	10 Ⓐ Ⓑ Ⓒ Ⓓ Ⓔ	18 Ⓐ Ⓑ Ⓒ Ⓓ Ⓔ	26 Ⓐ Ⓑ Ⓒ Ⓓ Ⓔ
3 Ⓐ Ⓑ Ⓒ Ⓓ Ⓔ	11 Ⓐ Ⓑ Ⓒ Ⓓ Ⓔ	19 Ⓐ Ⓑ Ⓒ Ⓓ Ⓔ	27 Ⓐ Ⓑ Ⓒ Ⓓ Ⓔ
4 Ⓐ Ⓑ Ⓒ Ⓓ Ⓔ	12 Ⓐ Ⓑ Ⓒ Ⓓ Ⓔ	20 Ⓐ Ⓑ Ⓒ Ⓓ Ⓔ	28 Ⓐ Ⓑ Ⓒ Ⓓ Ⓔ
5 Ⓐ Ⓑ Ⓒ Ⓓ Ⓔ	13 Ⓐ Ⓑ Ⓒ Ⓓ Ⓔ	21 Ⓐ Ⓑ Ⓒ Ⓓ Ⓔ	29 Ⓐ Ⓑ Ⓒ Ⓓ Ⓔ
6 Ⓐ Ⓑ Ⓒ Ⓓ Ⓔ	14 Ⓐ Ⓑ Ⓒ Ⓓ Ⓔ	22 Ⓐ Ⓑ Ⓒ Ⓓ Ⓔ	30 Ⓐ Ⓑ Ⓒ Ⓓ Ⓔ
7 Ⓐ Ⓑ Ⓒ Ⓓ Ⓔ	15 Ⓐ Ⓑ Ⓒ Ⓓ Ⓔ	23 Ⓐ Ⓑ Ⓒ Ⓓ Ⓔ	
8 Ⓐ Ⓑ Ⓒ Ⓓ Ⓔ	16 Ⓐ Ⓑ Ⓒ Ⓓ Ⓔ	24 Ⓐ Ⓑ Ⓒ Ⓓ Ⓔ	

Subtest 4: Spatial Apperception

1 Ⓐ Ⓑ Ⓒ Ⓓ Ⓔ	8 Ⓐ Ⓑ Ⓒ Ⓓ Ⓔ	15 Ⓐ Ⓑ Ⓒ Ⓓ Ⓔ	22 Ⓐ Ⓑ Ⓒ Ⓓ Ⓔ
2 Ⓐ Ⓑ Ⓒ Ⓓ Ⓔ	9 Ⓐ Ⓑ Ⓒ Ⓓ Ⓔ	16 Ⓐ Ⓑ Ⓒ Ⓓ Ⓔ	23 Ⓐ Ⓑ Ⓒ Ⓓ Ⓔ
3 Ⓐ Ⓑ Ⓒ Ⓓ Ⓔ	10 Ⓐ Ⓑ Ⓒ Ⓓ Ⓔ	17 Ⓐ Ⓑ Ⓒ Ⓓ Ⓔ	24 Ⓐ Ⓑ Ⓒ Ⓓ Ⓔ
4 Ⓐ Ⓑ Ⓒ Ⓓ Ⓔ	11 Ⓐ Ⓑ Ⓒ Ⓓ Ⓔ	18 Ⓐ Ⓑ Ⓒ Ⓓ Ⓔ	25 Ⓐ Ⓑ Ⓒ Ⓓ Ⓔ
5 Ⓐ Ⓑ Ⓒ Ⓓ Ⓔ	12 Ⓐ Ⓑ Ⓒ Ⓓ Ⓔ	19 Ⓐ Ⓑ Ⓒ Ⓓ Ⓔ	
6 Ⓐ Ⓑ Ⓒ Ⓓ Ⓔ	13 Ⓐ Ⓑ Ⓒ Ⓓ Ⓔ	20 Ⓐ Ⓑ Ⓒ Ⓓ Ⓔ	
7 Ⓐ Ⓑ Ⓒ Ⓓ Ⓔ	14 Ⓐ Ⓑ Ⓒ Ⓓ Ⓔ	21 Ⓐ Ⓑ Ⓒ Ⓓ Ⓔ	

Answer Sheet
ASTB #1

Subtest 5: Aviation/Nautical Information

1 Ⓐ Ⓑ Ⓒ Ⓓ Ⓔ	9 Ⓐ Ⓑ Ⓒ Ⓓ Ⓔ	17 Ⓐ Ⓑ Ⓒ Ⓓ Ⓔ	25 Ⓐ Ⓑ Ⓒ Ⓓ Ⓔ
2 Ⓐ Ⓑ Ⓒ Ⓓ Ⓔ	10 Ⓐ Ⓑ Ⓒ Ⓓ Ⓔ	18 Ⓐ Ⓑ Ⓒ Ⓓ Ⓔ	26 Ⓐ Ⓑ Ⓒ Ⓓ Ⓔ
3 Ⓐ Ⓑ Ⓒ Ⓓ Ⓔ	11 Ⓐ Ⓑ Ⓒ Ⓓ Ⓔ	19 Ⓐ Ⓑ Ⓒ Ⓓ Ⓔ	27 Ⓐ Ⓑ Ⓒ Ⓓ Ⓔ
4 Ⓐ Ⓑ Ⓒ Ⓓ Ⓔ	12 Ⓐ Ⓑ Ⓒ Ⓓ Ⓔ	20 Ⓐ Ⓑ Ⓒ Ⓓ Ⓔ	28 Ⓐ Ⓑ Ⓒ Ⓓ Ⓔ
5 Ⓐ Ⓑ Ⓒ Ⓓ Ⓔ	13 Ⓐ Ⓑ Ⓒ Ⓓ Ⓔ	21 Ⓐ Ⓑ Ⓒ Ⓓ Ⓔ	29 Ⓐ Ⓑ Ⓒ Ⓓ Ⓔ
6 Ⓐ Ⓑ Ⓒ Ⓓ Ⓔ	14 Ⓐ Ⓑ Ⓒ Ⓓ Ⓔ	22 Ⓐ Ⓑ Ⓒ Ⓓ Ⓔ	30 Ⓐ Ⓑ Ⓒ Ⓓ Ⓔ
7 Ⓐ Ⓑ Ⓒ Ⓓ Ⓔ	15 Ⓐ Ⓑ Ⓒ Ⓓ Ⓔ	23 Ⓐ Ⓑ Ⓒ Ⓓ Ⓔ	
8 Ⓐ Ⓑ Ⓒ Ⓓ Ⓔ	16 Ⓐ Ⓑ Ⓒ Ⓓ Ⓔ	24 Ⓐ Ⓑ Ⓒ Ⓓ Ⓔ	

Subtest 6: Aviation Supplemental Test

1 Ⓐ Ⓑ Ⓒ Ⓓ Ⓔ	10 Ⓐ Ⓑ Ⓒ Ⓓ Ⓔ	19 Ⓐ Ⓑ Ⓒ Ⓓ Ⓔ	28 Ⓐ Ⓑ Ⓒ Ⓓ Ⓔ
2 Ⓐ Ⓑ Ⓒ Ⓓ Ⓔ	11 Ⓐ Ⓑ Ⓒ Ⓓ Ⓔ	20 Ⓐ Ⓑ Ⓒ Ⓓ Ⓔ	29 Ⓐ Ⓑ Ⓒ Ⓓ Ⓔ
3 Ⓐ Ⓑ Ⓒ Ⓓ Ⓔ	12 Ⓐ Ⓑ Ⓒ Ⓓ Ⓔ	21 Ⓐ Ⓑ Ⓒ Ⓓ Ⓔ	30 Ⓐ Ⓑ Ⓒ Ⓓ Ⓔ
4 Ⓐ Ⓑ Ⓒ Ⓓ Ⓔ	13 Ⓐ Ⓑ Ⓒ Ⓓ Ⓔ	22 Ⓐ Ⓑ Ⓒ Ⓓ Ⓔ	31 Ⓐ Ⓑ Ⓒ Ⓓ Ⓔ
5 Ⓐ Ⓑ Ⓒ Ⓓ Ⓔ	14 Ⓐ Ⓑ Ⓒ Ⓓ Ⓔ	23 Ⓐ Ⓑ Ⓒ Ⓓ Ⓔ	32 Ⓐ Ⓑ Ⓒ Ⓓ Ⓔ
6 Ⓐ Ⓑ Ⓒ Ⓓ Ⓔ	15 Ⓐ Ⓑ Ⓒ Ⓓ Ⓔ	24 Ⓐ Ⓑ Ⓒ Ⓓ Ⓔ	33 Ⓐ Ⓑ Ⓒ Ⓓ Ⓔ
7 Ⓐ Ⓑ Ⓒ Ⓓ Ⓔ	16 Ⓐ Ⓑ Ⓒ Ⓓ Ⓔ	25 Ⓐ Ⓑ Ⓒ Ⓓ Ⓔ	34 Ⓐ Ⓑ Ⓒ Ⓓ Ⓔ
8 Ⓐ Ⓑ Ⓒ Ⓓ Ⓔ	17 Ⓐ Ⓑ Ⓒ Ⓓ Ⓔ	26 Ⓐ Ⓑ Ⓒ Ⓓ Ⓔ	
9 Ⓐ Ⓑ Ⓒ Ⓓ Ⓔ	18 Ⓐ Ⓑ Ⓒ Ⓓ Ⓔ	27 Ⓐ Ⓑ Ⓒ Ⓓ Ⓔ	

Practice Navy/Marine Corps/Coast Guard Aviation Selection Test Battery (ASTB) #1

TEST FORMAT

The Aviation Selection Test Battery (ASTB) is used by the U.S. Navy, Marine Corps, and Coast Guard to select flight training candidates from those officers and officer applicants who wish to become aviators. It is also used for all U.S. Navy Officer Candidate School applicants.

The ASTB consists of six subtests with a total of 176 questions; examinees have 140 minutes (two hours and 20 minutes) to complete the test.

The first subtest, Math Skills, has 30 questions, which you have 25 minutes to answer. The Math Skills subtest evaluates your knowledge of basic arithmetic and your problem-solving ability using math.

The Reading Skills subtest consists of 27 questions, which you will have 25 minutes to answer. This subtest will measure your basic vocabulary and reading skills. Read the passage associated with each question carefully, then choose the response that best answers the question based on the passage.

The third subtest, Mechanical Comprehension, has 30 questions, which you will have 15 minutes to answer. It tests your ability to comprehend and reason with mechanical applications and simple physics rules.

The Spatial Apperception subtest, which has 25 questions that you will have 10 minutes to answer, measures your ability to determine the position of an aircraft in flight relative to the view the pilot would see when looking out of the cockpit. For each question, you will see first a view of the landscape that the pilot would see when looking forward out of the cockpit. Your task is to determine whether the aircraft is banking, diving, climbing, or in level flight; then you must choose the one illustration (from a series of five) that best represents how that same aircraft would look when viewed from the outside.

The fifth subtest, Aviation/Nautical Information, has 30 questions, which you will have 15 minutes to answer. It measures your general aviation and nautical knowledge, especially as it applies to U.S. Navy nautical practices and terminology.

The Aviation Supplemental Test—the last subtest of the six—has 34 questions, which you will have 25 minutes to answer. It consists of a review of the preceding five subtests; you may see questions that are exactly the same as you've already answered, or they may be slightly or completely different—or, of course, a combination of the three, which is usually the case. Your results from this subtest will be run through a custom-made algorithm that calculates the composite scores used for the pilot and flight officer selection process.

SUBTEST 1: MATH SKILLS

1. You need eight barrels of water to sprinkle $\frac{1}{2}$ mile of roadway. How many barrels of water do you need to sprinkle $3\frac{1}{2}$ miles of roadway?

   (A) 7
   (B) 15
   (C) 50
   (D) 56
   (E) 28

2. A snapshot 8 inches long and 6 inches wide is to be enlarged so that its length will be 12 inches. How many inches wide will the enlarged snapshot be?

   (A) 8
   (B) 6
   (C) 9
   (D) 10
   (E) 12.5

3. Heather Marie has an ordinary life insurance policy with a face value of $10,000. At her age, the annual premium is $24.00 per thousand. What is the total premium paid for this policy every six months?

   (A) $100
   (B) $120
   (C) $240
   (D) $400
   (E) $480

4. If 2 pounds of cottage cheese cost $3.20, what is the cost of a 3-ounce portion of cottage cheese?

   (A) $0.30
   (B) $0.20
   (C) $0.25
   (D) $0.15
   (E) $0.45

5. Jonathan drove for 12 hours at an average speed of 55 miles per hour. If his car covered 22 miles for each gallon of gas consumed, how many gallons of gas did he use?

   (A) 32 gals.
   (B) 34 gals.
   (C) 36 gals.
   (D) 30 gals.
   (E) 28 gals.

6. Gus earns $7.50 per hour. If he works from 8:45 A.M. until 5:15 P.M., with one hour off for lunch, how much does he earn in one day?

   (A) $58.50
   (B) $56.25
   (C) $55.00
   (D) $53.75
   (E) $63.75

7. If five shirts and three ties cost $52 and each tie costs $4, what is the cost of a shirt?

   (A) $6.00
   (B) $8.00
   (C) $10.00
   (D) $7.50
   (E) $10.40

8. What is the fifth term in this series: 5; 2; 9; 6; ____?

   (A) 16
   (B) 15
   (C) 14
   (D) 13
   (E) 3

9. In a theater audience of 500 people, 80% were adults. How many children were in the audience?

   (A) 20
   (B) 50
   (C) 100
   (D) 125
   (E) 140

10. A brand-name dining room table usually sells for $240, but because it has been the display model and is a little shopworn, the store manager lets it go for $210. What is the percent of reduction?

    (A) $12\frac{1}{2}\%$

    (B) $14\frac{2}{7}\%$

    (C) $16\frac{2}{3}\%$

    (D) $18\frac{3}{4}\%$

    (E) $19\frac{1}{4}\%$

11. Mr. and Mrs. Bailey bought a repossessed house for an investment for $55,000. It was assessed at 80% of the purchase price. If the real estate tax was $4.74 per $100, how much tax did the Baileys pay?

    (A) $2,085.60
    (B) $1,985.60
    (C) $2,607.00
    (D) $285.60
    (E) $2,805.60

12. The scale on a particular map is 1 inch = 50 miles. On this map, two cities are $2\frac{1}{2}$ inches apart. What is the actual distance between the two cities?

    (A) 75 miles
    (B) 100 miles
    (C) 225 miles
    (D) 125 miles
    (E) 175 miles

13. A shipment of 2,200 pounds of fertilizer is packed in 40-ounce bags. How many bags are needed for the shipment?

    (A) 800
    (B) 880
    (C) 780
    (D) 640
    (E) 680

14. A TV set priced at $400 was reduced 25% during a weekend sale. In addition, there was a 10% discount for cash. What was the cash price of the TV set during the sale?

    (A) $130
    (B) $260
    (C) $270
    (D) $320
    (E) $330

15. In a store, four clerks each receive $255 per week, and two part-timers each earn $120. What is the average weekly salary paid to these six workers?

    (A) $200.00
    (B) $210.00
    (C) $187.50
    (D) $190.00
    (E) $192.00

16. The perimeter of a rectangle is 40 feet. If the length is 15 feet, 6 inches, what is the width of the rectangle?

    (A) 4 ft., 6 in.
    (B) 9 ft., 6 in.
    (C) 5 ft., 6 in.
    (D) 5 ft.
    (E) 6 ft.

17. What is the result of dividing 0.675 by 0.9?

    (A) 7.5
    (B) 0.075
    (C) 75
    (D) 0.75
    (E) 1.75

18. Two planes leave the same airport, traveling in opposite directions. One is flying at a speed of 340 miles per hour, the other at 260 miles per hour. In how many hours will the two planes be 3,000 miles apart?

    (A) 5
    (B) 3.75
    (C) 6
    (D) 10
    (E) 37.5

19. What is the cost of 5 feet, 3 inches of plastic slipcover material that sells for $8 per foot?

    (A) $14.00
    (B) $42.00
    (C) $23.00
    (D) $21.12
    (E) $42.40

20. If 1 gallon of milk costs $3.84, what is the cost of 3 pints?

    (A) $1.44
    (B) $2.82
    (C) $2.04
    (D) $1.96
    (E) $1.69

21. A man left $72,000 in his will to his wife and son. The ratio of the wife's share to the son's share was 5:3. How much did his wife receive?

    (A) $27,000
    (B) $14,000
    (C) $45,000
    (D) $54,000
    (E) $56,000

22. A recipe calls for $2\frac{1}{2}$ ounces of chocolate and $\frac{1}{2}$ cup of corn syrup. If only 2 ounces of chocolate are available, how much corn syrup should be used?

    (A) $\frac{1}{2}$ cup

    (B) $\frac{1}{3}$ cup

    (C) $\frac{2}{5}$ cup

    (D) $\frac{3}{10}$ cup

    (E) $\frac{3}{5}$ cup

23. A ship sails x miles the first day, y miles the second day, and z miles the third day. What was the average distance covered per day?

    (A) $3(x+y+z)$
    (B) $(x+y+z) \div 3$
    (C) $3xyz$
    (D) $(xyz) \div 3$
    (E) none of the above

24. A man invests $6,000 at 5% annual interest. How much more must he invest at 6% annual interest so that his annual income from both investments is $900?

    (A) $3,000
    (B) $5,000
    (C) $8,000
    (D) $10,000
    (E) $12,400

25. Which of these is an example of similar figures?

    (A) a plane and a scale model of that plane
    (B) a pen and a pencil
    (C) a motorcycle and a car
    (D) an equilateral triangle and a right triangle
    (E) an isosceles triangle and a right triangle

26. Find the numerical value of $5a^2b - 3ab^2$ if $a = 7$ and $b = 4$.

    (A) 846
    (B) 644
    (C) 488
    (D) 224
    (E) 248

27. If the circumference of a circle is divided by the length of its diameter, what is the result?

    (A) 2
    (B) 27
    (C) π
    (D) 7
    (E) 14

28. A businesswoman spends $\frac{1}{5}$ of her small company's gross income for office rent, and $\frac{3}{8}$ of the remainder of the company's income for salaries. What part of her income does she spend for salaries?

    (A) $\frac{23}{40}$

    (B) $\frac{3}{10}$

    (C) $\frac{1}{2}$

    (D) $\frac{3}{4}$

    (E) $\frac{5}{40}$

29. Using the following formula, find the value of C when $F = 50$.

    $$C = \frac{5}{9}(F\text{-}32)$$

    (A) 10
    (B) 18
    (C) 90
    (D) 40
    (E) 45

30. What is the average of these temperature readings, taken on a cold day last winter?

6:00 A.M.	−12 degrees
7:00 A.M.	−7 degrees
8:00 A.M.	−2 degrees
9:00 A.M.	0 degrees
10:00 A.M.	+6 degrees

    (A) 0 degrees
    (B) 2 degrees
    (C) −1 degree
    (D) −3 degrees
    (E) −2 degrees

SUBTEST 2: READING SKILLS

Specialized warships, even ships suitable for war, are relatively recent in origin. They have always been expensive to build and they require handling by specialist crews. Their construction and operation therefore demand considerable disposable wealth, probably the surplus of a ruler's revenue; and if the earliest form of fighting at sea was piratical rather than political in motive, we must remember that even the pirate needs capital to start in business. The first navies may or may not have been anti-piratical in purpose—the advantages conferred by the ability to move forces or supplies along rivers or coasts may have first prompted rulers to maintain warships—but navies are, by definition, more costly than individual ships. Whichever way it is looked at, fighting on water has cost more than fighting on land from the start.

1. According to this passage, navies

    (A) are necessary to project power.
    (B) are more expensive to have and maintain than individual ships.
    (C) were always piratical in nature.
    (D) are an ancient invention that brought revenue to rulers.
    (E) are suitable to build by specialists.

Dr. Albert Mehrabian, a noted researcher in the field of nonverbal communication (UCLA), found that only 7 percent of our feelings and attitudes are communicated with words, 38 percent via tone of voice, and a whopping 55 percent through nonverbal expressions. These numbers are astonishing, but that's only part of the picture . . . the communications channels over which we have the most control, and understand the best, have the least amount of impact. And the channels over which we have the least control, and understand the least, have the most impact.

2. According to the above passage,

    (A) 55 percent of what we say is understood through tone of voice.
    (B) verbal communication is what gets the message understood.
    (C) we have the most control over the most important aspects of how we communicate.
    (D) written communication is more precise than verbal communication.
    (E) more than half of our communication is through nonverbal expressions.

3. Conflagration most nearly means

    (A) a secret or conspiratorial message.
    (B) a seizure by a higher authority.
    (C) a large and destructive fire.
    (D) the act of letting the air out of an inflatable object.
    (E) a restraining of strong forces.

4. Inurbane most nearly means

    (A) rude or uncouth.
    (B) nonsensical.
    (C) smooth and polished.
    (D) having great value.
    (E) covered with water.

5. Alluvial most nearly means

    (A) dating to ancient times.
    (B) covered with sediment deposited by flowing water.
    (C) small, insignificant.
    (D) referring to land held in absolute ownership.
    (E) mixed with other metals.

Genghis Khan; original name Temujin, c. 1162–1227. Mongol conqueror. Became leader of a destitute clan; defeated other clan leaders; proclaimed Universal Ruler (Genghis Khan) of all the Mongols (1206); consolidated his authority among Mongols (1206–12); made his capital at Karakorum. Invaded northern China (1211), capturing Peking (1215); made conquests in west (c. 1216–23), overcoming Khwārezm while his generals subdued what is now Iran, Iraq, and part of Russia; died on campaign (1226–27) against Tangut kingdom of Hsi Hsia. A conciliatory leader and military genius. Father of Ögödei (his successor) and Chagatai.

6. In the passage above, what word is used incorrectly?

    (A) destitute
    (B) subdued
    (C) capital
    (D) conciliatory
    (E) consolidated

The process by which the legions came to serve at such a distance from the Roman army's birthplace and to embrace so wide a range of recruits as members began during the Punic wars with Carthage. That city, a colony of the Phoenicians, first fell into conflict with the Romans when the latters' success in subduing their Italian neighbors drew them south to Sicily, which Carthage regarded as within its sphere of influence; Rome's confrontation with Pyrrhus, also an enemy of Carthage, weakened its position in the island. In 265 B.C. the two powers found themselves at war over it, and the war rapidly extended, by both land and sea, until the Carthaginians had to concede defeat and the establishment of Roman control over Sicily. While Rome added Corsica and Sardinia to these beginnings of its overseas empire, and made its first inroads into the land of the Gauls, Carthage responded by campaigning along the Mediterranean coast of Spain against cities that were Rome's allies. The siege of Saguntum in 219 B.C. brought on war afresh; it lasted for seventeen years, ended in Carthaginian defeat only after Rome had stared catastrophe in the face, and established the Romans as the dominant power in the Mediterranean world.

7. What area were the Romans and Carthaginians fighting over in 265 B.C.?

(A) Gaul
(B) Sicily
(C) Carthage
(D) Saguntum
(E) Spain

8. Rhetoric most nearly means

(A) the persuasive use of language to influence listeners or readers.
(B) a painful pathological condition of the joints.
(C) a regulated pattern of long and short notes or beats.
(D) referring to a continuously variable electrical resistor.
(E) referring to a parallelogram with unequal adjacent sides.

9. Exemplify most nearly means

(A) to test or measure for quality.
(B) worthy of being imitated.
(C) to illustrate by example.
(D) to breathe out.
(E) to tear or wear the skin off of something.

In any planning, especially strategic planning, it is vitally important to select the "right" objectives. In fact, some would suggest that this is the primary role of strategic planning. In addition to setting the "right" objectives, part of the job of planning is to determine the best means of achieving the objectives and, further, to facilitate effective communication and review of the means as the plan is executed. In order to select the "right" objectives, the planners must, among other things, do their work in the context of the higher-order purposes of the organization.

10. According to the passage above, how must strategic planners choose appropriate goals?

(A) by selecting the "right" objectives
(B) by facilitating effective communication
(C) in the context of the higher-order purposes of the organization
(D) by reviewing the means as the plan is executed
(E) by determining the best means of achieving the strategic plan objectives

The traditions of Freemasonry have evolved over many centuries and from many sources. They are a powerful source of the cement that gels a Lodge and Freemasons into one sacred band. Often, the traditions are never codified into law but are taught from mouth to ear. They can be modified (slowly) to fit the needs of the organization. Most Lodges adhere to the same traditions, but some may have adopted some of their own. As members become aware of the traditions, they soon learn that they are part of something larger than themselves.

11. According to the passage above, the traditions of Freemasonry teach new members that

(A) they are part of something larger than themselves.
(B) new members can quickly change traditions to meet the organization's needs.
(C) traditions are never written in concrete.
(D) there is only one source for traditional laws of Freemasonry.
(E) changing tradition bonds members of a Lodge together.

12. Captain Agnew had located the Italian convoy—and brought his "Force K" into the most favorable attacking position—by means of radar; for the Italians, who possessed no such weapon, the darkness remained <u>impenetrable</u>, and their surprise was consequently complete.

    Impenetrable most nearly means

    (A) not perceptible to the touch.
    (B) unprejudiced.
    (C) free from blemish.
    (D) not capable of being pierced or entered.
    (E) incapable of being moved.

Texas A&M University, located in College Station, Texas, is one of only a few select academic institutions to hold triple federal designation as a Land Grant, Sea Grant, and Space Grant university. Offering more than 150 courses of study, it has awarded more than 320,000 degrees since its establishment in 1876, including more than 70,000 graduate and professional degrees. The first public institution of higher learning established in Texas, it is the nation's sixth-largest in enrollment, with more than 49,000 students for the 2010–2011 year and a campus of some 5,200 acres. It was listed among the top 25 public universities by *US News and World Report*'s 2011 "America's Best Colleges" issue. Home to the George Bush Presidential Library and Museum, which opened in 1997, it conducts research valued at more than $500 million annually and has an endowment valued at $4.4 billion, placing it third among U.S. public universities and seventh overall.

13. According to the passage above, what is Texas A&M University's enrollment ranking nationally?

    (A) 46,000
    (B) 320,000
    (C) $4.4 billion
    (D) Top 5
    (E) Top 6

14. <u>Drogue</u> most nearly means

    (A) a one-humped domesticated camel widely used in northern Africa.
    (B) to slobber or drool.
    (C) a male bee who performs no work and produces no honey.
    (D) a funnel-shaped device at the end of a hose of a tanker aircraft.
    (E) to make a continuous, low, humming sound.

Babe Ruth was much more than simply the quintessential slugger who reigned over the great revolution in hitting. No modern athletic hero has exceeded Ruth's capacity to project multiple images of brute power, the natural, uninhibited man, and the fulfillment of the legendary American success formula. Ruth was living proof that the lone individual could still rise from mean, vulgar beginnings to fame and fortune, to a position of public recognition equaled by few men in American history. His mighty home runs represented a dramatic finality, a total clearing of the bases with one mighty swat.

15. According to this passage, the reader can infer that Babe Ruth's childhood was

    (A) privileged, upper economic class.
    (B) focused on teamwork.
    (C) uninhibited.
    (D) poor, lower economic class.
    (E) publicly recognized, middle economic class.

16. Aircraft carriers provide a credible, sustainable, independent forward presence and conventional _____ in peacetime.

    (A) appearance
    (B) assimilation
    (C) obscuration
    (D) insipience
    (E) deterrence

Most drivers try to drive safely. A major part of safe driving is driving at the right speed. But what is the "right" speed? Is it 20 miles per hour, or 35, or 60? That question may be hard to answer. On some city streets and in heavy traffic, 20 miles per hour could be too fast, even if it's within the posted speed limit. On a superhighway, 35 miles per hour could be too slow. Of course, a good driver must follow the speed limit, but he must also use good judgment. The "right" speed will vary depending on the number of cars, the road surface and its condition, and the driver's visibility.

17. The general theme of this passage is that a good driver

    (A) drives at 35 miles an hour.
    (B) adjusts to different driving conditions.
    (C) always drives at the same speed.
    (D) always follows the speed limit.
    (E) never exceeds the speed limit.

18. "Negotiation in the classic _____ sense assumes parties more anxious to agree than to disagree." [Dean Acheson]

    (A) diplomatic
    (B) aggressive
    (C) automatic
    (D) attacking
    (E) mathematical

About three-fourths of the surface of the earth is water. Of the 336 million cubic miles of water, most (97.2%) is found in the oceans and is salty. Glaciers at both poles hold to themselves another 2 percent of the total. Less than 1 percent (0.8%) is available as fresh water for people to use—and much of that is not near people who need it.

19. The amount of fresh water available for people to use is

(A) 97.2%.
(B) 0.8%.
(C) two-tenths.
(D) 2%.
(E) eight one-hundredths.

20. <u>Transmogrify</u> most nearly means

(A) to change into a different or bizarre shape or form.
(B) to displace an object from one position to another.
(C) to reverse or interchange the order of two or more objects.
(D) to pass beyond a human limit.
(E) someone or something that passes away or decreases with time.

There are a number of different varieties of quarks: there are thought to be at least six "flavors," which we call up, down, strange, charmed, bottom, and top. Each flavor comes in three "colors," red, green, and blue. (It should be emphasized that these terms are just labels: quarks are much smaller than the wavelength of visible light and so do not have any color in the normal sense. It is just that modern physicists seem to have more imaginative ways of naming new particles and phenomena—they no longer restrict themselves to Greek!) A proton or neutron is made up of three quarks, one of each color. A proton contains two up quarks and one down quark; a neutron contains two down and one up. We can create particles made up of the other quarks (strange, charmed, bottom, and top), but these all have a much greater mass and decay very rapidly into protons and neutrons.

21. According to the passage above, how many different types of "flavors" of quarks are there?

(A) 2
(B) 3
(C) 6
(D) 12
(E) 18

Nucleic acids are found in all living organisms, from viruses to man. They received their name because of their discovery in the nuclei of white blood cells and fish sperm by Swiss physiologist Johann Miescher (who founded the first physiological institute in Switzerland) in 1869. However, it is now well established that nucleic acids occur outside the cell nucleus as well.

22. Nucleic acids are found

(A) only in human cells.
(B) only in viruses.
(C) in all living cells.
(D) only in the cell nucleus.
(E) only in the laboratory.

23. Galley navies, with their oared ships and limited carrying capacities, were never <u>autonomous</u> instruments of strategy but extensions—or, more accurately, partners—of armies on land.

Autonomous most nearly means

(A) catalytic.
(B) independent.
(C) native to a particular place.
(D) operating without human involvement.
(E) superior.

The War of 1812 was in many ways one of the most unfortunate events in American history. For one reason, it was needless; the British Orders in Council that had caused the worst irritation were being unconditionally repealed just as Congress declared war. For another, the United States suffered from internal divisions of the gravest kind. While the South and West favored war, New York and New England in general opposed it, and toward its end important New England groups went to the very edge of disloyalty. For a third reason, the war was far from glorious in a military sense. The American army . . . was in wretched shape to fight.

24. The above passage characterizes the War of 1812 as

(A) a war for which the military was unprepared.
(B) an unnecessary conflict.
(C) a generally opposed war.
(D) an unfortunate event.
(E) A, B, and D above.

25. Abusive excise taxes burdened agriculture and mining, while the tariff gave Spanish manufacturers and traders an exclusive _____, which they exploited by charging ruinous prices for goods.

    (A) advertisement
    (B) insouciance
    (C) diversification
    (D) remembrance
    (E) monopoly

The Tao-te-ching (The Way and Its Power) is the basic text of the Chinese philosophy and religion known as Taoism. It is made up of 81 short chapters or poems that describe a way of life marked by quiet effortlessness and freedom from desire. This is thought to be achieved by following the creative, spontaneous life force of the universe, called the Tao. The book is attributed to Lao-tzu, but it was probably written in the third century B.C.

26. The Tao-te-ching

    (A) is the basic text of the Chinese universe.
    (B) describes a life way marked by effortless desire.
    (C) is made up of 81 chapters and a short poem.
    (D) was probably not written by Lao-tzu, even though it is attributed to him.
    (E) describes a creative way of finding your life's desire.

27. In the first land <u>skirmish</u> of the Cuban campaign, the Marines quickly overcame enemy resistance and established the base at Guantanamo Bay.

    Skirmish most nearly means

    (A) long siege.
    (B) negotiation.
    (C) small battle.
    (D) reconnaissance.
    (E) logistics resupply.

SUBTEST 3: MECHANICAL COMPREHENSION

1. Gear B is intended to mesh with

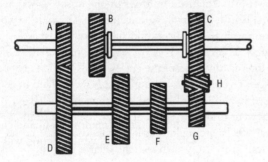

    (A) gear A only.
    (B) gear D only.
    (C) gear E only.
    (D) gear F only.
    (E) all of the above gears.

2. As cam A makes one complete turn, the setscrew hits the contact point how many times?

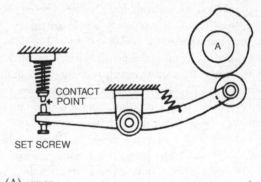

    (A) once
    (B) twice
    (C) three times
    (D) four times
    (E) not at all

3. If gear A makes 14 revolutions, gear B will make

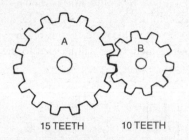

15 TEETH   10 TEETH

(A) 21 revolutions.
(B) 28 revolutions.
(C) 14 revolutions.
(D) 17 revolutions.
(E) 9 revolutions.

4. Which of the other gears is moving in the same direction as Gear 2?

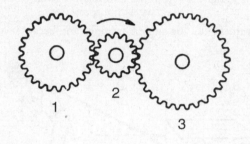

1   2   3

(A) gear 1
(B) gear 3
(C) neither of the other gears
(D) gears 1 and 3
(E) both of the other gears

5. Floats X and Y are measuring the specific gravity of two different liquids. Which float indicates the liquid with the highest specific gravity?

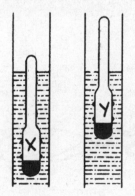

(A) Y
(B) X
(C) neither X nor Y
(D) both X and Y are the same
(E) cannot be determined from the information given

6. The wheelbarrow is an example of a

(A) first-class lever.
(B) second-class lever.
(C) third-class lever.
(D) load-bearing mechanism.
(E) first- and third-class lever.

7. Most of the lift on an aircraft's wings is because of

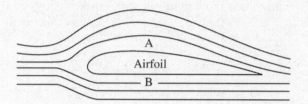

(A) a decrease in pressure on the upper side of the wing (A).
(B) a decrease in pressure on the bottom side of the wing (B).
(C) a vacuum created under the wing at point B.
(D) an increase in pressure on the upper side of the wing (A).
(E) none of the above.

8. You balance a wooden beam on a fulcrum at its center of gravity (CG). If you then mark the CG and cut the beam in two at that point, which section will weigh more?

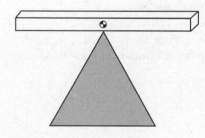

(A) the lefthand portion
(B) the righthand portion
(C) the bigger segment
(D) the smaller segment
(E) both segments will weigh the same

ASTB #1

9. In the depicted arrangement of pulleys and belts, which pulley will have the highest number of revolutions per minute (rpm)?

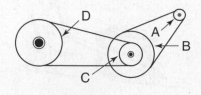

(A) pulley A
(B) pulley B
(C) pulley C
(D) pulley D
(E) unable to tell from information given

10. If gear B is the drive gear and makes 12 revolutions, how many revolutions will gear A make?

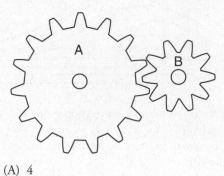

(A) 4
(B) 8
(C) 18
(D) 24
(E) 36

11. In the diagram above, if gear B is the drive gear and it is turning clockwise, what direction will gear A turn?

(A) clockwise
(B) counterclockwise
(C) gear A is free spinning
(D) none of the above
(E) cannot tell from the information given

12. Two cylinders containing hydraulic fluid, A and B, are connected by a hydraulic line as shown. If the diameter of cylinder A is 3 inches and the diameter of cylinder B is 6 inches, and the piston in cylinder B presses down 1 inch, what will happen to the piston in cylinder A?

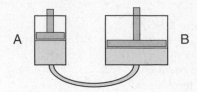

(A) It will rise one-half inch.
(B) It will rise one inch.
(C) It will rise two inches.
(D) Nothing; the fluid will compress.
(E) cannot tell from the information given

13. In the figure, the angle θ is important, because when it is

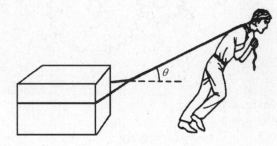

(A) 0 (zero) degrees, the entire force is dragging the box.
(B) 90 degrees, the entire force is lifting the box.
(C) 45 degrees, it is equally lifting and dragging the box.
(D) both lifting and dragging to some extent between 0 and 90 degrees.
(E) all of the above

14. Pliers are an example of a

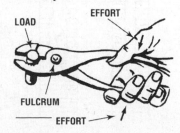

(A) first-class lever.
(B) second-class lever.
(C) third-class lever.
(D) first- and second-class lever.
(E) second- and third-class lever.

15. The follower is at its highest position between points

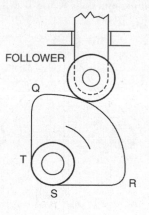

(A) Q and R.
(B) R and S.
(C) S and T.
(D) T and Q.
(E) T and R.

16. If pulley A is the driver and turns in direction 1, which pulley turns faster?

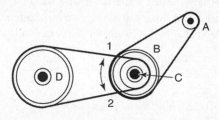

(A) A
(B) B
(C) C
(D) D
(E) A and D are equal.

17. The greatest amount of mechanical advantage of power is attained when an 11-tooth gear drives a(n)

(A) 29-tooth gear.
(B) 11-tooth gear.
(C) 47-tooth gear.
(D) 15-tooth gear.
(E) 22-tooth gear.

18. Which shaft or shafts are turning in the same direction as shaft X?

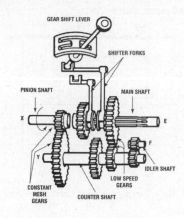

(A) Y
(B) Y and E
(C) F
(D) E and F
(E) E, F, and Y

19. The human arm as depicted below is an example of a

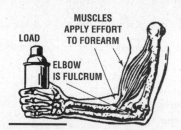

(A) first-class lever.
(B) second-class lever.
(C) third-class lever.
(D) second- and third-class lever.
(E) first- and second-class lever.

20. If arm H is held fixed as gear B turns in direction 2, gear

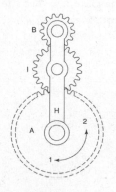

(A) A will turn in direction 1.
(B) A will turn in direction 2.
(C) I must turn in direction 2.
(D) A must be held fixed.
(E) B will spin freely.

21. Two 30-pound blocks are attached to the ceiling using ropes, as shown below. Which of the following statements are true?

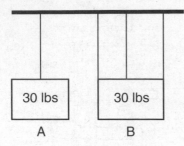

30 lbs   30 lbs

A   B

(A) All the ropes are under the same amount of tension.

(B) The rope holding block A is under $\frac{1}{3}$ of the tension of the ropes holding block B.

(C) The ropes supporting block B are under $\frac{1}{3}$ of the tension of the rope holding block A.

(D) The rope supporting block A is under twice the tension of the ropes holding block B.

(E) The ropes supporting block B are under $\frac{1}{6}$ of the tension of the rope holding block A.

22. An ax is what type of mechanical device?

(A) cutting
(B) inclined plane
(C) chopping
(D) gravitational
(E) first-class lever

23. A 400-pound pallet needs to be moved into a trailer whose floor is 3 feet off the ground. In order to reduce by $\frac{1}{3}$ the amount of effort needed to move the pallet by lifting it straight up, we need an inclined plane _____ feet long.

(A) 4
(B) 9
(C) 12
(D) 15
(E) 18

24. As the shaft in the illustration below spins faster in a clockwise direction, balls A and B will

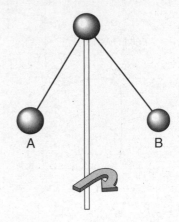

A   B

(A) move outward and downward.
(B) move outward and upward.
(C) move up.
(D) move down.
(E) stay at the same level.

25. Water flows into a water tower at a rate of 120 gallons per hour and flows out at the rate of 2 gallons per minute. The level of water in the tower will

(A) remain the same.
(B) lower.
(C) rise.
(D) rise initially, then lower.
(E) lower initially, then rise.

26. In the illustration below, if the fulcrum is moved farther away from the weight on the resistance arm, the result will be that

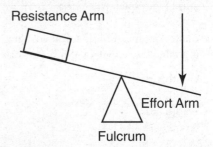

Resistance Arm

Effort Arm

Fulcrum

(A) the weight will be easier to lift, and will travel higher.
(B) the weight will be easier to lift, and will not travel as high.
(C) the weight will take more effort to lift, and will travel higher.
(D) the weight will take more effort to lift, and will not travel as high.
(E) the weight will take the same amount of effort to lift, and will travel the same height.

ASTB #1

27. In the diagram below, if gear A is the driving gear turning clockwise, what directions will gears B, C, and D turn?

(A) B counterclockwise, C counterclockwise, and D counterclockwise.
(B) B clockwise, C clockwise, and D clockwise.
(C) B clockwise, C counterclockwise, and D clockwise.
(D) B counterclockwise, C clockwise, and D counterclockwise.
(E) B counterclockwise, C counterclockwise, and D clockwise.

28. In the diagram above, what is the mechanical advantage of gear A to gear D?

(A) 1:1
(B) 1:2
(C) 1:4
(D) 1:8
(E) 1:24

29. In the illustration below, if pulley A is rotating in the direction indicated, then pulley C will

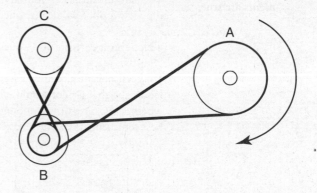

(A) rotate in the same direction as pulley B.
(B) rotate in the same direction as pulleys A and B.
(C) rotate in the opposite direction of pulleys A and B.
(D) rotate in the same direction as pulley A.
(E) none of the above

30. In the pulley system shown in problem 29, which pulley will rotate the fastest?

(A) pulley A
(B) pulley B
(C) pulley C
(D) They will all rotate at the same speed.
(E) This depends on the speed of the drive pulley.

SUBTEST 4: SPATIAL APPERCEPTION

This subtest measures your ability to determine the position of an aircraft in flight in relation to the view a pilot would see when looking out the front of the cockpit.

This subtest consists of 25 questions, which must be answered in 10 minutes.

For each question, you will see a series of six pictures. The first picture will depict a view of the landscape that a pilot would see when looking out the front of the cockpit. You are to determine whether the aircraft is climbing, diving, banking, or in level flight, and choose the picture that best represents the same aircraft when viewed from the outside.

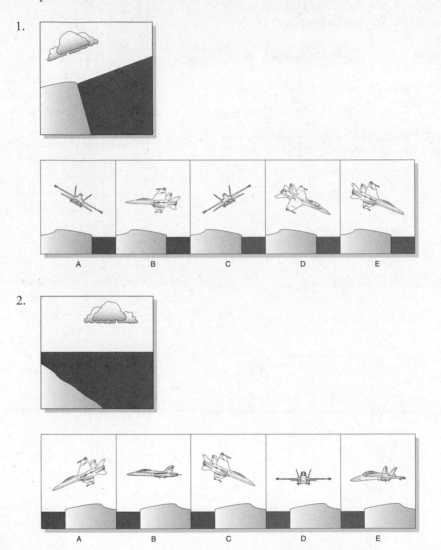

3.

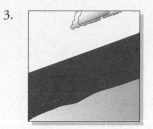

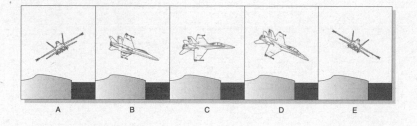

4.

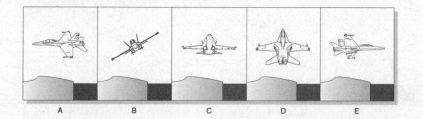

5.

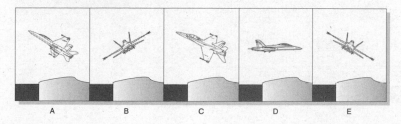

ASTB #1

6.

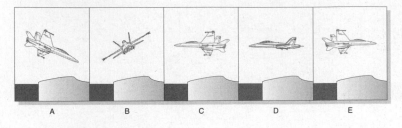

A	B	C	D	E

7.

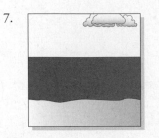

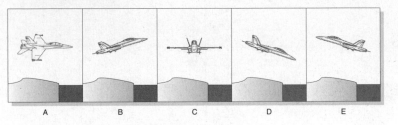

A	B	C	D	E

8.

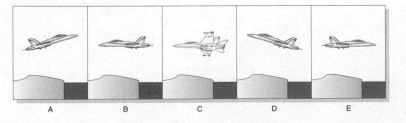

A	B	C	D	E

9.

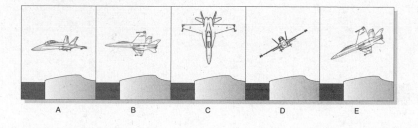

10.

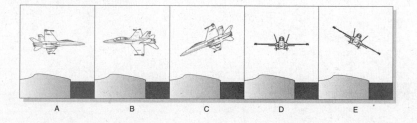

11.

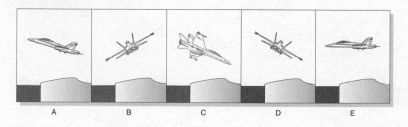

12.

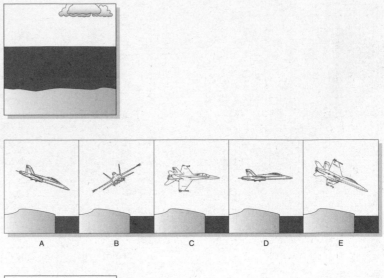

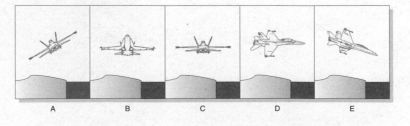

13.

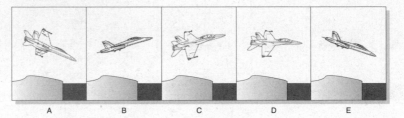

14.

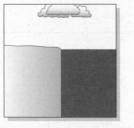

ASTB #1

15.

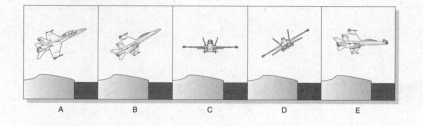

A   B   C   D   E

16.

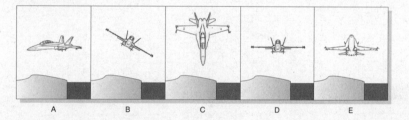

A   B   C   D   E

17.

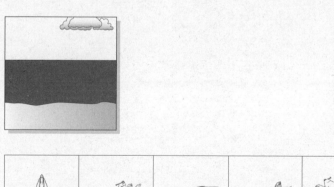

A   B   C   D   E

18.

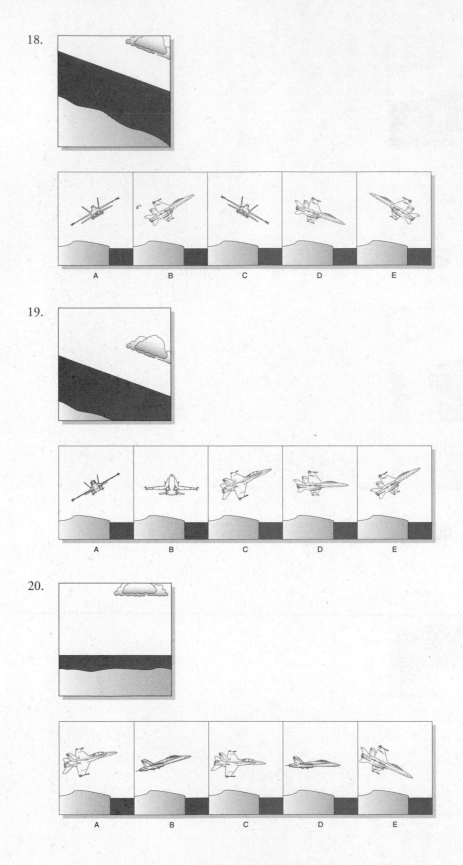

19.

20.

21.

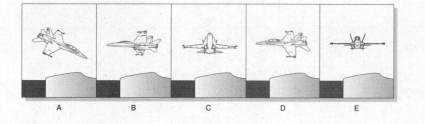

22.

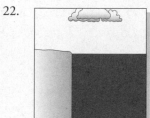

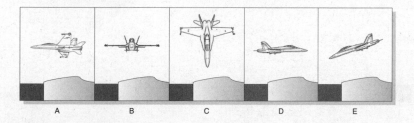

23.

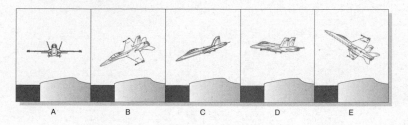

24.

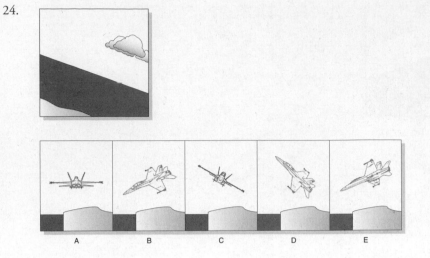

25.

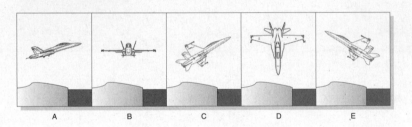

SUBTEST 5: AVIATION/NAUTICAL INFORMATION

1. What do the terms *port*, *starboard*, *fore*, and *aft* mean?

   (A) left, right, up, and down
   (B) right, left, above, and below
   (C) left, right, in front, and behind
   (D) right, left, behind, and in front
   (E) left, right, above, and beyond

2. On an aircraft carrier deck, what color shirt would a plane handler or tractor driver wear?

   (A) green
   (B) blue
   (C) purple
   (D) yellow
   (E) red

3. The angle between the chord line of a wing or airfoil and the direction of the relative wind or airflow is called the

   (A) angle of pitch.
   (B) degree of roll.
   (C) angle of deflection.
   (D) angle of attack.
   (E) degree of yaw.

4. A wall or vertical surface within a ship is called a

   (A) bulkhead.
   (B) bilgeway.
   (C) gangway.
   (D) keel.
   (E) frame.

5. A conventional fixed-wing aircraft is controlled around its longitudinal axis by means of the

   (A) ailerons.
   (B) elevators.
   (C) rudder.
   (D) trim tab.
   (E) flaps.

6. Two statute miles are equal to

   (A) 2.0 nautical miles.
   (B) 1.74 nautical miles.
   (C) 2.3 nautical miles.
   (D) 2.3 knots.
   (E) 2.0 knots.

7. The altimeter typically shows the height of the aircraft above a particular pressure level in

   (A) feet.
   (B) hundreds of feet.
   (C) thousands of feet.
   (D) hundreds of meters.
   (E) thousands of meters.

8. The time of 7 P.M. would be expressed using the 24-hour clock as

   (A) 0700.
   (B) 1400.
   (C) 1700.
   (D) 1900.
   (E) none of the above

9. When a pilot pulls back on the control stick, the elevators will

   (A) extend.
   (B) retract.
   (C) move upward.
   (D) move downward.
   (E) assume a neutral position.

10. The order given to the helmsman to align the rudder with the keel of the ship is

    (A) "Ease the rudder."
    (B) "Rudder amidships."
    (C) "Steady as you go."
    (D) "Align your rudder."
    (E) "Steady the rudder."

11. If one end of a runway was numbered 09, what number would designate the other end of the same runway?

    (A) 90
    (B) 27
    (C) 18
    (D) 10
    (E) 36

12. The coordinates of latitude and longitude are used to express _____ in _____.

    (A) direction, degrees.
    (B) position, degrees.
    (C) distance, time.
    (D) location, meridians.
    (E) heading, mils.

13. Which of the following engines could operate outside the earth's atmosphere?

    (A) jet engine
    (B) turbofan engine
    (C) rocket engine
    (D) four-stroke diesel engine
    (E) two-stroke gasoline engine

14. The bridge of a ship is where

    (A) all orders and commands affecting the ship originate.
    (B) the lookout is stationed.
    (C) the captain has his quarters.
    (D) the ship's officers meet and consume their meals.
    (E) the superstructure and the mast are joined together.

15. Which of the following is a flight instrument?

    (A) tachometer
    (B) fuel flow indicator
    (C) control column
    (D) trim tab
    (E) altimeter

16. The tailhook of a carrier-borne aircraft is used to

    (A) catch one of four arresting cables stretched across the deck.
    (B) position the aircraft on the deck for launch.
    (C) engage with the catapult T-bar before launch.
    (D) stabilize the aircraft on the deck elevator.
    (E) designate to the bridge when an aircraft is ready for launch.

17. *VFR* stands for

    (A) Velocity Flight Resistance.
    (B) Venturi Flight Resonance.
    (C) Vertical Flight Rules.
    (D) Visual Flight Rules.
    (E) Visual Front Resolution.

18. A nautical mile is approximately

    (A) 1,760 yds.
    (B) 5,280 ft.
    (C) 6,076 ft.
    (D) 7,676 ft.
    (E) 9,082 ft.

19. The four aerodynamic forces acting on an aircraft in flight are

    (A) gravity, lift, thrust, and friction.
    (B) lift, gravity, thrust, and drag.
    (C) velocity, drag, lift, and thrust.
    (D) lift, gravity, velocity, and drag.
    (E) attitude, pitch, lift, and drag.

20. A flashing green air traffic control directed to an aircraft on the ground is a signal that the pilot

    (A) should radio the tower.
    (B) should stop taxiing.
    (C) should hold his position.
    (D) has clearance to take off.
    (E) has clearance to taxi.

21. The Latin phrase *Semper Paratus* is the motto of the

    (A) U.S. Navy Submarine Service.
    (B) U.S. Marine Corps.
    (C) U.S. Marine Air Wing.
    (D) U.S. Coast Guard.
    (E) U.S. Air Force Air Combat Command.

22. The *empennage* of an airplane is usually referred to as the

    (A) vertical stabilizer.
    (B) horizontal stabilizer.
    (C) main body.
    (D) wing root.
    (E) tail section.

23. On an aircraft carrier, the standard watch length for the Officer of the Deck is

    (A) two hours
    (B) four hours
    (C) six hours
    (D) eight hours
    (E) 12 hours

24. _____ are designed to help minimize a pilot's workload by aerodynamically assisting movement and position of the flight control surfaces to which they are attached.

    (A) Labor-saving devices
    (B) Secondary flight controls
    (C) Trim systems
    (D) Spoilers
    (E) Adverse yaw deflectors

25. The Carrier Strike Group could be employed in a variety of roles, such as

    (A) protection of commercial and/or military shipping.
    (B) protection of a Marine amphibious force.
    (C) establishing a naval presence in support of national interests.
    (D) all of the above.
    (E) none of the above.

26. Ailerons

    (A) extend from the midpoint of the wing outward toward the tip.
    (B) create aerodynamic forces that cause the airplane to roll.
    (C) move in opposite directions.
    (D) all of the above
    (E) none of the above

27. "Pri-Fly" is

    (A) the facility where U.S. military aircraft are designed.
    (B) the control tower for flight operations on an air-craft carrier.
    (C) the two-aircraft section that has priority for launch from a carrier.
    (D) where carrier aircraft get refueled and serviced.
    (E) the prime runway for takeoff from an airport.

28. The two types of turn indicators used in an aircraft are

    (A) turn-and-slip indicator and attitude indicator.
    (B) attitude indicator and automatic gyroscope.
    (C) turn-and-slip indicator and turn coordinator.
    (D) left and right indicators.
    (E) turn coordinator and vertical speed indicator.

29. In the Navy, the term *Bravo Zulu* has come to tradi-tionally mean

    (A) well done.
    (B) two hours later than Greenwich Mean (Zulu) time.
    (C) two hours earlier than Greenwich Mean (Zulu) time.
    (D) beyond the zone.
    (E) below the zone.

30. When an airplane banks into a turn,

    (A) the horizontal lift component acts parallel to the earth's surface and opposes inertia.
    (B) the horizontal lift component acts parallel to the earth's surface and opposes gravity.
    (C) the horizontal lift component acts perpendicular to the earth's surface and opposes inertia.
    (D) the horizontal lift component acts perpendicular to the earth's surface and opposes gravity.
    (E) none of the above.

SUBTEST 6: AVIATION SUPPLEMENTAL TEST

1. If 2 pounds of cottage cheese cost $3.00, what is the cost of a 2-ounce portion of cottage cheese? Round off to the nearest cent.

    (A) $0.18
    (B) $0.19
    (C) $0.37
    (D) $0.10
    (E) $0.21

Dr. Albert Mehrabian, a noted researcher in the field of nonverbal communication (UCLA), found that only 7 per-cent of our feelings and attitudes are communicated with words, 38 percent via tone of voice, and a whopping 55 percent through nonverbal expressions. These numbers are astonishing, but that's only part of the picture . . . the com-munications channels over which we have the most control, and understand the best, have the least amount of impact. And the channels over which we have the least control, and understand the least, have the most impact.

2. According to the above passage,

    (A) 55 percent of what we say is understood through tone of voice.
    (B) verbal communication is what gets the message understood.
    (C) we have the most control over the most important aspects of how we communicate.
    (D) written communication is more precise than ver-bal communication.
    (E) more than half of our communication is through nonverbal expressions.

3. Aberration most nearly means

    (A) a deviation from the standard.
    (B) the sprouting of a fruit-bearing tree.
    (C) the end of an ursine hibernation period.
    (D) the middle part of a 1-mile horse race.
    (E) the edge of a machine-cut page of paper.

4. If pulley A is the driver and turns in direction 1, which pulley turns faster?

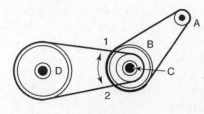

(A) A
(B) B
(C) C
(D) D
(E) A and D are equal.

5. What is the product of $(3a - 2)$ and $(a + 3)$?

(A) $4a + 2$
(B) $3a^2 - 6$
(C) $3a^2 - 2a + 6$
(D) $3a^2 + 7a - 6$
(E) $3a^2 - 4a + 2$

6. What is the difference between weight and mass?

(A) Weight can be changed by buoyancy, but mass is relative to gravity.
(B) Mass remains constant, but weight depends on altitude.
(C) Weight remains constant, but mass depends on altitude.
(D) Mass can be changed by buoyancy, but weight is relative to gravity.
(E) There is no difference between mass and weight.

7. Amanda drove for three hours through different traffic conditions. Her average speed was 50 mph for the first hour, 72 mph for the second hour, and 46 mph for the third hour. If her car gets an average of 23 miles per gallon of gas, how many gallons of gas did she use?

(A) 2.4 gals.
(B) 4.8 gals.
(C) 7.3 gals.
(D) 5.3 gals.
(E) 9.7 gals.

8.

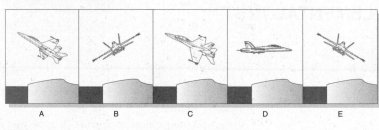

9. How much effort must be exerted at point A to lift the weight at point B?

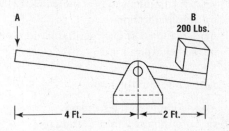

(A) 200 pounds
(B) 400 pounds
(C) 800 pounds
(D) 100 pounds
(E) 600 pounds

10. <u>Alacrity</u> most nearly means

(A) a general alarm
(B) an undeserved criticism
(C) the speed of academic doctrinal change
(D) the pendulum speed of a fully wound spring-driven clock
(E) a cheerful willingness or ready response

11. You need eight barrels of water to sprinkle $\frac{1}{2}$ mile of roadway. How many barrels of water do you need to sprinkle $3\frac{1}{2}$ miles of roadway?

    (A) 24
    (B) 32
    (C) 64
    (D) 56
    (E) 40

12.

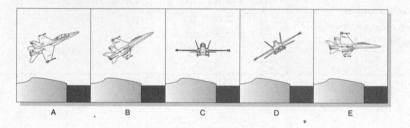

13. <u>Conundrum</u> most nearly means

    (A) a cone-shaped high-toned orchestra drum.
    (B) a perplexing puzzle or riddle.
    (C) "with a slow drumbeat" in Latin.
    (D) the hot exhaust from a jet engine.
    (E) a muffled drumbeat used to march in Revolutionary War–era battles.

14.

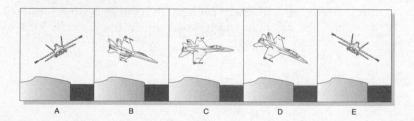

15. A fence that had been installed around a small rectangular parking lot 40 feet long and 36 feet wide is torn down. The entire fence is then reused to completely enclose a square garden. What is the length in feet of a side of the square garden?

(A) 76 ft.
(B) 18 ft.
(C) 42 ft.
(D) 38 ft.
(E) 32 ft.

9 September 1943—ITALY—U.S. Fifth Army, under Gen. Mark Clark, invades Italy, landing at H Hour (0330) south of Salerno with U.S. VI Corps south of the Sele River and British 10 Corps north of the river. Landings and operations ashore are closely supported by aircraft and naval gunfire. By end of day, VI and 10 Corps each hold a bridgehead on shallow Salerno plain but gap exists between them. 36th Division's RCTs [Regimental Combat Teams] 141 and 142, making initial assault, secure beachhead and withstand at least four strong tank counterattacks as enemy makes futile attempts to push the RCTs back into the sea. RCT 141, on right, is particularly hard pressed but retains shallow beachhead. Reserve—RCT 143—is committed in center upon landing. By end of day, initial objectives, except on right flank, are secured.

16. According to this passage, Regimental Combat Team 143 was

(A) held in reserve.
(B) pushed back into the sea.
(C) committed on the right flank.
(D) landed in the center of the Sele River.
(E) committed between RCT 141 and 142.

17. Refer to the passage for Question 16. If we know that the 36th Division was an American division, where did it land?

(A) north of Salerno
(B) to the left of RCT 142
(C) north of the Sele River
(D) south of the Sele River
(E) to the right of RCT 141

18.

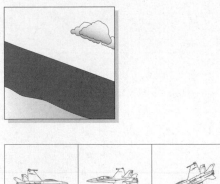
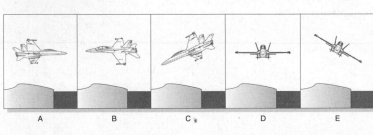

19. June's beauty, grace, and style—as well as her integrity, wisdom, and strength of character—mark her as the _____ of virtue.

(A) perigee
(B) facet
(C) facsimile
(D) epitome
(E) exposition

20. Two planes leave the same airport, traveling in opposite directions. One is flying at a speed of 340 miles per hour, the other at 260 miles per hour. In how many hours will the two planes be 3,000 miles apart?

(A) 5
(B) 3.75
(C) 6
(D) 10
(E) 37.5

21. Heather had to dismiss an employee because he displayed too much _____ and had too many _____ in his sales receipts.

    (A) initiative, remunerations
    (B) helpfulness, failures
    (C) lethargy, discrepancies
    (D) effluvium, heresies
    (E) morale, overtures

22.

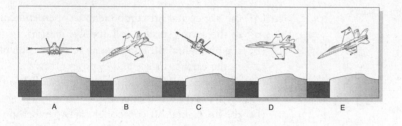

23. Jaycie had to ask her grandparents to put the Christmas angel at the _____ of the Christmas tree.

    (A) apex
    (B) apogee
    (C) atlas
    (D) beacon
    (E) crux

24. The brakes on your car use the same force that stops your car if you just let it coast. This force is called

    (A) joules.
    (B) gravity.
    (C) friction.
    (D) velocity.
    (E) acceleration.

25. Aircraft carriers provide a credible, sustainable, independent forward presence and conventional _____ in peacetime.

    (A) appearance
    (B) assimilation
    (C) obscuration
    (D) insipience
    (E) deterrence

26.

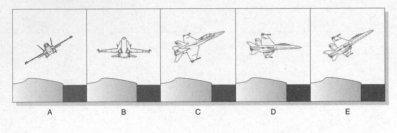

27. The _____ of several different scientific theories was judged to be a _____ by religious leaders.

    (A) hypothesis, heresy
    (B) electrification, anomaly
    (C) desecration, benevolence
    (D) elevation, heresy
    (E) automation, presentation

28. The amount of magnification that a machine produces is referred to as the

    (A) work load.
    (B) effort arm.
    (C) mechanical advantage.
    (D) efficiency factor.
    (E) force multiplier.

29. In a 3rd Battalion, 144th Infantry muster formation of 574 people, about 92% were enlisted personnel. How many officers were in the formation?

    (A) 44
    (B) 45
    (C) 46
    (D) 528
    (E) 529

30. When an airplane banks into a turn,

    (A) the horizontal lift component acts perpendicular to the earth's surface and opposes inertia.
    (B) the horizontal lift component acts perpendicular to the earth's surface and opposes gravity.
    (C) the horizontal lift component acts parallel to the earth's surface and opposes inertia.
    (D) the horizontal lift component acts parallel to the earth's surface and opposes gravity.
    (E) none of the above

31. Force is something that can change the velocity of an object by making it

    (A) start moving.
    (B) stop moving.
    (C) speed up.
    (D) slow down.
    (E) do all of the above.

32. A ground radar set is capable of detecting objects within the area around it within a radius of 10 miles. If the radar is used to cover a 36-degree segment of the circle around the radar set, how many square miles of area will it cover? Use 3.14 as the value of π.

    (A) 360 sq. mi.
    (B) 12.56 sq. mi.
    (C) 6.28 sq. mi.
    (D) 31.4 sq. mi.
    (E) 62.8 sq. mi.

33. When a pilot pushes forward on the control stick, the elevators will

   (A) extend.
   (B) retract.
   (C) move upward.
   (D) move downward.
   (E) assume a neutral position.

34. If pulley 1 in the diagram below is turning clockwise, how many pulleys will be rotating counterclockwise?

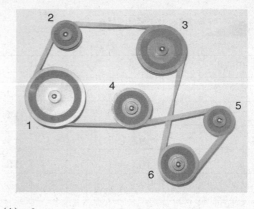

   (A) 0
   (B) 1
   (C) 2
   (D) 3
   (E) 4

ANSWERS AND EXPLANATIONS

Subtest 1: Math Skills

	✔	✘		✔	✘		✔	✘		✔	✘		✔	✘
1. D			7. B			13. B			19. B			25. A		
2. C			8. D			14. C			20. A			26. B		
3. B			9. C			15. B			21. C			27. C		
4. A			10. A			16. A			22. C			28. B		
5. D			11. A			17. D			23. B			29. A		
6. B			12. D			18. A			24. D			30. D		

1. **D** You need eight barrels of water to sprinkle $\frac{1}{2}$ mile. You need 16 barrels to sprinkle 1 mile. You need 3×16 (or 48) barrels to sprinkle 3 miles. Therefore, you need 48 + 8 (or 56) barrels to sprinkle $3\frac{1}{2}$ miles.

2. **C** Because the picture and its enlargement are similar figures, the lengths have the same ratio as the widths.

$$\frac{\text{length of picture}}{\text{length of enlargement}} = \frac{\text{width of picture}}{\text{width of enlargement}}$$

$$\frac{8}{12} = \frac{6}{\text{width of enlargement } (x)}$$

To solve this, cross-multiply the measurements, using x for the one you don't know.

$$8 \times x = 12 \times 6 = 72$$
$$x = \frac{72}{8} = 9 \text{ (width)}$$

3. **B** There are ten units of $1,000 in $10,000. Thus, Heather pays $10 \times $24 (or $240) each year in premiums. That means that every six months, Heather pays $\frac{1}{2}$ of $240, or $120.

4. **A** There are 16 ounces in a pound. Therefore, if 2 pounds of cottage cheese cost $3.20, then 1 pound of cottage cheese costs $1.60. One ounce costs ($1.60 ÷ 16) = $0.10, so 3 ounces cost $3 \times $0.10 = $0.30.

5. **D** To find the distance Jonathan drove, multiply the hours by the miles per hour. Thus,

$$12 \times 55 = 660 \text{ (distance covered)}$$

To find the number of gallons he used, divide the distance by the miles for each gallon. Thus,

$$660 \div 22 = 30 \text{ (gallons used)}$$

6. **B** From 8:45 A.M. to 4:45 P.M. is 8 hours; from 4:45 P.M. to 5:15 P.M. is $\frac{1}{2}$ hour. Subtract Gus' lunch hour:

$$8\frac{1}{2} - 1 = 7\frac{1}{2} \text{ (or 7.5 hours)}$$

Multiply his work hours by his hourly rate.

$$7.5 \times \$7.50 = \$56.25 \text{ (day's salary)}$$

7. **B** Find the cost of three ties: $3 \times $4 = $12 Subtract $12 (cost of three ties) from the total cost, $52:

$$\$52 - \$12 = \$40$$

Divide $40 (cost of all five shirts) by the number of shirts to find the cost of one shirt:

$$\$40 \div 5 = \$8$$

8. **D** Find the relationship between each pair of numbers in the series. Thus,

$$(5; 2) \; 5 - 3 = 2$$
$$(2; 9) \; 2 + 7 = 9$$
$$(9; 6) \; 9 - 3 = 6$$

The pattern so far is $-3, +7, -3$. To continue the series, add 7 to the fourth number in the series: $6 + 7 = 13$

9. **C** If 80% of the audience was adults, then the percentage of children was

$$100\% - 80\% = 20\% \; (0.2)$$

To find the number of children, multiply

$$500 \times 0.2 = 100.0 = 100 \text{ children}$$

10. **A** Find the amount of reduction by subtracting.

$$\$240 - \$210 = \$30$$

To find the percentage of reduction, divide the amount of the reduction by the original price.

$$\frac{\$30}{\$240} = \frac{1}{8}$$

Multiply the numerator, 1, by 100 and then divide by the denominator, 8, to get the percentage.

$$\frac{100}{8} = 12\frac{1}{2}\%$$

11. **A** Multiply the cost of the home by the assessment rate.

$$\$55,000 \times 80\% = \$55,000 \times 0.8 = \$44,000$$

The property tax is $4.74 for each $100 in $44,000.

$$\$44,000 \div 100 = 440 \text{ (hundreds)}$$
$$\$4.74 \times 440 = \$2,085.60 \text{ (tax)}$$

12. **D** If 1 inch equals 50 miles, then $2\frac{1}{2}$ inches (or 2.5 inches) equal $2.5 \times 50 = 125$ miles.

13. **B** One pound equals 16 ounces. Find the number of ounces in 2,200 pounds by multiplying.

$$2,200 \times 16 = 35,200 \text{ (ounces)}$$

Find the number of 40-ounce bags needed to pack 35,200 ounces by dividing.

$$35,200 \div 40 = 880 \text{ (bags)}$$

14. **C** Find the first reduction and the weekend sale price. (25% is the same as .25).

$$\$400 \times .25 = \$100 \text{ (first reduction)}$$
$$\$400 - \$100 = \$300 \text{ (weekend sale price)}$$

Use the weekend sale price to find the reduction for paying cash and the final price (10% = 0.1).

$$\$300 \times 0.1 = \$30 \text{ (second reduction)}$$
$$\$300 - \$30 = \$270 \text{ (cash price)}$$

15. **B** Find the combined salaries of the four clerks.

$$\$255 \times 4 = \$1,020$$

Find the combined salaries of the part-timers.

$$\$120 \times 2 = \$240$$

Add both totals and divide by 6 for the average.

$$\$1,020 + \$240 = \$1,260$$
$$\$1,260 \div 6 = \$210 \text{ (average salary)}$$

16. **A** The perimeter of a rectangle is equal to the sum of the two lengths and two widths. If 15 feet, 6 inches ($15\frac{1}{2}$ feet) equal 1 length, then

$$2 \times 15\frac{1}{2} = 31 \text{ ft. (2 lengths)}$$
$$40 - 31 = 9 \text{ ft. (both widths)}$$
$$9 \div 2 = 4\frac{1}{2} \text{ ft. (1 width)}$$

17. **D** Before dividing by a decimal, do what is needed to clear the decimal point in the divisor—and then, of course, you have to perform the same operation to the dividend to have the same number. In this case, to make 0.9 a whole number, we multiply it by 10, and then multiply the top number by the same amount.

$$\frac{0.675}{0.9} = \frac{6.75}{9} = 0.75$$

18. **A** In the first hour, the two planes will be a combined distance of 340 + 260 miles apart. Thus,

$$340 + 260 = 600 \text{ miles apart in 1 hour}$$

Find how many hours it will take them to be 3,000 miles apart by dividing.

$$3,000 \div 600 = 5 \text{ (hours)}$$

19. **B** Multiply the cost per foot by the length of the material. 12 inches equal 1 foot and 3 inches equal $\frac{1}{4}$ foot, therefore 5 feet, 3 inches equal $5\frac{1}{4}$ feet (or 5.25 feet).

$$\$8 \times 5.25 = \$42$$

20. **A** Find the cost of one pint. (There are 8 pints in 1 gallon.)

$$\$3.84 \div 8 = \$0.48$$

Find the cost of 3 pints.

$$\$0.48 \times 3 = \$1.44$$

21. **C** Begin by letting x equal one share of the inheritance. According to the ratio, the widow received 5 shares ($5x$), and the son received 3 shares ($3x$). Together, they inherited $72,000. This can be written as an equation.

$$5x + 3x = \$72,000$$

Solve for x by combining similar terms.

$$8x = \$72,000$$
$$x = \$9,000 \text{ (one share)}$$

Multiply the value of one share by the number of shares the mother received.

$$5x = \$45,000 \text{ (mother's share)}$$

22. **C** Begin by setting up a statement of proportion.

$$\frac{\text{chocolate}}{\text{chocolate}} = \frac{\text{corn syrup (recipe)}}{\text{corn syrup (amount available)}}$$

$$\frac{2\frac{1}{2}}{2} = \frac{\frac{1}{2}}{x} \quad \text{(or)} \quad \frac{\frac{5}{2}}{2} = \frac{\frac{1}{2}}{x}$$

Simplify each side of the proportion.

(a) $\dfrac{5}{2} \div \dfrac{2}{1} = \dfrac{5}{2} \times \dfrac{1}{2} = \dfrac{5}{4}$

(b) $\dfrac{1}{2} \div \dfrac{x}{1} = \dfrac{1}{2} \times \dfrac{1}{x} = \dfrac{1}{2x}$

Then solve the proportion by cross-multiplying

$$\frac{5}{4} = \frac{1}{2x} \quad \text{(or)} \quad 10x = 4$$

Divide each side of the equation by 10 to find the value of x.

$$10x = 4$$
$$x = \frac{4}{10}$$
$$= \frac{2}{5} \text{ cup of corn syrup}$$

23. **B** To find the average of three numbers, divide their sum by 3.

$x + y + z$ (sum of three numbers)

$\dfrac{x + y + z}{3}$ (sum of numbers, divided by 3)

24. **D** First find the income he gets on the $6,000 at 5% annual interest.

$$\$6,000 \times 0.05 = \$300.00 \text{ (income)}$$

Next, find how much more interest he wants to earn in a year.

$$\$900 - \$300 = \$600 \text{ (additional interest)}$$

This $600 will equal 6% of the amount (x) he has to invest. Write this as an equation.

$$\$600 = 0.06\,x$$

To solve for x, divide each side of the equation by 0.06 (clear the decimal in the divisor).

$$\frac{\$600.00}{0.06} = \left(\frac{0.06}{0.06}\right)x$$

$$\$10,000 = x$$
(new amount needed) $x = \$10,000$

25. **A** Two figures are similar if they have the same shape. They may or may not have the same size. A plane and a scale model of that plane have the same shape and are therefore similar.

26. **B** Solve by substituting the given number values for the algebraic letters and then working out the arithmetic operations.

$$a = 7,\ b = 4$$
$$5a^2b - 3ab^2 =$$
$$5(7^2)(4) - 3(7)(4^2) =$$
$$5(49)(4) - 3(7)(16) =$$
$$245(4) - 21(16) =$$
$$980 - 336 = 644$$

27. **C** The formula for the circumference (C) of a circle can be written in terms of its radius (R) or its diameter (D).

$$C = 2 \times R \times \pi \quad \text{or} \quad C = D \times \pi$$

Therefore, if you divide the circumference of a circle by its diameter, you are left with π.

28. **B** If the businesswoman spends $\dfrac{1}{5}$ of her income for rent, she has $\dfrac{4}{5}$ of her income left. She then spends $\dfrac{3}{8}$ of the remainder on salaries. To calculate what that amount is, cross-multiply the remaining income $\left(\dfrac{4}{5}\right)$ by the fraction spent on salaries:

$$\frac{4}{5} \times \frac{3}{8} = \frac{12}{40} = \frac{3}{10} \text{ (salaries)}$$

29. **A** Solve by substituting the number value for F, and then doing the arithmetic operations.

$$C = \frac{5}{9}(F - 32)$$
$$C = \frac{5}{9}(50 - 32)$$
$$C = \frac{5}{9} \times (18)$$
$$C = 10$$

30. **D** To obtain the average, add the five temperatures and divide the total by 5.

Add: $-12 + (-7) + (-2) + 0 + 6$
$= -21 + 6$
$= -15$

Divide: $-15 \div 5 = -3$

Subtest 2: Reading Skills

	✔	✘		✔	✘		✔	✘		✔	✘		✔	✘
1. B			7. B			13. E			19. B			25. E		
2. E			8. A			14. D			20. A			26. D		
3. C			9. C			15. D			21. C			27. C		
4. A			10. C			16. E			22. C					
5. B			11. A			17. B			23. B					
6. D			12. D			18. A			24. E					

1. **B** According to this passage, navies **are more expensive to have and maintain than individual ships.** The passage says that "navies are, by definition, more costly than individual ships."

2. **E** According to the passage, **more than half of our communication is through nonverbal expressions.** The passage says that 55 percent of our feelings and attitudes are communicated with nonverbal expressions.

3. **C** Conflagration, a noun, most nearly means **a large and destructive fire.** A "secret or conspiratorial message" might be a *confidential communication*; a "seizure by a higher authority" would be a *confiscation*; and "the act of letting the air out of an inflatable object" is *deflation*.

4. **A** Inurbane, an adjective, most nearly means **rude or uncouth.** Another word for "nonsensical" is *inane*; an *urbane* person is smooth and polished (the opposite of inurbane); and another word for "covered with water" is *inundated*.

5. **B** Alluvial, an adjective, most nearly means **covered with sediment deposited by flowing water.** Something that dates to ancient times could be called *antediluvian* ("before the flood"); something small or insignificant is *trivial*; land that is held in absolute ownership, without any obligation to a feudal lord, is known as *allodium* (a noun); and an *alloy* (a noun) is one metal mixed with others.

6. **D** In the passage, the word **conciliatory** is used incorrectly to describe the leadership of a "conqueror" who, by military conquest and force of arms, subdued much of the Asian continent. The word **conciliatory** applies to someone who makes peace through friendly, calming negotiations, rather than someone who uses warfare to conquer new territory.

7. **B** The passage says that "Carthage . . . first fell into conflict with the Romans when the [Romans'] success . . . drew them south to **Sicily** . . . In 265 B.C., the two powers found themselves at war over it."

8. **A** Rhetoric, a noun, most nearly means **the persuasive use of language to influence listeners or readers.** A pathological condition of the joints is *rheumatism*; a regulated pattern of long and short notes or beats is a *rhythm*; a continuously variable electrical resistor is a *rheostat*; and a parallelogram with unequal adjacent sides is a *rhombus*.

9. **C** Exemplify, a verb, most nearly means **to illustrate by example.** To test or measure for quality is to *examine*; something worthy of being imitated may be called *exemplary* (an adjective); to breathe out is to *exhale*; and to tear or wear the skin off of something is to *excoriate* it.

10. **C** The passage says that "in order to select the 'right' objectives, the planners must, among other things, do their work in the context of the higher-order purposes of the organization."

11. **A** The passage says, "As members become aware of the traditions, they soon learn that they are part of something larger than themselves."

12. **D** Captain Agnew had located the Italian convoy—and brought his "Force K" into the most favorable attacking position—by means of radar; for the Italians, who possessed no such weapon, the darkness remained **impenetrable**, and their surprise was consequently complete. *Impenetrable* means "not capable of being pierced or entered," so the correct choice here is D; the Italians, with no radar, had no way to pierce or see through the darkness of night, and so were surprised by Captain Agnew's British fleet. If something is not perceptible to the touch, it is *impalpable*; something or

someone who is unprejudiced is said to be *impartial*; something free from blemish is *immaculate*; and something that is incapable of being moved is (you've guessed it by now) *immovable*.

13. **E** The passage says that Texas A&M's enrollment is "sixth-largest"—a ranking relative to other schools, rather than a stand-alone number—which places it in the top six.

14. **D** Drogue, a noun, most nearly means **a funnel-shaped device at the end of a hose of a tanker aircraft.** A one-humped domesticated camel widely used in northern Africa is a *dromedary*; to slobber or drool is to *drivel* (a verb); a male bee who performs no work and produces no honey is a *drone*; and the verb that means to make a continuous, low, humming sound is also to *drone*.

15. **D** The passage says that "Ruth was living proof that the lone individual could still rise from mean, vulgar beginnings to fame and fortune." *Rising* from *mean, vulgar beginnings* shows that Ruth started his life in lower-level economic circumstances and rose higher as an adult.

16. **E** "Aircraft carriers provide a credible, sustainable, independent forward presence and conventional deterrence in peacetime." *Deterrence* means to prevent or discourage someone (in this case, other nations) from doing something—in this example, to discourage them from attacking us by showing strength and thereby persuading other countries that they will not be able to attack us successfully. *Appearance* does not make sense as an answer in this context; *assimilation* means absorbing and incorporating something; *obscuration* is making something hidden, unclear, or indistinct; and *insipience* is foolishness or a lack of wisdom.

17. **B** The general theme of this passage is that a good driver **adjusts to different driving conditions.**

18. **A** Negotiation in the classic diplomatic sense assumes parties more anxious to agree than to disagree [Dean Acheson]. None of the other choices presented make sense in the context given.

19. **B** The amount of fresh water available for people to use is, as stated in the passage, 0.8%. Choice **E**, eight one-hundredths, is equivalent to 8.0%—still 10 times the correct amount of 0.8%.

20. **A** Transmogrify most nearly means **to change into a different or bizarre shape or form.** To displace an object from one position to another is to *transport* it; to reverse or interchange the order of two or more objects is to *transpose* them; to pass beyond a human limit is to *transcend* that limit; and someone or something that passes away or decreases with time is a *transient*.

21. **C** According to the passage, there are six different "flavors" of quarks: up, down, strange, charmed, bottom, and top.

22. **C** Nucleic acids are found in all living organisms, as stated in the first sentence of the passage.

23. **B** "Galley navies, with their oared ships and limited carrying capacities, were never autonomous instruments of strategy but extensions—or, more accurately, partners—of armies on land." The correct answer is **B**, because *autonomous* means "independent" or "self-sustaining."

24. **E** The passage calls the War of 1812 "unfortunate," says that one of the chief causes of the war was being repealed even as Congress was declaring war (making it unnecessary), and further says that the army was in "wretched shape," clearly implying unpreparedness.

25. **E** "Abusive excise taxes burdened agriculture and mining, and the tariff gave Spanish manufacturers and traders an exclusive monopoly, which they exploited by charging ruinous prices for goods." The critical clue here is the word *exclusive* before the blank to be filled in; none of the other choices presented make sense in the context given.

26. **D** The passage says that the Tao-te-ching "is attributed to Lao-tzu, but it was probably written in the third century B.C." This clearly implies that Lao-tzu (who lived during the sixth century B.C.) did not write the book.

27. **C** In the first land skirmish of the Cuban campaign, the Marines quickly overcame enemy resistance and established the base at Guantanamo Bay. A *skirmish* is a small battle, so the correct answer is **C**.

Subtest 3: Mechanical Comprehension

	✔	✘		✔	✘		✔	✘		✔	✘		✔	✘
1. C			7. A			13. E			19. C			25. A		
2. A			8. E			14. A			20. B			26. C		
3. A			9. A			15. A			21. C			27. D		
4. C			10. B			16. A			22. B			28. A		
5. A			11. B			17. C			23. B			29. D		
6. B			12. C			18. D			24. B			30. B		

1. **C** Gears A and D are in constant mesh, and F is too small.

2. **A** When the lobe (high spot) on cam A makes contact with the follower (roller) on the contact arm, the contact will close. Because cam A has only one lobe, the contacts will close one time per revolution.

3. **A** To calculate the revolutions of gear B, use this formula: $r = \dfrac{(D \times R)}{d}$ where

   D = number of teeth on gear A;
   R = revolutions of gear A;
   d = number of teeth on gear B;
   r = revolutions of gear B;

   $r = \dfrac{(D \times R)}{d}$

   $r = \dfrac{(15 \times 14)}{10}$

   $r = \dfrac{210}{10}$

   $r = 21$

4. **C** Gears that are meshed turn in opposite directions. Gear 2 is turning clockwise; gears 1 and 3 are turning counterclockwise.

5. **A** Hydrometers use floats to measure specific gravity. Specific gravity is the weight of a liquid compared with the weight of the water. The liquid with the highest specific gravity will cause the float to rise higher in the glass tube.

6. **B** On a second-class lever, the fulcrum is at one end, the effort is at the other end, and the load is in between.

7. **A** When oncoming air meets the leading edge of the airfoil (wing), part goes over the top and part flows underneath. The air flowing over the top of the wing has to go farther than the air underneath, because it must meet again at the far side of the wing—physical laws act together to prevent or minimize vacuums in most cases. Because the air flowing over the top must go faster than that underneath, the pressure on the top of the wing is decreased, whereas the pressure underneath the wing remains relatively unchanged. Therefore, most of the lift on an aircraft's wing is because of a decrease in pressure on the wing's upper side.

8. **E Both segments will weigh the same.** If this were not the case, then you would not have been able to balance the beam at its CG because gravity would have been acting unequally on the two (still-joined) segments of the beam; the center of gravity wouldn't have been the center of gravity at all if you couldn't balance the beam there. Also, if the beam was regularly proportioned, both segments will be very close to the same size, allowing only for density variations in the wood itself.

9. **A Pulley A will have the highest number of RPMs (i.e., will turn the fastest).** In any arrangement of connected pulleys, the smaller pulley will turn faster than the larger pulley—it has to "keep up" and therefore turns faster. Pulleys B and D appear to be of the same size, while pulley A is the smaller of the connected pulleys and therefore turns fastest.

10. **B** Gear A has 15 teeth and Gear B has 10 teeth, so the gear ratio is 3:2. This means that for every three turns that the smaller drive gear B makes, the larger drive gear A only makes two. So, if Gear B makes 12 revolutions (the "3" part of the gear ratio), divide that by one-third to find out what "1" is, then multiply by the "2" part of the gear ratio to get the number of revolutions that Gear A will make. $12 \div 3 = 4$; $4 \times 2 = 8$.

11. **B** Regardless of gear ratio, when two meshing gears turn and the drive wheel turns one way (in this example, clockwise), the driven gear turns the other way (counterclockwise).

12. **C The piston in cylinder A will rise two inches.** The formula for mechanical advantage in this kind of problem is

$$\frac{a_2}{a_1} = \frac{d_2}{d_1}$$

where a_1 is the area of the smaller cylinder and a_2 is the area of the bigger cylinder, and d_1 is the vertical distance moved by the smaller cylinder and d_2 is the vertical distance moved by the larger cylinder. In this case the smaller cylinder is 3 inches in diameter and the bigger one is 6 inches Therefore, the mechanical advantage is $\left(\frac{6}{3}\right)$ = 2. Therefore we take the one inch moved by the larger cylinder and multiply it by the mechanical advantage to see that the piston in the smaller cylinder A will be forced upwards by two inches.

13. **E** The angle of the rope, θ, determines if the box is being pulled or dragged along the floor or being lifted from the floor. That means it can be both lifted and pulled along any angle that is more than 0 degrees and less than 90 degrees.

14. **A** The fulcrum is positioned between the effort and the load on a first-class lever.

15. **A** The shaft of the pivot is at T and S. The high spot (lobe) of the cam is between Q and R.

16. **A** When a series of pulleys is connected by drive belts, the pulley with the smallest diameter rotates at the highest speed; the smallest pulley will turn the fastest.

17. **C** The greater the difference between the number of teeth of the two meshed gears, the greater the torque.

18. **D** When gears are meshed, they turn in opposite directions. X and Y are therefore turning in opposite directions. However, because both E and F are meshed with Y, they are both turning in the same direction as X.

19. **C** On a third-class lever, the fulcrum is at one end, the load is at the other, and the effect is between the fulcrum and the load.

20. **B** Two meshed gears turn in opposite directions. When an idler gear (gear I is the idler in this example) is placed between the two, both turn in the same direction. The idler gear turns in direction 1.

21. **C** Because there are three ropes supporting block B, they are under $\frac{1}{3}$ the tension as the rope supporting block A.

22. **B** The correct answer is "inclined plane." An ax is classified as a wedge, which is a type of inclined plane.

23. **B** To reduce by $\frac{1}{3}$ the effort of moving an object to a height of 3 feet, we need an inclined plane or ramp that is three times the amount of the height: $3 \times 3 = 9$

24. **B** Centrifugal force from the spin (it doesn't matter which direction) will cause the balls to move outward, and the tension on the strings holding them will result in the balls moving upward.

25. **A** Water is flowing into the water tower at 120 gallons per hour. To convert that to gallons per minute, we divide 120 gallons by the 60 minutes in an hour, resulting in a rate of 2 gallons per minute coming into the water tower. Therefore, the level of water in the tower will remain the same.

26. **C** The farther away the fulcrum is from the resistance arm, the greater the amount of force that is required to lift the weight and the higher the resistance arm will travel.

27. **D B counterclockwise, C clockwise, and D counterclockwise.** Each driven gear in succession turns in the opposite direction from the gear that is driving it.

28. **A** The mechanical ratio of gear A to gear D is 1:1 because all four gears have the same number of teeth and will therefore turn at the same rate.

29. **D** Pulley C will rotate in the same direction as pulley A. Pulley A causes pulley B to rotate in the opposite direction from pulley A, and pulley B causes pulley C to rotate in the opposite direction from pulley B—which (there being only two directions of rotation available) is the same direction as pulley A.

30. **B** Pulley B will rotate the fastest. In the same way as meshing gears, the smaller the pulley in a system, the faster it rotates.

Subtest 4: Spatial Apperception

	✔	✘			✔	✘			✔	✘			✔	✘			✔	✘			✔	✘
1. A			6. C				11. B				16. B				21. D			
2. E			7. D				12. A				17. D				22. C			
3. D			8. E				13. C				18. D				23. B			
4. B			9. E				14. C				19. E				24. C			
5. A			10. A				15. D				20. B				25. A			

Answer	Pitch	Bank	Heading		Answer	Pitch	Bank	Heading
1. A	level flight	right	coastline left		14. C	level flight	wings level	coastline left
2. E	level flight	wings level	45° right of the coastline		15. D	level flight	left	coastline left
3. D	diving	right	out to sea		16. B	level flight	left	coastline right
4. B	level flight	right	coastline right		17. D	diving	wings level	out to sea
5. A	climbing	right	out to sea		18. D	diving	left	out to sea
6. C	level flight	right	out to sea		19. E	climbing	left	out to sea
7. D	diving	wings level	out to sea		20. B	climbing	wings level	out to sea
8. E	level flight	wings level	out to sea		21. D	level flight	left	out to sea
9. E	diving	right	out to sea		22. C	diving	wings level	coastline right
10. A	level flight	left	out to sea		23. B	diving	left	out to sea
11. B	level flight	left	coastline left		24. C	climbing	left	out to sea
12. A	diving	wings level	out to sea		25. A	climbing	wings level	out to sea
13. C	climbing	right	out to sea					

Subtest 5: Aviation/Nautical Information

	✔	✘			✔	✘			✔	✘			✔	✘			✔	✘
1. C			7. C				13. C				19. B				25. D		
2. B			8. D				14. A				20. E				26. D		
3. D			9. C				15. E				21. D				27. B		
4. A			10. B				16. A				22. E				28. C		
5. A			11. B				17. D				23. B				29. A		
6. B			12. B				18. C				24. C				30. A		

1. **C** *Port* is nautical terminology for "left," *starboard* means "right," *fore* means "in front (of)," and *aft* means "behind."

2. **B** On an aircraft carrier deck, blue shirts are worn by plane handlers, tractor drivers, aircraft elevator operators, messengers, and phone talkers.

3. **D** The angle between the chord line of a wing or airfoil and the direction of the relative wind or airflow is called the **angle of attack.**

4. **A** A wall or vertical surface within a ship is called a **bulkhead.**

5. **A** A conventional fixed-wing aircraft is controlled around its longitudinal axis (roll) by means of the **ailerons.** Elevators control movement around the lateral axis (pitch); the rudder controls movement around the vertical axis (yaw). Flaps increase both lift and drag, and are normally used during takeoffs and landings.

6. **B** Two statute miles are equal to **1.74 nautical miles.** A nautical mile is equal to 1.15 statute miles—so, to convert from statute miles to nautical miles, you must divide by 1.15. A knot is a measure of speed of one nautical mile per hour.

7. **C** The altimeter typically shows the height of the aircraft above a particular pressure level in **thousands of feet.**

8. **D** The time of 7 P.M. would be expressed using the 24-hour clock as **1900.**

9. **C** When a pilot pulls back on the control stick, the elevators will **move upward.** This pushes the tail of the aircraft downward and the nose upward.

10. **B** The order given to the helmsman to align the rudder with the keel of the ship is "**Rudder amidships.**"

11. **B** If one end of a runway was numbered 09, what number would designate the other end of the same runway? The correct answer is **27.** Runways are given two-digit numbers based on the magnetic compass heading or azimuth of the runway in tens of degrees. Runway 09 would therefore be the runway facing 90 degrees or due east; the opposite direction, due west, would have a designation of 27, for 270 degrees.

12. **B** The coordinates of latitude and longitude are used to express **position** in **degrees.**

13. **C** Which of the following engines could operate outside the earth's atmosphere? A **rocket engine** is the only choice that could operate outside the atmosphere because all the other engines require oxygen to operate.

14. **A** The bridge of a ship is where **all orders and commands affecting the ship originate.**

15. **E** Which of the following is a flight instrument? An **altimeter** is a flight instrument. The tachometer and fuel flow indicator are engine instruments; the control column isn't an instrument; and the trim tab is a secondary flight control.

16. **A** The tailhook of a carrier-borne aircraft is used to **catch one of four arresting cables stretched across the deck.**

17. **D** *VFR* stands for **Visual Flight Rules,** which means visually establishing the aircraft's attitude with reference to the natural horizon.

18. **C** A nautical mile is approximately **6,076 feet,** or about 1.15 statute miles.

19. **B** The four aerodynamic forces acting on an aircraft in flight are **lift, gravity, thrust, and drag.**

20. **E** A flashing green air traffic control directed to an aircraft on the ground is a signal that the pilot **has clearance to taxi.**

21. **D** The Latin phrase *Semper Paratus* is the motto of the **U.S. Coast Guard.** The meaning of the phrase is "Always Ready." The Marine Corps motto is *Semper Fidelis* ("Always Faithful").

22. **E** The *empennage* of an airplane is usually referred to as the **tail section.**

23. **B** On an aircraft carrier, the standard watch length for the Officer of the Deck is **four hours.**

24. **C** Trim Systems are designed to help minimize a pilot's workload by aerodynamically assisting movement and position of the flight control surfaces to which they are attached.

25. **D** The Carrier Strike Group could be employed in a variety of roles, such as **all of the above.** The CSG's mission can be protection of commercial and/or military shipping, protection of a Marine amphibious force, or establishing a naval presence in support of national interests.

26. **D** Ailerons extend from the midpoint of the wing outward toward the tip (choice A), create aerodynamic forces that cause the airplane to roll (Choice B), and move in opposite directions (Choice C), so the answer is **D, all of the above.**

27. **B** "Pri-Fly" is **the control tower for flight operations on an aircraft carrier.**

28. **C** The two types of turn indicators used in an aircraft are the **turn-and-slip indicator and turn coordinator.** The turn-and-slip indicator shows the rate of turn in degrees per second; the turn coordinator can initially show the roll rate (because the gyroscope is canted), and then shows rate of turn. Both instruments indicate turn direction and coordination of the turn, and also serve as a backup source of bank information in the circumstance where an attitude indicator fails.

29. **A** In the Navy, the term *Bravo Zulu* has come to traditionally mean **well done.** Although the phrase's origin is uncertain, the most common explanation is that it is a signal sent by Admiral William F. Halsey to members of his naval task force after defeating the Japanese in the Battle of the Solomon Islands during World War II.

30. **A** When an airplane banks into a turn, **the horizontal lift component acts parallel to the earth's surface and opposes inertia.** The vertical lift component continues to act perpendicular to the Earth's surface and opposes gravity.

Subtest 6: Aviation Supplemental Test

	✔	✘		✔	✘		✔	✘		✔	✘		✔	✘
1. B			8. A			15. D			22. C			29. C		
2. E			9. D			16. E			23. A			30. C		
3. A			10. E			17. D			24. C			31. E		
4. A			11. D			18. A			25. E			32. D		
5. D			12. D			19. D			26. E			33. D		
6. B			13. B			20. A			27. D			34. C		
7. C			14. D			21. C			28. C					

1. **B** There are 16 ounces in a pound. Therefore, if 2 pounds of cottage cheese cost $3.00, then 1 pound of cottage cheese costs $1.50. One ounce costs ($1.50 ÷ 16) = $0.09375, so 2 ounces cost 2 × $0.09375 = $0.1875, or, rounded off, $0.19.

2. **E** According to the above passage, **more than half of our communication is through nonverbal expressions.** The passage says that 55 percent of our feelings and attitudes are communicated with nonverbal expressions.

3. **A** An <u>aberration</u> most nearly means "a deviation from the standard."

4. **A** When a series of pulleys is connected by drive belts, the pulley with the smallest diameter rotates at the highest speed; the smallest pulley will turn the fastest.

5. **D** Set this up like a basic multiplication problem. Multiply each term of $(3a - 2)$ by a and write the results as the first line of partial products (remember that the product of multiplying a positive number and a negative number is always negative). Next, multiply each term of $(3a - 2)$ by $+3$ and write the results as the second line of partial products. Add the partial products as you would do in any multiplication problem to get the final answer.

$$
\begin{array}{r}
3a - 2 \\
a + 3 \\
\hline
3a^2 - 2a \\
+ 9a - 6 \\
\hline
3a^2 + 7a - 6
\end{array}
$$

6. **B** Mass remains constant, but the weight of an object depends on its altitude—or, said differently, its distance from the gravitational pull of the earth.

ASTB #1

7. **C** First we must calculate how far Amanda traveled, so we add the average speed for each of the three hours Amanda drove (since she drove for only an hour at each average speed, we don't have to calculate the average speed for the whole trip):

$$50 + 72 + 46 = 168$$

Then divide the total miles driven by how many miles per gallon Amanda's vehicle gets:

$$168 \div 23 = 7.3 \text{ gals.}$$

8. **A** Climbing, right bank, out to sea.

9. **D** To calculate the effort needed to lift the load of 200 pounds, use this formula: The effort multiplied by the effort arm equals the load multiplied by the load arm—stated mathematically like this:

E = effort needed to lift the load
$E \times e = L \times w$
e = length of the effort arm
$E \times 4 = 200 \times 2$
w = load arm
$E \times 4 = 400; L$ = load
$E = \dfrac{400}{4}$
$E = 100 \text{ lbs.}$

10. **E** <u>Alacrity</u> most nearly means "a cheerful willingness or ready response."

11. **D** You need eight barrels of water to sprinkle $\frac{1}{2}$ mile. You need 16 barrels of water to sprinkle 1 mile. You need 3×16 (or 48) barrels to sprinkle 3 miles. Therefore, you need 48 + 8 (or 56) barrels to sprinkle $3\frac{1}{2}$ miles.

12. **D** Level flight, left bank, coastline left.

13. **B** <u>Conundrum</u> most nearly means "a perplexing puzzle or riddle."

14. **D** Diving, right bank, out to sea.

15. **D** If the same fence fits around the rectangular lot and the square garden, then their perimeters are equal. The perimeter of a rectangle is the sum of the lengths of its four sides.

$$P = 40 + 36 + 40 + 36$$
$$= 152 \text{ ft.}$$

The perimeter of a square is the sum of its four equal sides, so the length of one side is the perimeter divided by four.

$$152 \div 4 = 38 \text{ ft.}$$

16. **E** According to this passage, Regimental Combat Team 143 was <u>committed between RCT 141 and 142</u>. The last sentence of the passage says that RCT 143 was "committed in center upon landing." Because the last half of the passage deals with the landing of the three RCTs of the 36th Division, with RCTs 141 and 142 making the initial assault and RCT 141 on the right withstanding strong counterattacks, the inference is clear that RCT 143, being landed in the center, is between RCTs 141 and 142.

17. **D** If we know that the 36th Division was an American division, then we can safely conclude that it and its three RCTs were part of the U.S. VI Corps that landed <u>south of the Sele River</u>. Since the RCTs are part of the 36th Division and not the other way around, the division can't land to the left or right of one of its own subunits.

18. **A** Level flight, left bank, out to sea.

19. **D** "June's beauty, grace, and style—as well as her integrity, wisdom, and strength of character—mark her as the <u>epitome</u> of virtue." *Epitome* means a top-level representation of a quality; by praising her for both internal and external qualities, the writer has identified her as the very best in all categories of virtue. *Perigee* means a low point; a *facet* is one side of a gem or other many-sided object; a *facsimile* is an exact copy; and an *exposition* is an explanation.

20. **A** In the first hour, the two planes will be a combined distance of 340 + 260 miles apart. Thus,

$$340 + 260 = 600 \text{ miles apart in 1 hour}$$

Find how many hours it will take them to be 3,000 miles apart by dividing.

$$3,000 \div 600 = 5 \text{ (hours)}$$

21. **C** "Heather had to dismiss an employee because he displayed too much <u>lethargy</u> and had too many <u>discrepancies</u> in his sales receipts." *Lethargy* means laziness or slowness, and *discrepancies* are mistakes or flaws; this is the only answer where both words make sense fitting into the sentence. *Initiative, helpfulness,* and *morale,* for instance, are all positive things that would be unlikely to get someone fired.

22. **C** Climbing, left bank, out to sea.

23. **A** "Jaycie had to ask her grandparents to put the Christmas angel at the <u>apex</u> of the Christmas tree." The implication here is clearly that the Christmas angel is going to be put at the top, or *apex*, of the tree. *Apogee* does mean the highest point, but of an orbit or ballistic trajectory, not a Christmas tree; an *atlas* is a book of maps; a *beacon* shows the way with its light; and the *crux* or center of the tree would not be the place to put the ornament.

24. **C** The brakes on your car use the same force that stops your car if you just let it coast. This force is called <u>friction.</u>

25. **E** "Aircraft carriers provide a credible, sustainable, independent forward presence and conventional <u>deterrence</u> in peacetime." *Deterrence* means to prevent or discourage someone (in this case, other nations) from doing something—in this example, to discourage them from attacking us by showing strength and thereby persuading other countries that they will not be able to attack us successfully. *Appearance* does not make sense as an answer in this context; *assimilation* means absorbing and incorporating something; *obscuration* is making something hidden, unclear, or indistinct; and *insipience* is foolishness or a lack of wisdom.

26. **E** Climbing, left bank, out to sea.

27. **D** "The <u>elevation</u> of several different scientific theories was judged to be a <u>heresy</u> by religious leaders." Throughout history, many people have perceived that science and religion are conflicting ideas or forces, so it is not uncommon to think that religious leaders might think that the increased prominence or *elevation* of several scientific theories constituted *heresy*, an opinion opposed to established religious beliefs.

28. **C** The amount of magnification that a machine produces is referred to as the <u>mechanical advantage</u>, or the ratio of load to effort.

29. **C** If 92% of the formation consisted of enlisted personnel, then the percentage of children was

$$100\% - 92\% = 8\% \text{ or } 0.08$$

To find the number of officers, then, multiply

$$574 \times 0.08 = 45.92 \text{ officers}$$

And, since we can't have .92 of a person—also, notice that the equation said "about 92%"—we round that up to 46 officers for the correct answer.

30. **C** When an airplane banks into a turn, **the horizontal lift component acts parallel to the earth's surface and opposes inertia.** The vertical lift component continues to act perpendicular to the earth's surface and opposes gravity.

31. **E** Force is something that can change the velocity of an object by making it <u>do all of the above</u>.

32. **D** The ground radar set can cover a complete circle with a radius of 10 miles. First, find the area of this circle, using the formula $A = \pi \times R^2$, where R is the radius.

$$A = 3.14 \times 10^2 = 3.14 \times 100 = 314 \text{ square miles}$$

We know that there are 360 degrees in a circle; if the radar is used to cover part of this, then that amount would be represented by the fraction

$$\frac{\text{number of degrees covered}}{\text{number of degrees in a circle}}$$

$$\frac{36 \text{ degrees}}{360 \text{ degrees}} = \frac{1}{10}$$

$$\frac{1}{10} \times 314 \text{ sq. mi.} = 31.4 \text{ sq. mi.}$$

33. **D** When a pilot pushes forward on the control stick, the elevators will <u>move downward</u>. This pushes the tail of the aircraft upward and the nose downward.

34. **C** Pulleys 5 and 6 will be rotating counterclockwise.

Answer Sheet
ASTB #2

Subtest 1: Math Skills

1 Ⓐ Ⓑ Ⓒ Ⓓ Ⓔ	9 Ⓐ Ⓑ Ⓒ Ⓓ Ⓔ	17 Ⓐ Ⓑ Ⓒ Ⓓ Ⓔ	25 Ⓐ Ⓑ Ⓒ Ⓓ Ⓔ
2 Ⓐ Ⓑ Ⓒ Ⓓ Ⓔ	10 Ⓐ Ⓑ Ⓒ Ⓓ Ⓔ	18 Ⓐ Ⓑ Ⓒ Ⓓ Ⓔ	26 Ⓐ Ⓑ Ⓒ Ⓓ Ⓔ
3 Ⓐ Ⓑ Ⓒ Ⓓ Ⓔ	11 Ⓐ Ⓑ Ⓒ Ⓓ Ⓔ	19 Ⓐ Ⓑ Ⓒ Ⓓ Ⓔ	27 Ⓐ Ⓑ Ⓒ Ⓓ Ⓔ
4 Ⓐ Ⓑ Ⓒ Ⓓ Ⓔ	12 Ⓐ Ⓑ Ⓒ Ⓓ Ⓔ	20 Ⓐ Ⓑ Ⓒ Ⓓ Ⓔ	28 Ⓐ Ⓑ Ⓒ Ⓓ Ⓔ
5 Ⓐ Ⓑ Ⓒ Ⓓ Ⓔ	13 Ⓐ Ⓑ Ⓒ Ⓓ Ⓔ	21 Ⓐ Ⓑ Ⓒ Ⓓ Ⓔ	29 Ⓐ Ⓑ Ⓒ Ⓓ Ⓔ
6 Ⓐ Ⓑ Ⓒ Ⓓ Ⓔ	14 Ⓐ Ⓑ Ⓒ Ⓓ Ⓔ	22 Ⓐ Ⓑ Ⓒ Ⓓ Ⓔ	30 Ⓐ Ⓑ Ⓒ Ⓓ Ⓔ
7 Ⓐ Ⓑ Ⓒ Ⓓ Ⓔ	15 Ⓐ Ⓑ Ⓒ Ⓓ Ⓔ	23 Ⓐ Ⓑ Ⓒ Ⓓ Ⓔ	
8 Ⓐ Ⓑ Ⓒ Ⓓ Ⓔ	16 Ⓐ Ⓑ Ⓒ Ⓓ Ⓔ	24 Ⓐ Ⓑ Ⓒ Ⓓ Ⓔ	

Subtest 2: Reading Skills

1 Ⓐ Ⓑ Ⓒ Ⓓ Ⓔ	9 Ⓐ Ⓑ Ⓒ Ⓓ Ⓔ	17 Ⓐ Ⓑ Ⓒ Ⓓ Ⓔ	25 Ⓐ Ⓑ Ⓒ Ⓓ Ⓔ
2 Ⓐ Ⓑ Ⓒ Ⓓ Ⓔ	10 Ⓐ Ⓑ Ⓒ Ⓓ Ⓔ	18 Ⓐ Ⓑ Ⓒ Ⓓ Ⓔ	26 Ⓐ Ⓑ Ⓒ Ⓓ Ⓔ
3 Ⓐ Ⓑ Ⓒ Ⓓ Ⓔ	11 Ⓐ Ⓑ Ⓒ Ⓓ Ⓔ	19 Ⓐ Ⓑ Ⓒ Ⓓ Ⓔ	27 Ⓐ Ⓑ Ⓒ Ⓓ Ⓔ
4 Ⓐ Ⓑ Ⓒ Ⓓ Ⓔ	12 Ⓐ Ⓑ Ⓒ Ⓓ Ⓔ	20 Ⓐ Ⓑ Ⓒ Ⓓ Ⓔ	
5 Ⓐ Ⓑ Ⓒ Ⓓ Ⓔ	13 Ⓐ Ⓑ Ⓒ Ⓓ Ⓔ	21 Ⓐ Ⓑ Ⓒ Ⓓ Ⓔ	
6 Ⓐ Ⓑ Ⓒ Ⓓ Ⓔ	14 Ⓐ Ⓑ Ⓒ Ⓓ Ⓔ	22 Ⓐ Ⓑ Ⓒ Ⓓ Ⓔ	
7 Ⓐ Ⓑ Ⓒ Ⓓ Ⓔ	15 Ⓐ Ⓑ Ⓒ Ⓓ Ⓔ	23 Ⓐ Ⓑ Ⓒ Ⓓ Ⓔ	
8 Ⓐ Ⓑ Ⓒ Ⓓ Ⓔ	16 Ⓐ Ⓑ Ⓒ Ⓓ Ⓔ	24 Ⓐ Ⓑ Ⓒ Ⓓ Ⓔ	

Subtest 3: Mechanical Comprehension

1 Ⓐ Ⓑ Ⓒ Ⓓ Ⓔ	9 Ⓐ Ⓑ Ⓒ Ⓓ Ⓔ	17 Ⓐ Ⓑ Ⓒ Ⓓ Ⓔ	25 Ⓐ Ⓑ Ⓒ Ⓓ Ⓔ
2 Ⓐ Ⓑ Ⓒ Ⓓ Ⓔ	10 Ⓐ Ⓑ Ⓒ Ⓓ Ⓔ	18 Ⓐ Ⓑ Ⓒ Ⓓ Ⓔ	26 Ⓐ Ⓑ Ⓒ Ⓓ Ⓔ
3 Ⓐ Ⓑ Ⓒ Ⓓ Ⓔ	11 Ⓐ Ⓑ Ⓒ Ⓓ Ⓔ	19 Ⓐ Ⓑ Ⓒ Ⓓ Ⓔ	27 Ⓐ Ⓑ Ⓒ Ⓓ Ⓔ
4 Ⓐ Ⓑ Ⓒ Ⓓ Ⓔ	12 Ⓐ Ⓑ Ⓒ Ⓓ Ⓔ	20 Ⓐ Ⓑ Ⓒ Ⓓ Ⓔ	28 Ⓐ Ⓑ Ⓒ Ⓓ Ⓔ
5 Ⓐ Ⓑ Ⓒ Ⓓ Ⓔ	13 Ⓐ Ⓑ Ⓒ Ⓓ Ⓔ	21 Ⓐ Ⓑ Ⓒ Ⓓ Ⓔ	29 Ⓐ Ⓑ Ⓒ Ⓓ Ⓔ
6 Ⓐ Ⓑ Ⓒ Ⓓ Ⓔ	14 Ⓐ Ⓑ Ⓒ Ⓓ Ⓔ	22 Ⓐ Ⓑ Ⓒ Ⓓ Ⓔ	30 Ⓐ Ⓑ Ⓒ Ⓓ Ⓔ
7 Ⓐ Ⓑ Ⓒ Ⓓ Ⓔ	15 Ⓐ Ⓑ Ⓒ Ⓓ Ⓔ	23 Ⓐ Ⓑ Ⓒ Ⓓ Ⓔ	
8 Ⓐ Ⓑ Ⓒ Ⓓ Ⓔ	16 Ⓐ Ⓑ Ⓒ Ⓓ Ⓔ	24 Ⓐ Ⓑ Ⓒ Ⓓ Ⓔ	

Subtest 4: Spatial Apperception

1 Ⓐ Ⓑ Ⓒ Ⓓ Ⓔ	8 Ⓐ Ⓑ Ⓒ Ⓓ Ⓔ	15 Ⓐ Ⓑ Ⓒ Ⓓ Ⓔ	22 Ⓐ Ⓑ Ⓒ Ⓓ Ⓔ
2 Ⓐ Ⓑ Ⓒ Ⓓ Ⓔ	9 Ⓐ Ⓑ Ⓒ Ⓓ Ⓔ	16 Ⓐ Ⓑ Ⓒ Ⓓ Ⓔ	23 Ⓐ Ⓑ Ⓒ Ⓓ Ⓔ
3 Ⓐ Ⓑ Ⓒ Ⓓ Ⓔ	10 Ⓐ Ⓑ Ⓒ Ⓓ Ⓔ	17 Ⓐ Ⓑ Ⓒ Ⓓ Ⓔ	24 Ⓐ Ⓑ Ⓒ Ⓓ Ⓔ
4 Ⓐ Ⓑ Ⓒ Ⓓ Ⓔ	11 Ⓐ Ⓑ Ⓒ Ⓓ Ⓔ	18 Ⓐ Ⓑ Ⓒ Ⓓ Ⓔ	25 Ⓐ Ⓑ Ⓒ Ⓓ Ⓔ
5 Ⓐ Ⓑ Ⓒ Ⓓ Ⓔ	12 Ⓐ Ⓑ Ⓒ Ⓓ Ⓔ	19 Ⓐ Ⓑ Ⓒ Ⓓ Ⓔ	
6 Ⓐ Ⓑ Ⓒ Ⓓ Ⓔ	13 Ⓐ Ⓑ Ⓒ Ⓓ Ⓔ	20 Ⓐ Ⓑ Ⓒ Ⓓ Ⓔ	
7 Ⓐ Ⓑ Ⓒ Ⓓ Ⓔ	14 Ⓐ Ⓑ Ⓒ Ⓓ Ⓔ	21 Ⓐ Ⓑ Ⓒ Ⓓ Ⓔ	

Answer Sheet
A S T B # 2

Subtest 5: Aviation/Nautical Information

1 Ⓐ Ⓑ Ⓒ Ⓓ Ⓔ   9 Ⓐ Ⓑ Ⓒ Ⓓ Ⓔ   17 Ⓐ Ⓑ Ⓒ Ⓓ Ⓔ   25 Ⓐ Ⓑ Ⓒ Ⓓ Ⓔ
2 Ⓐ Ⓑ Ⓒ Ⓓ Ⓔ   10 Ⓐ Ⓑ Ⓒ Ⓓ Ⓔ   18 Ⓐ Ⓑ Ⓒ Ⓓ Ⓔ   26 Ⓐ Ⓑ Ⓒ Ⓓ Ⓔ
3 Ⓐ Ⓑ Ⓒ Ⓓ Ⓔ   11 Ⓐ Ⓑ Ⓒ Ⓓ Ⓔ   19 Ⓐ Ⓑ Ⓒ Ⓓ Ⓔ   27 Ⓐ Ⓑ Ⓒ Ⓓ Ⓔ
4 Ⓐ Ⓑ Ⓒ Ⓓ Ⓔ   12 Ⓐ Ⓑ Ⓒ Ⓓ Ⓔ   20 Ⓐ Ⓑ Ⓒ Ⓓ Ⓔ   28 Ⓐ Ⓑ Ⓒ Ⓓ Ⓔ
5 Ⓐ Ⓑ Ⓒ Ⓓ Ⓔ   13 Ⓐ Ⓑ Ⓒ Ⓓ Ⓔ   21 Ⓐ Ⓑ Ⓒ Ⓓ Ⓔ   29 Ⓐ Ⓑ Ⓒ Ⓓ Ⓔ
6 Ⓐ Ⓑ Ⓒ Ⓓ Ⓔ   14 Ⓐ Ⓑ Ⓒ Ⓓ Ⓔ   22 Ⓐ Ⓑ Ⓒ Ⓓ Ⓔ   30 Ⓐ Ⓑ Ⓒ Ⓓ Ⓔ
7 Ⓐ Ⓑ Ⓒ Ⓓ Ⓔ   15 Ⓐ Ⓑ Ⓒ Ⓓ Ⓔ   23 Ⓐ Ⓑ Ⓒ Ⓓ Ⓔ
8 Ⓐ Ⓑ Ⓒ Ⓓ Ⓔ   16 Ⓐ Ⓑ Ⓒ Ⓓ Ⓔ   24 Ⓐ Ⓑ Ⓒ Ⓓ Ⓔ

Subtest 6: Aviation Supplemental Test

1 Ⓐ Ⓑ Ⓒ Ⓓ Ⓔ   10 Ⓐ Ⓑ Ⓒ Ⓓ Ⓔ   19 Ⓐ Ⓑ Ⓒ Ⓓ Ⓔ   28 Ⓐ Ⓑ Ⓒ Ⓓ Ⓔ
2 Ⓐ Ⓑ Ⓒ Ⓓ Ⓔ   11 Ⓐ Ⓑ Ⓒ Ⓓ Ⓔ   20 Ⓐ Ⓑ Ⓒ Ⓓ Ⓔ   29 Ⓐ Ⓑ Ⓒ Ⓓ Ⓔ
3 Ⓐ Ⓑ Ⓒ Ⓓ Ⓔ   12 Ⓐ Ⓑ Ⓒ Ⓓ Ⓔ   21 Ⓐ Ⓑ Ⓒ Ⓓ Ⓔ   30 Ⓐ Ⓑ Ⓒ Ⓓ Ⓔ
4 Ⓐ Ⓑ Ⓒ Ⓓ Ⓔ   13 Ⓐ Ⓑ Ⓒ Ⓓ Ⓔ   22 Ⓐ Ⓑ Ⓒ Ⓓ Ⓔ   31 Ⓐ Ⓑ Ⓒ Ⓓ Ⓔ
5 Ⓐ Ⓑ Ⓒ Ⓓ Ⓔ   14 Ⓐ Ⓑ Ⓒ Ⓓ Ⓔ   23 Ⓐ Ⓑ Ⓒ Ⓓ Ⓔ   32 Ⓐ Ⓑ Ⓒ Ⓓ Ⓔ
6 Ⓐ Ⓑ Ⓒ Ⓓ Ⓔ   15 Ⓐ Ⓑ Ⓒ Ⓓ Ⓔ   24 Ⓐ Ⓑ Ⓒ Ⓓ Ⓔ   33 Ⓐ Ⓑ Ⓒ Ⓓ Ⓔ
7 Ⓐ Ⓑ Ⓒ Ⓓ Ⓔ   16 Ⓐ Ⓑ Ⓒ Ⓓ Ⓔ   25 Ⓐ Ⓑ Ⓒ Ⓓ Ⓔ   34 Ⓐ Ⓑ Ⓒ Ⓓ Ⓔ
8 Ⓐ Ⓑ Ⓒ Ⓓ Ⓔ   17 Ⓐ Ⓑ Ⓒ Ⓓ Ⓔ   26 Ⓐ Ⓑ Ⓒ Ⓓ Ⓔ
9 Ⓐ Ⓑ Ⓒ Ⓓ Ⓔ   18 Ⓐ Ⓑ Ⓒ Ⓓ Ⓔ   27 Ⓐ Ⓑ Ⓒ Ⓓ Ⓔ

Practice Navy/Marine Corps/Coast Guard Aviation Selection Test Battery (ASTB) #2

Please turn to the beginning of Chapter 13, page 441, for more information about the breakdown and scoring attributes of the Aviation Selection Test Battery (ASTB).

SUBTEST 1: MATH SKILLS

1. Jonathan earns $350 (before taxes) every two weeks at his part-time job. His withholdings are $27.75 for federal income taxes, $5.65 for Social Security (FICA), and $12.87 for Medicare tax. How much will his net paycheck be?

    (A) $314.73
    (B) $304.73
    (C) $303.73
    (D) $313.73
    (E) $307.73

2. A computer-generated award certificate 9 inches long and 6 inches wide has to be enlarged so that its length will be 12 inches. How many inches wide will the enlarged certificate be?

    (A) 8
    (B) 6
    (C) 9
    (D) 10
    (E) 12.5

3. June C. has a certificate of deposit for $10,000 at an annual interest percentage rate of six percent. How much interest will she gain if she does not touch the CD for two years?

    (A) $11,236
    (B) $10,636
    (C) $1,200
    (D) $1,236
    (E) $10,636

4. If 2 pounds of jellybeans cost $3.20, what is the cost of 3 ounces?

    (A) $0.30
    (B) $0.20
    (C) $0.25
    (D) $0.15
    (E) $0.45

5. Mrs. H.B. drove her Volvo S80 four-door sedan from Waco to San Antonio at an average speed of 60 miles per hour, including two rest stops of 10 minutes each. Her car gets average highway mileage of 30 miles per gallon. If her car used 7 gallons of gas, how many hours did she travel?

    (A) 3 hrs.
    (B) 3.5 hrs.
    (C) 2.1 hrs.
    (D) 7.0 hrs.
    (E) none of the above

6. Mike earns $17.50 per hour. If he works from 7:45 A.M. until 5:30 P.M., with 1 hour off for lunch, about how much does he earn in one day?

    (A) $170.63
    (B) $163.37
    (C) $147.88
    (D) $153.13
    (E) $135.63

7. A basketball team won 70% of the 40 games it played. How many games did it lose?

    (A) 28
    (B) 30
    (C) 22
    (D) 12
    (E) 7

8. EconoAir Flight 1776 is scheduled for departure at 3:50 P.M. If the flight takes 2 hours and 55 minutes, at what time is it scheduled to arrive at its destination?

    (A) 5:05 P.M.
    (B) 6:05 P.M.
    (C) 6:15 P.M.
    (D) 6:45 P.M.
    (E) 6:50 P.M.

9. How many 4-ounce candy bars are there in a 3-pound package of candy?

    (A) 12
    (B) 16
    (C) 48
    (D) 9
    (E) 24

10. What is the fifth term of the series $2\frac{5}{6}$, $3\frac{1}{2}$, $4\frac{1}{6}$, $4\frac{5}{6}$, ... ?

    (A) $5\frac{1}{6}$

    (B) $5\frac{1}{2}$

    (C) $5\frac{5}{6}$

    (D) $6\frac{1}{6}$

    (E) $5\frac{1}{4}$

11. In a steakhouse, a guest orders a small steak entree with vegetables for $12.50, dessert for $3.50, and coffee for $1.25. If the tax on meals is 8%, what tax should be added to his check?

    (A) $0.68
    (B) $0.80
    (C) $1.00
    (D) $1.28
    (E) $1.38

12. A mechanic's warehouse is going to use a 55-gallon drum of oil to fill cans that hold 2 quarts each. How many cans can be filled from the drum?

    (A) 55
    (B) $27\frac{1}{2}$
    (C) 110
    (D) 220
    (E) 165

13. On production line 2A in the Lee County wooden product factory, a lathe operator takes 45 minutes to do the finish work on 9 spindles. How many hours will it take him to finish 96 spindles at the same rate?

    (A) 8
    (B) 72
    (C) 10
    (D) 10
    (E) 45

14. A triangle has two equal sides. The third side has a length of 13 feet, 2 inches. If the perimeter of the triangle is 40 feet, what is the length of one of the equal sides?

    (A) 13 ft., 4 in.
    (B) 26 ft., 10 in.
    (C) 13 ft., 11 in.
    (D) 13 ft., 5 in.
    (E) 10 ft., 3 in.

15. A lawn is 21 feet wide and 39 feet long. How much will it cost Jan to weed and feed it if a gardening service charges $0.40 per square yard for this treatment?

    (A) $109.20
    (B) $36.40
    (C) $327.60
    (D) $24.00
    (E) $218.40

16. The perimeter of a rectangle is 40 feet. If the length is 15 feet, 6 inches, what is the width of the rectangle?

    (A) 4 ft., 6 in.
    (B) 9 ft., 6 in.
    (C) 5 ft., 6 in.
    (D) 5 ft.
    (E) 6 ft.

17. Two partners operate a business that shows a profit for the year equal to $63,000. Their partnership agreement calls for them to share the profits in the ratio 5:4. How much of the profit should go to the partner who gets the larger share?

    (A) $35,000
    (B) $28,000
    (C) $32,000
    (D) $36,000
    (E) $24,000

18. A purchaser paid $17.16 for an article that had recently been increased in price by 4%. What was the price of the article before the increase?

    (A) $17.00
    (B) $17.12
    (C) $16.50
    (D) $16.47
    (E) $17.20

19. In a clothing factory, 5 workers finish production of 6 garments each per day, 3 others turn out 4 garments each per day, and one worker turns out 12 per day. What is the average number of garments produced per worker per day?

    (A) $2\frac{2}{9}$
    (B) 6
    (C) 4
    (D) $7\frac{1}{3}$
    (E) $5\frac{1}{9}$

20. Travis makes a 255-mile trip by car. He drives the first 2 hours at 45 miles per hour. At what speed must he travel for the remainder of the trip in order to arrive at his destination 5 hours after he started the trip?

    (A) 31 mph
    (B) 50 mph
    (C) 51 mph
    (D) 55 mph
    (E) 49 mph

21. A contractor bids $300,000 as his price for erecting a building. He estimates that $\frac{1}{10}$ of this amount will be spent for masonry materials and labor, $\frac{1}{3}$ for lumber and carpentry, $\frac{1}{5}$ for plumbing and heating, and $\frac{1}{6}$ for electrical and lighting work. The remainder will be his profit. How much profit does he expect to make?

    (A) $24,000
    (B) $80,000
    (C) $60,000
    (D) $50,000
    (E) $48,000

22. The list price of a TV set is $325, but the retailer offers successive discounts of 20% and 30%. What price does a customer actually pay?

    (A) $182.00
    (B) $270.00
    (C) $162.50
    (D) $176.67
    (E) $235.50

23. A certain brand of motor oil is regularly sold at a price of 2 quart cans for $1.99. On a special sale, a carton containing 6 of the quart cans is sold for $5.43. What is the saving per quart if the oil is bought at the special sale?

    (A) $0.27
    (B) $0.09
    (C) $0.54
    (D) $0.5425
    (E) $0.18

24. A worker earns $7.20 an hour. She is paid time and a half for overtime beyond a 40-hour week. How much will she earn in a week in which she works 43 hours?

    (A) $295.20
    (B) $320.40
    (C) $432.00
    (D) $464.40
    (E) $465.12

25. A tree 36 feet high casts a shadow 8 feet long. At the same time, another tree casts a shadow 6 feet long. How tall is the second tree?

    (A) 30 ft.
    (B) 27 ft.
    (C) 24 ft.
    (D) 32 ft.
    (E) 28 ft.

26. Find the numerical value of $5a2b - 3ab2$ if $a = 7$ and $b = 4$.

    (A) 244
    (B) 124
    (C) 112
    (D) 224
    (E) 248

27. If the circumference of a circle is divided by the length of its diameter, what is the result?

    (A) 2
    (B) 27
    (C) π
    (D) 7
    (E) 14

28. For a special mission, 1 soldier is to be chosen at random from among 3 infantrymen, 2 artillerymen, and 5 tank crewmen. What is the probability that an infantryman will be chosen?

    (A) $\frac{3}{10}$

    (B) $\frac{1}{10}$

    (C) $\frac{1}{3}$

    (D) $\frac{3}{7}$

    (E) $\frac{1}{7}$

29. A naval task force is to be made up of a destroyer, a supply ship, and a submarine. If 4 destroyers, 2 supply ships, and 3 submarines are available from which to choose, how many different combinations are possible for the task force?

    (A) 9
    (B) 24
    (C) 8
    (D) 12
    (E) 16

30. The base of a cylindrical can is a circle whose diameter is 2 inches. Its height is 7 inches. How many cubic inches are there in the volume of the can? (Use $\frac{22}{7}$ for the value of *pi*).

    (A) $12\frac{4}{7}$ cu. in.

    (B) 22 cu. in.

    (C) 44 cu. in.

    (D) 88 cu. in.

    (E) 66 cu. in.

SUBTEST 2: READING SKILLS

The tactical effect of speech is not only that it improves cohesion—from which comes unified action—but that it is the vital spark in all maneuver. Speech galvanizes the desire to work together. It is the beginning of the urge to get something done. Until there is speech, each soldier is likely to think of his situation in purely negative terms; with the coming of speech, he starts to face up to it. If you doubt this, put yourself in the middle of a group of men who have just been pinned down by close-range sniper fire. What happens? These men will hug the dirt or snuggle up to the nearest log or boulder or building remnant, but they won't do anything constructive about their situation until one of them makes a specific suggestion: "It's too hot; let's get out of here," or "You cover me while I work my way up to that treeline."

1. According to this passage, soldiers

   (A) like to take cover from snipers.
   (B) have to communicate first before they get anything done.
   (C) are more likely to get pinned down if they don't communicate.
   (D) think only in negative terms.
   (E) are basically cowards until someone they respect gives them orders.

By September 23, the Communists were in obvious retreat. The 1st Cavalry Division received the mission of pushing up the central corridor toward the X Corps beachhead at Inchon. The division commander organized Task Force 777 (built mostly around elements of Custer's onetime unit, the 7th Cavalry), which was to drive north—disregarding flanks and lateral contact—avoid decisive engagement with the retreating enemy, and move night and day to effect a linkup. The 3rd Battalion, 7th Cavalry, under Lt. Col. James H. Lynch, was reinforced and designated "Task Force Lynch"— this was the pointy end of the 1st Cavalry Division's spearhead. By midmorning of September 26, with little more than a hundred miles to go, Lynch's troopers were bypassing gaggles of disorganized, leaderless North Korean People's Army soldiers, and were cheered by villagers whose homes were still on fire in the wake of the retreating invaders. Lynch's lead group of three Pershing tanks plowed ahead so far and so fast that they outran even radio contact. By ten that night, they had made contact with the 31st Infantry Regiment north of Osan—but only after a blaze of hair-trigger American antitank fire at the unexpected visitors took off the head of a tank crewman in one of the Pershings.

2. According to the above passage,

   (A) the 7th Cavalry was commanded by Custer during the Civil War.
   (B) Task Force 777 reached Inchon on September 26.
   (C) the 31st Infantry Regiment reached Inchon on September 26.
   (D) Task Force Lynch linked up with the 31st Infantry but suffered a friendly fire casualty.
   (E) Task Force Lynch's mission was to hold their position and await linkup.

3. <u>Anomaly</u> most nearly means

   (A) bitter hostility or open hatred.
   (B) an abnormality or irregularity.
   (C) a collection of songs or stories.
   (D) boldness.
   (E) indifference.

4. <u>Cacophony</u> most nearly means

   (A) a sound made by a chicken or other domesticated bird.
   (B) bad handwriting.
   (C) a winged staff symbolizing the medical profession.
   (D) a jarring, discordant sound or noise.
   (E) automatic electronic communication.

5. <u>Xenophobe</u> most nearly means

   (A) a person who is afraid of foreigners or strangers.
   (B) a person who does not like foreigners or strangers.
   (C) a person who has a deep hated of women.
   (D) a light that flashes at rapid, predetermined intervals.
   (E) an element that does not mix with inert gases.

A credibility check has its roots in a leader's history as it is known by other people; it has to do with reputation. Reputation is human collateral—the security we pledge to guarantee the performance of our obligations as leaders, friends, colleagues, and citizens. It is what supports the (usually natural) human instinct to *want* to trust. Reputation is to be derided and cared for—a damaged one lowers people's perceptions of a leader's worth and hence their motivation to follow.

6. In the passage above, what word is used incorrectly?

   (A) collateral
   (B) security
   (C) derided
   (D) obligations
   (E) instinct

During the Battle of the Bulge, the town of Bastogne was occupied by the American 101st Airborne Division to control the vital crossroads there, but surrounded by the German Army as it tried to unexpectedly slice through a lightly held sector to the port of Antwerp. On December 22, 1944, four Germans under a flag of truce, carrying a surrender demand, approached the lines of the 327th Infantry Regiment on the outskirts of Bastogne. The message cited the progress of attacking German forces farther west as evidence of the futility of holding out at Bastogne, and demanded the surrender of the encircled town within two hours. The surrender demand was delivered to acting division commander Brig. Gen. Anthony C. McAuliffe as he was about to leave his headquarters to congratulate the defenders of a roadblock who had driven off a heavy attack. He dropped the message on the floor, said "Nuts," and left. When he returned, his staff reminded him of the message, which he at first had not taken seriously; McAuliffe asked his staff what they thought should be the reply. The division operations officer said, "That first remark of yours would be hard to beat." So the message delivered to the Germans read, "To the German Commander: Nuts! The American Commander." The confused German major asked if this was affirmative or negative; he was told by the 327th's regimental commander that it was "decidedly not affirmative."

7. Why was the 101st Airborne Division holding out at Bastogne?

    (A) To protect the vital nut and berry agricultural center at Bastogne.
    (B) To set up a roadblock.
    (C) To deny the Germans an important crossroads.
    (D) To serve as an affirmative symbol of Allied resistance.
    (E) To keep the Germans from reaching the crossroads at Antwerp.

8. What news did the German major have to take back to his commander?

    (A) The Americans would surrender within two hours.
    (B) The Americans would surrender, but not within two hours.
    (C) The Americans would not surrender.
    (D) The Americans would not surrender the nut plantations west of Bastogne.
    (E) The passage is not clear.

9. Incentive most nearly means

    (A) a motivation or benefit for doing something.
    (B) capable of producing new ideas.
    (C) copied or adapted from something else.
    (D) moderate or cautious.
    (E) unaware of the thoughts or feelings of others.

Our current understanding of the motion of objects dates back to Newton and Galileo. Before then, people held to Aristotle's ideas that the "natural state" of an object was to be at rest, and that it moved only if it was caused to move by some force. Aristotle also thought one could figure out all the principles governing the universe by reason alone; there was no need to physically verify those conclusions by experimentation or observation—so no one until Galileo checked to see if bodies of differing weights *actually* fell at different velocities. The story goes that Galileo dropped weights from the leaning tower of Pisa, but whether or not this is actually true, we know that he did roll balls of differing weights down a smooth slope (an easier experiment because the speeds are less). Galileo's experiment showed that each body increased its speed at the same rate, no matter what its weight. His work was then used by Newton to deduce his three laws of motion.

10. According to the passage above,

    (A) Aristotle's experiments formed the basis of Galileo's and Newton's work.
    (B) different weights fall at different speeds from the Leaning Tower of Pisa.
    (C) different weights fall at the same speed from the Leaning Tower of Pisa.
    (D) balls of differing weights roll downhill at the same rate.
    (E) balls of the same weight roll downhill at different rates.

The least considerable man among us has an interest equal to the proudest nobleman in the laws and constitution of his country, and is equally called upon to make a generous contribution in support of them—whether it be the heart to conceive, the understanding to direct, or the hand to execute.

11. According to the passage above,

    (A) every citizen has an obligation to do what they can to make their country better.
    (B) all citizens should make an equal contribution to running their country.
    (C) rich people should contribute more to their nation since they have more.
    (D) poor people should contribute more to their country since there are more of them.
    (E) only noblemen are capable of fulfilling positions of leadership.

As a citizen, you are to be a quiet and peaceable subject, true to your government, and just to your country; you are not to <u>countenance</u> disloyalty or rebellion, but patiently submit to legal authority, and conform with cheerfulness to the government of the country in which you live.

12. <u>Countenance</u> most nearly means

  (A) face
  (B) start
  (C) enumerate
  (D) consider
  (E) impair

The "zero tolerance on fighting" policy many of our schools have instituted sounds great at first, but it's actually a smokescreen that lets school leaders avoid tough decisions while teaching kids the wrong lessons. The biggest problem happens when the student who is attacked gets swept up in the punishment net along with the one who started the fight—unless he doesn't fight back and lets himself get pummeled. It is morally wrong to teach our kids that the attacked person is invariably as much in the wrong as the attacker. The correct solution, instead, is a balanced application of reasonable judgment by administrators, backed up by a determination to tell the truth to parents. Parents, too, have an obligation—to recognize that their little angel may not be perfect, and not to sue the school because a teacher or principal told them an unpleasant truth.

13. The author of this passage believes that

  (A) "zero tolerance on fighting" policies sound great.
  (B) administrators should sue parents whose children get into fights.
  (C) parents should sue school personnel who tell them something they don't want to hear.
  (D) zero tolerance policies call for sound judgment by school administrators.
  (E) the student who defends himself should be viewed differently than the attacker.

14. <u>Posterity</u> most nearly means

  (A) the back side of an object or person.
  (B) a series of small signs or posters.
  (C) great honor or recognition.
  (D) future descendants or generations.
  (E) the angle of a helicopter's tail rotor.

It is either exceptionally naïve or depressingly cynical to equate an analysis of incomplete facts that turns out to be wrong with knowing untruths (otherwise known as "lies"). Military, political, and economic intelligence—information about a known or potential adversary or competitor—is especially open to gaps, misinterpretation, and other confusion. Perfect information seldom if ever exists even in non-adversarial situations, much less when the adversary is actively trying to deny you the facts—or sell you the wrong ones. The quest for perfectly complete and accurate information results in analysis paralysis: the inability to make a decision until you have all the information, which is never going to happen.

15. According to this passage, the reader can infer that the author

  (A) likes to make decisions based on 100% accurate information.
  (B) knows that complete information will eventually be available.
  (C) believes that acting on incomplete information is often necessary.
  (D) wants to give accurate information to potential adversaries or competitors.
  (E) supports the quest for non-adversarial interpretation.

16. <u>Quandary</u> most nearly means

  (A) a swampy area that impedes the movement of people or vehicles.
  (B) a stanza of four lines in poetry.
  (C) divided into four sections.
  (D) a search for new knowledge.
  (E) deep uncertainty about a choice; a dilemma.

After Texas broke away from Mexico and became a republic, the new nation's government made halting but significant steps toward a public education system. In 1839, the Texas House passed a law calling for three leagues (13,285 acres) to be set aside in each county for a "primary school or academy," and 50 leagues to be set aside for two colleges. However, the official system of public schools did not even begin to become a reality until after Texas was admitted to the Union as a state in 1845.

17. The passage primarily discusses

  (A) the relationship of leagues to acres.
  (B) early steps toward public education in Texas.
  (C) steps taken by private organizations to improve public education.
  (D) how Texas became a republic and then a state in the Union.
  (E) opposition to public education in the Republic of Texas.

18. There is no room in this _____ for hyphenated Americanism. The one absolutely certain way of bringing this nation to ruin, of preventing all possibility of its continuing to be a nation at all, would be to permit it to become a tangle of squabbling nationalities. [Theodore Roosevelt]

    (A) improbability
    (B) country
    (C) diversity
    (D) science
    (E) object

Perhaps the most valuable result of all education is the ability to make yourself do the thing you have to do, when it ought to be done, whether you like it or not; it is the first lesson that ought to be learned; and however early a man's training begins, it is probably the last lesson that he learns thoroughly. [Thomas Henry Huxley]

19. If the passage above had to be summarized, it would be

    (A) Don't Procrastinate.
    (B) Support Early Childhood Education.
    (C) If You Think Education Is Expensive, Try Ignorance.
    (D) Don't Put Off Till Tomorrow What You Can Do Today.
    (E) A Smart Man Does What He's Supposed to Do.

20. Discernment most nearly means

    (A) to treat differently due to race or color.
    (B) a preference for always being at the center of events.
    (C) insight; the ability to see things clearly.
    (D) scientific knowledge of natural phenomena.
    (E) passion for a just cause.

An ultimate British victory was certain for three main reasons. First, the 1.5 million inhabitants of the British colonies in 1754 were tenacious, resourceful, and growing quickly—while New France had fewer than 100,000 people, brave but scattered and deficient in initiative. Second, the British held a better strategic geographical position. While operating on interior lines of communication and transportation, they could effectively strike westward at what is now Pittsburgh, northwestward toward Niagara, and northward toward Quebec and Montreal. They also had a better navy, could more quickly reinforce and supply their troops, and could lay siege to Quebec by water. Finally, they proved able to produce better leaders in both the civilian and military realms.

21. What does the author of the passage state were the three main reasons why the British victory in North America was "certain"?

    (A) More people, more land, more ships.
    (B) More people, better commerce, better military.
    (C) Fewer people, better geographical position, more leaders.
    (D) Fewer people, more land, better leaders.
    (E) More people, better geographical position, better leaders.

Chlorophyll can be any one of almost a dozen kinds of green pigments present in most plant cells. Chlorophyll is able to convert the energy from sunlight into carbohydrates, which plants form from carbon dioxide and water from the environment. The carbohydrates in turn become a source of energy for animals and humans when the plant material is eaten.

22. Chlorophyll uses _____ to make carbohydrates.

    (A) water and carbon dioxide.
    (B) pigments, water, and carbon dioxide.
    (C) animal waste, water, and carbon dioxide.
    (D) sunlight, carbon dioxide, and water.
    (E) water, carbon dioxide, and plant cells.

The most common cold weather injury is frostbite. Severe cold, especially for a prolonged period, can severely constrict the blood vessels, reducing the normal flow of warm blood to exposed body parts. The symptoms usually include a very cold feeling in the exposed skin area, followed by full or partial loss of feeling. The skin may appear flushed or reddish at first, but later it becomes white or grayish yellow. Because of the loss of feeling, the victim is often unaware of the injury.

23. The best remedy for frostbite is

    (A) vigorous rubbing of the affected area to create friction and therefore heat.
    (B) removal of tight clothing and gradual warming of the area.
    (C) immediate heating of the affected area, followed by vigorous exercise.
    (D) immediate warming of the affected area with immersion in warm water.
    (E) not addressed in this passage.

Far better it is to dare mighty things, to win glorious triumphs, even though checkered by failure, than to take rank with those poor spirits who neither enjoy much nor suffer much, because they live in the gray twilight that knows not victory nor defeat. [Theodore Roosevelt]

24. The above passage encourages the reader to

(A) make the effort to accomplish challenging goals.
(B) live in the gray twilight so as not to suffer much.
(C) dare to outrank the poor.
(D) devote one's life to public service.
(E) avoid failure at all costs.

25. Leaders demonstrate that they value other people when they listen to them, trust them, and are _____ and willing to listen to reports of unproductive or unpleasant information—even when it involves the leader himself.

(A) spontaneous
(B) receptive
(C) disarming
(D) characteristic
(E) diaphanous

In 1949, the Federal Communications Commission (FCC) instituted its Fairness Doctrine, which required broadcasters to "afford reasonable opportunity for the discussion of conflicting views of public importance." The Personal Attack rule in that Doctrine required broadcasters to provide rebuttal time to anyone of whom a less-than-complimentary opinion had been spoken on the air. This resulted in self-imposed inhibitions on political speech to avoid federal prosecution, as well as loss of income by trying to comply. By 1987, however, it was recognized that the Doctrine was "antagonistic to the freedom of expression guaranteed by the First Amendment," and the speech-stifling regulation was itself stifled—or rather, gleefully strangled by those who were willing to engage in the give-and-take of a fair public debate.

26. The Fairness Doctrine was

(A) instituted in 1987 and is still in effect today.
(B) recognized as antagonistic to freedom of expression.
(C) a reasonable opportunity to respond to broadcast attacks.
(D) a vast right-wing conspiracy.
(E) a precisely defined effort at regulating the airwaves.

27. If a nation expects to be ignorant and free, in a state of _____, it expects what never was and never will be. [Thomas Jefferson]

(A) siege
(B) negotiation
(C) civilization
(D) nature
(E) declaration

SUBTEST 3: MECHANICAL COMPREHENSION

1. If gear B is the driving gear and it makes 10 revolutions, how many revolutions will gear A make?

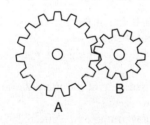

(A) 10
(B) 14
(C) 15
(D) 20
(E) 21

2. The wheels below are connected by a belt as shown. If the larger wheel makes 2 revolutions, how many revolutions will the smaller wheel make?

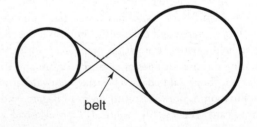

belt

(A) less than one
(B) one
(C) two
(D) more than two
(E) none of the above

ASTB #2

3. In the diagram on page 498, if the wheel on the left turns counterclockwise, which way will the wheel on the right turn?

    (A) clockwise
    (B) counterclockwise
    (C) unable to tell from the information given

4. If block A, on which the lever is resting, is moved closer to block B,

    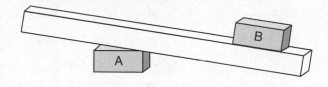

    (A) there will be no change in the effort required to lift block B to the same height.
    (B) it will be harder to lift block B but it will go higher.
    (C) it will be easier to lift block B and it will go higher.
    (D) it will be harder to lift block B and it will not be lifted to the same height.
    (E) it will be easier to lift block B but it will not be lifted as high.

5. A gear system derives the greatest amount of mechanical advantage if a 7-tooth gear drives a

    (A) 27-tooth gear.
    (B) 7-tooth gear.
    (C) 28-tooth gear.
    (D) 14-tooth gear.
    (E) 5-tooth gear.

6. Recruit Highspeed is assigned to cross a fast-moving stream by swimming it while facing at a right angle to the banks. If he maintains his perpendicular orientation correctly during his swim, where will he arrive on the far bank?

    (A) upstream of his departure point
    (B) downstream of his departure point
    (C) directly across from his departure point
    (D) it is impossible to do this; he will grow tired and drown
    (E) not enough information given to answer

7. If pulley C is rotating clockwise, what direction will pulley A rotate?

    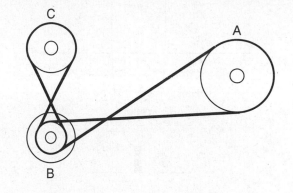

    (A) clockwise
    (B) counterclockwise
    (C) insufficient information to answer
    (D) pulley A will not rotate

8. In the pulley system above, which pulley will rotate the fastest?

    (A) pulley A
    (B) pulley B
    (C) pulley C
    (D) all will rotate at the same speed

9. If the cisterns of both water towers A and B are the same size and the same height above the ground, and both begin with a full water level, which water tower will be able to provide more water to the thirsty troops below?

    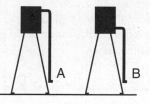

    (A) water tower A
    (B) water tower B
    (C) both will provide the same amount
    (D) unable to tell from the information provided

10. If a bullet from a rifle is fired at a 1 degree angle above the horizontal, at what point will it have the highest velocity?

    (A) when it leaves the muzzle
    (B) midway between the muzzle and the top of its arc
    (C) at the top of its arc
    (D) midway between the top of its arc and the target
    (E) when it hits the target in the 10 ring

11. When the plug in the tube is removed, water will flow

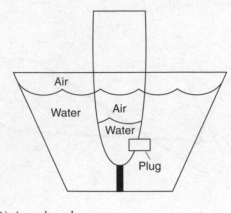

(A) into the tube.
(B) out of the tube.
(C) in neither direction.
(D) impossible to tell

12. Which weight exerts more pull on the horizontal bar from which both weights hang by strings as shown?

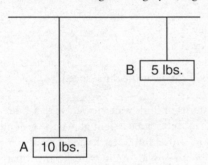

(A) A
(B) B
(C) both exert the same pull
(D) cannot tell from the information given
(E) none of the above

13. The force required to balance the lever shown below would be

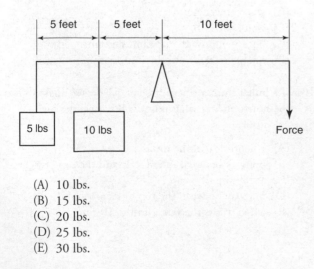

(A) 10 lbs.
(B) 15 lbs.
(C) 20 lbs.
(D) 25 lbs.
(E) 30 lbs.

14. An experimental miniature submarine is traveling through the ocean when it develops a crack in its outer hull and pressurized air pushes out of its lower right side. In which direction must the rudder be turned for the sub to maintain its original heading?

(A) A
(B) B
(C) no rudder correction is necessary
(D) cannot tell from the information given
(E) none of the above

15. In the water system below, assume that the main tank begins in an empty state and that all the valves are closed. In order for the tank to fill approximately halfway and maintain that level, which valves would have to be open?

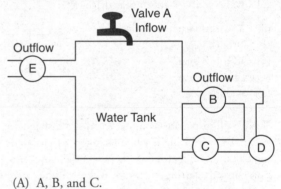

(A) A, B, and C.
(B) A, B, and D.
(C) A, E, and B.
(D) A, E, and C.
(E) B, C, and D.

16. Which pendulum takes more time to make one complete swing?

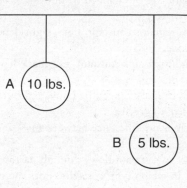

(A) A
(B) B
(C) both take the same amount of time
(D) insufficient information to answer

17. In the diagram above, if pendulum A was the same length as pendulum B, which pendulum would take less time to make one swing?

(A) A
(B) B
(C) both would take the same amount of time
(D) insufficient information to answer

18. If two resistors and a battery are arranged as shown in each circuit, which circuit arrangement has a greater resistance?

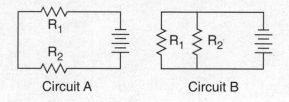

(A) Circuit A
(B) Circuit B
(C) both circuits have the same resistance
(D) insufficient information to answer

19. When two or more forces act in such a way that their combination has a net effect of zero, what is this condition called?

(A) similarity
(B) equilibrium
(C) equilateral
(D) notionality
(E) equestrianism

20. The descent of an airborne paratrooper is primarily affected by what physical forces?

(A) Gravity and thrust.
(B) Gravity and temperature.
(C) Thrust and temperature.
(D) Drag and gravity.
(E) Lift and drag.

21. Heat is transferred from one location to another by conduction, convection, and

(A) condensation.
(B) evaporation.
(C) radiation.
(D) thermal inertia.
(E) cooling.

22. When a salt is dissolved in water, it causes

(A) an increase in the freezing point of the solution.
(B) a decrease in the freezing point of the solution.
(C) no significant difference in the freezing point of the solution.
(D) the water to freeze and separate from the salt.
(E) none of the above.

23. When a liquid is changed to vapor, the process is called

(A) evaporation.
(B) distillation.
(C) dehydration.
(D) condensation.
(E) pressurization.

24. When water that is being heated is confined to a closed container so that the steam cannot escape, the pressure inside the container increases and the temperature of the boiling water

(A) decreases.
(B) increases.
(C) stays the same.
(D) varies according to the cosine of the temperature.
(E) none of the above

25. If pulley A is the driver and turns counterclockwise, which pulley will turn the slowest?

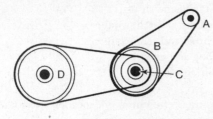

    (A) pulley A
    (B) pulley B
    (C) pulley C
    (D) pulley D
    (E) all pulleys will turn at the speed dictated by the driver

26. Compressing the air in a closed space will

    (A) increase the volume and raise the temperature.
    (B) increase the volume and lower the temperature.
    (C) decrease the volume and raise the temperature.
    (D) decrease the volume and lower the temperature.
    (E) decrease the volume and not affect the temperature.

27. When two magnets have opposite poles facing each other,

    (A) the magnets will not have any reaction to each other.
    (B) the magnets will push apart.
    (C) the magnets will pull together.
    (D) the magnets will spark if they are close enough.
    (E) the magnets will generate a one-time electrical charge.

28. What is the difference between weight and mass?

    (A) Weight can be changed by buoyancy, but mass is relative to gravity.
    (B) Mass remains constant, but weight depends on altitude.
    (C) Weight remains constant, but mass depends on altitude.
    (D) Mass can be changed by buoyancy, but weight is relative to gravity.
    (E) There is no difference between mass and weight.

29. The water in a stream flows through narrow and wide sections. In which type of section does the water flow fastest?

    (A) wide sections
    (B) narrow sections
    (C) sections that are neither narrow nor wide
    (D) speed of the water does not change
    (E) insufficient information to answer

30. Static electricity is

    (A) battery current.
    (B) direct currect (DC).
    (C) alternating current (AC).
    (D) a theoretical concept used to balance equations.
    (E) none of the above.

SUBTEST 4: SPATIAL APPERCEPTION

This subtest measures your ability to determine the position of an aircraft in flight in relation to the view a pilot would see when looking out the front of the cockpit.

This subtest consists of 25 questions, which must be answered in 10 minutes.

For each question, you will see a series of six pictures. The first picture will depict a view of the landscape that a pilot would see when looking out the front of the cockpit. You are to determine whether the aircraft is climbing, diving, banking, or in level flight, and choose the picture that best represents the same aircraft when viewed from the outside.

1.

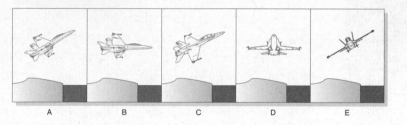

2.

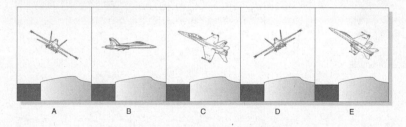

3.

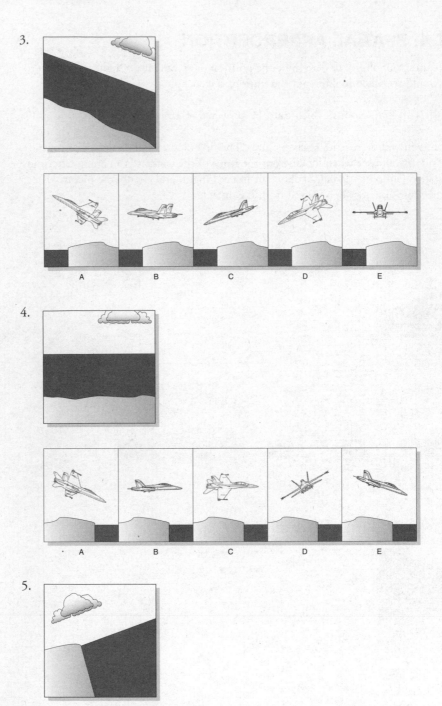

4.

5.

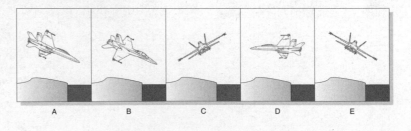

6.

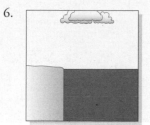

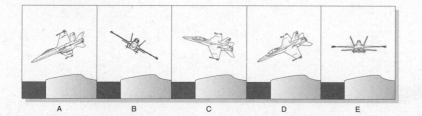

A   B   C   D   E

7.

A   B   C   D   E

8.

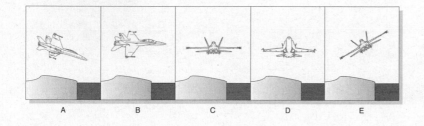

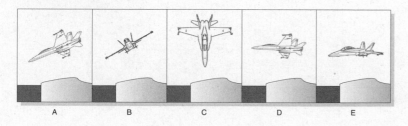

A   B   C   D   E

9.

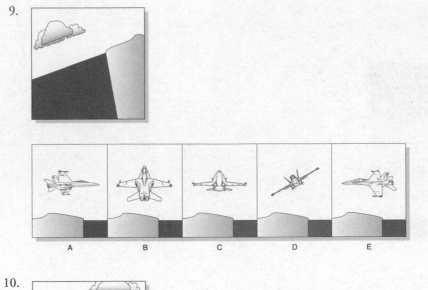

10.

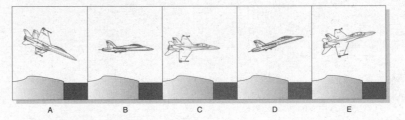

11.

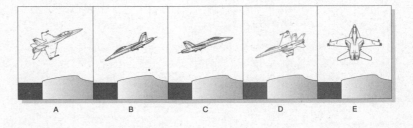

12.

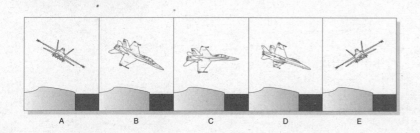

A   B   C   D   E

13.

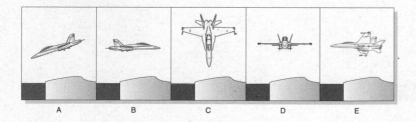

A   B   C   D   E

14.

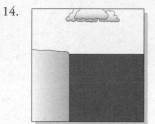

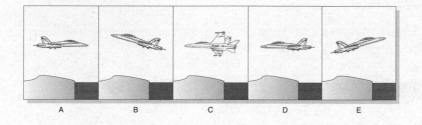

A   B   C   D   E

15.

16.

17.

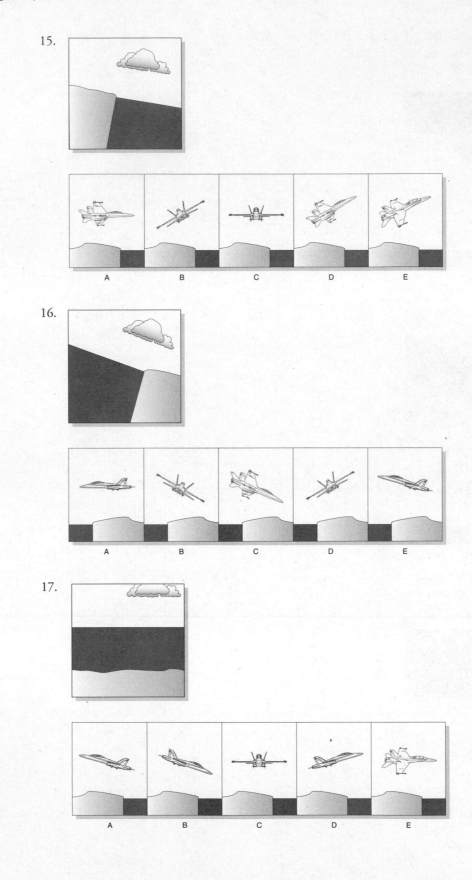

18.

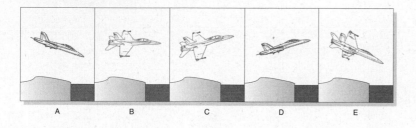

19.

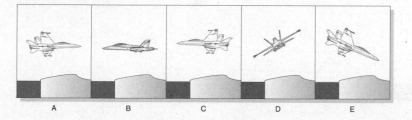

20.

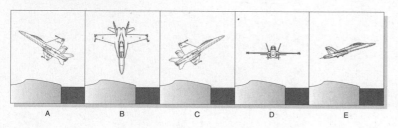

21.

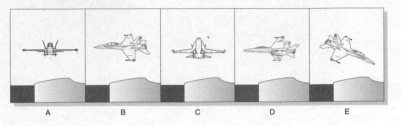

22.

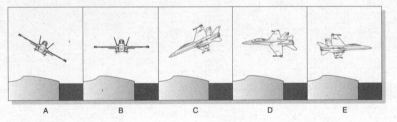

23.

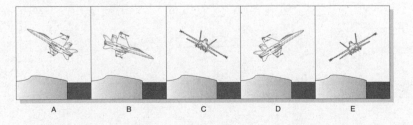

24.

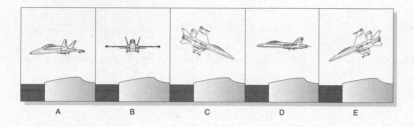

A   B   C   D   E

25.

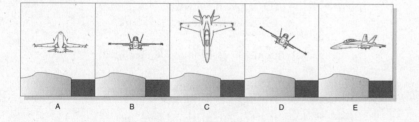

A   B   C   D   E

SUBTEST 5: AVIATION/NAUTICAL INFORMATION

1. If a fixed-wing aircraft has tricycle landing gear, it

   (A) has landing gear supporting the nose of the aircraft.
   (B) has three sets of landing gear evenly spaced under the aircraft.
   (C) has three sets of landing gear mounted closely together.
   (D) has three sets of landing gear spaced longitudinally along the fuselage.
   (E) none of the above

2. A floor or horizontal surface on a ship is called a

   (A) divider.
   (B) gangway.
   (C) deck.
   (D) spewcatcher.
   (E) bulkhead.

3. What is the nickname for the EA-6B?

   (A) Growler
   (B) Prowler
   (C) Tomcat
   (D) Hornet
   (E) Avenger

4. Who was Yuri Gagarin?

   (A) inventor of the helicopter
   (B) Father of the Navy
   (C) first man into space
   (D) first woman into space
   (E) first man to fly a jet airplane

5. The wings of an airplane design are angled upwards. This is called

   (A) armature.
   (B) angulation.
   (C) attitude of attack.
   (D) positive pitch.
   (E) dihedral.

6. Who is considered to be the Father of the Navy?

   (A) John Paul Jones
   (B) John Paul Sartre
   (C) John Paul
   (D) Albert Thayer Mahan
   (E) Thaddeus Kosczowski

7. Where is the bow of a ship?

   (A) in the back
   (B) below decks
   (C) underneath
   (D) in the front
   (E) on the left side

8. The time of 5 A.M. would be expressed using the 24-hour clock as

   (A) 0500.
   (B) 0700.
   (C) 1500.
   (D) 1700.
   (E) none of the above.

9. When a pilot pushes forward on the control stick, the elevators will

   (A) extend.
   (B) retract.
   (C) move upward.
   (D) move downward.
   (E) assume a neutral position.

10. From where is longitude measured?

    (A) the prime meridian
    (B) the equator
    (C) the international date line
    (D) Greenwich Village
    (E) the North Pole

11. If one end of a runway was numbered 10, what number would designate the other end of the same runway?

    (A) 11
    (B) 28
    (C) 12
    (D) 20
    (E) 36

12. From where is latitude measured?

    (A) the prime meridian
    (B) the equator
    (C) the international date line
    (D) Greenwich, England
    (E) the South Pole

13. Who was the first American to complete an orbital space mission?

    (A) Alan Shepard
    (B) John Glenn, Jr.
    (C) Neil Armstrong
    (D) Deke Slayton
    (E) Gus Grissom

14. What were the names, in chronological order, of the three primary American manned space programs?

    (A) Gemini, Apollo, Challenger
    (B) Dynasoar, Redstone, Saturn
    (C) Redstone, Gemini, Mercury
    (D) Mercury, Gemini, Apollo
    (E) Mercury, Apollo, Gemini

15. For the F/A-18 aircraft, what does "F/A" stand for?

    (A) fighter, advanced
    (B) fighter/attack
    (C) fueler, airborne
    (D) fighter/assault
    (E) flying arsenal

16. What is hypoxia?

    (A) too much oxygen in the bloodstream, resulting in euphoria
    (B) too little oxygen in the bloodstream, resulting in blackout
    (C) too much smallpox vaccine, resulting in mild smallpox symptoms
    (D) an early stage of rust below the waterline of a ship
    (E) a malfunction of the aircraft oxygen delivery system

17. A ship's gunwales are

    (A) the upper edges of the vessel's sides.
    (B) the mounts where machine guns are mounted.
    (C) the areas where fire can be observed.
    (D) the fire control direction center.
    (E) able to be unscrewed and dismounted if needed.

18. Above what altitude would you normally need oxygen?

    (A) 5,500 ft.
    (B) 10,000 ft.
    (C) 12,000 ft.
    (D) 14,200 ft.
    (E) 20,700 ft.

19. Who first broke the sound barrier, and in what year?

    (A) Billy Mitchell, 1942
    (B) Charles Lindbergh, 1952
    (C) Robert Goddard, 1949
    (D) Chuck Yeager, 1947
    (E) Frank Whittle, 1939

20. Who was the first man to walk on the moon?

    (A) Neil Young
    (B) Tip O'Neal
    (C) Neil Armstrong
    (D) Lance Armstrong
    (E) Edwin "Buzz" Aldrin

21. The Latin phrase *Semper Fidelis* is the motto of the

    (A) U.S. Navy.
    (B) U.S. Central Command.
    (C) U.S. Air Force.
    (D) U.S. Marine Corps.
    (E) U.S. Army.

22. Who was the first American woman in space and in what year?

    (A) Sally Wright, 1981
    (B) Sally Forth, 1985
    (C) Sally Ride, 1983
    (D) June Cleaver, 1982
    (E) Jane Thomas, 1984

23. A ship designated with a hull number starting with "CGN" is what kind of ship?

    (A) combat logistics, special weapons (nuclear)
    (B) battleship, cruise missile
    (C) carrier, nuclear-propelled
    (D) missile cruiser, nuclear-propelled
    (E) multi-purpose cruiser

24. The first conflict to see widespread use of the helicopter was the

    (A) Korean War.
    (B) Vietnam War.
    (C) Cuban Missile Crisis.
    (D) Persian Gulf War.
    (E) Second World War.

25. Aircraft position lights

    (A) should be on from dusk till dawn.
    (B) show red on the left wing.
    (C) show green on the right wing.
    (D) show white on the tail.
    (E) all of the above

ASTB #2

26. The first American spacecraft to explore the outer solar system was the

    (A) *Pioneer 1.*
    (B) *Pioneer 10.*
    (C) *Freedom 7.*
    (D) *Voyager 2.*
    (E) *Sputnik.*

27. The four types of airspeed are

    (A) instrument, calibrated, equilibrium, and true.
    (B) indicated, calculated, equivalent, and temperature-dependent.
    (C) indicated, calibrated, equivalent, and true.
    (D) instrument, calibrated, equivalent, and true.
    (E) indicated, calculated, equilibrium, and technical.

28. The airspeed indicator measures and shows the difference between

    (A) equivalent and indicated airspeed.
    (B) true airspeed and equivalent groundspeed.
    (C) above-ground altitude and altitude above mean sea level (MSL).
    (D) indicated and calculated airspeed.
    (E) impact and static pressure.

29. The typical air wing aboard a U.S. Navy aircraft carrier usually includes

    (A) one F-14 squadron, a helicopter squadron, and an E-2C squadron.
    (B) no more than two F/A-18 squadrons and at least two helicopter squadrons.
    (C) six to seven F/A-18 squadrons, as well as S-3 and EA-6B squadrons.
    (D) F/A-18, E-2C, EA-6B, S-3, and helicopter squadrons.
    (E) F/A-18, F-14, EA-6B, S-3, and helicopter squadrons.

30. A nuclear-powered aircraft carrier has what designation?

    (A) CV
    (B) CVN
    (C) CGN
    (D) CVA
    (E) CGA

SUBTEST 6: AVIATION SUPPLEMENTAL TEST

1. Above what altitude would you normally need oxygen?

    (A) 8,500 ft.
    (B) 10,000 ft.
    (C) 15,000 ft.
    (D) 20,000 ft.
    (E) 24,700 ft.

2. Who was the first American astronaut to walk in space?

    (A) Ed White
    (B) Gus Grissom
    (C) Alan Shepard
    (D) John Glenn
    (E) Deke Slayton

3. What is the difference between weight and mass?

    (A) Weight can be changed by buoyancy, but mass is relative to gravity.
    (B) Mass remains constant, but weight depends on altitude.
    (C) Weight remains constant, but mass depends on altitude.
    (D) Mass can be changed by buoyancy, but weight is relative to gravity.
    (E) There is no difference between mass and weight.

4. An experimental miniature submarine is traveling through the ocean when it develops a crack in its outer hull and pressurized air pushes out of its lower right side. In which direction must the rudder be turned for the sub to maintain its original heading?

    (A) A
    (B) B
    (C) no rudder correction is necessary
    (D) cannot tell from the information given
    (E) none of the above

5.

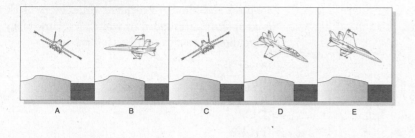

6. Mrs. H.B. drove her Volvo S70 four-door sedan from Waco to Corpus Christi at an average speed of 68 miles per hour, including two rest stops of ten minutes each. Her car, on average, gets highway mileage of 30 miles per gallon. If her car used 9.5 gallons of gas, about how many hours did she travel?

(A) 4 hr., 45 min.
(B) 3 hr., 30 min.
(C) 4 hr., 12 min.
(D) 4 hr., 2 min.
(E) none of the above

7. A naval task force is to be made up of a destroyer, a supply ship, and a submarine. If 4 destroyers, 2 supply ships, and 3 submarines are available from which to choose, how many different combinations are possible for the task force?

(A) 9
(B) 24
(C) 8
(D) 12
(E) 16

Far better it is to dare mighty things, to win glorious triumphs, even though checkered by failure, than to take rank with those poor spirits who neither enjoy much nor suffer much, because they live in the gray twilight that knows not victory nor defeat. [Theodore Roosevelt]

8. In the passage above, the phrase "take rank" means

(A) become bad-smelling.
(B) join a group.
(C) get promoted.
(D) to not be checkered.
(E) to win triumphs.

9. When a pilot pushes forward on the control stick, the elevators will

(A) extend.
(B) retract.
(C) move upward.
(D) move downward.
(E) assume a neutral position.

10. From where is longitude measured?

(A) the prime meridian
(B) the equator
(C) the international date line
(D) Greenwich Village
(E) the North Pole

11. Jaycie Marie has a 20-year term life insurance policy for $100,000. The annual premium is $12.00 per thousand. What is the total premium paid for this policy every six months?

(A) $600
(B) $1,200
(C) $100
(D) $2,400
(E) $24,000

12. Centripetal most nearly means

(A) away from a center or axis.
(B) relating to the feet.
(C) having more than 100 petals.
(D) toward a center or axis.
(E) circular.

13. An F/A-18 is flying a circular or "racetrack" orbit around a 4,000-meter-high mountaintop. Assume the pilot flies a perfectly circular course. What is the distance in kilometers he travels each orbit if it is 40 kilometers from the mountaintop to the outer edge of his orbit? (use $\pi = \frac{22}{7}$)

    (A) 13 km.
    (B) 25 km.
    (C) 126 km.
    (D) 251 km.
    (E) 503 km.

14. When in the down (extended) position, wing flaps provide

    (A) increased lift and decreased drag.
    (B) decreased lift and increased drag.
    (C) increased lift and increased drag.
    (D) increased lift only.
    (E) decreased wing camber (curvature).

15. Municipal airports often provide at least one extended or unusually long runway to facilitate the take-off of

    (A) heavily loaded aircraft in calm conditions.
    (B) lightly-loaded aircraft taking off in a crosswind.
    (C) small aircraft in rainy weather.
    (D) aircraft with higher than average climbing speeds.
    (E) rotary-wing aircraft in trail formation.

16. The small hinged section on the elevator of most airplanes is known as the

    (A) aileron.
    (B) flap.
    (C) stabilator.
    (D) elevon.
    (E) trim tab.

17. The rearward retarding force on the airplane known as drag is opposed by

    (A) lift.
    (B) thrust.
    (C) weight.
    (D) laminar air flow.
    (E) compression.

18. At night, airport taxiways are identified by omni-directional edge lights that are _____ in color.

    (A) red
    (B) white
    (C) alternating red and white
    (D) blue
    (E) green

19. Envisage most nearly means

    (A) conceive.
    (B) wrap around.
    (C) articulate.
    (D) designate.
    (E) paint one's face.

20. A floor is made up of hexagonal tiles, some of which are black and some of which are white. Every black tile is completely surrounded by white tiles. How many white tiles are there around each black tile?

    (A) 4
    (B) 5
    (C) 6
    (D) 8
    (E) 12

21. The straight line joining the ends of the mean camber line is called the

    (A) lower camber curve.
    (B) mean airfoil throughpoint.
    (C) wing chord.
    (D) angle of attack.
    (E) relative lift threshold line.

22. The wheels below are connected by a belt as shown. If the larger wheel makes two revolutions, how many revolutions will the smaller wheel make?

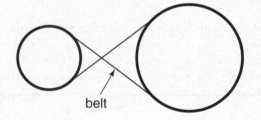

belt

    (A) less than one
    (B) one
    (C) two
    (D) more than two
    (E) none of the above

23. In the diagram above, if the wheel on the left turns counterclockwise, which way will the wheel on the right turn?

    (A) clockwise
    (B) counterclockwise
    (C) unable to tell from the information given

ASTB #2

24.

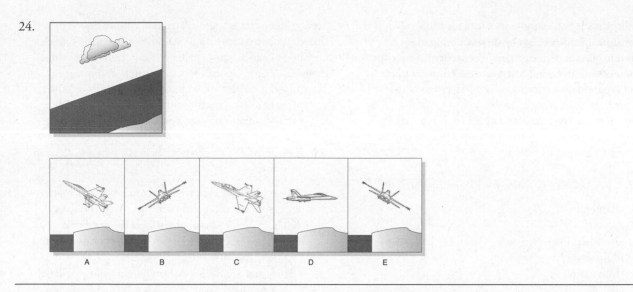

---

25. If two resistors and a battery are arranged as shown in each circuit, which circuit arrangement has less resistance?

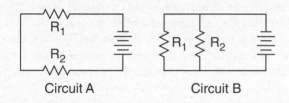

(A) circuit A
(B) circuit B
(C) both circuits have the same resistance
(D) insufficient information to answer

26. Two 30-lb. blocks are attached to the ceiling using ropes, as shown below. Which of the following statements is true?

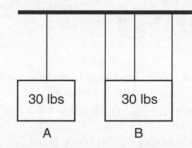

(A) All the ropes are under the same amount of tension.

(B) The rope holding block A is under $\frac{1}{3}$ of the tension of the ropes holding block B.

(C) The ropes supporting block B are under $\frac{1}{3}$ of the tension of the rope holding block A.

(D) The rope supporting block A is under twice the tension of the ropes holding block B.

(E) The ropes supporting block B are under $\frac{1}{6}$ of the tension of the rope holding block A.

A credibility check has its roots in a leader's history as it is known by other people; it has to do with reputation. Reputation is human disincentive—the security we pledge to guarantee the performance of our obligations as leaders, friends, colleagues, and citizens. It is what supports the (usually natural) human instinct to *want* to trust. Reputation is to be cherished and cared for—a damaged one lowers people's perceptions of a leader's worth and hence their motivation to follow.

27. In the passage above, what word is used incorrectly?

(A) collateral
(B) security
(C) cherished
(D) obligations
(E) disincentive

28. If block A, on which the lever is resting, is moved farther away from block B,

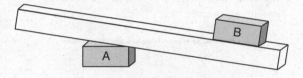

(A) there will be no change in the effort required to lift block B to the same height.
(B) it will be harder to lift block B but it will go higher.
(C) it will be easier to lift block B and it will go higher.
(D) it will be harder to lift block B and it will not be lifted to the same height.
(E) it will be easier to lift block B but it will not be lifted as high.

Leaders must create an organizational culture driven by actual, shared values that are calls to action, not just high-sounding platitudes. Leaders must challenge assumptions, take courageous risks, and inspire others by example and integrity. They must, however, still be humble, give credit to others, and follow through. In this way they create a legacy that shows the organization's members what "right" looks like.

29. The author of this passage believes that a leadership position

(A) is a reward for previous hard work and service.
(B) is founded on maintaining current policies.
(C) is a time to finally let others do the work.
(D) is an obligation to challenge the status quo and take measured risks.
(E) shows organizational members what privilege looks like.

Carthage first came into conflict with the Romans when the latter started subduing their Italian neighbors to the south including Sicily, which Carthage regarded as within its sphere of influence. Rome's confrontation with Pyrrhus, also an enemy of Carthage, weakened its position on the island. In 265 B.C. the two powers found themselves at war over it, and the war rapidly extended, by both land and sea, until the Carthaginians had to concede defeat and let the Romans control Sicily. While Rome added Corsica and Sardinia to these beginnings of its overseas empire, and made its first inroads into the land of the Gauls, Carthage responded by campaigning along the Mediterranean coast of Spain against cities that were Rome's allies. The siege of Saguntum in 219 B.C. brought war on again; this one lasted for seventeen years, ended in Carthaginian defeat only after Rome had almost lost, and established the Romans as the dominant power in the Mediterranean area.

30. What area were the Romans and Carthaginians fighting over in 219 B.C.?

(A) Gaul
(B) Sicily
(C) Carthage
(D) Saguntum
(E) Spain

31. <u>Conflagration</u> most nearly means

   (A) a secret or conspiratorial message
   (B) a seizure by a higher authority
   (C) the joining together of two verbs of the same tense
   (D) a large and destructive fire
   (E) opponents moving toward each other in order to fight

32. Water flows into a water tower at a rate of 120 gallons per hour and flows out at the rate of two gallons per minute. The level of water in the tower will

   (A) remain the same.
   (B) lower.
   (C) rise.
   (D) rise initially, then lower.
   (E) lower initially, then rise.

33. Aircraft carrier battle groups, as they travel the world's oceans, conduct exercises, and sometimes merely cruise back and forth in a certain area, are a visible symbol of _____ for America's allies and _____ for potential adversaries.

   (A) degradation, deterrence
   (B) friendliness, calmness
   (C) support, deterrence
   (D) technocentrism, colonialism
   (E) deterrence, reminder

34. <u>Scrutiny</u> most nearly means

   (A) a point of conscience or ethics.
   (B) obligation.
   (C) revolt of a ship's crew.
   (D) careful inspection.
   (E) a room adjoining the kitchen.

ANSWERS AND EXPLANATIONS

Subtest 1: Math Skills

	✔	✘		✔	✘		✔	✘		✔	✘		✔	✘
1. C			7. D			13. A			19. B			25. B		
2. A			8. D			14. D			20. D			26. C		
3. D			9. A			15. B			21. C			27. C		
4. A			10. B			16. A			22. A			28. A		
5. B			11. E			17. A			23. B			29. B		
6. D			12. C			18. C			24. B			30. B		

1. **C** First, total up all the withholding amounts.

$$\$27.75 + \$5.65 + \$12.87 = \$46.27$$

Jonathan's net pay is his salary for the pay period minus the total of all the withholdings.

$$\text{Net pay} = \$350.00 - \$46.27 = \$303.73$$

2. **A** Because the certificate and its enlargement are similar (i.e., proportional) figures, the lengths will have the same ratio as the widths; if the length is increased by a given proportion, then the width will be increased by the same proportion or percentage of its original size.

$$\frac{\text{length of original}}{\text{length of enlargement}} = \frac{\text{width of original}}{\text{width of enlargement}}$$

$$\frac{9}{12} = \frac{6}{\text{width of enlargement}}$$

To solve this, cross-multiply the measurements, using x for the one you don't know.

$$9 \times x = 12 \times 6$$
$$9x = 72$$
$$\frac{9x}{9} = \frac{72}{9}$$
$$x = 8$$

The width of the enlarged certificate is 8 inches.

3. **D** There is a standard equation to calculate compound interest, but you don't need to remember it to work this problem. You can work it as a simple multiplication problem (interest rate times the amount in the CD at that time) and repeat it for each time period in the problem (in this case only two years).

$$\$10,000 \times .06 = 600 \text{ (first year's interest)}$$
$$(10,000 + 600) \times .06 = \text{second year's interest}$$
$$10,600 \times .06 = 636 \text{ (second year's interest)}$$

So, the total interest—make sure you pay attention to what the question asks for—for the two years is $600 + $636 = $1,236.

4. **A** There are 16 ounces in a pound. Therefore, if two pounds of jellybeans cost $3.20, then one pound costs $1.60. The cost of one ounce is ($1.60 ÷ 16) = $0.10, so three ounces cost 3 × $0.10 = $0.30.

5. **B** We are given a lot of numbers and information here, so the first thing to do is identify what we need and what we don't. It doesn't matter what model of car Mrs. H.B. drove, and it doesn't matter that she stopped twice for 10 minutes each, since we are given her average speed for the trip. So, the way to attack this problem is

7 gallons of gas × 30 miles per gallon = 210 miles traveled
210 miles ÷ 60 miles per hour = 3.5 hours

6. **D** From 7:45 A.M. to 5:30 P.M. with an hour off for lunch is 8 hours and 45 minutes, or 8.75 hours. Multiply Mike's work hours by his hourly rate.

$$8.75 \times \$17.50 = \$153.13 \text{ (one day's salary)}$$

7. **D** The number of games won is 70% (or 0.70) of the number of games played, 40.

$$\text{Number of games won} = 0.70(40) = 28$$

The number of games lost is the total number played minus the number won.

$$\text{Number of games lost} = 40 - 28 = 12$$

8. **D** The time of arrival is 2 hours and 55 minutes after the departure time of 3:50 P.M. By 4:00 P.M., the flight has taken 10 minutes of the total flight time of 2 hours and 55 minutes. 2 hours and 45 minutes remain, and 2 hours and 45 minutes after 4:00 P.M. is 6:45 P.M.

9. **A** There are 16 oz. in 1 lb. Therefore, 4 of the 4-oz. candy bars will make 1 pound. A 3-lb. package will hold 3 times 4 or 12 bars.

10. **B** Find the relationship between each pair of successive numbers in the series. It is helpful to change $3\frac{1}{2}$ to $3\frac{1}{6}$ in order to see the relationships. Each term of the series is obtained by adding $\frac{4}{6}$ to the preceding term. The fifth term is $5\frac{3}{6}$ or $5\frac{1}{2}$.

11. **E** First add the prices of the three items ordered to get the cost of the meal before the tax.

$$\$12.50 + \$3.50 + \$1.25 = \$17.25$$

The tax is 8% (or 0.08) of the cost of the meal.

$$0.08 \times \$17.25 = \$1.38$$

12. **C** There are four quarts in one gallon; therefore, a 55-gallon drum holds 4×55 quarts.

$$4 \times 55 \text{ quarts} = 220 \text{ quarts}$$

If each can holds two quarts, the number of cans filled is 220 divided by 2.

$$220 \div 2 = 110 \text{ cans}$$

13. **A** Since it takes 45 minutes to finish nine spindles, it takes five minutes to finish each spindle ($45 \div 9 = 5$). So, the number of minutes it takes to finish 96 spindles is

$$5 \times 96 = 480$$
$$480 \text{ minutes} \div 60 \text{ minutes} = 8 \text{ hours}$$

14. **D** The perimeter, 40 feet, is the sum of the lengths of all three sides. The sum of the lengths of the two equal sides is the difference between the perimeter and the length of the third side. The sum of the lengths of two equal sides

$$= 40 \text{ ft.} - 13 \text{ ft., 2 in.}$$
$$= 39 \text{ ft., 12 in.} - 13 \text{ ft., 2 in.}$$
$$= 26 \text{ ft., 10 in.}$$

The length of one side is obtained by dividing the sum by 2. The length of one equal side

$$= 13 \text{ ft., 5 in.}$$

15. **B** Since 3 feet = 1 yard, convert the length and width to yards by dividing their dimensions in feet by 3. The area of a rectangle is the product of its length and width.

Area = $7 \times 13 = 91$ sq. yds.

The cost for the entire lawn is obtained by multiplying the area in square yards by the cost per square yard.

$$91 \times \$.40 = \$36.40$$

16. **A** The perimeter of a rectangle is equal to the sum of the two lengths and two widths. If 15 feet, 6 inches ($15\frac{1}{2}$ feet) equal 1 length, then

$$2 \times 15\frac{1}{2} = 31 \text{ ft. (2 lengths)}$$
$$40 - 31 = 9 \text{ ft. (both widths)}$$
$$9 \div 2 = 4\frac{1}{2} \text{ ft. (1 width)}$$

17. **A** First add both partners' shares together to find the value of one share ($5 + 4 = 9$), then divide the total profit by nine: $\$63,000 \div 9 = \$7,000$. Then multiply the value of one share by the number of shares held by the partner who holds the most shares to find out how much he gets: $\$7,000 \times 5 = \$35,000$.

18. **C** The current (recently increased) price is 4% more than the previous price, so it is 104% of that amount; we want to find out what 100% (the old price) was. Set up a proportion with x representing the unknown original price over 100 (for its percentage) and the new price over 104, then cross-multiply and solve for x:

$$\frac{x}{100} = \frac{17.16}{104}$$
$$104x = 17.16 \times 100$$
$$104x = 1716$$
$$\frac{104x}{104} = \frac{1716}{104}$$
$$x = 16.50$$

The original price was $16.50.

19. **B** First find the total number of garments produced in a day by all nine workers:

$$(5 \times 6) + (3 \times 4) + 12 = 30 + 12 + 12 = 54$$

Now divide the total garments produced per day (54) by the total number of workers (9) to find out that the average number of garments produced per day per worker is 6.

20. **D** After driving the first two hours at 45 mph, Travis has covered 90 miles (45 mph × 2 hours = 90 miles). Subtract this from the total distance of 255 and we see that he has 165 miles remaining to go in three hours (five hours total trip time minus the two hours he already drove). Divide 165 miles by those three hours and we see that Travis must travel at 55 mph to make it to his destination on time.

21. **C** Break down the contractor's costs by applying the fractional costs to the total:

Masonry materials: $300,000 × $\frac{1}{10}$ = $30,000

Lumber and carpentry: $300,000 × $\frac{1}{3}$ = $100,000

Plumbing and heating: $300,000 × $\frac{1}{5}$ = $60,000

Electrical and lighting: $300,000 × $\frac{1}{6}$ = $50,000

Total costs $240,000

Subtract the contractor's costs ($240,000) from his bid ($300,000) and we see that his profit will be $60,000.

22. **A** The key to getting the right answer here is careful reading: the discounts are *successive*—they follow one after the other. We apply the first discount of 20% by multiplying $325 by 20% or 0.2, reaching the intermediate step answer of $65, and then subtracting that $65 from the $325 original price to get a price of $260 after the first discount. Now do the same thing for the second discount of 30%:

$260 × 0.3 = $78
$260 − $78 = $182

So we see that the final price paid by the customer after two successive discounts is $182.

23. **B** First find the price *per quart* at the regular price (notice that the regular price is $1.99 for *two* cans, not just one). $1.99 divided by two is $0.995; hold onto that and don't round it off yet. Now, for the sale price *per quart*, divide $5.43 by the six quart cans to get $0.905 per quart. Subtract the sale price *per quart* from the regular price *per quart* and we see that the savings on the sale is $0.09 per quart.

24. **B** First find how much she makes for her regular 40-hour work week: 40 × $7.20 = $288. Now, for the three hours beyond 40 that she worked, her pay per hour is 1.5 × $7.20 = $10.80. Add the overtime pay for three hours (3 × $10.80 = $32.40) to her regular pay of $288 and we see that $288 + $32.40 = $320.40.

25. **B** Since light rays are parallel to each other and the angle from the light source (the sun) would be the same, the shadows will be proportionate to the height of the tree. Set up a proportion where x is the height of the second tree:

$$\frac{8}{36} = \frac{6}{x}$$
$$8x = 36 × 6$$
$$8x = 216$$
$$x = 27$$

The height of the second tree is 27 ft.

26. **C** All you have to do here is substitute the values for *a* and *b* listed and follow the order of operations:

$5a2b − 3ab2$
$(5 × 7 × 2 × 4) − (3 × 7 × 4 × 2)$
$(280) − (168) = 112$

27. **C** The definition of π is the circumference of a circle divided by the length of its diameter.

28. **A** The probability of a particular event occurring is the number of favorable outcomes divided by the total possible number of outcomes. Since there are three possible infantrymen to choose, there are three possible favorable outcomes for choosing an infantryman. Since a choice may be made from among three infantrymen, two artillerymen, and five tank crewmen, there are 3 + 2 + 5, or 10, possible outcomes in total. The probability of choosing an infantryman is, therefore, $\frac{3}{10}$.

29. **B** There are four possible choices for the destroyer. Each of these choices may be coupled with any of the two choices for the supply ship. Each such destroyer-supply ship combination may in turn be coupled with any of the three possible choices for the submarine. Thus, there are 4 × 2 × 3, or 24, different combinations possible.

30. **B** The volume of a cylinder is equal to the product of its height and the area of its base. The base is a circle. The area of a circle is $π r^2$, where $π = \frac{22}{7}$ and r is the radius. Since the diameter is 2 inches, the radius (which is one-half the diameter) is 1 inch.

A = Area of the base
A = $π(r^2)$
A = $\frac{22}{7}(1^2)$
A = $\frac{22}{7}$

V = Volume of the cylinder
h = height of the cylinder
V = A · h
V = $\frac{22}{7}$ sq. in. · 7 in.
V = 22 cu. in.

Subtest 2: Reading Skills

	✔	✘		✔	✘		✔	✘		✔	✘		✔	✘
1. B			7. C			13. E			19. E			25. B		
2. D			8. C			14. D			20. C			26. B		
3. B			9. A			15. C			21. E			27. C		
4. D			10. D			16. E			22. D					
5. A			11. A			17. B			23. E					
6. C			12. D			18. B			24. A					

1. **B** According to this passage, soldiers **have to communicate first before they get anything done.** The passage states that "speech [communication] is the vital spark in all maneuver" and "speech is the beginning of the urge to get something done."

2. **D** According to this passage, **Task Force Lynch linked up with the 31st Infantry but suffered a friendly fire casualty.**

3. **B** Anomaly most nearly means **an abnormality or irregularity**. "Bitter hostility or open hatred" is *animosity*; "a collection of songs or stories" is an *anthology*; another word for "boldness" is *audacity*; and a synonym for "indifference" is *apathy*.

4. **D** Cacophony most nearly means **a jarring, discordant sound or noise.** "Bad handwriting" is *cacography*; and a "winged staff symbolizing the medical profession" is a *caduceus* (it also usually has two serpents twined around the staff).

5. **A** Xenophobe most nearly means **a person who is afraid of foreigners or strangers.** A person who has a deep hated of women is a *misogynist*; and a light that flashes at rapid, predetermined intervals is a *strobe* light.

6. **C** In the passage, the word **derided** is used incorrectly. **Derided** refers to treating something with ridicule or contemptuous humor. The passage makes the point strongly that a good reputation is something that is worth a lot, especially to a leader.

7. **C** The 101st Airborne Division was holding out at Bastogne **to deny the Germans an important crossroads.**

8. **C** The German major who approached the American lines with a German surrender demand had to tell his commander that **the Americans would not surrender.** The passage states that the American slang reply was clarified for the German officer as "decidedly not affirmative."

9. **A** Incentive most nearly means **a motivation or benefit for doing something.** Someone who is "capable of producing new ideas" could be said to be *inventive* or *innovative*; something that is "copied or adapted from something else" is *derivative*; someone who is "moderate or cautious" could be said to be *conservative*; and someone who is "unaware of the thoughts or feelings of others" would be *insensitive*.

10. **D** The passage explains that Galileo's experiment showed that **balls of differing weights roll downhill at the same rate.** The passage casts doubt on whether Galileo actually dropped different weights from the Leaning Tower of Pisa, which rules out choice **C**.

11. **A** The gist of the passage is that **every citizen has an obligation to do what they can to make their country better.** It states that "the least considerable man...has an interest equal to the proudest nobleman...and is equally called upon..."

12. **D** *Countenance* in this context most nearly means **consider** or agree with. In a different context, *countenance* does in fact refer to one's face or expression, but not here.

13. **E** The author of this passage believes that **the student who defends himself should be viewed differently than the attacker**. The passage states that "the biggest problem happens when the student who is attacked gets swept up in the punishment net along with the one who started the fight," and "it is morally wrong to teach our kids that the attacked person is invariably as much in the wrong as the attacker."

14. **D** Posterity most nearly means **future descendants or generations**. The "back side of an object or person" would be the *posterior*.

15. **C** According to this passage, the reader can infer that the author **believes that acting on incomplete information is often necessary.** The passage states that "the quest for perfectly complete…information results in…the inability to make a decision until you have all the information, *which is never going to happen* [emphasis added]." Therefore, we can conclude that the author believes the opposite, giving us our answer.

16. **E** Quandary most nearly means **deep uncertainty about a choice; a dilemma**. A swampy area that impedes the movement of people or vehicles can be called a *quagmire*; a stanza of four lines is a *quatrain*; and something consisting of four parts can be called *quarternary*.

17. **B** The passage *primarily* discusses **early steps toward public education in Texas**. The passage touches on how many acres are in a league, as well as the fact that Texas was a republic and then became a state—but those are not the *primary* points made in the passage. Although it would be relevant, the passage does not even mention steps taken by private organizations to improve public education, nor opposition to public education in the Republic of Texas.

18. **B** "There is no room in this country for hyphenated Americanism. The one absolutely certain way of bringing this nation to ruin, of preventing all possibility of its continuing to be a nation at all, would be to permit it to become a tangle of squabbling nationalities." [Theodore Roosevelt] It is clear in this quote—both from the context and the other references to the "nation"—that President Roosevelt was speaking of the entire **country** or nation. Of the choices given, **country** is the only one that makes sense in the context given.

19. **E** The author's *main* point in this passage is that education (resulting in a "smart man") enables us to do what we have to do at the appropriate time, whether we want to or not. The other choices make valid points, but they are not the main point of this passage.

20. **C** Discernment most nearly means **insight** or **the ability to see things clearly**.

21. **E** The author of the passage maintains that the three main reasons why the British victory in North America was "certain" were **more people, better geographical position,** and **better leaders**.

22. **D** Chlorophyll uses **sunlight, carbon dioxide, and water** to make carbohydrates.

23. **E** The best remedy for frostbite is **not addressed in this passage**.

24. **A** The passage encourages the reader to **make the effort to accomplish challenging goals**.

25. **B** Leaders demonstrate that they value other people when they listen to them, trust them, and are **receptive** and willing to listen to reports of unproductive or unpleasant information—even when it involves the leader himself. **Receptive** is the only choice that makes sense in the context given.

26. **B** The Fairness Doctrine was **recognized as antagonistic to freedom of expression** in 1987 and is no longer public policy.

27. **C** "If a nation expects to be ignorant and free, in a state of **civilization**, it expects what never was and never will be." [Thomas Jefferson] This is the only choice that makes sense in the given context.

Subtest 3: Mechanical Comprehension

	✔	✘		✔	✘		✔	✘		✔	✘		✔	✘
1. C			7. A			13. A			19. B			25. D		
2. D			8. B			14. A			20. D			26. C		
3. A			9. B			15. B			21. C			27. C		
4. E			10. A			16. B			22. B			28. B		
5. C			11. A			17. C			23. A			29. B		
6. B			12. A			18. A			24. B			30. E		

1. **C** Gear A will turn **15** times. Counting the number of teeth in the two gears tells us that the mechanical advantage of the larger gear A is 3:2, since gear A has 15 teeth and gear B has 10 teeth. Knowing that and knowing that gear B will make 10 revolutions, we divide 10 by 2 to get 5, then multiply that 5 by 3 to get 15.

2. **D** We are not told the sizes of the two wheels, but we can see that one is larger than the other. If the two wheels are connected by a belt, the small wheel will be forced to turn faster and complete more turns than the larger wheel.

3. **A** If the wheel on the left turns counterclockwise, the wheel on the right will turn **clockwise**.

4. **E It will be easier to lift block B but it will not be lifted as high.** If block A under the lever beam is moved toward block B on top of the lever beam, the moment for a particular force exerted will increase, since the fulcrum is now further from the force; this will make block B easier to lift. However, the height to which block B on the end of the lever beam can be raised decreases the closer block A is moved toward block B.

5. **C** The greater the difference between the number of teeth of the two meshed gears, the greater the torque or mechanical advantage

6. **B** Recruit Highspeed will arrive on the far bank **downstream of his departure point**, because he will be pushed downstream while he swims at right angles to the banks. If he wanted to arrive directly across the stream from his departure point, he would have to swim upstream at a sufficient angle to compensate for the force of the water pushing him downstream.

7. **A** By rotating clockwise, pulley C will cause pulley B to rotate counterclockwise, which will in turn cause pulley A to rotate **clockwise**.

8. **B** Pulley B will rotate the fastest because it is the smallest.

9. **B** Water tower B will be able to provide the most water, because its outlet pipe is near the bottom and can let almost all of its contents out, while the outlet pipe on tower A is near the top and will stop providing water as soon as A's water level drops below where the pipe leaves the cistern.

10. **A** The bullet will have its highest velocity at the point where it **leaves the muzzle** of the rifle. After that, gravity and friction will combine to continually slow it down until it hits its target.

11. **A** When the plug is removed, water will flow **into the tube** to equalize the water level both inside and outside the tube.

12. **A** The string holding the 10-pound weight exerts more pull; the fact that that string is longer makes no difference.

13. **A** The force required to balance the lever shown would be **15 pounds** because the sum of the moments on each side of the fulcrum must be zero. To calculate this, we would set it up like this:

$$F \times d = F \times d$$

Where F is the force or weight involved and d is the distance from the fulcrum. Therefore,

$$(5 \text{ lb.} \times 10 \text{ ft.}) + (10 \text{ lb.} \times 5 \text{ ft.}) = F \times 10 \text{ ft.}$$
$$50 \text{ ft.-lb.} + 50 \text{ ft.-lb.} = F \times 10 \text{ ft.}$$
$$100 \text{ ft.-lb.}/10 \text{ ft.} = F$$
$$10 \text{ lb.} = F$$

14. **A** The air pushing out of the crack in the hull will tend to push the rear of the sub to the left and hence the nose of the sub will veer to the right. To compensate for this, a left rudder correction must be used.

15. **B Valves A, B, and D must be open for the tank to fill halfway and maintain that level.** Water flows in through valve A (so any choice not including valve A is a non-starter), and flows out when the tank is half full through valve B—but, for that water to leave the system, valve D must also be open.

16. **B** The length of time taken for one swing depends on the length of the string, not the weight.

17. **C** Both would take the same amount of time to make one swing; the length of time taken for one swing depends on the length of the string, not the weight at the end of it.

18. **A Circuit A would have the greater resistance.** As the electrical current makes its trip from one polarity of the battery to the other on circuit A, it has no choice but to pass through two resistors. However, on circuit B, the current will follow the path of least resistance and take a "shortcut" that only passes through one resistor.

19. **B** When two or more act in such a way that their combination has a net effect of zero (i.e., they cancel each other out), the condition is called **equilibrium.**

20. **D** The descent of a paratrooper under his parachute is **primarily** affected by **drag** (air resistance) **and gravity**.

21. **C** There are three ways of transferring heat from one place to another: conduction, convection, and **radiation**.

22. **B** Putting salt into the water increases the specific gravity of the solution and lowers its freezing point.

23. **A** Changing a liquid to a gas or vapor is called **evaporation**. Boiling is one method of accomplishing this process.

24. **B** Heating a closed container of boiling water increases the pressure of the water vapor (steam) inside the container and **increases** the temperature of the water.

25. **D** The largest pulley will turn the slowest.

26. **C** Compressing the air in a closed space will **decrease the volume and raise the temperature**. The diesel engine—which does not use a spark plug—is an example of this principle. As a piston moves up on its compression stroke, air in the cylinder is compressed, and then ignition takes place when fuel is injected into the cylinder. The increased temperature of the compressed air provides the heat needed for combustion, so no spark plug is needed.

27. **C** When two magnetic objects have opposite poles facing each other, they will attract each other.

28. **B Mass remains constant, but the weight of an object depends on its altitude**—or, said differently, its distance from the gravitational pull of the earth.

29. **B** The water will flow fastest through the narrowest sections.

30. **E** Static electricity is definitely not theoretical, and is also neither AC nor DC—hence its accurately descriptive name, *static* electricity.

Subtest 4: Spatial Apperception

	✔	✘		✔	✘		✔	✘		✔	✘		✔	✘
1. A			6. C			11. B			16. D			21. B		
2. E			7. C			12. A			17. B			22. E		
3. D			8. A			13. B			18. C			23. B		
4. E			9. D			14. C			19. C			24. A		
5. E			10. D			15. B			20. E			25. D		

Answer	Pitch	Bank	Heading	Answer	Pitch	Bank	Heading
1. A	climbing	left	out to sea	14. C	diving	wings level	coastline right
2. E	climbing	right	out to sea	15. B	level flight	left	coastline left
3. D	diving	left	out to sea	16. D	level flight	left	coastline left
4. E	diving	wings level	out to sea	17. B	diving	wings level	out to sea
5. E	level flight	right	coastline left	18. C	climbing	right	out to sea
6. C	level flight	wings level	coastline left	19. C	level flight	right	out to sea
7. C	climbing	left	out to sea	20. E	climbing	wings level	out to sea
8. A	diving	right	out to sea	21. B	level flight	left	out to sea
9. D	level flight	right	coastline right	22. E	level flight	left	out to sea
10. D	climbing	wings level	out to sea	23. B	diving	left	out to sea
11. B	diving	wings level	out to sea	24. A	level flight	wings level	out to sea at an angle
12. A	level flight	wings level	out to sea	25. D	level flight	left	coastline right
13. B	diving	right	out to sea				

Subtest 5: Aviation/Nautical Information

	✔	✘		✔	✘		✔	✘		✔	✘		✔	✘
1. A			7. D			13. B			19. D			25. E		
2. C			8. A			14. D			20. C			26. B		
3. B			9. D			15. B			21. D			27. C		
4. C			10. A			16. B			22. C			28. E		
5. E			11. B			17. A			23. D			29. D		
6. A			12. B			18. B			24. A			30. B		

ASTB #2

1. **A** If a fixed-wing aircraft has tricycle landing gear, it **has landing gear supporting the nose of the aircraft.**

2. **C** A floor or horizontal surface on a ship is called a **deck.**

3. **B** The official nickname for the EA-6B is the **Prowler.**

4. **C** Yuri Gagarin, a Soviet cosmonaut, was the **first man into space** in 1961.

5. **E** When the wings of an airplane design are angled upwards, it is called **dihedral.**

6. **A** **John Paul Jones** is considered to be the Father of the U.S. Navy.

7. **D** The bow of a ship is the most forward part, i.e., the front.

8. **A** The time of 5 A.M. would be expressed using the 24-hour clock as **0500.**

9. **D** When the pilot pushes forward on the control stick, the elevators will **move downward**, causing the nose to pitch down, following which the aircraft usually descends.

10. **A** Longitude is measured from the **prime meridian** in Greenwich, England.

11. **B** If one end of a runway was numbered 10 (meaning its orientation was 100 degrees by the compass), the other end of the same runway would be numbered 28 for 280 degrees.

12. **B** Latitude is measured from the **equator.**

13. **B** The first American to complete an orbital space mission was **John Glenn, Jr.** Alan Shepard was the first American into space, but his mission was suborbital (i.e., his capsule did not travel a complete orbit around the earth).

14. **D** The three primary American manned space programs, in chronological order, were **Mercury, Gemini, and Apollo.**

15. **B** The dual-role F/A-18 Hornet and SuperHornet are designated as **fighter/attack** aircraft.

16. **B** Hypoxia is **too little oxygen in the bloodstream, resulting in blackout.**

17. **A** A ship's gunwales are **the upper edges of the vessel's sides.**

18. **B** You would normally need oxygen if you were going to fly above **10,000 feet.**

19. **D** The first man to verifiably break the sound barrier was **Chuck Yeager** in the Bell X-1 rocketplane, in **1947.**

20. **C** **Neil Armstrong** was the first man to walk on the moon, July 21, 1969.

21. **D** The Latin phrase *Semper Fidelis* ("Always Faithful") is the motto of the **U.S. Marine Corps.**

22. **C** The first American woman in space was **Sally Ride** in **1983.**

23. **D** A ship designated with a hull number starting with "CGN" is a **guided missile cruiser, nuclear-propelled.**

24. **A** The first conflict to see widespread use of the helicopter was the **Korean War**, where the helicopter first began to be used for medical evacuation and command and control.

25. **E** Aircraft position lights should be on from dusk till dawn and show red on the left wing, green on the right, and white on the tail (**all of the above**).

26. **B** The first American spacecraft to explore the outer solar system was the **Pioneer 10.**

27. **C** The four types of airspeed are: **indicated, calibrated, equivalent, and true.**

28. **E** The airspeed indicator is a sensitive differential pressure gauge that measures and promptly shows the difference between *pitot* (impact) pressure, and **static pressure**, the undisturbed atmospheric pressure at level flight.

29. **D** The typical air wing aboard a U.S. Navy aircraft carrier usually contains three to four F/A-18 squadrons, one S-3 squadron, one EA-6B squadron, one E-2C squadron, and one helicopter squadron.

30. **B** A nuclear-powered aircraft carrier has a **CVN** designation starting its hull number.

ASTB #2

Subtest 6: Aviation Supplemental Test

	✔	✘		✔	✘		✔	✘		✔	✘		✔	✘
1. B			8. B			15. A			22. D			29. D		
2. A			9. D			16. E			23. A			30. D		
3. B			10. A			17. B			24. A			31. D		
4. A			11. A			18. D			25. B			32. A		
5. A			12. D			19. A			26. C			33. C		
6. C			13. D			20. C			27. E			34. D		
7. B			14. C			21. C			28. B					

1. **B** When flying in an aircraft, you would normally need oxygen above **10,000 ft.**

2. **A Ed White** was the first American to walk in space.

3. **B** Mass remains constant, but the weight of an object depends on its altitude—or, said differently, its distance from the gravitational pull of the earth.

4. **A** The air pushing out of the crack in the hull will tend to push the rear of the sub to the left; therefore, the nose of the sub will veer to the right. To compensate for this, a left rudder correction must be used.

Answer	**Pitch**	**Bank**	**Direction**
5. **A**	level flight	right bank	coastline left

6. **C** We are given a lot of numbers and information here, so the first thing to do is identify what we need and what we don't. It doesn't matter what model of car Mrs. H.B. drove, and it doesn't matter that she stopped twice for ten minutes each, since we are given her average speed for the trip. So, the way to attack this problem is

$$9.5 \text{ gals. of gas} \times 30 \text{ miles per gal.} =$$
$$285 \text{ miles traveled}$$

$$285 \text{ miles} \div 68 \text{ miles per hr.} =$$
$$4.2 \text{ hrs.} = 4 \text{ hr., } 12 \text{ min.}$$

7. **B** There are four possible choices for the destroyer. Each of these choices may be coupled with any of the two choices for the supply ship. Each such destroyer-supply ship combination may in turn be coupled with any of the three possible choices for the submarine. Thus, there are $4 \times 2 \times 3$, or 24, different combinations possible.

8. **B** In the passage above, the phrase "take rank" means to **join a group**, as in when one becomes part of a military formation standing in ranks or some orderly arrangement.

9. **D** When the pilot pushes forward on the control stick, the elevators will **move downward**, causing the nose to pitch down, following which the aircraft usually descends.

10. **A** Longitude is measured from the **prime meridian** in Greenwich, England.

11. **A** There are 100 units of $1,000 in $100,000. Thus, Jaycie Marie pays $100 \times \$12$ (or $1,200) every year in premiums, or $100 every month. Therefore, every six months, Jaycie Marie pays $\frac{1}{2}$ of $1,200 (or six times $100), which equals $600.

12. **D** <u>Centripetal</u> most nearly means **toward a center or axis.**

13. **D** The formula for the circumference of a circle is:

$$d \text{ (diameter)} \times \pi \text{ } (pi) = \text{circumference}$$

The pilot flies in a circle with a radius of 40 km and therefore a diameter of 80 km.

$$80 \text{ km} \times \frac{22}{7} = \text{circumference}$$

$$\frac{80 \times 22}{7} = \text{circumference}$$

$$\frac{1760}{7} = \text{circumference}$$

$$251 \text{ km} = \text{circumference}$$

14. **C** Being in the down or extended position means that the wing flaps are pivoted downward from hinged points on the trailing edge of the wing. This effectively increases the wing camber or curvature, resulting in increased lift and increased drag; this allows the airplane to climb or descend at a steeper angle or a slower airspeed.

15. **A** Heavily-loaded aircraft are slower and therefore take longer to achieve flying speed, so a longer runway is needed to develop the lift required for take-off. Also, a take-off in calm or nearly calm air takes away the increased wind speed advantage derived from taking off into the wind. Therefore, many municipal or regional airports have a longer runway to accommodate airplanes needing a longer take-off roll due to one or both of these conditions.

16. **E** The small hinged section on the elevator of most airplanes is called the **trim tab**. The trim tab helps prevent or minimize pilot fatigue by relieving control pressure at the desired flight angle—in other words, the pilot does not have to spend physical and mental energy keeping the elevator at a certain angle to maintain a certain attitude (climbing, level flight, or diving).

17. **B** The rearward retarding force on the airplane known as drag is opposed by **thrust**, which propels the aircraft through the air.

18. **D** At night, airport taxiways are identified by omnidirectional edge lights that are **blue** in color.

19. **A** Envisage most nearly means to **conceive** or conceptualize an idea or plan.

20. **C** A hexagon has six sides. Each of the six sides of the black tile must touch a side of a white tile, so there are six (6) white tiles surrounding each black tile.

21. **C** The straight line joining the ends of the mean camber line is called the **wing chord**.

22. **D** We are not told the sizes of the two wheels, but we can see that one is larger than the other. If the two wheels are connected by a belt, the small wheel will be forced to turn faster and complete more turns than the larger wheel.

23. **A** If the wheel on the left turns counterclockwise, the wheel on the right will turn **clockwise**.

Answer	Pitch	Bank	Direction
24. **A**	climbing	right	out to sea

25. **B Circuit B would have less resistance.** As the electrical current makes its trip from one polarity of the battery to the other on circuit A, it has no choice but to pass through *two* resistors, whereas on circuit B the current will follow the path of least resistance and take a "shortcut" that only passes through one resistor—thereby giving circuit B less resistance.

26. **C** Because there are three ropes supporting block B, they are under $\frac{1}{3}$ the tension as the rope supporting block A.

27. **E** In the passage, **disincentive** does not fit in the context and, in fact, runs counter or opposite to the original meaning of the sentence.

28. **B** If block A, on which the lever is resting, is moved farther away from block B, **it will be harder to lift block B but it will go higher.**

29. **D** The author of this passage believes that a leadership position **is an obligation to challenge the status quo and take measured risks.**

30. **D** In 219 B.C., the passage states that the Romans and Carthaginians were fighting over the city of **Saguntum.**

31. **D** Conflagration most nearly means **a large and destructive fire**.

32. **A** Water is flowing into the water tower at 120 gallons per hour. To convert that to gallons per minute, we divide 120 gallons by the 60 minutes in an hour, resulting in a rate of two gallons per minute coming into the water tower. Therefore, the level of water in the tower will **remain the same**.

33. **C** "Aircraft carrier battle groups, as they travel the world's oceans, conduct exercises, and sometimes merely cruise back and forth in a certain area, are a visible symbol of **support** for America's allies and **deterrence** for potential adversaries." This is the only pair of words that make sense given the context of the rest of the sentence.

34. **D** Scrutiny means a **careful inspection**, often at close range or with a critical attitude. A point of conscience or ethics is a *scruple*; an obligation is a *duty*; a revolt of a ship's crew is a *mutiny*; and the room adjoining the kitchen—especially in a large, older-style house or mansion—is a *scullery*.

Abbreviations and Acronyms

ACT	A college entrance exam (formerly the American College Test)
AETC	Air Education and Training Command
AFAST	Alternate Flight Aptitude Selection Test (Army)
AFB	Air Force Base
AFI	Air Force Instruction (service regulation)
AFOQT	Air Force Officer Qualifying Test
AFROTC	Air Force Reserve Officer Training Corps
ANG	Air National Guard
AR	Army Regulation
ARNG	Army National Guard
ASCP	Airman Scholarship and Commissioning Program
ASTB	Aviation Selection Test Battery (Navy/Marine Corps/Coast Guard)
ASVAB	Armed Services Vocational Aptitude Battery
ASW	Anti-Submarine Warfare
AWACS	Airborne Warning and Control System
C2 (C^2)	Command and Control
CPG	Copilot/gunner
CRRC	Combat Rubber Raiding Craft
DA	Department of the Army
ENJJPT	Euro-NATO Joint Jet Pilot Training
EW	Electronic warfare
GPA	Grade point average
GRE	Graduate Record Exam
GWOT	Global War on Terror/Terrorism
HARM	High-speed Anti-Radiation Missile
IFF	Identification Friend or Foe
IFR	Instrument Flight Rules
JPATS	Joint Primary Aircraft Training System
JSUPT	Joint Specialized Undergraduate Pilot Training
Kg	Kilograms, a measure of weight
Lbs.	Pounds, a measure of weight
MEDEVAC	Medical evacuation

MEPS	Military Entrance Processing Station
NAS	Naval Air Station
NATO	North Atlantic Treaty Organization
NCO	Noncommissioned officer (sergeant in the Army, Air Force, and Marine Corps; petty officer in the Navy and Coast Guard)
NFO	Naval Flight Officer
nm	Nautical miles
NROTC	Navy Reserve Officer Training Corps
OCC	Officer Candidate Course (USMC)
OCS	Officer Candidate School (Army, Navy)
OEF	Operation Enduring Freedom (Afghanistan)
OIF	Operation Iraqi Freedom (Iraq)
OND	Operation New Dawn (Iraq)
OTS	Officer Training School (Air Force)
PLC	Platoon Leaders' Course (USMC)
PSI	Pounds (of pressure) per Square Inch
RIO	Radar Intercept Officer
ROTC	Reserve Office Training Corps (usually Army ROTC when not designated)
SAT	A college entrance exam (formerly the Scholastic Aptitude Test)
SNO	Student Naval Aviator
TACAMO	Take Charge and Move Out
TBS	The Basic School (USMC)
UAV	Unmanned Aerial Vehicle
USA	United States of America; United States Army
USAF	United States Air Force
USAFA	United States Air Force Academy at Colorado Springs, Colorado
USAFR	United States Air Force Reserve
USAR	United States Army Reserve
USASOC	United States Army Special Operations Command
USCG	United States Coast Guard
USMA	United States Military Academy at West Point, New York
USMC	United States Marine Corps
USMCR	United States Marine Corps Reserve
USN	United States Navy
USNA	United States Naval Academy at Annapolis, Maryland
USNR	United States Navy Reserve
VFR	Visual Flight Rules
V/STOL	Vertical/Short Takeoff and Landing
WOCS	Warrant Officer Candidate School (Army)

Bibliography

Anderson, John D., Jr. *Introduction to Flight*. New York: McGraw-Hill, Inc., 1978.

Bekker, Cajus. *Hitler's Naval War*. New York: Kensington Publishing Corp., 1974.

Carretta, Thomas R. "US Air Force Pilot Training and Selection Methods," *Aviation & Space Environmental Medicine*, 2000.

Charlton, James (editor). *The Military Quotation Book*. New York: St. Martin's Press, 1990.

Clancy, Tom. *Carrier: A Guided Tour of an Aircraft Carrier*. New York: Berkley Publishing Group, 1999.

Cowley, Michael, and Domb, Ellen. *Beyond Strategic Vision*. Newton, MA: Butterworth-Heinemann, 1997.

Duran, Terry L. *Barron's ASVAB, 9th Edition*. Hauppauge, NY: Barron's Educational Series, 2009.

Federal Aviation Administration. *Aeronautical Information Manual: Official Guide to Basic Flight Information and ATC Procedures*. St. Louis, MO: U.S. Government Printing Office, 2010.

Federal Aviation Administration. *Flight Training Handbook*. St. Louis, MO: U.S. Government Printing Office, 1980.

Foss, Joe, and Brennan, Matthew. *Top Guns*. New York: Simon & Schuster, 1991.

Fredriksen, John C. *Warbirds: An Illustrated Guide to U.S. Military Aircraft 1915–2000*. Santa Barbara, CA: ABC-Clio, 1999.

Grossnik, Roy A. *Dictionary of American Naval Aviation Squadrons*. Washington, DC: Naval Historical Center, Department of the Navy, 1995.

Gschwandtner, Gerhard, with Garnett, Pat. *Nonverbal Selling Power*. Upper Saddle River, NJ: Prentice Hall, Inc., 1985.

Guest, Tom. "Tradition: A Primary Pillar of Freemasonry." *Texas Mason Magazine*, Vol. XV, Issue 4, Fall 2006.

Hardison, Chaitra M., Sims, Carra S., and Wong, Eunice C. "The Air Force Officer Qualifying Test: Validity, Fairness, and Bias." Santa Monica, CA: RAND Corporation, 2010.

Hastings, Max (editor). *The Oxford Book of Military Anecdotes*. New York: Oxford University Press, 1985.

Hawking, Stephen W. *A Brief History of Time*. New York: Bantam Books, 1988.

Heinl, Robert D., Jr. *Victory at High Tide: the Inchon-Seoul Campaign*. New York: J. B. Lippincott Co., 1968.

Hibbeler, R. C. *Statics and Dynamics, 12th Edition*. Upper Saddle River, NJ: Pearson Prentice Hall, 2010.

HQ, Department of the Air Force. *AFOQT Information Pamphlet*, 2005.

HQ, Department of the Air Force. Air Force Instruction (AFI) 11-202, Volume 3, Flying Operations: General Flight Rules, 5 April 2006.

HQ, Department of the Army. Department of the Army Pamphlet 611-256-2, Alternate Flight Aptitude Selection Test (AFAST) Information Pamphlet. Washington, DC: HQ, Department of the Army, 1987.

HQ, Department of the Navy. Department of the Navy Flight Training Instruction, Contact, TH-57, CNATRA P-457 (Rev. 02-04). Corpus Christi, TX: Chief of Naval Air Training, 2004.

Keegan, John. *A History of Warfare*. New York: Alfred A. Knopf, 1993.

Kern, Florence, and Voulgaris, Barbara. *Traditions of the United States Coast Guard*. Washington, DC: Office of the Historian, U.S. Coast Guard, 1990.

Kotter, John P. *Leading Change*. Boston, MA: Harvard Business School Press, 1996.

Kouzes, James M., and Posner, Barry Z. *Credibility*. San Francisco, CA: Jossey-Bass, Inc., 1993.

Marshall, S.L.A. *Men Against Fire: The Problem of Battle Command in Future War*. Gloucester, MA: Peter Smith, 1947.

Matloff, Maurice (editor). *American Military History, Vol. 1: 1775–1902*. Conshohocken, PA: Combined Books, 1996.

Merriam-Webster, Inc. *Webster's New Biographical Dictionary*. Springfield, MA: Merriam-Webster, Inc., 1988.

Murray, Williamson, and Millett, Allan R. *Military Innovation in the Interwar Period*. New York: Cambridge University Press, 1996.

Nevins, Allan, and Commager, Henry Steele, with Morris, Jeffrey. *A Pocket History of the United States, 9th Revised Edition*. New York: Simon & Schuster, 1992.

The New York Public Library Desk Reference. New York: Simon & Schuster, 1989.

Powers, Rod. *Barron's Officer Candidate School Tests*. Hauppauge, NY: Barron's Educational Series, 2006.

Rader, Benjamin G. *Baseball: A History of America's Game*. Chicago: University of Illinois Press, 1992.

Weissmuller, Johnny J., Schwartz, Kenneth L., Kenney, Stanley D., Shore, C. Wayne, and Gould, R. Bruce. PowerPoint briefing, "Recent Developments in USAF Officer Testing and Selection," October 25, 2004.

Williams, Mary H. *The U.S. Army in World War II: Chronology 1941–1945*. Washington, DC: Center of Military History, 1958.

Young, Hugh D., Freedman, Roger A., and Ford, A. Lewis. *University Physics, 12th Edition*. San Francisco: Pearson Addison-Wesley, 2008.

Websites

http://www.af.mil, United States Air Force "Air Force Link" Factsheets, *Air Force Reserve Officer Training Corps.mht*

http://cfr.vlex.com/vid/91-211-supplemental-oxygen-19562365

http://en.wikipedia.org/wiki/Aviation_Selection_Test_Battery

http://en.wikipedia.org/wiki/Air_Education_and_Training_Command

http://en.wikipedia.org/wiki/Eugene_Burton_Ely

http://en.wikipedia.org/wiki/rotorcraft

http://en.wikipedia.org/wiki/US_military

http://navy.com/careers/officerplanner/officerprograms/

http://physics.about.com/

http://www.med.navy.mil/sites/navmedmpte/nomi/nami/Pages/ASTBOverview.aspx

http://www.navy.mil/navydata/

http://www.afrotc.com/U_S_Air_Force_ROTC_General_Requirements/mht

https://www.cnatra.navy.mil/

http://www.grc.nasa.gov/WWW/K-12/airplane/

http://www.globalsecurity.org/Chief_of_Naval_Air_Training_(CNATRA)

http://www.randolph.af.mil/library/factsheets/

http://www-rucker.army.mil/

http://www.tamu.edu

Index

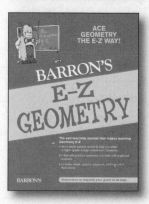

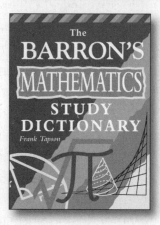
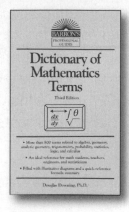

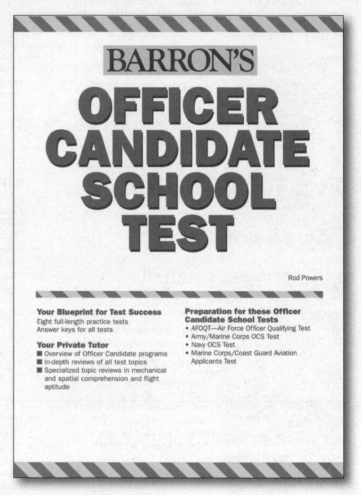

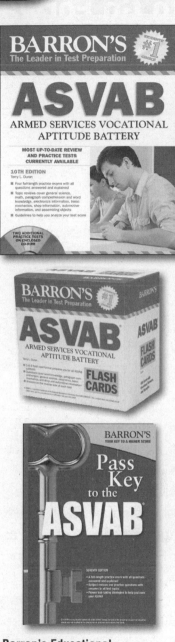